Macmillan/McGraw-Hill Edition

McGRAW-HILL READING

McGraw-Hill
School Division

New York   Farmington

Contributors

The Princeton Review, Time Magazine, Accelerated Reader

The Princeton Review is not
affiliated with Princeton
University or ETS.

McGraw-Hill School Division

A Division of The McGraw·Hill Companies

McGraw-Hill School Division
Two Penn Plaza
New York, New York 10121

Printed in the United States of America

ISBN 0-02-184766-5/4, U.2

3 4 5 6 7 8 9   006   04 03 02 01 00

McGRAW-HILL READING

McGraw-Hill
School Division

New York   **Farmington**

Selected Quizzes Prepared by  Accelerated Reader®

McGraw-Hill Reading
Authors
Make the Difference...

Dr. James Flood

Ms. Angela Shelf Medearis

Dr. Jan E. Hasbrouck

Dr. Scott Paris

Dr. James V. Hoffman

Dr. Steven Stahl

Dr. Diane Lapp

Dr. Josefina Villamil Tinajero

Dr. Karen D. Wood

Contributing
Authors

Dr. Barbara Coulter

Ms. Frankie Dungan

Dr. Joseph B. Rubin

Dr. Carl B. Smith

Dr. Shirley Wright

Part 1
START TOGETHER

Focus on Reading and Skills

All students start with the SAME:
- Read Aloud
- Pretaught Skills
  Phonics
  Comprehension
- Build Background
- Selection Vocabulary

...Never hold a child back. Never leave a child behind.

Part 2
MEET INDIVIDUAL NEEDS

Read the Literature

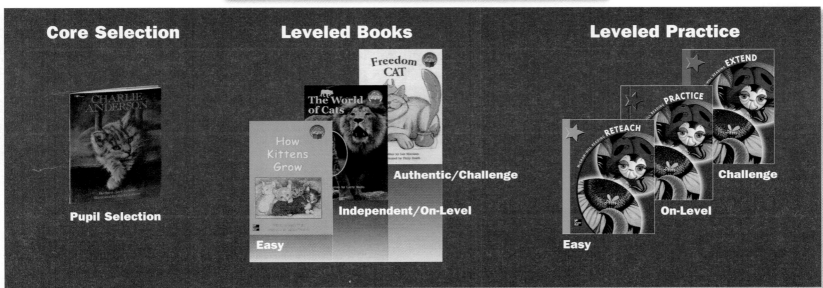

Core Selection

Pupil Selection

Leveled Books

Easy

Independent/On-Level

Authentic/Challenge

Leveled Practice

Easy

On-Level

Challenge

Examples Taken From Grade 2

Part 3
FINISH TOGETHER

Build Skills

All students finish with the SAME:
- Phonics
- Comprehension
- Vocabulary
- Study Skills
- Assessment

McGraw-Hill Reading
Applying the Research

Phonological Awareness

Phonological awareness is the ability to hear the sounds in spoken language. It includes the ability to separate spoken words into discrete sounds as well as the ability to blend sounds together to make words. A child with good phonological awareness can identify rhyming words, hear the separate syllables in a word, separate the first sound in a word (onset) from the rest of the word (rime), and blend sounds together to make words.

Recent research findings have strongly concluded that children with good phonological awareness skills are more likely to learn to read well. These skills can be improved through systematic, explicit instruction involving auditory practice. McGraw-Hill Reading develops these key skills by providing an explicit Phonological Awareness lesson in every selection at grades K-2. Motivating activities such as blending, segmenting, and rhyming help to develop children's awareness of the sounds in our language.

Guided Instruction/ Guided Reading

Research on reading shows that guided instruction enables students to develop as independent, strategic readers. *The reciprocal-teaching model* of Anne-Marie Palincsar encourages teachers to model strategic-thinking, questioning, clarifying, and problem-solving strategies for students as students read together with the teacher. In McGraw-Hill Reading, guided instruction for all Pupil Edition selections incorporates the Palincsar model by providing interactive questioning prompts. *The guided-reading model* of Gay Su Pinnell is also incorporated into the McGraw-Hill Reading program. Through the guided-reading lessons provided for the leveled books offered with the program, teachers can work with small groups of students of different ability levels, closely observing them as they read and providing support specific to their needs.

By adapting instruction to include successful models of teaching and the appropriate materials to deliver instruction, McGraw-Hill Reading enables teachers to offer the appropriate type of instruction for all students in the classroom.

Phonics

Our language system uses an alphabetic code to communicate meaning from writing. Phonics involves learning the phonemes or sounds that letters make and the symbols or letters that represent those sounds. Children learn to blend the sounds of letters to decode unknown or unfamiliar words. The goal of good phonics instruction is to enable students to read words accurately and automatically.

Research has clearly identified the critical role of phonics in the ability of readers to read fluently and with good understanding, as well as to write and spell. Effective phonics instruction requires carefully sequenced lessons that teach the sounds of letters and how to use these sounds to read words. The McGraw-Hill program provides daily explicit and systematic phonics instruction to teach the letter sounds and blending. There are three explicit Phonics and Decoding lessons for every selection. Daily Phonics Routines are provided for quick reinforcement, in addition to activities in the Phonics/Phonemic Awareness Practice Book and technology components. This combination of direct skills instruction and applied practice leads to reading success.

Curriculum Connections

As in the child's real-world environment, boundaries between disciplines must be dissolved. Recent research emphasizes the need to make connections between and across subject areas. McGraw-Hill Reading is committed to this approach. Each reading selection offers activities that tie in with social studies, language arts, geography, science, mathematics, art, music, health, and physical education. The program threads numerous research and inquiry activities that encourage the child to use the library and the Internet to seek out information. Reading and language skills are applied to a variety of genres, balancing fiction and nonfiction.

Integrated Language Arts

Success in developing communication skills is greatly enhanced by integrating the language arts in connected and purposeful ways. This allows students to understand the need for proper writing, grammar, and spelling. McGraw-Hill Reading sets the stage for meaningful learning. Each week a full writing-process lesson is provided. This lesson is supported by a 5-day spelling plan, emphasizing spelling patterns and spelling rules, and a 5-day grammar plan, focusing on proper grammar, mechanics, and usage.

Meeting Individual Needs

Every classroom is a microcosm of a world composed of diverse individuals with unique needs and abilities. Research points out that such needs must be addressed with frequent intensive opportunities to learn with engaging materials. McGraw-Hill Reading makes reading a successful experience for every child by providing a rich collection of leveled books for easy, independent, and challenging reading. Leveled practice is provided in Reteach, Practice, and Extend skills books. To address various learning styles and language needs, the program offers alternative teaching strategies, prevention/intervention techniques, language support activities, and ESL teaching suggestions.

Assessment

Frequent assessment in the classroom makes it easier for teachers to identify problems and to find remedies for them. McGraw-Hill Reading makes assessment an important component of instruction. Formal and informal opportunities are a part of each lesson. Minilessons, prevention/intervention strategies, and informal checklists, as well as student self-assessments, provide many informal assessment opportunities. Formal assessments, such as weekly selection tests and criterion-referenced unit tests, help to monitor students' knowledge of important skills and concepts. McGraw-Hill Reading also addresses how to adapt instruction based on student performance with resources such as the Alternate Teaching Strategies. Weekly lessons on test preparation, including test preparation practice books, help students to transfer skills to new contexts and to become better test takers.

McGraw-Hill School
TECHNOLOGY

*inter***NET** **CONNECTION** For information on research that supports this program, visit **www.mhschool.com/reading**

McGraw-Hill Reading

Theme Chart

MULTI-AGE Classroom

Using the same global themes at each grade level facilitates the use of materials in multi-age classrooms.

GRADE LEVEL	Experience Experiences can tell us about ourselves and our world.	Connections Making connections develops new understandings.
Kindergarten	**My World** We learn a lot from all the things we see and do at home and in school.	**All Kinds of Friends** When we work and play together, we learn more about ourselves.
Sub-theme 1	At Home	Working Together
Sub-theme 2	School Days	Playing Together
1	**Day by Day** Each day brings new experiences.	**Together Is Better** We like to share ideas and experiences with others.
2	**What's New?** With each day, we learn something new.	**Just Between Us** Family and friends help us see the world in new ways.
3	**Great Adventures** Life is made up of big and small experiences.	**Nature Links** Nature can give us new ideas.
4	**Reflections** Stories let us share the experiences of others.	**Something in Common** Sharing ideas can lead to meaningful cooperation.
5	**Time of My Life** We sometimes find memorable experiences in unexpected places.	**Building Bridges** Knowing what we have in common helps us appreciate our differences.
6	**Pathways** Reflecting on life's experiences can lead to new understandings.	**A Common Thread** A look beneath the surface may uncover hidden connections.

Themes: Kindergarten – Grade 6

Six Units IN EVERY GRADE

Expression	Inquiry	Problem-Solving	Making Decisions
There are many styles and forms for expressing ourselves.	By exploring and asking questions, we make discoveries.	Analyzing information can help us solve problems.	Using what we know helps us evaluate situations.
Time to Shine We can use our ideas and our imagination to do many wonderful things.	**I Wonder** We can make discoveries about the wonders of nature in our own backyard.	**Let's Work It Out** Working as part of a team can help me find a way to solve problems.	**Choices** We can make many good choices and decisions every day.
Great Ideas	**In My Backyard**	**Try and Try Again**	**Good Choices**
Let's Pretend	**Wonders of Nature**	**Teamwork**	**Let's Decide**
Stories to Tell Each one of us has a different story to tell.	**Let's Find Out!** Looking for answers is an adventure.	**Think About It!** It takes time to solve problems.	**Many Paths** Each decision opens the door to a new path.
Express Yourself We share our ideas in many ways.	**Look Around** There are surprises all around us.	**Figure It Out** We can solve problems by working together.	**Starting Now** Unexpected events can lead to new decisions.
Be Creative! We can all express ourselves in creative, wonderful ways.	**Tell Me More** Looking and listening closely will help us find out the facts.	**Think It Through** Solutions come in many shapes and sizes.	**Turning Points** We make new judgments based on our experiences.
Our Voices We can each use our talents to communicate ideas.	**Just Curious** We can find answers in surprising places.	**Make a Plan** Often we have to think carefully about a problem in order to solve it.	**Sorting It Out** We make decisions that can lead to new ideas and discoveries.
Imagine That The way we express our thoughts and feelings can take different forms.	**Investigate!** We never know where the search for answers might lead us.	**Bright Ideas** Some problems require unusual approaches.	**Crossroads** Decisions cause changes that can enrich our lives.
With Flying Colors Creative people help us see the world from different perspectives.	**Seek and Discover** To make new discoveries, we must observe and explore.	**Brainstorms** We can meet any challenge with determination and ingenuity.	**All Things Considered** Encountering new places and people can help us make decisions.

Something in Common

Contents

Sharing ideas can lead to meaningful cooperation.

"The Arrow and the Song"
a poem by *Henry Wadsworth Longfellow*

written by **Mildred Pitts Walter**
illustrated by **Floyd Cooper**

SKILLS			
Comprehension	**Vocabulary**	**Study Skill**	**Phonics**
• **Introduce** Make Predictions	• **Introduce** Context Clues	• **Reference Sources:** Use a Dictionary	• **Review** Syllable Patterns
• **Review** Make Predictions			
• **Introduce** Form Generalizations			

REALISTIC FICTION

written and illustrated by **Chris Van Allsburg**

SKILLS			
Comprehension	**Vocabulary**	**Study Skill**	**Phonics**
• **Introduce** Sequence of Events	• **Introduce** Compound Words	• **Reference Sources:** Use a Thesaurus	• **Review** Consonant Clusters
• **Review** Sequence of Events			
• **Review** Form Generalizations			

FANTASY

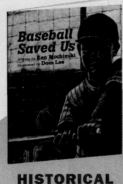
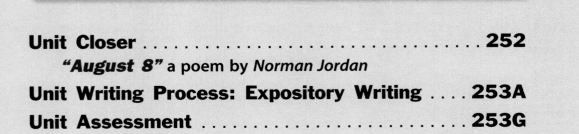

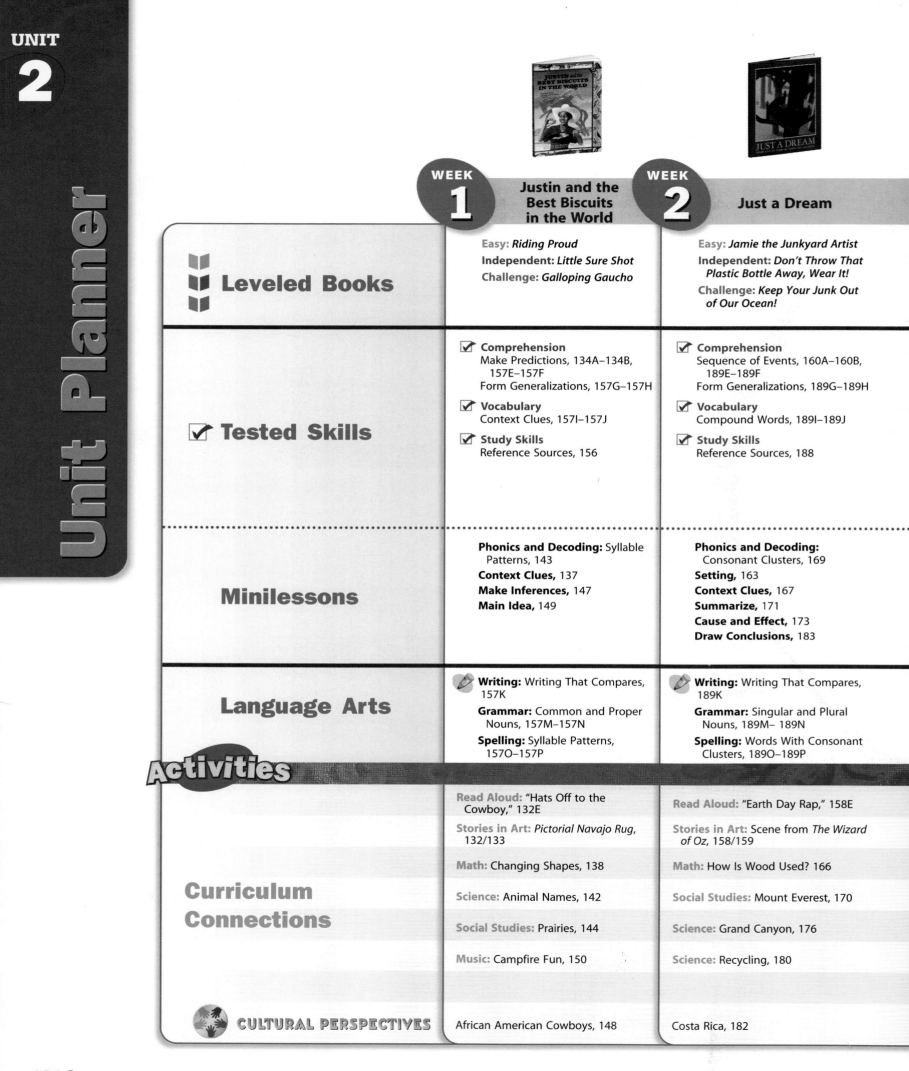

Leveled Books

Justin and the Best Biscuits in the World	Just a Dream
Easy: *Riding Proud*	**Easy:** *Jamie the Junkyard Artist*
Independent: *Little Sure Shot*	**Independent:** *Don't Throw That Plastic Bottle Away, Wear It!*
Challenge: *Galloping Gaucho*	**Challenge:** *Keep Your Junk Out of Our Ocean!*

✓ Tested Skills

☑ **Comprehension** Make Predictions, 134A–134B, 157E–157F Form Generalizations, 157G–157H	☑ **Comprehension** Sequence of Events, 160A–160B, 189E–189F Form Generalizations, 189G–189H
☑ **Vocabulary** Context Clues, 157I–157J	☑ **Vocabulary** Compound Words, 189I–189J
☑ **Study Skills** Reference Sources, 156	☑ **Study Skills** Reference Sources, 188

Minilessons

Phonics and Decoding: Syllable Patterns, 143	**Phonics and Decoding:** Consonant Clusters, 169
Context Clues, 137	**Setting,** 163
Make Inferences, 147	**Context Clues,** 167
Main Idea, 149	**Summarize,** 171
	Cause and Effect, 173
	Draw Conclusions, 183

Language Arts

Writing: Writing That Compares, 157K	**Writing:** Writing That Compares, 189K
Grammar: Common and Proper Nouns, 157M–157N	**Grammar:** Singular and Plural Nouns, 189M– 189N
Spelling: Syllable Patterns, 157O–157P	**Spelling:** Words With Consonant Clusters, 189O–189P

Activities

Curriculum Connections

Read Aloud: "Hats Off to the Cowboy," 132E	Read Aloud: "Earth Day Rap," 158E
Stories in Art: *Pictorial Navajo Rug*, 132/133	Stories in Art: Scene from *The Wizard of Oz*, 158/159
Math: Changing Shapes, 138	Math: How Is Wood Used? 166
Science: Animal Names, 142	Social Studies: Mount Everest, 170
Social Studies: Prairies, 144	Science: Grand Canyon, 176
Music: Campfire Fun, 150	Science: Recycling, 180

CULTURAL PERSPECTIVES

African American Cowboys, 148	Costa Rica, 182

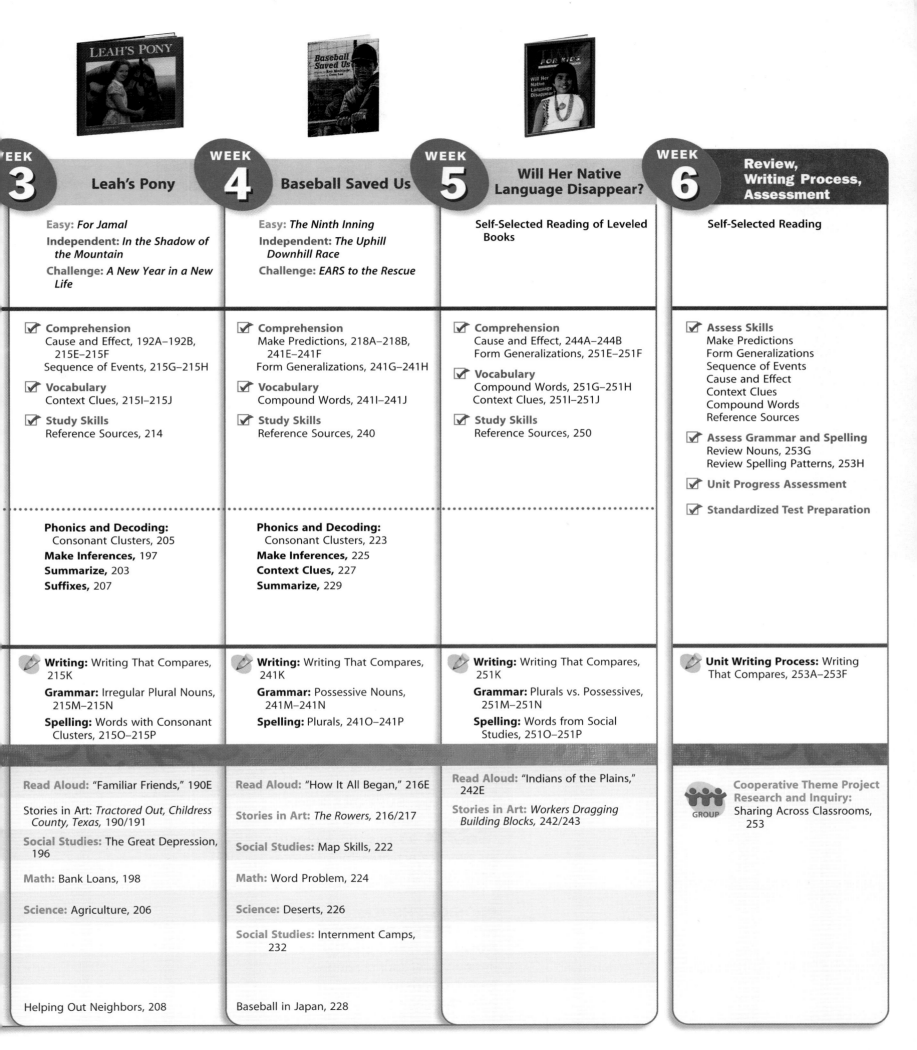

WEEK 3 — Leah's Pony	WEEK 4 — Baseball Saved Us	WEEK 5 — Will Her Native Language Disappear?	WEEK 6 — Review, Writing Process, Assessment
Easy: *For Jamal* **Independent:** *In the Shadow of the Mountain* **Challenge:** *A New Year in a New Life*	**Easy:** *The Ninth Inning* **Independent:** *The Uphill Downhill Race* **Challenge:** *EARS to the Rescue*	**Self-Selected Reading of Leveled Books**	**Self-Selected Reading**
☑ **Comprehension** Cause and Effect, 192A–192B, 215E–215F Sequence of Events, 215G–215H ☑ **Vocabulary** Context Clues, 215I–215J ☑ **Study Skills** Reference Sources, 214	☑ **Comprehension** Make Predictions, 218A–218B, 241E–241F Form Generalizations, 241G–241H ☑ **Vocabulary** Compound Words, 241I–241J ☑ **Study Skills** Reference Sources, 240	☑ **Comprehension** Cause and Effect, 244A–244B Form Generalizations, 251E–251F ☑ **Vocabulary** Compound Words, 251G–251H Context Clues, 251I–251J ☑ **Study Skills** Reference Sources, 250	☑ **Assess Skills** Make Predictions Form Generalizations Sequence of Events Cause and Effect Context Clues Compound Words Reference Sources ☑ **Assess Grammar and Spelling** Review Nouns, 253G Review Spelling Patterns, 253H ☑ **Unit Progress Assessment** ☑ **Standardized Test Preparation**
Phonics and Decoding: Consonant Clusters, 205 **Make Inferences,** 197 **Summarize,** 203 **Suffixes,** 207	**Phonics and Decoding:** Consonant Clusters, 223 **Make Inferences,** 225 **Context Clues,** 227 **Summarize,** 229		
Writing: Writing That Compares, 215K **Grammar:** Irregular Plural Nouns, 215M–215N **Spelling:** Words with Consonant Clusters, 215O–215P	**Writing:** Writing That Compares, 241K **Grammar:** Possessive Nouns, 241M–241N **Spelling:** Plurals, 241O–241P	**Writing:** Writing That Compares, 251K **Grammar:** Plurals vs. Possessives, 251M–251N **Spelling:** Words from Social Studies, 251O–251P	**Unit Writing Process:** Writing That Compares, 253A–253F
Read Aloud: "Familiar Friends," 190E Stories in Art: *Tractored Out, Childress County, Texas,* 190/191 Social Studies: The Great Depression, 196 Math: Bank Loans, 198 Science: Agriculture, 206	Read Aloud: "How It All Began," 216E Stories in Art: *The Rowers,* 216/217 Social Studies: Map Skills, 222 Math: Word Problem, 224 Science: Deserts, 226 Social Studies: Internment Camps, 232	Read Aloud: "Indians of the Plains," 242E Stories in Art: *Workers Dragging Building Blocks,* 242/243	**Cooperative Theme Project Research and Inquiry:** Sharing Across Classrooms, 253
Helping Out Neighbors, 208	Baseball in Japan, 228		

Unit Resources

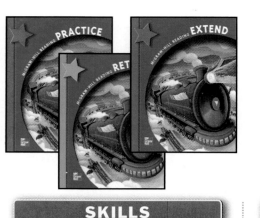

LITERATURE

LEVELED BOOKS

📕 **Easy:**
- *Riding Proud*
- *Jamie the Junkyard Artist*
- *For Jamal*
- *The Ninth Inning*

📖 **Independent:**
- *Little Sure Shot*
- *Don't Throw That Plastic Bottle Away, Wear It!*
- *In the Shadow of the Mountain*
- *The Uphill Downhill Race*

📕 **Challenge:**
- *Galloping Gaucho*
- *Keep Your Junk Out of Our Ocean!*
- *A New Year in a New Life*
- *EARS to the Rescue*

📼 **LISTENING LIBRARY AUDIOCASSETTES** Recordings of the student book selections and poetry.

SKILLS

LEVELED PRACTICE

Practice Book: Student practice for comprehension, vocabulary, and study skills; plus practice for instructional vocabulary and story comprehension. Take-Home Story included for each lesson.

Reteach: Reteaching opportunities for students who need more help with assessed skills.

Extend: Extension activities for vocabulary, comprehension, story, and study skills.

 TEACHING CHARTS Instructional charts for modeling vocabulary and tested skills. Also available as transparencies.

WORD BUILDING MANIPULATIVE CARDS Cards with words and structural elements for word building and practicing vocabulary.

LANGUAGE SUPPORT BOOK

ESL Parallel teaching lessons and appropriate practice activities for students needing language support.

PHONICS/PHONEMIC AWARENESS PRACTICE BOOK Additional practice focusing on vowel sounds, phonograms, blends, digraphs, and key phonetic elements.

LANGUAGE ARTS

GRAMMAR PRACTICE BOOK
Provides practice for grammar and mechanics lessons.

SPELLING PRACTICE BOOK
Provides practice with the word list and spelling patterns. Includes home involvement activities.

DAILY LANGUAGE ACTIVITIES
Sentence activities that provide brief, regular practice and reinforcement of grammar, mechanics, and usage skills. Available as blackline masters and transparencies.

McGraw-Hill School
TECHNOLOGY

*inter*NET **CONNECTION** extends lesson activities through Research and Inquiry Ideas.

Visit **www.mhschool.com/reading**

Resources for **Meeting Individual Needs**

	EASY	ON-LEVEL	CHALLENGE	LANGUAGE SUPPORT
UNIT 2				
Justin and the Best Biscuits in the World	**Leveled Book:** *Riding Proud* **Reteach,** 38–44 **Alternate Teaching Strategies,** T60–T66 **Writing:** Captions and Labels, 157L	**Leveled Book:** *Little Sure Shot* **Practice,** 38–44 **Alternate Teaching Strategies,** T60–T66 **Writing:** Journal Entry, 157L	**Leveled Book:** *Galloping Gaucho* **Extend,** 38–44 **Writing:** Rodeo Report, 157L	**Teaching Strategies,** 134C, 135, 136, 139, 157L **Language Support,** 41–48 **Alternate Teaching Strategies,** T60–T66 **Writing:** Write a Report, 157K–157L
Just a Dream	**Leveled Book:** *Jamie the Junkyard Artist* **Reteach,** 45–51 **Alternate Teaching Strategies,** T60–T66 **Writing:** Make a Diagram, 189L	**Leveled Book:** *Don't Throw That Plastic Bottle Away, Wear It!* **Practice,** 45–51 **Alternate Teaching Strategies,** T60–T66 **Writing:** Write a Brochure, 189L	**Leveled Book:** *Keep Your Junk Out of Our Ocean!* **Extend,** 45–51 **Writing:** Interview an Expert, 189L	**Teaching Strategies,** 160A, 160C, 161, 164, 167, 172, 179, 189L **Language Support,** 49–56 **Alternate Teaching Strategies,** T60–T66 **Writing:** Write an Essay, 189K–189L
Leah's Pony	**Leveled Book:** *For Jamal* **Reteach,** 52–58 **Alternate Teaching Strategies,** T60–T66 **Writing:** Diary, 215L	**Leveled Book:** *In the Shadow of the Mountain* **Practice,** 52–58 **Alternate Teaching Strategies,** T60–T66 **Writing:** Letter, 215L	**Leveled Book:** *A New Year in a New Life* **Extend,** 52–58 **Writing:** Speech, 215L	**Teaching Strategies,** 192A, 192C, 193, 195, 200, 207, 215I, 215L **Language Support,** 57–64 **Alternate Teaching Strategies,** T60–T66 **Writing:** Write a Newspaper Article, 215K–215L
Baseball Saved Us	**Leveled Book:** *The Ninth Inning* **Reteach,** 59–65 **Alternate Teaching Strategies,** T60–T66 **Writing:** Certificate of Award, 241L	**Leveled Book:** *The Uphill Downhill Race* **Practice,** 59–65 **Alternate Teaching Strategies,** T60–T66 **Writing:** Interview Ken, 241L	**Leveled Book:** *EARS to the Rescue* **Extend,** 59–65 **Writing:** Letter, 241L	**Teaching Strategies,** 218A, 218C, 219, 220, 231, 233, 235, 241L **Language Support,** 65–72 **Alternate Teaching Strategies,** T60–T66 **Writing:** Write a Sports Column, 241K–241L
Will Her Native Language Disappear?	**Review** **Reteach,** 66–72 **Alternate Teaching Strategies,** T60–T66 **Writing:** Chart, 251L	**Review** **Practice,** 66–72 **Alternate Teaching Strategies,** T60–T66 **Writing:** Interview, 251L	**Review** **Extend,** 66–72 **Writing:** School Story, 251L	**Teaching Strategies,** 244C, 245, 251L **Language Support,** 73–80 **Alternate Teaching Strategies,** T60–T66 **Writing:** Write an Interview, 251K–251L

INFORMAL

Informal Assessment

- Comprehension, 134B, 152, 153, 157F, 157H; 160B, 184, 185, 189F, 189H; 192B, 210, 211, 215F, 215H; 218B, 236, 237, 241F, 241H; 244B, 247, 251F
- Vocabulary, 157J, 189J, 215J, 241J, 251H, 251J

Performance Assessment

- Scoring Rubrics, 157L, 189L, 215L, 241L, 251L, 253F
- Research and Inquiry, 131, 253
- Writing Process, 157K 189K, 215K, 241K, 251K
- Listening, Speaking, Viewing Activities, 132E, 132/133, 134C, 134–155, 157D, 157L; 158E, 158/159, 160C, 160–187, 189D, 189L; 190E, 190/191, 192C, 192–213, 215D, 215L; 216E, 216/217, 218C, 218–239, 241D, 241L; 242E, 242/243, 244C, 244–249, 251D, 251L
- Portfolio, 157L, 189L, 215L, 241L, 251L
  Writing, 157K–157L, 189K–189L, 215K–215L, 241K–241L, 251K–251L, 253A–253F
- Cross Curricular Activities, 138, 142, 144, 150, 166, 170, 176, 180, 196, 198, 206, 222, 224, 226, 232

Leveled Practice

Practice, Reteach, Extend

- **Comprehension**
  Make Predictions, 38, 42, 59, 63
  Form Generalizations, 43, 50, 64, 70
  Sequence of Events, 45, 49, 57
  Cause and Effect, 52, 56, 66
- **Vocabulary Strategies**
  Context Clues, 44, 58, 72
  Compound Words, 51, 65, 71
- **Study Skills**
  Reference Sources, 41, 48, 55, 62, 69

FORMAL

Selection Assessments

- **Skills and Vocabulary Words**
  Justin and the Best Biscuits in the World, 11–12
  Just a Dream, 13–14
  Leah's Pony, 15–16
  Baseball Saved Us, 17–18
  Will Her Native Language Disappear? 19–20

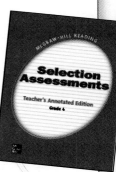

Unit 2 Test

- **Comprehension**
  Make Predictions
  Form Generalizations
  Sequence of Events
  Cause and Effect
- **Vocabulary Strategies**
  Context Clues
  Compound Words
- **Study Skills**
  Reference Sources

Grammar and Spelling Assessment

- **Grammar**
  Nouns, 37, 43, 49, 55, 61, 63, 64
- **Spelling**
  Syllable Patterns, 38
  Words with Consonant Clusters, 44
  Words with Consonant Clusters, 50
  Plurals, 56
  Words from Social Studies, 62
  Unit Review, 63–64

Diagnostic/Placement Evaluations

- Individual Reading Inventory, 1–2
- Running Record, 3–4
- Grade 4 Diagnostic/Placement
- Grade 5 Diagnostic/Placement
- Grade 6 Diagnostic/Placement

Test Preparation

- Test Power in Teacher's Edition, 157, 189, 215, 241, 251
- TAAS Preparation and Practice Book

Something in Common

The Arrow and the Song

I shot an arrow into the air,
It fell to earth, I knew not where;
For, so swiftly it flew, the sight
Could not follow it in its flight.

I breathed a song into the air,
It fell to earth, I knew not where;
For who has sight so keen and strong,
That it can follow the flight of song?

Long, long afterward, in an oak
I found the arrow, still unbroke;
And the song, from beginning to end,
I found again in the heart of a friend.

by Henry Wadsworth Longfellow

131

LEARNING ABOUT POETRY

Literary Devices: Rhythm Read the poem aloud, emphasizing the rhythm. Have students read it aloud and nod their heads up and down to the rhythm. Point out that just like songs, some poems have a definite beat or rhythm. Divide the class into three groups and ask each group to read a stanza of the poem aloud while the other two groups clap the rhythm.

Response Activity Ask partners to work together to dramatize this poem. One student can read the poem while the other student performs the actions. Have pairs perform for each other.

Activity

Research and Inquiry

Theme Project: Sharing Across Classrooms Have students work in teams to brainstorm things to share with another class. Examples might include sharing extra books or sports equipment, knowledge and skills, something they have built, like a game of "Schoolopoly." Have teams present their ideas then chose one project.

List What They Know Have them list what they already know about the interests and needs of another class.

Ask Questions and Identify Resources Ask students to brainstorm questions they need to answer in order to prepare their presentations. Have them list possible resources.

QUESTIONS	POSSIBLE RESOURCES
• What skills or knowledge do we have that we could share? • How can we share information with each other? • How can we learn about others' needs and interests?	• Take a survey. • Create questionnaires. • Look at books about hobbies, sports, animals.

interNET CONNECTION Have students visit **www.mhschool.com/reading** to learn about projects of other schools.

Remind students to take notes.

Create a Presentation When their research is complete, students will present their plan for sharing across classrooms. Encourage students to create displays, surveys, and reports about their activities. See Wrap Up the Theme, page 253.

131

Justin and the Best Biscuits in the World

Selection Summary   On a visit to Grandpa's ranch, Justin learns all about cowboys. His special connection with Grandpa also teaches him a few things he never would have guessed about chores—or himself.

**Listening
Library
Audiocassette**

INSTRUCTIONAL
Pages 134–157

About the Author   Mildred Pitts Walter grew up in Louisiana, but moved to Los Angeles to become a teacher. As a teacher, she observed a need for children's books about African Americans and their cultural heritage, so she decided to try writing some herself.

About the Illustrator   Floyd Cooper's realistic illustrations are full of details that contribute to the reader's understanding of cowboy life and African American history. At the same time, they have a gentle quality that captures the warm feelings Grandpa and Justin share.

Resources for Meeting Individual Needs

LEVELED BOOKS

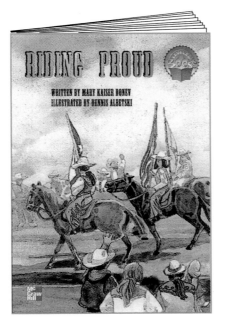

EASY
Pages 157A, 157D

INDEPENDENT
Pages 157B, 157D

CHALLENGE
Pages 157C, 157D

LEVELED PRACTICE

Reteach 38–44
blackline masters with reteaching opportunities for each assessed skill

Practice 38–44
workbook with Take-Home stories and practice opportunities for each assessed skill and story comprehension

Extend 38–44
blackline masters that offer challenge activities for each assessed skill

ADDITIONAL RESOURCES

- **Language Support Book,** 41–48
- **Take-Home Story, Practice,** p. 39a
- **Alternate Teaching Strategies,** T60–T66
- **Selected Quizzes Prepared by** Accelerated Reader®

McGraw-Hill School TECHNOLOGY

interNET CONNECTION Research and Inquiry Ideas. Visit *www.mhschool.com/reading*

Suggested Lesson Planner

READING AND LANGUAGE ARTS	DAY 1 — Focus on Reading and Skills	DAY 2 — Read the Literature
• Comprehension • Vocabulary • Phonics/Decoding • Study Skills • Listening, Speaking, Viewing, Representing	**Read** **Read Aloud and Motivate,** 132E *Hats Off to the Cowboy* **Develop Visual Literacy,** 132/133 ☑ **Introduce Make Predictions,** 134A–134B **Teaching Chart 31** Reteach, Practice, Extend, 38	**Build Background,** 134C Develop Oral Language **Vocabulary,** 134D *festival inspecting pranced* *guilt lingered resounded* **Teaching Chart 32** Word Building Manipulative Cards Reteach, Practice, Extend, 39 **Read** **Read the Selection,** 134–153 ☑ Make Predictions **Minilessons,** 137, 143, 147, 149 **Cultural Perspectives,** 148
• Curriculum Connections	**Link** Works of Art, 132/133	**Link** Social Studies, 134C
• Writing	**Writing Prompt:** On a recent trip out West, you met a cowboy. Write a postcard to a friend to tell why you admire him.	**Writing Prompt:** Write a work schedule for a cowhand. Show jobs for a whole week. **Journal Writing,** 153 Quick-Write
• Grammar	**Introduce the Concept: Common and Proper Nouns,** 157M Daily Language Activity 1. My friend is a Cowboy. cowboy 2. His name is ringo. Ringo 3. My buddy drives a Truck. truck **Grammar Practice Book,** 33	**Teach the Concept: Common and Proper Nouns,** 157M Daily Language Activity 1. We all work hard the month of july. July 2. Rick lives in new mexico. New Mexico 3. His day off is monday. Monday **Grammar Practice Book,** 34
• Spelling	**Pretest: Syllable Patterns,** 157O **Spelling Practice Book,** 33, 34	**Explore the Pattern: Syllable Patterns,** 157O **Spelling Practice Book,** 35

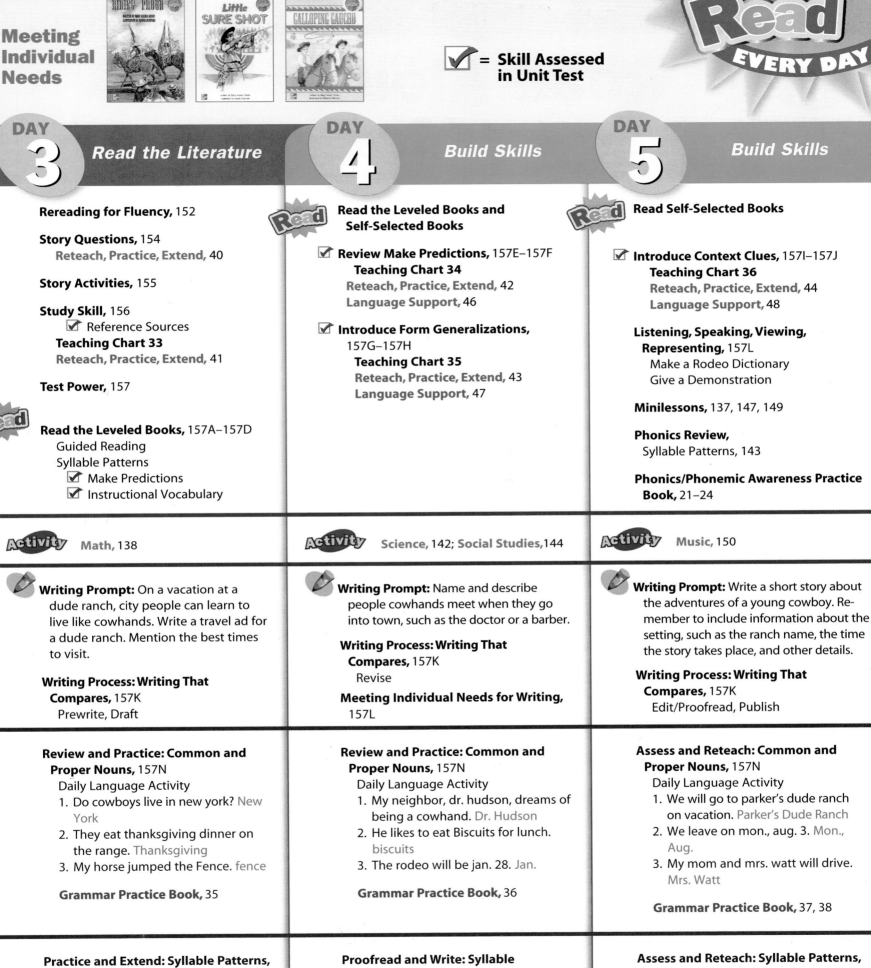
DAY 3 *Read the Literature*	**DAY 4** *Build Skills*	**DAY 5** *Build Skills*
Rereading for Fluency, 152	**Read** **Read the Leveled Books and Self-Selected Books**	**Read** **Read Self-Selected Books**
Story Questions, 154 Reteach, Practice, Extend, 40	☑ **Review Make Predictions,** 157E–157F **Teaching Chart 34** Reteach, Practice, Extend, 42 Language Support, 46	☑ **Introduce Context Clues,** 157I–157J **Teaching Chart 36** Reteach, Practice, Extend, 44 Language Support, 48
Story Activities, 155		**Listening, Speaking, Viewing, Representing,** 157L Make a Rodeo Dictionary Give a Demonstration
Study Skill, 156 ☑ Reference Sources **Teaching Chart 33** Reteach, Practice, Extend, 41	☑ **Introduce Form Generalizations,** 157G–157H **Teaching Chart 35** Reteach, Practice, Extend, 43 Language Support, 47	
Test Power, 157		**Minilessons,** 137, 147, 149
		Phonics Review, Syllable Patterns, 143
Read **Read the Leveled Books,** 157A–157D Guided Reading Syllable Patterns ☑ Make Predictions ☑ Instructional Vocabulary		**Phonics/Phonemic Awareness Practice Book,** 21–24
Activity Math, 138	**Activity** Science, 142; Social Studies, 144	**Activity** Music, 150
Writing Prompt: On a vacation at a dude ranch, city people can learn to live like cowhands. Write a travel ad for a dude ranch. Mention the best times to visit. **Writing Process: Writing That Compares,** 157K Prewrite, Draft	**Writing Prompt:** Name and describe people cowhands meet when they go into town, such as the doctor or a barber. **Writing Process: Writing That Compares,** 157K Revise **Meeting Individual Needs for Writing,** 157L	**Writing Prompt:** Write a short story about the adventures of a young cowboy. Remember to include information about the setting, such as the ranch name, the time the story takes place, and other details. **Writing Process: Writing That Compares,** 157K Edit/Proofread, Publish
Review and Practice: Common and Proper Nouns, 157N Daily Language Activity 1. Do cowboys live in new york? New York 2. They eat thanksgiving dinner on the range. Thanksgiving 3. My horse jumped the Fence. fence **Grammar Practice Book,** 35	**Review and Practice: Common and Proper Nouns,** 157N Daily Language Activity 1. My neighbor, dr. hudson, dreams of being a cowhand. Dr. Hudson 2. He likes to eat Biscuits for lunch. biscuits 3. The rodeo will be jan. 28. Jan. **Grammar Practice Book,** 36	**Assess and Reteach: Common and Proper Nouns,** 157N Daily Language Activity 1. We will go to parker's dude ranch on vacation. Parker's Dude Ranch 2. We leave on mon., aug. 3. Mon., Aug. 3. My mom and mrs. watt will drive. Mrs. Watt **Grammar Practice Book,** 37, 38
Practice and Extend: Syllable Patterns, 157P **Spelling Practice Book,** 36	**Proofread and Write: Syllable Patterns,** 157P **Spelling Practice Book,** 37	**Assess and Reteach: Syllable Patterns,** 157P **Spelling Practice Book,** 38

Read Aloud and Motivate

Language Arts

Hats Off to the Cowboy

a poem by Red Steagall

The city folks think that it's over.
The cowboy has outlived his time—
An old worn-out relic, a thing of the
    past,
But the truth is, he's still in his prime.

The cowboy's image of freedom,
The hard-ridin' boss of the range.
His trade is a fair one, he fights for
    what's right,
And his ethics aren't subject to
    change.

He still tips his hat to the ladies,
Lets you water first at the pond.
He believes a day's pay is worth a
    day's work,
And his handshake and word are his
    bond.

Oral Comprehension

LISTENING AND SPEAKING Read the poem's title aloud. Elicit from students that taking off one's hat is a way to show respect. To motivate students to make predictions about what they will hear, ask, "What reasons can you think of for showing someone respect?" After you have finished reading the poem, ask, "Which of your reasons for showing respect did the poet mention? Did the poet include any ideas that you didn't expect to hear?"

Activity Organize the class into pairs and ask students to imagine that a cowhand has come to talk to them on Career Day. Have one partner play a job applicant and describe features that he or she would like to find in a career, such as an outdoor work environment, working with animals, or a corner office and regular work hours. Have the other partner take the role of the cowhand and predict whether or not the applicant would be happy working as a cowhand. ▶ **Oral/Interpersonal**

Anthology pages 132–133

Stories in Art

Some artists work with cloth and colored yarn instead of paint. They are called textile artists.

Look at this Navajo rug. What details do you notice? How do these details describe life in a Navajo village?

Look at this rug again. How can you tell that weaving wool is important to the Navajo way of life? What do you think will happen to the wool on the sheep? Notice the car near the center. Do you think it will change life in this Navajo village? How?

Pictorial Navajo Rug
by Betty Patterson

132   133

Objective: Make Predictions

VIEWING The scene in this rug tells a story of Navajo life in the West, including the Navajo tradition of weaving that led to the creation of the rug itself. Ask students to point out details that help them understand the Navajo way of life. Then have them find one detail that does not seem to fit in with the traditional Navajo lifestyle. (the car)

Read the page with students, encouraging individual interpretations of the scene.

Encourage students to use details from the rug to predict whether or not life might change for these people in the near future. For example:

• The car is shown very small in comparison to other things in the rug. Maybe that means the artist believes the Navajo have been able to experience modern things like cars wihout losing their traditional lifestyle and culture.

REPRESENTING Have students draw or paint the scene as it might appear in the future.

132/133

OBJECTIVES
Students will make predictions about a story.

Introduce Make Predictions

TEACHING TIP

INSTRUCTIONAL Point out that checking predictions to confirm or revise them is an important part of the prediction process. Also, discuss why stories with surprising twists are sometimes more enjoyable to read than stories with plots that are easy to predict.

OBJECTIVES
Students will make predictions about a story.

PREPARE

Discuss Making Predictions

Ask students if they have ever made a prediction about what is going to happen next in a movie. Tell them that such predictions are generally based on two things: what has happened in the story so far and what they know from their own experience.

TEACH

Define Making Predictions

Explain that readers can use the same kinds of clues to make predictions about a story. They can use what they know from experience, along with what they read, to guess what might happen next.

On the Trail

As soon as the sun rose, Barney woke up. He stretched. He shivered a little as he crawled out of his tent. His stomach rumbled.

"Time's a-wastin'," Barney thought to himself. After all, a cowboy's life was a busy one. He had a long day's ride ahead and miles of fences to mend. He'd better get started.

Barney lit the fire. While the fire grew bigger and hotter, Barney searched through his pack. He took out a pan and some flour and shortening. He brought water from a nearby stream.

Teaching Chart 31

Read the Story and Model the Skill

Display **Teaching Chart 31.** Model making predictions.

MODEL I know from the story that Barney is a cowboy who is out on the trail by himself. It is early morning and he is hungry. When I'm hungry, I get something to eat. In the morning, I eat breakfast. Barney has everything he needs to make a meal. I think he will make breakfast now.

PRACTICE

Create a Predictions Chart

ONE

Have students underline and discuss clues that helped them predict what Barney would do next. Then point out that making a Predictions chart can help readers keep track of their predictions and what happens in the story. ▶ **Linguistic/Visual**

PREDICTIONS	WHAT HAPPENED
Barney will make breakfast.	

Finish the Story

GROUP

Have groups write two different endings for "On the Trail": one ending in which what they predicted happens and one in which something else happens instead. ▶ **Interpersonal/Linguistic**

ASSESS/CLOSE

Use Clues to Make More Predictions

Ask students to predict what the rest of Barney's day might be like. (Sample answer: He will ride and fix fences. Then he will find a place to camp and make dinner.) **What clues did you use to make your predictions?** (Students should mention both story clues and clues that are based on their own experience.)

SELECTION Connection

Students will make predictions when they read *Justin and the Best Biscuits in the World* and the Leveled Books.

ALTERNATE TEACHING STRATEGY

MAKE PREDICTIONS

For a different approach to teaching this skill, see page T60.

Meeting Individual Needs for Comprehension

EASY	ON-LEVEL	CHALLENGE

EASY

Name_____ Date_____ Reteach **38**

Make Predictions

When you think ahead about what may or may not happen next in a story, you **make a prediction.**

Read the sentences. Then circle what you think will happen.

1. Annette gives the cashier a $10 bill for a movie ticket that costs $8.50. What do you think Annette will do next?
   a. look for a place to sit
   (b.) wait for change from the cashier
   c. buy candy

2. Roger loves to be outdoors and to exercise. Today, he is going to the movies. The theater is 1 mile away from home. How do you think he will get there?
   (a.) walk   b. take a bus   c. ask his mother for a ride

3. Traci wants to buy a special CD as a gift for a friend. It costs $16 but she has only $10. What do you think Traci might do?
   a. forget about the whole idea
   (b.) find a way to earn the money that she needs
   c. buy a cheaper CD

4. Nick just remembered that Mia's birthday party is tomorrow. He knows a store that is open for another hour. What do you think Nick will do?
   a. not go to the party
   b. buy a present after the party
   (c.) hurry to the store

5. Nadine decided to walk rather than take the bus home from school. When she had walked one block, it began to rain. What do you think Nadine will do?
   a. continue walking home
   b. call a friend for a ride
   (c.) go back and take the bus

Book 4/Unit 2
Justin and the Best Biscuits in the World   **38**

At Home: Have students watch a favorite television show. At a commercial break, have them predict what will happen next.

Reteach, 38

ON-LEVEL

Name_____ Date_____ Practice **38**

Make Predictions

As you read a story, you often ask yourself what will happen next. To answer your question, you think about clues in the story and your own experience. Then you **make a prediction,** or a guess, about what will happen.

Read the first part of the story, and make a prediction. Then check your prediction by reading the next part of the story. Answers may vary.

   Mike's aunt often told him not to read scary books before going to bed. But tonight Mike wanted to finish his book. He had to find out what happened next. Mike was well into the final chapter when he heard something. Was it his aunt downstairs? Was it something in the closet? "Probably just the wind," he thought.
   "Lights out, Mike!" called his aunt. Mike put the book down and turned off the light.

1. Why do you think Mike's aunt doesn't want him to read scary stories before going to bed? Possible answers: Mike will have a hard time going to sleep. Mike will have bad dreams.

2. What do you predict will happen after Mike turns off the light? Possible answer: He will lie awake listening for noises.

3. List the clues in the story that helped you make your prediction. Answers will vary, but should mention story clues.

4. Write your own ending to the story using predictions you have made. Possible answers: Mike's aunt warns him not to read scary stories before going to bed; Mike thinks he hears something scary.

Book 4/Unit 2
Justin and the Best Biscuits in the World   **38**

At Home: Have students write the beginning of a one-paragraph story that includes a predictable situation.

Practice, 38

CHALLENGE

Name_____ Date_____ Extend **38**

Make Predictions

A **prediction** is a guess about something that will happen in the future. Use the information in the paragraph below to make predictions about how the students will do on their spelling test Friday.

   Carlos reviewed the spelling words every night. Taylor, Natalie, and Julia formed a study group to quiz each other on the words. Jonathan looked over the spelling list on Monday. Chris played video games instead of studying.

Predict who you think will do well on the spelling test.
Carlos, Taylor, Natalie, and Julia

Predict who you think will not do well on the spelling test.
Jonathan and Chris

Predict what you will do to earn a living when you are an adult. Explain how you made your prediction.
Answers will vary.

Book 4/Unit 2
Justin and the Best Biscuits in the World   **38**

At Home: Have students make predictions about every day events and how they affect their actions and/or decisions.

Extend, 38

Build Background

Link

Social Studies

Anthology and Leveled Books

Evaluate Prior Knowledge

CONCEPT: COWBOYS In these stories, the characters are cowboys. Invite students to tell what they know about the history of cowboys, their jobs, and their daily lives.

SHARE INFORMATION Create a class K-W-L chart and invite students to fill in the first two columns together. Explain they will be adding to the chart as they learn more about cowboys. ▶ **Logical/Visual**

Know	**W**ant to Know	**L**earn
Old West	What do cowboys do?	
care for cattle	How do cowboys live?	
live on ranch work hard	What do rodeos have to do with cowboys?	

Graphic Organizer 27

DESCRIBE A DAY Have small groups discuss cowboy life. Then have them work together on a cowboy's diary, with each student writing an entry for one day.

GROUP · WRITING

Develop Oral Language

DISCUSS COWBOY LIFE If possible, show pictures from reference books or magazines of historic or modern-day cowboys at work or performing in rodeos. Ask students to describe what the cowboys are doing.

ESL

Using the students' ideas, write sentences on the chalkboard. Next, make a list of key vocabulary words they used that also appear in the story. Then add other cowboy-related words from the story, such as *ranch, mending fences, plains, mounted, foothills,* and *bales of hay*. Help students write a definition for each one and use it in a sentence. Leave the list of definitions on the chalkboard so they can refer back to it as they read the story.

TEACHING TIP

MANAGEMENT Post the K-W-L chart in the classroom and leave it on display. Set aside a few minutes each day to discuss, add to, and revise the chart.

Use the Develop Oral Language activity to make concepts about cowboy life concrete for students who need help with oral language facility.

LANGUAGE SUPPORT

See Language Support Book, pages 41–44, for teaching suggestions for Build Background and Vocabulary.

Vocabulary

Key Words

The Cowboy Festival

1. Both the cowboys and their horses seemed happy about celebrating at the festival. 2. Cheerful echoing shouts resounded through the fairgrounds. 3. The horses pranced and danced with excitement. 4. Justin walked through the barn, looking over the ponies and carefully inspecting the ones he liked best. 5. He stopped walking and lingered for a little while to pet one pony that he wished he could ride. 6. Justin was glad he had finished his chores early in the morning, because now he wouldn't have to feel any guilt about enjoying this great day.

Teaching Chart 32

Vocabulary in Context

IDENTIFY VOCABULARY WORDS
Display **Teaching Chart 32** and read the passage with students. Have volunteers circle each vocabulary word and underline other words that are clues to its meaning.

DISCUSS MEANINGS Ask questions like these to help clarify word meanings:

- Is a festival a sad event or a happy one?
- What word do you get if you cover the prefix and suffix in *resounded?*
- How would a horse that is prancing move? Show me.
- What are you doing when you examine something very carefully?
- If you lingered on the way to class, would you be likely to arrive on time?
- Would a person who felt guilt look sad?

Practice

DEMONSTRATE WORD MEANING Have students take turns choosing a vocabulary card and using the word as they tell a partner about an experience from their own life.
▶ **Oral/Linguistic**

Word Building Manipulative Cards

WRITE SYNONYM SENTENCES Ask students to write sentences with synonyms for each vocabulary word. Students can exchange papers, find the synonyms, and hold up the correct vocabulary card. ▶ **Linguistic**

Definitions

festival (p.137) a special celebration, often held yearly

resounded (p. 144) echoed, or filled with sound

pranced (p. 143) walked with high, lively steps

inspecting (p. 138) looking at closely and carefully

lingered (p. 140) stayed in one place for a long time

guilt (p. 136) a feeling of shame

SPELLING/VOCABULARY CONNECTIONS

See Spelling Challenge Words, pages 157O–157P.

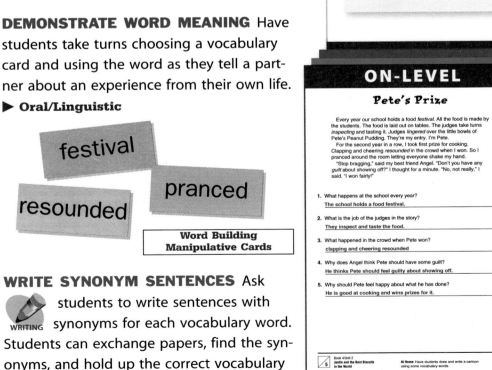

ON-LEVEL

Pete's Prize

Every year our school holds a food *festival*. All the food is made by the students. The food is laid out on tables. The judges take turns *inspecting* and tasting it. Judges *lingered* over the little bowls of Pete's Peanut Pudding. They're my entry. I'm Pete.

For the second year in a row, I took first prize for cooking. Clapping and cheering *resounded* in the crowd when I won. So I pranced around the room letting everyone shake my hand.

"Stop bragging," said my best friend Angel. "Don't you have any *guilt* about showing off?" I thought for a minute. "No, not really," I said. "I won fairly!"

1. What happens at the school every year?
   The school holds a food festival.

2. What is the job of the judges in the story?
   They inspect and taste the food.

3. What happened in the crowd when Pete won?
   clapping and cheering resounded

4. Why does Angel think Pete should have some guilt?
   He thinks Pete should feel guilty about showing off.

5. Why should Pete feel happy about what he has done?
   He is good at cooking and wins prizes for it.

Book 4/Unit 2
Justin and the Best Biscuits in the World

At Home: Have students draw and write a cartoon using some vocabulary words. 39a

Take-Home Story 39a
Reteach 39
Practice 39 • Extend 39

Guided Instruction

Preview and Predict

Display the title page and ask a volunteer to read aloud the title and the names of the author and illustrator. Have students page through the story to look at the illustrations.

- The story seems to have two settings. What are they?
- How can you tell how the man and the boy might feel about each other?
- What kinds of things do the boy and the man do together?
- Do you think this story is realistic or a fantasy? Why? (It is realistic because the characters look like real people and the settings look like real places.) *Genre*

Let students read the introduction to find out what happened before the story begins. Then invite students to make predictions about the kinds of things that Justin will learn from his grandfather.

Set Purposes

Ask students to tell what they want to learn from the story. For example:

- What kinds of things do cowboys do?
- How do you make the "best biscuits in the world"?

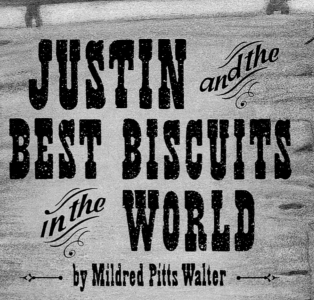

JUSTIN and the BEST BISCUITS in the WORLD

by Mildred Pitts Walter

Ten-year-old Justin lives with his mother and two sisters. Justin's family expects him to help with the household chores, but he thinks cooking and cleaning are women's work. He would rather play ball with his friend Anthony. When Justin's cowboy grandfather invites him to visit his ranch, Justin is delighted. Justin is certain that he and his grandfather will do real men's work together, like riding the range. But Justin's grandfather is full of surprises. Before his visit is over, Justin learns a lot more from his grandfather than he ever imagined.

Illustrated by Floyd Cooper

134

Meeting Individual Needs • Grouping Suggestions for Strategic Reading

EASY	ON-LEVEL	CHALLENGE
Read Together Students may read along with the **Listening Library Audiocassette** or read the story together with the class. Stop periodically to let students predict what will happen next. Use Guided Instruction and Intervention prompts to help with vocabulary and comprehension.	**Guided Reading** Introduce the story words on page 135. Then use the Guided Instruction questions as you read the story with students, or let students read along with the **Listening Library Audiocassette** before discussing the questions. Have students stop periodically to make and confirm predictions.	**Read Independently** Before students read the story on their own, remind them that making predictions as they read will help them understand the story. Suggest that they stop occasionally to jot down predictions. After reading, students can check their predictions.

135

Guided Instruction

☑ **Make Predictions**

Strategic Reading Before we start, let's make a chart to keep track of our predictions.

PREDICTIONS	WHAT HAPPENED

① **MAKE PREDICTIONS** We learn on page 134 that Justin thinks of some chores as "women's work." We also find that Justin will learn things from his grandfather. What kinds of things do you predict Justin will learn from his grandfather?

MODEL I suspect that Justin's grandfather does many of the things Justin thinks are "women's work," and does them well. Because Justin seems to respect his grandfather, I predict Justin may learn to cook and do other housework, too.

Story Words

The words below may be unfamiliar. Have students check their meanings and pronunciations in the Glossary beginning on page 726 or in a dictionary.

- ranch, p. 134
- soapsuds, p. 136
- foothills, p. 140
- utensils, p. 144
- skillet, p. 145

LANGUAGE SUPPORT

A blackline master of the Predictions chart is available in the **Language Support Book.**

Name_____ Date_____
Make Predictions

Predictions	What Happened

Grade 4   Language Support / Blackline Master 21 • Justin and the Best Biscuits in the World 45

LANGUAGE SUPPORT, 45

135

Guided Instruction

2 How does Grandpa feel about doing "women's work"? How do you know? (Grandpa must think it is all right to do any kind of chore because he does household chores like cooking and cleaning up without stalling or complaining.) *Make Inferences*

3 **MAKE PREDICTIONS** Justin feels "a strange feeling of guilt" about not helping with the household chores. What do you think Justin will do the next time a household chore needs to be done?

MODEL I read that Justin feels guilty because he didn't help Grandpa. I know how he feels. Sometimes I feel guilty about things I've left undone, too. I don't like that feeling, so I try to avoid it by doing the right thing the next time. I predict Justin will try to avoid feeling guilty by helping out the next time a household chore needs to be done.

The smell of coffee and home-smoked ham woke Justin. His grandpa was already up and downstairs cooking breakfast. Justin jumped out of bed and quickly put on his clothes.

Grandpa had hot pancakes, apple jelly, and ham all ready for the table. Justin ate two stacks of pancakes with two helpings of everything else.

After breakfast, Grandpa cleared the table, preparing to wash the dishes. "Would you rather wash or dry?" he asked Justin.

"Neither," Justin replied, quickly thinking how little success he had with dishes.

Grandpa said nothing as he removed the dishes from the table. He took his time, carefully measuring liquid soap and letting hot water run in the sink. Then he washed each dish and rinsed it with care, too. No water splashed or spilled. Soapsuds were not all over. How easy it looked, the way Grandpa did it.

After washing the dishes, Grandpa swept the floor and then went upstairs.

Justin stood around downstairs. He had a strange feeling of guilt and wished he had helped with the dishes. He heard Grandpa moving about, above in his room. Justin thought of going outside, down into the meadow, but he decided to see what was going on upstairs.

When he saw his grandpa busy making his own big bed, Justin went into his room. His unmade bed and his pajamas on the floor bothered him. But he decided that the room didn't look too bad. He picked

136

LANGUAGE SUPPORT

ESL Pantomime several of the actions described on these pages and ask students to guess what you are doing. For example, you might mime cooking breakfast, washing the dishes, and making the bed. Help them find the correct phrase to describe each task.

Then invite students to take turns pantomiming some of the other actions. For example, they might act out picking up clothes, unpacking clothes, and hanging clothes on hangers. Have the rest of the class guess what they are doing.

up his pajamas and placed them on the bed and sat beside them. He waited.

Finally Grandpa came in and said, "Are you riding fence with me today?"

"Oh yes!"

"Fine. But why don't you make your bed? You'll probably feel pretty tired tonight. A well-made bed can be a warm welcome."

Justin moved slowly, reluctant to let Grandpa see him struggle with the bed. He started. What a surprise! Everything was tightly in place. He only had to smooth the covers. The bed was made. No lumps and bumps. Justin looked at Grandpa and grinned broadly. "That was easy!" he shouted.

④

"Don't you think you should unpack your clothes? They won't need ironing if you hang them up. You gotta look razor sharp for the festival." He gave Justin some clothes hangers.

"Are we *really* going to the festival every day?" Justin asked.

"You bet, starting with the judging early tomorrow and the dance tomorrow night." Grandpa winked at him.

137

Guided Instruction

④ Why did Justin hesitate before making his bed? (He was afraid he would do a clumsy job.) *Cause and Effect*

Minilesson

REVIEW/MAINTAIN

Context Clues

Remind students that they can often figure out the meaning of an unfamiliar word by reading the words around it, or its context.

- Point out *reluctant* in the fifth paragraph.
- Ask them to find words or phrases in the sentences around the word that give clues to its meaning. (moved slowly, struggle)
- Help students use the clues to determine what *reluctant* means.

Activity Have each student find a difficult word in the dictionary, write a sentence including both the word and context clues, and trade sentences with a partner, who should try to determine the word's meaning.

137

Guided Instruction

5 What, according to Grandpa, are the steps for folding a shirt neatly? (1. Turn it so the buttons face down. 2. Bring the sleeves to the back. 3. Turn in the sides of the shirt so the sleeves are on top of the facedown shirt. 4. Fold the tail of the shirt over the cuffs. 5. Fold the shirt again to bring the bottom of the shirt up to the collar.) *Steps in a Process*

6 Think about the generalization that Grandpa just made. Do you agree with him? Why or why not? *Critical Thinking*

5 Justin's excitement faded when he started unpacking his rumpled shirts. "They sure are wrinkled, Grandpa," he said.

"Maybe that's because they weren't folded."

"I can't ever get them folded right," Justin cried.

"Well, let's see. Turn it so the buttons face down." Grandpa showed Justin how to bring the sleeves to the back, turning in the sides so that the sleeves were on top. Then he folded the tail of the shirt over the cuffs, and made a second fold up to the collar. "Now you try it."

Justin tried it. "Oh, I see. That was easy, Grandpa." Justin smiled, pleased with himself.

6 "Everything's easy when you know how."

Justin, happy with his new-found skill, hurriedly placed his clothes on the hangers. He hoped the wrinkles would disappear in time for the festival.

"Now you'll look sharp," Grandpa said.

Justin felt a surge of love for his grandpa. He would always remember how to make a bed snug as a bug and fold clothes neatly. He grabbed Grandpa's hand. They walked downstairs, still holding hands, to get ready to ride fence.

7 Riding fence meant inspecting the fence all around the ranch to see where it needed mending. Riding fence took a great deal of a rancher's time. Justin and Grandpa planned to spend most of the day out on the plains. Grandpa said he'd pack a lunch for them to eat on the far side of the ranch.

138

Activity

Cross Curricular: Math

CHANGING SHAPES Reread Grandpa's directions for folding a shirt into a neat rectangular shape. Then give pairs of students four paper triangles and model how to use the triangles to form a square with all four right angles meeting at a center point.

One partner can hide his or her puzzle behind a book and form a new shape. Then that student can give directions for forming the shape to the partner. Afterward, let students remove the book to see how well the shapes match.

▶ **Kinesthetic/Visual**

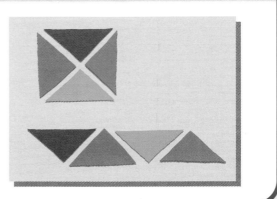

Guided Instruction

7 How does Justin feel about himself after doing several chores well? (He is happy and no longer afraid of making a mistake because he knows he will remember how to do them well.) *Character*

LANGUAGE SUPPORT

ESL For students who have difficulty following Grandpa's directions for folding a shirt to pack it or visualizing the steps, bring in a child's shirt and demonstrate how to fold it. Follow the directions from page 138, and talk about each step as you do it. Then let students repeat the demonstration, following your model by demonstrating and talking through the steps.

Guided Instruction

8 **MAKE PREDICTIONS** Justin was surprised at the things Grandpa packed for lunch. What do you think Grandpa plans to do about lunch? (He will cook lunch out on the trail. Because of the story's title, students should predict that lunch would probably include biscuits.)

Let's look at some of the predictions we've made so far and see how they turned out. We can keep track by filling out our chart.

PREDICTIONS	WHAT HAPPENED
Justin will learn about household chores and learn to help out more.	So far Justin has learned to make his bed neatly and fold shirts.
Since Grandpa brought ingredients instead of a finished lunch, he probably plans to cook out.	

COMPOUND WORDS Read the first sentence in the third paragraph. What two smaller words do you see in the word *hilltops*? (*hill* and *tops*) What do you think the word *hilltops* means? (the tops of hills)

Justin was surprised when Grandpa packed only flour, raisins, shortening, and chunks of smoked pork. He also packed jugs of water and makings for coffee.

The horses stood in the meadow as if they knew a busy day awaited them. While Grandpa saddled Pal, he let Justin finish the saddling of Black Lightning. Justin tightened the cinches on Black,

feeling the strong pull on his arm muscles. With their supplies in their saddlebags, they mounted Pal and Black, leaving Cropper behind to graze in the meadow.

The early sun shone fiery red on the hilltops while the foothills were cast in shades of purple. The dew still lingered heavily on the morning. They let their horses canter away past the house through the tall green grass. But on the outer edge of the ranch where the fence started, they walked the horses at a steady pace.

The fence had three rows of taut wire. "That's a pretty high fence," Justin said.

"We have to keep the cattle in. But deer sometimes leap that fence and eat hay with the cattle." When it got bitter cold and frosty, Grandpa rode

140

PREVENTION/INTERVENTION

COMPOUND WORDS Tell students that *hilltops* is a compound word, or a long word that is made up of two smaller complete words. Explain that breaking the compound word into its two parts, *hill* and *tops,* can help them read the word more easily and determine its meaning. Have students reread the sentence and find another compound word. (foothills) Then ask students to find the compound word in the second paragraph. (saddlebags) Guide them to break the compound word into its two parts. Help them use the two smaller words to determine the meaning of *saddlebags.* (bags that are attached to a saddle)

around the ranch dropping bales of hay for the cattle. It took a lot of hay to feed the cattle during the winter months.

"I didn't think a cow could jump very high," Justin said.

"Aw, come on. Surely you know that a cow jumped over the moon." Grandpa had a serious look on his face.

"I guess that's a joke, eh?" Justin laughed.

Justin noticed that Grandpa had a map. When they came to a place in the fence that looked weak, Grandpa marked it on his map. Later, helpers who came to do the work would know exactly where to mend. That saved time.

Now the sun heated up the morning. The foothills were now varying shades of green. Shadows dotted the plains. Among the blackish green trees on the rolling hills, fog still lingered like lazy clouds. Insects buzzed. A small cloud of mosquitoes swarmed just behind their heads, and beautiful cardinals splashed their redness on the morning air. Justin felt a surge of happiness and hugged Black with his knees and heels.

Suddenly he saw a doe standing close to the fence. "Look, Grandpa!" he said. She seemed alarmed but did not run away. Doe eyes usually look peaceful and sad, Justin remembered. Hers widened with fear. Then Justin saw a fawn caught in the wire of the fence.

Quickly they got off their horses. They hitched them to a post and moved cautiously toward the fawn.

(9)

141

Guided Instruction

(9) MAKE PREDICTIONS A fawn is caught in the fence. What do you think will happen next?

MODEL The fawn really seems to be in danger. I know that Grandpa is very good at housework, but he seems like someone who'd be good at anything. I think the doe might try to attack him, but that Grandpa will save the fawn.

TEACHING TIP

INSTRUCTIONAL Children whose cultural background does not include Western nursery rhymes may not understand Grandpa's joke about the cow that jumped over the moon.

Invite a volunteer to recite "Hey, Diddle, Diddle":
Hey, diddle, diddle, the cat and the fiddle.
The cow jumped over the moon.
The little dog laughed to see such sport,
And the dish ran away with the spoon.

Invite volunteers to share familiar nursery rhymes from their own cultures.

Guided Instruction

10 **MAKE PREDICTIONS** Look carefully at the illustration on this page. What does it tell you about what will happen to the fawn? Does the information the picture adds make you want to change your prediction? (Sample answer: No, I thought Grandpa would help the fawn.)

142

<Activity>

Cross Curricular: Science

ANIMAL NAMES Have students read paragraph 7 on page 143 to find two animal names. Help them use context to determine that doe is the name for a female deer and that fawn is the name for a baby deer. Ask what we call a male deer. (buck or stag)

Work with students to make a chart of the different names given adult male, adult female, and baby animals of the same species. Begin with animals in the story, such as cattle and horses. Extend the activity to other kinds of animals. ▶
Interpersonal/Linguistic

Animal Names

	Male	Female	Baby
Deer	Stag	Doe	Fawn
Horse	Stallion	Mare	Colt
Bovine	Bull	Cow	Calf

The mother rushed to the fence but stopped just short of the sharp wire. "Stay back and still," Grandpa said to Justin. "She doesn't know we will help her baby. She thinks we might hurt it. She wants to protect it."

The mother pranced restlessly. She pawed the ground, moving as close to the fence as she could. Near the post the fence had been broken. The wire curled there dangerously. The fawn's head, caught in the wire, bled close to an ear. Whenever it pulled its head the wire cut deeper.

Grandpa quickly untangled the fawn's head.

Blood flowed from the cut.

"Oh, Grandpa, it will die," Justin said sadly.

"No, no," Grandpa assured Justin. "Lucky we got here when we did. It hasn't been caught long."

The fawn moved toward the doe. The mother, as if giving her baby a signal, bounded off. The baby trotted behind.

As they mounted their horses, Justin suddenly felt weak in the stomach. Remembering the blood, he trembled. Black, too, seemed uneasy. He moved his nostrils nervously and strained against the bit. He arched his neck and sidestepped quickly. Justin pulled the reins. "Whoa, boy!"

"Let him run," Grandpa said.

Justin kicked Black's sides and off they raced across the plain. They ran and ran, Justin pretending he was rounding up cattle. Then Black turned and raced back toward Grandpa and Pal.

"Whoa, boy," Justin commanded. Justin felt better and Black seemed calm, ready now to go on riding fence.

143

Guided Instruction

(11) MAKE PREDICTIONS Both Justin and Black seem uneasy. What do you think will happen next? (Students may say that the horse will throw Justin off or that Justin will be able to control the horse.)

PREFIXES Find the words *untangled* in the third paragraph and *uneasy* five paragraphs later. How are the two words alike? What do the words mean?

Minilesson

REVIEW/MAINTAIN

Syllable Patterns

Review these syllable patterns:

- A two-syllable word with the VCCV pattern is usually divided between the consonants. The vowel sound in the first syllable is short: **bet ter   sig nal.**
- If a two-syllable word with the VCV pattern is divided after the consonant, the vowel sound in the first syllable is short: **giv ing.**
- If a two-syllable word with the VCV pattern is divided before the consonant, the vowel sound in the first syllable is long: **ba by.**

Activity Have students syllabicate and pronounce these words: *broken, center, female, doctor, magic, tiger, punish.*

PREVENTION/INTERVENTION

PREFIXES Write *untangled* and *uneasy* on the board, and invite a volunteer to circle the word part that the words have in common. (*un-*)

Explain that *un-* is a prefix. A prefix is a word part that is added at the beginning of a word. Adding a prefix gives a new meaning to the word. Help students conclude that the prefix *un-* means "not", so *untangled* means "not tangled," and *uneasy* means "not easy." Have students find other familiar prefixes in the story.

143

Guided Instruction

(12) MAKE PREDICTIONS What prediction did you make about lunch? Let's add to our Predictions chart.

PREDICTIONS	WHAT HAPPENED
Justin will learn about household chores and learn to help out more.	So far Justin has learned to make his bed neatly and fold shirts.
Since Grandpa brought ingredients instead of a finished lunch, he probably plans to cook out.	Grandpa makes biscuits.

SELF-MONITORING

STRATEGY

REREAD There are many reasons why a story event may not happen the way readers predicted. When readers make a wrong prediction, rereading can help them find clues they missed on the first reading.

he sun beamed down and sweat rolled off Justin as he rode on with Grandpa, looking for broken wires in the fence. They were well away from the house, on the far side of the ranch. Flies buzzed around the horses and now gnats swarmed in clouds just above their heads. The prairie resounded with songs of the bluebirds, the bobwhite quails, and the mockingbirds mimicking them all. The cardinal's song, as lovely as any, included a whistle.

Justin thought of Anthony and how Anthony whistled for Pepper, his dog.

It was well past noon and Justin was hungry. Soon they came upon a small, well-built shed, securely locked. Nearby was a small stream. Grandpa reined in his horse. When he and Justin dismounted, they hitched the horses, and unsaddled them.

"We'll have our lunch here," Grandpa said. Justin was surprised when Grandpa took black iron pots, other cooking utensils, and a table from the shed. Justin helped him remove some iron rods that Grandpa carefully placed over a shallow pit. These would hold the pots. Now Justin understood why Grandpa had brought uncooked food. They were going to cook outside.

First they collected twigs and cow dung. Grandpa called it cowchips. "These," Grandpa said, holding up a dried brown pad, "make the best fuel. Gather them up."

There were plenty of chips left from the cattle that had fed there in winter. Soon they had a hot fire.

Justin watched as Grandpa carefully washed his hands and then began to cook their lunch.

144

Activity

Cross Curricular: Social Studies

PRAIRIES On this page, students will find the word *prairie*, along with a description of some of the sights and sounds of a prairie. Have students make an illustration for this page, showing the geography of a prairie environment.

If necessary, students may look for photos of prairies in encyclopedias, social studies texts, or magazines. They may also find clues in the story illustrations.

"When I was a boy about your age, I used to go with my father on short runs with cattle. We'd bring them down from the high country onto the plains."

"Did you stay out all night?"

"Sometimes. And that was the time I liked most. The cook often made for supper what I am going to make for lunch."

Grandpa put raisins into a pot with a little water and placed them over the fire. Justin was surprised when Grandpa put flour in a separate pan. He used his fist to make a hole right in the middle of the flour. In that hole he placed some shortening. Then he added water. With his long delicate fingers he mixed the flour, water, and shortening until he had a nice round mound of dough.

⑫

Soon smooth circles of biscuits sat in an iron skillet with a lid on top. Grandpa put the skillet on the fire with some of the red-hot chips scattered over the lid.

Justin was amazed. How could only those ingredients make good bread? But he said nothing as Grandpa put the chunks of smoked pork in a skillet and started them cooking. Soon the smell was so delicious, Justin could hardly wait.

⑬

Finally, Grandpa suggested that Justin take the horses to drink at the stream. "Keep your eyes open and don't step on any snakes."

145

Guided Instruction

⑬ **What are the directions for making** "the best biscuits in the world"? List the steps in order. (Put flour in a pan and make a hole in the middle of the flour. Place shortening in the hole. Add water. Mix. Cut into circle shapes. Cook in a skillet over a fire. Serve with stewed raisins.) **Who would like to role-play Justin and Grandpa? Pantomime Justin watching Grandpa make the biscuits, and make up some dialogue.** *Steps in a Process; Role-Play*

CONTEXT CLUES **What is a** *skillet?* **What clues to its meaning can you find?**

⚫ᵖ/ᵢ **PREVENTION/INTERVENTION**

CONTEXT CLUES Explain that when students are unclear about the exact meaning of a word—even if they get the general meaning— context clues can help.

• Guide students to see that from what they know of the situation, or context, they should be able to tell that a skillet is something used for cooking.

• Students may guess that because the skillet must survive rough treatment on the prairie and sit directly on hot fires, it is probably made of a heavy, strong metal.

• Knowing the nuances of a word can help readers enjoy the flavor of a story.

145

Guided Instruction

(14) MAKE PREDICTIONS What warning did Grandpa give Justin just before he went off to the stream? ("Don't step on any snakes.") Do you think Justin will see a snake? Why or why not? (Some students may say that the warning foreshadows a problem with a snake. Others may say that since Grandpa teases a lot, he's probably teasing now, too.)

TEACHING **TIP**

INSTRUCTIONAL To explain the reference on page 147 to "egg on the floor . . . rice burning," have students look back at the introduction on page 134. Point out that this selection is an excerpt from a novel. Explain that earlier in the novel, Justin had tried to prepare some eggs and rice in his kitchen at home. He had made a mess, and his sister had yelled at him for his failure. Later, Justin had cried and complained about housework being "women's work" in front of his grandfather, who was visiting.

146

Justin knew that diamondback rattlers sometimes lurked around. They were dangerous. He must be careful. He watered Black first.

While watering Pal, he heard rustling in the grass. His heart pounded. He heard the noise again. He wanted to run, but was too afraid. He looked around carefully. There were two black eyes staring at him. He tried to pull Pal away from the water, but Pal refused to stop drinking. Then Justin saw the animal. It had a long tail like a rat's. But it was as big as a cat. Then he saw something crawling on its back. They were little babies, hanging on as the animal ran.

A mama opossum and her babies, he thought, and was no longer afraid.

By the time the horses were watered, lunch was ready. *"M-mm-m,"* Justin said as he reached for a plate. The biscuits were golden brown, yet fluffy inside. And the sizzling pork was now crisp. Never had he eaten stewed raisins before.

"Grandpa, I didn't know you could cook like this," Justin said when he had tasted the food. "I didn't know men could cook so good."

"Why, Justin, some of the best cooks in the world are men."

Justin remembered the egg on the floor and his rice burning. The look he gave Grandpa revealed his doubts.

"It's true," Grandpa said. "All the cooks on the cattle trail were men. In hotels and restaurants they call them chefs."

"How did you make these biscuits?"

(14)

(15)

147

Guided Instruction

(15) **Before eating the biscuits, what does Justin think about male cooks in general?** (He didn't think men could be good cooks.) **What does Justin learn from Grandpa about male cooks?** (Some of the best cooks, both on the trail and in hotels and restaurants, are men.) *Form Generalizations*

Minilesson

REVIEW/MAINTAIN

Make Inferences

Remind students they can make inferences as they read by putting together evidence from the text with facts they already know.

- With student's books closed, read aloud the first three paragraphs.

- Pause after *He heard the noise again; two black eyes staring at him;* and *refused to stop drinking* to let students make inferences about whether or not the animal in the grass is really a snake.

Activity Ask volunteers to tell what they were thinking after each pause. Ask when they realized the animal was harmless.

147

Guided Instruction

(16) MAKE PREDICTIONS How do you know that Justin is beginning to believe that cooking is not just "women's work"? (When Grandpa offers to let Justin make biscuits, Justin does not say no.) Check your predictions. Did you predict that this would happen?

(17) Why do you think the author may have included information about African American cowboys? (The author wants the reader to learn from Grandpa's story, too.) *Author's Purpose/Critical Thinking*

(16) "That's a secret. One day I'll let you make some."

"Were you a cowboy, Grandpa?"

"I'm still a cowboy."

"No, you're not."

"Yes, I am. I work with cattle, so I'm a cowboy."

"You know what I mean. The kind who rides bulls, broncobusters. That kind of cowboy."

"No, I'm not that kind. But I know some."

"Are they famous?"

"No, but I did meet a real famous Black cowboy once. When I was eight years old, my grandpa took me to meet his friend Bill Pickett. Bill Pickett was an old man then. He had a ranch in Oklahoma."

"Were there lots of Black cowboys?"

"Yes. Lots of them. They were hard workers, too. They busted broncos, branded calves, and drove cattle. My grandpa tamed wild mustangs."

"Bet they were famous."

"Oh, no. Some were. Bill Pickett created the sport of bulldogging. You'll see that at the rodeo. One cowboy named Williams taught Rough Rider Teddy Roosevelt how to break horses; and another one named Clay taught Will Rogers, the comedian, the art of roping." Grandpa offered Justin the last biscuit.

When they had finished their lunch they led the horses away from the shed to graze. As they watched the horses, Grandpa went on, "Now, there were some more very famous Black cowboys. Jessie Stahl. They say he was the best rider of wild horses in the West."

(17) "How could he be? Nobody ever heard about him. I didn't."

(148)

CULTURAL PERSPECTIVES

AFRICAN AMERICAN COWBOYS On the chalkboard, list the African American cowboys mentioned on pages 148–149: Bill Pickett, Williams, Clay, Jessie Stahl, and Nate Love.

RESEARCH AND INQUIRY Ask students to research the life of an African American cowboy. Suggest they role-play the cowboy they researched.
▶ **Oral/Kinesthetic**

inter NET CONNECTION Students can learn more about African American cowboys by visiting **www.mhschool.com/reading**

PRESENTING BILL PICKETT

"Oh, there're lots of famous Blacks you never hear or read about. You ever hear about Deadwood Dick?"

Justin laughed. "No."

"There's another one. His real name was Nate Love. He could outride, outshoot anyone. In Deadwood City in the Dakota Territory, he roped, tied, saddled, mounted, and rode a wild horse faster than anyone. Then in the shooting match, he hit the bull's-eye every time. The people named him Deadwood Dick right on the spot. Enough about cowboys, now. While the horses graze, let's clean up here and get back to our men's work."

Justin felt that Grandpa was still teasing him, the way he had in Justin's room when he had placed his hand on Justin's shoulder. There was still the sense of shame whenever the outburst about women's work and the tears were remembered.

As they cleaned the utensils and dishes, Justin asked, "Grandpa, you think housework is women's work?"

(18)

"Do you?" Grandpa asked quickly.

"I asked you first, Grandpa."

"I guess asking you that before I answer is unfair. No, I don't. Do you?"

"Well, it seems easier for them," Justin said as he splashed water all over, glad he was outside.

149

Guided Instruction

(18) What further evidence can you find that Justin is now ready to stop thinking that some kinds of work are for women only? (Justin pitches in to help clean up without complaint.) *Make Inferences*

Minilesson

REVIEW/MAINTAIN

Main Idea

Remind students that the main idea is the key idea in a paragraph, section, or story.

- Have students reread pages 148–149, from "No, but I did meet a real famous Black cowboy once " to "let's clean up and get back to our men's work."

- Ask them to state the main idea of the passage in one sentence. (There were many Black cowboys.)

- Then ask them to cite supporting details.

Activity Have students make a simple outline of the main idea and its supporting details.

149

Guided Instruction

(19) Grandpa makes this generalization about work: "The better you do it, the easier it becomes, and we seem not to mind doing things that are easy." What things that used to be hard for you are things you enjoy doing now? (Answers will vary.) *Form Generalizations*

"Easier than for me?"

"Well, not for you, I guess, but for me, yeah."

"Could it be because you don't know how?"

"You mean like making the bed and folding the clothes."

"Yes." Grandpa stopped and looked at Justin. "Making the bed is easy now, isn't it? All work is that way. It doesn't matter who does the work, man or woman, when it needs to be done. What matters is that we try to learn how to do it the best we can in the most enjoyable way."

"I don't think I'll ever like housework," Justin said, drying a big iron pot.

(19) "It's like any other kind of work. The better you do it, the easier it becomes, and we seem not to mind doing things that are easy."

With the cooking rods and all the utensils put away, they locked the shed and went for their horses.

"Now, I'm going to let you do the cinches again. You'll like that."

There's that teasing again, Justin thought. "Yeah. That's a man's work," he said, and mounted Black.

"There are some good horsewomen. You'll see them at the rodeo." Grandpa mounted Pal. They went on their way, riding along silently, scanning the fence.

Finally Justin said, "I was just kidding, Grandpa." Then without planning to, he said, "I bet you don't like boys who cry like babies."

(20) "Do I know any boys who cry like babies?"

"Aw, Grandpa, you saw me crying."

150

Activity

Cross Curricular: Music

CAMPFIRE FUN Explain cowboys on the range in the old West had to learn to entertain themselves as they sat around the campfire in the evenings. They could talk, as Grandpa and Justin do, or tell stories like the ones that Grandpa tells about the African American cowboys.

Sometimes they sang cowboy songs. With students, sing a few familiar cowboy songs like *Home on the Range*, *The Yellow Rose of Texas,* and *Good-bye Old Paint*. You might like to play old recordings of singing cowboys, like Roy Rogers and Gene Autry.

HOME ON THE RANGE

Oh, give me a home...

151

Guided Instruction

20 **MAKE PREDICTIONS** From what you now know about Grandpa, what do you think that he'll say about Justin's crying? Pretend you are Grandpa. Tell us what you might say. (Students may say that just as Grandpa feels it's okay for anyone to do any kind of work, it's also okay for anyone to cry.) *Role-Play*

Fluency

DIALOGUE This story provides an opportunity for students to practice fluent reading of narrative dialogue. Student volunteers can assume the roles of the characters and of the author's voice.

You may want to model fluent reading of the conversation between Grandpa and Justin on page 151. Have students practice reading the parts. Encourage them to give one another helpful suggestions about how they can improve accuracy, rate, and expressiveness.

Guided Instruction

(21) MAKE PREDICTIONS Let's complete our Predictions chart. Did you predict what would happen in the story? Why may some of your predictions have been different from what happened?

PREDICTIONS	WHAT HAPPENED
Justin will learn about household chores and learn to help out more.	So far Justin has learned to make his bed neatly and fold shirts.
Since Grandpa brought ingredients instead of a finished lunch, he probably plans to cook out.	Grandpa makes biscuits.
Justin will decide there is no such thing as "women's work."	Justin helps Grandpa clean up after lunch without complaining.

RETELL THE STORY Invite students to name the major events in the story. Students may refer to their Predictions charts. Let students work with partners to write a brief summary focusing on ways Justin changed. *Summarize*

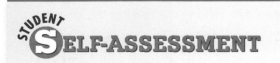 SELF-ASSESSMENT

- How did making predictions as I read help me better understand the story?
- Did making predictions make the story more interesting?

TRANSFERRING THE STRATEGY

- When might I try using this strategy again?

"Oh, I didn't think you were crying like a baby. In your room, you mean? We all cry sometime."

"You? Cry, Grandpa?"

"Sure."

They rode on, with Grandpa marking his map. Justin remained quiet, wondering what could make a man like Grandpa cry.

As if knowing Justin's thoughts, Grandpa said, "I remember crying when you were born."

"Why? Didn't you want me?"

"Oh, yes. You were the most beautiful baby. But, you see, your grandma, Beth, had just died. When I held you I was flooded with joy. Then I thought, *Grandma will never see this beautiful boy.* I cried."

The horses wading through the grass made the only sound in the silence. Then Grandpa said, "There's an old saying, son. 'The brave hide their fears, but share their tears.' Tears bathe the soul."

Justin looked at his grandpa. Their eyes caught. A warmth spread over Justin and he lowered his eyes. He wished he could tell his grandpa all he felt, how much he loved him.

(21)

152

REREADING FOR *Fluency*

GROUP Have groups of three students read a section with dialogue, taking the roles of Grandpa, Justin, and narrator.

READING RATE You may want to evaluate a student's reading rate. Have the student read aloud from *Justin and the Best Biscuits in the World* for one minute. Ask the student to place a stick-on note after the last word read. Then count the number of words he or she read.

Alternatively, you could assess small groups or the whole class together by having students count words and record their own scores.

A Running Record form provided in **Diagnostic/Placement Evaluation** will help you evaluate reading rate(s).

meet

MILDRED PITTS WALTER

Mildred Pitts Walter wrote her first book, *Lillie of Watts*, when she was a teacher in Los Angeles. Since then she has written a number of award-winning books about African-American children, including *Justin and the Best Biscuits in the World*, which won the Coretta Scott King Award.

African-American traditions are often a part of Walter's stories. In *Have a Happy . . .*, for example, Chris, a boy whose birthday falls on December 25 and whose father is looking for work, fears his birthday won't seem very important to anyone. But as the family prepares for Kwanzaa, the seven-day celebration of African-American heritage, Chris begins to feel that his birthday may not be so disappointing after all.

Speaking about her stories, Walter says, "I like to think that the images I create will make all young people thoughtful and African Americans aware of themselves as well."

153

Guided Instruction

Return to Predictions and Purposes

With students, review predictions they made as they read. Which predictions were correct? When the author did not write what students expected, could students find reasons for the differences?

INFORMAL ASSESSMENT

MAKE PREDICTIONS

HOW TO ASSESS

- Have students predict how Justin might act differently when he returns home.
- Ask students to support their predictions with ideas from the text and from their own experiences.

Students should recognize that Justin will probably be more willing to help with chores and might also feel more comfortable expressing his feelings.

FOLLOW UP If students have trouble citing evidence, suggest that they reread the introduction and pages 149–152. Discuss what they think Justin has learned from Grandpa.

LITERARY RESPONSE

QUICK-WRITE Invite students to record their thoughts about the story. These questions may help them get started:

JOURNAL

- What do you think of Justin? Of Grandpa? Would you like to have either of them as friends? Why?
- What do you think of the way Grandpa and Justin communicate with each other?

ORAL RESPONSE Have students share journal writings and discuss what parts they enjoyed most.

VIEWING If possible, have students compare an interactive electronic version of *Justin and the Best Biscuits in the World* with the written story. See page T76 for information.

Story Questions

Have students discuss or write answers to the questions on page 154.

Answers:

1. He thinks it is "women's work," and he doesn't want to do it. *Literal/Character*

2. Yes. Justin watched Grandpa cheerfully do household chores, and listened when Grandpa said, "It doesn't matter who does the work . . . when it needs to be done." *Inferential/Make Predictions*

3. Grandpa listens and patiently shows Justin how to do things. *Inferential/Evaluate*

4. Justin grows and changes during his visit with Grandpa. *Critical/Summarize*

5. Students should identify a character who is age appropriate. *Critical/Reading Across Texts*

Write a Letter For a full writing process lesson, see pages 157K–157L.

Story Questions & Activities

1. How does Justin feel about doing housework at the beginning of the story?

2. Did you expect him to change his mind about doing chores at the end? Why or why not?

3. What makes Grandpa such a good grandfather? Explain.

4. What is this story mostly about?

5. Imagine that Grandpa was asked to play a part in a movie or a television show. What character could he play? Explain your choice.

Write a Letter

Imagine you are Justin. Write a letter to your family about the chores you have done on Grandpa's ranch. Compare these chores to the chores that need to be done at home. Give supporting details.

Meeting Individual Needs

EASY	ON-LEVEL	CHALLENGE

EASY — Reteach 39

Name_____ Date_____ Reteach **39**

Vocabulary

Write a word from the list to complete each sentence.

festival	guilt	inspecting	lingered	pranced	resounded

1. We were _____inspecting_____ the boat to make sure it was safe.
2. Ellen _____lingered_____ at the table long after she had finished her dinner.
3. Jack felt a sense of _____guilt_____ because of the unkind things he had said to his brother.
4. The horses _____pranced_____ restlessly in the corral.
5. The sound of the explosion _____resounded_____ through the night.
6. There will be many bands and good food at the _____festival_____.

Story Comprehension Reteach **40**

Write a ✔ next to every sentence that tells about "Justin and the Best Biscuits in the World." For help you may look back at the story.

1. _____ Justin has always liked housework.
2. _____ Justin cleared the table and washed the dishes without being asked.
3. __✔__ Justin learned to fold his shirts and make his bed.
4. __✔__ Justin was impressed by his grandfather's cooking.
5. __✔__ Justin helped his grandfather inspect the house.
6. _____ Justin was bored by stories about Black cowboys.
7. __✔__ Justin's grandfather was a cowboy but not a broncobuster.
8. __✔__ Justin learned that it doesn't matter whether women or men do the work when it needs to be done.

39–40 *At Home: Have students recall two more details from "Justin and the Best Biscuits in the World."*

ON-LEVEL — Practice 40

Name_____ Date_____ Practice **40**

Story Comprehension

Read statements 1 to 6 below. Write **T** for true if the statement describes "Justin and the Best Biscuits in the World." Write **F** for false if it does not.

1. __T__ Justin felt guilty when he didn't help Grandpa wash the dishes.
2. __F__ Justin couldn't make his bed, even though he tried.
3. __F__ "Riding the fence" means "sitting on the fence."
4. __T__ A baby deer was in trouble and needed Grandpa's help.
5. __F__ The mother deer attacked Grandpa.
6. __T__ Grandpa learned to cook the biscuits when he was a boy.

Write to tell why the following statements are not true. Answers will vary.

7. Grandpa told Justin that one thing cowboys never do is cry.
   Grandpa is a cowboy and he cries. He cried when Justin was born.

8. Justin loves Grandpa, but he didn't learn anything new from him.
   Justin learned that there is no such thing as women's work.
   Everyone has to cook, clean, and make their beds. He also learned that everyone cries, even cowboys.

40 *At Home: Have students write a report about their experiences helping with household chores.*

CHALLENGE — Extend 39

Name_____ Date_____ Extend **39**

Vocabulary

festival	guilt	inspecting
lingered	pranced	resounded

Make your own crossword puzzle using the vocabulary words above. Remember to start with **Across** clues and then give the **Down** clues. Then draw numbered boxes for the answers. Exchange your puzzle with a partner's puzzle and try to solve it.

Across
_____
_____
_____
_____

Down
_____
_____
_____
_____

Extend **40**

Story Comprehension

Review "Justin and the Best Biscuits in the World." Predict what kind of a grandfather you think that Justin will be. Tell how you used the story to help you make your prediction.

Answers will vary. Possible answer: I think Justin will try to model himself after his own grandfather. He loves his grandfather and learns many things from him.

39–40 *At Home: Have students discuss what they think the good and the more difficult aspects of a cowboy's life would be.*

Reteach, 40   Practice, 40   Extend, 40

Trace the Trail

An important job for cowboys was a cattle drive. They drove herds of cattle long distances from Texas and the Southwest to railroad towns in Kansas and Nebraska. Use an encyclopedia to learn more about cattle drives. Then draw a map showing one of the trails. Include a scale of miles to show distance.

Write a Song

Cowboys, or cowhands, often sang songs on the trail. Their songs were about freedom and loneliness, the empty range, and cattle drives. Listen to cowboy songs in the library. Then write a short song that a cowboy might sing.

Find Out More

In the story, Justin's grandfather had once been a cowboy. Cowboys had special clothing and equipment for their work. Find out more about cowboy gear. Start by looking in an encyclopedia. Use what you learn to draw a picture of a cowboy or a cowgirl. Then label the special gear.

155

Story Activities

Trace the Trail

Materials: drawing paper, markers, ruler, encyclopedias, atlases

GROUP You may want to review maps and map scale before students begin. As students present their maps to the class, they can share stories about adventures and hardships that occurred on the trail in their illustrations.

Write a Song

GROUP Ask students to listen for the simple melodies, harmonies, and story lines in traditional cowboy songs. Suggest that they may wish to set their words to a familiar tune so everyone can easily sing along.

Find Out More

RESEARCH AND INQUIRY Suggest that students consult nonfiction and fiction books about cowhands and the old West, along with the Internet, to find photographs and illustrations of real cowhands. Talk about why cowboys needed each piece of equipment.

interNET CONNECTION For more information about cowboy gear, students can visit **www.mhschool.com/reading**

FORMAL ASSESSMENT

After page 155, see the Selection Assessment.

Study Skills

REFERENCE SOURCES

OBJECTIVES Students will use a dictionary to understand the meanings of unfamiliar words.

PREPARE Display **Teaching Chart 33.** Elicit from students that the chart shows a dictionary entry.

TEACH Ask volunteers to read the introduction and point out the parts of a dictionary entry.

PRACTICE Have students answer questions 1–5. Review the answers with them. **1.** a long rope with a loop at one end used to catch animals **2.** three **3.** noun **4.** Yes; *lasso* is listed as a synonym for *lariat*. **5.** when you can't figure out its meaning by using context clues

ASSESS/CLOSE Have students look up other words associated with cowhands, such as *bronco, dogie, rustler, brand,* and *corral.*

Meeting Individual Needs

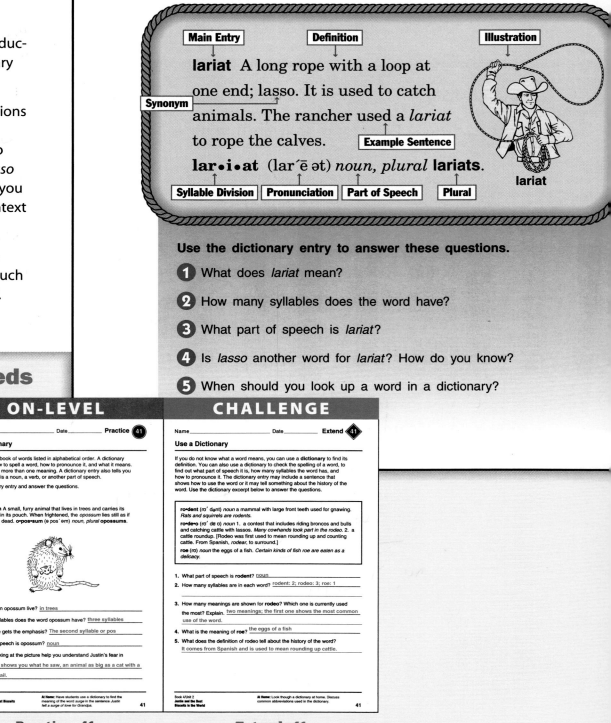

Study SKILLS

Use a Dictionary

Grandpa uses some things in the story that you may not know. Grandpa's *lariat*, for example, is an important piece of cowboy gear. What is a lariat? You can look up this word in a dictionary.

A **dictionary** tells you what the word means and how to pronounce it. It also gives you the word's part of speech. Sometimes a dictionary shows you how to use the word in a sentence. It may even show you a picture of the word.

Main Entry	Definition	Illustration

lariat A long rope with a loop at one end; lasso. It is used to catch animals. The rancher used a *lariat* to rope the calves.

Synonym / Example Sentence

lar•i•at (lar´ē ət) *noun, plural* **lariats**.

Syllable Division	Pronunciation	Part of Speech	Plural

lariat

Use the dictionary entry to answer these questions.

1 What does *lariat* mean?

2 How many syllables does the word have?

3 What part of speech is *lariat*?

4 Is *lasso* another word for *lariat*? How do you know?

5 When should you look up a word in a dictionary?

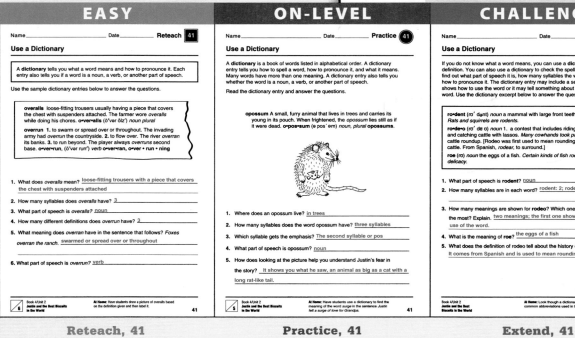

Reteach, 41   Practice, 41   Extend, 41

TEST POWER

THE PRINCETON REVIEW

Test Tip

A FACT is something that is true in the passage.

DIRECTIONS

Read the sample story. Then read each question about the story.

SAMPLE

Paul's Puppy

Paul's friend Jinnie received a puppy for her birthday. The puppy had white fur and a patch of black fur over its right eye. Whenever Jinnie picked it up, it would wag its tail and lick her face.

Paul asked his mother if he could get a puppy, too. His mother thought about it for a moment and said, "A dog is a big responsibility, Paul. Dogs are fun, but they also need a lot of care. They can be great friends, but only if you are a good friend to them. Are you willing to take on that kind of challenge?"

Paul agreed that he was up to the responsibility.

1 Which of these is the best summary of this story?

  A Paul liked Jinnie's puppy.

  B The puppy wagged its tail.

  C Jinnie's puppy was cute.

  Ⓓ Paul agreed to take care of a puppy.

2 Which of these is a FACT in this story?

  F Dogs are great friends.

  Ⓖ Jinnie's puppy has white fur.

  H Dogs are always cute.

  J Puppies are fun.

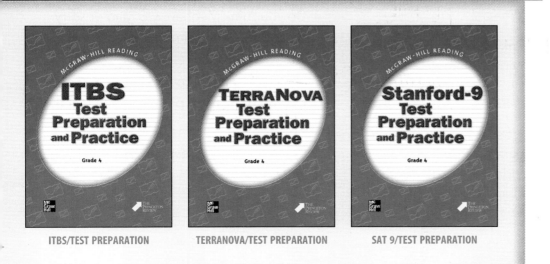

How do you know which are facts in the story? Explain.

157

Test Power

THE PRINCETON REVIEW

Read the Page

Direct students to read the passage and, before looking at the questions, have them say in their own words what the passage was mostly about.

Discuss the Questions

Question 1: This question requires students to determine which is the best summary of the story. For each incorrect answer choice, ask "What makes this choice incorrect?" Remind students that a correct answer must summarize the *whole* passage.

Question 2: This question requires students to determine which of the four choices is a FACT in the story. The three incorrect answer choices in this question are OPINIONS. Read each of the answer choices as a group. Students must be able to distinguish between what is a FACT and what is an OPINION. Eliminate OPINIONS.

ITBS Test Preparation and Practice — Grade 4

TERRANOVA Test Preparation and Practice — Grade 4

Stanford-9 Test Preparation and Practice — Grade 4

ITBS/TEST PREPARATION

TERRANOVA/TEST PREPARATION

SAT 9/TEST PREPARATION

EASY

Answers to Story Questions

1. Krystal had always been there when she needed her, so Meghan felt she should do the same for Krystal.

2. Answers vary, but may include: Meghan was proud because, even though the parade was important to her, she knew she had done the right thing by staying behind to help her friend.

3. Answers will vary but may include: Meghan wouldn't have enjoyed being in the parade as much knowing that her best friend wasn't there.

4. A girl is willing to miss her chance to ride her horse in a parade in order to help her best friend get there.

5. Answers will vary.

Story Questions and Activity

1. Why did Meghan agree to help Krystal catch her horse?

2. Why is the story called *Riding Proud*?

3. What might have happened if Meghan had not helped Krystal?

4. What is the story mostly about?

5. If Justin from *Justin and the Best Biscuits in the World* were in this story, how might he have helped the girls get to the rodeo?

Rodeo Time

Meghan and Krystal are on their way to a rodeo. What will happen when the Grand Parade reaches the rodeo grounds? Do some research about rodeos today and make a program for the day, describing what events will take place and who will compete. Illustrate your program with drawings of the events.

from Riding Proud

Leveled Books

EASY

Riding Proud

Syllable Patterns

☑ **Make Predictions**

☑ **Instructional Vocabulary:** *festival, guilt, inspecting, lingered, pranced, resounded*

RIDING PROUD

written by Mary Kaiser Donev
illustrated by Dennis Albetski

Guided Reading

PREVIEW AND PREDICT Have students preview the pictures through page 8 and then record predictions about how the girls will catch the horse in their journals.

SET PURPOSES Allow time for students to write their purposes for reading the story. For example: *I want to know what it's like to have a horse of my own.*

READ THE BOOK Use questions such as the following to guide a group reading or in a follow-up discussion.

Pages 2–3: Why was *inspecting* Starlight so important to Meghan? (The parade was very important to Meghan; Starlight had to look her best.) *Vocabulary*

Page 5: Do you think Meghan will help Krystal? Why or why not? (Sample answer: No, since Meghan has to get ready for the parade.) *Make Predictions*

Page 9: If you aren't sure how to say *m-o-m-e-n-t* in the last paragraph, what strategy can you try? (Divide the word after the first vowel. Try pronouncing the first syllable with both a long and short vowel. See which pronunciation sounds familiar.) *Phonics and Decoding*

Page 14: Do you think the girls can find a way to join the parade? (Yes, since the presence of the people shows that the riders have just left.) *Make Prediction*

RETURN TO PREDICTIONS AND PURPOSES Lead students in a discussion about their predictions. Were they accurate? Have students review their purposes for reading. Did they learn what they wanted to learn?

LITERARY RESPONSE Discuss these questions:

- Do you think Meghan was glad or sorry that she took the time to help Krystal catch Ginger? Why?

- How would it feel to ride in the parade? Do you think most people would feel the same way?

Also see the story questions and activity in *Riding Proud*.

Leveled Books

INDEPENDENT

Little Sure Shot

written by Mary Kaiser Donev
illustrated by Leslie Bowman

☑ **Make Predictions**

☑ **Instructional Vocabulary:**
festival, guilt, inspecting, lingered, pranced, resounded

INDEPENDENT

Guided Reading

PREVIEW AND PREDICT Have students look at the pictures through page 13. Then have students predict how the audience will like Annie's act. Ask them to record their predictions in their journals.

SET PURPOSES Have students write reasons for reading this book. For example: *I want to know how people reacted to a woman doing "men's work."*

READ THE BOOK Ask questions such as the ones below as you read the story together, or ask the questions after students have read independently.

Page 2: How was Annie different from most women of her time? (Most women didn't shoot guns, but Annie did.) *Form Generalization*

Pages 4–5: Will Annie get the job? (Sample answer: She will since she has shown her talent for target shooting.) *Make Predictions*

Page 8: Find the word *pranced*. What pranced? (horses) Demonstrate how the horses moved as they pranced around the arena. *Vocabulary*

Page 12: What do you think Annie did after her accident? (Sample answer: Annie worked to recover and perform again.) *Make Predictions*

Pages 13–15: Summarize Annie's other accomplishments. (Annie taught women to shoot, gave generously to charity, and built a hospital for children.) *Summarize*

RETURN TO PREDICTIONS AND PURPOSES Have students look back at their predictions and reasons for reading. Did they find out how the people reacted to Annie's work?

LITERARY RESPONSE Discuss these questions:

- How do you know that this is a true story?

- If Annie were alive today, what do you think she'd be doing?

Also see the story questions and activity in *Little Sure Shot*.

Answers to Story Questions

1. When her father died, she started shooting at game to feed her family.
2. Annie Oakley practiced shooting over and over again until she could hit anything she aimed at.
3. Answers will vary.
4. Anyone can succeed if they keep trying, no matter how difficult the task, even if the odds are against them.
5. Answers will vary.

Story Questions and Activity

1. Why did Phoebe Anne Moses first start shooting a gun?
2. How did Annie Oakley's motto help her become such a good shooter?
3. Predict what Annie Oakley might do today to impress a modern audience at the Wild West Show.
4. What is the main idea of the book?
5. If the grandfather from *Justin and the Best Biscuits in the World* and Annie Oakley could write a book together, what would it be about and what would its title be?

Practice Makes Perfect

Remember a time when you had a difficult task to master that required you to spend many hours practicing. What was a typical week like for you then? Make a chart showing what your schedule was like and share your experience with another person in your class. Let that person know what you learned from the experience.

from Little Sure Shot

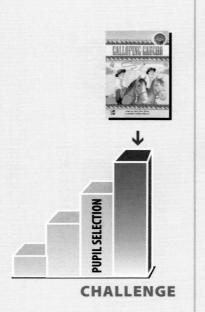

PUPIL SELECTION

CHALLENGE

Answers to Story Questions

1. The most important thing to a *gaucho* is his horse.
2. Nathan thought it would be boring in Argentina.
3. Accept all reasonable responses.
4. No one can predict what he or she will or will not like, or what he or she can or cannot do until an attempt is made.
5. Answers will vary.

Story Questions and Activity

1. What was the most important thing to a *gaucho*?
2. Why didn't Nathan want to go to Argentina?
3. Predict how Nathan would describe his galloping gaucho adventure to his parents.
4. What is the main idea of the book?
5. If Nathan had a conversation with Justin from *Justin and the Best Biscuits in the World*, what do you think they would talk about?

Adventuring into the Unknown

Think about something that you have never tried to do. Write a paragraph about why you would like to try it and why you think you'd be good at it.

from Galloping Gaucho

Leveled Books

LEVELED Books

GALLOPING GAUCHO

written by Mary Kaiser Donev
illustrated by Rebecca Rayman

CHALLENGE

Galloping Gaucho

☑ **Make Predictions**

☑ **Instructional Vocabulary:**
festival, guilt, inspecting, lingered, pranced, resounded

Guided Reading

PREVIEW AND PREDICT Guide students to preview the story through page 4. Ask why Nathan's father might have removed the CDs. Then record students' predictions about what Nathan might do on his vacation without the things he is used to playing with.

SET PURPOSES Ask students to write their purposes for reading the story. For example: *I want to see how Nathan copes without things like CDs and a skateboard.*

READ THE BOOK Use questions such as the following to guide a group reading or in a follow-up discussion.

Pages 3–4: Nathan thinks the vacation will be boring. How do you think it will turn out? (Sample answer: I predict Nathan will find new things to do.) *Make Predictions*

Page 10: Do you think Nathan will find a way to avoid learning to ride like a *gaucho*? (Sample answer: Yes, I think he will think of an excuse.) *Make Predictions*

Page 14: Why might riding a horse that *pranced* be scary? (A prancing horse makes bouncy movements.) *Vocabulary*

Page 15: "A *gaucho* does not know what he can do until he tries." Do you think this is true of other people, too? Why or why not? (Yes, because many people are afraid to try something new, but often find that they like it after they try it.) *Form Generalizations*

RETURN TO PREDICTIONS AND PURPOSES Have students check their predictions to see whether the vacation turned out the way they thought it would. Were their predictions accurate? Invite students to talk about their purposes for reading and if they found out what they wanted to learn.

LITERARY RESPONSE Discuss these questions:

- Would you have been scared to ride the horse? Why or why not?
- What did Nathan learn about himself?

Also see the story questions and activity in *Galloping Gaucho*.

Activities
Anthology and Leveled Books

Connecting Texts

RANCH AND RODEO CHART
Write the story titles on a chart. Discuss with students life on a ranch. Have students from each reading level suggest information to add to the chart. Use the charts to help students summarize the stories.

Justin and the Best Biscuits in the World	Riding Proud	Little Sure Shot	Galloping Gaucho
• Cowboys worked in the Old West. • Cowboys do all kinds of work.	• It's important to take good care of the horses. • Ranchers may show off their horses in parades.	• Ranchers entertained people. • Annie Oakley was one of the most skillful Wild West performers.	• Ranchers are an important part of some cultures. • Horses are very important to ranchers.

Viewing/Representing

PERFORM SKITS Divide the class into groups according to the books they read. (For *Justin and the Best Biscuits in the World* combine students of different reading levels.) Tell students in each group to pretend they are playwrights and make up skits based on characters in their book. Groups can act out the skits during a "cowboy campfire."

COWBOY CAMPFIRE Ask the audience to sit in a circle to view the skits as if they were around a campfire on the range. When audience members ask questions, presenters should answer them as the character they played in the skit.

Research and Inquiry

RODEO FRIEZE Remind students that a rodeo is a chance for cowhands to show off the skills they use every day, as well as a sport. Encourage students to find out more about rodeos by:

• researching rodeo events.

• choosing an event and drawing a picture of it.

• making a wall frieze for everyone to view by taping their pictures on the walls at eye level.

interNET CONNECTION To find out more about ranches and rodeos, have students visit *www.mhschool.com/reading*

ᴛᴇsᴛᴇᴅ
☑OBJECTIVES
Students will make
predictions about a story.

Review Make Predictions

PREPARE

Discuss Making Predictions

Review: Pausing during reading to make predictions can help readers better understand what they are reading. To make a prediction, use information from the text, along with things you already know to guess what may happen next. Good predictions will be supported with evidence from the story and from the reader's experience.

TEACH

Read "Justin Goes Home" and Model the Skill

Read the **Teaching Chart 34** passage with students. Tell students they will be asked to make a prediction when they have finished.

Justin Goes Home

"Welcome back, Justin," his mother said. "You're just in time to help with the dishes."

Justin's sisters laughed. "Sure, after all that time on the ranch, Justin's going to love doing 'women's work.' Anyway, he'd get soapsuds all over. He might break the dishes, too. Forget it, Mom. He'd only slow us down."

Justin remembered making his bed neatly and learning to fold his shirts. He remembered all the times he helped Grandpa clean up. And most of all, he remembered all the things Grandpa had said about work.

Teaching Chart 34

Ask students to tell what they think happened next and why.

MODEL I think Justin surprised them all by doing the dishes without complaining and doing a great job. The sisters remember the way Justin was before he stayed with Grandpa. But I remember all the things Grandpa taught Justin, too. And I know that when I learn something new, I can't wait to show it off.

PRACTICE

Make Predictions

GROUP

Have students underline clues in the story that helped them predict what Justin would do next. Have groups compare predictions. Then ask students to relate experiences from their own lives that helped them make their predictions. ▶ **Logical/Interpersonal**

ASSESS/CLOSE

Make Up a New Story

PARTNERS

Have pairs of students work together to make up more stories about Justin that show how he grew and changed during the story. Then let the partners read their story to another pair of students, stopping at a crucial point to let the listeners predict how the story will end.

ALTERNATE TEACHING STRATEGY

MAKE PREDICTIONS
For a different approach to teaching this skill, see page T60.

SELF-SELECTED Reading

Students may choose from the following titles.

ANTHOLOGY
- Justin and the Best Biscuits in the World

LEVELED BOOKS
- Riding Proud
- Little Sure Shot
- Galloping Gaucho

Bibliography, pages T76–T77

Meeting Individual Needs for Comprehension

EASY	ON-LEVEL	CHALLENGE	LANGUAGE SUPPORT

EASY

Name _____ Date _____ Reteach **42**

Make Predictions

You can use what you know about story characters to **predict**, or think ahead about, what the characters may do.

Read each story below. Then answer the questions.

The horseback riding teacher was curious about why Sandra Sanchez had missed her last three lessons. He knew that the lessons were very important to Sandra's mother. Mrs. Sanchez wanted Sandra to start entering riding contests soon. One day, the riding teacher saw Mrs. Sanchez on the street.

1. What do you think the riding teacher will do?
He may ask Mrs. Sanchez why Sandra missed her lessons.

2. How do you think Sandra's mother will react?
Answers will vary. Mrs. Sanchez may be totally surprised to hear about the missed lessons, or she may say that Sandra was sick.

Noah liked every subject but art. Noah's pictures just never looked the way he wanted them to. But a funny thing happened when Noah started painting. Mr. Vass thought that Noah's paintings were very good, and asked if Noah would enter them in a contest! Noah smiled with pride. When Noah came home, Noah's parents could see that he was very happy.

3. Do you think that Noah will enter the contest? Explain why.
Possible answer: Yes. Noah is proud the teacher likes his paintings.

4. Do you think Noah will stop painting when the art class moves on to a different topic? Explain.
Possible answer: No. Noah probably feels differently about art class now that he has done well.

At Home: Have students make another prediction based on one of the stories.

Book 4/Unit 2 Justin and the Best Biscuits in the World 4

42

Reteach, 42

ON-LEVEL

Name _____ Date _____ Practice **42**

Make Predictions

When you make a **prediction**, you make a logical guess about what will happen next, based on story clues and your own experiences. As you read on, you find out if you were right. Making and confirming predictions can help you understand why characters act as they do.

Think back to your first reading of "Justin and the Best Biscuits in the World." Then answer these questions about predictions you made or might have made at different points in the story. *Answers may vary.*

1. At the beginning of the story, did you think Justin and Grandpa were going to get along? Why? They wouldn't get along. Justin let Grandpa wash all the dishes.

2. What did you think would happen when Justin started making his bed while Grandpa watched? He was going to do a bad job of it. Justin was not used to making beds and didn't know how.

3. What happened with Justin and the bed? How did it change what you predicted would happen in the rest of the story? Justin found that making a bed was not hard. Maybe he would try other things.

4. What did you think Justin would do when he saw the blood from the doe? Possible answer: He would want to go back to the ranch. He would be upset.

5. Write a prediction about Justin's future visits to Grandpa's ranch. Justin will look forward to going. Justin will have a good time visiting Grandpa.

At Home: Have students write a prediction about what will happen at school tomorrow including information used to base their prediction.

Book 4/Unit 2 Justin and the Best Biscuits in the World 5

42

Practice, 42

CHALLENGE

Name _____ Date _____ Extend **42**

Make Predictions

Look back at "Justin and the Best Biscuits in the World" to help you answer the questions.

The first morning that Justin was at his grandfather's ranch he did not help prepare breakfast, wash the dishes, or sweep the floor. He also did not have his bed made when his grandfather came into his room.

1. Predict what you think Justin will do on the second morning of his visit. Explain.
Answers will vary. Possible answer: Justin will get up early and make his bed. He'll help with breakfast. He will wash or dry the dishes and offer to sweep the floor. Justin admires his grandfather and will want to be more like him and help out.

Justin did not like to help with household chores at home. He considered them women's work.

2. What do you predict Justin will do about household chores when he returns home? Explain.
Answers will vary. Possible answer: He will probably be more willing to help. Justin's grandfather explained to him that there were no chores that were "women's work."

At Home: Have students discuss a favorite story in which they were able to predict the outcome. What clues led to the prediction.

Book 4/Unit 2 Justin and the Best Biscuits in the World

42

Extend, 42

LANGUAGE SUPPORT

Name _____ Date _____

Can You Predict the Future?

1. Read the sentences in the crystal ball to see what might happen to Justin.
2. Write what you think might happen. 3. Share your idea with a partner.

Justin will refuse to help out. **1**	Justin will cook all the meals. **2**
Justin will start helping out around the house. **3**	Justin will get his own apartment. **4**

Story Events:

1. _____
2. _____
3. _____
4. _____

46 Justin and the Best Biscuits in the World • Language Support / Blackline Master 22 Grade 4

Language Support, 46

✓ **OBJECTIVES**

Students will identify and
form generalizations.

TEACHING TIP

INSTRUCTIONAL You
may want to take this opportunity to point out that very
broad generalizations about
a whole group of people, or
stereotypes, are examples of
invalid generalizations.

Introduce Form Generalizations

PREPARE

Discuss Forming
Generalizations

Explain: People can't know everything in the world. So we usually
form conclusions from a small group of examples. These conclusions
are called generalizations. Since we can't know about every example,
we need to use words like *most* and *usually* to make our generalization true, or valid. Generalizations should not include words like *all*
or *never,* since there probably are exceptions.

TEACH

Read "Women's
Work?" and
Model the Skill

Read the **Teaching Chart 35** passage with students. Ask students to
pay attention to generalizations.

Women's Work?

Justin said, "When I make the bed, it has lumps. When I try
to cook, I spill things. A man can never cook a good meal or
make a bed well."

"Well," said Grandpa. "Who do you think made the bed you
slept in last night? And how did you like the biscuits I made?"

"That's right, Grandpa," Justin said, surprised. "Most men
can probably learn to do household chores very well. I'll bet I
can, too."

Teaching Chart 35

Model identifying generalizations and determining if they are valid.

MODEL Justin had some strange ideas in the beginning. He made a
statement about all men based on what he could do himself. That
generalization was not valid. Grandpa pointed out some exceptions right away. When Justin used words like *some, many, most,*
and *probably*, he made correct generalizations.

PRACTICE

Identify Generalizations

GROUP

Have students underline the generalizations in the story. For each generalization, have them tell whether it is valid or not and why. Have small groups work together to make a chart showing their conclusions. ▶ **Interpersonal/Linguistic**

GENERALIZATION	VALID?
A man can never cook a good meal or make a bed well.	No, because there are many exceptions.
Most men can probably learn to do household chores very well.	Yes, because it tells about "most men."

ASSESS/CLOSE

Form Generalizations

PARTNERS

Have pairs of students work together to write two generalizations from examples they know about. Let the partners read their generalizations to another pair of students, who will tell whether the generalizations seem valid or not.

LOOKING AHEAD

Students will apply this skill as they read the next selection, *Just a Dream.*

ALTERNATE TEACHING STRATEGY
....

FORM GENERALIZATIONS

For a different approach to teaching this skill, see page T62.

Meeting Individual Needs for Comprehension

EASY

Name_____ Date_____ **Reteach** 43

Form Generalizations

A **generalization** is a broad statement. It can be about many people, many animals, or many things.

Read the paragraphs below. Put a ✔ next to each generalization that you can make from the facts in the paragraph.

Braille is a system of reading that is used by blind people. It is named for its inventor, Louis Braille. The idea came to him when he noticed a system of sending coded wartime messages by using raised dots on cardboard. By placing raised dots in different positions, Braille made an alphabet, a system of punctuation, and music, that blind people read by running their fingers over the dots. Braille was not accepted officially right away. Today, however, it is used in all written languages.

1. _____ All people accepted the Braille system right away.
2. ✔ Today, Braille is widely used in all written languages.
3. _____ There is no system for blind people to read music.

Owning a pet can be a rewarding experience. However you should choose a pet carefully. For example, a large dog might be unhappy in a small apartment. A bird or some fish might be a good choice for someone who wants a pet that does not need to be walked or played with. People who are unwilling or unable to take responsibility for a pet are better off choosing not to have one. A pet is a living being that must be cared for.

4. ✔ Owning a pet is a responsibility.
5. _____ There is only one correct pet for each owner.
6. ✔ To choose a pet, you need to think about how the pet will fit into your home and your life.

Book 4/Unit 2
Justin and the Best Biscuits in the World
At Home: Have students make a generalization about an article they have read or a television show they have watched.
6 / 43

Reteach, 43

ON-LEVEL

Name_____ Date_____ **Practice** 43

Form Generalizations

A **generalization** is a broad statement about something. Generalizations often include words such as *always, many, most, almost, all, no,* or *none.*

Complete each sentence starter below by writing a generalization based on details from "Justin and the Best Biscuits in the World."
Answers will vary.

1. Washing dishes _can be easy._
2. A well-made bed _is always a warm welcome._
3. None of the wrinkled shirts _had been folded correctly._
4. The morning sun on the hilltops always _made the foothills appear purple._
5. A doe's eyes usually _look peaceful and sad._
6. When Justin's grandpa was a boy, he _helped his father with the cattle._
7. Cowchips _make the best fuel for a fire._
8. Diamondback rattlers _are dangerous snakes._
9. Some of the best cooks in the world _are men._
10. On the cattle trail _all cooks were men._

Book 4/Unit 2
Justin and the Best Biscuits in the World
At Home: Have students write three sentences beginning: Most students in our class.
10 / 43

Practice, 43

CHALLENGE

Name_____ Date_____ **Extend** 43

Form Generalizations

Think about "Justin and the Best Biscuits in the World." When Justin's grandfather showed him how to fold his shirt, Justin was willing to try it on his own. When his grandfather told him to try to make his bed, Justin did so and found that it was not very hard to do.
Do you think that Justin would have responded with the same willingness to similar suggestions from his mother at home? You can use the story to help you form a **generalization**, or a general conclusion, about how Justin might have responded to his mother.

Answers will vary. Possible answer: Probably not, since Justin considered such chores to be women's work. Justin saw that his grandfather did these kinds of chores willingly. His way of showing Justin the importance of this kind of work helped Justin see things differently.

Grandpa told Justin about many African American cowboys. Use the story to form a generalization about the lives of African American cowboys.
Answers will vary. Possible answer: The contributions of African American cowboys went unrecognized for a long time, but now people are finding out more about them.

Book 4/Unit 2
Justin and the Best Biscuits in the World
At Home: Have students make generalizations about what their life will be like years from now.
43

Extend, 43

LANGUAGE SUPPORT

Name_____ Date_____

Fill up the Plate

1. Read this sentence:

   Men and boys are good at housework and cooking.

2. Which four biscuits below the plate go together to make this sentence true?
3. Cut out the biscuits and paste them on the plate.

1 Grandpa made delicious biscuits.
2 Grandpa showed Justin how to make a bed neatly.
Jessie Stahl was a famous Black cowboy.
3 Justin saw how well Grandpa washed the dishes.
Grandpa and Justin were going to a rodeo.
4 Justin quickly learned how to fold up his clothes.

Grade 4 Language Support/Blackline Master 23 • Justin and the Best Biscuits in the World 47

Language Support, 47

Introduce Context Clues

TEACHING TIP

INSTRUCTIONAL You may want to teach context clues to some students with materials that are below reading level. This will help insure that they can read and understand the context words they need to know to deduce the meanings of unfamiliar words.

PREPARE

Discuss Context   Explain: Students can often figure out the meanings of unfamiliar words by reading the words around the unfamiliar word. The sentences and paragraphs around an unfamiliar word are called its context.

TEACH

Read "Rodeo Day" and Model the Skill   Read the **Teaching Chart 36** passage with students. Ask students to use the words they know to figure out the meanings of the words in dark type.

Rodeo Day

The cowboys were excited about the rodeo. If they were the best, they might win a prize!

Deadwood couldn't wait for his turn. To get rid of extra weight, he removed his bulging **saddlebags** from behind the saddle. Then he tightened the **cinches** around the horse's belly. He wouldn't want the saddle to fall off.

Deadwood would ride on a horse that had never been ridden before. He was sure that at the end of the day he would be the champion **broncobuster.**

Teaching Chart 36

Model using context clues for specialized vocabulary.

MODEL   I'm not sure what *saddlebags* are, but there are some clues in the passage about the rodeo. I know they are right behind the saddle. They are bulging. Maybe that's because they are full of supplies. They must be like little suitcases that a cowboy uses to carry supplies.

PRACTICE

**Identify and Use
Context Clues**

ONE

Ask volunteers to use context to define the boldfaced words on the
chart. Then ask other volunteers to underline the words that gave
clues to the meanings of the unfamiliar words. ▶ **Linguistic**

ASSESS/CLOSE

Draw a Definition

Ask students to draw a picture that shows the meaning of one of the
boldfaced words in the passage. Then have them look up other
words related to horses or the rodeo and draw pictures to show
what those words mean.

ALTERNATE TEACHING STRATEGY
....

CONTEXT CLUES

**For a different approach to
teaching this skill, see page
T63.**

Meeting Individual Needs for Vocabulary

EASY	ON-LEVEL	CHALLENGE	LANGUAGE SUPPORT

EASY

Name_____ Date_____ **Reteach** 44

Use Context Clues

Sometimes when you read, you will come to a word that you don't know.
You can use **context clues**, or other words or sentences around the
unfamiliar word, to help you figure out the meaning of the word.

Circle the letter beside the meaning of the underlined word in each
sentence.

1. Grandfather warmed stew and even fried some bread in the skillet.
   (a.) cooking pan   b. type of wagon

2. They see for miles across the treeless, even plains.
   a. hilly green areas   (b.) stretch of flat land

3. Fred searched everywhere, scanning the area for stray cattle.
   (a.) looking carefully   b. ignoring

4. The foreman told the ranch hands what each should do.
   (a.) boss of a crew   b. stranger

5. After tiring, the horse began to canter, and the rider could catch her breath.
   a. run wildly   (b.) move at a slow, steady pace

6. On some ranches, calves are branded to let people know who owns them.
   (a.) marked with sign   b. kept indoors

At Home: Have students tell what context clues they found
to help them identify the meanings of skillet and foreman.
44
Book 4/Unit 2 *Justin and the Best Biscuits in the World* 6

ON-LEVEL

Name_____ Date_____ **Practice** 44

Context Clues

There may be words you don't know in a story you are reading. Sometimes
the sentence, or **context** surrounding a word, holds clues that can help you
understand the word's meaning.

Write a word from the list that makes sense in each sentence.

shallow	resounded	mustangs	chores	outburst
broadly	cautiously	lingered	surge	assured

1. The night air ____resounded____ with sounds of crickets and bat wings.

2. Hannah ____lingered____ in the yard after her parents went into the house.

3. Kevin raked the leaves and finished other outdoor ____chores____.

4. Dad showed all his teeth when he smiled ____broadly____.

5. Antonio felt a ____surge____ of happiness as he rode the horse.

6. Mei-Li tiptoed ____cautiously____ so she wouldn't frighten the kittens.

7. When Consuelo spelled the word, she felt ____assured____ of the prize.

8. Keeshawn dug ____shallow____ holes near the surface for the flower seeds.

9. Tamara used to tame wild ponies called ____mustangs____.

10. That was quite an ____outburst____ when Chad yelled without thinking.

At Home: Have students write sentences with strong
context clues for four words.
44
Book 4/Unit 2 *Justin and the Best Biscuits in the World* 10

CHALLENGE

Name_____ Date_____ **Extend** 44

Context Clues

cinch	saddlebags	broncobuster
bale	hitched	branded

Sometimes you can figure out the meaning of a word from its setting and the way
it is used in a sentence. The words above are usually used in a western or ranch-
related context.

Read each sentence in the box. Use the **context clues** in them to help you
match the words with their meaning's below.

He pulled on the leather strap to *cinch* the saddle.
The *bales* of hay were stacked on the truck.
They *hitched* the horses to a post while they had lunch.
They *branded* the calves with the symbol of the ranch.
The cowboy put his rain gear and a map in the *saddlebags*.
The wild mustang was calmed by the *broncobuster*.

1. marked to indicate identity or ownership _branded_

2. large bundles tied tightly together _bales_

3. fastened with a rope _hitched_

4. a cowboy who tames wild horses _broncobuster_

5. to tighten a saddle girth _cinch_

6. Pouches, usually of leather, hung across a saddle _saddlebags_

Use another sheet of paper to draw a picture that illustrates some of the
words above.

At Home: What words do you associate with the
American West? Discuss the reasons why.
44
Book 4/Unit 2 *Justin and the Best Biscuits in the World*

LANGUAGE SUPPORT

Name_____ Date_____

Get the Picture

1. Read each sentence below. 2. Study the underlined words. These words
appear in the story, *Justin and the Best Biscuits in the World*. 3. Look at the circled words. These words are clues to help you learn what the underlined words
mean. 4. Cut out the underlined story words. 5. Paste them next to the thing in
the picture each word tells about.

The cowboy's saddlebags are
on his horse full of supplies.
With his reins he pulls up on
the bit in the horse's mouth to
signal the horse to stop.

The broncobuster is riding a
kicking Brahma bull.

broncobuster

bit
saddlebags

48 *Justin and the Best Biscuits in the World* • Language Support /Blackline Master 24   Grade 4

Reteach, 44   **Practice, 44**   **Extend, 44**   **Language Support, 48**

GRAMMAR/SPELLING CONNECTIONS

See the 5-Day Grammar and Usage Plan on common and proper nouns, pages 157M–157N.

See the 5-Day Spelling Plan on syllable patterns, pages 1570–157P.

TECHNOLOGY TIP

Tell students: When you use the Internet for research, pay special attention to the source of the information. Be sure it's a source you can trust.

Writing That Compares

Prewrite

WRITE A LETTER Present the following assignment: Imagine you are Justin. Write a letter to your family about the chores you have done on Grandpa's ranch. Compare these chores to the chores that need to be done at home.

BRAINSTORM LISTS Guide students to brainstorm the chores mentioned in the selection. List these on the board. Discuss which of these chores Justin may have to do at home and which he does with Grandpa. Discuss how these chores are similar and different.

Strategy: Make a Chart Have students organize their lists into a chart. Help students list the chores under headings marked *At Grandpa's* and *At Grandpa's and At Home.*

AT GRANDPA'S	AT GRANDPA'S AND AT HOME
cook out on the trail	cook
ride fence	wash dishes
rescue animals	make the bed
build a fire	fold clothes
saddle the horses	
water the horses	

Draft

USE THE CHART Guide students to write a strong introduction expressing the main idea of their letter. Have them mark off specific details from their chart as they make their comparisons. Remind them to use the correct format for a friendly letter.

Revise

SELF-QUESTIONING Have students assess their drafts for revisions.

• Is a clear comparison made between chores done in the two places?

• Have I shown enough similarities and differences?

• Does this sound like a friendly letter?

PARTNERS Have each student read his or her letter aloud to a partner and ask the listener to tell whether any parts are unclear.

Edit/Proofread

CHECK FOR ERRORS Let students read their work aloud, checking punctuation by exaggerating pauses at periods and commas. Be sure they check for correct letter format.

Publish

GIVE ORAL READINGS Have students read their letters aloud in small groups.

Dear Mom,

I'm having a swell time on Grandpa's ranch. Grandpa showed me how to saddle and water the horses, mend fences, and build a fire. One day we rescued a fawn caught in a fence.

Even some chores we do at home—like folding clothes, washing dishes, and making beds—seem different when Grandpa does them. I always thought they were women's work, but I guess I was wrong. When I get home, I'll show you what a great dishwasher I can be!

Love from your son,
Justin

Presentation Ideas

MAKE A POSTER Students can make a poster to illustrate the similarities and differences between chores at home and chores on the ranch. Have them label their drawings. ▶ **Viewing/Representing**

LISTEN CRITICALLY As students share their letters aloud, instruct the audience to listen for similarities and differences between the speaker's comparison and their own. ▶ **Speaking/Listening**

Consider students' creative efforts, possibly adding a plus (+) for originality, wit, and imagination.

Scoring Rubric

Excellent	Good	Fair	Unsatisfactory
4: The writer	**3:** The writer	**2:** The writer	**1:** The writer
• has a strong opening indicating the main idea.	• states the point of the comparison.	• attempts to compare chores in both places.	• does not compare chores in both places.
• gives detailed comparisons of chores in both places.	• clearly compares chores in both places.	• does not clearly state differences and similarities.	• gives disorganized or inappropriate information.
• has a logical sequence.	• has an easy-to-follow sequence.	• does not elaborate fully on comparisons.	• has problems with writing conventions.
• uses the correct format for a friendly letter.	• uses a friendly-letter format.	• may not use a friendly-letter format.	• does not use friendly-letter format.

0: The writer leaves the page blank or fails to respond to the writing task. The student does not address the topic or simply paraphrases the prompt. The response is illegible or incoherent.

For a 6-point or an 8-point scale, see pages T105–T106.

Meeting Individual Needs for Writing

EASY

Captions and Labels Have students draw a picture of Justin doing a chore. Then have them make a drawing of Grandpa doing the same chore correctly. They should add appropriate labels and write a caption describing how each character is doing the chore.

ON-LEVEL

Journal Entry Have students write a journal entry from Justin's point of view, comparing himself before and after living on Grandpa's ranch. Have them concentrate on describing Justin's feelings about doing chores and about learning from Grandpa.

CHALLENGE

Rodeo Report Have a small group of students work together on a rodeo report. Have them write a group outline and then divide up the outline topics for individual research and writing. To complete the report, they can bind their pages together.

5 Day Grammar and Usage Plan

DAILY LANGUAGE ACTIVITIES

Write the Daily Language Activities on the chalkboard or use **Transparency 6.** Have students name the nouns and describe capitalization errors orally. For answers, see the transparency.

Day 1
1. My friend is a Cowboy.
2. His name is ringo.
3. My buddy drives a Truck.

Day 2
1. We all work hard the month of july.
2. Rick lives in new mexico.
3. His day off is monday.

Day 3
1. Do cowboys live in new york?
2. They eat thanksgiving dinner on the range.
3. My horse jumped the Fence.

Day 4
1. My neighbor, dr. hudson, dreams of being a cowhand.
2. He likes to eat Biscuits for lunch.
3. The rodeo will be jan. 28.

Day 5
1. We will go to parker's dude ranch on vacation.
2. We leave on mon., aug. 3.
3. My mom and mrs. watt will drive.

Daily Language Transparency 6

DAY 1 Introduce the Concept

Oral Warm-Up Say *biscuit, Justin,* and *Kansas.* Summarize by saying that those three words name a thing, a person, and a place.

Introduce Nouns A noun is one kind of word. Present the following:

> **Common and Proper Nouns**
>
> - A **noun** names a person, place, or thing.
> - A **common noun** names any person, place, or thing.
> - A **proper noun** names a particular person, place, or thing.
> - A proper noun begins with a capital letter.

Present the Daily Language Activity. Then ask small groups to list more nouns and categorize them as people, places, and things.

 Assign the daily Writing Prompt on page 132C.

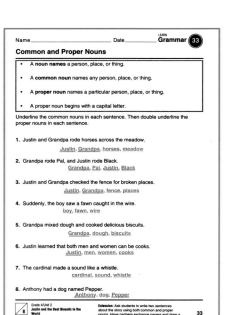

GRAMMAR PRACTICE BOOK, PAGE 33

DAY 2 Teach the Concept

Review Nouns Have students explain how a common noun differs from a proper noun.

Introduce Special Proper Nouns Some proper nouns follow special rules. Present the following:

> **Special Rules for Proper Nouns**
>
> - Some proper nouns contain more than one word. Each important word begins with a capital letter.
> - The name of a day, month, or holiday begins with a capital letter.

Present the Daily Language Activity. Then have students write a sentence or two about a place with a two-word name that they would like to visit on a holiday. Ask them to include the day and date of the holiday.

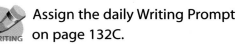 Assign the daily Writing Prompt on page 132C.

GRAMMAR PRACTICE BOOK, PAGE 34

Common and Proper Nouns

Learn from the Literature
Review common and proper nouns. Read the fourth sentence in paragraph 3 on page 149 of *Justin and the Best Biscuits in the World*.

> **In Deadwood City in the Dakota Territory**, he roped, tied, saddled, mounted, and rode a wild <u>horse</u> faster than anyone.

Ask students to identify the nouns and tell why some are capitalized and one is not.

List Common and Proper Nouns
Model how to make a noun chart with two columns headed *Common Nouns* and *Proper Nouns* and three rows for *Persons*, *Places*, and *Things*. Have students write nouns from the story in the correct boxes on the chart.

 Assign the daily Writing Prompt on page 132D.

Review Nouns
Write sentences from the Daily Language Activities for Days 1–3 on the board. Have volunteers identify the nouns. Then present the Daily Language Activity for Day 4.

Mechanics and Usage Discuss:

Abbreviations

- An **abbreviation** is the shortened form of a word.
- An abbreviation begins with a capital letter and ends with a period.
- Abbreviate titles of people before names.
- You can abbreviate days of the week.
- You can also abbreviate most months.

Provide students with the following examples: *Mrs., Mr., Dr., Sun., Sept.*

 Assign the daily Writing Prompt on page 132D.

Assess Use the Daily Language Activity and page 37 of the **Grammar Practice Book** for assessment.

Reteach Have volunteers point to each noun or abbreviation in the Daily Language Activity sentences. Have the rest of the class stand if the noun should be capitalized and remain seated if it should not. For each proper noun, ask one of the standing students to explain the capitalization rule.

Have students work together to make a word wall with lists of common and proper nouns.

Use page 38 of the **Grammar Practice Book** for additional reteaching.

Assign the daily Writing Prompt on page 132D.

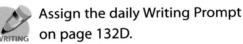

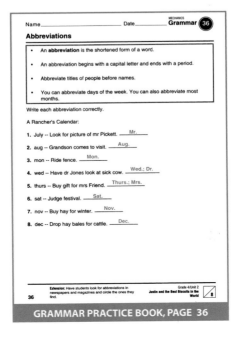

5 Day Spelling Plan

Say *cabin, mitten, sofa, and clover*. Have students repeat the words and snap their fingers to determine the number of syllables in each word.

DICTATION SENTENCES

Spelling Words

1. This biscuit is good.
2. The horse ate the clover.
3. We can swim at the public beach.
4. Father put the meat in the oven.
5. A bandage will keep the cut clean.
6. We stayed in a log cabin in the forest.
7. The toy is made of plastic.
8. The plane came into sight on the radar screen.
9. My little brother left one mitten at school.
10. I put everything in my knapsack.
11. The book fair will be at the local library.
12. Please give me some mustard.
13. My little sister is a pupil in the first grade.
14. All three of us can sit on the sofa.
15. Visitors are welcome any time.
16. Mother cut my hair with a razor.
17. These fancy boots are pretty.
18. The limit is two books a week.
19. We saw a famous star at the party.
20. She bought only one item today.

Challenge Words

21. We all had a good time at the festival.
22. All the clues point to his guilt.
23. The baby was inspecting the new toy.
24. After the party, a few people lingered.
25. The shout resounded around the canyon.

DAY 1 — Pretest

Assess Prior Knowledge Use the Dictation Sentences at the left and **Spelling Practice Book** page 33 for the pretest. Allow students to correct their own papers. Students who require a modified list may be tested on the first ten words.

Spelling Words		Challenge Words
1. **biscuit**	11. local	21. **festival**
2. clover	12. mustard	22. **guilt**
3. public	13. pupil	23. **inspect-ing**
4. oven	14. sofa	
5. bandage	15. **welcome**	24. **lingered**
6. cabin	16. **razor**	25. **resounded**
7. plastic	17. fancy	
8. radar	18. limit	
9. mitten	19. **famous**	
10. **knapsack**	20. item	

*Note: Words in **dark type** are from the story.*

Word Study On page 33 of the **Spelling Practice Book** are word study steps and an at-home activity.

DAY 2 — Explore the Pattern

Sort and Spell Words Say *cabin* and *razor*. Ask students to listen for the vowel sound in the first syllable of each word. (/a/, /ā/) Have students read the spelling words aloud and sort them as below.

Long vowel sound in the first syllable

clover	sofa	famous
radar	pupil	item
local	razor	

Short vowel sound in the first syllable

biscuit	cabin	mustard
public	plastic	welcome
oven	mitten	fancy
bandage	knapsack	limit

Syllable Patterns Have students divide the words into syllables. If the first syllable has a long vowel sound *(open syllable)*, divide after the vowel. *(lo-cal)* If it has a short vowel sound *(closed syllable)*, divide after the next consonant *(lim-it, pub-lic)*.

Syllable Patterns

Practice and Extend

Proofread and Write

Assess and Reteach

Day 3 — Practice and Extend

Word Meaning: Antonyms Remind students that an antonym has the opposite meaning of another word. Have students think of antonyms for *public*, *cabin*, *pupil*, *welcome*, *fancy*, and *famous*. Then have them write a sentence using one set of antonyms.

If students need extra practice, have partners give each other a midweek test.

Glossary Elicit from students that a *synonym* is a word that means almost the same thing as another word. The Glossary shows synonyms for some entry words. Have students

- look up *inspect* in the Glossary.

- find the synonym for *inspect*.

- write *inspecting* and write the synonym beside it, using the same form as the form of the Challenge Word.

(examining)

Day 4 — Proofread and Write

Proofread Sentences Write these sentences on the chalkboard, including the misspelled words. Ask students to proofread, circling incorrect spellings and writing the correct spellings. There are two spelling errors in each sentence.

The (biscits) are baking in the (uven).
(biscuits, oven)

Dad packed his (razer) in his (napsack).
(razor, knapsack)

Have students create additional sentences with errors for partners to correct.

WRITING Have students use as many Spelling Words as possible in the daily Writing Prompt on page 132D. Remind students to proofread their writing for errors in spelling, grammar, and punctuation.

Day 5 — Assess and Reteach

Assess Students' Knowledge Use page 56 of the **Spelling Practice Book** or the Dictation Sentences on page 157O for the posttest.

JOURNAL **Personal Word List** Students can add troublesome words to their personal lists in their journals. Suggest that they write the words in syllables and mark the vowel in the first syllable as either long or short.

Students should refer to their word lists during later writing activities.

SPELLING PRACTICE BOOK, PAGE 36

SPELLING PRACTICE BOOK, PAGE 37

SPELLING PRACTICE BOOK, PAGE 38

Just a Dream

Selection Summary Students will read a fantasy account of one boy's trip into a future shaped by the present day's disregard for the environment. When he awakes, the boy is glad to discover that his trip was "just a dream."

Listening Library Audiocassette

INSTRUCTIONAL
Pages 160–189

About the Author/Illustrator Chris Van Allsburg has explored flights of

fancy in several of his much-loved books. Van Allsburg has won numerous awards for his stories and illustrations, among them the Caldecott Medal in 1982, for *Jumanji*, and in 1986, for *The Polar Express*. He has also won *New York Times Best Illustrated Children's Book* citations for seven different books. Van Allsburg's illustrations appear highly realistic, but often his stories take characters on amazing voyages.

Resources for Meeting Individual Needs

LEVELED BOOKS

EASY
Pages 189A, 189D

INDEPENDENT
Pages 189B, 189D

CHALLENGE
Pages 189C, 189D

LEVELED PRACTICE

Reteach 45–51
blackline masters with reteaching opportunities for each assessed skill

Practice 45–51
workbook with Take-Home stories and practice opportunities for each assessed skill and story comprehension

Extend 45–51
blackline masters that offer challenge activities for each assessed skill

ADDITIONAL RESOURCES

- **Language Support Book,** 49–56
- **Take-Home Story, Practice,** p. 46a
- **Alternate Teaching Strategies,** T60–T66
- **Selected Quizzes Prepared by** Accelerated Reader

McGraw-Hill School
TECHNOLOGY
interNET CONNECTION Research and Inquiry Ideas. Visit www.mhschool.com/reading

Suggested Lesson Planner

🔵 **Available on CD-ROM**

READING AND LANGUAGE ARTS	DAY 1 — Focus on Reading and Skills	DAY 2 — Read the Literature
● **Comprehension** ● **Vocabulary** ● **Phonics/Decoding** ● **Study Skills** ● **Listening, Speaking, Viewing, Representing**	**Read** **Read Aloud and Motivate,** 158E *Earth Day Rap* **Develop Visual Literacy,** 158/159 ☑ **Introduce Sequence of Events** 160A–160B **Teaching Chart 37** Reteach, Practice, Extend, 45	**Build Background,** 160C Develop Oral Language **Vocabulary,** 160D bulging foul shrieking crumpled haze waddled **Teaching Chart 38** Word Building Manipulative Cards Reteach, Practice, Extend, 46 **Read** **Read the Selection,** 160–185 ☑ Sequence of Events ☑ Form Generalizations **Minilessons,** 163, 167, 169, 171, 173, 183 **Cultural Perspectives,** 182
● **Curriculum Connections**	**Link** Works of Art, 158/159	**Link** Science, 160C
● **Writing**	✏️ **Writing Prompt:** Make a list of things that you could recycle at home.	✏️ **Writing Prompt:** Write an ad for trees, bushes, and flowers, telling how they can improve a neighborhood. 📓 **Journal Writing,** 185 Quick-Write
● **Grammar**	**Introduce the Concept: Singular and Plural Nouns,** 189M Daily Language Activity 1. My father planted many tree. trees 2. That tree has lots of apple. apples 3. This tree has many flower. flowers **Grammar Practice Book,** 39	**Teach the Concept: Singular and Plural Nouns,** 189M Daily Language Activity 1. Plant bushs to cut down on noise. bushes 2. Babys should have clean air to breathe. Babies 3. Will children in the future have toy? toys **Grammar Practice Book,** 40
● **Spelling**	**Pretest: Words with Consonant Clusters,** 189O **Spelling Practice Book,** 39, 40	**Explore the Pattern: Words with Consonant Clusters,** 189O **Spelling Practice Book,** 41

DAY 3 Read the Literature	**DAY 4** Build Skills	**DAY 5** Build Skills
Rereading for Fluency, 184	**Read** **Read the Leveled Books and Self-Selected Books**	**Read** **Read Self-Selected Books**
Story Questions, 186 Reteach, Practice, Extend, 47	☑ **Review Sequence of Events,** 189E–189F **Teaching Chart 40** Reteach, Practice, Extend, 49 Language Support, 54	☑ **Introduce Compound Words,** 189I–189J **Teaching Chart 42** Reteach, Practice, Extend, 51 Language Support, 56
Story Activities, 187		
Study Skill, 188 ☑ Reference Sources **Teaching Chart 39** Reteach, Practice, Extend, 48	☑ **Review Form Generalizations,** 189G–189H **Teaching Chart 41** Reteach, Practice, Extend, 50 Language Support, 55	**Listening, Speaking, Viewing, Representing,** 189L Prepare Photography Displays Make Speeches
Test Power, 189		**Minilessons,** 163, 167, 171, 173, 183
		Phonics Review Consonant Clusters, 169
Read **Read the Leveled Books,** 189A–189D Guided Reading Consonant Clusters ☑ Sequence of Events ☑ Instructional Vocabulary		**Phonics/Phonemic Awarness Practice Book,** 25–28
Activity **Math,** 166	**Activity** **Social Studies,** 170	**Activity** **Science,** 176, 180
Writing Prompt: Write a set of directions for painting benches or planting bushes. **Writing Process: Writing That Compares,** 189K Prewrite, Draft	**Writing Prompt:** Write a paragraph listing things you would expect to see if you visited the future. **Writing Process: Writing That Compares,** 189K Revise **Meeting Individual Needs for Writing,** 189L	**Writing Prompt:** Imagine that you had a wild dream. Write about the things you saw in your dream. **Writing Process: Writing That Compares,** 189K Edit/Proofread, Publish
Review and Practice: Singular and Plural Nouns, 189N Daily Language Activity 1. The park has many bench. benches 2. Duck like to swim in the pond. Ducks 3. Some foxs live in the park, too. foxes **Grammar Practice Book,** 41	**Review and Practice: Singular and Plural Nouns,** 189N Daily Language Activity 1. The air is cleaner on some day than others. days 2. City bus make a lot of noise. buses 3. The sky has patchs of smog. patches **Grammar Practice Book,** 42	**Assess and Reteach: Singular and Plural Nouns,** 189N Daily Language Activity 1. Librarys have books about recycling. libraries 2. Those bin are for litter. bins 3. Recycle those bottle. bottles **Grammar Practice Book,** 43, 44
Practice and Extend: Words with Consonant Clusters, 189P **Spelling Practice Book,** 42	**Proofread and Write: Words with Consonant Clusters,** 189P **Spelling Practice Book,** 43	**Assess and Reteach: Words with Consonant Clusters,** 189P **Spelling Practice Book,** 44

Music

Read Aloud and Motivate

Earth Day Rap
words and music
by Doug Goodkin

The sky is high and the ocean is
deep,
But we can't treat the planet like a
garbage heap.
Don't wreck it, protect it, keep part
of it wild,
And think about the future of your
great-grandchild.

Recycle, bicycle, don't you drive by
yourself,
Don't buy those plastic products on
the supermarket shelf.

Boycott, petition, let the big
bus'ness know,
That if we mess it up here, there's
nowhere else we can go.

Don't shrug your shoulders, say,
"What can I do?"
Only one person can do it and that
person is you!

Oral Comprehension

LISTENING AND SPEAKING Motivate students to begin thinking about the sequence of events that leads to environmental problems by reading this rap song aloud. Ask students, "What can you do to protect the environment?" Then ask, "What will happen if you don't take care of the environment?" You might consider organizing students into three groups, distributing a copy of one stanza to each group, and having each group read its part of the whole poem.

Activity Encourage groups to create new stanzas for the rap. They can begin by brainstorming ideas to create a topic for the stanza and then experiment with different word combinations. Have them write down the final version, practice it, and present it to the class.
▶ **Musical/Linguistic**

Develop Visual Literacy

Anthology pages 158–159

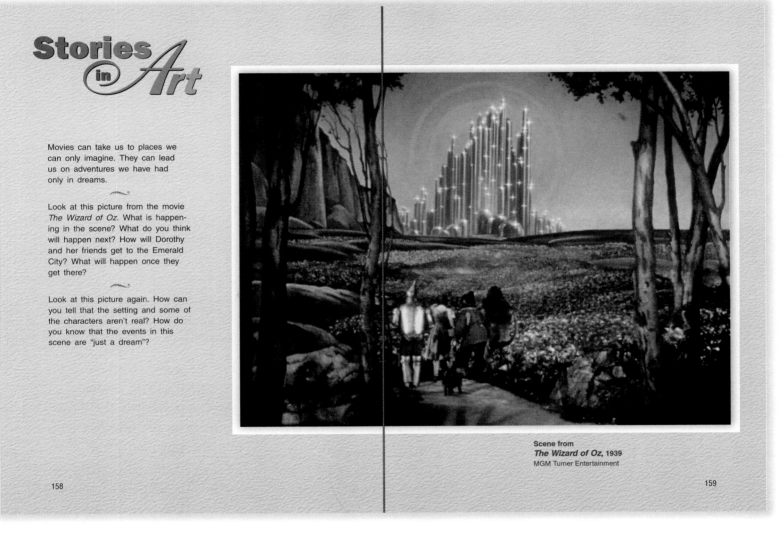

Stories in Art

Movies can take us to places we can only imagine. They can lead us on adventures we have had only in dreams.

Look at this picture from the movie *The Wizard of Oz*. What is happening in the scene? What do you think will happen next? How will Dorothy and her friends get to the Emerald City? What will happen once they get there?

Look at this picture again. How can you tell that the setting and some of the characters aren't real? How do you know that the events in this scene are "just a dream"?

Scene from
The Wizard of Oz, 1939
MGM Turner Entertainment

158

159

Objective: Identify Sequence of Events

VIEWING Tell students that this is a picture of a scene from the movie *The Wizard of Oz*. Explain that in photographs and paintings, objects that appear to be nearer the viewer (foreground) are larger. Objects that appear to be in the distance (background) are smaller. Have students describe in order objects that are in the foreground, middle, and background of the photo.

Read the page with students. Be sure students understand that the characters will follow a path to get to the Emerald City. Ask them to use visual clues in the picture (as well as incidents they may recall from the movie) to list a sequence of three or four events that might happen along the way.

Have them compare how the characters' ideas about the city may change the closer they get to it.

REPRESENTING Have students make a map of the path from the forest through the field of poppies to the Emerald City. Have them add brief numbered captions to the map to describe what might happen at three or four locations along the route.

Students will identify the sequence of events.

LANGUAGE SUPPORT

ESL Write the words *first, next, then, after that,* and *finally* on the chalkboard. Ask a student to describe what he or she did before school today using one of these words to begin each sentence. Point out how the words are used to clarify the order things happened in a sequence of events.

Introduce Sequence of Events

PREPARE

Discuss Sequence of Events

Have students think of the things they did to get ready for school today. Have volunteers list the series of events in the order they occurred.

TEACH

Define Sequence of Events

Explain: You can learn to identify a series of events by listening carefully or thinking about the order in which things happen. Writers and speakers often use clue words such as *then, later, next,* or *first, second, last* to signal the order of events.

Amy Recycles

Every Tuesday and Friday Amy sorts and takes out the trash. First, she stacks up the newspapers and makes another pile of magazines. Next, she places the dog food cans and other metals in one bag. Then she dumps the milk bottles and other plastics in another bag. After that, she carefully places the glass jars in a third bag. Finally, she carries the compost bucket to the garden, holding her nose with her clean hand.

Teaching Chart 37

Read the Story and Model the Skill

Display **Teaching Chart 37.** Have students look for clues about the sequence of events as they read the story.

MODEL The first sentence tells me that this story is about how Amy sorts the garbage. Clue words such as *first* and *next* throughout the story show the order in which she does each step.

Identify Sequence of Events

Have students circle the words that signal the order of events and underline each action in the sequence.

PRACTICE

Create a Sequence Chart

GROUP

Using a Sequence of Events chart, have students list the steps Amy follows as she sorts the garbage. Guide them in filling in the first step and then call on volunteers to complete the rest of the chart.

▶ **Linguistic/Logical**

Sequence of Events

First, Amy stacks up newspapers and magazines.

▼

Next, she places the dog food cans and other metal in one bag.

ASSESS/CLOSE

Identify Sequence of Events

Ask students to write these events in the most logical sequence:

- Jackie removes the plastic wrapper from the CD-ROM.
- Jackie buys a new CD-ROM.
- Jackie goes to the computer store to look at CD-ROMs.
- Jackie throws the wrapper in the trash.

SELECTION Connection

Students will apply sequence of events as they read *Just a Dream* and the Leveled Books.

ALTERNATE TEACHING STRATEGY

SEQUENCE OF EVENTS
For a different approach to teaching this skill, see page T64.

Meeting Individual Needs for Comprehension

EASY

Name_____ Date_____ Reteach **45**

Sequence of Events

Sequence is the order in which things happen. Words such as *before*, *first*, and *then* can help you understand sequence.

Read the story. Circle the letter beside the answer to each question.

Jed won the marathon by 10 minutes. But it wasn't as easy as it seemed. Before Jed began running, he read about training. Then he started to run short distances. Jed increased the number of miles he ran each week. After 4 months, Jed ran a half-marathon, or 13 miles. Although Jed lost his first race, he trained for another 8 months until he was ready for a full marathon.

1. Which of these events happened first?
   a. Jed won the marathon.
   b. Jed began running.
   c. Jed read all about training.

2. Which of these events happened last?
   a. Jed trained for another 8 months.
   b. Jed won the marathon.
   c. Jed ran a half-marathon.

3. What is the first thing Jed did after he read about training?
   a. Jed increased the number of miles he ran each week.
   b. Jed ran a half-marathon.
   c. Jed started to run short distances.

4. What did Jed do after he lost the half-marathon?
   a. Jed trained for another 8 months.
   b. Jed read about training.
   c. Jed increased the number of miles that he ran each week.

5. How many months of training did Jed need until he won a marathon?
   a. 4   b. 8   **c.** 12

Book 4/Unit 2
Just a Dream   **At Home:** Have students describe five things they have done during the day in the order in which the things happened.   **45**

Reteach, 45

ON-LEVEL

Name_____ Date_____ Practice **45**

Sequence of Events

The **sequence of events** is the order in which things happen in a story. Keeping track of the order helps you understand the plot. Read this story and then number the events 1 to 5 in the order in which they occurred.

It happened a long time ago on a distant planet called Evergreen. This planet took its name from the beautiful trees that covered much of its land. The special thing about the people on Evergreen was that everything they had was made of paper. The paper was made from trees. They had paper clothes, paper toys, paper houses, and paper cars. The people on Evergreen used a lot of trees.

After a thousand years, great bare spots began to appear in the forests of Evergreen. Many trees had been cut down, but none had been replanted. Next, deer, fox, and other animals disappeared from Evergreen. They had no place to live. Finally, the air began to go bad. The great forests had always cleaned the air. There were no more large forests on the planet. It wouldn't be long until all life on Evergreen disappeared.

___3___ Deer, fox, and other animals disappeared.

___1___ Evergreen was covered with beautiful trees.

___5___ It would not be long before all life on Evergreen would die.

___2___ Houses, clothes, toys, and cars were made of paper.

___4___ The air on Evergreen went bad.

Book 4/Unit 2
Just a Dream   **At Home:** Have students write their own tale and sequence the events in it.   **45**

Practice, 45

CHALLENGE

Name_____ Date_____ Extend **45**

Sequence of Events

Think about a typical day at school. Do you usually have the same subject at the same time each day? Are recesses and lunch at the same time? Outline a typical day at school. Write each event in the order in which it occurs during the day. Compare the **sequence of events** in your school day with those of classmates. Discuss any differences.

Answers will vary, but events should be in the correct sequence.

_____

_____

_____

_____

_____

_____

_____

_____

Book 4/Unit 2
Just a Dream   **At Home:** Compare and contrast the sequence of events on a weekday with the sequence of events on a Saturday.   **45**

Extend, 45

Build Background

Link
Science

Anthology and Leveled Books

Evaluate Prior Knowledge

CONCEPT: ECOLOGY These selections highlight the importance of taking care of the environment. Encourage students to share what they know about how things in nature, including humans, are interdependent.

MAKE A CHART ABOUT ECOLOGICAL RESPONSIBILITY Brainstorm with students actions some people take that can damage the environment. Talk about responsible actions that people can take to improve the environment. List their ideas in a chart. ▶ **Logical/Visual**

IRRESPONSIBLE	RESPONSIBLE
leave water running	turn off water
waste food	take only what you need
leave car running while you wait	walk or bike to places

PLAN A PROJECT Show students a video such as *The Garbage Dump Dilemma*. (See page T76.) Then have them work with partners to brainstorm a list of places in the community that need cleaning up. Have them discuss and list ways that people could work together to improve these places.

PARTNERS   WRITING

Develop Oral Language

TALK ABOUT POLLUTION Show students pictures that depict environmental pollution, such as a factory smokestack belching smoke and a lawn mower making a lot of noise. Also display some actual objects that pollute the environment, such as empty soda cans, fast-food wrappers, and foam trays. Ask students to describe each example of pollution.

Then look at these items again and help students describe ways they can help prevent or lessen environmental pollution. For example, they can be sure to recycle soda cans and throw fast-food wrappers in trash cans. Then ask them what factory owners and others can do to help. Give language support as needed.

TEACHING TIP

MANAGEMENT As pairs of students work together on the Plan a Project activity, use the Develop Oral Language activity to work with students who need to develop oral language facility.

LANGUAGE SUPPORT

See **Language Support Book,** pages 49–52, for teaching suggestions for Build Background and Vocabulary.

Vocabulary

Key Words

Pollution in the Park

1. Walter held a tissue to his nose to <u>keep from breathing</u> the (foul) air. **2.** <u>Many more tissues</u> filled his (bulging) pockets. **3.** He picked up a <u>dirty,</u> (crumpled) piece of paper and put it in the trash. **4.** He could <u>barely see</u> through the <u>thick gray</u> (haze) **5.** He didn't even see a <u>duck</u> until it (waddled) right up to him and quacked. **6.** Walter was so <u>surprised,</u> he <u>ran</u> (shrieking) from the park.

Teaching Chart 38

Definitions

foul (p. 168) dirty and smelly

bulging (p. 164) swelling out

crumpled (p. 161) crushed together

haze (p. 176) misty or smoky air

waddled (p. 179) walked with short, swaying steps

shrieking (p. 174) giving off a loud, shrill sound

SPELLING/VOCABULARY CONNECTIONS

See Spelling Challenge Words, pages 189O–189P.

Vocabulary in Context

IDENTIFY VOCABULARY WORDS Display **Teaching Chart 38** and read the passage with students. Have volunteers circle each vocabulary word and underline words that provide clues to its meaning.

DISCUSS MEANINGS Use prompts like these to help clarify word meanings:

• What might make the air foul?

• What is the base word of *bulging?* What might make your pockets bulge?

• How would you crumple a tissue or piece of paper? Show us.

• Where have you ever seen a haze before? Describe it.

• How does a duck waddle? Show us.

• What things might make you shriek?

Practice

DEMONSTRATE WORD MEANING Have partners act out the story on the chart, holding up vocabulary words as they occur in the role-play. ▶ **Kinesthetic/Linguistic**

Word Building Manipulative Cards

WRITE CLOZE STORIES Have partners write a story using blanks to indicate the vocabulary words. They can then exchange stories with another pair who will complete the blanks.

▶ **Linguistic/Interpersonal**

ON-LEVEL

In Early Spring

A misty *haze* filled the morning sky. The fresh spring air seemed sweet compared to the *foul* air of winter. Baby birds were *shrieking* for food and attention. Baby ducks *waddled* behind their mothers toward the river. A slight breeze blew the fallen and *crumpled* flowers from last year. At the market, people's shopping bags were *bulging* with garden tools, boxes of tiny plants, and flower and vegetable seeds. Spring was really here.

1. What is another name for *haze?* _mist_
2. How is the winter air described? _The air was foul compared to spring air._
3. How are shopper's bags described? _They were bulging with garden tools, boxes of tiny plants, and flower and vegetable seeds._
4. How did the baby ducks walk? _They waddled._
5. Why do you think this story is called "In Early Spring"? _Because it tells of things that occur at that time of year._

Book 4/Unit 2 *Just a Dream*
At Home: Have students draw a picture to illustrate the story.
46a

Take-Home Story 46a
Reteach 46
Practice 46 • Extend 46

Guided Instruction

Preview and Predict

Have students preview the pictures, looking for clues to the sequence of events.

- What do you think happens after the main character falls asleep?
- Where do you think the beginning of this story takes place?
- What is this story most likely about?
- What clue does the title give that this story might be a fantasy? (A fantasy describes things that can't really happen. The title implies the story events didn't really take place.) *Genre*

Have students record their predictions about the story events.

PREDICTIONS	WHAT HAPPENED
The boy has a dream.	
The boy learns something in his dream.	

Set Purposes

What do students want to learn as they read the story? For example:

- What does the boy dream about?
- What does the boy learn?

160

Meeting Individual Needs • Grouping Suggestions for Strategic Reading

EASY

Read Together Read the story with students or have them read along with the **Listening Library Audiocassette**. Have students use the Sequence of Events chart to record details about the order in which events occur. Guided Instruction and Intervention prompts offer additional help with decoding, vocabulary, and comprehension.

ON-LEVEL

Guided Reading Preview the story words listed on page 161. Then select from the Guided Instruction questions as you read the story with students. You may wish to have students play the **Listening Library Audiocassette.** Have students use the Sequence of Events chart to track key events as they read.

CHALLENGE

Read Independently Have students read independently. Remind them that paying attention to the sequence of events will help them understand the story. Have students begin a Sequence of Events chart as on page 161. After reading, have them use their chart to review the story and retell the events.

𝔄s usual, Walter stopped at the bakery on his way home from school. He bought one large jelly-filled dough-nut. He took the pastry from its bag, eating quickly as he walked along. He licked the red jelly from his fingers. Then he crumpled up the empty bag and threw it at a fire hydrant.

①

JUST A DREAM

Written and Illustrated by
Chris Van Allsburg

161

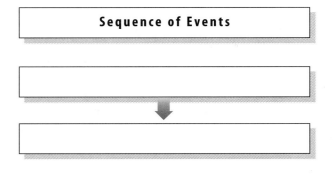
Guided Instruction

☑ **Sequence of Events**
☑ **Form Generalizations**

Strategic Reading Sometimes a story moves around in time and place. These stories can be confusing if you lose track of what happens when. Before we begin reading, let's prepare Sequence of Events charts so that we can keep track of the events in the story as they happen.

Sequence of Events

⬇

① **SEQUENCE OF EVENTS** What events begin this story? (A boy named Walter buys a doughnut, eats it, and throws away the bag.)

Story Words

The words below may be unfamiliar. Have students check their meanings and pronunciations in the Glossary beginning on page 726 or in a dictionary.

- garbage, p. 162
- robot, p. 163
- machine, p. 163
- traveled, p. 163
- foggy, p. 176
- smog, p. 176

Guided Instruction

2 What does Walter think of the present that Rose got for her birthday? (He thinks a tree is a foolish choice for a present.) *Make Inferences*

3 **FORM GENERALIZATIONS** Why doesn't Walter usually separate the trash into the three cans next to the garage?

MODEL I have already seen how Walter litters, like when he threw away the doughnut bag. I can also tell he doesn't care about trees. Using these things I've learned I can make the generalization that Walter doesn't care about the environment.

$\mathcal{A}$t home Walter saw Rose, the little girl next door, watering a tree that had just been planted. "It's my birthday present," she said proudly. Walter couldn't understand why anyone would want a tree for a present. His own birthday was just a few days away, "And I'm not getting some dumb plant," he told Rose.

2 After dinner Walter took out the trash. Three cans stood next to the garage. One was for bottles, one for cans, and one for everything else. As usual, Walter dumped everything into one can. He was too busy to sort through garbage, especially when there was something good on television.

3 The show that Walter was so eager to watch was about a boy who lived in the future. The boy flew around in a tiny airplane that he parked on the roof of his house.

162

Guided Instruction

4 **SEQUENCE OF EVENTS** What happens after Walter gets into bed?

MODEL I'm a little confused. This story has been very realistic up to now, but suddenly Walter's bed is flying and he's traveling to the future. Let me think about the sequence of events. First, Walter goes to bed. Then he falls asleep. Then his wish for a plane and doughnut machine comes true. Wait. Now I understand. Walter is dreaming. The author left that step out of the sequence, but that must be what happened.

He had a robot and a small machine that could make any kind of food with the push of a button.

Walter went to bed wishing he lived in the future. He couldn't wait to have his own tiny plane, a robot to take out the trash, and a machine that could make jelly doughnuts by the thousands. When he fell asleep, his wish came true. That night Walter's bed traveled to . . .

4 the future.

163

163

Guided Instruction

5 Has anyone ever wanted to drive a bulldozer? Would someone act out how a bulldozer driver might push a heap of trash bags and then put the bulldozer in neutral? *Pantomime*

$\mathbf{W}$alter woke up in the middle of a huge dump. A bulldozer was pushing a heap of bulging trash bags toward him. "Stop!" he yelled.

5 The man driving the bulldozer put his machine in neutral. "Oh, sorry," he said. "Didn't see you."

Walter looked at the distant mountains of trash and saw half-buried houses. "Do people live here?" he asked.

"Not anymore," answered the man.

A few feet from the bed was a rusty old street sign that read

164

LANGUAGE SUPPORT

ESL Use the illustrations to help students understand terms such as *huge dump, bulldozer, mountains of trash, half-buried,* and *the covers.* Ask them to define each term in their own words and to use it in an original sentence. For example, they might say: *There is a huge dump out on highway 63 near Watkins* or *A bulldozer is used to dig holes in the ground or to move around piles of dirt.*

Guided Instruction

 6 **SEQUENCE OF EVENTS** Where is Walter now? What exactly is happening?

MODEL Restating each new event in my own words helps me keep track of what is happening. Before this, Walter went to sleep. Now he's in the same place, Floral Avenue, but somewhere in the future or in a dream. He doesn't like what he sees so he goes back to sleep.

7 Why do you think Walter hopes that this is a dream, and not the future?
(Sample answer: Walter doesn't like what he sees. He had a different idea of how the future would look.) *Make Inferences*

FLORAL AVENUE. "Oh no," gasped Walter. He lived on Floral Avenue.

6

The driver revved up his bulldozer. "Well," he shouted, "back to work!"

Walter pulled the covers over his head. This can't be the future, he thought. I'm sure it's just a dream. He went back to sleep.

7

But not for long . . .

165

165

Guided Instruction

8 Let's act out what happens on these two pages. Who wants to be Walter? Who will be the woodcutters? Woodcutters, show all the actions described. Walter, show how you feel when you find out the important reason they are cutting down the tree.
Role-Play

TEACHING TIP

MANAGEMENT To involve more students in the role-playing, for pages 166–167, organize students into groups of three and have each group act out the dramatization.

8 Walter peered over the edge of his bed, which was caught in the branches of a tall tree. Down below, he could see two men carrying a large saw. "Hello!" Walter yelled out.

"Hello to you!" they shouted back.

"You aren't going to cut down this tree, are you?" Walter asked.

But the woodcutters didn't answer. They took off their jackets, rolled up their sleeves, and got to work. Back and forth they pushed the saw, slicing through the trunk of Walter's tree. "You must need

166

Activity

Cross Curricular: Math

HOW IS WOOD USED? Explain to students that trees are a valuable resource with many uses. On the chalkboard, write the following information about how wood is used:
- fuel (17.6%)
- lumber (44.2%)
- paper (29.3%)
- plywood (8.9%).

Have students use this information to create a pie chart.

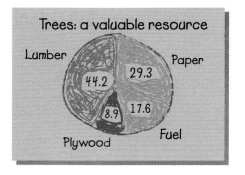

Trees: a valuable resource
Lumber 44.2, Paper 29.3, Fuel 17.6, Plywood 8.9

Guided Instruction

(9) SEQUENCE OF EVENTS Let's add to our Sequence of Events charts to show the events that have taken place since the story began.

Sequence of Events

Walter litters and does not bother trying to recycle trash.

⬇

Walter falls asleep and starts dreaming of the future.

⬇

He dreams he sees his house buried under trash, and trees cut down just to make toothpicks.

this tree for something important," Walter called down.

"Oh yes," they said, "very important." Then Walter noticed lettering on the wood- *stop* cutters' jackets. He could just make out the words: QUALITY TOOTHPICK COMPANY. Walter sighed and slid back under the blankets.

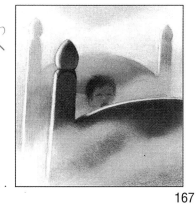

(9)

Until . . .

167

LANGUAGE SUPPORT

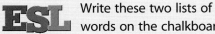 Write these two lists of words on the chalkboard.

1: peer, slice, notice, sigh, slide

2: cut, be able to see, groan, slip, see something suddenly

Ask students to read pages 166–167 independently. Then have them try to write one of the definitions from list 2 after each of the words in list 1. Discuss their answers and finish matching up all the words. Then ask them to reread the pages, using the word list as a guide if they have difficulty understanding.

Minilesson

REVIEW/MAINTAIN

Context Clues

Remind students that looking for context clues can help them understand unfamiliar words.

• Point out the word *peered* on page 166. Have students identify context clues in the surrounding sentences, such as the phrase "could see."

• Have them guess what the word means and then check the illustration on pages 166–167 for more clues. Would they like to revise their guess?

Activity Have students write three sentences using *peered*. Each should contain a different context clue.

167

Guided Instruction

(10) In what ways does the illustration create a feeling that supports the text on these pages? (The smoke looks really red and irritating; the boy in the bed seems very exposed.) *Critical Thinking*

(p/i) DECODING/WORD STRUCTURE How many syllables do you hear in the words *filled, belched,* and *climbed?* (Each word is pronounced as one syllable; the inflectional ending *-ed* is not pronounced as a separate syllable.)

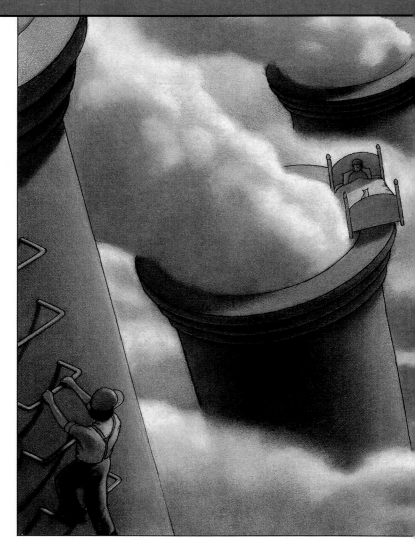

(10)

Walter couldn't stop coughing. His bed was balanced on the rim of a giant smokestack. The air was filled with smoke that burned his throat and made his eyes itch. All around him, dozens of smokestacks belched thick clouds of hot, foul smoke. A workman climbed one of the stacks.

"What is this place?" Walter called out.

"This is the Maximum Strength Medicine Factory," the man answered.

"Gosh," said Walter, looking at all the smoke, "what kind of medicine do they make here?"

"Wonderful medicine," the

168

(p/i) PREVENTION/INTERVENTION

DECODING/WORD STRUCTURE
Explain to students that adding an ending such as *-ed* to a word may or may not change the number of syllables in the word.

Have students list a number of words with the inflectional ending *-ed*. Then have them say the words, listening for each syllable, and sort the words based on whether the ending becomes a new syllable. Have students form a generalization about what they observe. For example, they might notice that in words ending with *-t* or *-d*, adding *-ed* forms another syllable.

workman replied, "for burning throats and itchy eyes."

Walter started coughing again.

"I can get you some," the man offered.

"No thanks," said Walter. He buried his head in his pillow and, when his coughing stopped, fell asleep.

But then . . .

169

Guided Instruction

11 What is funny about the man's response when Walter asks what kind of medicine is made in the factory? (The factory makes medicine; if the factory weren't there, there wouldn't be smoke to make people cough, and they wouldn't need the medicine.) *Critical Thinking*

Minilesson

REVIEW/MAINTAIN

Consonant Clusters

Remind students that consonants often appear in pairs. List these examples:

- *fl, cl, cr, br* (at the beginning of a word)
- *ng, nk* (at the end of a word)

Explain that in these consonant clusters each letter keeps its own sound, but in the other pairs, such as *ph*, the two letters combine to form one sound.

Activity Students can make a chart of words with each of the consonant clusters above. Have them start by looking through *Just a Dream.*

169

Guided Instruction

(12) SEQUENCE OF EVENTS How does Walter end up on Mount Everest after he was just at the Maximum Strength Medicine Factory? (He has another dream.)

Snowflakes fell on Walter. He was high in the mountains. A group of people wearing snowshoes and long fur coats hiked past his bed.

"Where are you going?" Walter asked.

"To the hotel," one of them replied.

Walter turned around and saw an enormous building. A sign on it read HOTEL EVEREST. "Is that hotel," asked Walter, "on the top of Mount Everest?"

170

Activity

Cross Curricular: Social Studies

MOUNT EVEREST At 29,028 feet, Mount Everest is the world's tallest mountain. Since Sir Edmund Hillary and Tenzing Norgay first scaled it, Everest has become a popular climbing destination. Today many tons of climbing equipment litter the slopes of the mountain.

RESEARCH AND INQUIRY Have students investigate how climbers prepare for Mount Everest and what special equipment they need. If possible, they should find out what equipment gets left behind. Have them make a poster showing what they learn. ▶ **Visual**

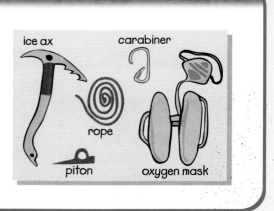

"Yes," said one of the hikers. "Isn't it beautiful?"

"Well," Walter began. But the group didn't wait for his answer. They waved goodbye and marched away. Walter stared at the flashing yellow sign, then crawled back beneath his sheets.

But there was more to see . . .

171

Guided Instruction

 FORM GENERALIZATIONS Why do people like to go to places like Mount Everest? Would many people want to climb Mount Everest if it had a hotel with a flashing sign on top? (People like to go there because it is a place of natural beauty, removed from busy, noisy modern life. A hotel with flashing lights would probably disturb people.)

Minilesson

REVIEW/MAINTAIN

Summarize

Tell students that summarizing is a good way to check whether they have understood what they read.

• Have students give a short summary of the events on pages 170–171.

Activity Students can write a paragraph summarizing another story they have read recently.

171

Guided Instruction

(14) Why are the fishermen so excited to catch one small fish? (It seems that there are few fish left at all, so they are glad to find even a small one.) *Draw Conclusions*

SELF-MONITORING

STRATEGY

SEARCH FOR CLUES Looking for clues can help readers understand things that the writer doesn't say directly.

MODEL At first I couldn't understand why the fishermen were so excited about catching one tiny fish. But the clue that it was only the second fish they caught this week helped me realize that not many fish live in this water.

Walter's hand was wet and cold. When he opened his eyes, he found himself floating on the open sea, drifting toward a fishing boat. The men on the boat were laughing and dancing.

"Ship ahoy!" Walter shouted. The fishermen waved to him.

"What's the celebration for?" he asked.

"We've just caught a fish," one of them yelled back. "Our second one this week!" They held up their small fish for Walter to see.

(14) "Aren't you supposed to throw the little ones back?" Walter asked.

172

But the fishermen didn't hear him. They were busy singing and dancing.

Walter turned away. Soon the rocking of the bed put him to sleep. **(15)**

But only for a moment . . .

173

Guided Instruction

(15) **SEQUENCE OF EVENTS** Let's act out the events that take place on the open sea. Who would like to help show the actions? We need someone to be Walter and several people to be the fishermen. Now show what the characters say and do. *Role-Play*

173

Guided Instruction

16 **SEQUENCE OF EVENTS** Where does Walter find himself next? (He is stuck in traffic on a noisy, crowded highway.)

p/i **SYNTACTIC CLUES** Look at the words *shrieking, creeping,* and *honking.* What is the same in these words? (They end in *-ing.*) How can you tell if these words are verbs, nouns, or adjectives? (You must think about how the word is used in the sentence.)

A loud, shrieking horn nearly lifted Walter off his mattress. He jumped up. There were cars and trucks all around him, horns honking loudly, creeping along inch by inch. Every driver had a car phone in one hand and **16** a big cup of coffee in the other.

When the traffic stopped completely, the honking grew even louder. Walter could not get back to sleep.

Hours passed, and he wondered if he'd be stuck on this highway forever. He pulled his pillow tightly around his head.

174

SYNTACTIC CLUES Tell students that words can sometimes act as more than one part of speech.

Write the words *shrieking, creeping,* and *honking* on the chalkboard. Have students read these sentences and think about whether *shrieking* is a noun, a verb, or an adjective in each sentence.

- A horn was shrieking loudly.
- The shrieking horn could be heard for blocks.
- The horn's shrieking hurt his ears.

Then have students write sentences of their own, using *creeping* and *honking* each as two different parts of speech.

This can't be the future, he thought. Where are the tiny airplanes, the robots? The honking continued into the night, until finally, one by one, the cars became quiet as their drivers, and Walter, went to sleep.

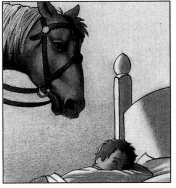

But his bed traveled on . . .

175

Guided Instruction

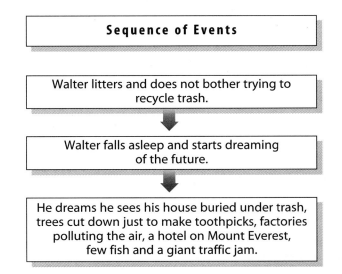

17 **SEQUENCE OF EVENTS** Let's update our Sequence of Events charts. First, let's list everything Walter has seen in his dreams so far:

1. He saw a huge garbage dump where the trash buried his home.

2. He saw men cutting down big trees just to make toothpicks.

3. He saw factories polluting the air with foul smoke.

4. Walter saw that people had built a hotel on the world's tallest mountain.

5. He learned few fish were left in the sea.

6. Then he sat in a giant traffic jam.

Now let's sum up his dreams and add to our chart.

Sequence of Events

Walter litters and does not bother trying to recycle trash.

⬇

Walter falls asleep and starts dreaming of the future.

⬇

He dreams he sees his house buried under trash, trees cut down just to make toothpicks, factories polluting the air, a hotel on Mount Everest, few fish and a giant traffic jam.

Guided Instruction

18 Do you know what the Grand Canyon looks like? How is it different from this picture? What do you think could have caused so much smog? (Sample answer: The Grand Canyon is a beautiful place. Smoke from factories and cars could have caused this smog.) *Make Inferences*

18

Walter looked up. A horse stood right over his bed, staring directly at him. In the saddle was a woman wearing cowboy clothes. "My horse likes you," she said.

"Good," replied Walter, who wondered where he'd ended up this time. All he could see was a dull yellow haze.

"Son," the woman told him, spreading her arms in front of her, "this is the mighty Grand Canyon."

Walter gazed into the foggy distance.

"Of course," she went on, "with all this smog, nobody's gotten a good look at it for years." The woman offered to sell Walter some

176

Activity

Cross Curricular: Science

GRAND CANYON Explain that the Grand Canyon is one of the natural wonders of the world. Show students a picture of it or have them locate one.
RESEARCH AND INQUIRY Have students research what kinds of plants and animals are found at the Grand Canyon.

Groups can create murals depicting the area's various plant and animal species.
▶ **Visual/Interpersonal**

*inter*NET **CONNECTION** Students can learn about the Grand Canyon by visiting *www.mhschool.com/reading*

See the Grand Canyon!

Guided Instruction

 19 How is this setting similar to the one at the cough medicine factory? (There is a lot of air pollution in both places.) *Compare and Contrast*

MULTIPLE-MEANING WORDS Reread the last sentence, which contains the word *back*. What is one meaning of the word *back*? What do you think the word *back* means in this sentence?

postcards that showed the canyon in the old days. "They're real pretty," she said.

But he couldn't look. It's just a dream, he told himself. I know I'll wake up soon, back in my room.

But he didn't . . .

177

PREVENTION/INTERVENTION

MULTIPLE-MEANING WORDS
Write *back* on the chalkboard. Tell students that this is a multiple-meaning word. Ask volunteers to suggest different meanings. (the part of a person's body opposite the front; part of a chair; behind in space or time; in the place from which something or someone came)

Play a game in which you give students a number of directions using different meanings of the word *back*. Have them respond using gestures. For example:
- Point to your back.
- Touch the back of your chair.
- Step back from your desk.
- Go back to your seat.

Guided Instruction

(20) **SEQUENCE OF EVENTS** What is Walter's next adventure? Show how you might react if a duck started talking to you. *Pantomime*

Visual Literacy

VIEWING AND REPRESENTING

Ask students to look at the picture on pages 178–179. Point out the different shades of blue in the illustration, and then encourage students to describe how it makes them feel. Invite students to look at the illustrations that accompany the dream sequences on pages 164–179. Help them notice that each illustration is dominated by one color. Encourage students to tell how they react to certain colors. Do Chris Van Allsburg's color choices portray the mood he's trying to convey?

Walter looked out from under his sheets. His bed was flying through the night sky. A flock of ducks passed overhead. One of them landed on the bed, and to Walter's surprise, he began to speak. "I hope you don't mind," **(20)** the bird said, "if I take a short rest here." The ducks had been flying for days, looking for the pond where they had always stopped to eat.

"I'm sure it's down there somewhere," Walter said, though he suspected something awful might have happened. After a

178

while the duck waddled to the edge of the bed, took a deep breath, and flew off. "Good luck," Walter called to him. Then he pulled the blanket over his head. "It's just a dream," he whispered, and wondered if it would ever end.

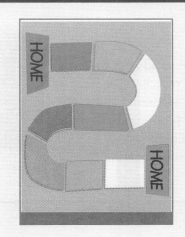

Then finally . . .

179

Guided Instruction

 Based on the other events in the story, what could have happened to the pond? (Possible responses: The air could be too smoggy for the ducks to see it; people might have filled it in and built houses where it used to be.) *Draw Conclusions*

LANGUAGE SUPPORT

ESL The many sudden changes of setting in this story may be confusing for students needing language support. To help them keep track, distribute a game board outline like the one at right. Have students write a simple label on each square for each place Walter visits in a dream—for example, clouds. Also use the outline to discuss the story's pattern.

179

Guided Instruction

22 SEQUENCE OF EVENTS Now where does Walter find himself? (He has returned to his room; he is back in the present.)

Walter's bed returned to the present. He was safe in his room again, but he felt terrible. The future he'd seen was not what he'd expected. Robots and little airplanes didn't seem very important now. He looked out his window at the trees and lawns in the early morning light, then **22** jumped out of bed.

He ran outside and down the block, still in his pajamas. He found the empty jelly doughnut bag he'd thrown at the fire hydrant the day before. Then Walter went back home and, before the sun came up, sorted all the trash by the garage.

A few days later, on Walter's birthday, all his friends came over for cake and ice cream. They loved his new toys: the laser gun set, electric yo-yo, and inflatable dinosaurs. "My best present,"

180

Activity

Cross Curricular: Science

RECYCLING Walter decides recycling is worth the effort. If your school does not have a recycling program, you may want the class to help start one.

You may want to begin by inviting a speaker from your local government or a community volunteer to address the class on setting up a recycling program. You could also place separate barrels in the school lunchroom for recyclable plastics, metals cans, and glass.

▶ **Interpersonal/Kinesthetic**

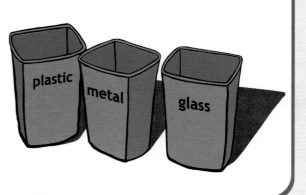

Walter told them, "is outside." Then he showed them the gift that he'd picked out that morning—a tree.

After the party, Walter and his dad planted the birthday present. When he went to bed, Walter looked out his window. He could see his tree and the tree Rose had planted on her birthday. He liked the way they looked, side by side. Then he went to sleep, but not for long, because that night Walter's bed took him away again.

181

Guided Instruction

(23) **FORM GENERALIZATIONS** In what ways do Walter's actions show the lessons he learned from his adventures? (He picks up litter he had dropped and says that his best present is a tree. These actions show that he has learned the value of caring for the environment.)

Guided Instruction

24 Why does Walter think that he is in the past rather than the future? (People are not using modern conveniences such as clothes dryers and power lawn mowers.) *Make Inferences*

When Walter woke up, his bed was standing in the shade of two tall trees. The sky was blue. Laundry hanging from a clothesline flapped in the breeze. A man pushed an old motorless lawn **24** mower. This isn't the future, Walter thought. It's the past.

"Good morning," the man said. "You've found a nice place to sleep."

"Yes, I have," Walter agreed. There was something very peaceful about the huge trees next to his bed.

182

CULTURAL PERSPECTIVES

COSTA RICA Costa Rica, in Central America, covers less than 0.03% of the planet's surface, yet it is home to 5% of the plant and animal species on Earth. The government of Costa Rica has recognized the importance of its rain forests. Today it protects the rain forests, which form the basis of an important tourist-based economy.

Activity Students can make a poster about preserving a plant, animal, or natural area in their community.
▶ **Interpersonal/Spatial**

The man looked up at the rustling leaves. "My great-grandmother planted one of these trees," he said, "when she was a little girl."

183

Guided Instruction

25 **SEQUENCE OF EVENTS** If the man's great-grandmother planted one of the trees, where is Walter at this point in the story? (He is in the future.)

Minilesson

Draw Conclusions

Remind students that they can use information from a story, as well as what they know from their own experience, to draw conclusions about a story.

• Ask students what conclusions they can draw about the trees that Walter is discussing with the man.

Activity Have students review the story and draw and support other conclusions, such as whether Walter travels into the past or the future, or whether he is just dreaming.

Guided Instruction

26 **SEQUENCE OF EVENTS** Let's complete the Sequence of Events chart.

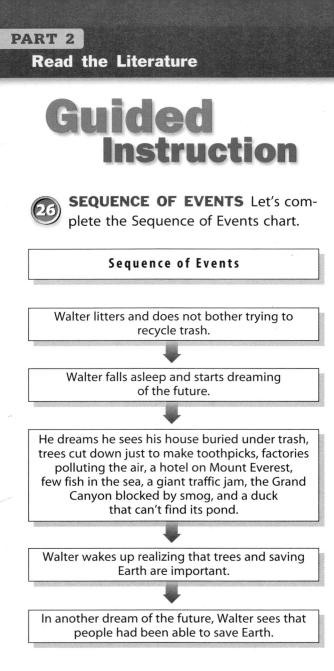

Sequence of Events

Walter litters and does not bother trying to recycle trash.

Walter falls asleep and starts dreaming of the future.

He dreams he sees his house buried under trash, trees cut down just to make toothpicks, factories polluting the air, a hotel on Mount Everest, few fish in the sea, a giant traffic jam, the Grand Canyon blocked by smog, and a duck that can't find its pond.

Walter wakes up realizing that trees and saving Earth are important.

In another dream of the future, Walter sees that people had been able to save Earth.

RETELL THE STORY Ask volunteers to retell the story using the chart. Then ask partners to summarize what Walter learned from his experiences. *Summarize*

STUDENT SELF-ASSESSMENT

- How did analyzing sequence of events help me understand the story?
- How did the Sequence of Events chart help me?

TRANSFERRING THE STRATEGY

- When might I try using this strategy again? In what other reading could a chart like this help me?

184   *Just a Dream*

---

26 Walter looked up at the leaves too, and realized where his bed had taken him. This was the future, after all, a different kind of future. There were still no robots or tiny airplanes. There weren't even any clothes dryers or gas-powered lawn mowers. Walter lay back and smiled. "I like it here," he told the man, then drifted off to sleep in the shade of the two giant trees—the trees he and Rose had planted so many years ago.

MEET
Chris Van Allsburg

184

REREADING FOR *Fluency*

PARTNERS Partners can choose a section about one of Walter's dreams to read aloud. Invite students to read with expression.

READING RATE You may want to evaluate a student's reading rate. Have the student read aloud from *Just a Dream* for one minute and place a self-stick note after the last word he or she reads. Then count the number of words read.

You might also assess several students at one time by having them count the words they read and record their own scores.

A Running Record form provide in **Diagnostic/Placement Evaluation** will help you evaluate reading rate(s).

Chris Van Allsburg is often asked where he gets the ideas for his books. Sometimes he says they are sent through the mail or beamed in from outer space. The truth, admits Van Allsburg, is that he isn't sure where he gets them. They just seem to arrive.

For Van Allsburg, who is both an artist and a writer, a story often begins with an image. He had just such an image in mind when he began *The Polar Express,* a book that won the Caldecott Medal. Van Allsburg pictured a boy looking at a train in front of his house and then taking trips on the train. Eventually, the train rolled all the way to the North Pole.

For *Just a Dream,* Van Allsburg pictured a polluted environment. How could he make this real problem into a good story? He decided to have a boy named Walter travel in his bed to various places. "Bed, with the covers up, is supposed to be a safe place," says the author. "But it's not safe to be in bed in a garbage dump."

Van Allsburg writes before he draws pictures for his stories. He can usually see the pictures in his mind as he writes, though. Creating a story, he says, is a little like making a film. He has to decide which parts to show in his drawings.

185

Guided Instruction

Return to Predictions and Purposes

Review with students their story predictions and reasons for reading the story. Did they predict correctly? Did they find answers to what they wanted to learn?

PREDICTIONS	WHAT HAPPENED
The boy has a dream.	The boy has a dream about the future.
The boy learns something in his dream.	He learns about the importance of taking care of the environment.

INFORMAL ASSESSMENT

SEQUENCE OF EVENTS

HOW TO ASSESS

- Can students identify the sequence of events in the realistic part of the story (not the dreams)?

Students should understand that this story has three major parts: the events before Walter's dream, the dream itself, and the events that occur after Walter wakes up.

FOLLOW UP If students have trouble recalling the sequence of events in the story, encourage them to use the pictures in the story to help them.

LITERARY RESPONSE

QUICK-WRITE Invite students to jot down their responses about the story. Use these questions to help them get started:

JOURNAL

- Which event do you think is most important in making Walter think about the environment?
- How would you like to be Walter?

ORAL RESPONSE Have students share with the class some of their journal entries and discuss the parts of the story they liked best.

Story Questions

Have students discuss or write answers to the questions on page 186.

Answers:

1. He is asleep in his bed. *Literal/Setting*

2. At first, he doesn't care. By the end, he does. *Inferential/Character*

3. They teach him to care for the environment. *Inferential/Main Idea*

4. Walter litters. Then, he travels to the future, where he sees the results of not taking care of the environment. Back in the present, he changes his behavior. Then he visits a different future, one that results from people having cared for the planet. *Critical/Summarize*

5. What you see may not actually be real. *Critical/Reading Across Texts*

Write an Essay For a full writing process lesson, see the lesson on pages 189K–189L.

Story Questions & Activities

for test give?

1. Where is Walter during most of the story?

2. How does Walter feel about the environment at the beginning of the story? At the end?

3. Why are Walter's dreams important?

4. What are the major events in the story? List them in order.

5. Imagine that Walter stepped into the picture from *The Wizard of Oz* on pages 158–159. What do you think he would say to Dorothy and her friends?

Write an Essay

Walter's dreams show him the importance of saving the environment. Write an essay to compare what the world may be like if we do not protect the environment and what it may be like if we do. Suggest a way you and your classmates can help bring about the better future.

Meeting Individual Needs

EASY

Name_____ Date_____ **Reteach** 46

Vocabulary

Choose the word that matches the meaning. Fill in the crossword puzzle.

| bulging | crumpled | foul | haze | shrieking | waddled |

Across
4. crushed; wrinkled
5. mist, smoke, or dust in the air
6. swelling outwards

Down
1. having a bad smell
2. making a shrill noise
3. walked with short steps, swayed from side to side

Story Comprehension **Reteach** 47

Circle the letter beside the words that correctly complete each sentence about "Just a Dream." You may look back at the story for help.

1. The wish that started Walter's dream trip was _____.
   (a.) to live in the future   b. to live in the past

2. At the beginning of the story, Walter _____.
   a. cared about litter   (b.) didn't sort garbage

3. When Walter fell asleep, he dreamt about a world that _____.
   (a.) was dirty and noisy   b. was wonderfully clean

4. Walter's dreams made him change how he _____.
   a. cleaned his room   (b.) felt about the environment

At Home: Have students retell "Just a Dream" in their own words.
46–47   Book 4/Unit 2 *Just a Dream* 4

Reteach, 47

ON-LEVEL

Name_____ Date_____ **Practice** 47

Story Comprehension

Complete each sentence with the correct word or phrase. Look back at "Just a Dream" for help.

1. His bed was balancing on the edge of a giant ___smokestack___
2. After the party, Walter and his dad planted the ___birthday___ present.
3. Walter ___crumpled___ up the empty bag and threw it at the fire hydrant.
4. The sign read Hotel ___Everest___
5. Walter bought a large jelly-filled ___doughnut___
6. This can't be the ___future___, Walter thought.
7. The ducks had been looking for the ___pond___ for days.
8. Walter couldn't understand why anyone would want a ___tree___ for a present.
9. When Walter first woke up, he was in the middle of a huge ___dump___
10. The huge trees seemed very ___peaceful___ next to his bed.

At Home: Have students take responsibility for a chore at home that involves recycling.
47   Book 4/Unit 2 *Just a Dream* 10

Practice, 47

CHALLENGE

Name_____ Date_____ **Extend** 46

Vocabulary

| bulging | crumpled | foul |
| haze | shrieking | waddled |

Make a comic strip in the boxes below. Use the vocabulary words in speech bubbles or in captions in the comic strip. Answers will vary but should show correct use of vocabulary.

Extend 47

Story Comprehension

In "Just a Dream," Walter's dreams highlight environmental problems. Select two of Walter's dreams that affected you the most. Explain why. Answers will vary.

At Home: Have students write about ways they can help the environment.
46–47   Book 4/Unit 2 *Just a Dream*

Extend, 47

Do a Science Experiment

In Walter's dream, the air became so polluted that no one could see through it. How clean is your air? To find out, hang a clean white cloth from your window. Leave it there for at least a full day. Then take it in. Is it still clean? Report the results to the class.

Draw a Cartoon

Walter's dreams showed him a pollution-filled world. Draw your own cartoon that shows what will happen if people continue to hurt the environment. Write a clever caption for your cartoon.

Find Out More

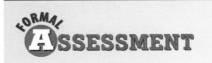

In the story, Walter's town had a plan for recycling bottles and cans. What kind of recycling plan does your community have? Start by looking in the yellow pages of your telephone book under recycling to find out the items you can recycle. Then use what you learn to make a flyer. Tell people *what*, *when*, *where*, and *how* to recycle.

187

Story Activities

Do a Science Experiment

Materials: squares of clean white cotton cloth, magnifying glasses (optional)

GROUP Have students examine the cloth before and after it is placed outdoors. You may want to keep a clean sample for comparison. Have each group write a paragraph summarizing their observations.

Draw a Cartoon

Materials: pencil, drawing paper, fine point black marker, colored pencils

ONE Check students' pencil sketches for appropriateness and correctness before they create a final draft in ink and color.

Find Out More

RESEARCH AND INQUIRY For more information on local recycling efforts, students can contact the town or city government. Before they do so, have them write a list of questions they would like to have answered.

*inter*NET CONNECTION To learn more about other recycling ideas, have students visit **www.mhschool.com/reading**

FORMAL

(A)SSESSMENT

After page 187, see the Selection Assessment.

Study Skills

REFERENCE SOURCES

OBJECTIVES Students will use a thesaurus to find synonyms.

PREPARE Explain that students can use a thesaurus or synonym finder to find synonyms when they write. Display **Teaching Chart 39.**

TEACH Have students examine the sample thesaurus entry. Explain that the sample in the middle of the page shows what a typical thesaurus entry might look like. Have students find synonyms for the word *small*.

PRACTICE Have students answer questions 1–5. Review the answers with them. **1.** It shows synonyms for words. **2.** *little, tiny, petite* **3.** look for the word in alphabetical order **4.** *Small* is an adjective. **5.** Unlike a dictionary, a thesaurus does not show pronunciations or definitions, just synonyms.

ASSESS/CLOSE Have students suggest when they might use a thesaurus or synonym finder and what information they could get.

STUDY SKILLS

Use a Thesaurus

Walter is eager to watch a TV program. The show is about a boy who flies around in a *tiny* airplane. This boy also has a *small* machine that can make food with the press of a button. Look at the words *tiny* and *small*. They are synonyms. A **synonym** is a word that has the same or almost the same meaning as another word. You can find synonyms in a book called a *thesaurus*. A **thesaurus** is often arranged alphabetically, like a dictionary. After each main word is a list of synonyms.

> **small** *adj.* **1.** *Are you small enough to squeeze through this door?*: little, tiny, petite. **2.** *Even the small details should be checked*: minor, unimportant. **3.** *The puppy uttered a small cry*: weak, faint.

Use the sample thesaurus to answer these questions.

1 What information does a thesaurus have?

2 What are three synonyms for the first meaning of *small*?

3 How would you look up a word in a thesaurus arranged like a dictionary?

4 What part of speech is the word *small*?

5 How is a thesaurus different from a dictionary?

Meeting Individual Needs

EASY	ON-LEVEL	CHALLENGE

EASY

Name_____ Date_____ Reteach **48**

Use a Thesaurus

A **thesaurus** is a book that gives synonyms for a word. If you want to add interest to your writing, use a thesaurus.

Use the thesaurus entries to choose the best synonym for the underlined word in each sentence. Circle the correct letter.

> **clean** verb. 1. Volunteers helped *clean* the park.
> Synonyms: wash, cleanse, scrub, spruce up, tidy

> **environment** noun. 1. Littering fouls our *environment*.
> Synonyms: surroundings, habitat, setting, world, atmosphere

> **trash** noun. 1. Put the *trash* in the can.
> Synonyms: waste, garbage, junk, litter
> 2. The expert called the ideas in the report *trash*.
> Synonyms: nonsense, foolishness, drivel

1. Norah ignored the article because she thought it was <u>trash</u>.
   a. waste b. litter **c.** nonsense
2. The government will <u>clean</u> Wild River.
   a. scrub **b.** cleanse c. litter
3. People know that recycling helps the <u>environment</u>.
   a. world b. setting c. waste
4. The dump was filled with mountains of <u>trash</u>.
   a. nonsense **b.** garbage c. foolishness
5. We had to use a brush to <u>clean</u> the oil off the floor.
   a. tidy **b.** scrub c. spruce up

Book 4/Unit 2
Just a Dream   At Home: Have students explain why scrub is not the best synonym for clean in the second item.   48

Reteach, 48

ON-LEVEL

Name_____ Date_____ Practice **48**

Use a Thesaurus

A **thesaurus** is a book that lists the synonyms of words. You can use a thesaurus when you want to find different words that have the same, or nearly the same meaning.

Below are two thesaurus entries. Read them, then answer the questions.

> **ridiculous** *adjective* absurd, foolish, laughable, preposterous, unbelievable, silly
> **said** *verb* asked, bragged, complained, demanded, exclaimed, mentioned, muttered, questioned, whined, yelled

1. When would you find a thesaurus helpful? <u>when you want to find a synonym for a word</u>
2. What are three synonyms for the word ridiculous? <u>absurd, foolish, preposterous</u>
3. What part of speech is the word said? <u>verb</u>
4. What do we call words that have the same, or nearly the same meaning? <u>synonyms</u>
5. What do we call a book that lists synonyms? <u>thesaurus</u>
6. Write a sentence using different words for ridiculous and said.
   <u>Sentences will vary.</u>

Book 4/Unit 2
Just a Dream   At Home: Have students write a thesaurus entry for a word of their choice.   48

Practice, 48

CHALLENGE

Name_____ Date_____ Extend **48**

Use a Thesaurus

A **thesaurus** is a list of synonyms, or words that have the same or nearly the same meaning. It is usually arranged with words in alphabetical order. Use the thesaurus excerpt below to answer the questions.

> **event** *noun* 1. incident, occasion, affair. 2. outcome, result.
> **eventful** *adjective* 1. busy. 2. significant, important.
> **eventually** *adverb* finally, at last.
> **ever** *adverb* 1. always, forever. 2. continuously, constantly.
> **everyone** *pronoun* everybody, all.

1. A thesaurus usually tells what part of speech each entry is. Which words above are adjectives? adverbs? <u>adjectives—eventful; adverb—ever, eventually</u>
2. Write a sentence using an adjective and a sentence using an adverb. **Answers will vary.**
3. There are two listings for *event*. Why? <u>Synonyms are given for the two different meanings of the word.</u>
4. Write a sentence using a synonym for *event*. <u>Answers will vary.</u>
5. What are two synonyms for *everyone*? <u>everybody, all</u>
6. Write a short 4-line poem using both synonyms. <u>Answers will vary.</u>

Book 4/Unit 2
Just a Dream   At Home: Have students write a thesaurus entry for a word of their choice.   48

Extend, 48

TEST POWER

DIRECTIONS

Read the sample story. Then read each question about the story.

SAMPLE

Timothy's Gift for Matt

All of the things in Timothy's house were packed in boxes. Timothy's parents had been <u>transferred</u>, and Timothy and his family were moving away. Both Timothy and his best friend, Matt, were very upset. They had been friends since the second grade when they played on the same Little League team. It was hard for Matt to think about going to school the next day and not seeing Timothy there.

Matt blurted out, "I wish you didn't have to move!"

Timothy looked down at the box at his feet marked "baseball." He leaned down and pulled from the box his favorite baseball and gave it to his best friend, Matt.

1 What is this story mostly about?

   A Being in Little League

   (B) The friendship of two boys

   C Packing boxes

   D Going to school

2 In this story, the word <u>transferred</u> means—

   F lied to

   (G) moved to a different place

   H asked to do a favor

   J given a lot of money

189

Test Power

Read the Page

Have students read *all* the information in the story. Instruct students to summarize the story in their own words. This process will help students come up with the answer to summary type questions.

Discuss the Questions

Question 1: This question asks students what the passsage is *mostly* about. Teach students to be careful not to quickly choose the answer to this type of question. Wrong answer choices often give information that *is stated* in the passage but this information is not what the passage is *mostly* about.

Question 2: This question asks students to define a word in context. Remind students to look for clues in the surrounding sentences. The rest of the sentence following the vocabulary word says ". . . Timothy and his family were moving away."

ITBS/TEST PREPARATION   TERRANOVA/TEST PREPARATION   SAT 9/TEST PREPARATION

EASY

Leveled Books

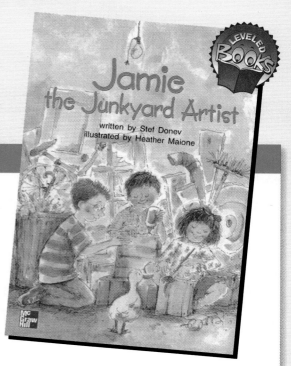

Jamie the Junkyard Artist
written by Stef Donev
illustrated by Heather Maione

EASY

Jamie the Junkyard Artist

Consonant Clusters
☑ **Sequence of Events**
☑ **Instructional Vocabulary:**
bulging, crumpled, foul, haze, shrieking, waddled

Guided Reading

PREVIEW AND PREDICT Have students discuss the illustrations up to page 7 and write their thoughts about the problem that Jamie faces. Have them predict what they think will happen in the story.

SET PURPOSES Have students think about what they want to learn from this story. Ask them to write a few questions that they hope the story will answer.

READ THE BOOK Have students read the story independently. Then use the questions below to emphasize reading strategies.

Page 4: By what day does Jamie have to have all his stuff out of the garage? (Monday) *Sequence of Events*

Pages 4–5: Which words on these pages begin with *cl* or *cr*? (crumpled, clean) *Phonics*

Page 7: How did George move as he followed Jamie and Suzie? (He waddled.) What does the word *waddled* mean? (moved in a slow rocking way) *Vocabulary*

Pages 10–11: Which words on these pages end with *ng* or *nk*? (junk, pink, stink[s], burning, shrieking) *Phonics and Decoding*

Pages 13–14: When did Jamie and his friends begin work on the duck house? When did they finish the job? (They began work on Friday and finished late Sunday.) *Sequence of Events*

RETURN TO PREDICTIONS AND PURPOSES Discuss students' predictions. Ask them to describe how close they came to guessing what would happen in the story. Also ask them to review their purposes for reading. Did they find out what they wanted to know?

LITERARY RESPONSE Discuss these questions:

- Can you think of another good title for this story? What would it be?
- Why do you think the author decided to write about a "junkyard artist"?

Also see the story questions and activity in *Jamie the Junkyard Artist*.

Answers to Story Questions

1. Jamie's idea was to use the neat stuff in his garage to build a nice house for Suzie's duck, George.
2. Suzie went to get her brother, Jamie went to get his friends, and they all worked on the duck house until bedtime.
3. At first Jamie's mother thought the junk should be thrown away, but by the end of the story she was convinced that "junk" could be recycled.
4. A young boy decides to recycle some "junk" in order to help out a friend.
5. Answers will vary.

Story Questions and Activity

1. What was Jamie's idea?
2. What were the first three things that happened after Suzie agreed to the idea?
3. Describe Jamie's mother's feeling about the "junk" at the beginning of the story and then at the end of the story.
4. What is this story mostly about?
5. Do you think Walter from *Just a Dream* would have helped Jamie and his friends with their project? Explain your answer.

Your Own Junk

What could you build out of "junk" that you find around your home, school or neighborhood? Think about how it might be used and draw a picture of what you would want it to look like. Then build it!

from Jamie the Junkyard Artist

Leveled Books

INDEPENDENT

Don't Throw That Plastic Bottle Away, Wear It!

☑ **Sequence of Events**

☑ **Instructional Vocabulary:**
bulging, crumpled, foul, haze, shrieking, waddled

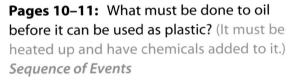

Guided Reading

PREVIEW AND PREDICT Have students discuss the illustrations up to page 5 and their thoughts about the overall topic of this book. Have them predict what types of information the author will present. Chart their predictions.

SET PURPOSES Have students think about what they want to learn from this book. Ask them to write a few questions that they hope the book will answer.

READ THE BOOK Have students read the book independently. Then use the questions below to emphasize reading strategies.

Pages 4–5: What generalization might you make about recycling, based on the information on pages 4 and 5? (There are many surprising and unusual ways to recycle glass, plastic, and old tires.) *Form Generalizations*

Page 10: Find the word *shrieking*. What clues did the author provide to help you know the meaning of this word? (alarm, buzzer) *Vocabulary*

Pages 10–11: What must be done to oil before it can be used as plastic? (It must be heated up and have chemicals added to it.) *Sequence of Events*

Pages 14–15: When did Americans first begin to collect cans? (in 1972) *Sequence of Events*

RETURN TO PREDICTIONS AND PURPOSES Discuss students' predictions. Ask them to describe how close they came to guessing what the author would describe. Also ask them to review their purposes for reading. Did they find out what they wanted to know?

LITERARY RESPONSE Discuss these questions:

• Why do you think the author chose to write this book?

• How do you know that this book is non-fiction?

Also see the story questions and activity in *Don't Throw That Plastic Bottle Away, Wear It!*

Answers to Story Questions

1. Recycling uses less new material, saves energy, and reduces pollution.
2. Answers will vary, but may include: drinking containers, windows, and mirrors.
3. Metal is taken from rocks and clay; the can is made; the product is bought and used; the can is recycled; the new can is made.
4. The book is about many things that we use that can be recycled to help the environment.
5. Answers will vary.

Story Questions and Activity

1. What are the three main benefits of recycling?
2. List at least three products made from glass.
3. Explain the sequence of events in making and using an aluminum can.
4. What is the main idea of the book?
5. If Walter from *Just a Dream* had written this book, what other information might have been included?

Make a Flow Chart

Pick a product in this book, or any other product that you think can be recycled. Do a little research using a library book or an encyclopedia to show how this product is used and reused. Make a flow chart, illustrating each step of the process. Your steps might include the material being made from natural resources; the material being turned into a product in a factory or workshop; the product being used; the product being collected for recycling; and the product being turned into something new.

from *Don't Throw That Plastic Bottle Away, Wear It!*

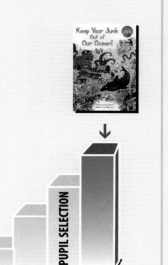

PUPIL SELECTION

↓

CHALLENGE

Answers to Story Questions

1. King Sharky called a meeting.
2. Accept all reasonable responses.
3. The sea creatures returned the junk to the shore, the dry land creatures threw it back in the ocean, and the sea creatures forced the debris onto land.
4. It is a fantasy story but one with an important message about how polluted waters can affect sea life.
5. Answers will vary.

Story Questions and Activity

1. Why did all the sea creatures meet by the sunken barge?
2. Do you think that Moe's plan was fair to the dry land creatures living on the island? Why do you think so?
3. List two events that occurred after Moe came up with his suggestion.
4. What is the story mostly about?
5. If Walter's next dream took him down to King Sharkey's kingdom, what do you think might happen?

Up Close and Personal

Find out about water pollution in your own area by doing research on the Internet or in the periodicals and microfiche sections of your local library. Then write a brief report on the problem you found and what is currently being done to correct it.

from *Keep Your Junk Out of Our Ocean!*

Leveled Books

CHALLENGE

Keep Your Junk Out of Our Ocean!

☑ **Sequence of Events**

☑ **Instructional Vocabulary:**
bulging, crumpled, foul, haze, shrieking, waddled

written by Stef Donev
illustrated by Jared Lee

Guided Reading

PREVIEW AND PREDICT Preview the book up to page 5. Have students discuss the illustrations and write their thoughts about the problem facing the sea animals. Have them predict what events might happen in the story and record them in a chart.

SET PURPOSES Ask students to write a few questions that they hope the book will answer. For example, they may want to know what genre this book belongs in.

READ THE BOOK Have students read the book independently. Then use the questions below to emphasize reading strategies.

Page 4: What did all the animals do just before the meeting began? (They looked around at all the garbage that had been dumped in the ocean.) *Sequence of Events*

Page 6: What word describes the taste of the sea water due to the dumping that has taken place? (foul) *Vocabulary*

Page 12: What solution to the problem did the animals consider first? (They thought about moving all the garbage into deeper water.) *Sequence of Events*

Pages 14–15: Think about how the humans react when the animals return the garbage. What generalization might you form about people and their garbage? (Sample answer: Most people generally aren't willing to take responsibility for the garbage they create.) *Form Generalizations*

RETURN TO PREDICTIONS AND PURPOSES Discuss students' predictions. Ask them to describe how close they came to guessing what would happen in the story. Also ask them to review their purposes for reading. Did they find out what they wanted to know?

LITERARY RESPONSE Discuss these questions:

* What other title might be a good one for this story?

* What elements of this story are fantasy?

* How might a realistic story about the effects of dumping on sea life be different?

Also see the story questions and activity in *Keep Your Junk Out of Our Ocean!*

Activities
Anthology and Leveled Books

Connecting Texts

ISSUES CHARTS Write the story titles on a chart. Discuss with students how each story deals with the issues of garbage and pollution. Then have students note what the author of each story seems to say about these issues. Have students add their suggestions to the chart.

Just a Dream	Jamie the Junkyard Artist	Don't Throw That Plastic Bottle Away, Wear It!	Keep Your Junk Out of Our Ocean!
• If we continue to pollute, the world will be dirty and unhealthy. • We need to simplify our lifestyles to cut down on pollution.	• It's possible to recycle garbage into useful products. • Communities should recycle garbage.	• People need to recycle garbage since burning is unhealthy and space is too limited for landfills. • New uses have been found for worn-out tires and old glass and paper.	• Dumping garbage in the ocean is not acceptable. • Due to ocean dumping, sea life is less healthy than it might be.

Viewing/Representing

MAKE POSTERS Organize the class into groups, one for each of the four stories read in the lesson. (For *Just a Dream*, combine students of different reading levels.) Have each group create anti-pollution or recycling posters to show the issues and opinions that each story addresses. Encourage groups to share their posters.

SMALL GROUP DISCUSSION Have students study each group's posters. Allow time for students to ask questions about the information on the posters.

Research and Inquiry

MORE ABOUT POLLUTION AND RECYCLING ISSUES Have students research information about how their own community is dealing with pollution and recycling. Suggest that they use local newspapers or interview a local official to find out the following:

• How much of the community's trash is recycled?

• What types of pollution are a problem in the community?

Students might make Community Recycling or Community Pollution cards to display the information they find.

interNET CONNECTION Have students log on to **www.mhschool.com/reading** to find out more about pollution and recycling.

OBJECTIVES

Students will identify the sequence of events in a story.

TEACHING TIP

INSTRUCTIONAL After students have identified the events and clue words in "One Too Many," call on volunteers to number the sentences to show the order in which the events actually took place.

Review Sequence of Events

PREPARE

Discuss Sequence of Events

Review: Recognizing the order in which things happen in a story makes it easier to understand the story. Writers sometimes use clue words to signal the order of events. These clue words help readers understand what happened even if the events are not described in the order they occur. Talk about how understanding the sequence of events in *Just a Dream* helped students understand the story better.

TEACH

Read "One Too Many" and Model the Skill

Ask students to listen carefully to the sequence of events as you read the **Teaching Chart 40** passage together.

One Too Many

Walter's stomach felt funny as (he climbed into bed) one night. Probably (he had eaten one jelly doughnut too many) that day. When he woke up, (he found himself in a factory.) "Here's your seat," said one of the workers. "Make sure you keep up with the machines."

Just then a (jelly doughnut appeared in front of Walter.) "Go on, you're supposed to taste them and make sure our customers will like them," said the woman next to him. Walter had just finished tasting the doughnut when (another one) (rolled onto the table) in front of him.

Teaching Chart 40

Discuss clues in the passage that help readers follow the sequence of events.

MODEL Paying attention to clue words in a story helps me follow the order of events more easily. Clue words show me that first Walter ate too many doughnuts and then he got into bed. The words *When he woke up* signal the next event.

PRACTICE

Identify Sequence of Events

Have students underline the clues in "One Too Many" that help point out the sequence of events. Have them circle the events that these clues indicate. Have them then list each event in the order it happened.

PARTNERS

Have students work with partners to make a story map for the events in "One Too Many," showing the sequence in which they occurred. ▶ **Logical/Interpersonal**

ASSESS/CLOSE

Recap the Sequence of Events in Another Story

Have students work in small groups to chart the sequence of events in another story they have read recently, clearly indicating the order in which the events took place.

ALTERNATE TEACHING STRATEGY

SEQUENCE OF EVENTS

For a different approach to teaching this skill, see page T64.

SELF-SELECTED Reading

Students may choose from the following titles.

ANTHOLOGY

- Just a Dream

LEVELED BOOKS

- Jamie the Junkyard Artist
- Don't Throw That Plastic Bottle Away, Wear It!
- Keep Your Junk Out of Our Ocean

Bibliography, pages T76–T77

Meeting Individual Needs for Comprehension

EASY	ON-LEVEL	CHALLENGE	LANGUAGE SUPPORT

EASY — Reteach, 49

Name _____ Date _____ Reteach **49**

Sequence of Events

Keeping track of **sequence**, or the order in which things happen, can help you better understand and enjoy a story. Look for time clue words to help you identify the sequence.

Read the story and the sentences below. Next to each sentence, write a number from 1 to 8 to show the order in which events happened.

The living room was such a mess! When Mrs. Roper walked in, she couldn't believe that Sam and Janet had cleaned it that afternoon. But they had. Unfortunately, right after they had finished, the first accident happened. Spot jumped up on a table and knocked over the flower pot. That led to the second accident. When Sam tried to vacuum the dirt, the vacuum bag ripped open. Dirt and dust fell all over the floor. Next, Janet slipped on the dirt, and dropped a vase she'd been carrying. A few seconds later, Mrs. Roper walked in.

7 Janet dropped a vase.
8 Mrs. Roper walked in.
1 Sam and Janet cleaned the living room.
5 The vacuum bag ripped open.
3 Spot knocked over the flower pot.
4 Sam tried to vacuum the dirt.
2 Spot jumped up on a table.
6 Janet slipped on the dirt.

At Home: Have students think of a few events from "Just a Dream" and list the events in the order in which they happened.

49   Book 4/Unit 2 *Just a Dream* 8

Reteach, 49

ON-LEVEL — Practice, 49

Name _____ Date _____ Practice **49**

Sequence of Events

The **sequence of events** in a story is the order in which things happen. Keeping track of the sequence of events can help you understand what is happening in a story. Ten events from "Just a Dream" are listed out of order below. Number each event to show the correct sequence.

3 1. Walter watched a television show about the future.
8 2. Walter planted a tree on his birthday.
1 3. Walter threw an empty bag at a fire hydrant.
6 4. Walter saw the fishermen catch one small fish.
7 5. Walter got stuck in traffic on the highway.
10 6. Walter went back to sleep in the shade of two trees.
2 7. Walter dumped all the trash into one can.
5 8. Walter woke up on a mountain of trash.
4 9. Walter wished he had robots to work for him.
9 10. Walter saw a man pushing a motorless lawn mower.

At Home: Have students tell a family member the sequence of events in "Just a Dream."

49   Book 4/Unit 2 *Just a Dream* 10

Practice, 49

CHALLENGE — Extend, 49

Name _____ Date _____ Extend **49**

Sequence of Events

The **sequence of events** in a story refers to the order in which the events occurred. Think about the sequence of events in "Just a Dream," and answer the questions.

1. At the beginning of the story Walter litters on his way home from school. What did this tell you about Walter? Answers will vary. Possible answer: He was careless about littering.

2. Why do you think Walter's dream had so many parts? Answers will vary. Possible answer: So he could see the seriousness of the different effects of pollution.

3. What types of pollution does Walter dream about? Answers should include air, water, and noise pollution.

4. How did the illustrations make Walter's dream seem more real to you? Explain. Answers will vary. Possible answer: The pictures show the terrible effects of pollution.

5. At the beginning of the story Walter thinks that Rose's tree is a silly birthday present. By the end of the story, Walter has changed his mind. When do you think Walter asked for his tree? The morning after his first dream when his parents got up.

6. How do you feel about Walter's dreams? How do they make you feel about the environment? Answers will vary but should express an awareness of the problem of environmental pollution.

At Home: Have students design a poster showing the sequence of events leading to the pollution of a park.

49   Book 4/Unit 2 *Just a Dream*

Extend, 49

LANGUAGE SUPPORT — Language Support, 54

Name _____ Date _____

Up a Tree

1. Cut out the places where Walter goes in his dreams. 2. Paste them on the ladder in the order they happened in the story. 3. Stop when you get to the top of the tree.

In his dream, Walter finds himself:

at the dump	at the Grand Canyon	on the ocean	at a factory
in the sky with ducks	on Mt. Everest	on a highway	in a tree

in the sky with ducks
at the Grand Canyon
on a highway
on the ocean
on Mt. Everest
at a factory
in a tree
at the dump

54 *Just a Dream* • Language Support /Blackline Master 26   Grade 4

Language Support, 54

Review Form Generalizations

TEACHING TIP

INSTRUCTIONAL

Students may have difficulty
understanding the term *valid
generalization*. In this case,
you may prefer to ask if
a generalization is true
or false.

PREPARE

Discuss Forming Generalizations

Explain: A generalization is a broad statement that can be supported with specific examples. A valid generalization is always true and often contains words such as *often, most,* and *rarely*. If some examples do not fit the generalization, it is an invalid generalization.

TEACH

Read "Back to Nature" and Model the Skill

Read "Back to Nature." Focus students' attention on examples that can be used to support a generalization.

Back to Nature

(Often modern progress isn't really progress at all.) Many household chores used to be done by hand. They used less energy and were more satisfying than the ways we do them now. For example, hanging sheets to dry on a line uses no energy at all. The sheets smell nice and fresh, and you get a little exercise hanging them out to dry. Another example is mowing the lawn. Gas and electric mowers make noise, use energy, and create pollution. Mowing lawns with a hand mower is quiet, satisfying, and clean.

Teaching Chart 41

Ask a volunteer to find and circle the generalization stated in the beginning of the passage. Then ask students to find and underline examples that support the generalization.

MODEL The passage states that often modern progress isn't really progress at all. What examples support this generalization? One example is people hanging their clothes on the line, instead of using electric or gas dryers. Another example is people using hand-powered lawn mowers instead of electric or gas mowers.

PRACTICE

Create a Generalization Chart

GROUP

Have students create a generalization chart for "Back to Nature." Help them get started.

GENERALIZATION	EXAMPLES
Often modern progress isn't really progress at all.	• Hanging sheets instead of using a dryer saves energy. • Using a hand mower instead of a gas or electric mower can be more satisfying.

ASSESS/CLOSE

Form and Support Other Generalizations

Have students work with partners to form other generalizations about selection-related topics such as ecology and progress. Have them identify some examples that support their generalization. They can then record their information in a Generalization chart.

ALTERNATE TEACHING STRATEGY

FORM GENERALIZATIONS

For a different approach to teaching this skill, see page T62.

LOOKING AHEAD

Students will apply this skill as they read the next selection, *Leah's Pony*.

Meeting Individual Needs for Comprehension

EASY	ON-LEVEL	CHALLENGE	LANGUAGE SUPPORT

EASY

Name_____ Date_____ **Reteach** 50

Form Generalizations

A **generalization** is a broad statement based on a set of facts.

Read the sentences below. Circle the letter next to the generalization that can be drawn from the facts.

1. Mark plays baseball from April to September. He plays football from October to December. However, Mark likes to play basketball year round.
   a. Mark enjoys many sports.
   b. Mark likes baseball better than football.
   c. Mark wants to be a professional basketball player.

2. After school every day, Paige walks dogs for her neighbors. On some weekends, Paige babysits. Paige also does errands for pay.
   a. Paige spends a lot of money.
   b. Paige does little when she is not in school.
   c. Paige is a hard-working girl.

3. When I told a scary story, Onida yawned. She laughs at horror movies and would skydive, if her mother would let her.
   a. Onida is not easy to scare.
   b. Onida likes movies.
   c. Onida is frightened of many things.

4. Mr. Potter built his own computer. After that, he made an alarm system for his house. He also fixed my broken watch.
   a. Mr. Potter breaks a lot of things.
   b. Mr. Potter spends a lot of time at home.
   c. Mr. Potter is good at making and fixing mechanical things.

5. Manuel writes in his journal every night. He writes stories for his younger brother all the time. He answers letters from his pen pal every week.
   a. Manuel doesn't like sports.
   b. Manuel likes to write.
   c. Manuel does well in math.

Book 4/Unit 2
Just a Dream

At Home: Have students write some facts about themselves and then use the list to make a few generalizations about themselves.

50

ON-LEVEL

Name_____ Date_____ **Practice** 50

Form Generalizations

A **generalization** is a broad statement about something. Generalizations often include words such as *most, none, everything,* or *all.* Read each passage. Then write a generalization about "Just a Dream" on the line below. Answers may vary.

1. When Walter took out the trash, he dumped everything into one can. He didn't care that there were three cans for three different kinds of trash. He wanted to get back to watching television.
   Generalization: Walter never took the time to sort the garbage.

2. In the story, Walter wished that he had his own plane, robot, and a machine to make jelly doughnuts.
   Generalization: Walter wished he had machines to do all the work.

3. Walter saw houses buried under huge piles of trash. He gasped when he saw the street sign that had the name of his street on it. A man told him no one lived there anymore.
   Generalization: No one lived on Floral Avenue anymore because of the mountain of trash.

4. When Walter was on the edge of a smokestack, he coughed and the smoke burned his throat and made his eyes itch.
   Generalization: All the smoke made it almost impossible to breathe.

5. When Walter awoke, he ran outside in his pajamas to find the jelly doughnut wrapper he had discarded earlier that day.
   Generalization: Walter changed all of his old bad habits and stopped polluting.

Book 4/Unit 2
Just a Dream

At Home: Have students write to complete this generalization: The best stories are the ones that _____

50

CHALLENGE

Name_____ Date_____ **Extend** 50

Form Generalizations

To **form a generalization** means to think about something in a general way. Form generalizations about "Just a Dream" to answer the questions below. Answers will vary.

1. Using Walter's first dream, what generalization can you form about littering?
   _____
   _____

2. What can you say about most people who like to plant trees?
   _____
   _____

3. After reading the story, what generalization can you form about pollution?
   _____
   _____

4. How do you think most people will feel after reading "Just a Dream"?
   _____
   _____

5. Why do you think the author of "Just a Dream" used dreams to make his points?
   _____
   _____

Book 4/Unit 2
Just a Dream

At Home: What would you do if clean water did not come out of your faucet at home? Form a generalization about what you would do and how it might affect your life.

50

LANGUAGE SUPPORT

Name_____ Date_____

What Would Happen?

Fill in the blank in each sentence with a word or words from the list below.

forest	polluted	garbage dump	stopped

1. If everyone threw trash on the ground, the earth would soon be a huge garbage dump.

2. If everyone cut down a tree, the earth would soon not have one forest.

3. If everyone drove cars, traffic on the highways would soon be stopped.

4. If every car and factory made bad smoke, the air would soon be polluted.

Grade 4   Language Support /Blackline Master 27 • *Just a Dream* 55

Reteach, 50   Practice, 50   Extend, 50   Language Support, 55

Students will identify and determine the meanings of compound words.

TEACHING TIP

INSTRUCTIONAL If students have difficulty isolating individual words within a compound word, use a visual clue such as a colored slash or a word mask to highlight the separate parts of the word.

Introduce Compound Words

PREPARE

Discuss Compound Words

Explain: Compound words are new words formed by joining two smaller words. The compound word has a different meaning from the meanings of the two individual words.

TEACH

Read the Passage and Model the Skill

Have students read the passage on **Teaching Chart 42.**

> ### Stuck in Traffic
>
> Walter wasn't sure if this was a dream or a trip into the future. Walter was on the <u>freeway</u>, stuck in traffic. He was trying to get to the world <u>headquarters</u> of the Pollution Control Committee. Garbage had piled up so high in the city dump that it had begun to <u>overflow onto</u> the <u>highway</u>, blocking traffic. Horns blared around Walter, but nothing moved.
> Walter looked through his <u>windshield</u> at the piles of trash. Green grass and trees were <u>nowhere</u> to be found.
>
> **Teaching Chart 42**

Model identifying and explaining a compound word.

MODEL The word freeway is a compound word. I can tell because it is formed by two smaller words, *free* and *way*. A *freeway* is a big busy road. The meaning comes from the two words that form it, but the compound has a somewhat different meaning.

Find the Meaning of a Compound Word

Have students identify the two words that make up the compound word *headquarters*. Ask how the meaning of *headquarters* is related to the meanings of the two words from which it is formed. (A meaning of *head* is *leading* or *main*; a meaning of *quarters* is *assigned section* or *office; headquarters* means *main office.*)

PRACTICE

Identify Compound Words and Discuss Their Meanings

GROUP

Have volunteers underline the compound words in the passage. Have other students identify the two words that make up each compound word. Then have groups discuss what each compound means. Have them check meanings in a dictionary.

▶ **Interpersonal/Linguistic**

ASSESS/CLOSE

Use Compound Words

PARTNERS

Have students work with partners to brainstorm at least three compound words. Then have them use the words to write a paragraph. They can read their paragraphs to the class and have others listen for the compound words.

Meeting Individual Needs for Vocabulary

EASY	ON-LEVEL	CHALLENGE	LANGUAGE SUPPORT

EASY

Name_____ Date_____ **Reteach** 51

Compound Words

When two words are put together to make one word, the new word is called a **compound word**. You can usually use the meaning of each of the small words to help you figure out the meaning of the compound word.

Look at the compound words below. Write the two smaller words that make up each compound word. Then write the meaning of the compound word.

clothesline
1. Word 1: clothes
2. Word 2: line
3. Meaning: line that you hang clothes up on

hairbrush
4. Word 1: hair
5. Word 2: brush
6. Meaning: brush used to arrange your hair

underground
7. Word 1: under
8. Word 2: ground
9. Meaning: under the surface or under the ground

shamefaced
10. Word 1: shame
11. Word 2: faced
12. Meaning: showing shame on one's face

51 At Home: Ask students to name the small words in the compounds storefront, crosswalk, and foghorn and write the meanings for them.
Book 4/Unit 2 *Just a Dream* 12

Reteach, 51

ON-LEVEL

Name_____ Date_____ **Practice** 51

Compound Words

A **compound word** is made up of two short words. The two words together may mean something different than what they meant separately. An example would be *head* and *light* making *headlight*.

Put two words from the list together to make a compound word to fill in the blank in each sentence.

skate	book	note	ball	back
flash	thunder	camp	pack	noon
storm	after	fire	board	scraper
basket	sky	brush	light	tooth

1. Ivan wrote stories in her ____notebook____.
2. Bonita delivered papers every ____afternoon____ after school.
3. Teresa carries her books in her ____backpack____.
4. You often have lightning along with a ____thunderstorm____.
5. That ____skyscraper____ has 47 floors.
6. Chan's brother plays guard on the ____basketball____ team.
7. Spyros uses his ____toothbrush____ after every meal.
8. A ____flashlight____ is a good thing to have in the dark.
9. We put more wood on the ____campfire____.
10. I can move really fast when I'm on my ____skateboard____.

51 At Home: Have students make a list of five new compound words.
Book 4/Unit 2 *Just a Dream* 10

Practice, 51

CHALLENGE

Name_____ Date_____ **Extend** 51

Compound Words

A **compound word** is a word that is formed by putting two other words together. For example, the word *everyone* is made up of the words *every* and *one*.

Use the words below to write as many compound words as you can on the lines.

birth	be	time	day
air	high	where	light
bed	side	plane	every

Possible answers: birthday, beside, bedtime, airplane, highlight, everywhere, everyday, bedside

Use some of the compound words that you made to write a story about the future.
Answers will vary.

51 At Home: Play a compound word game. Have students think of a compound word. Tell a partner half of the word and give clues as needed. How many clues does it take before your partner guesses the word?
Book 4/Unit 2 *Just a Dream*

Extend, 51

LANGUAGE SUPPORT

Name_____ Date_____

All Together Now

1. Look at the pictures. 2. Find the word below that goes with each picture.
3. Write a line connecting two pictures that go together to make one compound word. (Hint: All the pictures in the left column show the first part of a word.)
4. Write the compound word on the line next to the pictures.

wood	birth	pick	cutter
smoke	boy	day	cow
post	card	tack	tooth

cowboy

woodcutter

birthday

postcard

toothpick

56 Just a Dream • Language Support/Blackline Master 28
Grade 4

Language Support, 56

Writing That Compares

GRAMMAR/SPELLING CONNECTIONS

See the 5-Day Grammar and Usage Plan on singular and plural nouns, pages 189M–189N.

See the 5-Day Spelling Plan on words with consonant clusters, pages 1890–189P.

TECHNOLOGY TIP

Tell students that they can make notes on the computer and then develop their notes into a rough draft.

TEACHING TIP

MANAGEMENT Have students work with partners during the prewriting step to share ideas for their essays.

Prewrite

WRITE AN ESSAY Present the following assignment: Walter's dreams show him the importance of saving the environment. Write an essay to compare two possible futures: what the world may be like if we do not protect the environment, and what it may be like if we do. At the end of your essay, suggest a way you and your classmates can help bring about the better future.

BRAINSTORM LISTS Have students brainstorm the effects of air, water, and litter pollution. Then have them list the effects of an unpolluted environment.

Strategy: Use a Graphic Organizer Have students organize their lists in a two-column chart. Help students to use their charts effectively by separating ideas under headings marked *A Clean World* and *A Polluted World*.

A CLEAN WORLD	A POLLUTED WORLD
• Air: fresh and clear; you can breathe easily	• Air: dirty and smells of gas or factory fumes
• Litter: collected and recycled when possible	• Litter: wastes recyclable objects and destroys the land
• Water: clean and drinkable	• Water: toxic and kills plant and animal life

Draft

USE THE GRAPHIC ORGANIZER In their essays, students should begin with a main idea statement and then describe at least two causes and effects of pollution. In a closing statement, they should list ways that they can make a difference locally.

Revise

SELF-QUESTIONING Ask students to assess their drafts for improvement.

• Does my opening tell what my essay is about?

• Did I compare the effects of a polluted and a clean environment?

• Did I include a suggestion about ways my friends and I could make a difference in our community?

PARTNERS Students may trade essays with a partner to get feedback on interest level and clarity.

Edit/Proofread

CHECK FOR ERRORS After students finish revising their essays, have them proofread for final corrections and changes.

Publish

MAKE AN ANTHOLOGY Make a class anthology titled "Future World: Make It Clean!"

Possible Futures

What will happen if we do not save the environment? And what would a cleaner world be like?

If we do not clean up the world's air and water supplies, toxic waste will continue to harm rivers, lakes, and animals. There may not be enough drinking water, and people could become very sick from gas and factory fumes.

With stricter laws, however, we could help to clean up the air and water. Nature could recover from pollution. And people would have a cleaner, healthier world to live in.

In our community, we can send letters to the mayor and the governor asking them to make laws for pollution control. We can also organize local recycling and clean-up crews. A clean future could be ours.

Presentation Ideas

MAKE A PHOTO DISPLAY Have students take photos of places in the community where pollution is a problem. Then have them make drawings showing how they think the places could look if the problem were cleaned up. ▶ **Viewing/Representing**

MAKE SPEECHES Have students work in teams to create an anti-pollution town meeting. They can present speeches based on their essays and invite other classes to hear them. ▶ **Speaking/Listening**

Consider students' creative efforts, possibly adding a plus (+) for originality, wit, and imagination.

For a 6-point or an 8-point scale, see pages T105–T106.

Meeting Individual Needs for Writing

EASY	ON-LEVEL	CHALLENGE
Make a Diagram Students can diagram a method for lessening one type of pollution in the community, adding numbers and captions to describe the steps in some detail.	**Write a Brochure** Students can prepare a brochure for community members on ways they can recycle and help lessen pollution in the community.	**Interview an Expert** Students can write questions to ask a local scientist or health department official about sources and solutions to community pollution problems.

5 Day Grammar and Usage Plan

DAILY LANGUAGE ACTIVITIES

Write the Daily Language Activities on the chalkboard each day or use **Transparency 7.** Have students correct the sentences orally. For answers, see the transparency.

Day 1
1. My father planted many tree.
2. That tree has lots of apple.
3. This tree has many flower.

Day 2
1. Plant bushs to cut down on noise.
2. Babys should have clean air to breathe.
3. Will children in the future have toy?

Day 3
1. The park has many bench.
2. Duck like to swim in the pond.
3. Some foxs live in the park, too.

Day 4
1. The air is cleaner on some day than others.
2. City bus make a lot of noise.
3. The sky has patchs of smog.

Day 5
1. Librarys have books about recycling.
2. Those bin are for litter.
3. Recycle those bottle.

Daily Language Transparency 7

DAY 1 — Introduce the Concept

Oral Warm-Up Hold up a single book and say: *I have a book.* Then hold up two and say: *I have two books.* Ask students what they can tell by the endings of the two nouns.

Introduce Singular and Plural Nouns A noun can name one or more than one person, place, or thing.

Singular and Plural Nouns

- A **singular noun** names one person, place, or thing.

- A **plural noun** names more than one person, place, or thing.

- Add -*s* to form the plural of most singular nouns.

Present the Daily Language Activity. Then have students form the plurals of *bed, toothpick,* and *paper,* and use each in a sentence.

 Assign the daily Writing Prompt on page 158C.

Name _____ Date _____ LEARN Grammar **39**

Singular and Plural Nouns

- A **singular noun** names one person, place, or thing.
- A **plural noun** names more than one person, place, or thing.
- Add -*s* to form the plural of most singular nouns.

Decide whether each underlined word is a singular or plural noun. Then write an "S" for singular or a "P" for plural on the line.

1. There were three trash <u>cans</u> in the garage. **P**
2. One can had only <u>bottles</u> in it. **P**
3. Walter traveled to the future in his <u>bed</u>. **S**
4. Walter did not like the <u>dream</u> he had. **S**
5. He put his head under the <u>blankets</u>. **P**
6. Smoke poured from the <u>smokestack</u> by Walter's bed. **S**
7. <u>Trucks</u> honked loudly all around the bed. **P**
8. A woman showed Walter <u>postcards</u> of the Grand Canyon. **P**
9. A <u>duck</u> that could talk landed on Walter's bed. **S**
10. Walter was glad to get back to his <u>room</u>. **S**

Grade 4/Unit 2
Just a Dream   **10**   Extension: Have students make a list of the underlined singular nouns. Then ask students to add -*s* to each word and write its plural form.   **39**

GRAMMAR PRACTICE BOOK, PAGE 39

DAY 2 — Teach the Concept

Review Singular and Plural Nouns Ask students how to form the plurals of most nouns.

Introduce Plurals for Some Words Words with certain endings follow different patterns in forming plurals.

Singular and Plural Nouns

- Add -*es* to form the plural of singular nouns that end in *s, sh, ch,* or *x.*

- To form the plural of nouns ending in a consonant and *y,* change *y* to *i* and add -*es.*

- To form the plural of nouns ending in a vowel and *y,* add -*s.*

Present the Daily Language Activity. Then have students write the plural forms of *bush, baby,* and *toy.*

 Assign the daily Writing Prompt on page 158C.

Name _____ Date _____ LEARN AND PRACTICE Grammar **40**

Forming Plural Nouns

- Add -*es* to form the plural of singular nouns that end in *s, sh, ch,* or *x.*
- To form the plural of nouns ending in a consonant and *y,* change *y* to *i* and add -*es.*
- To form the plural of nouns ending in a vowel and *y,* add -*s.*

Find the plural noun in the box for each underlined singular noun in the sentences below. Write the plural noun on the line.

| gases | wishes | branches | boxes |
| bakeries | parties | toys | highways |

1. Doughnuts and other sweets are made in <u>bakery</u> **bakeries**
2. There were <u>box</u> **boxes** of trash in the huge dump.
3. Walter's bed landed on <u>branch</u> **branches** in a tree.
4. Deadly <u>gas</u> **gases** filled the air.
5. The <u>highway</u> **highways** in the future were crowded.
6. Walter's birthday <u>wish</u> **wishes** all came true.
7. He got many new <u>toy</u> **toys** and a tree.
8. Of all his birthday <u>party</u> **parties** he liked this one best.

Extension: Have students make a Singular and Plural chart. Ask students to list singular nouns ending in *s, sh, ch, x,* and *y* and then write the plurals of these words.   **40**   Grade 4/Unit 2 *Just a Dream*   **8**

GRAMMAR PRACTICE BOOK, PAGE 40

Singular and Plural Nouns

Learn from the Literature Review singular and plural nouns. Ask students to read the second sentence of the last paragraph on page 180 of *Just a Dream*.

> They loved his new <u>toys</u>: the laser gun set, electric yo-yo, and inflatable <u>dinosaurs</u>.

Ask students to identify the plural nouns and tell how they were formed.

Form Plurals Present the Daily Language Activity and have students correct the nouns orally.

Have students make a four-column chart and write one of the rules from Days 1 and 2 at the top of each column. Then have them brainstorm plural nouns and record them in the column that has the appropriate rule.

 Assign the daily Writing Prompt on page 158D.

Review Singular and Plural Nouns Write the incorrect nouns from the Daily Language Activities for Days 1–3 on the chalkboard. Have students correct the nouns and name the rule that is used to form each plural. Then present the Daily Language Activity for Day 4.

Mechanics and Usage Before students begin the daily Writing Prompt, review the use of commas in a series.

Commas in a Series

- A comma tells the reader to pause between the words that it separates.
- Use commas to separate three or more words in a series.
- Do not use a comma after the last word in a series.

Display: *Walter saw smokestacks, cars, and drivers from his bed.*

 Assign the daily Writing Prompt on page 158D.

Assess Use the Daily Language Activity and page 43 of the **Grammar Practice Book** for assessment.

Reteach Have students write each plural rule as a heading on a sheet of paper. Then they should draw a picture of objects that adhere to each rule (for example, a *set of dishes* for the *-es* rule), and write the plural forms of the nouns underneath their drawings.

Have students create a word wall of plurals that follow each pattern.

Use page 44 of the **Grammar Practice Book** for additional reteaching.

 Assign the daily Writing Prompt on page 158D.

---

5 Day Spelling Plan

Some students may find clusters with the letter *l* difficult to pronounce, since the sound may not exist in their primary languages. Pronounce each word and have students repeat it. Write each word, substituting a blank for each letter in the cluster. Have students fill in the missing letters.

DICTATION SENTENCES

Spelling Words

1. This paper is blank.
2. That was a daring jump.
3. Who will claim this mitten?
4. You need flour to make bread.
5. Open the window a crack.
6. Take the bridge across the river.
7. Can you float on your back?
8. Walk up the plank to the boat.
9. Find a job on the classified page.
10. Don't rock the cradle.
11. What brand of soup do you like?
12. Is he among your friends?
13. You flatter me!
14. Put this skirt on the clothesline.
15. Grab the horse by its bridle.
16. Did I get credit on the test?
17. That is a darling baby.
18. What made the curtain flutter?
19. The dish made a loud clatter.
20. I want to take a cruise.

Challenge Words

21. Books were bulging from the bag.
22. Who crumpled up this paper?
23. There is a dark haze in the sky.
24. The children were shrieking with joy.
25. The duck waddled to the pond.

DAY 1 Pretest

Assess Prior Knowledge Use the Dictation Sentences at the left and **Spelling Practice Book** page 39 for the pretest. Allow students to correct their own papers. Students who require a modified list may be tested on the first ten words.

Spelling Words		Challenge Words
1. blank	12. among	21. **bulging**
2. daring	13. flatter	22. **crum-**
3. claim	14. **clothes-**	**pled**
4. **flour**	**line**	23. **haze**
5. crack	15. bridle	24. **shrieking**
6. bridge	16. credit	25. **waddled**
7. **float**	17. darling	
8. plank	18. flutter	
9. classified	19. clatter	
10. cradle	20. cruise	
11. brand		

*Note: Words in **dark type** are from the story.*

Word Study On page 40 of the **Spelling Practice Book** are word study steps and an at-home activity.

SPELLING PRACTICE BOOK, PAGE 39

WORD STUDY STEPS AND ACTIVITY, PAGE 40

DAY 2 Explore the Pattern

Sort and Spell Words Say *flatter* and *clatter*. Ask students to tell how the words are different. Then have students read the Spelling Words aloud and sort them as below.

Words beginning with

fl	cl	cr	br
flour	claim	crack	bridge
float	classified	cradle	brand
flatter	clothes-	credit	bridle
flutter	line	cruise	
	clatter		

Words ending with

nk	ng
blank	daring
plank	among
	darling

Word Wall Have students create a word wall based on the word sort and add more words from their reading.

SPELLING PRACTICE BOOK, PAGE 41

Words with Consonant Clusters

DAY 3 Practice and Extend

Word Meaning: Endings Remind students that common endings can be added to many words. These endings may change the meaning somewhat or form a new part of speech. Ask students to identify Spelling Words that can add the ending *-s* or *-ing*. Discuss how the new ending changes the meaning of each word.

If students need extra practice, have partners give each other a midweek test.

Glossary Review how inflected forms of words are shown in the Glossary. Have partners

- write the base word of each Challenge Word.

- look up the Challenge Words.

- write the different inflected forms.

- note whether there are any changes to the spelling of the base word when the ending is added.

DAY 4 Proofread and Write

Proofread Sentences Write these sentences on the chalkboard, including the misspelled words. Ask students to proofread, circling incorrect spellings and writing the correct spellings. There are two spelling errors in each sentence.

There is a crak in the base of the brige. (crack, bridge)

See the butterfly flote and fluter over the flowers. (float, flutter)

Have students create additional sentences with errors for partners to correct.

Have students use as many spelling words as possible in the daily Writing Prompt on page 158D. Remind students to proofread their writing for errors in spelling, grammar, and punctuation.

DAY 5 Assess and Reteach

Assess Students' Knowledge Use page 44 of the **Spelling Practice Book** or the Dictation Sentences on page 189O for the posttest.

Personal Word List If students have trouble with any words in the lesson, have them add the words to their personal word lists of troublesome words in their journals. Have students underline the consonant cluster in each word.

Students should refer to their word lists during later writing activities.

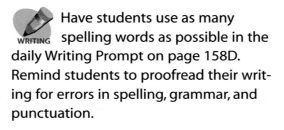

SPELLING PRACTICE BOOK, PAGE 42

SPELLING PRACTICE BOOK, PAGE 43

SPELLING PRACTICE BOOK, PAGE 44

Leah's Pony

Selection Summary Students will read about Leah, a Depression-era girl whose favorite possession is a pony. When drought destroys her family's crops, Leah must sell her pony to raise money. Her sacrifice inspires her neighbors to help her family keep their farm.

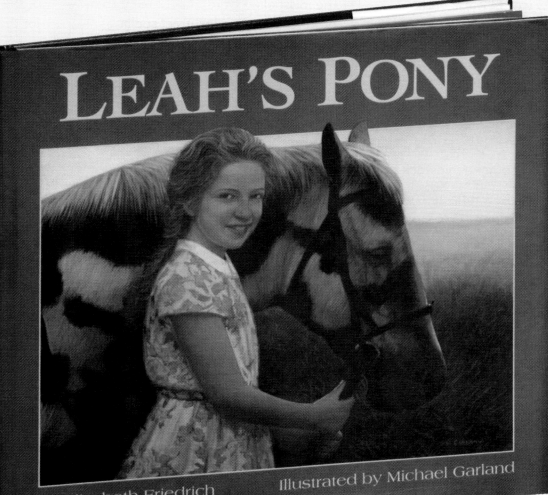

LEAH'S PONY

by Elizabeth Friedrich   Illustrated by Michael Garland

Listening Library Audiocassette

INSTRUCTIONAL
Pages 192–215

About the Author Elizabeth Friedrich spent summers on a farm when she was a child, and today she lives on a farm in New Hampshire. Her love of farm animals, her interest in the Great Depression, and her strong commitment to family led her to write this story.

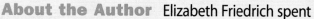

About the Illustrator An author as well as an illustrator, Michael Garland's other books include *Dinner at Magritte's, Circus Girl, Angel Cat,* and *My Cousin Katie.* He lives with his family in New York State.

Resources for
Meeting Individual Needs

EASY
Pages 215A, 215D

INDEPENDENT
Pages 215B, 215D

CHALLENGE
Pages 215C, 215D

LEVELED PRACTICE

Reteach 52–58
blackline masters with reteaching opportunities for each assessed skill

Practice 52–58
workbook with Take-Home stories and practice opportunities for each assessed skill and story comprehension

Extend 52–58
blackline masters that offer challenge activities for each assessed skill

ADDITIONAL RESOURCES

- **Language Support Book,** 57–64
- **Take-Home Story, Practice,** p. 53a
- **Alternate Teaching Strategies,** T60–T66
- **Selected Quizzes Prepared by** Accelerated Reader

McGraw-Hill School
TECHNOLOGY

inter**NET**
CONNECTION Research and Inquiry Ideas. Visit
www.mhschool.com/reading

🔘 **Available on CD-ROM**

Suggested Lesson Planner

READING AND LANGUAGE ARTS

- ⚫ Comprehension
- ⚫ Vocabulary
- ⚫ Phonics/Decoding
- ⚫ Study Skills
- ⚫ Listening, Speaking, Viewing, Representing

- ⚫ Curriculum Connections

- ⚫ Writing

- ⚫ Grammar

- ⚫ Spelling

DAY 1 — *Focus on Reading and Skills*

Read **Read Aloud and Motivate,** 190E
Familiar Friends

Develop Visual Literacy, 190/191

☑ **Introduce Cause and Effect,** 192A–192B
Teaching Chart 43
Reteach, Practice, Extend, 52

Link Works of Art, 190/191

✏️ **Writing Prompt:** Imagine you lived on the farm shown on pages 196–197. Tell about farm animals, such as mice, geese, oxen, and sheep, that you might encounter there.

Introduce the Concept: Irregular Plural Nouns, 215M
Daily Language Activity
1. Leah's cat landed on both foots. feet
2. Her cat lost two tooths. teeth
3. Leah found two mouses in the barn. mice

Grammar Practice Book, 45

Pretest: Words with Consonant Clusters, 215O
Spelling Practice Book, 45, 46

DAY 2 — *Read the Literature*

Build Background, 192C
Develop Oral Language

Vocabulary, 192D

| bidding | county | overflowing |
| clustered | glistened | sturdy |

Teaching Chart 44
Word Building Manipulative Cards
Reteach, Practice, Extend, 53

Read **Read the Selection,** 192–211
☑ Cause and Effect
☑ Form Generalizations

Minilessons, 197, 203, 205, 207

Cultural Perspectives, 208

Link Social Studies, 192C

✏️ **Writing Prompt:** Your area of the country has gone through a long drought. Tell how the dry weather affects the men, women and children in your community.

📓 **Journal Writing,** 211
Quick-Write

Teach the Concept: Irregular Plural Nouns, 215M
Daily Language Activity
1. Not many childs live near Leah. children
2. Do we have to sell the sheeps? sheep
3. Four deers ate the apples. deer

Grammar Practice Book, 46

Explore the Pattern: Words with Consonant Clusters, 215O
Spelling Practice Book, 47

DAY 3 — Read the Literature

Rereading for Fluency, 210

Story Questions, 212
Reteach, Practice, Extend, 54

Story Activities, 213

Study Skill, 214
☑ Reference Sources
Teaching Chart 45
Reteach, Practice, Extend, 55

Test Power, 215

Read the Leveled Books, 215A–215D
Guided Reading
Consonant Clusters
☑ Cause and Effect
☑ Instructional Vocabulary

Activity Social Studies, 196

✎ **Writing Prompt:** Imagine you live on a farm near a forest. Write about your reaction to seeing animals such as deer or moose on the edge of your farm.

Writing Process: Writing That Compares, 215K
Prewrite, Draft

Review and Practice: Irregular Plural Nouns, 215N
Daily Language Activity
1. Some womans helped Leah's family.
   women
2. A herd of mooses ran by the barn.
   moose
3. Four oxes pulled the wagon. oxen

Grammar Practice Book, 47

Practice and Extend: Words with Consonant Clusters, 215P
Spelling Practice Book, 48

DAY 4 — Build Skills

Read the Leveled Books and Self-Selected Books

☑ **Review Cause and Effect,** 215E–215F
Teaching Chart 46
Reteach, Practice, Extend, 56
Language Support, 62

☑ **Review Sequence of Events,** 215G–215H
Teaching Chart 47
Reteach, Practice, Extend, 57
Language Support, 63

Activity Math, 198

✎ **Writing Prompt:** Pretend you were at the auction at Leah's farm. Write a diary entry that tells what happened and names the people who were there.

Writing Process: Writing That Compares, 215L
Revise
Meeting Individual Needs for Writing, 215L

Review and Practice: Irregular Plural Nouns, 215N
Daily Language Activity
1. Two mans bought the tractor. men
2. The gooses flew away. geese
3. Leah's dad caught four trouts. trout

Grammar Practice Book, 48

Proofread and Write: Words with Consonant Clusters, 215P
Spelling Practice Book, 49

DAY 5 — Build Skills

Read Self-Selected Books

☑ **Review Context Clues,** 215I–215J
Teaching Chart 48
Reteach, Practice, Extend, 58
Language Support, 64

Listening, Speaking, Viewing, Representing, 215L
Illustrate the Scene
Present a Play

Minilessons, 197, 203, 207

Phonics Review
Consonant Clusters, 205

Phonics/Phonemic Awareness Practice Book, 25–28

Activity Science, 206

✎ **Writing Prompt:** You spent a day with Leah and a veterinarian learning about ponies at her farm. Write a paragraph telling about ponies, including their manes, teeth, feet, and tails.

Writing Process: Writing That Compares, 215K
Edit/Proofread, Publish

Assess and Reteach: Irregular Plural Nouns, 215N
Daily Language Activity
1. Leah counted sheeps last night.
   sheep
2. Three bisons were hurt by the fire.
   bison
3. A neighbor bought both swines.
   swine

Grammar Practice Book, 49, 50

Assess and Reteach: Words with Consonant Clusters, 215P
Spelling Practice Book, 50

Link

Language Arts

Read Aloud and Motivate

Familiar Friends

a poem by James S. Tippett

The horses, the pigs,
And the chickens,
The turkeys, the ducks
And the sheep!
I can see all my friends
From my window
As soon as I waken
From sleep.

The cat on the fence
Is out walking.
The geese have gone down
For a swim.
The pony comes trotting

Right up to the gate;
He knows I have candy
For him.

The cows in the pasture
Are switching
Their tails to keep off
The flies.
And the old mother dog
Has come out in the yard
With five pups to give me
A surprise.

Oral Comprehension

LISTENING AND SPEAKING Motivate students to think about the strong feelings of friendship that people often develop for their animals by reading them this poem. When you have finished reading, ask: "How does the speaker of the poem feel about the animals on his farm?" Then ask, "Which of the farm animals do you think the speaker has a close friendship with?" Have students think about the words in the poem that show this friendship. For example, students should consider what causes the pony to trot right up to the gate.

Activity Encourage students to find photographs in magazines and other sources that show people with their pets. Students can work together to create a "Pets and People" booklet. They can include favorite animal and pet poems in the booklet, too. As students share their booklets, encourage them to discuss the effects that pets have on their owners and the effects owners have on their pets. Have students identify causes for these effects. ▶ **Visual**

Develop Visual Literacy

Link

Works of Art

Anthology pages 190–191

Stories in Art

When you look at this photograph, you can almost feel the empty setting. What do you think has caused the people to leave?

Study this black-and-white photograph. What do you see? What effect does the deserted house have on you? How do the empty fields make you feel?

Look at the picture again. If you could take the same photograph, would you use color film? Explain your reasons.

Tractored Out
Childress County, Texas, 1938

190

191

Objective: Identify Cause and Effect

VIEWING This photograph expresses a mood of emptiness or loneliness. The photographer's subject— an abandoned farmhouse in the middle of a field—and use of black and white film help create this mood. Have students close their eyes to visualize the photograph. Afterward, ask them if the starkness of the picture helped them remember what was in it. Discuss what students remember in relation to how the photograph made them feel.

Read the page with students, encouraging individuals to share their reactions.

Ask students to suggest some cause-and-effect relationships that might explain some of the details in the photograph. For example:

• The house is empty because the farm was sold to another nearby farmer.

• In order to grow the most crops, the new owner has plowed right up to the walls of the old empty house.

• The land is dry because of a severe drought.

REPRESENTING Have students sketch or paint scenes that express a mood of loneliness.

190/191

Introduce Cause and Effect

LANGUAGE SUPPORT

 Point out that clue words such as *because, since,* and *in order to,* can often help us recognize cause-and-effect relationships in texts. Write the clue words on the chalkboard in a sentence. Help students identify the cause-and-effect relationships found in the sentences. Invite students to use the clue words to write their own sentences showing cause-and-effect relationships.

PREPARE

Discuss Cause and Effect   Discuss everyday examples of cause-and-effect relationships. Have students tell what might happen if they overslept one day.

TEACH

Define Cause and Effect   Explain that the reason something happens is called a *cause*. The thing that happens as a result of a cause is called an *effect*.

The Hot, Dry Summer

Papa and Mama stared sadly at the sky. The sun was hot and bright again today. <u>The sun had been hot and bright every day for more than a month. It hadn't rained a drop in five weeks.</u>

Mama and Papa looked out over the cornfields they had planted in the spring. They had worked so hard to plant and tend the fields. <u>Now most of the small corn plants had turned brown and died.</u>

Papa shook his head. <u>This year's corn crop has been lost. Now the family would have little money to buy the things they would need to live.</u> Mama and Papa looked at each other and wondered, "What can we do?"

Teaching Chart 43

Read the Story and Model the Skill   Display **Teaching Chart 43.** Model identifying cause and effect.

MODEL   As I read this paragraph, I learn that because of the hot sun and lack of rain, the corn crop Mama and Papa had planted died. In this case, the heat and dry weather are the cause. The dead corn crop is the effect.

Identify Cause and Effect   Have students draw one line under each cause in the paragraph and two lines under each effect.

PRACTICE

Create a Cause
and Effect Chart

ONE

Have students identify the cause-and-effect relationships
in the paragraph. Help volunteers fill in the chart.

▶ **Linguistic/Logical**

CAUSE (Why It Happens)	EFFECT (What Happens)
There is no rainfall for many weeks.	The corn crop dies.
Papa loses his corn crop.	The family will not have money.

ASSESS/CLOSE

Explain Cause
and Effect
Relationships

Have students review the cause-and-effect relationships shown on
the chart. Encourage students to continue writing the story by providing additional examples of cause-and-effect relationships. For
example: Because the family needed money (cause), Mama found a
job in town (effect).

ALTERNATE TEACHING
STRATEGY

CAUSE AND EFFECT

For a different approach to
teaching this skill, see page
T66.

Meeting Individual Needs for Comprehension

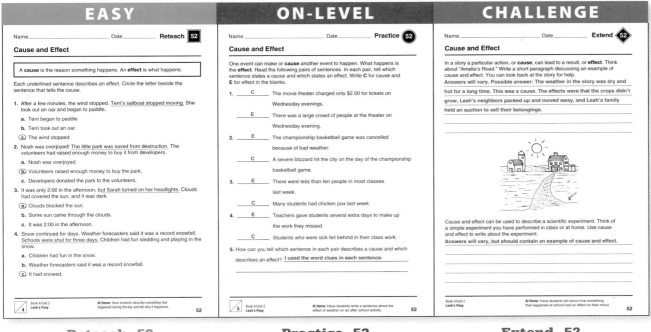

Reteach, 52   Practice, 52   Extend, 52

Build Background

Social Studies

Anthology and Leveled Books

Evaluate Prior Knowledge

CONCEPT: HELPING EACH OTHER The characters in *Leah's Pony* help each other during a time of hardship. Have students share experiences or knowledge they have of neighbors working together to help a family or individual facing hardship.

IDENTIFY HELPERS AND WAYS THEY HELP Have students create a chart in which they list the people and the organizations in their communities that help people in need. Have them identify the service each person or organization offers.

▶ **Logical/Visual**

PERSON OR ORGANIZATION	TYPE OF HELP
job counselor	helps people find work
public health nurse	helps families stay healthy
summer day camp	provides a place where kids can vacation
homeless shelter	provides a place for the homeless to sleep

Graphic Organizer 31

PLAN A DAY Have students write a schedule of what they might do during a day spent visiting various individuals and groups that help people in their community. Ask them to suggest what they might see during each visit they make.

PARTNERS   WRITING

Develop Oral Language

DISCUSS COMMUNITIES If possible,

ESL provide pictures of people involved in community organizations. Use the pictures to discuss ways people in a community help each other. Ask questions such as: "What kind of help does this person offer? How is this person helping?" Emphasize the word *help* each time it is used. Also discuss ways students are or can be involved in helping.

Ask students to brainstorm a list of small, everyday ways people in a community show they care about each other. Suggestions can range from giving a person directions to picking up litter. When possible, have students act out their suggestions. Write the list on the chalkboard.

Discuss the meanings of key words and ask volunteers to use them in sentences. You might suggest that students sketch a scene of people helping one another.

TEACHING TIP

MANAGEMENT After you complete the chart, explain the Plan-a-Day activity. Suggest that students work on this activity in pairs. While partners are working, present the Develop Oral Language activity to students who need help with oral language facility.

LANGUAGE SUPPORT

See **Language Support Book**, pages 57–60, for teaching suggestions for Build Background and Vocabulary.

Vocabulary

Key Words

Reynaldo's New Bike

1. Last summer, Reynaldo and his dad drove across a bridge into another county for an auction. **2.** When they got there, a crowd of people were clustered around the auctioneer. **3.** The man was holding up a sturdy bike for the people to see and buy. **4.** The strong, well-made bike was painted bright red, and it glistened in the sun. **5.** The auctioneer started the bidding for the bicycle at $5. **6.** When his dad got the bike for $10, Reynaldo was so happy his heart began overflowing with joy!

Teaching Chart 44

Vocabulary in Context

IDENTIFY VOCABULARY WORDS
Display **Teaching Chart 44** and read the passage. Have volunteers circle each vocabulary word and underline other words that are clues to its meaning. If necessary, explain the words *auction* and *auctioneer*.

DISCUSS MEANINGS Ask questions like these to help clarify word meanings:

- What county do you live in?
- Tell about a time you and your friends clustered around a person or thing. Why?
- What sorts of things are sturdy? Why?
- What might glisten in sunlight?
- What is the base word of *bidding*? Use the word in a sentence.
- What two smaller words together make up the word *overflowing*?

Practice

DEMONSTRATE WORD MEANING Have volunteers choose a vocabulary card and say a sentence using the word—but have them pause in silence where the word belongs. Invite listeners to complete each sentence. ▶ **Linguistic/Oral**

Word Building Manipulative Cards

WRITE CONTEXT SENTENCES Have students write context sentences using a synonym for each vocabulary word. Have them exchange papers and write each vocabulary word above its synonym. ▶ **Linguistic/Oral**

Definitions

county (p. 195) one of the sections into which a state is divided

clustered (p. 204) formed into a group

sturdy (p. 194) strong; not likely to break

glistened (p. 195) shone or sparkled

bidding (p. 206) offering to pay a price

overflowing (p. 198) being very full

SPELLING/VOCABULARY CONNECTIONS

See Spelling Challenge Words, pages 2150–215P.

ON-LEVEL

Auction

The *county* decided to hold an auction to raise money for a swimming pool. The morning of the auction, groups of people clustered near the auctioneer. The stage was *overflowing* with furniture, paintings, and a skateboard. "What will you bid for this used but *sturdy* old skateboard?" called the auctioneer. "I'll start the *bidding* at one dollar."

Tyrone clutched the money he had saved. The quarters *glistened* in the sun. "I bid two dollars," he shouted. Tyrone was hoping to take it home.

"Three dollars," a woman shouted from the crowd.

"Four!" cried Tyrone. That was all the money he had.

Suddenly from the back of the room, a man yelled, "Five hundred dollars,"

Tyrone had lost. As he was about to leave, the man spoke. "This *county* needs a swimming pool. Five hundred dollars is my donation." Then he handed the skateboard to Tyrone. "Enjoy your new skateboard," he said. "And enjoy the new pool."

1. Which part of the government held the auction? _____ the county
2. Which word describes the auction stage? _____ overflowing
3. At what amount did the auctioneer start the *bidding*? _____ one dollar
4. What was the skateboard like? _____ used but sturdy
5. Why do you think the stage was *overflowing* with so many items?
Possible answer: The people of the county wanted a pool and probably donated a lot of things to be auctioned.

Book 4/Unit 2
Leah's Pony

At Home: Have students use the vocabulary words to write a follow up to the story.

53a

Take-Home Story 53a
Reteach 53
Practice 53 · Extend 53

Guided Instruction

Preview and Predict

Have students read the title and preview the selection by looking at the illustrations.

- When and where might this story take place?

- Will the story be about something that could have happened in the past? How can you tell? (The clothing suggests that this story takes place long ago. The characters and setting are realistic.) *Genre*

- Do the pictures give clues about what might cause a problem for the main character? What are the clues?

- What is this story most likely about?

Have students record their predictions.

PREDICTIONS	WHAT HAPPENED
The story takes place long ago.	
Something happens to Leah's pony.	

Set Purposes

What do students want to find out by reading the story? For example:

- When does the story take place?

- What happens to Leah's pony?

MEET ELIZABETH FRIEDRICH

Elizabeth Friedrich was born in San Francisco, California. As a child, she loved to visit her aunt and uncle's farm in Missouri. To her, the farm was a magical place. *Leah's Pony* is based in part on what she learned there.

Today, Friedrich and her family live on a 150-year-old farm in New Hampshire, where she has a horse and six sheep. When she is not writing or working on her farm, she enjoys collecting antiques, reading, and traveling.

MEET MICHAEL GARLAND

Michael Garland was born and raised in New York City. No stranger to children's books, Garland has both written and illustrated many books for young people. His books include *Dinner at Magritte's*, *Circus Girl*, *Angel Cat*, and *My Cousin Katie*.

In his spare time Garland enjoys painting. He lives with his wife and three children in Patterson, New York.

192

Meeting Individual Needs • Grouping Suggestions for Strategic Reading

EASY	ON-LEVEL	CHALLENGE
Read Together Read the story together with students. You may wish to invite students to use the **Listening Library Audiocassette** first. Help students complete the Cause and Effect chart from page 193 to record information in the story. Guided Instruction and Intervention prompts offer additional help with vocabulary and comprehension.	**Guided Reading** Review the story words listed on page 193. Choose from the Guided Instruction questions as you read the story with students or after they have listened to the **Listening Library Audiocassette.** Have students chart cause-and-effect relationships in the story.	**Read Independently** Remind students that identifying cause-and-effect relationships will help them better understand the events in the story. Have students set up a Cause and Effect chart as on page 193. After reading the story, students can use their charts to sum up the story.

LEAH'S PONY

Written by Elizabeth Friedrich   Illustrated by Michael Garland

Guided Instruction

☑ **Cause and Effect**
☑ **Form Generalizations**

Strategic Reading Looking for cause-and-effect relationships can help us understand and appreciate a story. Before we begin reading, let's make a Cause and Effect chart. We can use the chart to keep track of what happens in the story and why it happens.

CAUSE (Why It Happens)	EFFECT (What Happens)

1 **CAUSE AND EFFECT** Look at the picture of Leah and her pony. Why do you think Leah looks so happy? (Leah might be happy because she has a pony to ride.)

Story Words

The words below may be unfamiliar. Have students check their meanings and pronunciations in the Glossary beginning on page 726 or in a dictionary.

- girth, p. 194
- tractor, p. 199
- windowpanes, p. 203
- whinny, p. 209

LANGUAGE SUPPORT

A blackline master of the Cause and Effect chart is available in the **Language Support Book.**

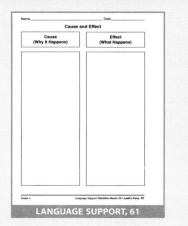

Guided Instruction

② **CAUSE AND EFFECT** Read the first sentence of the story carefully. Why do you think Leah's father bought her a pony the year the corn grew tall and straight?

MODEL Let me think about the phrase "The year the corn grew tall and straight." That probably means it was a very good year for growing and so the family made a lot of money. Growing lots of corn was the cause. The effect was Papa could afford to buy Leah a pony.

CONTEXT CLUES Look at the word *girth* near the end of the first paragraph. What do you think it means? Can you find any clues?

② THE YEAR THE CORN GREW TALL AND STRAIGHT, Leah's papa bought her a pony. The pony was strong and swift and sturdy, with just a snip of white at the end of his soft black nose. Papa taught Leah to place her new saddle right in the middle of his back and tighten the girth around his belly, just so.

194

℗/ℹ PREVENTION/INTERVENTION

CONTEXT CLUES Write the word *girth* on the chalkboard. Ask:

- What does the beginning of the sentence describe Papa doing? (teaching Leah how to put a saddle on her horse)

- How might a *girth* relate to a saddle? (It may be part of a saddle.)

- What does Leah do to the girth? (She tightens it around the horse's belly.)

- What kind of object might be tightened around a horse's belly? (some kind of belt or strap)

- Think about these clues. What do you think a *girth* is? (a belt or strap used to hold a saddle in place)

That whole summer, Leah and her pony crossed through cloud-capped cornfields and chased cattle through the pasture.

Leah scratched that special spot under her pony's mane and brushed him till his coat glistened like satin.

Each day Leah loved to ride her pony into town just to hear Mr. B. shout from the door of his grocery store, "That's the finest pony in the whole county."

3

195

Guided Instruction

3 **FORM GENERALIZATIONS** What does Mr. B. say about Leah's pony? (He says, "That's the finest pony in the whole county.") What details does the story offer that support the idea that Leah's pony might be the finest in the county?

MODEL Mr. B.'s comment, "That's the finest pony in the whole county," tells about a large group of things—all the ponies in the area. Let me think about that generalization. The author says that Leah's pony was "strong and swift and sturdy." Also, the pony's coat "glistened like satin." Those details back up Mr. B's statement. The point he was making—that Leah's pony is wonderful—seems true.

195

Guided Instruction

4 **CAUSE AND EFFECT** One cause can often have two or more effects. The author explains that during one growing season, the sky was black with dust. What were some of the effects? (It was hard for Leah to keep her pony's coat shining. It was hard for Mama to keep the house clean. It was hard for Papa to carry buckets of water for the sow and piglets.)

The year the corn grew no taller than a man's thumb, Leah's house became very quiet. Sometimes on those hot, dry nights, Leah heard Papa and Mama's hushed voices whispering in the kitchen. She couldn't understand the words but knew their sad sound.

Some days the wind blew so hard it turned the sky black with dust. It was hard for Leah to keep her pony's coat shining. It was hard for Mama to keep the house clean. It was hard for Papa to carry buckets of water for the sow and her piglets.

4

196

Activity

Cross Curricular: Social Studies

THE GREAT DEPRESSION *Leah's Pony* is set in the United States during the 1930s, the time of the Great Depression. Ask students what they know about this time of economic hardship. Write their responses on the chalkboard.

RESEARCH AND INQUIRY Invite students to learn about the drought and dust storms that affected many farming regions of the Middle West during the Great Depression. Suggest students look at videos or in reference or history books. ▶ **Linguistic**

Soon Papa sold the pigs and even some of the cattle. "These are hard times," he told Leah with a puzzled look. "That's what these days are, all right, hard times."

Mama used flour sacks to make underwear for Leah. Mama threw dishwater on her drooping petunias to keep them growing. And, no matter what else happened, Mama always woke Leah on Saturday with the smell of fresh, hot coffee cake baking.

(5)

197

Guided Instruction

5 **FORM GENERALIZATIONS** Papa forms a generalization when he says, "These are hard times." What details in the story support this generalization? (The corn did not grow; the weather is hot and dry; the sky is black with dust.)

p/i **DECODING/CONTEXT CLUES** Look at the word after *drooping* in the second sentence of the second paragraph. How do you say that word? What do you think it means? Can you find any clues?

Minilesson

REVIEW/MAINTAIN
Make Inferences

Remind students that authors don't tell readers everything. Sometimes readers have to make inferences based on details in the story and on what they know from real life.

Read aloud the first four sentences on page 197. Discuss what these details suggest about the family's finances. (They must have little or no money.)

Activity Ask what students can infer based on Mama

- throwing dishwater on the petunias (There is a water shortage and no water can be wasted.)

- making coffee cake every Saturday (Mama still tries to give Leah treats.)

p/i PREVENTION/INTERVENTION

DECODING/CONTEXT CLUES
Write the word *petunias* on the chalkboard. Point out both the first and last syllables have the /ə/ sound. Help students sound it out. Then ask:

- What kind of things might droop in hot weather?

- What kind of things need water to keep growing?

- What kind of things might Mama want growing near her house?

- Think about these clues. What do you think petunias are? (a type of flower)

197

Guided Instruction

6 **CAUSE AND EFFECT** The author of a story might not state clearly the reason something happens. What do you think causes Leah's neighbors to move to Oregon? (The hot dry weather, the poor crops, and the grasshoppers made the neighbors decide to leave.)

Let's add this information to our chart.

CAUSE (Why It Happens)	EFFECT (What Happens)
Dry weather and grasshoppers destroy the crops.	The neighbors leave their farm.

One hot, dry, dusty day grasshoppers turned the day to night. They ate the trees bare and left only twigs behind.

The next day the neighbors filled their truck with all they owned and stopped to say good-bye. "We're off to Oregon," they said. "It must be better there." Papa, Mama, and Leah waved as their neighbors wobbled down the road in an old truck overflowing with chairs and bedsprings and wire.

The hot, dry, dusty days kept coming. On a day you could almost taste the earth in the air, Papa said, "I have something to tell you, Leah, and I want you to be brave.

198

Activity

Cross Curricular: Math

BANK LOANS Explain that banks charge people who borrow money a fee called interest. Share this example: For every $100 someone borrows from Student Bank, they must pay $6 interest. Pose problems based on the example:

• André borrows $500 from Student

Bank. Sarah borrows $1,000 from Student Bank. How much interest will each of them have to pay?

• How much interest would there be on a loan of $2,100?

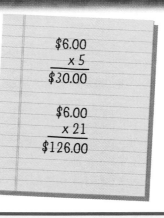

$6.00
x 5
$30.00

$6.00
x 21
$126.00

I borrowed money from the bank. I bought seeds, but the seeds dried up and blew away. Nothing grew. I don't have any corn to sell. Now I can't pay back the bank," Papa paused. "They're going to have an auction, Leah. They're going to sell the cattle and the chickens and the pickup truck."

Leah stared at Papa. His voice grew husky and soft. "Worst of all, they're going to sell my tractor. I'll never be able to plant corn when she's gone. Without my tractor, we might even have to leave the farm. I told you, Leah, these are hard times."

7

199

Guided Instruction

7 **CAUSE AND EFFECT** Why is the bank going to auction off Papa's belongings? (Papa borrowed money from the bank to plant, grow, and sell corn. But the corn did not grow. As a result, Papa did not make money and cannot pay the bank what he owes. To get its money back, the bank will take the things Papa owns and sell them.)

Let's add this information to our chart.

CAUSE (Why It Happens)	EFFECT (What Happens)
Dry weather and grasshoppers destroy the crops.	The neighbors leave their farm.
Papa cannot pay the bank the money he owes.	The bank is going to auction off the things Papa owns.

p/i **COMPOUND WORDS** Read the next-to-last word in the first paragraph on page 199. (pickup) Sound out the word. What smaller words do you see in this word?

199

Guided Instruction

(8) **FORM GENERALIZATIONS** Leah makes a generalization when she says that people who come to auctions have "eager faces." Why might the people at an auction often appear eager? (Many auction goers hope to find a bargain; they are eager to buy things cheaply.)

Leah knew what an auction meant. She knew eager faces with strange voices would come to their farm. They would stand outside and offer money for Papa's best bull and Mama's prize rooster and Leah's favorite calf.

(8)

200

LANGUAGE SUPPORT

ESL Pause to monitor the comprehension of students needing language support. Help them summarize the story so far by asking simple questions requiring short answers. For example:

- Where do Leah and her family live? (on a farm)

- What is the main thing they grow? (corn)

- What happened to all their corn? (It died.)

- Who is making the family sell what they own? (the bank)

Pair students who have difficulty with proficient readers. Have partners identify characters, settings, and events shown in the illustrations and paraphrase each page of text.

All week Leah worried and waited and wondered what to do. One morning she watched as a man in a big hat hammered a sign into the ground in front of her house.

9

201

Guided Instruction

9 **CAUSE AND EFFECT** Losing the farm would have serious effects on Leah's whole family. What effect in particular might Leah be most worried about?

MODEL I know Leah loves her pony very much. If her family has to leave the farm and move away, Leah may not be able to keep her pony. That's probably what Leah worries about most.

Ⓢelf-monitoring

STRATEGY

SEARCH FOR CLUES Explain: Readers can better understand a story by looking for clues that tell why something is happening.

MODEL When I saw the picture on page 201 I didn't really understand why there was going to be an auction at Papa's farm. So I read pages 198–200 again and searched for clues. I learned that the bank is auctioning off Papa's farm equipment to get its money back.

Guided Instruction

 Look at the picture on pages 202–203. Where do you think Leah and her pony might ride? What might she do? (Sample answer: Leah will ride to meet a friend with whom she can share her feelings about the auction; perhaps she might ask someone to help her find a way to save the farm.) *Make Predictions*

202

Visual Literacy

VIEWING AND INTERPRETING

Explain that artists often take special care to capture the changing mood of a story in their illustrations. Have students look closely at the illustration on pages 202–203.

- What is the mood at this point of the story? (sad, anxious)

- In what ways does this picture suggest how Leah might be feeling? (The land looks empty and dry; Leah might be feeling empty because her family may lose its farm. The old, run-down house in the background looks lonely and sad, which is how Leah may be feeling.)

Leah wanted to run away. She raced her pony past empty fields lined with dry gullies. She galloped past a house with rags stuffed in broken windowpanes. She sped right past Mr. B. sweeping the steps outside his store.

At last Leah knew what she had to do. She turned her pony around and rode back into town. She stopped in front of Mr. B.'s store. "You can buy my pony," she said. **(11)**

203

Guided Instruction

(11) CAUSE AND EFFECT Why do you think Leah offers to sell her pony to Mr. B.? (Perhaps she wants to raise money to help her family.) Pretend you are Leah. Explain why you did this. *Role-Play*

TEACHING TIP

INSTRUCTIONAL Guide students to consider the importance of Leah's pony in her life. Discuss how places in farm country are often very spread out and how during the Great Depression bicycles and cars were rarer and more expensive. Ask:

- **How might Leah get from place to place without her pony?** (She might have to walk.)
- **Why might giving up her pony mean giving up some of her freedom?** (It might mean she has to spend more time at home since it will be harder for her to get around.)

Minilesson

REVIEW/MAINTAIN

Summarize

Remind students that stopping from time to time to summarize what they have read will help them remember and appreciate a story better.

- Ask students to think about what they have learned about Leah and her family up to page 203.
- Suggest students use the pictures to help them summarize the story to this point.

Activity Have students choose one of the following topics to summarize:

- why times are hard in Leah's county
- why there is an auction at Leah's farm

Guided Instruction

(12) **CAUSE AND EFFECT** Leah says she wants to sell her pony because she is too big for him. Is this the real cause of Leah's actions? (No. She is selling her pony to raise money for her family.)

Let's add this to our Cause and Effect chart.

CAUSE (Why It Happens)	EFFECT (What Happens)
Dry weather and grasshoppers destroy the crops.	The neighbors leave their farm.
Papa cannot pay the bank the money he owes.	The bank is going to auction off the things Papa owns.
Leah needs money to help her family.	Leah decides to sell her pony.

Fluency

READ WITH EXPRESSION Invite groups of four children to read page 204 together. One student can read the part of Mr. B., another can read the part of Leah, the third can read the part of the auctioneer, while the fourth can read the running narration. Suggest students first practice reading their parts alone and then run through the passage with the other readers. Remind students that:

- Mr. B. should sound surprised.
- Leah should sound sad.
- The auctioneer should be loud and fast, trying to get people's interest.
- The narrator should sound thoughtful.

Mr. B. stopped sweeping and stared at her. "Why would you want to sell him?" he asked. "That's the finest pony in the county."

(12) Leah swallowed hard. "I've grown a lot this summer," she said. "I'm getting too big for him."

Sunburned soil crunched under Leah's feet as she walked home alone. The auction had begun. Neighbors, friends, strangers—everyone clustered around the man in the big hat. "How much for this wagon?" boomed the man. "Five dollars. Ten dollars. Sold for fifteen dollars to the man in the green shirt."

Papa's best bull.
Sold.
Mama's prize rooster.
Sold.
Leah's favorite calf.
Sold.

204

205

Guided Instruction

(13) **CAUSE AND EFFECT** What has happened so far in the story to make Leah look so sad? (A lost corn crop left her family without money. The bank is auctioning off Papa's farm equipment. Leah has tried to raise money by selling her dearest possession, her pony.)

Minilesson

REVIEW/MAINTAIN

Consonant Clusters

Have students find and pronounce *stared* and *strangers* on page 204.

- Write *st* and *str* as column heads on the board. Have volunteers write the words in the correct columns.

- Add *sp, spr,* and *thr* as column heads. Have volunteers name words that begin with these clusters, such as *spine, spring,* and *thread*.

Activity Have students list words beginning with each consonant cluster in the correct column.

Guided Instruction

14 **CAUSE AND EFFECT** What will happen if no one else bids for the tractor? *(Leah will get the tractor for just one dollar.)*

TEACHING TIP

INSTRUCTIONAL Point out that one way to understand what happens in a story is to imagine themselves in the story. If the students were at the auction and saw Leah bid one dollar for her father's tractor, how would they feel? If no one bid on the things being auctioned, would the students bid on the items? Why or why not?

Leah clutched her money in her hand. "It has to be enough," she whispered to herself. "It just has to be."

"Here's one of the best items in this entire auction," yelled the man in the big hat. "Who'll start the bidding at five hundred dollars for this practically new, all-purpose Farmall tractor? It'll plow, plant, fertilize, and even cultivate for you."

It was time. Leah's voice shook. "One dollar."

The man in the big hat laughed. "That's a low starting bid if I ever heard one," he said. "Now let's hear some serious bids."

14

No one moved. No one said a word. No one even seemed to breathe.

206

Activity

Cross Curricular: Science

AGRICULTURE The auctioneer says the tractor can "plow, plant, fertilize, and cultivate." Ask what students know about these steps in raising a crop.

RESEARCH AND INQUIRY Invite students to find out what crops grow on farms in their state. They may want to write to their state's department of agriculture for information. Students can create a flow chart of steps that local farmers must follow to raise each crop.
▶ **Visual**

IRRIGATION

"Ladies and gentlemen, this tractor is a beauty! I have a bid of only one dollar for it. One dollar for this practically new Farmall tractor! Do I hear any other bids?"

Again no one moved. No one said a word. No one even seemed to breathe.

"This is ridiculous!" the man's voice boomed out from under his hat into the silence. "Sold to the young lady for one dollar."

The crowd cheered. Papa's mouth hung open. Mama cried. Leah proudly walked up and handed one dollar to the auctioneer in the big hat. **(15)**

207

Guided Instruction

(15) CAUSE AND EFFECT Why does the crowd cheer when the bank sells Leah the tractor for just one dollar? (The people are happy that Leah has outwitted the bank and is making it possible for her family to keep the farm.)

Minilesson

REVIEW/MAINTAIN
Suffixes

Remind students that suffixes are word parts that are added to the end of a word to create a new word with a new meaning. Point out the word *auctioneer* on page 207. Have students identify its base word. (auction) Explain that the suffix *-eer* means "one who is involved with or runs." Then have students suggest the meaning of *auctioneer*. (one who runs an auction)

Activity Invite students to identify the base word in each of the following words and then define each of the words using the meanings of the base words and the suffix *-eer*. (*puppeteer, engineer, electioneer*)

LANGUAGE SUPPORT

 If necessary, explain the concept of an auction. Tell students that all the people at an auction have a chance to say what they are willing to pay for an item. The person who offers the highest price gets the item. Then review some of the phrases that are used at the auction in the story:

• Who'll start the bidding at (five hundred dollars)?

• I have a bid of only (one dollar) for it. Do I hear any other bids?

• Sold to (the young lady) for (one dollar).

You may wish to conduct a mock auction to review these phrases. For example, you might pretend to auction off your briefcase or your coat.

207

Guided Instruction

(16) CAUSE AND EFFECT Why does the auctioneer become angry? (He becomes angry because no one offers to pay the real value of the objects being auctioned; he will not make much money from the auction; the bank will not recover its money from the auction.)

Let's add this to our Cause and Effect chart.

CAUSE (Why It Happens)	EFFECT (What Happens)
Dry weather and grasshoppers destroy the crops.	The neighbors leave their farm.
Papa cannot pay the bank the money he owes.	The bank is going to auction off the things Papa owns.
Leah needs money to help her family.	Leah decides to sell her pony.
No one offers the real value of the objects being auctioned.	The auctioneer becomes angry.

"That young lady bought one fine tractor for one very low price," the man continued. "Now how much am I bid for this flock of healthy young chickens?"

"I'll give you ten cents," offered a farmer who lived down the road.

(16) "Ten cents! Ten cents is mighty cheap for a whole flock of chickens," the man said. His face looked angry.

208

Again no one moved. No one said a word. No one even seemed to breathe.

"Sold for ten cents!"

The farmer picked up the cage filled with chickens and walked over to Mama. "These chickens are yours," he said.

The man pushed his big hat back on his head. "How much for this good Ford pickup truck?" he asked.

"Twenty-five cents," yelled a neighbor from town.

Again no one moved. No one said a word. No one even seemed to breathe.

"Sold for twenty-five cents!" The man in the big hat shook his head. "This isn't supposed to be a penny auction!" he shouted.

The neighbor paid his twenty-five cents and took the keys to the pickup truck. "I think these will start your truck," he whispered as he dropped the keys into Papa's shirt pocket.

Leah watched as friends and neighbors bid a penny for a chicken or a nickel for a cow or a quarter for a plow. One by one, they gave everything back to Mama and Papa.

The crowds left. The sign disappeared. Chickens scratched in their coop, and cattle called for their corn. The farm was quiet. Too quiet. No familiar whinny greeted Leah when she entered the barn. Leah swallowed hard and straightened her back.

That night in Leah's hushed house, no sad voices whispered in the kitchen. Only Leah lay awake, listening to the clock chime nine and even ten times. Leah's heart seemed to copy its slow, sad beat.

209

Guided Instruction

17 **FORM GENERALIZATIONS** What generalization might you make based on what happened at the farm auction? (Sample answer: When ordinary people work together they can often overcome powerful institutions.)

18 **CAUSE AND EFFECT** With the help of neighbors, Leah has saved her family's farm. Why then is Leah's heart so sad? Show us how Leah's face might look and then explain why she feels that way. (Leah feels sad because she has sold her beloved pony to Mr. B.) *Pantomime*

Guided Instruction

19 **CAUSE AND EFFECT** Let's complete our Cause and Effect chart.

CAUSE (WHY IT HAPPENS)	EFFECT (WHAT HAPPENS)
Dry weather and grasshoppers destroy the crops.	The neighbors leave their farm.
Papa cannot pay the bank the money he owes.	The bank is going to auction the things Papa owns.
Leah needs money to help her family.	Leah decides to sell her pony.
No one offers the real value of the objects being auctioned.	The auctioneer becomes angry.
Neighbors return Mama and Papa's belongings.	Mama and Papa are able to keep their farm.

RETELL THE STORY Have volunteers recount the major events of the story by referring to their Cause and Effect charts. Students may also write one or two sentences that summarize the story. Have them focus on the causes and effects behind the events in the story. *Summarize*

STUDENT SELF-ASSESSMENT

- How did using the strategy of recognizing cause-and-effect relationships help me understand the events in the story?

TRANSFERRING THE STRATEGY

- How might recognizing cause-and-effect relationships help me when I read science and social studies books?

210

REREADING FOR *Fluency*

PARTNERS Have students choose one page of the story to read aloud to a partner. Encourage the students to read with expression.

READING RATE You may want to assess students' rate of reading. Have a student read aloud from *Leah's Pony* for one minute. Ask the student to place a stick-on note after the last word read. Then count the total number of words read.

Alternatively, you could assess small groups or the whole class by having students count words and record their own scores.

A Running Record form provided in **Diagnostic/Placement Evaluation** will help you evaluate reading rate(s).

The next morning Leah forced open the heavy barn doors to start her chores. A loud whinny greeted her. Leah ran and hugged the familiar furry neck and kissed the white snip of a nose. "You're back!" she cried. "How did you get here?"

Then Leah saw the note with her name written in big letters:

Dear Leah,
    This is the finest pony in the county. But he's a little bit small for me and a little bit big for my grandson. He fits you much better.

                      Your friend,
                      Mr. B.

P.S. I heard how you saved your family's farm. These hard times won't last forever.

And they didn't.

(19)

211

LITERARY RESPONSE

QUICK-WRITE Invite students to record their thoughts about the story. These questions may help them get started:

- How would you describe Leah?
- What do you think of the way Leah solved her problem?

- Why do you think Mr. B. returned the pony to Leah?

ORAL RESPONSE Invite students to share their journal writing and discuss what they liked most about the story.

Guided Instruction

Return to Predictions and Purposes

Review with students their story predictions and reasons for reading the story. Were their predictions correct? Did they find out what they wanted to know?

PREDICTIONS	WHAT HAPPENED
The story takes place long ago.	The story takes place during the Great Depression of the 1930s.
Something happens to Leah's pony.	Leah sells the pony to save the family's farm, but the buyer gives the pony back to Leah.

CAUSE AND EFFECT

HOW TO ASSESS

- Have students work in pairs to identify a cause-and-effect relationship in the story that is not listed on the chart on page 211. One partner should identify causes, the other partner the effects.

Students should recognize that the cause of an event is a reason something happens, and an effect is what happens. Students should be able to discuss one cause-and-effect relationship that influences the events in the story about Leah and her family.

FOLLOW UP If students have trouble identifying cause-and-effect relationships, have them write "because" in large letters on a sheet of paper. Direct students to write an event from in the story in front of the word *because* and write why it happened after the word *because*.

Story Questions

Have students discuss or write answers to the questions on page 212.

Answers:

1. The weather is dry. The grasshoppers eat everything. *Literal/Cause and Effect*

2. They have to sell their belongings at auction to pay off a bank loan. *Inferential/Cause and Effect*

3. Sample answer: The neighbors bid low at the auction; they give the items back to Leah's family so they can stay on the farm. *Inferential/Form Generalizations*

4. This story is mainly about a girl who saves her family's farm by selling her pony. *Critical/Summarize*

5. Sample answer: Leah might dream heavy rains fall, the crops grow, and hard times end. *Critical/Reading Across Texts*

Write a Newspaper Article For a full writing process lesson related to this writing suggestion, see pages 215K–215L.

Story Questions & Activities

1. What causes the family's crops to fail?

2. What effect does the crop failure have on Leah and her family?

3. How do you know that Leah's neighbors are helpful?

4. What would you say to sum up this story?

5. Imagine that Leah was the main character in "Just a Dream." What kind of dream do you think she would have? Give reasons for your answer.

Write a Newspaper Article

Good times will return to Leah's family's farm. Imagine you are a newspaper reporter. Write an article about the way life improves for the farmers in the county. In the article, compare the good times with the hard times that came before.

Meeting Individual Needs

EASY

Name_____ Date_____ Reteach 53

Vocabulary

Write a word from the list to complete each sentence.

| bidding | clustered | county | glistened | overflowing | sturdy |

1. Reporters ___clustered___ around the baseball star.
2. Meg's eyes ___glistened___ with tears.
3. The laundry hamper was ___overflowing___ with clothes.
4. Mr. Polanski owns the largest farm in the ___county___.
5. The ___bidding___ for the house began at $98,000.
6. Although the table was old and used, it was still ___sturdy___.

Story Comprehension Reteach 54

Write a ✔ next to every sentence that tells something true about "Leah's Pony." You may look back at the story for help.

1. ____ Leah's family were factory workers.
2. ____ Leah's family always had money problems.
3. ✔ Some neighbors moved away to find a better place.
4. ✔ Leah's family had to sell animals and machines.
5. ____ Leah sold her pony because she was told to.
6. ✔ Neighbors helped buy back the family's things.
7. ✔ Leah's family was surprised and pleased by her actions.
8. ____ Leah never got back her pony.

At Home: Have students identify their favorite part of "Leah's Pony."

Book 4/Unit 2
Leah's Pony 8

53–54

Reteach, 54

ON-LEVEL

Name_____ Date_____ Practice 54

Story Comprehension

Answer the questions about "Leah's Pony." Answers may vary.

1. How did the crops grow in the year that Leah got the pony?
   They grew tall and straight.

2. What would Mr. B say when Leah rode the pony into town?
   That's the finest pony in the whole county.

3. How tall did the corn grow the year the wind was black with dust?
   The corn grew no taller than a man's thumb.

4. How did grasshoppers make conditions worse for the farmers?
   They ate the trees bare and left only twigs behind.

5. Papa borrowed money from the bank and couldn't pay it back. Why?
   He had no corn to sell because of the dust and grasshoppers.

6. What was going to be sold at auction?
   The tractor and farm animals including a bull, rooster, and calf.

7. How does Leah try to help?
   She sells her pony and uses the money to bid for Papa's tractor.

8. Why was Leah's pony back in the barn the next morning?
   Mr. B said it was too small for him or his grandson and that it was the right size for Leah.

54 At Home: Have students retell Leah's story.

Book 4/Unit 2
Leah's Pony 8

Practice, 54

CHALLENGE

Name_____ Date_____ Extend 53

Vocabulary

| bidding | clustered | county |
| glistened | overflowing | sturdy |

Suppose that you are at an auction and overhear a conversation between two people discussing the auction. Write the dialogue between the two people below. Remember to include quotation marks and identify each speaker. Use as many of the vocabulary words from the box as you can.
Answers will vary, but should include some of the vocabulary words and proper use of grammar.

Extend 54

Story Comprehension

In "Leah's Pony," Leah's parents sell many things even before they have the auction. Why do you think that they never ask Leah to sell her pony?
Answers will vary. Possible answer: They know how important the pony is to Leah, and selling it might not have made much difference anyway.

At Home: Discuss how unpredictable the weather can be and the long-term effects of different weather conditions.

Book 4/Unit 2
Leah's Pony

53–54

Extend, 54

Make a Chart

A farm is a busy place, and so is a city. Use details from the story to make a chart. Draw three columns. In the column at the left, list some things about city life. In the column at the right, list some things about farm or country life. In the middle column, list the things that are about the same in the city and the country.

Draw a Diagram

Farmers like Leah's father have to know about their crops. Find out how a corn plant grows. Draw a diagram that shows its life cycle. Include the seed, the new plant, the flower, and the mature corn. On your diagram, write what the corn plant needs in order to grow.

Find Out More

In the story, there is a long dry spell, or drought, that causes everything to die. This drought really happened in the "Dust Bowl," an area in parts of Kansas, Texas, and Oklahoma. Use an encyclopedia to find out more about what happened in the Dust Bowl in the 1930s. Share what you learn with your classmates.

213

Story Activities

Make a Chart

GROUP You may want to display a sample chart so students can see how to set up theirs. Show students where the labels **City Life, Farm Life,** and **Same** should appear. Have groups of students brainstorm lists of farm activities and city activities to include in their charts.

Draw a Diagram

Materials: science book or encyclopedia

PARTNERS Working in pairs, students can use reference sources to find information. Encourage them to include labels, drawings, and captions whenever possible to make their diagrams clear. Also remind them that they will need to use arrows and numbers to show the steps in the process.

Find Out More

RESEARCH AND INQUIRY Suggest topics students may look up to learn more about the setting of *Leah's Pony*. Topics might include "the Dust Bowl," "the Great Depression," and "drought." Students might also look for music by Woody Guthrie, who wrote many songs about his experiences during the Dust Bowl era. After students research their topics, suggest they write a journal entry about what it must have been like to live on a farm during that time.

interNET CONNECTION To learn more about the Dust Bowl, have students visit **www.mhschool.com/reading**

FORMAL ASSESSMENT

After page 213, see Selection Assessment.

213

Study Skills

REFERENCE SOURCES

OBJECTIVES Students will identify when to use different reference sources.

PREPARE Read the opening paragraph and identify any reference sources in the classroom. Display **Teaching Chart 45.**

TEACH Point to each reference source shown and have a volunteer read its description. Ask students to relate situations in which they have used or would use this reference source.

PRACTICE Have students answer questions 1–5. Review the answers with them.
1. dictionary; **2.** encyclopedia; **3.** almanac; **4.** thesaurus; **5.** Knowing which reference source is most likely to have the information you need will help you avoid wasting time.

ASSESS/CLOSE Have partners play a game in which one states the information sought and the other suggests the best reference source.

Study Skills

Choose Reference Sources

Suppose that you wanted to write a report about the Dust Bowl. Where would you look? You could start with the **dictionary**. From there, you could look in an **encyclopedia** for more information. For maps of the area, you could look in an **atlas**. Here is a description of some reference sources you could use for your report.

Almanac: has up-to-date information about people, places, and events. The information often appears in a table or a chart.
Atlas: has many different kinds of maps.

Dictionary: lists words in alphabetical order. A dictionary gives the meaning, pronunciation, and part of speech of a word.
Encyclopedia: has articles on many topics, arranged in alphabetical order.

Thesaurus: lists words with the same or almost the same meaning.

Use the reference sources to answer these questions.

1 Where would you look to find out what *glisten* means?

2 Where would you look to find out about raising chickens?

3 Where would you look to find an up-to-date chart showing how many people live in each state of the United States?

4 In which book would you look to find other words for *big*?

5 How does knowing which reference book to use save you time?

Meeting Individual Needs

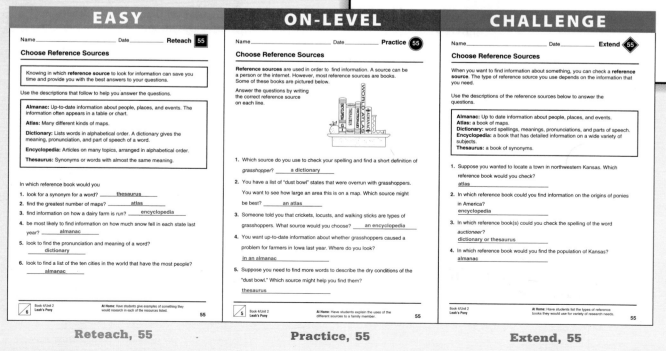

Reteach, 55   Practice, 55   Extend, 55

TEST POWER

Test Tip

Tell yourself the story again in your own words.

DIRECTIONS

Read the sample story. Then read each question about the story.

SAMPLE

Achilles' Pottery

One day, Achilles looked up at a row of his best pots lined up on a shelf, and said, "I have exhausted all of the possibilities for my pottery. I have made round pots, square pots, big pots and small pots. I can mold the clay into any form I wish, but there isn't another pot for me to make."

"Perhaps," his father suggested, "you should consider painting your pots. Some of the best pots are painted with figures, animals, and landscapes."

Achilles smiled as he sprang to his feet. "I'll be right back!" he cried. "I must get to the painter's shop before it closes!"

1 In the future, Achilles' pots will probably be—

A the same as before

B painted with figures, animals, or landscapes

C painted all the same color

D have only animals painted on them

2 How did Achilles feel when he looked at his best pots on the shelf?

F Furious

G Lively

H Excited

J Frustrated

215

Test Power

THE PRINCETON REVIEW

Read the Page

When students finish reading the story, have them ask themselves, "What might happen next?"

Discuss the Questions

Question 1: This question asks students to determine what Achilles' pots will *probably* look like in the future. Two clues are given in the passage—Achilles' father said, ". . . you should consider painting your pots," and Achilles said, "I must get to the painter's shop before it closes!"

Question 2: This question requires that students understand Achilles' feelings. The first answer choice is *furious*. Ask students if it is likely, given the information in the story, that Achilles was *furious* when he looked at his best pots. Have students eliminate answers that don't make sense.

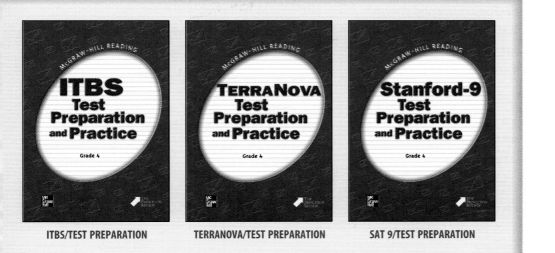

ITBS/TEST PREPARATION   TERRANOVA/TEST PREPARATION   SAT 9/TEST PREPARATION

EASY

Answers to Story Questions

1. Jamal had not been completely awake for two days; when he finally woke up, he didn't realize he had been asleep so long.

2. Jamal couldn't go back to school while his leg was healing. He needed help during the day with his schoolwork and just taking care of himself. Since both his parents were at work, they couldn't be home to care for him.

3. When he was injured, many people came to help him and his family. If he had not had the accident, he would not have known how many people cared about him and would help him.

4. Many people in a community were needed and were willing to help a young boy throughout his recovery from an accident.

5. Answers will vary.

Story Questions and Activity

1. How come Jamal didn't know how long he had been in the hospital?

2. Why did Jamal's parents need help taking care of him when he came home from the hospital?

3. What happened that caused Jamal to understand that many people were connected to his life?

4. What is this story mostly about?

5. If Leah from *Leah's Pony* lived in Jamal's neighborhood, how might she have offered to help him?

Sending Good Wishes

People need doctors and medicine to get better when they are sick or injured, but the good wishes of a friend or family member are important, too. Make a card or picture to send to someone you know who is sick, injured, or who just might need a friendly greeting.

from *For Jamal*

Leveled Books

EASY

For Jamal

Consonant Clusters
☑ **Cause and Effect**
☑ **Instructional Vocabulary:** *bidding, clustered, county, glistened, overflowing, sturdy*

Guided Reading

PREVIEW AND PREDICT Have students discuss the illustrations up to page 5 and write their thoughts about these pictures in their journals. Have them predict what they think will happen in the rest of the story.

SET PURPOSES Have students think about what they want to find out as they read *For Jamal*. Ask them to write a few questions that they hope the story will answer.

READ THE BOOK After students have read the story, use the questions that follow to check understanding.

Page 2: Reread the sentence with the word *glistened*. What does *glistened* mean? (shined brightly) What context clues helped you figure out the meaning? (metallic, sun) *Vocabulary*

Page 7: Why was Jamal's mother grateful that he was wearing a bike helmet? (He had hit his head really hard during the accident and probably would have had head injuries without the helmet.) *Cause and Effect*

Pages 12–14: Which words on these pages begin with *sp, st,* or *str*? (street, stairs, sturdy, spending, spend, started) What other words can you name that begin with these sounds? *Phonics and Decoding*

Page 16: Why do you think the author wrote this story? (It is an interesting way to show how the people of a community join together to help someone in need.) *Author's Purpose*

RETURN TO PREDICTIONS AND PURPOSES Review students' predictions and reasons for reading. Were their predictions correct? Did they find out what they wanted to know?

LITERARY RESPONSE Discuss these questions with students.

- Do you think the events in this story could really have happened?

- Why do you think the title of the story is *For Jamal*?

Also see the story questions and activity in *For Jamal*.

Leveled Books

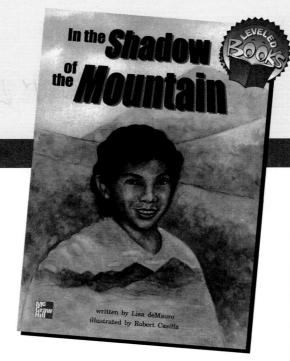

In the Shadow of the Mountain

written by Lisa deMauro
illustrated by Robert Casilla

INDEPENDENT

In the Shadow of the Mountain

☑ **Cause and Effect**

☑ **Instructional Vocabulary:** *bidding, clustered, county, glistened, overflowing, sturdy*

INDEPENDENT

Guided Reading

PREVIEW AND PREDICT Have students preview and discuss the illustrations up to page 8. Have them write their thoughts about the pictures in their journals. Have them predict what they think will happen in the story.

SET PURPOSES Have students think about the story title, as well as what they want to learn from this story. Ask them to write a few questions that they hope the story will answer.

READ THE BOOK Have students read the story independently. Then use the questions that follow to emphasize reading strategies.

Page 3: What caused the school in Victor's village to be destroyed? (a huge mudslide off the mountain) *Cause and Effect*

Page 7: What picture clues help you know the meaning of *sturdy*? What other items can you name that are sturdy? (Answers will vary.) *Vocabulary*

Page 10: Why did Victor suggest sending the crafts to the countries where the tourists lived? (Because of the heavy rains, the tourists were not visiting and not buying the crafts. If the crafts were sent to the tourists, they could buy them without leaving their countries.) *Cause and Effect*

Page 15: What generalization might you make about the business experiences of Victor and the other villagers? (Sample answer: Pooling resources and working collectively often results in good financial rewards.) *Form Generalizations*

RETURN TO PREDICTIONS AND PURPOSES Discuss students' predictions and how close they were to what happened in the story. Also ask them to review their purposes for reading. Did they find out what they wanted to know?

LITERARY RESPONSE Discuss these questions:

• What conflict did the people of the community solve by working together?

• How might the arrangement for selling their products improve life in the village in the future?

Also see the story questions and activity in *In the Shadow of the Mountain.*

Answers to Story Questions

1. The people of Victor's village used the wool from the sheep for knitting and weaving.
2. There are a lot more people in the United States who might buy the crafts, but who might never take a trip to Victor's village.
3. The rain created a mudslide, which destroyed the school; the villagers needed to make money to replace books and school supplies so they started selling more crafts.
4. The people in a mountain community worked together to replace books and rebuild a school destroyed in a mudslide.
5. Answers will vary.

Story Questions and Activity

1. How were the sheep useful to the people of Victor's village?
2. Why would the villagers be likely to sell more crafts by sending them to the United States instead of selling them only to tourists who visited the village?
3. How did the heavy rain lead to the community's need to sell more crafts?
4. What is story mostly about
5. How was Victor's community like the one in *Leah's Pony*? How was it different? Use examples to explain your answer.

Community Pride

Each mountain village in the Andes has its own *manta,* which is a flat weaving that looks like a flag. It is usually made up of bands of solid color with patterned stripes. Design and draw a *manta* for your town or city. Color it using crayons, paints, or markers.

from *In the Shadow of the Mountain*

PUPIL SELECTION

CHALLENGE

Answers to Story Questions

1. The Hmong had to leave their villages in Asia because war destroyed their homes and it was dangerous for them to stay.
2. The Hmong children learned what they needed to know from older relatives. When they got to this country, they were unfamiliar with our educational system.
3. It might be hard to order food in a restaurant if you didn't know the language, were not familiar with the food, and could not read the menu. You might end up ordering something you would not wish to eat.
4. The Hmong have tried to hold on to tradition even though they have had to get used to a new way of life.
5. Answers will vary.

Story Questions and Activity

1. Why did the Hmong leave their villages in Asia?
2. Why didn't the Hmong children go to school when they lived in Asia? What was the cause? Identify its effect.
3. Why might it be difficult to order a meal in a restaurant in a foreign country?
4. What is the main idea of the book?
5. If Leah from *Leah's Pony* could tell a Hmong family about what her community did for her, what words of encouragement might she add?

Share a Tradition

Different families have different traditions. Some are part of a religious or national holiday. Some come from the countries of our parents, grandparents, or other relatives. Draw a picture showing one of your family's traditions.

from A New Year in a New Life

Leveled Books

CHALLENGE

A New Year in a New Life

- ☑ **Cause and Effect**
- ☑ **Instructional Vocabulary:** *bidding, clustered, county, glisten, overflowing, sturdy*

written by Lisa deMauro
illustrated by Dom Lee

Guided Reading

PREVIEW AND PREDICT Have students discuss the illustrations up to page 6. Have them predict what they think the story will be about. Ask them to record their predictions in their journals.

SET PURPOSES Have students write a few questions that they hope the story will answer.

READ THE BOOK After students read the story independently, use the questions below to emphasize reading strategies.

Page 2: Why did many Hmong leave Laos and come to the United States? (Their villages were destroyed in a war, and it was not safe for them there.) *Cause and Effect*

Page 2: Point out the word *country* and *county*. Discuss how their meanings are similar and different. (Both have geographic boundaries and their own governments. A country is a nation, and a county is one of the sections into which a country or a state is divided.) *Vocabulary*

Page 7: What do the problems that the Hmong faced tell you about the difficulties of immigrants in general? (Sample answer:

Most immigrants have to adjust to speaking a new language and living in communities quite different from those in their homelands.) *Form Generalizations*

Page 16: Why are holidays, like the Hmong New Year, especially important for newcomers to this land? (Most immigrants use holidays to preserve traditions and customs.) *Form Generalizations*

RETURN TO PREDICTIONS AND PURPOSES Have students compare their predictions to story events. Also ask them to review their purposes for reading. Did they find out what they wanted to know?

LITERARY RESPONSE Discuss these questions:

- What are some ways in which the Hmong people help each other solve their problems?

- How do the people of the Hmong community maintain their heritage?

Also see the story questions and activity in *A New Year in a New Life*.

Activities

Anthology and Leveled Books

Connecting Texts

THEME CHARTS Write the story titles on a chart. Discuss with students how these stories have something in common. Point out that each story develops the concept of *Community Members Helping Each Other*. Have students from each reading level summarize the events in their story that illustrate this concept.

Use the chart to talk about how people in a community often come together to help one another in times of need.

Leah's Pony	For Jamal	In the Shadow of the Mountain	A New Year in a New Life
• Leah's family is about to lose their farm. • Leah's neighbors bid low prices at the auction. • Leah's family is able to save their farm. • Mr. B. gives Leah back her pony.	• Jamal is badly hurt in an accident. • Relatives and friends come to the hospital. • Neighbors volunteer to watch Jamal and help do the chores.	• A mudslide has destroyed the village. • The villagers work together to clean up their village. • They also work out a plan and work together to rebuild the school.	• The Hmong people struggle to keep their traditions while adapting to life in the United States. • To preserve their traditions, the Hmong make and sell story cloths.

Viewing/Representing

GROUP PRESENTATIONS Divide the class into groups, one for each of the four stories read in the lesson. (For *Leah's Pony*, combine students of different reading levels.) Have each group create a Cause and Effect chart to show why things happened the way they did in their story. Have each group present its Cause and Effect chart.

AUDIENCE RESPONSE After students listen to each group's presentation, allow time for questions.

Research and Inquiry

MORE ABOUT COMMUNITIES These four stories are about communities that have come together to help people in need. Have students research real-life situations in which this is happening today. Suggest they do the following:

• Find articles in newspapers and magazines that show communities at work.

• Make a Community Helpers wall display about community organizations and the services they provide.

• Post news items they find.

interNET CONNECTION Have students visit **www.mhschool.com/reading** to find out more about community organizations.

OBJECTIVES

Students will identify and explain cause-and-effect relationships.

TEACHING TIP

MANAGEMENT Have pairs of volunteers work to identify the cause-and-effect relationships in the passage. One partner might use a yellow marker to highlight all causes and the other partner might use a pink marker to high-light all effects.

Review Cause and Effect

PREPARE

Discuss Cause and Effect

Review: To recognize cause-and-effect relationships in a story, pay attention to what happens and why it happens. What happens is usually an effect. Why it happens is usually a cause. Ask students to name one cause-and-effect relationship that they identified in *Leah's Pony*.

TEACH

Read "The Race" and Model the Skill

Ask students to pay close attention to cause-and-effect relationships as you read the **Teaching Chart 46** passage with them.

The Race

As she rode her pony across the plains, Leah (smelled) (smoke.) Then she saw that a field of dry grass had caught fire. The wind was blowing the fire toward town. Leah had to ride faster than wildfire to warn the people about the fire! In town, Leah rang the big fire bell. The (firefighters ran to get) (their fire-fighting equipment ready to go.)

Suddenly, the unexpected happened! The clouds in the sky grew dark and heavy drops of rain began to fall. This was the first rain in weeks. (The people began to cheer.) The rain came down faster and faster and soon (put out the fire.)

Teaching Chart 46

Discuss one example of a cause-and-effect relationship in the passage.

MODEL As I read the passage I understand that Leah smelled smoke because the dry grass was on fire. The fire's the cause. The smoke is the effect.

PRACTICE

Identify and Explain Cause and Effect

GROUP

Have students identify other examples of cause and effect in "The Race." Have them circle the effects and underline the causes. For example, students might note that the fire fighters went into action (effect) because Leah rang the fire bell. (cause) Students might also note that heavy rain caused the fire to go out. (effect) Have small groups discuss how each cause and effect they identified go together. Did any cause have more than one effect?

▶ **Interpersonal/Linguistic**

ASSESS/CLOSE

Identify More Causes and Effects

PARTNERS

Have students work in pairs to create a paragraph about another adventure Leah and her pony might have. Ask them to include at least one cause-and-effect relationship in the story. Have each pair of students read their paragraph and ask the listeners to identify a cause and its effect.

ALTERNATE TEACHING STRATEGY

CAUSE AND EFFECT

For a different approach to teaching this skill, see page T66.

SELF-SELECTED Reading

Students may choose from the following titles.

ANTHOLOGY
- Leah's Pony

LEVELED BOOKS
- For Jamal
- In the Shadow of the Mountain
- A New Year in a New Life

Bibliography, pages T76–T77

Meeting Individual Needs for Comprehension

EASY	ON-LEVEL	CHALLENGE	LANGUAGE SUPPORT

EASY

Name_____ Date_____ Reteach 56

Cause and Effect

In stories one thing often **causes** something else to happen. The result is an **effect**. As you read, look for what happens and why.

Read each story. Then write the missing cause or effect.

Mr. Bumper read an article that said "Fish food is brain food!" For four weeks he cooked fish each night. Though Mr. Bumper didn't feel any smarter, he was willing to continue this fish diet. However, Mr. Bumper finally stopped preparing fish. His family simply refused to keep eating fish every night.

1. Cause: Mr. Bumper thought that eating fish would make him smarter.
   Effect: Mr. Bumper prepared fish every night.

2. Cause: Mr. Bumper's family finally refused to eat more fish.
   Effect: Mr. Bumper stopped making fish.

A magazine article said that doing a headstand for 10 minutes each day was good for a person's health. As a result, Mr. Andreas did a headstand each morning when he got to his office. After a month Mr. Andreas didn't feel much healthier. But now everyone in his company knew who he was. The company newsletter had printed a picture of Mr. Andreas standing on his head.

3. Cause: An article said headstands were good for your health.
   Effect: Mr. Andreas did a headstand each morning at his office.

4. Cause: A picture was printed that showed Mr. Andreas standing on his head.
   Effect: Everyone in the company recognized Mr. Andreas.

At Home: Have students think of a famous person. Then have students think of causes for that fame.

56   Book 4/Unit 2 Leah's Pony 4

ON-LEVEL

Name_____ Date_____ Practice 56

Cause and Effect

One event can cause another to happen. This kind of relationship is called a **cause and effect** relationship. Read the summary below. Then write an effect for each cause.

Leah's story takes place in the 1930s. During this time the Great Plains of the central United States was called the Great Dust Bowl. There was little or no rain, a condition called a drought. The grass and land dried up.

Heavy winds blew across the dry land — where corn and wheat once grew. The sky filled with dust. Grasshoppers ate the trees bare of leaves.

People piled their families and a few belongings into their old cars and headed west. They had abandoned their farms, leaving the only homes most of them had ever known. The families hoped to find better land for planting crops. They settled in different states. Some of the people had a difficult time, but others created new and successful lives.

Cause	Effect
1. There was little or no rain.	The land dried up.
2. Wind blew across the land.	The air filled with dust.
3. Grasshoppers ate tree leaves.	The trees were bare.
4. Families abandoned their farms.	Families got into their cars and headed west.
5. Families settled in different states.	Some found better lives.

At Home: Have students write two pairs of sentences illustrating cause and effect.

56   Book 4/Unit 2 Leah's Pony 5

CHALLENGE

Name_____ Date_____ Extend 56

Cause and Effect

Cause and effect can be used to describe several different situations in "Leah's Pony." Think about cause and effect to answer the questions below.

1. How does the weather make it possible for Leah to get a pony? When the weather is good the crops are good, and there is money for a pony.

2. How is the weather a cause of the auction? When the weather is so hot, dry, and dusty that crops do not grow, there will be no money from the farm to pay the bills. Then an auction might be held to raise money.

3. What does Leah do when she learns about the auction, and why? She sells her horse to help save the farm.

4. What is the effect of Leah's bidding at the auction? The neighbors decide to bid low and give the items back to Leah's parents.

5. What caused the neighbors to make low bids at the auction? They followed Leah's example.

6. Do you think that Leah intended for the neighbors to bid low prices at the auction? Explain. No. Although she knew how little money she had, Leah did not know that she was setting the example.

At Home: Have students recall experiences when their family or school plans were changed because of a cause, such as bad weather.

56   Book 4/Unit 2 Leah's Pony 6

LANGUAGE SUPPORT

Name_____ Date_____

What Happened on the Farm

1. Fill in the blanks in the chart using the words shown below.

rains	auctioned	saved	sold	lose	crops	money

The rains didn't come.

The crops did not grow.

The farm animals and tractor had to be auctioned

To buy the tractor back, Leah sold her pony.

Without crops to sell, Leah's family lost money

Without a tractor, Leah's family would lose the farm.

By buying the tractor, Leah saved the farm.

62 Leah's Pony • Language Support/Blackline Master 30   Grade 4

Reteach, 56   Practice, 56   Extend, 56   Language Support, 62

Review Sequence of Events

TEACHING TIP

INSTRUCTIONAL Write each step in the process of making hay on sentence strips. Invite volunteers to select a sentence strip and arrange themselves in the order that shows the sequence for making hay. Have them read aloud their sentences. Encourage them to use words such as *first, next,* and *then* to introduce their sentences.

PREPARE

Discuss Sequence of Events

Explain: The sequence of events is the order in which things happen in a story. Events in a story often follow time order, but sometimes authors do not describe events in the exact order they happened. Words such as *first, then, next, before, after, finally,* and *last* can indicate the sequence of events in a story.

TEACH

Read "Making Hay" and Model the Skill

Read "Making Hay." Focus students' attention on the sequence of events in the passage.

Making Hay

Each summer, Leah helps Papa make hay for the farm animals. *(1)* First, Papa attaches a long cutter to the big tractor and drives around in circles, cutting down all the hay. *(2)* They then leave the hay on the ground for three days to dry in the sun. *(3)* When the hay is dry, Leah attaches a hay rake to the small tractor. She rakes the hay into long narrow rows. *(4)* Then Papa uses another machine to bale, or bundle, the hay. *(5)* Leah picks up the heavy bales and puts them in a wagon. *(6)* Finally, Leah and Papa stack the hay bales in the barn.

Teaching Chart 47

Ask a volunteer to number the first step in making hay. List the first step on the board. Ask another volunteer to note the second step. Reread the steps in order and use the words *first, second, third* to introduce each step.

MODEL As I read this passage, I learn that the first step in making hay is to attach a special cutter to a tractor and cut down the hay in the field. The clue word *First* helps me figure this out. Then they let the hay dry out for three days. Once the cut hay is dry, the third step is raking. The clue word *Next* helps me here.

PRACTICE

Create a Sequence Chart

GROUP

Have students work in small groups to list the steps in hay-making on a chart. Have students identify the clue words that help them sequence the steps. Have students use the chart to pantomime the actions involved in making hay. ▶ **Kinesthetic/Linguistic**

STEP	HAY-MAKING SEQUENCE
1	Cut the hay.
2	Let the hay dry.
3	Rake the dry hay.
4	Bale the hay.
5	Load the bales into a wagon.
6	Stack the hay bales in the barn.

ASSESS/CLOSE

Identify a Sequence of Events

Have students create a sequence chart to describe part of their day yesterday. For example, they can chart what they did after their last class yesterday.

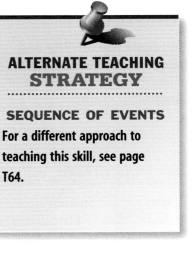

ALTERNATE TEACHING STRATEGY

SEQUENCE OF EVENTS

For a different approach to teaching this skill, see page T64.

LOOKING AHEAD

Students will apply this skill as they read the next selection, *Baseball Saved Us.*

Meeting Individual Needs for Comprehension

EASY	ON-LEVEL	CHALLENGE	LANGUAGE SUPPORT

EASY

Name_____ Date_____ **Reteach** 57

Sequence of Events

Sequence is the order in which things happen. Picturing the events in your mind often helps you understand the order in which events happen.

Each group of sentences below tells a story. The sentences are in the wrong order. Decide the correct order. Write the numbers 1 to 3 on the lines before the sentences to show the order in which events happened.

1. __3__ Nora planted a garden.
   __2__ Nora ordered seeds and got them through the mail.
   __1__ Nora decided to plant a garden.

2. __3__ Ed used his savings to buy a CD player.
   __2__ Ed saved money from the movie theater paycheck.
   __1__ The movie theater hired Ed to collect tickets.

3. __2__ Yolanda started doing extra math homework every night.
   __1__ Yolanda got low grades on two math tests in a row.
   __3__ Yolanda's math grades improved.

4. __3__ Ned used the note cards to give his speech.
   __1__ Ned was asked to talk about his after-school computer business.
   __2__ Ned put the major points of his speech on note cards.

Book 4/Unit 2
Leah's Pony
At Home: Have students list the steps in making a scrapbook. 57

Reteach, 57

ON-LEVEL

Name_____ Date_____ **Practice** 57

Sequence of Events

Keeping track of the order in which things happen in a story helps you to understand the plot. Read this story and then number the **sequence of events** 1 to 5 in the order in which they occurred.

Curt bounced along in the back seat of the old car his father was driving. Curt's mother comforted his crying little sister. Looking out the window at the flat, dry, dusty land, Curt wondered if they'd ever get to the new home they were looking for.

At sundown, Curt's father pulled into a grove of trees near a stream. There was soft grass and clean air. Maybe things were looking up. Curt helped his father set up the tent. Then they built a campfire and cooked the evening meal. In this fresh, green place, the food tasted delicious.

Curt's mother and his sister went to sleep in the tent. His father stayed by the campfire. "Almost there now," said his father. "It's green like this place. We'll have a good life from now on." Curt smiled. He should have known his father would take care of everything.

__2__ Curt and his father built a campfire and cooked a meal.
__4__ Curt's father says they will have a good life.
__1__ Curt looks at the dry land outside the car window.
__5__ Curt realizes that his father will take care of everything.
__3__ Curt's mother and his sister go to sleep in the tent.

Book 4/Unit 2
Leah's Pony
At Home: Have students write four sentences in sequence that describe what happens when Curt gets to his new home. 57

Practice, 57

CHALLENGE

Name_____ Date_____ **Extend** 57

Sequence of Events

Think about the **sequence of events** in "Leah's Pony." Were you surprised when Leah sold her pony? Write a paragraph describing the sequence of events that made Leah decide to sell her pony.

Answers will vary, but key events in the story should appear in sequence.

_____
_____
_____
_____
_____
_____
_____

Leah's bid at the auction changed the entire course of the auction. Explain how you know this is true.

Answers will vary. Possible answer: Some of the items had already been sold. If Leah had not made the low bid, the neighbors would not have done
_____
_____
_____
_____

Book 4/Unit 2
Leah's Pony
At Home: Discuss situations in which your own actions have been influenced by another person's actions. 57

Extend, 57

LANGUAGE SUPPORT

Name_____ Date_____

Make a Movie

Grade 4
Language Support/Blackline Master 31 • Leah's Pony 63

Language Support, 63

215H

OBJECTIVES

Students will identify and use context clues to help determine the meanings of unfamiliar words.

LANGUAGE SUPPORT

ESL Students acquiring English may need special support to identify and use context clues. Pair them with native English speakers for the Practice and Assess/Close activities, and encourage their partners to paraphrase the passage and suggest simpler synonyms for any additional words they do not know.

PREPARE

Discuss the Meaning of Context and Context Clues

Review: The context is the words and sentences around a new or unfamiliar word. Often the context contains clues that help you figure out the meaning of a word. Learning to use context clues will help you become a better reader.

TEACH

Read the Passage and Model the Skill

Have students read the passage on **Teaching Chart 48.**

Cultivating the Cornfields

Growing corn takes lots of hard work and planning. In May, Papa plants corn in long rows in the cornfields. The corn grows, and many weeds grow between the rows of corn. Weeds can kill the tiny corn plants.

Papa cultivates the fields to kill the weeds. He drags a wide piece of equipment over the places in the cornfield where the weeds grow. The equipment digs up the weeds but leaves the corn plant. It also loosens the soil, which helps the corn plants grow.

Teaching Chart 48

Demonstrate how to use context clues to determine the meanings of unfamiliar words.

MODEL I'm not sure what the word *cornfields* in the second sentence means. I can use other words in the sentence to help me understand the word. For example, the rest of sentence says that Papa planted corn there. The context clue makes it easy to see that cornfields are places where corn is grown.

Identify and Use Context Clues

PARTNERS

Have students circle the unfamiliar words *cornfields* and *cultivates* in the story. Then have them underline context clues that they can use to help them figure out the meanings of the words. Invite students working in pairs to use the context clues to create a definition for each of the circled words. ▶ **Linguistic/Logical**

ASSESS/CLOSE

Write Sentences with Context Clues

Ask students to find the words *petunias* and *all-purpose* on pages 197 and 206 respectively. Have them record the context clues the author included to help the reader figure out the meanings of these words.

ALTERNATE TEACHING STRATEGY

···

CONTEXT CLUES

For a different approach to teaching this skill, see page T63.

Meeting Individual Needs for Vocabulary

EASY	ON-LEVEL	CHALLENGE	LANGUAGE SUPPORT

EASY

Name_____ Date_____ Reteach **58**

Use Context Clues

When you read a word you don't know, look at the words and sentences around that word to learn its meaning. This is called using **context clues**.

Read each sentence. Circle the context clues that help you figure out the meaning of each underlined word. Then write the meaning on the line.

1. We work hard to (put the cut hay into piles.) The result is a field filled with haystacks. _____ **piles of cut hay**

2. Mr. Roth and his sons toil in the fields all day. This (hard work) keeps them fit. _____ **to work hard**

3. Every fall, the farmers harvest their crops. After this (gathering of the food) they have a celebration. _____ **gathering of food crops**

4. A century ago farmers used a horse to pull a plow through the field (to turn up) (the soil for planting.) _____ **machine used for turning up the soil**

5. The cows are in the pasture. They eat (that grassy field) until they are full. _____ **grassy field**

6. The Beckley farm has pipes and sprinklers (to water) its crops. Many other farms use a similar system to irrigate their land. _____ **to bring water to crops**

At Home: Have students write a sentence with a context clue for the word *farm*.

58   Book 4/Unit 2 Leah's Pony **6**

Reteach, 58

ON-LEVEL

Name_____ Date_____ Practice **58**

Context Clues

Sometimes the **context**, or words surrounding a word you may not know, will hold clues to help you understand the word's meaning.

Fill in the blanks with the correct word from the choices in parentheses.

1. The mother bought a used bike at the _____ **auction** . (theater, auction)

2. The fire blackened the grass and _____ **scorched** the trees. (scratched, scorched)

3. The _____ **windowpanes** are made of glass. (windowpanes, windowsills)

4. Juanita _____ **hammered** the nails. (hammered, hummed)

5. The gardener _____ **cultivates** the flowers. (captures, cultivates)

6. The horses _____ **stampeded** across the Plains. (stampeded, stranded)

7. Carlita's birthday was a great _____ **celebration** . (cantaloupe, celebration)

8. The building rose to a _____ **tremendous** height. (tremendous, transfer)

9. That boy never says anything _____ **ridiculous** . (recommend, ridiculous)

10. That girl never _____ **hesitates** to help others. (hesitates, haunts)

At Home: Using the words above, have students play the guessing game, I'm thinking of a word that means _____.

58   Book 4/Unit 2 Leah's Pony **10**

Practice, 58

CHALLENGE

Name_____ Date_____ Extend **58**

Context Clues

Words work together to give meaning to a sentence. If you look closely at how words are used, you can often figure out the meaning of a word from clues in the sentence. These clues are called **context clues**.

All the words below can be used in a country or farm-related context. Use as many of the words as you can to write a short story about what you think a typical day on a farm would be like. Use context clues in your writing.

cornfields	tractor	fertilize	county
cultivate	pasture	gullies	flock
whinny	coop	drooping	galloped

Answers will vary, but should make correct use of the words.

_____

_____

_____

_____

_____

_____

Write a title for your story. Try to include a context clue in your title.
Answers will vary.

At Home: Have students explain the context clues in the story they wrote.

58   Book 4/Unit 2 Leah's Pony

Extend, 58

LANGUAGE SUPPORT

Name_____ Date_____

Finish the Story

1. Read the story. 2. Use the words below to fill in the blanks.

tractor	cornfield	pasture	cultivate

Leah and her family live on a 🏠 . On their farm, 🌽 grows in a big open space called a _____ **cornfield** . Leah's father has a Farmall _____ **tractor** that he uses for most of the important work on the farm. He uses it to pull machines that _____ **cultivate** , or get the soil ready for planting.

On the farm, Leah's family also raises 🐄 and 🐔 . The 🐄 spend every day out in the _____ **pasture** eating grass. Leah's favorite animal, her 🐴 , nibbles grass there, too.

64 Leah's Pony • Language Support / Blackline Master 32   Grade 4

Language Support, 64

GRAMMAR/SPELLING CONNECTIONS

See the 5-Day Grammar and Usage Plan on irregular plural nouns, pages 213M–213N.

See the 5-Day Spelling Plan on words with consonant clusters, pages 213O–213P.

TECHNOLOGY TIP

Tell students: the thesaurus on a word processing program suggests synonyms for words you tend to use too often. Use the thesaurus to find exactly the right word.

Writing That Compares

Prewrite

WRITE A NEWSPAPER ARTICLE Present this writing assignment: Good times will return to Leah's family's farm. Imagine you are a newspaper reporter. Write an article about the way life improves for the farmers in the county. In the article, compare the good times with the hard times that came before.

BRAINSTORM IDEAS Have students brainstorm ideas about what the county may be like when the good times return.

Strategy: Make Two Word Webs Have students write Hard Times in the center of one web and Good Times in the center of the other. Point out that they may get some ideas from *Leah's Pony*. Others they will have to imagine for themselves.

```
  ( corn no higher        ( farms sold
    than a man's            at auction )
    thumb )
              \           /
              ( HARD TIMES )
              /           \
  ( hot, dry,             ( no money for
    black dust )            clothes )
```

Draft

USE THE WEBS To begin their articles, students should write a headline and lead sentence that will grab the reader's interest. They can make up names for Leah's family and for their county.

Revise

SELF-QUESTIONING Ask students to assess their drafts. Have them develop their writing by adding ideas and details.

- Did I begin with a lead sentence that will get the reader's attention?
- Did I make my comparisons point by point?
- Does my article clearly describe the events that did happen and will happen?
- What would make my news article better?

Have students trade news articles with classmates to get another point of view.

Edit/Proofread

CHECK FOR ERRORS Students should reread their news articles for spelling, grammar, and punctuation.

Publish

SHARE THE NEWS ARTICLES Students can read their articles or post them on a bulletin board. Classmates may want to compare their articles to news articles in a local paper.

Good Times Return to Cooks County

August 7. The corn is growing again in Cooks County—tall and straight and high as a man's shoulder. Local farmers can remember a few years ago when the corn was no higher than a man's thumb. The reason, of course, is water. Lots of it has poured from the skies this year and last, unlike past years when winds blew black dust over everything and no rain fell. Now crops and flowers are flourishing.

"I used to have to throw my dirty dishwater on my garden," says Ms. Lander, a resident of the county. "We were so poor I made my family's underwear out of flour sacks." Like Ms. Lander's family, many farmers had their belongings sold at auction. But now that better days are here, farmers have money to buy clothes and improve their farms. "No matter how bad things got," Ms. Lander's daughter, Leah, said, "I always had faith that the good times would return."

Presentation Ideas

ILLUSTRATE THE ARTICLE Have students draw a picture to illustrate their newspaper article. Tell them to make it look as much like a photograph as possible.
▶ **Viewing/Representing**

TAPE INTERVIEWS Have students take the part of Leah and other members of the community to record what they would tell a reporter about the good times and the hard times. ▶ **Speaking/Listening**

Consider students' creative efforts, possibly adding a plus (+) for originality, wit, and imagination.

Scoring Rubric

Excellent	Good	Fair	Unsatisfactory
4: The writer • provides an attention-grabbing lead sentence. • clearly contrasts the hard times and the good times. • has a logical sequence, linked by transition words.	**3:** The writer • provides a lead sentence. • contrasts the hard times and good times. • has an easy-to-follow sequence.	**2:** The writer • may not provide a lead sentence. • does not contrast or show clear differences. • may have vague or inaccurate story details.	**1:** The writer • provides no lead sentence. • does not compare or contrast. • presents disorganized ideas and irrelevant observations.

0: The writer leaves the page blank or fails to respond to the writing task. The student does not address the topic or simply paraphrases the prompt. The response is illegible or incoherent.

For a 6-point or an 8-point scale, see pages T105–T106.

LANGUAGE SUPPORT

ESL Display some sample headlines and have English-fluent partners help second-language learners write their own. Point out that headlines use language in a unique way—articles are omitted and only the simple present tense is used.

PORTFOLIO Invite students to include their newspaper articles or another writing project in their portfolios.

Meeting Individual Needs for Writing

EASY	ON-LEVEL	CHALLENGE
Diary Have students write a diary entry that Leah might write on the day that her father harvests a good crop of corn. They should have her compare this harvest with the previous poor harvest as described in the story.	**Letter** Students can write a letter from Leah to her best friend. They should have Leah discuss what she likes best about having the good times return and what made her most unhappy during the hard times.	**Speech** Have students write short speeches in which Leah addresses local farmers about ways to protect themselves from future hard times. They should have Leah compare her suggestions with the way things are usually done.

5 Day Grammar and Usage Plan

Hold up one object, such as a book or pencil, and have students name it. Review that this is a singular noun. Then hold up two of the same object and have students name it. Review that this is a plural noun.

DAILY LANGUAGE ACTIVITIES

Write the Daily Language Activities on the chalkboard each day or use **Transparency 8.** Have students respond orally, using the correct plural noun. For answers, see the transparency.

Day 1
1. Leah's cat landed on both foots.
2. Her cat lost two tooths.
3. Leah found two mouses in the barn.

Day 2
1. Not many childs live near Leah.
2. Do we have to sell the sheeps?
3. Four deers ate the apples.

Day 3
1. Some womans helped Leah's family.
2. A herd of mooses ran by the barn.
3. Four oxes pulled the wagon.

Day 4
1. Two mans bought the tractor.
2. The gooses flew away.
3. Leah's dad caught four trouts.

Day 5
1. Leah counted sheeps last night.
2. Three bisons were hurt by the fire.
3. A neighbor bought both swines.

| **Daily Language Transparency 8** |

DAY 1 — Introduce the Concept

Oral Warm-Up Read aloud: *The boys rode ponies past the bushes.* Ask students to identify the plural nouns. Review that these nouns were formed by adding -s or -es.

Introduce Irregular Plural Nouns Some plural nouns are formed differently. Present and discuss:

> **Irregular Plural Nouns**
> * Some nouns have special plural forms.

Write the following on the board: *man/men, woman/women, child/children, tooth/teeth, foot/feet, mouse/mice, goose/geese, ox/oxen.*

Present the Daily Language Activity. Then have students form the plurals of *man* (men), *woman* (women), and *child* (children) and use each in a sentence.

 Assign the daily Writing Prompt on page 190C.

Name_____ Date_____ **LEARN Grammar 45**

Irregular Plural Nouns

| * Some nouns have special plural forms. |

| calves | children | feet | geese | gentlemen |
| lives | men | oxen | teeth | women |

Look in the above box for the plural form of each singular noun. Write it on the line provided.

1. man _____men_____
2. child _____children_____
3. woman _____women_____
4. life _____lives_____
5. calf _____calves_____
6. goose _____geese_____
7. ox _____oxen_____
8. foot _____feet_____
9. tooth _____teeth_____
10. gentleman _____gentlemen_____

Grade 4/Unit 2
Leah's Pony

Extension: Have partners take turns using the singular and plural nouns on this page in oral sentences.

45

GRAMMAR PRACTICE BOOK, PAGE 45

DAY 2 — Teach the Concept

Review Irregular Plurals Ask students what familiar nouns form their plurals in special ways. List them on the chalkboard.

More About Irregular Plurals Some nouns do not change their spelling to form the plural. Present the following:

> **Irregular Plural Nouns**
> * A few nouns have the same singular and plural forms.

Write the following singular and plural forms on the chalkboard: *sheep/sheep, deer/deer, moose/moose.*

Present the Daily Language Activity. Then have students use the plural forms of *sheep, deer,* and *moose* in sentences.

 Assign the daily Writing Prompt on page 190C.

Name_____ Date_____ **LEARN AND PRACTICE Grammar 46**

Irregular Plural Nouns

| * A few nouns have the same singular and plural forms. |

Read the sentences below. Then decide whether the underlined word is a singular noun or plural noun and write singular or plural on the line.

1. There was not one <u>sheep</u> on Papa's farm. _____singular_____
2. There was no grass in his dry field for <u>sheep</u> to eat. _____plural_____
3. Some farms have ponds with <u>fish</u> in them. _____plural_____
4. Have you ever seen a <u>fish</u> in a pond? _____singular_____
5. Farmers in Maine may see a <u>moose</u> drink from a pond. _____singular_____
6. <u>Moose</u> are much bigger animals than cows. _____plural_____
7. Moose and <u>deer</u> are not farm animals. _____plural_____
8. A <u>deer</u> could jump over a farmer's fence. _____singular_____

46

Extension: Ask students to draw pictures illustrating the singular and plural forms of the words sheep, fish, moose, and deer. Have students write captions for their pictures.

Grade 4/Unit 2
Leah's Pony

GRAMMAR PRACTICE BOOK, PAGE 46

Irregular Plural Nouns

DAY 3 — Review and Practice

Learn from the Literature Review irregular plural nouns. Read the first sentence of the last paragraph on page 206 of *Leah's Pony:*

> **"Ladies and gentlemen, this tractor is a beauty!"**

Ask students to identify the noun in the sentence that is an irregular plural. Have students name the singular form of this noun. (gentleman)

Form Irregular Plurals Present the Daily Language Activity. Then have students make a two-column chart and write rules from Day 1 and Day 2 at the top of the columns. Then ask them to list in each column the singular and plural forms of nouns that follow the column rule.

 Assign the daily Writing Prompt on page 190D.

DAY 4 — Review and Practice

Review Irregular Plural Nouns Ask students to write sentences using irregular plural nouns. Then present the Daily Language Activity.

Mechanics and Usage Before students begin the daily Writing Prompt on page 190D, discuss:

Capitalization

- A proper noun begins with a capital letter.
- The name of a day, month, or holiday begins with a capital letter.
- Capitalize family names.
- Capitalize titles of people before names.

Write the following on the board:

I will visit Mother next week.

Today I visited Dr. Lewis.

 Assign the daily Writing Prompt on page 190D.

DAY 5 — Assess and Reteach

Assess Use the Daily Language Activity and page 49 of the **Grammar Practice Book** for assessment.

Reteach Have students write each rule for irregular plurals on index cards. They should include examples of nouns that follow each rule.

Invite students to play a round-robin game in which the first player calls out the singular form of an irregular noun. The next student gives the plural form and then calls out a different singular noun, and so on.

Have students create a word wall with pairs of singular nouns and their irregular plurals.

Use page 50 of the **Grammar Practice Book** for additional reteaching.

 Assign the daily Writing Prompt on page 190D.

Grammar 47 — Practice and Review

Plural Nouns

- Some nouns have special plural forms.
- A few nouns have the same singular and plural forms.

Read each sentence. Draw a line under the word in parentheses that is the correct plural form.

1. Of all the (ponys, <u>ponies</u>) in the county, Leah's pony was the finest.
2. Leah waved to the (childs, <u>children</u>) in the truck.
3. (<u>Boxes</u>, Boxs) full of the family's things were piled into the truck.
4. The (lifes, <u>lives</u>) of farmers were hard in these times.
5. The land was too dry for farm animals like (<u>sheep</u>, sheeps) and cattle.
6. There were no (fishes, <u>fish</u>) because the streams had dried up.
7. Several (<u>men</u>, mans) came to the auction.
8. Sometimes (calfs, <u>calves</u>) were sold at an auction.
9. A man in a big hat called out, "Ladies and (gentlemans, <u>gentlemen</u>)."
10. A farmer gave Papa the (<u>keys</u>, keyes) to the truck.

Grade 4/Unit 2
Leah's Pony

GRAMMAR PRACTICE BOOK, PAGE 47

Grammar 48 — Mechanics

Capitalization

- A proper noun begins with a capital letter.
- The name of a day, month, or holiday begins with a capital letter.
- Capitalize family names if they refer to specific people.
- Capitalize titles of people before names.

Read the sentences below. Then correct the capitalization mistakes and rewrite the sentences on the line provided.

1. When leah went into town, she always rode by the grocery store.
   When Leah went into town, she always rode by the grocery store.
2. She knew mr. b. liked to see her pony.
   She knew Mr. B. liked to see her pony.
3. Leah's mother always baked coffee cake on saturday.
   Leah's mother always baked coffee cake on Saturday.
4. One day, the neighbors moved to oregon.
   One day, the neighbors moved to Oregon.
5. Because times were hard, papa had to sell his tractor.
   Because times were hard, Papa had to sell his tractor.
6. Papa's tractor was made by a company named farmall.
   Papa's tractor was made by a company named Farmall.
7. The family also had to sell mama's prize rooster.
   The family also had to sell Mama's prize rooster.
8. The story about leah and her pony was written by elizabeth friedrich.
   The story about Leah and her pony was written by Elizabeth Friedrich.

Grade 4/Unit 2
Leah's Pony

GRAMMAR PRACTICE BOOK, PAGE 48

Grammar 49 — Test

Irregular Plural Nouns

A. Write *yes* if the noun below has the same singular and plural forms.
Write *no* if the noun does not have the same singular and plural forms.

1. rooster _____ no
2. deer _____ yes
3. sheep _____ yes
4. pony _____ no
5. moose _____ yes
6. calf _____ no

B. Complete each sentence with the plural form of the singular noun in parentheses.

7. Leah's (foot) _____ feet _____ were dusty because she walked home.
8. It was hard for (woman) _____ women _____ to keep the houses clean.
9. Most (child) _____ children _____ on a farm have chores to do.
10. Even the (mouse) _____ mice _____ that lived in the fields had little to eat.

Grade 4/Unit 2
Leah's Pony

GRAMMAR PRACTICE BOOK, PAGE 49

5 Day Spelling Plan

LANGUAGE SUPPORT

Write the clusters *st, sp, str, spr,* and *thr* on the chalkboard, and have students say them aloud. Then ask volunteers to suggest familiar words that begin with each cluster.

DICTATION SENTENCES

Spelling Words

1. The new toys will thrill the children.
2. That tall tree is a spruce.
3. We had to stand on our own two feet.
4. The car was moving at high speed.
5. Stand up and stretch your legs.
6. The player began to sprint for home.
7. I have no money to spare now.
8. I threw the basketball to Tom.
9. We did not get to know the stranger.
10. In springtime, the daisies came out.
11. The stern teacher never tells jokes.
12. A crowd came to see the spectacle.
13. The strap on my dress broke.
14. You can save money by being thrifty.
15. Your school is at the end of the street.
16. The bee stung my arm.
17. The stars sparkle in the night sky.
18. I need a break from the stress.
19. Your birthday is a special time.
20. Dad served steak.

Challenge Words

21. A crowd clustered around me.
22. We can drive out of the county.
23. The new bike glistened in the sun.
24. The bowl was overflowing with water.
25. Put on sturdy boots to climb that hill.

DAY 1 — Pretest

Assess Prior Knowledge Use the Dictation Sentences at the left and **Spelling Practice Book** page 45 for the pretest. Allow students to correct their own papers. Students who require a modified list may be tested on the first ten words.

Spelling Words		Challenge Words
1. thrill	11. stern	21. **clustered**
2. spruce	12. spectacle	22. **county**
3. **stand**	13. strap	23. **glistened**
4. speed	14. thrifty	24. **over-flowing**
5. stretch	15. street	25. **sturdy**
6. sprint	16. stung	
7. spare	17. sparkle	
8. threw	18. stress	
9. **stranger**	19. special	
10. spring-time	20. steak	

*Note: Words in **dark type** are from the story.*

Word Study On page 46 of the **Spelling Practice Book** are word study steps and an at-home activity.

SPELLING PRACTICE BOOK, PAGE 45

WORD STUDY STEPS AND ACTIVITY, PAGE 46

DAY 2 — Explore the Pattern

Sort and Spell Words Say *thrill* and *spruce* and ask students what consonant clusters they hear at the beginning of each word. *(thr, spr)* Do the same with the clusters that begin other words on the list. Then have students read the Spelling Words aloud and sort them as below.

Words beginning with

st	sp	str
stand	speed	stretch
stern	spare	stranger
stung	spectacle	strap
steak	sparkle	street
	special	stress

spr	thr	
spruce	thrill	
sprint	threw	
springtime	thrifty	

Word Wall Have students create a word wall based on the word sort and add more words from their reading.

SPELLING PRACTICE BOOK, PAGE 47

Words with Consonant Clusters

DAY 3 — Practice and Extend

Word Meaning: Synonyms Remind students that a synonym is a word that has a similar meaning to another word. Ask students to think of synonyms for as many of the Spelling Words as they can. (examples: *thrill/delight, sprint/race, stern/serious, spare/extra, street/road, special/unusual*) Write sentences using the words.

If students need extra practice, have partners give each other a midweek test.

Glossary Review the pronunciation key in the Glossary. Have partners:

- write each Challenge Word.

- look up the respelling in the Glossary.

- find the symbol that stands for the first vowel sound in the word.

- write the word from the pronunciation key that contains the same vowel sound.

DAY 4 — Proofread and Write

Proofread Sentences Write these sentences on the chalkboard, including the misspelled words. Ask students to proofread, circling incorrect spellings and writing the correct spellings. There are two spelling errors in each sentence.

> It's always a (trill) to climb a (spuse) tree in springtime. (thrill, spruce)
>
> A (stanger) began to sprint down our (steet). (stranger, street)

Have students create additional sentences with errors for partners to correct.

WRITING Have students use as many Spelling Words as possible in the daily Writing Prompt on page 190D. Remind students to proofread their writing for errors in spelling, grammar, and punctuation.

DAY 5 — Assess

Assess Students' Knowledge Use page 50 of the **Spelling Practice Book** or the Dictation Sentences on page 215O for the posttest.

JOURNAL **Personal Word List** If students have trouble with words in the lesson, have them add the words to their personal lists of troublesome words in their journals. Have students underline the consonant cluster in each word.

Students should refer to their word lists during later writing activities.

Spelling Practice Book, Page 48

Name_____ Date_____ PRACTICE AND EXTEND **Spelling 48**

Words with Consonant Clusters

thrill	stretch	stranger	strap	sparkle
spruce	sprint	springtime	thrifty	stress
stand	spare	stern	street	special
speed	threw	spectacle	stung	steak

Finish the Word
Write the missing letters to correctly complete the words in the sentences.

"Hurry up," my parents called. "There's not a minute to 1. sp___are___. We don't want to be late. We'll wait for you in the car."

I grabbed my cap, tightened the 2. str___ap___ on my fanny pack, and ran out the door to the car.

Every April, our city holds a 3. spr___ingtime___ festival, beginning with a parade. It is always a very 4. sp___ecial___ event. This year's parade was an eye-popping 5. sp___ectacle___. It was a 6. thr___ill___ for children and adults alike. Dozens of bands and floats made their way down the one-mile 7. str___etch___ of Fifth Avenue, the main 8. str___and___ in our city. My brother and I like to 9. st___and___ along the curb near City Hall. That's where the parade will slow down for the mayor and then 10. sp___eed___ up again. This year my sister is in the high school marching band. We watched as she and the other twirlers 11. thr___ew___ their batons up in the air and then caught them. The sunlight hit the beads and sequins on their outfits and made them 12. sp___arkle___. What a sight! We cheered loudly as they marched past us.

Word Groups
Write the spelling word that belongs in each group.

13. pierced, pricked, ___stung___
14. fir, pine, ___spruce___
15. strain, pressure, ___stress___
16. economical, penny-wise, ___thrifty___
17. race, run, ___sprint___
18. alien, foreigner, ___stranger___
19. harsh, strict, ___stern___
20. chop, burger, ___steak___

48 Challenge Extension: Write a sentence for each Challenge Word. Grade 4/Unit 2 Leah's Pony 20

SPELLING PRACTICE BOOK, PAGE 48

Spelling Practice Book, Page 49

Name_____ Date_____ PROOFREAD AND WRITE **Spelling 49**

Words with Consonant Clusters

Proofreading Activity
There are six spelling mistakes in this short story. Circle the misspelled words. Write the words correctly on the lines below.

Leah was my best friend. I got a letter from her last month. She told me about the (speshal) way she saved her family's farm. I wish I could have seen the expression on the auctioneer's face when Leah offered him one dollar for her father's tractor!

We lost our farm in the (sprinktime) and then we moved to Oregon. I haven't seen Leah in a year. Whenever I have a few (spair) pennies for a stamp, I write to her.

Life has been difficult for farm families everywhere because of the drought. We had to be as (thirfty) as we could. We (thruw) nothing away, not even empty flour sacks. My mama used the material to make clothes for my sister and me. She could even make a pot of soup (strech) for three or four meals. Times were difficult, but they will get better.

1. ___special___ 3. ___spare___ 5. ___threw___
2. ___springtime___ 4. ___thrifty___ 6. ___stretch___

Writing Activity
What do you think Leah said in her letter? Pretend you are Leah. Write a letter telling about the auction. Use four spelling words in your writing.

_____

_____

_____

10 Grade 4/Unit 2 Leah's Pony 49

SPELLING PRACTICE BOOK, PAGE 49

Spelling Practice Book, Page 50

Name_____ Date_____ POSTTEST **Spelling 50**

Words with Consonant Clusters

Look at the words in each set below. One word in each set is spelled correctly. Use a pencil to fill in the circle next to the correct word. Before you begin, look at the sample sets of words. Sample A has been done for you. Do Sample B by yourself. When you are sure you know what to do, you may go on with the rest of the page.

Sample A (A) springkle (B) sprinkel (C) springle ● (D) sprinkle

Sample B ● (E) threaten (F) threatin (G) threten (H) threaton

1. (A) sturn (B) stren ● (C) stern (D) sternn
2. (E) springtime ● (F) springtime (G) sprinktime (H) sprngtime
3. ● (A) stranger (B) strangure (C) stanger (D) strangur
4. ● (E) specktakle (F) spektacle (G) specticle ● (H) spectacle
5. (A) thrugh (B) threw (C) thriew (D) thruw

6. (E) strapp (F) strape (G) starp ● (H) strap
7. ● (E) spare (F) spair (G) spayr (H) spar
8. (E) thirfty ● (F) thrifty (G) thirffy (H) thifty
9. ● (E) sprint (F) sprnt (G) sprint (H) spint
10. (E) streat (F) streit (G) stareet (H) street

11. (A) strech (B) stertch (C) stretch (D) sturetch
12. (E) spead (F) speed (G) spede (H) speide
13. ● (A) stung (B) stong (C) stug (D) stunge
14. (E) stande (F) stend (G) standed ● (H) stand
15. (A) spruce (B) spruse (C) sruce (D) sprooce

16. ● (E) thrill (F) thrill (G) thruill (H) thril
17. (E) stak (F) staik ● (G) steak (H) stacke
18. (E) sparkle (F) spearkle (G) sparckle (H) sprakle
19. (A) streass (B) streit (C) sterss (D) stres
20. (E) specail (F) spacial (G) speshal (H) sproose

50 Grade 4/Unit 2 Leah's Pony 20

SPELLING PRACTICE BOOK, PAGE 50

Baseball Saved Us

Selection Summary Students will read a story of how baseball improved morale for Japanese families confined in a WWII relocation camp and how it helped one boy discover his strengths. Students will also learn how people can use team spirit to overcome a bad situation.

Baseball Saved Us
Written by **Ken Mochizuki**
Illustrated by **Dom Lee**

Listening
Library
Audiocassette

INSTRUCTIONAL
Pages 218–241

About the Author Ken Mochizuki, the author of *Baseball Saved Us*, is a Japanese-American whose parents were forced to live in relocation camps during WWII. Ken Mochizuki's writing imagines what life in these camps must have been like and celebrates people's ability to overcome harsh conditions.

About the Illustrator Dom Lee is a Korean American. His family did not experience the relocation camps. For this story he relied on research materials such as famous photographs to help him visualize life in relocation camps.

Resources for Meeting Individual Needs

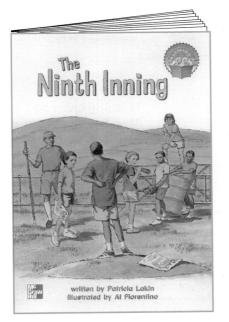

EASY
Pages 241A, 241D

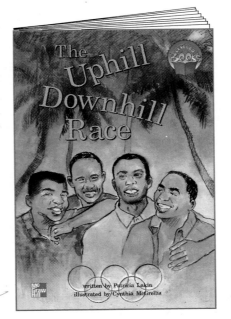

INDEPENDENT
Pages 241B, 241D

CHALLENGE
Pages 241C, 241D

LEVELED PRACTICE

Reteach 59–65

blackline masters with reteaching opportunities for each assessed skill

Practice 59–65

workbook with Take-Home stories and practice opportunities for each assessed skill and story comprehension

Extend 59–65

blackline masters that offer challenge activities for each assessed skill

ADDITIONAL RESOURCES

- **Language Support Book,** 65–72
- **Take-Home Story, Practice** p. 60a
- **Alternate Teaching Strategies,** T60–T66
- **Selected Quizzes Prepared by** Accelerated Reader

McGraw-Hill School
TECHNOLOGY

interNET CONNECTION Research and Inquiry Ideas. Visit **www.mhschool.com/reading**

Suggested Lesson Planner

● Available on CD-ROM

READING AND LANGUAGE ARTS

- ● Comprehension
- ● Vocabulary
- ● Phonics/Decoding
- ● Study Skills
- ● Listening, Speaking, Viewing, Representing

DAY 1 — Focus on Reading and Skills

Read **Read Aloud and Motivate,** 216E
How It All Began

Develop Visual Literacy, 216/217

☑ **Review Make Predictions,** 218A–218B
Teaching Chart 49
Reteach, Practice, Extend, 59

DAY 2 — Read the Literature

Build Background, 218C
Develop Oral Language

Vocabulary, 218D

| crate | endless | inning |
| ditches | glinting | mound |

Teaching Chart 50
Word Building Manipulative Cards
Reteach, Practice, Extend, 60

Read **Read the Selection,** 218–237
☑ Make Predictions
☑ Sequence of Events

Minilessons, 223, 225, 227, 229

Cultural Perspectives, 228

● Curriculum Connections

Link Works of Art, 216/217

Link Social Studies, 218C

● Writing

Writing Prompt: Write about a friend and his or her favorite sport. Describe the clothing and equipment your friend uses to play the sport.

Writing Prompt: Write sentences about several of the characters in the story. Tell which of their favorite possessions they may have taken to camp and which ones they were forced to leave at home.

Journal Writing, 237
Quick-Write

● Grammar

Introduce the Concept: Possessive Nouns, 241M
Daily Language Activity
1. They all liked Dads idea. Dad's
2. One guards face seemed scary. guard's
3. Kens team pulled together. Ken's

Grammar Practice Book, 51

Teach the Concept: Possessive Nouns, 241M
Daily Language Activity
1. Baseball is a fun childrens game. children's
2. The boys moms sewed uniforms. boys'
3. Babies cries kept Ken awake. Babies'

Grammar Practice Book, 52

● Spelling

Pretest: Plurals, 241O
Spelling Practice Book, 51, 52

Explore the Pattern: Plurals, 241O
Spelling Practice Book, 53

DAY 3 — Read the Literature

Rereading for Fluency, 236

Story Questions, 238
Reteach, Practice, Extend, 61

Story Activities, 239

Study Skill, 240
✓ Reference Sources
Teaching Chart 51
Reteach, Practice, Extend, 62

Test Power, 31

Read the Leveled Books, 241A–241D
Guided Reading
Consonant Clusters
✓ Make Predictions
✓ Instructional Vocabulary

Activity Social Studies, 222, 232

Writing Prompt: You are Ken, the main character. Write a postcard to a pal, describing a friend you've met in camp. Use your friend's name when you describe your friend's face or belongings.

Writing Process: Writing That Compares, 241K
Prewrite, Draft

Review and Practice: Possessive Nouns, 241N
Daily Language Activity
1. The kids shouts meant they won the game. kids'
2. Ken ran around the fields bases. field's
3. The womens sewing was excellent. women's

Grammar Practice Book, 53

Practice and Extend: Plurals, 241P
Spelling Practice Book, 54

DAY 4 — Build Skills

Read the Leveled Books and Self-Selected Books

✓ **Review Make Predictions,** 241E–241F
Teaching Chart 52
Reteach, Practice, Extend, 63
Language Support, 70

✓ **Review Form Generalizations,** 241G–241H
Teaching Chart 53
Reteach, Practice, Extend, 64
Language Support, 71

Activity Math, 224

Writing Prompt: Write a short biography of an athlete using the athlete's name to describe his or her abilities.

Writing Process: Writing That Compares, 241K
Revise
Meeting Individual Needs for Writing, 241L

Review and Practice: Possessive Nouns, 241N
Daily Language Activity
1. One players glove didn't fit. player's
2. Teddys mood was really bad. Teddy's
3. The mothers made both teams uniforms. teams'

Grammar Practice Book, 54

Proofread and Write: Plurals, 241P
Spelling Practice Book, 55

DAY 5 — Build Skills

Read Self-Selected Books

✓ **Review Compound Words,** 241I–241J
Teaching Chart 54
Reteach, Practice, Extend, 65
Language Support, 72

Listening, Speaking, Viewing, Representing, 241L
Illustrate a Sports Column
Dramatize the Game

Minilessons, 225, 227, 229

Phonics Review
Consonant Clusters, 223

Phonics/Phonemic Awareness Practice Book, 25–28

Activity Science, 226

Writing Prompt: You are Ken's dad or mom. Write a letter to the governor of your state telling about the people and the problems in the camp. Use singular and plural possessive nouns.

Writing Process: Writing That Compares, 241K
Edit/Proofread, Publish

Assess and Reteach: Possessive Nouns, 241N
Daily Language Activity
1. They all knew the games rules. game's
2. The campers lives were boring at first. campers'
3. Ken appreciated his fathers help. father's

Grammar Practice Book, 55, 56

Assess and Reteach: Plurals, 241P
Spelling Practice Book, 56

216D

Read Aloud and Motivate

How It All Began

nonfiction by
Lawrence S. Ritter

Baseball has been providing us with fun and excitement for more than a hundred years. The first *professional* baseball team was the Cincinnati Red Stockings, who toured the country in 1869 and didn't lose a game all year. Soon, baseball began to attract so many fans that in 1876 the National League was organized—the same National League that still exists today.

Although the game as it was played in 1876 was recognizable as baseball—nobody would confuse it with football or basketball—it was quite a bit different from baseball as we know it now. For example, pitchers had to throw underhand, the way they still do in softball; the batter could request the pitcher to throw a "high" or "low" pitch; it took nine balls, rather than four, for a batter to get a base on balls; and the pitching distance was only forty-five feet to home plate.

The rules were gradually changed over the following twenty years, until by about 1900 the game

Continued on pages T2–T5

Oral Comprehension

LISTENING AND SPEAKING Motivate students to think about making predictions by reading aloud this selection about the history of baseball. Have them take notes as they listen. Ask, "Do you think that the early baseball players could have predicted how the game is played today?" Then ask, "If you could make one change in baseball, what would it be?" Have students identify sentences that show the changes in baseball over time.

Activity Point out that the game of baseball has changed since 1869. Invite students to make predictions about what baseball will be like in the future. Have them brainstorm predictions, and then draw a scene from a baseball game of the future. Encourage partners to share their drawings and their predictions. ▶ **Visual/Oral**

Anthology pages 216–217

Some paintings hint at events. They do not tell the whole story. It is up to the viewer to predict what will happen.

Look at this painting. What can you tell about this race? Who is the man facing the rowers? Which team do you think will win? Why?

Look at this painting again. What do you think will happen to the winning team? How will the losers feel? If you could paint the next scene, how would it look?

The Rowers by Manuel Losada
Museo de Bellas Artes, Bilbao, Spain

216

217

Objective: Make Predictions

VIEWING In his painting, Manuel Losada depicts a rowing contest. Have students discuss why sports scenes can be exciting subjects for works of art. Ask them if the painting's use of line, shape, and color helped them see and "feel" the race. Invite students to conjecture about where the artist was when he painted this scene.

Read the page with students, asking them to make predictions about the race. Have them support their predictions. For example:

- The boat nearest to the viewer will win because it is ahead.

- The winning team may get a prize, like a trophy or ribbon, or the town may throw them a big party.

REPRESENTING Organize students into "teams" and "spectators" and dramatize the painting. Encourage "rowers" to practice the rowers' movements and facial expressions. Ask student spectators to predict the outcome of the race.

OBJECTIVES

Students will make predictions about a selection.

Review Make Predictions

PREPARE

Discuss Predicting the Weather

Have students look out the window. Ask: What do you think the weather might be like later this afternoon or evening? What clues help you to make this prediction?

TEACH

Define Make Predictions

Tell students: A story often has clues to help you predict, or guess beforehand, what will happen next. You can use these clues along with your background knowledge to make a prediction about a story's outcome.

The Obstacle Course

Bluto, the fastest runner in the whole camp, was set to run for the Rangers. No one on the Beavers thought they had a chance. Ken knew better. Though he was small and not very fast, Ken knew something the others had not thought of. It did not matter how fast Bluto was because there was no way he could fit through the tire swing. He was just too big. At the starting line, Ken gave his Beaver teammates a confident smile. Just then the starter's gun sounded. The race was on!

Teaching Chart 49

Read the Story and Model the Skill

Display **Teaching Chart 49**. Have students pay attention to clues that help them make predictions as the story is read.

MODEL I know that Ken is small and not very fast, but he might win anyway because of that tire.

Make Predictions Based on Clues

Have students underline clues that help them predict how Ken will do in the race.

PRACTICE

Create a Make Predictions Chart

GROUP

Have students use a Make Predictions chart to record their predictions about what will happen during the race. ▶ **Linguistic/Logical**

PREDICTIONS	WHAT HAPPENED
Bluto will have a big lead.	
Bluto will get stuck on the tire swing.	
Ken will win the race.	

Complete the Story

Have groups write an ending for "The Obstacle Course." Then have groups compare their endings, vote on the best, and complete the chart.

ASSESS/CLOSE

Make Predictions

Ask students what words they might use to describe Ken. (small, smart, clever) Ask students to predict how Ken might react in other activities where his team is having problems, such as another sport, a spelling bee, a debate, a chess match, or a class project. (He would probably use his brain to come up with clever ways to win; he would use his leadership skills to help his group make a plan.)

ALTERNATE TEACHING STRATEGY

MAKE PREDICTIONS
For a different approach to teaching this skill, see page T60.

Meeting Individual Needs for Comprehension

EASY

Name_____ Date_____ **Reteach** 59

Make Predictions

Reading titles can help you **predict** what a story will be about.

Read each title. Then read the predictions of what the story will be about. Put a ✔ next to the prediction that makes the most sense.

1. "My Life on Stage"
   ___ a history of movie theaters
   ✔ the life story of an actor
   ___ the life story of an athlete
2. "To the Top!"
   ✔ mountain climbing
   ___ toy making
   ___ ocean exploration
3. "All Aboard: Travel on the Iron Tracks"
   ✔ a history of train travel
   ___ a history of plane travel
   ___ a history of the highway system
4. "Beneath the Waves"
   ___ a man who flies a plane
   ___ a man who explores caves
   ✔ a woman who explores the sea
5. "Causes for Celebration"
   ___ math
   ___ pet care
   ✔ holidays

Book 4/Unit 2
Baseball Saved Us

At Home: Choose the title of an unfamiliar story, book, or movie and have students predict what it will be about.

59

Reteach, 59

ON-LEVEL

Name_____ Date_____ **Practice** 59

Make Predictions

When you **make a prediction,** you make a logical guess about what will happen next, based on story clues and your own experience. As you continue to read, you find out whether your prediction was right.
Read the story below and predict what will most likely happen to Pablo. Answers may vary.

It is rush hour and Pablo is waiting for the train. He has to meet his mother for dinner at 6:30 P.M. During nonrush hours, the train ride from work to the stop near his house is about 20 minutes. It is now 6:00 P.M. A train arrives at the stop, but it is too crowded to let new passengers on. No other trains are in sight.

1. What do you predict will most likely happen? _Possible answer: Pablo_
   will most likely be late.

2. What information did you use from the story to help make your
   prediction? _There is no room on the train and there are no trains in_
   sight.

As you read the following paragraph, think about what will most likely happen.

Kevin is thinking about leaving his homeland and moving to the United States. Like most of the men in his family, he has always been a coal miner. The mine in which he works is closing. His sister Kate lives in Florida and can get him a job in her company. His brother Tim has just moved to Pennsylvania where he has found work as a miner.

3. What do you predict will most likely happen? _Kevin will most likely_
   move to Pennsylvania and find a job as a miner.

4. What information did you use to make your prediction? _I thought about_
   the information in the story and thought about what I would do.

Book 4/Unit 2
Baseball Saved Us

At Home: Have students predict how they will spend their summer vacation.

59

Practice, 59

CHALLENGE

Name_____ Date_____ **Extend** 59

Make Predictions

Suppose that you and your classmates are getting together to play a game. Two classmates are the captains for the two teams. **Predict** how you would feel if you were the last one picked for either team. Explain why.

Answers will vary.
_____
_____
_____
_____
_____
_____

Now suppose that you are the captain of one of the teams. Write a paragraph describing how you would pick the members of your team. Predict how your team would do with those members on it.

Answers will vary.
_____
_____
_____
_____
_____
_____
_____

Book 4/Unit 2
Baseball Saved Us

At Home: Have students write a paragraph in which they predict whether they will become a better athlete, writer, or student.

59

Extend, 59

Build Background

Link

Social Studies

Anthology and Leveled Books

Evaluate Prior Knowledge

CONCEPT: TEAM SPIRIT The characters in these stories all learn how team spirit can help them to achieve their goals. Have students share their experiences with or knowledge of teamwork. Have them compare whether it was easier to reach a goal with or without teamwork.

COMPARE OUTCOMES Have students compare the possible outcomes of a team sport when they use teamwork and when they do not. Create a Venn diagram.

▶ Logical/Visual

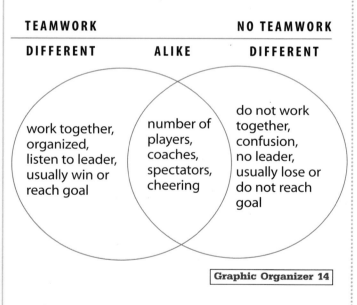

TEAMWORK		NO TEAMWORK
DIFFERENT	ALIKE	DIFFERENT
work together, organized, listen to leader, usually win or reach goal	number of players, coaches, spectators, cheering	do not work together, confusion, no leader, usually lose or do not reach goal

Graphic Organizer 14

GAME PLAN Have students write a list of the things they would do to prepare themselves for a team sporting event or group project. For example, they might plan how they could best win a football or baseball game or how they would complete a class project by working together.

Develop Oral Language

DISCUSS TEAM SPORTS Have students bring in pictures of people playing sports that are popular in their cultural backgrounds. If students have trouble, encourage them to research some cross-cultural sports, such as polo, cricket, soccer, lacrosse, and others.

Have students work in groups to write a how-to list for a sport. They should write each step in the sport in the correct sequence. Then students may want to read their how-to lists aloud as other students act out what the team members do at each step.

Alternatively, one student can tell the sequence in the game or activity orally as another volunteer writes the numbered sequence on a chart. Students may wish to display their charts in the gym so that physical education classes can learn the sports.

Vocabulary

Key Words

Baseball in the Desert

1. The huge desert where Ken lived seemed endless, stretching on for miles and miles. **2.** The landscape was covered with deep gullies and ditches, except for Ken's favorite place—the baseball field. **3.** During ballgames, Ken sat on a box—actually, a wooden crate—while awaiting his turn to bat. **4.** He loved to watch the pitcher throw the ball from high atop his mound in front of home plate. **5.** But sometimes the sun, glinting off the metal fence behind the pitcher, briefly blinded Ken, and he could not see the ball. **6.** This happened to Ken once when he went to bat in the ninth inning, or last period of the game.

Teaching Chart 50

Vocabulary in Context

IDENTIFY VOCABULARY WORDS
Display **Teaching Chart 50** and read the passage with students. Have volunteers circle each vocabulary word and underline other words that are clues to its meaning.

DISCUSS MEANINGS Ask questions like these to help clarify word meanings:

- How large is something that is endless?
- For what reasons do people dig ditches?
- What kinds of products are sometimes packed in crates?
- You see a mound on a baseball field. What other things might be mound-shaped?
- What are some objects that could be described as "glinting?"
- What happens at the start of each inning in a baseball game?

Practice

DEMONSTRATE WORD MEANING In groups, have students take turns drawing a vocabulary card, defining the word, and using it orally in a sentence.

▶ **Linguistic/Oral**

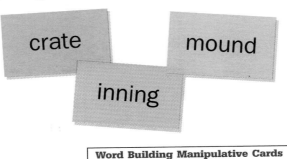

Word Building Manipulative Cards

WRITE CONTEXT SENTENCE CARDS

Have groups create cards with the beginnings and ends of sentences, so that the vocabulary cards fit in the middle. Then have groups exchange cards and match the cards to make sentences.

▶ **Linguistic/Oral**

 **efinitions**

endless (p. 220) without end; never stopping

ditches (p. 227) long, narrow holes, often dug beside roads

crate (p. 226) a wooden box used to transport products

mound (p. 236) the spot on a baseball field where the pitcher stands

glinting (p. 230) shining; glittering

inning (p. 228) one-ninth of a standard baseball game

SPELLING/VOCABULARY CONNECTIONS

See Spelling Challenge Words, pages 2410–241P.

ON-LEVEL

Jenelle's Baseball

"I don't know what the big deal is about baseball," said Jenelle. "It's so boring. One part of the game is called an *inning*. That's fine, but there are nine of those innings! I'm telling you, the game is *endless*. Then there's the pitcher who stands on a little hill of dirt called the *mound*. What's that all about? While a player is batting, the team sits down in one of those *ditches* called a dugout. The team keeps a *crate* of juice bottles down there. They never share it with the other team or with any of us watching the game. Sometimes, the game goes on forever. First it's the sun *glinting* off your glasses. Then, before you know it, it's the moon. As for me, I like kickball — no mounds, no ditches, no innings, just lots of fun!"

1. How many parts or *innings* are there in a game? nine innings
2. What is the *mound* used for? The pitcher stands on it to pitch.
3. Where does one team sit? in a ditch called a dugout
4. What's another word in the story for shining? glinting
5. How would you describe Jenelle's general feeling about the game of baseball? Jenelle finds the game boring, and she really doesn't understand it.

Book 4/Unit 2
Baseball Saved Us

At Home: Have students write a paragraph using the vocabulary words to explain baseball to a person who is unfamiliar with the game.

60a

Take-Home Story 60a
Reteach 60
Practice 60 • Extend 60

Guided Instruction

Preview and Predict

Have students preview the story, looking for pictures and other clues that might give them an idea of what happens in the story.

- Where do you think this story takes place?
- What clues do you find to identify one of the main character's favorite things to do?
- Do you think this story will be realistic fiction or a fantasy? How do you know? (Sample answer: Realistic fiction. The characters in the pictures look like real people, and they are doing the things real people would do. The setting looks like a real place.) *Genre*

Point out to students that as they answer these questions they are making predictions about the story.

Set Purposes

What do students want to find out by reading this story? For example:

- Why do the boy and his family look sad?
- How does baseball save the characters? From what are they saved?

Meet Ken Mochizuki

Baseball Saved Us has a personal meaning for Ken Mochizuki. During World War II, his Japanese-American parents were taken from their homes and forced to live in a government "camp." By showing the camp through the eyes of the boy in the story, Mochizuki describes how the game of baseball solved many of the problems of camp life.

From this book, Mochizuki hopes to show young readers "that they should actually get to know others, rather than to assume things about them." They should also believe in what they can do, instead of believing in what others have told them they cannot achieve.

Besides writing books for young people, Mochizuki works as an actor and a journalist.

Meet Dom Lee

Baseball Saved Us is a favorite of illustrator Dom Lee. He has worked with Ken Mochizuki on several books for young people, but he has a special feeling for this one.

Lee, who was born in South Korea, does a lot of research for his books. He often looks at photographs to get ideas. For *Baseball Saved Us*, he studied the photographs of one of these camps taken by the famous American photographer, Ansel Adams.

To make the illustrations for the book, Lee first put beeswax on paper, then scratched out the images he wanted. Finally, he added oil paint and colored pencil, with remarkable results!

218

Meeting Individual Needs • Grouping Suggestions for Strategic Reading

EASY	ON-LEVEL	CHALLENGE
Read Together Read the story with students or have them read along with the **Listening Library Audiocassette.** Have students use the Predictions chart to record clues that will help them predict story events. The Guided Instruction and Intervention prompts offer additional help with decoding, vocabulary, and comprehension.	**Guided Reading** Preview the story words on page 219. Choose questions from the Guided Instruction as you read the story with students or after they have played the **Listening Library Audiocassette.** Have them use the Predictions chart.	**Read Independently** Have students read independently. Have them construct a Predictions chart like the one on page 219. After reading, they can use the chart to summarize or retell the story.

Baseball Saved Us

Written by **Ken Mochizuki**
Illustrated by **Dom Lee**

Guided Instruction

☑ **Make Predictions**
☑ **Sequence of Events**

Strategic Reading Before we begin reading, let's prepare a Predictions chart so we can write down story notes.

PREDICTIONS	WHAT HAPPENED

(1) **MAKE PREDICTIONS** What is unusual about the setting shown in the picture? Make a prediction about where you think these boys might be. Can you make an inference about why the boys do not look very happy? (Sample answer: The fence has barbed wire on it. The setting is probably a baseball field, but it may be in a reform school for boys. The setting could be in Japan. Maybe the boys are not happy because they are losing the baseball game.)

Story Words

The words below may be unfamiliar. Have students check their meanings and pronunciations in the Glossary beginning on page 726 or in a dictionary.

• barbed-wire, p. 220
• barracks, p. 225
• sagebrush, p. 227
• irrigation, p. 227

LANGUAGE SUPPORT

A blackline master of the Predictions chart is available in the **Language Support Book.**

Name_____ Date_____
Make Predictions

Predictions	What Happens

Grade 4   Language Support /Blackline Master 33 • **Baseball Saved Us** 69

LANGUAGE SUPPORT, p. 69

Guided Instruction

(2) CONFIRM OR REVISE PREDICTIONS When a reader makes a prediction, he or she uses clues in the story and pictures to infer what could happen next. What did you predict about the setting? Does reading these pages and looking at the pictures make you want to change your predictions?

MODEL My earlier prediction was that the setting was in Japan. On this page, I find out that the setting is a camp—not a fun camp, but a camp with barbed-wire fences and soldiers with guns. I am going to change my prediction based on this information. I predict that these people did something wrong.

One day, my dad looked out at the endless desert and decided then and there to build a baseball field.

He said people needed something to do in Camp. We weren't in a camp that was fun, like summer camp. Ours was in the middle of nowhere, and we were behind a barbed-wire fence. Soldiers with guns made sure we stayed there, and the man in the tower saw everything we did, no matter where we were.

220

LANGUAGE SUPPORT

ESL To help students who may not be familiar with baseball and baseball terms, provide some baseball-related items for students to experience. As you present each item—*ball, bat, glove, hat*—emphasize its name. Help students associate each item with its name. Encourage students to use the words in sentences. Then invite them to find baseball words or pictures on page 220. (baseball, field, bat)

As Dad began walking over the dry, cracked dirt, I asked him again why we were here.

"Because," he said, "America is at war with Japan, and the government thinks that Japanese Americans can't be trusted. But it's wrong that we're in here. We're Americans too!" Then he made a mark in the dirt and mumbled something about where the infield bases should be.

221

Guided Instruction

③ CONFIRM OR REVISE PREDICTIONS When you make predictions, it is important to revisit them as new information becomes available. My last prediction was that the people in the picture did something wrong. Should I revise my prediction? Explain. (Yes. Dad explains that they are in the camp because they are Japanese Americans. I see now that they have done nothing wrong.)

WORD STRUCTURE What is the fourth word from the end on page 221? (infield) What two words are combined to make the word *infield*? (in, field) What does the word *infield* mean?

🅟/ᵢ PREVENTION/INTERVENTION

WORD STRUCTURE Remind students that a compound word is made up of two words put together. Write *in* on the chalkboard. Elicit that *in* is the opposite of *out* and can mean *inside* or *within*.

Write *field* on the chalkboard. Discuss different kinds of fields, including the one used in baseball. Have a volunteer draw a baseball diamond on the chalkboard, labeling the bases and pitcher's mound. Point out the field is divided into two main parts: the area inside the bases and the area beyond the bases. Have students label the area inside the bases as the *infield*. Ask what they think the area beyond the bases is called. (outfield)

221

Guided Instruction

(4) MAKE PREDICTIONS The opening picture shows Ken in a baseball uniform. Do you think Ken will make a good baseball player? Add your ideas to your Predictions chart.

PREDICTIONS	WHAT HAPPENED
Ken will not be a good ball player.	

(5) SEQUENCE OF EVENTS On page 222, the author provides a sequence of events that is out of order. The phrase *before camp* shows that the events described on this page happened before the beginning of the story. What is the sequence of events described here? (The boy was picked on in school because he was small. It got worse after the attack on Pearl Harbor. They had to leave their home and most of their things. They lived in horse stalls before they came to the camp.)

(4) Back in school, before Camp, I was shorter and smaller than the rest of the kids. I was always the last to be picked for any team when we played games. Then, a few months ago, it got even worse. The kids started to call me names and nobody talked to me, even though I didn't do anything bad. At the same time the radio kept talking about some place far away called Pearl Harbor.

(5) One day Mom and Dad came to get me out of school. Mom cried a lot because we had to move out of our house real fast, throwing away a lot of our stuff. A bus took us to a place where we had to live in horse stalls. We stayed there for a while until we came here.

222

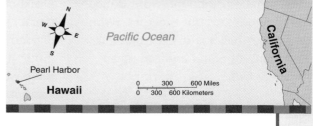

Activity

Cross Curricular: Social Studies

MAP SKILLS Provide students with atlases or world maps. Have students:

- locate Hawaii and California, then locate Pearl Harbor in the Hawaiian Islands.
- identify the scale of miles and calculate about how far Pearl Harbor is from the California coast.

RESEARCH AND INQUIRY Provide students with encyclopedias and have them research what happened at Pearl Harbor during World War II and what resulted from this event.

▶ **Visual/Mathematical**

CALIFORNIA AND HAWAII

Pacific Ocean

California

Pearl Harbor

Hawaii

| 0 | 300 | 600 Miles |
| 0 | 300 | 600 Kilometers |

223

Guided Instruction

Minilesson

REVIEW/MAINTAIN

Consonant Clusters

Review: Sometimes consonants join to make one sound, such as the *th* in *than*. At other times the consonants make more than one sound, such as the *st* in *started*.

- Ask students if the letters *thr* in *throwing* make one sound or more than one sound. (more than one; /th/ and /r/)

- Ask students to find other words on page 222 that begin with /st/. (stuff, stalls, stayed)

Activity Have students create a word wall of words that begin with the clusters *st, sp, str, spr,* and *thr.* Have students read the words aloud in unison as a volunteer points to each word.

Guided Instruction

6 **MAKE PREDICTIONS** Study the picture on these pages. Where do you think the people are going? Predict why.
(They are going inside the huge barracks, maybe to eat.)

6

This Camp wasn't anything like home. It was so hot in the daytime and so cold at night. Dust storms came and got sand in everything, and nobody could see a thing. We sometimes got caught outside, standing in line to eat or to go to the bathroom. We had to use the bathroom with everybody else, instead of one at a time like at home.

224

Activity

Cross Curricular: Math

WORD PROBLEM Have students look at the picture on pages 224–225. Ask:

- Are the people in the line moving quickly or slowly? How can you tell?
- How do you feel when you have to wait in line at a restaurant, store, bathroom, movie, or sporting event?

Have pairs solve the following problem:

- After reaching the front of the line, the first person still has to wait 3 minutes to get into the dining hall door. If you are the 12th person in line, how long will you have to wait to get in?

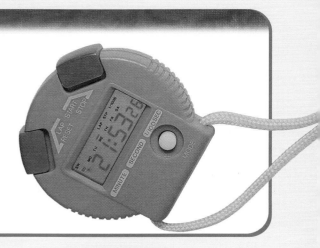

We had to eat with everybody else, too, but my big brother Teddy ate with his own friends. We lived with a lot of people in what were called barracks. The place was small and had no walls. Babies cried at night and kept us up.

7

225

Guided Instruction

7 **MAKE PREDICTIONS** At the end of these pages, the narrator writes about what it is like to live and sleep in those barracks. Predict how these living conditions might affect the children's mood and attitude. What clues lead you to make this prediction? Let's record another prediction on the Predictions chart.

PREDICTIONS	WHAT HAPPENED
Ken will not be a good ball player.	
The children will become very mean.	

Minilesson

REVIEW/MAINTAIN

Make Inferences

Remind students that making inferences means understanding ideas that the author does not state directly. Students should use details from the text and their experiences to make inferences.

- Have students reread the page and look at the picture.
- Ask them what they might infer about Ken's feelings in this camp.

Activity Ask students to imagine that they are in a camp like the one in this story. Have each student write a diary entry expressing his or her feelings about the camp. Remind students to include details that could be used to make an inference about their feelings.

225

Guided Instruction

8 Let's read page 226 aloud in groups of four. One of you can read the part of Dad, one the part of Teddy, one the old man, and one the part of the narrator. As you read aloud, act out the scene. Then, in each group, act out a scene of your own to show what might happen the next time Dad and Teddy get together. *Role-Play*

8

Back home, the older people were always busy working. But now, all they did was stand or sit around. Once Dad asked Teddy to get him a cup of water.

"Get it yourself," Teddy said.

"What did you say?" Dad snapped back.

The older men stood up and pointed at Teddy. "How dare you talk to your father like that!" one of them shouted.

Teddy got up, kicked the crate he was sitting on, and walked away. I had never heard Teddy talk to Dad that way before.

226

Activity

Cross Curricular: Science

DESERTS The camp where Ken and his family live is in the desert. Point out that a desert, like any other ecosystem, must have the following things: water, sunlight, soil, plants, and animals.

RESEARCH AND INQUIRY Have groups research desert ecosystems, and then make a terrarium. Encourage them to use sand, pebbles, small cacti, and so on. ▶ **Spatial/Interpersonal**

*inter***NET** **CONNECTION** Students can learn more about desert ecosystems by visiting **www.mhschool.com/reading**

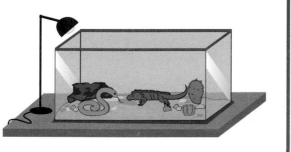

That's when Dad knew we needed baseball. We got shovels and started digging up the sagebrush in a big empty space near our barracks. The man in the tower watched us the whole time. Pretty soon, other grown-ups and their kids started to help.

We didn't have anything we needed for baseball, but the grown-ups were pretty smart. They funnelled water from irrigation ditches to flood what would become our baseball field. The water packed down the dust and made it hard. There weren't any trees, but they found wood to build the bleachers. Bats, balls and gloves arrived in cloth sacks from friends back home. My mom and other moms took the covers off mattresses and used them to make uniforms. They looked almost like the real thing. **9**

227

Guided Instruction

9 **SEQUENCE OF EVENTS** What steps did the people in the camp take to prepare a place for the children to play baseball?

MODEL Sometimes the steps in a sequence are not all given in the same paragraph or even on the same page. I remember earlier in the story, on page 221, Dad picked out a place for the baseball field. That was the first step in the sequence. The opening paragraph on page 227 gives the next step: the people clear the field by digging up the sagebrush. Now I'll continue reading page 227 to see which other steps are mentioned.

MULTIPLE-MEANING WORDS The word *hard* has more than one meaning. What do you think the word means as it is used on this page?

Minilesson

REVIEW/MAINTAIN

Context Clues

Remind students that they can often figure out the meaning of an unfamiliar word by looking at the words around it.

• Point out the word *funnelled*.

• Ask students to identify context clues that can be used to help them figure out what *funnelled* means.

Activity Ask students to write a sentence that defines *funnelled*. Then have them check a dictionary to verify the definition. Challenge them to find out what a funnel is and what its uses are.

PREVENTION/INTERVENTION

MULTIPLE-MEANING WORDS
Have students reread the sentence containing the words *hard*.

Point out that the context clue *packed down* can help students figure out how the word *hard* is used on this page. It means "solid; firm; not soft."

Also discuss how the words *tower* and *bats* are used on page 227. Then display the following sentences, and have students determine the meanings of the underlined words: Basketball players <u>tower</u> above most people. That test was really <u>hard</u>. <u>Bats</u> sometimes hang upside down in caves.

Guided Instruction

10 **MAKE PREDICTIONS** The suspense at the bottom of page 228 is great. What do you want to know? (whether or not Ken hits the ball) **What do you think will happen?** (Sample answer: Ken might get a hit.)

SELF-MONITORING

STRATEGY

SEARCH FOR CLUES Looking for clues to character traits can help a reader predict what a character might do later.

MODEL I know Ken does not have much confidence. In the first sentence on page 228 he says, "I wasn't that good." I might predict that Ken will never be a good player, but then I read that he practices often. He also knows the soldier and his friends are watching. I predict that Ken will try very hard because he doesn't want to be embarrassed.

I tried to play, but I wasn't that good. Dad said I just had to try harder. But I did know that playing baseball here was a little easier than back home. Most of the time, the kids were the same size as me.

All the time I practiced, the man in the tower watched. He probably saw the other kids giving me a bad time and thought that I was no good. So I tried to be better because he was looking.

Soon, there were baseball games all the time. Grown-ups played and us kids did, too. I played second base because my team said that was the easiest. Whenever I was at bat, the infield of the other team started joking around and moved in real close. The catcher behind me and the crowd for the other team would say, "Easy out." I usually grounded out. Sometimes I got a single.

Then came one of our last games of the year to decide on the championship. It was the bottom of the ninth inning and the other team was winning, 3 to 2. One of our guys was on second and there were two outs.

Two pitches, and I swung both times and missed. I could tell that our guy on second was begging me to at least get a base hit so somebody better could come up to bat. The crowd was getting loud. "You can do it!" "Strike out!" "No hitter, no hitter!" **10**

228

CULTURAL PERSPECTIVES

BASEBALL IN JAPAN Explain that even though baseball is often referred to as "America's National Pastime," this sport is extremely popular in many countries, such as Japan and Cuba.

RESEARCH AND INQUIRY Have students research Japanese baseball players and teams. Encourage them to work in small groups to use what they learn to design, illustrate, and write an article for a sports page. Post the finished articles on a bulletin board titled "Baseball in Japan." ▶ **Linguistic/Interpersonal**

11

229

Guided Instruction

11 **MAKE PREDICTIONS** Look at this picture of Ken. Do you think he will hit the ball successfully? Why or why not?

MODEL Looking at the picture, I see that there is an expression of determination on Ken's face. Some of the boys behind the fence appear to be teasing Ken. I have already read that Ken sometimes gets angry when he is being teased, and he does not want to be embarrassed in front of his friends. These clues lead me to predict that Ken will make an extra special effort and hit the ball.

Minilesson

REVIEW/MAINTAIN

Summarize

Remind students that a summary is a short retelling of a story and should only include the main events. Encourage students to refer to both the text and pictures to help them summarize.

• Have students recall three key events in the story to this point.

• Write their suggestions on the board.

• Then have them orally summarize what has happened in the story so far.

Activity Have students recall a story they have recently read and make a comic strip depicting the main events. Have them write brief captions to help summarize the story.

Guided Instruction

(12) **MAKE PREDICTIONS** Reread the first paragraph. What do you think will happen next? Why? Let's add to our Predictions chart. Let's also write what happened for our last prediction.

PREDICTIONS	WHAT HAPPENED
The children will become very mean.	Teddy treats his dad disrespectfully.
Ken will hit the ball.	

PHONICS AND DECODING Listen to these words: *I, behind, line, blinding, quiet, like.* How are these words alike?

Visual Literacy

VIEWING AND REPRESENTING

Help students compare the two illustrations on page 230: In the picture on the left, what do you see up close in the foreground? (the back of Ken's head and baseball cap) What do you see in the background? (a soldier in his tower) What do you imagine the look on Ken's face to be? Why? (He probably looks angry or scared because the soldier is looking at him.)

Why do you think the close-up of the soldier also appears on this page? (It shows how scary he looks.)

I glanced at the guardhouse behind the left field foul line and saw the man in the tower, leaning on the rail with the blinding sun glinting off his sunglasses. He was always watching, always staring. It suddenly made me mad.

I gripped the bat harder and took a couple of practice swings. I was gonna hit the ball past the guardhouse even if it killed me. Everyone got quiet and the pitcher threw.

I stepped into my swing and pulled the bat around hard. I'd never heard a crack like that before. The ball went even farther than I expected.

230

PREVENTION/INTERVENTION

PHONICS AND DECODING Write the words *I, behind, line, blinding, quiet,* and *like* on the chalkboard. Say each word slowly. emphasizing the long *i* sound. Point out that all these words appear on page 230. Have students say the words aloud and sort the words according to the spelling pattern that represents the long *i* sound in each word: *i* or *i-e.*

Challenge students to find a word on page 232 with the long *i* sound spelled a different way. (myself)

Invite students to suggest other words with the long *i.* Record their responses on the chalkboard, pointing out the spelling pattern that represents the long *i* sound in each word.

Against the hot desert sun, I could see the ball high in the air as I ran to first base. The ball went over the head of the left fielder.

I dashed around the bases, knowing for sure that I would get tagged out. But I didn't care, running as fast as I could to home plate. I didn't even realize that I had crossed it.

Before I knew it, I was up in the air on the shoulders of my teammates. I looked up at the tower and the man, with a grin on his face, gave me the thumbs-up sign. **13**

231

Guided Instruction

13 **SEQUENCE OF EVENTS** Pretend that you are a radio sports announcer. How would you announce the final at-bat of this game? *Role-Play*

Guided Instruction

(14) SEQUENCE OF EVENTS Notice that the story skips forward in time here. What exactly has happened? (The war has ended and Ken's family has returned home. Ken has started back at school.)

But it wasn't as if everything were fixed. Things were bad again when we got home from Camp after the war. Nobody talked to us on the street, and nobody talked to me at school, either. Most of my friends from Camp didn't come back here. I had to eat lunch by myself.

(14)

232

Activity

Cross Curricular: Social Studies

INTERNMENT CAMPS Have students discuss what happened to Ken's family. Have groups brainstorm ways to learn about the internment camps. (History books, the Internet, asking Japanese American neighbors, encyclopedias)

RESEARCH AND INQUIRY When they have finished their research, encourage groups to create a multimedia presentation for the class.
▶ **Kinesthetic/Interpersonal**

⑮

233

Guided Instruction

⑮ **MAKE PREDICTIONS** Look at this picture. Did things get better for Ken? (no) How does the picture help you know that? (The other children are laughing, talking, and having a good time. Ken is by himself.) What might happen to improve the situation?

MODEL I see a very quiet and thoughtful Ken in the picture on this page. Even though he is no longer forced to live in a camp, life is not back to the way it was before the war. Maybe Ken will start getting angry again and argue with the other boys or maybe he will make friends with them after all by being a baseball hero again.

LANGUAGE SUPPORT

ESL Have students look at the pictures on pages 232 and 233 as you read aloud the text on page 232. Ask students what feeling they get from the words and pictures on these two pages. (sad, lonely) Point out the words *bad, wasn't, didn't, nobody,* and *by myself* on page 232. Explain that all these negative words help create this mood.

Ask students to create an opposite mood by turning all the negatives in the paragraph into positives. For example, the paragraph would start: *And everything was fixed. Things were great again after we got home from camp.*

233

Guided Instruction

(16) SEQUENCE OF EVENTS Let's summarize the main events of the story so far. (During World War II, Ken's family was forced to live in an internment camp. There, Ken and other children played baseball to keep busy. Now, Ken's family is back home, but Ken feels different, even on the baseball team.) *Summarize*

Then baseball season came. I was the smallest guy again, but playing baseball in Camp had made me a lot better. The other guys saw that I was a pretty good player. They started calling me "Shorty," but they smiled when they said it.

By the time the first game came around, I felt almost like part of the team. Everyone was laughing and horsing around on the bus. But as soon as we got out there, it hit me: nobody on my team or the other team, or even **(16)** anybody in the crowd looked like me.

234

MAKE PREDICTIONS How does Ken feel when he comes to bat? (nervous) What happens that upsets him? (The crowd calls him "Jap.") Predict what will happen next.

Let's add to our Predictions chart. We can fill in what happened for our last prediction, too.

PREDICTIONS	WHAT HAPPENED
Ken will hit the ball.	He hit a home run.
He will get mad again and hit a home run.	

When we walked out onto the field, my hands were shaking. It felt like all these mean eyes were staring at me, wanting me to make mistakes. I dropped the ball that was thrown to me, and I heard people in the crowd yelling "Jap." I hadn't heard that word since before I went to Camp—it meant that they hated me.

My team came up to bat and I was up next. I looked down. I thought maybe I should pretend to be sick so I wouldn't have to finish the game. But I knew that would make things even worse, because I would get picked on at school for being a chicken. And they would use the bad word, too. (17)

235

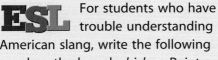

Guided Instruction

(18) MAKE PREDICTIONS Now that we have finished reading the story, let's complete our Predictions chart. Did you predict the final outcome?

PREDICTIONS	WHAT HAPPENED
Ken will not be a good ball player.	He practiced. He tried. He hit a home run.
The children will become very mean.	Teddy treats his dad disrespectfully.
Ken will hit the ball.	He hit a home run.
He will get mad again and hit a home run.	He did it!

RETELL THE STORY Have volunteers tell the major events of the story. Then have small groups work together to write one or two sentences to summarize the events. If they refer to their charts, remind them not to include in their summaries any predictions that turned out to be wrong. *Summarize*

SELF-ASSESSMENT

- How did the strategy of making predictions help me understand the story?
- How did the Predictions chart help me?

TRANSFERRING THE STRATEGY

- When might I try using this strategy again? In what other reading could the strategy help me?

Then it was my turn at bat. The crowd was screaming. "The Jap's no good!" "Easy out!" I heard laughing. I swung twice and missed. The crowd roared each time I missed, drowning out my teammates, who were saying, "C'mon, Shorty, you can do it!" I stepped back to catch my breath.

When I stepped back up to the plate, I looked at the pitcher. The sun glinted off his glasses as he stood on the mound, like the guard in the tower. We stared at each other. Then I blocked out the noise around me and got set. The pitcher wound up and threw.

236

REREADING FOR *Fluency*

PARTNERS Have students read a favorite section to a partner. Have partners listen for accuracy.

READING RATE You may want to evaluate a student's reading rate. Have the student read aloud from *Baseball Saved Us* for one minute. Ask the student to place a self-stick note after the last word read, and then count the number of words he or she has read.

Alternatively, you could assess small groups or the whole class together by having students count words and record their own scores.

A Running Record form provided in **Diagnostic/Placement Evaluation** will help you evaluate reading rate(s).

I swung and felt that solid whack again. And I could see that little ball in the air against the blue sky and puffy white clouds. It looked like it was going over the fence.

237

LITERARY RESPONSE

QUICK-WRITE Invite students to record their thoughts about the story in their journal. These questions may help them get started:

• How did the camp experience change Ken?

• How do you feel about the way the Japanese Americans were treated?

ORAL RESPONSE Have students share their journal writings and discuss their favorite passages.

Guided Instruction

Return to Predictions and Purposes

Review with students the purposes they set for reading. Ask them if they found out what they wanted to know.

Encourage students to share what surprised them about their predictions. Did they have to change any? Why? Did they find additional clues to help them support ones that were accurate?

Story Questions

Have students discuss or write answers to the questions on page 238.

Answers:

1. a place where Japanese-Americans were forced to stay during World War II. *Literal/Details*

2. Sample answer: Yes, because Ken was determined. *Inferential/Details*

3. It brought the people in the camp together and gave them a way to feel good about themselves in a harsh situation. *Inferential/Evaluate*

4. Sample answer: Ken develops his baseball skills to make friends and gain respect. *Critical/Summarize*

5. Leah and Ken are both determined to succeed and are both making their families proud. *Critical/Reading Across Texts*

Write a Sports Column For a full writing process lesson, see pages 241K–241L.

Story Questions & Activities

1. What is the "Camp" in the story?

2. Did you predict the ending of the story? Explain.

3. Why was baseball such a good idea for the people in the camp?

4. What would you tell a friend about this story?

5. Compare the boy in the story with Leah in "Leah's Pony." How are they alike? What makes them different?

Write a Sports Column

Imagine you are a wartime sportswriter reporting on games at the Japanese-American camp. Compare camp baseball to games played in other communities. Tell how and why the settings are different. Talk about how the games seem different and alike.

Meeting Individual Needs

EASY

Name_____ Date_____ **Reteach** 60

Vocabulary

Write a word from the list to complete each sentence.

crate	ditches	endless	glinting	inning	mound

1. The beach seemed ___endless___ in length.
2. The field was surrounded by deep ___ditches___.
3. Sun was ___glinting___ off the water.
4. My uncle sent us a ___crate___ that was full of oranges.
5. In the eighth ___inning___, Mandy hit a home run.
6. The pitcher stood on the ___mound___.

Story Comprehension **Reteach** 61

Write sentences to answer the questions about "Baseball Saved Us."

1. Why were the boy and his family sent to a government camp?
   They were Japanese and America was at war with Japan.

2. Why did the boy's father decide to build a baseball field?
   He felt the people needed something to do to get their minds off being at the camp.

3. Why did the boy get angry with the guard in the tower?
   The guard was always watching them. He reminded everyone they were in camp and couldn't leave.

4. After the boy got out of camp, how did baseball help the boy?
   His experience playing baseball and reacting to the guard helped him fit in at his new school.

At Home: Have students use three of the vocabulary words to tell a story of their own.
Book 4/Unit 2 **Baseball Saved Us** 4
60–61

Reteach, 61

ON-LEVEL

Name_____ Date_____ **Practice** 61

Story Comprehension

Read statements 1 to 6 below. Write **T** for true if the statement describes "Baseball Saved Us." Write **F** for false if it does not.

1. ___T___ Many of the Japanese Americans in California were born in the United States.

2. ___T___ The United States government thought that Japanese Americans couldn't be trusted.

3. ___T___ Many Japanese Americans were sent to the camp.

4. ___F___ The camp guards provided all the baseball equipment.

5. ___T___ The narrator, or person telling the story, hit a home run at the camp's championship game.

6. ___F___ The narrator's community welcomed him warmly when his family returned from the camp.

Write to tell why the following statements are not true. Answers may vary.

7. The narrator's family went happily to the camp, which was like a summer camp. The storyteller's mother cried the day they went to the camp. The camp was not like a summer camp. There were armed guards and barbed wire.

8. The narrator didn't experience any prejudice after he left the camp and returned to school. He had to eat lunch alone, no one would talk to him, and people called him names.

At Home: Have students tell the story to a family member.
Book 4/Unit 2 **Baseball Saved Us** 8
61

Practice, 61

CHALLENGE

Name_____ Date_____ **Extend** 60

Vocabulary

crate	ditches	endless
glinting	inning	mound

Suppose that you want to recruit some of your friends to play baseball. Write an advertisement that will attract their attention and make them want to play on your team. Use as many of the vocabulary words from the box as you can.
Answers will vary but should use vocabulary correctly.

_____

_____

_____

Extend 61

Story Comprehension

When the boy in "Baseball Saved Us" returned home, most of his friends from camp went to other places. Tell why.

Possible answers: The people in the camp were Japanese Americans from all over the country. People wanted to start their lives again someplace else.

Why did the boy eat lunch alone when he went back to school? Predict how you would feel in a similar situation.

Answers will vary. Possible answers: The other children still resented him for being Japanese. I would feel lonely and sad.

At Home: Discuss the meaning of the word prejudice.
Book 4/Unit 2 **Baseball Saved Us**
60–61

Extend, 61

Design a Baseball Uniform

Everyone in the story took part in the game. For example, mothers took the covers off mattresses and used them to make uniforms. Now design your own baseball uniform. You can do this by drawing it, sewing it, or by putting together a "baseball outfit." Then have a fashion show to show off your uniforms.

The people in the story built a baseball field. A baseball diamond has exact measurements. Look in an encyclopedia to find out what they are. Then draw a diagram of a baseball diamond. Include all of the measurements and angles.

Plan a Baseball Diamond

Find Out More

The narrator became a hero by hitting a home run. Who are some of the great heroes of baseball? Look at baseball cards, interview an older friend, look in an encyclopedia, or read the sports pages of a newspaper. Find out more about baseball "greats." Share your information with the class.

239

Story Activities

Design a Baseball Uniform

Materials: butcher paper, markers, sheet remnants, needles, thread

GROUP Have each student in the group make a pattern as follows: one student lies down on a piece of paper as others outline the student's upper and lower body to make shirt and pants patterns.

Plan a Baseball Diamond

Materials: drawing paper, ruler, calculator, protractor

PARTNERS After determining the correct measurements of a baseball diamond, have students work in pairs to figure out to what scale they will make their diagram. Remind them that their scale should allow their diagram to fit on their sheet of drawing paper.

Find Out More

RESEARCH AND INQUIRY Have students brainstorm interview questions for baseball heroes as part of their research. Encourage groups to make a multimedia presentation to the class—showing baseball souvenirs, old newspaper clippings, or videos, and sharing personal experiences they may have had with baseball and baseball players.

*inter*NET CONNECTION For more information on baseball, students can visit **www.mhschool.com/reading**

FORMAL ASSESSMENT

After page 239, see the Selection Assessment.

239

Study Skills

REFERENCE SOURCES

OBJECTIVES Students will locate information in an encyclopedia.

PREPARE Preview the illustration with students. Remind them that encyclopedias are helpful for looking up facts about a person, place, thing, or event. Display **Teaching Chart 51**.

TEACH Review how the information on the spine of an encyclopedia volume can help students do research.

PRACTICE Have students answer questions 1–5. Review the answers with them. **1.** Volume 2–*B* **2.** Volume 16–*R* **3.** Volume 2–*B* **4.** Volume 2–*B* **5.** You would look in the last volume—the index.

ASSESS/CLOSE Ask students to name some other baseball heroes: Babe Ruth, Willie Mays, and Hank Aaron, for example. Have students identify the volume where they could read about each player.

STUDY SKILLS

Use an Encyclopedia

Where would you look to find more information about baseball? You could look in an encyclopedia. An **encyclopedia** is a set of books with articles about people, places, things, events, and ideas. The articles are arranged in alphabetical order in volumes. When you use an encyclopedia, you need a **key word**. For example, for general facts about baseball you would look under *baseball*. You could also look in the **index**. This is the last book in the encyclopedia. It gives a listing of all the topics.

Use the set of encyclopedias to answer these questions.

1 In which volume would you find the rules of baseball?

2 In which volume would you find more information about Jackie Robinson?

3 Where would you find information about the history of World War II?

4 In which volume would you look for a picture of a diamond?

5 If you were not sure where to find a topic in the encyclopedia, where could you look it up?

Meeting Individual Needs

EASY

Reteach, 62

ON-LEVEL

Practice, 62

CHALLENGE

Extend, 62

TEST POWER

Test Tip

Look in the passage for clues about the character's feelings.

DIRECTIONS

Read the sample story. Then read each question about the story.

SAMPLE

What is Richie's new name?

Richard walked into the house, went straight to his bedroom, and closed the door.

His mother opened the door. "Richie," she asked, "is something wrong?"

"Kids are making fun of me, saying the name Richie is childish," he said sadly.

"Well, we can call you Richard or Rich, if you prefer," his mother suggested.

After his mother left his bedroom, Richard opened a book and looked through it. There he saw a famous race-car driver, Rick Astin. "Hey, Mom," Richard called, "I've found my new name."

1 What will Richard probably say next?

  A That he likes the name Bob

  (B) That he likes the name Rick

  C That "Richie" is okay

  D That he's hungry

2 How does Richard feel about the name "Richie"?

  F Happy

  G Enthusiastic

  H Proud

  (J) Embarrassed

241

Test Power

THE PRINCETON REVIEW

Read the Page

Have students read *all* the information on the page. Explain that short stories are often full of important details. Remind students to read *all* of the answer choices before choosing the best one.

Discuss the Questions

Question 1: This question asks students to determine what Richard will *probably* say next. What clue is given in the story? After reading about race-car driver Rick Astin, Richard says that he's "found his new name."

Question 2: This question requires that students understand how Richard feels about the name "Richie." Discuss what information in the story offers a clue. For example, the story characterizes Richard's comment "Kids are making fun of me, . . . the name Richie is childish" as something that is said *sadly*.

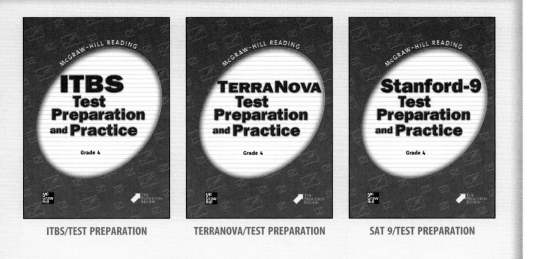

ITBS
Test Preparation and Practice
Grade 4

TerraNova
Test Preparation and Practice
Grade 4

Stanford-9
Test Preparation and Practice
Grade 4

ITBS/TEST PREPARATION   TERRANOVA/TEST PREPARATION   SAT 9/TEST PREPARATION

EASY

Answers to Story Questions

1. The Car Wash Fundraiser had to be cancelled because the extreme heat had caused a drought and the Mayor restricted water usage.
2. Coach Smith was suggesting that they all think about the people they knew who could help them.
3. The team might organize and assign tasks for buying the uniforms and equipment and getting the new field put in.
4. Friends work together to create a new fundraising event.
5. Answers will vary.

Story Questions and Activity

1. Why did the Car Wash Fund Raiser have to be cancelled?
2. What did Coach Smith mean by "using their resources"?
3. What do you predict the team will do next?
4. What is the main idea of the book?
5. What could the kids in this story have learned from the Japanese families in *Baseball Saved Us*?

Design a Race

Draw a map that depicts the route for a particular kind of race. For example, you could design a course for a marathon or bike race, or draw a track for a car race. Write a two-sentence description of your design.

from The Ninth Inning

Leveled Books

**written by Patricia Lakin
Illustrated by Al Florentino**

EASY

The Ninth Inning

Consonant Clusters
☑ **Make Predictions**
☑ **Instructional Vocabulary:**
crate, ditches, endless, glinting, inning, mound

Guided Reading

PREVIEW AND PREDICT Have students discuss the pictures through page 4 and predict what the story will be about. Ask them what they think the children's problem is and whether they will solve their problem.

SET PURPOSES Ask students to write questions they want answered as they read the book. For example: *Why do the children look sad on page 4?*

READ THE BOOK Use questions such as the following to guide students' as they read or use them after they have read the story on their own.

Page 4: What does Angela mean when she says, "But we've struck out"? (We weren't successful with the car wash.) *Make Inferences*

Page 5: Find the word *endless*. What does the base word *end* mean? What do you think *endless* means? (without end) *Vocabulary*

Page 6: Can you predict what ideas for raising money the kids will think of at their meeting? (Sample answers: They might

enter a race to win money; they might sell something.) *Make Predictions*

Page 9: Do you think the kids will be able to organize the derby by the weekend? Explain your answer. (Yes; because they have good ideas and are very determined.) *Make Predictions*

Page 13: Find the words *starting* and *stretched*. What do these words have in common? (They each begin with a consonant cluster.) How do they differ? (The consonant clusters are st- and str-.) *Phonics*

RETURN TO PREDICTIONS AND PURPOSES Review students' predictions and their purposes for reading. Were their predictions correct? Did they find out the answers to their questions?

LITERARY RESPONSE Discuss these questions:

• What lesson can be learned from reading this story?

• Who was your favorite character? Why?

Also see the story questions and activity in *The Ninth Inning*.

Leveled Books

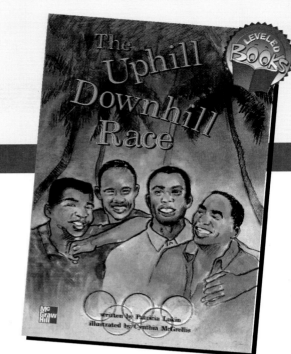

INDEPENDENT

The Uphill Downhill Race

☑ **Make Predictions**

☑ **Instructional Vocabulary:** *crate, ditches, endless, glinting, inning, mound*

PUPIL SELECTION

INDEPENDENT

Answers to Story Questions

1. Jamaicans raced pushcarts, which seemed similar to bobsleds to the Americans.
2. Bobsledders must be strong, fast, and cooperative team players.
3. Answers might include: The Jamaicans can win because they are a new team and they will keep getting better; they will never win because other teams will always have more experience on ice.
4. A group of Jamaicans proved that they could compete in the Winter Olympics.
5. Answers will vary.

Guided Reading

PREVIEW AND PREDICT Preview the book to page 9. Have students predict what the story will be about. Tell them to record their ideas in their journals.

SET PURPOSES Have students brainstorm questions they would like answered as they read the story. Have them write two questions in their journals.

READ THE BOOK Have students read the story independently. Then, use the guided reading questions for further teaching.

Pages 3: What does *glinting* mean? (shining, reflecting) What context clues help you figure out the meaning? ("sun," "waters") Off what other objects might you see the sun glinting? (diamonds, mirrors, tin cans) *Vocabulary*

Pages 4–5: Will the pushcart racers be good bobsledders? Explain. (Sample answer: Probably yes, because participants in both sports must have great speed and strength.) *Make Predictions*

Pages 6–11: Use the details and illustrations to make a general statement about the difficulty of bobsledding. (Sample

answer: Bobsledding is difficult and dangerous.) **What details did you use?** (Sample answers: Sleds may travel at 90 miles per hour; the men are wearing helmets; a sled can capsize.) *Form Generalizations*

Pages 12–13: What did the team have to do before they could compete in the 1988 Winter Olympics? (They had to qualify at the World Cup races.) *Sequence of Events*

RETURN TO PREDICTIONS AND PURPOSES Have students review their predictions and questions. Did they predict correctly? Were their questions answered?

LITERARY RESPONSE Discuss these questions with students:

• Is this selection fact or nonfact? How do you know?

• What is the most surprising fact you learned in this selection?

Also see the story questions and activity in *The Uphill Downhill Race.*

Story Questions and Activity

1. What made George Fitch and Bill Maloney think Jamaicans might be good bobsledders?
2. What are some important skills needed to be a successful bobsledder?
3. Do you think the Jamaican team can win an Olympic gold medal? Explain your answer.
4. What is the main idea of the book?
5. Baseball improved the morale of the Japanese families in "Baseball Saved Us." If Harris, White, and the Stokes brothers could have brought bobsledding to any group of people, where might they have organized a team?

Bobsledding in the 21st Century

Bobsleds were once made of wood. They have changed over time. Design a bobsled for the future. Then, write a short paragraph describing what your bobsled can do.

from *The Uphill Downhill Race*

PUPIL SELECTION

↓

CHALLENGE

Answers to Story Questions

1. EARS was created to rescue animals in natural disasters and accidents.

2. Terri Crisp feels that advanced training is necessary if animals are to be saved.

3. If EARS volunteers were on the scene, the bird would be rescued and treated for injuries. It would then be cared for until its original owner could come for it or another could be found.

4. Terri Crisp's love for animals led her to create EARS, an animal rescue organization.

5. Answers will vary but should include that people who work together of find themselves in similar circumstances often bond together and help each other.

Story Questions and Activity

1. Why was EARS created?

2. What does Terri Crisp feel is the key for a volunteer team to be successful?

3. Predict what would happen to the caged bird mentioned on page 3 if EARS volunteers were on the scene.

4. What is the main idea of this story?

5. How do the volunteers of EARS and the Japanese families in *Baseball Saved Us* show team spirit?

Save the Pets

Design a sticker that could be taped to a door to alert firefighters or other rescue workers that an animal is inside your home.

from EARS to the Rescue

Leveled Books

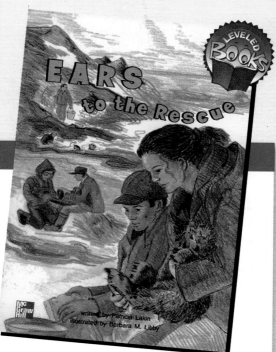

EARS to the Rescue

written by Patricia Lakin
illustrated by Barbara M. Libby

CHALLENGE

EARS to the Rescue

☑ **Make Predictions**

☑ **Instructional Vocabulary:** *crate, ditches, endless, glinting, inning, mound*

Guided Reading

PREVIEW AND PREDICT Preview the book to page 6. Have students predict what this selection will be about. Tell them to record their ideas in their journals.

SET PURPOSES Have students write a question about each picture that they hope will be answered in the text. For example, they may want to know what EARS is.

READ THE BOOK Encourage students to read independently, stopping periodically to predict what will happen next, and then reading on to check predictions. Use the questions that follow to apply strategies.

Page 2: Find a synonym for *ditches* on this page. (drains) Do you know another synonym for ditches? (Sample answers: holes, gullies) *Vocabulary*

Pages 6–7: The author tells you that "Crisp's life changed." Predict what changes you will read about, and then read on to find out if you were correct. (Sample answer: Terri Crisp spends her life volunteering with EARS.) *Make Predictions*

Pages 10–11: Make a general statement about the good and bad parts of working

with EARS. (The work is hard, but it is very rewarding.) *Form Generalization*

Pages 14–15: If a pet owner follows the pet safety rules, what do you think might happen in an emergency? (Sample answer: The pet will probably have a better chance of survival.) *Make Predictions*

RETURN TO PREDICTIONS AND PURPOSES Have students review their predictions and questions. Which predictions were accurate? If some of the students' questions weren't answered, encourage them to reread parts of the story or research the answers.

LITERARY RESPONSE Discuss these questions:

- What lesson can be learned by reading this selection?

- What can you do to help save a pet or person in a disaster?

Also see the story questions and activity in *EARS to the Rescue*.

Activities
Anthology and Leveled Books

Connecting Texts

TEAMWORK CHARTS
Write the four book titles on a chart. Discuss how people in each selection use teamwork to meet a goal. Have students identify the group or team goal and the effects of teamwork in each story. Write students' suggestions on the chart.

Use the chart to talk about the effectiveness of using teamwork to reach goals.

Baseball Saved Us	The Ninth Inning	The Uphill Downhill Race	EARS to the Rescue
• The Japanese-American families work together to make a baseball field. • The people at the camp are not bored. • The people stop fighting.	• Six kids work together to finish their baseball field. • They develop a plan to raise money at a duck derby. • They can pay for a new field, uniforms, and gloves.	• Four Jamaicans work together to form the first Jamaican Olympic bobsled team. • They placed 35th at the World Cup Races. • Their hard work and determination proves they are serious participants.	• EARS volunteers work together to rescue animals from disasters. • They set up animal shelters. • They care for the animals. • They find the owners of the lost pets.

Viewing/Representing

MAKE CHARTS Form a group for each of the four books based on reading levels. (For *Baseball Saved Us*, combine students of different reading levels.) Have each group discuss the sequence of events that resulted in the story characters meeting their goals. Have them chart the sequence and present their charts to the class.

SEQUENCE OF EVENTS Encourage students to pay close attention to the order of events in each sequence. Allow time for a question-and-answer session after each presentation.

Research and Inquiry

MORE ABOUT TEAMWORK Have students work in groups to research a sport or volunteer organization they have not read about in this lesson to find out the following:

• What qualities are essential to being a member of a team?

• How is teamwork important to the group's success?

You might invite a local leader or sports figure to speak with the class about their experiences with teamwork and about the importance of teamwork at work, school, and play. Have listeners take notes.

interNET CONNECTION Students can find out more about the importance of teamwork by visiting **www.mhschool.com/reading**

TESTED
OBJECTIVES

Students will use story clues to make predictions.

TEACHING TIP

MANAGEMENT As students read the story aloud with you, monitor reading for fluency. Review any vocabulary words, story words, or unfamiliar words that are causing problems orally. Then read the story in unison again.

Review Make Predictions

PREPARE

Discuss Making Predictions

Review: Paying attention to the small facts and details about a character or events in a story can help you predict what might happen next or what the character may do next.

TEACH

Read "A Long Line" and Model the Skill

Have students read **Teaching Chart 52** in unison with you, and encourage them to pay close attention to details that give clues about what the character will do next.

A Long Line

At the dining hall, Teddy stood at the end of a long line of people waiting to eat lunch. He had ignored his mother's warnings to get in line. Now the hot sun was beating down on him and he was definitely in a bad mood.

"My legs are sore," he moaned. "I think kids should be fed first," he said to an old man. Teddy started to push a younger boy out of the way and stepped on the feet of a girl behind him. Just then, Teddy's father arrived and told Teddy to stop. Teddy glared at his father. Time seemed to stop as they stared at each other.

Teaching Chart 52

Discuss clues in the passage that might help students make predictions about what will occur next.

MODEL The story tells me that Teddy is in a very bad mood. He has been very disrespectful to the people around him. At the end of the passage, he glares at his father. I predict that he will argue with his father and show his father disrespect, too.

PRACTICE

Make Predictions

ONE

Have students underline words or phrases in "A Long Line" that help them predict what might happen next.

Ask students to make other predictions about what could happen next in this passage. (Sample answers: Teddy will be sent to bed without his meal. The old man will complain to Teddy's parents about Teddy's bad behavior. Teddy's dad will tell Teddy to apologize to the people around him.) ▶ **Logical/Linguistic**

ASSESS/CLOSE

Write a Scene

GROUP

Have students predict what the dialogue between Teddy and his father might be like later that day. Then have them write a scene using this dialogue, and encourage them to include other characters in the dialogue as well. Encourage each group to perform its play scene for the class.

ALTERNATE TEACHING STRATEGY

MAKE PREDICTIONS

For a different approach to teaching this skill, see page T60.

SELF-SELECTED Reading

Students may choose from the following titles.

ANTHOLOGY
• **Baseball Saved Us**

LEVELED BOOKS
• **The Ninth Inning**
• **The Uphill Downhill Race**
• **EARS to the Rescue**

Bibliography, page T76–T77

Meeting Individual Needs for Comprehension

EASY	ON-LEVEL	CHALLENGE	LANGUAGE SUPPORT

EASY — Name _____ Date _____ **Reteach 63**

Make Predictions

You can use clues from the story to help you **predict** what may happen next.

Read each story. Then answer the questions.

Emily had always been shy. But her shyness grew worse after her family moved. She tried to avoid talking to any of the people she met. Emily never raised her hand in class, and she walked straight home after school, alone.

Emily had been in school for five weeks and still had no friends. Then one day, she was sitting alone at a small lunch table, when she noticed three girls heading for her table.

1. What do you think Emily will do? _She will probably try to avoid them._

2. Why? _Emily is very shy and has tried to avoid talking with people ever since her family moved._

Felicia liked her home in town. But sometimes, she thought about the house by the sea. When she was a child, Felicia spent many happy summers there. Felicia had been heartbroken when her grandparents sold the house.

One day, Felicia saw that the house by the sea was for sale. She had saved enough money to allow her to buy it. She hadn't been planning to move. Yet, she felt happier than she'd been in months.

3. What do you think Felicia will decide to do? _She will move to the house by the sea._

4. Why? _She was happy there long ago, and she was excited to be able to afford it._

At Home: Have students read the first paragraph of a story they choose and predict what will happen next. Book 4/Unit 2 **Baseball Saved Us** 4
63

ON-LEVEL — Name _____ Date _____ **Practice 63**

Make Predictions

To make a **prediction**, you can use story clues and your own experience. Read the following. Think about what might happen and answer the questions. Answers may vary.

Middle West Weather

Weather in the Middle West can change very quickly. A warm spring day can bring sudden hailstones of ice. Sometimes, during spring or early summer, tornadoes swirl quickly through the area, destroying objects in their paths. People in the Middle West know that when a tornado is sighted, they should seek shelter, preferably in the lowest level of their homes.

It is a clear, sunny Saturday afternoon in May. The Bates family decides to have a cookout. During lunch, Mrs. Bates notices a mass of dark clouds in the distance. The breeze turns brisk.

1. What are some of the things that could happen next? _There could be a tornado or rainstorm and the Bates will move inside. The Bates could wait out the storm._

2. What do you think will most likely happen next? _A storm will come through the area._

3. What clues from the above paragraphs helped you predict what would most likely happen next? _The spring weather in the Middle West can change quickly. Mrs. Bates notices the clouds and a change in the breeze._

4. What are some situations in and out of school when you might have predicted something would happen? _Answers will vary._

At Home: Have students write their predictions for tomorrow's weather including the clues they used to make the prediction. Book 4/Unit 2 **Baseball Saved Us** 4
63

CHALLENGE — Name _____ Date _____ **Extend 63**

Make Predictions

In "Baseball Saved Us," the boy made a home run after seeing the sun glinting off the guard's glasses. In the game back home, do you think the sun glinting off glasses helped him focus? Do you think the boy made a home run at the end of the story? Do you think that the glint of the sun on glasses will inspire the boy during other times? How do you think that the children at his school will treat the boy after the baseball game described at the end of the story? Write a paragraph explaining your **predictions**. Include reasons.

Answers will vary. Possible answers: I think that the glasses reminded him of his victory at the camp and made him feel that same determination. I think that he made a home run and helped win the game. The sun on glasses will probably always remind him of what he can do if he is determined. I think that the children will start to accept the boy and realize that he is like them in many ways. They will appreciate his skills at baseball.

At Home: Have students predict whether they will reach a goal important to them, then discuss things that might help them focus on a goal and avoid distractions that might interfere with achieving it. Book 4/Unit 2 **Baseball Saved Us** 4
63

LANGUAGE SUPPORT — Name _____ Date _____

What's Your Score?

1. Read the sentences below that describe events from the story, *How Baseball Saved Us*. 2. Circle the letter of what you think happened. 3. Look back at the story to compare what really happened with what you thought happened. 4. Keep score of your correct guesses on the scoreboard.

1. When the people in the camp start making a baseball diamond, the guards will:
a. make them stop
b. watch their every move
c. help them
d. throw things at them

2. When the boy in the story comes up to bat in the championship game, he will:
a. strike out
b. run away
c. hit a home run
d. start joking around

3. When the boy gets back home, other kids will:
a. welcome him
b. ignore him
c. beat him up
d. help him

4. When the boy plays baseball back home, he will:
a. be a failure
b. get sick
c. get thrown out
d. hit another home run

Scoreboard	
My Prediction	What Happens
1.	1. watch their every move
2.	2. hit a home run
3.	3. ignore him
4.	4. hit another home run

70 **Baseball Saved Us** • Language Support /Blackline Master 34 Grade 4

Reteach, 63	Practice, 63	Extend, 63	Language Support, 70

Students will review how to form generalizations based on details and clues.

Review **Form Generalizations**

INSTRUCTIONAL

Point out to students that they can use specific clues and details about a person, place, or event to form generalizations. For example, if Ken is 5 feet 6 inches tall, John is 5 feet 9 inches tall, Sheri is 5 feet tall, and Laura is 5 feet 2 inches tall, what generalization can you form about these students?
(The boys are taller than the girls.)

PREPARE

Discuss Forming Generalizations

Review: Pay attention to the specific details the author gives about people, places, and events in a story. Use these specific details or clues to form generalizations (broad general statements) about the characters, setting, and plot.

TEACH

Read "The Camp" and Model the Skill

Ask students to pay close attention to specific details or clues about the setting as you read the **Teaching Chart 53** passage with them.

The Camp

Ken looked around at his new home in a Japanese American camp. Tall barbed-wire fences surrounded him. Guard towers were placed at the corners of the camp, and guards in army uniforms watched every move of the people inside the camp. The guards had big guns slung over their shoulders, and they never said a kind word to any of Ken's family or friends. The huge wooden barracks were dirty and dusty on the outside and gloomy and crowded inside. Around the camp lay a hot and unwelcome desert that stretched for miles.

Teaching Chart 53

Discuss specific details and clues in the passage that help readers generalize about the setting and characters.

MODEL From the specific details the author gives about the setting, I can picture exactly what this camp looks like. For example, the camp has barbed-wire fences, gloomy buildings, guard towers, guards with guns, and a hot desert nearby. I could generalize that the camp is an unpleasant or scary setting.

PRACTICE

Form Generalizations Using Details

Have students underline details in "The Camp" that help them to form a generalization about the setting, that is, that the camp is an unpleasant, scary place.

Ask groups to form other generalizations based on details in "The Camp." (Sample answer: It would be very hard to escape from the camp.) Continue by asking students to use details in "The Camp" to form generalizations about the feelings of the Japanese Americans in the camp. (Sample answers: They are afraid of the guards. They hate living in the camp. They wish they could return to their homes.)

▶ **Interpersonal/Logical**

ASSESS/CLOSE

List Details and Generalize

Have small groups list specific details that describe a place with which they are very familiar. Have groups write their list of details on chart paper, draw the setting on butcher paper, and write their generalization about the setting at the bottom of the picture. Have each group display their drawing as they read their list of details. Invite volunteers from other groups to make oral general statements about the setting based on the details they hear and the picture they see. Ask them to point out details from the list or picture to support their generalizations.

LOOKING AHEAD

Students will apply this skill as they read the next selection, *Will Her Native Language Disappear?*

ALTERNATE TEACHING STRATEGY
· ·
FORM GENERALIZATIONS
For a different approach to teaching this skill, see page T62.

Meeting Individual Needs for Comprehension

EASY	ON-LEVEL	CHALLENGE	LANGUAGE SUPPORT

EASY

Name_____ Date_____ Reteach **64**

Form Generalizations

A **generalization** is a broad statement based on a set of facts. Read the facts carefully. Decide what is true based on the facts.

Read each set of facts. Then complete each generalization.

The Steiner Group constructs buildings all over the state. It owns 13 office buildings and 13 shopping malls. The Group also owns 1 apartment building. The company has been in business for 26 years.

1. The Steiner group is a well known company that constructs buildings _all over the state_

2. The Steiner Group is a builder that has been respected by businesses for _26 years_

Some people call Marina Del Sol a paradise. The daytime temperature is almost always between 70°F and 80°F, except in January and February. Then it is colder. Last month, there were only six days of rain. Most months, it rains less than that. If you want sunny days and a gentle ocean breeze, pack your bags and come to Marina Del Sol.

3. The daytime temperature in Marina Del Sol is almost never _too hot nor too cold_

4. In Marina Del Sol, rainy days _are rare; it is almost always sunny and pleasant_

Book 4/Unit 2
Baseball Saved Us | At Home: Have students list facts about the town in which they live and then make some generalizations. | 64

Reteach, 64

ON-LEVEL

Name_____ Date_____ Practice **64**

Form Generalizations

A **generalization** is a broad statement about something. Generalizations often include words such as always, all, everyone, none, everything. Read each passage. Then write a generalization. Answers may vary.

1. Every Saturday, Maisie goes grocery shopping for her family. As usual, she went next door to ask Mr. Hadley if he needed any milk or other things.
Generalization: _Maisie always asks Mr. Hadley if he needs anything._

2. Carlos picked up the newspapers and put them in the trash. He hung up his little brother's jacket and put away the toys. By the time Carlos' father got home from work, Carlos had straightened the whole house.
Generalization: _Carlos is very neat and always straightens things up._

3. My brother Bobby likes to eat. The other morning he ate breakfast, then crackers, fruit, and cheese just before lunch.
Generalization: _Bobby eats a lot._

4. The coach asked Lee if he would like to have a day off from practice, but Lee said no.
Generalization: _Lee would rather practice than take time off._

5. Each fourth grader in Mrs. Freewell's class has the habit of saying "please" and "thank you."
Generalization: _Everyone in Mrs. Freewell's class has good manners._

Book 4/Unit 2
Baseball Saved Us | At Home: Have students write generalizations using everyone, none, and all. | 64

Practice, 64

CHALLENGE

Name_____ Date_____ Extend **64**

Form Generalizations

In "Baseball Saved Us," some people **formed a generalization** about Japanese Americans. Tell what the generalization was and why you think people formed it.
Answers will vary. Possible answer: People formed a generalization that Japanese Americans couldn't be trusted. The United States was at war with Japan and some Americans were suspicious of Japanese Americans and thought they might be loyal to Japan rather than to the United States. Other Americans were angry that the Japanese bombed Pearl Harbor without warning, which made them think the Japanese couldn't be trusted.

Form a generalization about why the boy's father decided it was important to have a baseball field at the camp.
Answers will vary. Possible answer: He wanted there to be a positive activity to occupy the time. He was trying to make the best of a terrible situation.

Why was baseball so important to the boy after he returned home?
Answers will vary. Possible answer: He was able to show everyone that he was a valuable member of the team.

Book 4/Unit 2
Baseball Saved Us | At Home: Have students write a paragraph with generalizations on things to remember in order to. | 64

Extend, 64

LANGUAGE SUPPORT

Name_____ Date_____

Not All, Not Always

Color the baseballs next to the sentences that are generalizations in the story, *Baseball Saved Us*.

color in baseball

1. ⚾ All good baseball players are tall.

color in baseball

2. ⚾ All the camp guards were mean to the prisoners.

3. ⚾ The United States was at war with Japan.

4. ⚾ The camp guard was rooting for the boy in the story when he stepped up to bat.

5. ⚾ The small boy in the story hit a home run.

Grade 4 | Language Support / Blackline Master 35 • Baseball Saved Us **71**

Language Support, 71

Students will recognize and figure out meanings of compound words.

TEACHING TIP

INSTRUCTIONAL Students may think compound words are made up of only two smaller words. Point out that they can be made up of more than two words. Examples are *nevertheless* and *forevermore*.

Mention that the meanings of some compound words cannot be figured out by looking at their parts. *Sagebrush* in *Baseball Saved Us* is one example.

Review Compound Words

PREPARE

Discuss How to Identify Compound Words

Review: A compound word is made up of two or more words joined together. If you know the meaning of each smaller word, you can often figure out what the compound word means.

TEACH

Read the Passage and Model the Skill

Have students read the passage on **Teaching Chart 54**.

A Great Game!

It was the bottom of the eighth inning. The <u>sunlight</u> was glaring down into Ken's eyes as he stood in the <u>outfield</u>. Red, the best <u>sportsman</u> in camp, was at bat. Ken knew that Red would purposely hit a ball in his direction, just to see Ken fumble. Ken kept his <u>eyelids</u> <u>halfway</u> closed so that he could see the ball better. Suddenly, a crack rang out and the <u>baseball</u> came streaking toward Ken like a <u>rocketship</u>. In spite of <u>everyone's</u> doubts, Ken caught the fly and gave his team another chance at bat.

Teaching Chart 54

MODEL In the second sentence, I read the word *sunlight*. This word is made up of the words *sun* and *light,* I know what the sun is and I know what light is. So it is pretty easy to see that the word *sunlight* is used to describe the light that comes from the sun.

Have students use a similar process to figure out what the word *sportsman* means in the third sentence. (a man who plays sports)

Figure Out Meanings of Compound Words

ONE

Have volunteers underline each compound word in "A Great Game!" Then have them divide each word into its parts, tell the meanings of the separate parts, and figure out the meaning of the whole word. Have them reread the sentences to see if their meanings make sense.
▶ Linguistic/Logical

ASSESS/CLOSE

Find, Illustrate, and Use Compound Words

GROUP

Have students work in small groups to find five compound words in *Baseball Saved Us.* (Examples: sagebrush, endless, nobody, bathroom, outside, guardhouse, sunglasses, teammates)

Have groups illustrate or act out each word and challenge other groups to figure out what the compound words are. Then encourage groups to write a short paragraph or poem using their five words.

ALTERNATE TEACHING STRATEGY

COMPOUND WORDS
For a different approach to teaching this skill, see page T65.

Meeting Individual Needs for Vocabulary

EASY	ON-LEVEL	CHALLENGE	LANGUAGE SUPPORT

EASY

Name_____ Date_____ Reteach **65**

Compound Words

A **compound word** is made up of two smaller words. You can usually figure out the meaning of the compound word by looking at the two smaller words and putting their meanings together.

Make a compound word by joining a word in the list to the end of one of the numbered words. Then write a sentence using the compound word. Answers will vary.

brush	boat	pot	place	cloth	flake	coat	light

1. wash _____ cloth
Sample answer: I folded the washcloth over the towel rack.

2. snow _____ flake
Sample answer: The snowflakes fell gently.

3. fire _____ place
Sample answer: After sledding, we built a fire in the fireplace.

4. tooth _____ brush
Sample answer: I used an old toothbrush to clean grandpa's medal.

5. moon _____ light
Sample answer: The snow glistened in the moonlight.

6. motor _____ boat
Sample answer: The motorboat was faster and easier than the canoe.

7. rain _____ coat
Sample answer: When it started to rain, I remembered my raincoat.

8. flower _____ pot
Sample answer: He carefully planted tulips in the flowerpot.

At Home: Have students make compound words using each of the following words: horse, born, shoe, tag.
Book 4/Unit 2 Baseball Saved Us 8
65

ON-LEVEL

Name_____ Date_____ Practice **65**

Compound Words

Study the **compound words** below. Write each of the two smaller words that make up each compound. Then write a sentence using the compound word. Sentences will vary. Examples are given.

1. baseball ____ base ____ ball
Mom always picks us up after baseball practice.

2. everyone ____ every ____ one
Everyone was nervous about the spelling competition.

3. anything ____ any ____ thing
Would you like me to bring you anything from the store?

4. bathroom ____ bath ____ room
It's my job to clean the bathroom every Saturday.

5. flashlight ____ flash ____ light
We were glad we had a flashlight while counting.

6. teammates ____ team ____ mates
Each of our teammates is equally important.

7. sunglasses ____ sun ____ glasses
Sarah lost her sunglasses at the pool.

8. sidewalk ____ side ____ walk
The town has many sidewalk cafes.

9. weekend ____ week ____ end
Because of the holiday, we had a long weekend.

10. backyard ____ back ____ yard
Sometimes I help my sister garden in the backyard.

65
At Home: Have students write a paragraph using compound words.
Book 4/Unit 2 Baseball Saved Us 10

CHALLENGE

Name_____ Date_____ Extend **65**

Compound Words

Baseball is a **compound word**. It is made up of the words *base* and *ball*. Use the words below to make as many compound words as you can. Write them on the lines.

any	end	no	time
guard	thing	in	less
field	body	day	house
park	out	ball	fit

anybody, anytime, anything, endless, nobody, nothing, daytime, infield, guardhouse, ballpark, outfit

Suppose that you are a sportscaster for a radio show. You're going to interview a famous baseball player. Use some of the compound words you made above to write questions to ask the player.
Answers will vary, but should include some of the compound words formed above.

_____
_____
_____
_____
_____

65
At Home: Have students list five compound words from a newspaper, magazine, or story.
Book 4/Unit 2 Baseball Saved Us

LANGUAGE SUPPORT

Name_____ Date_____

Bases Loaded!

1. In the center of each baseball diamond is a word that can be put together with the words below to make several compound words. 2. See how many different compound words you can make. 3. Cut out the bases and paste each one on a base in the baseball diamonds. 4. Write the compound words on the lines below the baseball diamonds.

everything	nothing	everywhere	nowhere
anything	something	anywhere	somewhere

every	no	no	some
any	every	every	some

72 Baseball Saved Us • Language Support /Blackline Master 36 Grade 4

GRAMMAR/SPELLING CONNECTIONS

See the 5-Day Grammar and Usage Plan on possessive nouns, pages 241M–241N.

See the 5-Day Spelling Plan on plurals, pages 241O–241P.

TECHNOLOGY TIP

Point out that many newspaper articles are written in column format. Mention that some word-processing programs allow you to set up your page layout to accommodate column format. Have a volunteer show how to use the column format feature.

Writing That Compares

Prewrite

WRITE A SPORTS COLUMN Present this writing assignment: Imagine you are a wartime sports writer reporting on games at the Japanese American camp. Compare camp baseball to games played in other communities. Tell how and why the settings are different. Talk about how the games seem different and alike.

BRAINSTORM LISTS Ask students how they think baseball in the camp would have been different from games played outside camp. Have them make lists: How would the players feel? What would motivate them to win? How would spectators be alike and different?

Strategy: Make A Venn Diagram Have students organize their lists in a Venn diagram. Help students to use their diagrams effectively by separating ideas under headings marked **In Camp, Outside Camp,** and **Both Places.**

In Camp
People can't leave. Baseball is the main activity. Only people in the camp can watch. Players and spectators use baseball to keep up their spirits.

Both Places
Same rules. Spectators love the game. Players enjoy the excitement of competing. It takes practice to be good. People root for their favorite players.

Outside Camp
People can come and go. More activities than baseball. Anyone can go to a game. Players compete for fun and money.

Draft

Develop the Ideas Students should draw on their diagrams to show differences and similarities between baseball games inside and outside camp. Have them conclude by stating why camp games were unique.

Revise

SELF-QUESTIONING Ask students to assess their drafts for improvement.

- Did I begin with a strong statement?
- Did I compare baseball inside and outside camp?
- At the end, did I tell why the camp games were special?

Have students exchange their work to check for clear comparisons.

Edit/Proofread

CHECK FOR ERRORS AND DETAILS Have students recheck their papers for spelling, punctuation, and indentions.

Publish

SHARE THE SPORTS COLUMNS Students may wish to mount their typed columns on a piece of newsprint, add graphic design features of a sports page, and add a baseball picture cut out of a sports magazine.

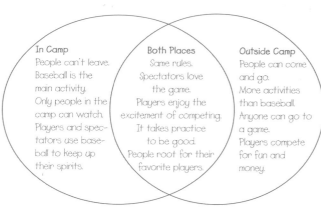

Camp Baseball

Japanese Americans in camps can't leave until the end of the war. To make their hard lives easier, they have organized baseball games. Their players are some of the best around!

Camp baseball games are different from games in other places, where people can go home after a game is over. Japanese American players and fans have to stay in the camps. In most places, people attend games for entertainment. They are just one of many fun things to do. In the camps, however, baseball is the only big event. Both players and fans use baseball to hold up their pride in a tough situation.

Still, some things about baseball are the same everywhere. Players practice a lot because they love to compete. The rules are the same. Fans are loyal to their teams and root for their favorite players. These things help Japanese Americans keep up their spirits as they wait to return to their homes.

Presentation Ideas

ILLUSTRATE A SPORTS COLUMN
Have students illustrate a suspenseful scene from Ken's game. Students can mount their illustrations on their facsimile newspaper sports page. ▶ **Viewing/Representing**

REPORT THE GAME Have students use their articles to create dramatic "radio" reports on the topic of Japanese American camp baseball.

▶ **Speaking/Listening**

Consider students' creative efforts, possibly adding a plus (+) for originality, wit, and imagination.

Scoring Rubric

Excellent	Good	Fair	Unsatisfactory
4: The writer • has a strong opening statement. • compares baseball inside and outside the camps in some detail. • ends by showing similarities of baseball everywhere and telling what makes camp games unique.	**3:** The writer • makes an opening statement. • compares baseball inside and outside the camps. • ends with a statement about the games' similarities, and why the camp games are special.	**2:** The writer • attempts to discuss baseball in Japanese American camps. • may not clearly show differences and similarities. • may not present accurate facts or detailed observations.	**1:** The writer • may not present a main idea or use comparisons. • may offer disorganized ideas and observations. • has problems with basic writing conventions.

0: The writer leaves the page blank or fails to respond to the writing task. The student does not address the topic or simply paraphrases the prompt. The response is illegible or incoherent.

For a 6-point or an 8-point scale, see pages T105–T106.

Meeting Individual Needs for Writing

EASY

Certificate of Award Have students design a Most Valuable Player certificate for Ken when he leads his team to victory. Remind them to include information about why Ken is receiving the award. They may decorate it with ribbons, gold seals, and stars.

ON-LEVEL

Interview Ken Have student partners write radio-interview dialogues with Ken. They can ask him to compare how he felt before and after winning the game.

CHALLENGE

Letter Have students write a letter from Ken's point of view. He can write to a sports editor, contrasting his experiences of playing ball in the camp and in his old neighborhood before the war.

COMMUNICATION TIPS

SPEAKING Before students present their sports columns orally, have them listen to actual radio or television sports reporters.

REPRESENTING Students can model baseball poses for each other's drawings.

LANGUAGE SUPPORT

ESL Second-language learners may need extra help using sports terminology and slang correctly. Have them share their first drafts with English-fluent partners who can help them figure out how to phrase their descriptions.

PORTFOLIO Invite students to include their sports columns in their writing portfolios.

5 Day Grammar and Usage Plan

ESL Some students may confuse plurals and possessives. Compare the formation of plurals with that of singular and plural possessives, and offer practice opportunities.

DAILY LANGUAGE ACTIVITIES

Write the Daily Language Activities on the chalkboard each day or use **Transparency 9.** Have students correct the sentences orally. For answers, see the transparency.

Day 1
1. They all liked Dads idea.
2. One guards face seemed scary.
3. Kens team pulled together.

Day 2
1. Baseball is a fun childrens game.
2. The boys moms sewed uniforms.
3. Babies cries kept Ken awake.

Day 3
1. The kids shouts meant they won the game.
2. Ken ran around the fields bases.
3. The womens sewing was excellent.

Day 4
1. One players glove didn't fit.
2. Teddys mood was really bad.
3. The mothers made both teams uniforms.

Day 5
1. They all knew the games rules.
2. The campers lives were boring at first.
3. Ken appreciated his fathers help.

Daily Language Transparency 9

DAY 1 — Introduce the Concept

Oral Warm-Up Read aloud: *The player's shirt was dirty.* Point out the singular possessive noun ending -'s.

Introduce Possessive Nouns Possessive nouns show ownership.

Possessive Nouns

- A **possessive noun** is a noun that shows who or what owns or has something.
- A **singular possessive noun** is a singular noun that shows ownership.
- Form a singular possessive noun by adding an **apostrophe (')** and an *s* to a singular noun.

Present the Daily Language Activity. Then have students write the possessives of *Dad, guard,* and *Ken* and use each word in a sentence.

 Assign the daily Writing Prompt on page 216C.

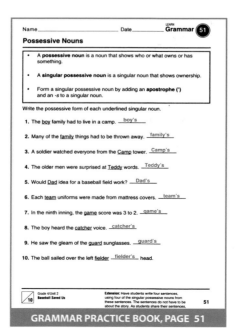

Name_____ Date_____ **Grammar 51**

Possessive Nouns

- A **possessive noun** is a noun that shows who or what owns or has something.
- A **singular possessive noun** is a singular noun that shows ownership.
- Form a singular possessive noun by adding an **apostrophe (')** and an *-s* to a singular noun.

Write the possessive form of each underlined singular noun.

1. The <u>boy</u> family had to live in a camp. ___boy's___
2. Many of the <u>family</u> things had to be thrown away. ___family's___
3. A soldier watched everyone from the <u>Camp</u> tower. ___Camp's___
4. The older men were surprised at <u>Teddy</u> words. ___Teddy's___
5. Would <u>Dad</u> idea for a baseball field work? ___Dad's___
6. Each <u>team</u> uniforms were made from mattress covers. ___team's___
7. In the ninth inning, the <u>game</u> score was 3 to 2. ___game's___
8. The boy heard the <u>catcher</u> voice. ___catcher's___
9. He saw the gleam of the <u>guard</u> sunglasses. ___guard's___
10. The ball sailed over the left <u>fielder</u> head. ___fielder's___

Grade 4/Unit 2 *Baseball Saved Us* — **Extension:** Have students write four sentences, using four of the singular possessive nouns from these sentences. The sentences do not have to be about the story. As students share their sentences, — 51

GRAMMAR PRACTICE BOOK, PAGE 51

DAY 2 — Teach the Concept

Review Possessive Nouns Read aloud: *The ball's cover flew off. The player's hat blew off.* Have students identify the possessive nouns.

Introduce Plural Possessives Plural possessives take different forms.

Plural Possessive Nouns

- A **plural possessive noun** is a plural noun that shows ownership.
- To form the possessive of a plural noun that ends in -*s*, add an apostrophe.
- To form the possessive of a plural noun that does not end in -*s*, add an apostrophe and -*s*.

Present the Daily Language Activity. Then have students write the singular and plural possessives for *child, boy,* and *baby.*

 Assign the daily Writing Prompt on page 216C.

Name_____ Date_____ **Grammar 52**

Plural Possessive Nouns

- A **plural possessive noun** is a plural noun that shows ownership.
- To form the possessive of a plural noun that ends in *s*, add an apostrophe.
- To form the possessive of a plural noun that does not end in *s*, add an apostrophe and an -*s*.

Write the possessive form of each underlined plural noun. Add an apostrophe or an apostrophe and -*s*.

1. In Camp, the <u>babies</u> cries kept people awake. ___babies'___
2. The <u>soldiers</u> job was to watch everyone. ___soldiers'___
3. The sound of the <u>women</u> sewing machines filled the room. ___women's___
4. The <u>men</u> work was building the bleachers. ___men's___
5. Soon the <u>families</u> children helped pack down the dust. ___families'___
6. There were bats, balls, and gloves in the <u>friends</u> sacks. ___friends'___
7. The <u>kids</u> teams played all the time. ___kids'___
8. After his home run, the boy rode on his <u>teammates</u> shoulders. ___teammates'___

Extension: Ask students to write sentences from the story. Have them use the possessive forms of these plural nouns: *players, parents, children, teams.* — Grade 4/Unit 2 *Baseball Saved Us* — 52

GRAMMAR PRACTICE BOOK, PAGE 52

Possessive Nouns

Learn from the Literature Review possessive nouns. Read the last sentence in the first paragraph on page 231 of *Baseball Saved Us*:

> **The ball went over the head of the left fielder.** (the left fielder's head)

Tell students that sometimes ownership is shown with the word *of*, as in *the head of the left fielder*. Have students rewrite the sentence to include a possessive noun.

Form Possessive Nouns Present the Daily Language Activity and have students correct the sentences orally. Then have students make a two-column chart. Ask them to write five singular and five plural nouns from the story in column one. Then, they should write the possessives for each in column two.

 Assign the daily Writing Prompt on page 216D.

Review Possessive Nouns Write the possessive nouns from the Daily Language Activity for Days 1–3 on the board. Ask students to name the rule that is used to create each possessive noun: (For example, *camp's*: a singular possessive noun adds -'s.) Then present the Daily Language Activity.

Mechanics and Usage Review the use of apostrophes in possessive nouns.

Apostrophes

- Add an apostrophe and an -s to a singular noun to make it possessive.

- Add an apostrophe to make most plural nouns possessive.

- Add an apostrophe and -s to form the possessive of plural nouns that do not end in -s.

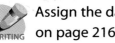 Assign the daily Writing Prompt on page 216D.

Assess Use the Daily Language Activity and page 55 of the **Grammar Practice Book** for assessment.

Reteach Have volunteers orally recite the rules about forming singular and plural possessive nouns. Write them as column heads on a chart.

Have pairs of students identify five examples of ownership from the selection. Invite partners to illustrate their examples. (Examples: *the boys' moms, Ken's baseball, the babies' cries*)

Have students display their illustrations on a bulletin board.

Use page 56 of the **Grammar Practice Book** for additional reteaching.

 Assign the daily Writing Prompt on page 216D.

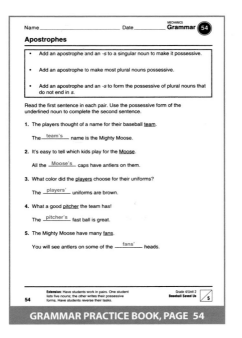

GRAMMAR PRACTICE BOOK, PAGE 53

GRAMMAR PRACTICE BOOK, PAGE 54

GRAMMAR PRACTICE BOOK, PAGE 55

5Day Spelling Plan

ESL If students are still having difficulty remembering when to add -es to form the plural, repeat the Language Support activity on page 198M. Encourage them to think of new words that end in -ses, -shes, -ches, and -xes.

DICTATION SENTENCES

Spelling Words

1. Cities are full of cars.
2. I made two mistakes on the test.
3. Foxes are fast animals.
4. The babies slept all night.
5. Don't play with sharp knives.
6. The drivers started their engines.
7. The soldiers fought bravely.
8. Ranches are huge farms.
9. One of my hobbies is baseball.
10. Don't hurt yourselves on the ice.
11. Deer have long eyelashes.
12. Our uniforms were covered with mud.
13. I bought batteries for my toy.
14. Calves are baby animals.
15. We were digging holes with shovels.
16. My sunglasses blocked the sun.
17. She bought groceries in the store.
18. We ate two loaves of bread.
19. The mattresses are soft and comfortable.
20. Ferries take cars across the river.

Challenge Words

21. He stood on a crate of wood.
22. In a storm, ditches fill with rain.
23. The sea is huge and endless.
24. The sun was glinting on the lake.
25. We scored a point in the first inning.

DAY 1 — Pretest

Assess Prior Knowledge Use the Dictation Sentences at the left and **Spelling Practice Book** page 51 for the pretest. Allow students to correct their own papers. Students who require a modified list may be tested on the first ten words.

Spelling Words		Challenge Words
1. cities	12. **uniforms**	21. **crate**
2. **mistakes**	13. batteries	22. **ditches**
3. foxes	14. calves	23. **endless**
4. **babies**	15. **shovels**	24. **glinting**
5. knives	16. **sun-**	25. **inning**
6. engines	**glasses**	
7. **soldiers**	17. groceries	
8. ranches	18. loaves	
9. hobbies	19. **mat-**	
10. yourselves	**tresses**	
11. eyelashes	20. ferries	

*Note: Words in **dark type** are from the story.*

Word Study On page 52 of the **Spelling Practice Book** are word study steps and an at-home activity.

SPELLING PRACTICE BOOK, PAGE 51
WORD STUDY STEPS AND ACTIVITY, PAGE 52

DAY 2 — Explore the Pattern

Sort and Spell Words Say *soldiers* and *ranches*. Ask students what endings are added to make each word plural. *(-s, -es)* Now say *cities* and *knives*. Discuss how each plural was formed. Have students read the Spelling Words aloud and sort them as below.

Words ending with

s	es	ies
mistakes	foxes	cities
engines	ranches	babies
soldiers	eyelashes	hobbies
uniforms	sunglasses	batteries
shovels	mattresses	groceries
		ferries

ves

knives
yourselves
calves
loaves

Word Wall Have students create a word wall based on the word sort and add more words from their reading.

SPELLING PRACTICE BOOK, PAGE 53

Plurals

DAY 3   Practice and Extend

Word Meaning: Base Words Remind students that a base word is a word without a suffix (*-ful*), word ending (*-s, -es*), or prefix (*dis-*) added to it. Remind them that their spelling words contain plural endings. Explain that sometimes the spelling of a base word changes when an ending is added. Have students identify the base word of each Spelling Word and tell what it means.

If students need extra practice, have partners give each other a midweek test.

Glossary Review the pronunciation key in the Glossary. Have partners:

- write each Challenge Word.

- look up their respellings in the Glossary or in a dictionary.

- circle each short vowel sound.

- draw a box around each long vowel sound.

DAY 4   Proofread and Write

Proofread Sentences Write these sentences on the chalkboard, including the misspelled words. Ask students to proofread, circling incorrect spellings and writing the correct spellings. There are two spelling errors in each sentence.

> The (babees) have pretty (ilashes).
> (babies, eyelashes)
>
> (Calfs) don't live in (citys).
> (calves, cities)

Have students create additional sentences with errors for partners to correct.

Have students use as many Spelling Words as possible in the daily Writing Prompt on page 216D. Remind students to proofread their writing for errors in spelling, grammar, and punctuation.

DAY 5   Assess

Assess Students' Knowledge Use page 56 of the **Spelling Practice Book** or the Dictation Sentences on page 241O for the posttest.

Personal Word List If students have trouble with any words in the lesson, have them add these to their personal lists in their journals. Have students list the words and their base (root) words. Then have them underline the spelling pattern of the plural form.

Students should refer to their word lists during later writing activities.

SPELLING PRACTICE BOOK, PAGE 54

SPELLING PRACTICE BOOK, PAGE 55

SPELLING PRACTICE BOOK, PAGE 56

Will Her Native Language Disappear?

Selection Summary Students will read about how the Choctaw language and many others are in danger of extinction and about efforts to keep them alive through the Endangered Language Fund and other educational efforts.

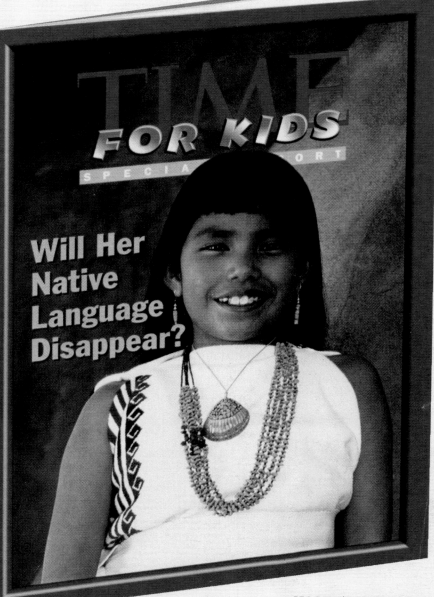

Listening
Library
Audiocassette

INSTRUCTIONAL
Pages 244–251

Resources for Meeting Individual Needs

LEVELED BOOKS

EASY
Pages 251A, 251D

INDEPENDENT
Pages 251B, 251D

CHALLENGE
Pages 251C, 251D

LEVELED PRACTICE

Reteach 66–72
blackline masters with reteaching opportunities for each assessed skill

Practice 66–72
workbook with Take-Home stories and practice opportunities for each assessed skill and story comprehension

Extend 66–72
blackline masters that offer challenge activities for each assessed skill

ADDITIONAL RESOURCES

- **Language Support Book,** 73–80
- **Take-Home Story, Practice,** p. 67a
- **Alternate Teaching Strategies,** T60–T66
- **Selected Quizzes Prepared by** ◢ Accelerated Reader

McGraw-Hill School **TECHNOLOGY**

interNET CONNECTION Research and Inquiry Ideas. Visit www.mhschool.com/reading

Suggested Lesson Planner

READING AND LANGUAGE ARTS

- Comprehension
- Vocabulary
- Phonics/Decoding
- Study Skills
- Listening, Speaking, Viewing, Representing

DAY 1 — Focus on Reading and Skills

Read **Read Aloud and Motivate,** 242E
Indians of the Plains

Develop Visual Literacy, 242/243

☑ **Review Cause and Effect,** 244A–244B
Teaching Chart 55
Reteach, Practice, Extend, 66

DAY 2 — Read the Literature

Build Background, 244C
Develop Oral Language

Vocabulary, 244D

backgrounds	extinct
century	generations
communicate	native

Teaching Chart 56
Word Building Manipulative Cards
Reteach, Practice, Extend, 67

Read **Read the Selection,** 244–247
☑ Cause and Effect
☑ Form Generalizations

- Curriculum Connections

Link Works of Art, 242/243

Link Social Studies, 244C

- Writing

Writing Prompt: Imagine that English is in danger of becoming an extinct language. Write a paragraph describing what you would do to prevent that from happening and why.

Writing Prompt: Write a paragraph describing one student's feelings on her or his first day of school. Include details about other students and their teachers.

Journal Writing, 247
Quick-Write

- Grammar

Introduce the Concept: Plurals vs. Possessives, 251M
Daily Language Activity
1. He reads many word's. words
2. Ask one of the student's. students
3. Many language's are endangered. languages

Grammar Practice Book, 57

Teach the Concept: Plurals vs. Possessives, 251M
Daily Language Activity
1. The groups job is to protect languages. group's
2. LeRoys day was lonely. LeRoy's
3. The picture's are of animals. pictures

Grammar Practice Book, 58

- Spelling

Pretest: Words from Social Studies, 251O
Spelling Practice Book, 57, 58

Explore the Pattern: Words from Social Studies, 251O
Spelling Practice Book, 59

DAY 3 — Read the Literature

Rereading for Fluency, 246

Story Questions, 248
  Reteach, Practice, Extend, 68

Story Activities, 249

Study Skill, 250
  ✔️ Reference Sources
  Teaching Chart 57
  Reteach, Practice, Extend, 69

Test Power, 251

 **Read the Leveled Books,** 251A–251D
  Guided Reading
  Phonics Review
  ✔️ Comprehension Review

Activity Social Studies, 249

Writing Prompt: Think about some skills you would like to learn from an older relative. Write a paragraph explaining how they might be useful.

Writing Process: Writing That Compares, 251K
  Prewrite, Draft

Review and Practice: Plurals vs. Possessives, 251N
  Daily Language Activity
  1. The group prints book's. books
  2. Jims book is here. Jim's
  3. Some teacher's speak Choctaw. teachers

  Grammar Practice Book, 59

Practice and Extend: Words from Social Studies, 251P
  Spelling Practice Book, 60

DAY 4 — Build and Review Skills

Read **Read the Leveled Books and Self-Selected Books**

✔️ **Review Form Generalizations,** 251E–251F
  Teaching Chart 58
  Reteach, Practice, Extend, 70
  Language Support, 78

✔️ **Review Compound Words,** 251G–251H
  Teaching Chart 59
  Reteach, Practice, Extend, 71
  Language Support, 79

Writing Prompt: Write a dialogue between LeRoy Sealy and his niece explaining why it is important to learn the language of one's ancestors.

Writing Process: Writing That Compares, 251K Revise

Meeting Individual Needs for Writing, 251L

Review and Practice: Plurals vs. Possessives, 251N
  Daily Language Activity
  1. Draw a horses body. horse's
  2. A hundred year's is not a long time. years
  3. I met LeRoy six month's ago. months

  Grammar Practice Book, 60

Proofread and Write: Words from Social Studies, 251P
  Spelling Practice Book, 61

DAY 5 — Build and Review Skills

Read **Read Self-Selected Books**

✔️ **Review Context Clues,** 251I–251J
  Teaching Chart 60
  Reteach, Practice, Extend, 72
  Language Support, 80

Listening, Speaking, Viewing, Representing, 251L
  Illustrate the Interview
  Tape the Interviews

Writing Prompt: Write a paragraph about a language other than English spoken by your friends or relatives. Tell about how it is like or unlike English.

Writing Process: Writing That Compares, 251K
  Edit/Proofread, Publish

Assess and Reteach: Plurals vs. Possessives, 251N
  Daily Language Activity
  1. LeRoy had many lonely day's. days
  2. Language's can become extinct. Languages
  3. He knows the words meaning. word's

  Grammar Practice Book, 61–62

Assess and Reteach: Words from Social Studies, 251P
  Spelling Practice Book, 62

Read Aloud and Motivate

Language Arts

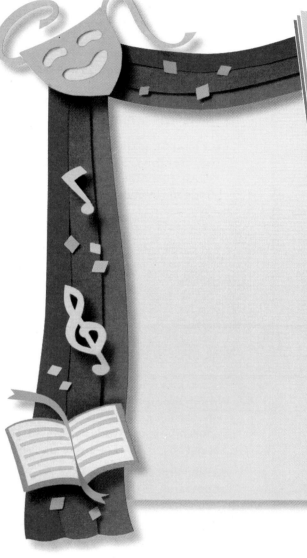

Indians of the Plains

a poem by
Myra Cohn Livingston

I like the names,
the way they sound—

Omaha, Iowa, Sioux,
Pawnee, Winnebago, Potawatomi,

Indian tribes who knew
these prairies before we came,
who lived with the buffalo—
Illinois, Osage, Sauk
                                    who lived

on plains of long ago.

Oral Comprehension

LISTENING AND SPEAKING Read the poem aloud. Encourage students to listen carefully to the names of the Native American groups that are mentioned. Ask: "Do you recognize any of these names?" Point out that many places in the United States are named for the Native American groups who first lived there.

Activity Have students paint a picture that illustrates the poem. Before they begin, point out that their painting does not have to be representational; that is, it does not have to show actual things such as buffalo, the plains, and so on. Instead, it could represent the feeling that the poem gives them. Encourage students to think about the colors, lines, and shapes that would express their feelings. ▶ **Visual/Spatial**

Develop **Visual Literacy**

Anthology pages 242–243

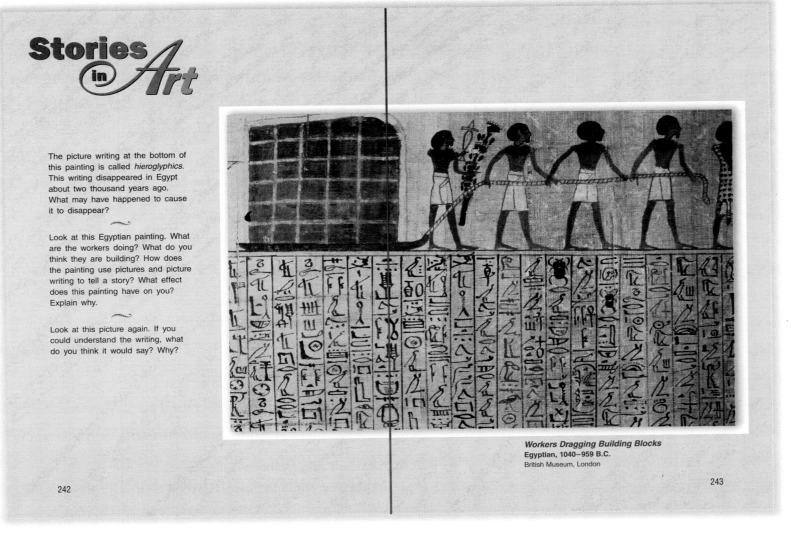

Stories in Art

The picture writing at the bottom of this painting is called *hieroglyphics*. This writing disappeared in Egypt about two thousand years ago. What may have happened to cause it to disappear?

Look at this Egyptian painting. What are the workers doing? What do you think they are building? How does the painting use pictures and picture writing to tell a story? What effect does this painting have on you? Explain why.

Look at this picture again. If you could understand the writing, what do you think it would say? Why?

Workers Dragging Building Blocks
Egyptian, 1040–959 B.C.
British Museum, London

242

243

Objective: Identify Cause and Effect

VIEWING Have students carefully view the wall painting and picture writing. Ask: "Was the artist probably painting to give information or to express feelings? Why do you think that?" Discuss with students the technique of painting one-dimensional figures in profile, used by ancient Egyptian artists, and the complex system of hieroglyphics, a form of picture writing used by the Egyptians.

Read the page with students, encouraging individual interpretations of the painting and picture writing.

Ask students to support inferences they make about cause-and-effect relationships in the picture. For example:

- Workers have been ordered to drag building blocks to build a structure for the pharaoh.

- The hieroglyphics may be explaining the picture, or the picture may be describing the writing.

REPRESENTING Have students draw or paint their own hieroglyphic message that explains what is happening in the picture and why it is taking place.

OBJECTIVES

Students will determine cause and effect based on text.

Review Cause and Effect

TEACHING TIP

INSTRUCTIONAL Point out to students that causes and effects are often signaled by clue words that come before or after them. For example, the word *because* is often found before a cause. The word *so* is often found before an effect.

PREPARE

Discuss a Familiar Case

Ask students: What happens when someone cuts in line? Write their answers on the chalkboard. Explain that cutting in line is a *cause*; it tells "why something happened." An *effect* tells "what happened."

TEACH

Read the Passage and Model the Skill

Tell students: You can understand the relationships among actions and events by noticing causes and effects.

The Choctaw

The Choctaw are a Native American people who formerly lived in what are now Alabama, Mississippi, and Louisiana. They were farmers who grew corn, beans, sweet potatoes, pumpkins, and tobacco. They also raised cattle, fished, and hunted for food.

Between the 1700s and the 1800s, the Choctaw were pushed farther and farther west (to make room for settlers from Europe.) By 1842, they were forced to give most of their land to the United States and settle on lands in Oklahoma. Today, the Choctaw still live mainly in Oklahoma.

Teaching Chart 55

Display **Teaching Chart 55.** Ask students to think about the questions *What happened to the Choctaw?* and *Why did it happen?* as you read the passage.

MODEL My first question is *What happened to the Choctaw?* My answer is *The Choctaw were forced to move west to Oklahoma.*

Identify Cause

Have students ask themselves "Why were the Choctaw forced to move?" Then ask students to circle the cause for the move.

Create a Cause and Effect Chart

Have groups brainstorm reasons why people might have to move today. Using a two-column Cause and Effect chart, students should record the reasons (causes) why each result (effect) occurred.

▶ **Logical/ Interpersonal**

CAUSE Why Something Happens	EFFECT What Happens
Parents got new jobs.	Family had to move to a new town.
Mother had another baby.	Family moved to bigger house.
Family got tired of living in the city.	They moved to a smaller town.

ASSESS/CLOSE

Make Cause and Effect Statements

Ask each student to make a cause-and-effect statement about a time when he or she had to change seats, classes, or schools. Students should identify the cause and the effect in each statement.

SELECTION Connection

Students will apply cause and effect when they read *Will Her Native Language Disappear?* and the Leveled Books.

ALTERNATE TEACHING STRATEGY

CAUSE AND EFFECT

For a different approach to teaching this skill, see page T66.

Meeting Individual Needs for Comprehension

EASY	ON-LEVEL	CHALLENGE

EASY — Reteach, 66

Name_____ Date_____ Reteach 66

Cause and Effect

Noting **cause** and **effect** relationships as you read will help you better understand and enjoy the selection.

Read the story. Then fill in the missing causes and effects in the chart.

Almost every day, Richard rode his horse around the edge of his ranch. Two months ago, Richard found a stray dog sleeping near the back gate. Someone had left the gate open by mistake.

The dog had no tags. Richard called his neighbors and the local sheriff. None of them knew about any dogs that were missing. So, Richard decided to take care of the dog himself.

At first, the dog was very weak. He must have been wandering for days without food. But Richard fed the dog and slowly the dog recovered. After a few weeks, the dog was running around and chasing birds. Richard decided to name the dog Birdman.

Effect, or what happened	Cause, or why it happened
1. A dog wandered into the ranch.	Someone left the back gate open by mistake.
2. Richard called his neighbors and the local sheriff.	Richard wanted to find out who the dog belonged to.
3. Richard decided to take care of the dog himself.	No one knew who the dog belonged to.
4. The dog became very weak.	The dog wandered for days without food.
5. Richard decided to name the dog Birdman.	The dog chased birds.

Book 4/Unit 2
Will Her Native Language Disappear?

At Home: Have students identify some effects of a storm, such as a hurricane or tornado.

66

ON-LEVEL — Practice, 66

Name_____ Date_____ Practice 66

Cause and Effect

One event can cause another event to happen. This kind of relationship is called cause and effect. Read the selection below. Then write an effect for each cause. Answers may vary.

The Catawba people lived in the region that is now the Southeastern part of the United States. The warm climate and plentiful forests made this area a good home. The Catawba celebrated the abundance of the land with ceremonies, customs, and skills that have survived for centuries.

One of these skills that has survived to this day is pottery-making. Before Columbus came to the Americas, Catawba women created clay cooking pots and special bowls for important ceremonies. Later on, when the English came, the Catawba traded these beautiful red clay pots for iron tools. Today, Catawba potters continue to use the same techniques that have been handed down from generation to generation for hundreds of years.

Cause	Effect
1. The climate was warm and the land was plentiful.	The area was a good home for those who lived there.
2. The Catawba celebrated the abundance of the land.	They celebrated the land with ceremonies, customs, and skills.
3. The Catawba used special bowls for important ceremonies.	Women created special clay bowls for these ceremonies.
4. Techniques were handed down from generation to generation.	Catawba pottery is made today with techniques that have been followed for hundreds of years.

Book 4/Unit 2
Will Her Native Language Disappear?

At Home: Have students create a cause and effect chart using information from their lives to fill in the columns.

66

CHALLENGE — Extend, 66

Name_____ Date_____ Extend 66

Cause and Effect

Have you ever read a story or watched a movie that was set in another time and place? What things about the characters seemed different to you? Think about **cause and effect** to help you write a description of the different ways of the characters. Tell why you think the characters dressed, acted, or behaved differently.

Answers will vary but should include cause and effect relationships.

Book 4/Unit 2
Will Her Native Language Disappear?

At Home: Talk with an adult family member about how he or she decided what to do to earn a living.

66

Reteach, 66   Practice, 66   Extend, 66

244B

Build Background

Link
Social Studies

TEACHING TIP

MANAGEMENT To help students gather information for "A Chance Meeting," set up a "Native American Information Center" with books and posters about Native Americans.

LANGUAGE SUPPORT

ESL See the Language Support Book, pages 73–76, for teaching suggestions for Build Background and Vocabulary.

Evaluate Prior Knowledge

CONCEPT: NATIVE AMERICAN CULTURES *Native Americans* is the name given to people who lived in North, Central, and South America before settlers from Europe arrived. Have students share knowledge of Native Americans. Point out that each native people has its own traditions, values, and language.

RECORD INFORMATION ABOUT NATIVE AMERICAN LANGUAGES Have students complete a K-W-L chart with information that they know and want to know about Native American languages. Ask students to leave the *L* column blank and complete it after they read the article.

▶ **Logical/Visual**

KNOW	WANT TO KNOW	LEARN
• Different groups spoke different languages. • Sometimes several groups spoke related languages.	• Do Native Americans still speak their languages today? • Are Native American languages written down?	

A CHANCE MEETING Have students suppose they are members of Native American groups who do not speak the same language and are meeting each other 200 years ago. How would they communicate? What would they want to know or say? Have student pairs write stories to describe the meeting.

Develop Oral Language

DISCUSS NATIVE AMERICANS Share pictures of traditional Native American homes, villages, and people with students. Ask them to tell what they know about traditional Native American life from the pictures. Record student ideas on the board.

Point out that each of the many different Native American peoples has a unique culture. Discuss what students know about the native groups in your area.

Explain that this selection focuses on the Choctaw people, who traditionally were farmers, raising corn and other crops. Discuss why their lifestyle may have changed from the time before European settlers arrived and why it might be difficult for them to keep alive some longstanding traditions.

Vocabulary

Key Words

A Visit to the Past

1. What if you could travel back in time <u>100 years</u> to the last (century?) **2.** Would you like to visit <u>people</u> of past (generations?) **3.** Would it be easy to (communicate) in ways <u>they could under-stand</u>? **4.** Would the people speak any languages that are (extinct,) or <u>no longer used</u> today? **5.** Would you want to know about the people's (backgrounds,) such as <u>where they come from</u>? **6.** Would even your (native) language, which you have been hearing <u>since you were born</u>, sound different?

Teaching Chart 56

Definitions

century (p. 247) period of 100 years

generations (p. 247) groups of people born around the same time

communicate (p. 245) send and receive information

extinct (p. 246) no longer existing

backgrounds (p. 247) people's experiences or learning

native (p. 245) belonging to a person by birth

SPELLING/VOCABULARY CONNECTIONS

See Spelling Challenge Words, pages 2510 –251P.

Vocabulary in Context

IDENTIFY VOCABULARY WORDS
Display **Teaching Chart 56** and read it with students. Have volunteers circle each vocabulary word and underline words that are clues to its meaning.

DISCUSS MEANINGS Ask questions like these to help students understand each word:

- How many years are in a century?

- What inventions do people enjoy today that past generations didn't have?

- What are some ways people can communicate without talking?

- What is one creature that is extinct?

- Do your parents share similar backgrounds?

- Is this your native state?

Practice

CREATE SENTENCES Ask students to make up a sentence that uses a vocabulary word. Have them write their sentences on pieces of paper, this time excluding the vocabulary word. Ask students to exchange papers with partners and try to complete the sentences. ▶ **Linguistic/Kinesthetic**

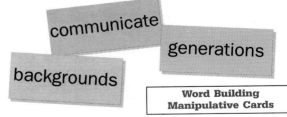

Word Building
Manipulative Cards

WRITE VOCABULARY WORDS Have students use vocabulary words to write brief paragraphs about grandparents or older friends.
▶ **Linguistic/Oral**

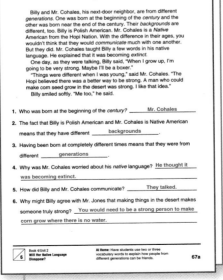

ON-LEVEL

Being Strong

Billy and Mr. Cohales, his next-door neighbor, are from different *generations*. One was born at the beginning of the *century* and the other was born near the end of the century. Their *backgrounds* are different, too. Billy is Polish American. Mr. Cohales is a *Native* American from the Hopi Nation. With the difference in their ages, you wouldn't think that they would *communicate* much with one another. But they did. Mr. Cohales taught Billy a few words in his native language. He explained that it was becoming *extinct*.

One day, as they were talking, Billy said, "When I grow up, I'm going to be very strong. Maybe I'll be a boxer."

"Things were different when I was young," said Mr. Cohales. "The Hopi believed there was a better way to be strong. A man who could make corn seed grow in the desert was strong. I like that idea."

Billy smiled softly. "Me too," he said.

1. Who was born at the beginning of the *century*? _____ Mr. Cohales

2. The fact that Billy is Polish American and Mr. Cohales is Native American means that they have different _____ backgrounds _____.

3. Having been born at completely different times means that they were from different _____ generations _____.

4. Why was Mr. Cohales worried about his *native* language? _____ He thought it was becoming extinct.

5. How did Billy and Mr. Cohales communicate? _____ They talked.

6. Why might Billy agree with Mr. Jones that making things in the desert makes someone truly strong? _____ You would need to be a strong person to make corn grow where there is no water.

Book 4/Unit 2 Will Her Native Language Disappear? **At Home:** Have students use two or three vocabulary words to explain how people from different generations can be friends. 67a

Take-Home Story 67a
Reteach 67
Practice 67 • Extend 67

Guided Instruction

Preview and Predict

Have students read the title and preview the selection, looking at the photographs, section headings, and captions for clues to cause-and-effect links.

- Based on what you see in the photos and drawings, who might the girl on page 244 be?
- Skim the chart on page 246. What language is being explored?
- What do you think this article is about?
- Will this selection be a made-up story or a nonfiction article? (The titles, captions, and photos all suggest a nonfiction article.) *Genre*

Set Purposes

What do students want to learn from this article? For example:

- How can a language die out?
- What happens to people whose language disappears?

TIME FOR KIDS
SPECIAL REPORT

Will Her Native Language Disappear?

Meeting Individual Needs • Grouping Suggestions for Strategic Reading

EASY	ON-LEVEL	CHALLENGE
Read Together Read the article with students or have them use the **Listening Library Audiocassette.** Have students use the Cause and Effect chart to record what happened as described in the article and why it happened. Guided Instruction prompts offer additional help with comprehension.	**Guided Reading** Introduce the story words listed on page 245. Have students read the article together first, or have them read the article independently. Use the Guided Instruction questions to aid in comprehension. Have students use the Cause and Effect chart to record what happens in the article and why it happened.	**Read Independently** Have students read the article independently. Remind them that identifying causes and effects will help them understand how events are related. Have students create a Cause and Effect chart as on page 244B.

Troubled Tongues

Even languages can be in danger of dying out

LeRoy Sealy's first day of first grade was probably the loneliest day of his life. He couldn't speak to any of the kids in his class. And he couldn't understand what they were saying. "I was pretty much alone, because I couldn't communicate," says Sealy, a Native American. "I didn't learn English until starting school." Sealy knew only the Choctaw language. No one else in his class could speak it.

Now grown up, Sealy teaches the Choctaw language at the University of Oklahoma. He still speaks Choctaw. So do about 12,000 other people. But Sealy worries about the future of his native language. Choctaw is on the endangered-language list.

①

②

Most Choctaw live in Oklahoma.

LeRoy Sealy helps his niece Patricia learn their native language, Choctaw.

245

Guided Instruction

☑ **Cause and Effect**
☑ **Form Generalizations**

Strategic Reading As we read, let's make a Cause and Effect chart to record what happened according to the article and why it happened. We can use the chart we created in our Cause and Effect lesson on page 244B as a model.

① **CAUSE AND EFFECT** Why was LeRoy Sealy's first day of first grade the loneliest day of his life? (He couldn't communicate because he couldn't speak English. He spoke Choctaw.)

② **FORM GENERALIZATIONS** Do you think it is scary for most children who don't speak English to go to an English-speaking school? Explain your answer. (Sample answer: Yes, because they can't understand any of the teacher's directions or the words of their classmates.)

Story Words

The words below may be unfamiliar. Have students check their meanings and pronunciations in the Glossary beginning on page 726 or in a dictionary.

• history, p. 247
• pottery, p. 247

LANGUAGE SUPPORT

A blackline master of the Cause and Effect chart is available in the **Language Support Book.**

Name_____ Date_____
Cause and Effect

Cause	Effect
Why Something Happens	What Happens

Grade 4   Language Support/Blackline Master 37 • Will Her Native Language Disappear? 77
LANGUAGE SUPPORT, 77

Guided Instruction

3 Do you think the Choctaw language will become extinct? Why or why not? (Sample answer: No, because people like LeRoy Sealy are working hard to keep it alive by teaching it to students and younger family members.) *Draw Conclusions*

4 **CAUSE AND EFFECT** Let's use our Cause and Effect chart to answer the following questions: What is happening to the Choctaw language? Why is it happening? How is the language being helped? Who is helping preserve it?

CAUSE Why Something Happens	EFFECT What Happens
A small group of Choctaw speakers live among a large group of English speakers, so	The Choctaw language is disappearing.
Native American children were told not to speak their native language, so	The Choctaw language is disappearing.
Many young Choctaw people don't want to speak the language of older relatives, so	The Choctaw language is disappearing.
Leroy Sealy teaches Choctaw at the University of Oklahoma, so	Young people can learn and carry on the Choctaw language.

ORGANIZE INFORMATION Ask volunteers to tell what they have learned about the Choctaw language. Then have volunteers complete the *L* column of their K-W-L charts. *Summarize*

When you hear the words *endangered* or extinct, you probably think of animals and other wildlife. But languages can also be endangered or extinct. People who study languages say about half the world's 6,500 languages may disappear in the next 100 years.

One group trying to change this is the Endangered Language Fund. The group prints books and makes recordings of languages that are dying out. By doing this, they may help keep some Native American languages alive.

How does a language become endangered? The most common way is that a small group of people who speak one language live among a large group of people who speak another language. The smaller group often starts to use the larger group's language and forgets its own. This has happened with Native Americans who have given up their own language to speak English.

3 Telephones, computers, and TV have spread languages spoken by a lot of people, such as English, across the planet.

Chat in Choctaw

Here is how to spell and say some common Choctaw words.

hello	halito (*ha*-li-to)
thank you	yakoke (*yay*-co-kee)
friend	ikana (n-*kah*-na)
good morning	onahinli achukma (o-na-*hin*-lee a-chuk-*ma*)
I'll see you later	chi pisala hakinli (chee pee-*sah*-la ha-*kin*-lee)

Loksi **is the Choctaw word for turtle.**

246

REREADING FOR *Fluency*

PARTNERS Have students reread "Picture This!" with a partner. Encourage them to pay careful attention to punctuation such as commas as they strive for smooth word flow.

READING RATE You may want to evaluate a student's reading rate. Have the student read aloud from *Will Her Native Language Disappear?* for one minute; ask the student to place a self-stick note after the last

word read. Then count the number of words he or she has read.

Alternatively, you could assess small groups or the whole class together by having students count words and record their own scores.

A Running Record form provided in **Diagnostic/Placement Evaluation** will help you evaluate reading rate(s).

Sealy believes that sometimes governments have hurt native languages. "Native American children sent to government schools in the 1950s and '60s were told not to speak their native languages," he says. Instead, these kids spoke English and forgot their native tongues.

Some endangered languages face another problem. Many young people don't want to speak the language of their older relatives. Sealy hopes young Native Americans will learn to value their backgrounds and their language.

Sealy has taught Choctaw to his niece, Patricia Sealy. "We encourage her," he says, "because the younger generations will be the ones to carry the language into the 21st century."

④

FIND OUT MORE
Visit our website:
www.mhschool.com/reading

*inter*NET
CONNECTION

Picture This!

Picture writing was used by Native Americans to record events about their lives, family histories, and the history of their tribes. Word signs were written on rocks, hides, bone, bark, and pottery. Picture writing made it possible for tribes who spoke different languages to communicate with each other.

Try picture writing yourself! Use some of the picture words here to make a story. Create your own pictures for words you would like to use.

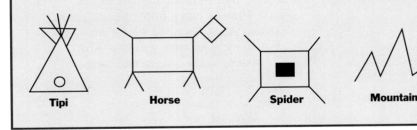

Up   Down

Sky

Tipi   Horse   Spider   Mountain

Based on an article in *TIME FOR KIDS*.

247

Guided Instruction

Return to Predictions and Purposes

Review with students their predictions about the article. Were they correct? Did they find out what they wanted to know?

CAUSE AND EFFECT

HOW TO ASSESS

• Ask: What happened to the Choctaw language? Why did it happen? Then have students identify which statement is a cause and which is an effect.

Students should recognize that the Choctaw language is threatened for several reasons. (fewer users, past educational rules which disallowed use of Choctaw, lack of interest among young Choctaw)

FOLLOW UP If students have trouble recognizing a cause-and-effect relationship regarding the status of the Choctaw language, guide them with a "cause" statement. For example: *Choctaw children went to school where they couldn't speak their own language, so . . .* Then have students complete the sentence.

LITERARY RESPONSE

QUICK-WRITE Ask students to record their thoughts about the Choctaw and their language. Suggest these questions as starters:

• Who were the Choctaw?

• What does Choctaw sound like when spoken aloud?

ORAL RESPONSE Have students share their journal responses with a group. Have groups discuss which parts of the article they found the most interesting.

*inter*NET
CONNECTION For more information about the Choctaw people today, have students go to **www.mhschool. com/reading** Then have groups begin a fact sheet about what they have learned.

Story Questions

Have students discuss or write answers to the questions on page 248.

Answers:

1. Choctaw *Literal/Details*

2. It could become extinct because few people learn and use it. *Inferential/Cause and Effect*

3. Sample answer: Language is an important tool for interpreting and handing down culture. *Inferential/Form Generalizations*

4. It is important to teach endangered languages to a new generation. *Critical/Summarize*

5. Sample answer: Yes. They both think it is important to pass along the culture.

Write a Diary Entry For a full writing process lesson related to this writing suggestion, see the lesson on Writing That Compares on pages 251K–251L.

Story Questions & Activities

1. What language did LeRoy Sealy speak as a child?

2. What might happen to the Choctaw language? Why?

3. Why is saving Native American languages important?

4. What is the main idea of this article?

5. Imagine that LeRoy Sealy met Justin's grandfather in "Justin and the Best Biscuits in the World." Do you think they would agree on why it is important to teach young people about the past? Explain.

Write a Diary Entry

LeRoy Sealy's first day of school was perhaps the loneliest day of his life. He couldn't speak English and couldn't understand anyone in his class. Write a diary entry about your first day at school. Compare how you felt then with how you feel now. Clearly state similarities and differences.

Meeting Individual Needs

EASY

Name_____ Date_____ **Reteach 67**

Vocabulary

Choose the word that matches the meaning. Then fill in the crossword puzzle.

communicate	extinct	native
backgrounds	generations	century

Across
2. exchange information; make known
4. gone; dead
5. experiences; environments

Down
1. stages in family history
2. period of 100 years
3. relating to a certain person or place

(crossword puzzle: c o m m u n i c a t e / e x t i n c t / b a c k g r o u n d s / g e n e r a t i o n)

Reteach 68

Story Comprehension

Write **True** or **False** next to each statement about "Will Her Native Language Disappear?" Look back at the article for help.

1. **True** Not being able to communicate makes people lonely.
2. **False** All Native American children speak their native languages.
3. **True** Some people still speak Choctaw.
4. **True** Languages can become endangered or extinct.
5. **True** Many young people do not value their native language.
6. **True** The Endangered Language Fund prints books in languages that are dying out.

At Home: Have students write a short story using at least four vocabulary words.

67–68   Will Her Native Language Disappear?   Book 4/Unit 2

Reteach, 68

ON-LEVEL

Name_____ Date_____ **Practice 68**

Story Comprehension

Answer the questions about "Will Her Native Language Disappear?" You may look back at the article.

1. What does the expression "native language" mean? __A person's native language is the first language he or she speaks.__

2. What is the endangered-language list and why is Choctaw on it? ___ Endangered languages are those that may disappear completely. Only about 12,000 people speak Choctaw now, and the number might become smaller.

3. What does LeRoy Sealy do to keep the Choctaw language from becoming extinct? __He teaches the Choctaw language at the University of Oklahoma.__

4. What does one picture caption tell you about how LeRoy Sealy is keeping the Choctaw language alive in his family? __One picture and caption shows him teaching Choctaw to his niece.__

5. What does the group called the Endangered Language Fund do? __The group makes books and recordings of endangered languages.__

6. How do you say, "Good morning, Friend. I'll see you later," in Choctaw? __onahinli achukma, ikana. chi pisala hakinli.__

At Home: Have students write another Choctaw sentence using the chart in "Will Her Native Language Disappear?"

68   Will Her Native Language Disappear?   Book 4/Unit 2

Practice, 68

CHALLENGE

Name_____ Date_____ **Extend 67**

Vocabulary

communicate	extinct	native
backgrounds	generations	century

Language allows us to communicate. Use the vocabulary words to write a paragraph about how you think language and communication might change in the next century.
Answers will vary but should include some vocabulary words.

Extend 68

Story Comprehension

What are some of the reasons a language may become endangered? Refer to "Will Her Native Language Disappear?" to help you answer.
Answers will vary. Possible answers: People move to a place where another language is spoken and they stop using their own language. As people lose interest in their original language they stop teaching it to their children. Children may not want to learn the language.

At Home: Discuss why it is important to preserve cultures.

67–68   Will Her Native Language Disappear?   Book 4/Unit 2

Extend, 68

Make a Chart

LeRoy Sealy showed you how to spell and say some common Choctaw words. Now it's your turn.

Interview a friend or a family member who speaks another language. Write down in that language how to say words for such ordinary things as *school*, *coat*, and *pencil*. Make a poster illustrating the words in the other language and in English. Be sure you tell what the other language is!

Prepare a Welcome

The first day in a new school can be a lonely experience. How would you make a new student feel welcome? Get together with a small group of classmates to make a list of the things you would do to welcome the student.

Find Out More

LeRoy Sealy is a Choctaw Indian. Learn more about the Choctaw by reading about them in an encyclopedia or a book about Native Americans. What is their history? What games did they play? How did they farm? Share your information with the class.

249

Story Activities

Make a Chart

Materials: poster board, crayons or markers

ONE Have each student share his or her poster with the class and lead a lesson on the language he or she studied.

Prepare a Welcome

GROUP Have groups share their lists. As a whole group, vote for one suggestion from each group's list to implement throughout the year as new students arrive.

Find Out More

RESEARCH AND INQUIRY Have students brainstorm interesting ways to present their information, such as through a fact sheet, mural, poster, skit, or poem.

 For more information on the Choctaw people, students can visit **www.mhschool.com/reading**

FORMAL **A**SSESSMENT

After page 251, see the Selection Assessment and Unit Assessment.

Study Skills

REFERENCE SOURCES

OBJECTIVES Students will identify techniques for conducting an interview.

PREPARE Read the opening paragraph and discuss the questions with students. Display **Teaching Chart 57.**

TEACH Point out that the note card on the teaching chart lists helpful tips for conducting an interview. Have volunteers read the tips aloud.

PRACTICE Have students answer questions 1–5. Review the answers with them. **1.** make a note card of questions **2.** *Who? What? When? Where? Why?* and *How?* **3.** clearly, simply, and politely **4.** to make notes about it; to ask follow-up questions **5.** if you wanted more information about an answer; if a new question occurred to you

ASSESS/CLOSE Have students write five questions to ask LeRoy Sealy's niece Patricia during an interview for an article about learning Choctaw.

Conduct an Interview

The writer had to interview Le Roy Sealy to get information for this article. What makes a good interview? Why is it important to know the right questions to ask? Here are some interviewing tips for you to follow.

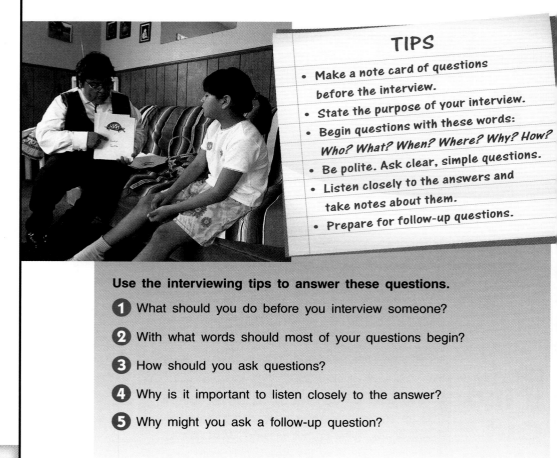

TIPS

- Make a note card of questions before the interview.
- State the purpose of your interview.
- Begin questions with these words: Who? What? When? Where? Why? How?
- Be polite. Ask clear, simple questions.
- Listen closely to the answers and take notes about them.
- Prepare for follow-up questions.

Use the interviewing tips to answer these questions.

1 What should you do before you interview someone?

2 With what words should most of your questions begin?

3 How should you ask questions?

4 Why is it important to listen closely to the answer?

5 Why might you ask a follow-up question?

Meeting Individual Needs

EASY	ON-LEVEL	CHALLENGE

EASY

Name_____ Date_____ **Reteach** 69

Conduct an Interview

The purpose of an **interview** is to gather information about a person. The person who asks the questions is the *interviewer.* The person who answers the questions is the *interviewee.*

Below are some words to remember when preparing to interview someone.

Key Words for Conducting an Interview:
Purpose—Know It
Prepare
Questions: *Who? What? Where? When? Why? How?*
Listen
Take Notes

A famous Olympic skating champion is coming to your school. You have been chosen to interview her at a school assembly. Answer the following questions about your interview with the champion.

1. How would you begin the interview? Introduce myself and the skater to the audience. Tell the purpose of the interview.

2. What would be the purpose of the interview? Possible responses: to learn how the skater became a champion; to learn about her training and experience; to inspire others to work towards their goals.

3. Write three questions you could ask in the interview. Possible responses: When did you start to skate? Who has helped you in your career? What is the most important thing you have learned from skating?

4. If the skater mentions the jumps and turns she does, but you don't understand the skating terms, what should you do? Possible answer: Ask her to explain more in a follow-up question.

Book 4/Unit 2
Will Her Native Language Disappear?
At Home: Have students think of someone they would like to interview, and then have them write four questions for the interview.
69

ON-LEVEL

Name_____ Date_____ **Practice** 69

Conduct an Interview

An **interview** is a meeting between an interviewer who asks questions and a person who is being interviewed. That person has information or an interesting story that the interviewer wants to know more about.

Read the interview plan below. Then answer the questions.
Answers will vary but should be in the correct context.

a. Choose a person to interview who you think is interesting.
b. Think about the person you will interview and what he or she knows. Write good questions to ask that person.
c. Begin the interview by stating your purpose for interviewing.
d. Ask polite, clear questions that use words such as *what? why? where? when? how?*
e. Listen carefully to the answers to your questions and take good notes.

1. On each blank line below write the name of someone you would like to interview:
Family member: _____ Famous person: _____
Neighbor: _____ Owner of a business: _____

2. Choose one person from above. Write what you think would be the most interesting question you could ask that person.
Person: _____
Question: _____

3. Write three questions you would like to ask this person in your interview.
_____
_____

4. State your purpose for interviewing this person. _____

Book 4/Unit 2
Will Her Native Language Disappear?
At Home: Have students write a list of questions for an interview with a family member or a neighbor.
69

CHALLENGE

Name_____ Date_____ **Extend** 69

Conduct an Interview

In an **interview** usually one person asks another person questions to gain information. To conduct a good interview, it is important to plan carefully before you begin. It's also important to be polite and listen carefully during the interview. Taking notes during it will help you organize what you learn from the interview.

Work with a partner. Suppose you were a talk show host who wanted to do a profile, or a short biography, of a guest. What would you want to know? Write a list of questions on an index card. Then interview your partner in the role of guest. Take notes on a separate sheet of paper. Use the notes to write a paragraph telling what you found out about your guest.

Questions:
Answers will vary but should give a clear biographical profile.

Paragraph:
Answers will vary.

Book 4/Unit 2
Will Her Native Language Disappear?
At Home: Have students listen to an interview. Discuss whether or not the interview was a success.
69

Reteach, 69   **Practice, 69**   **Extend, 69**

TEST POWER

Test Tip

Enjoy what you are reading.

DIRECTIONS

Read the sample story. Then read each question about the story.

SAMPLE

The Lucky Day

Every day, Kali's bus passed the stables on its way to take her home. She hoped she would have an opportunity to learn how to ride a horse someday. She loved the way the horses charged around inside the white fence of the <u>corral</u>.

When Kali finished her homework, she rode her bike to the stables. She had been doing this every day for a month. Today she noticed a new woman working with the horses. The woman walked over toward Kali. "Would you like to help me groom Marco?" she asked.

"That would be great," Kali said. This was Kali's lucky day.

1 The word <u>corral</u> in this passage means—

(A) pen

B race

C kitchen

D telephone

2 What is the main idea of this passage?

F Kali enjoyed riding her bicycle.

G Kali did her homework right after school.

H Kali was a daydreamer.

(J) Kali wanted to learn how to ride a horse.

Did you use clues in the story to find the right answer? How?

251

Test Power

Read the Page

Have students read the story. Instruct them to pay close attention to what the characters say.

Discuss the Questions

Question 1: This question asks students to define a word in context. Have students look for clues. The story refers to "inside the white fence of the <u>corral</u>." Ask, "Could the horses be 'inside the white fence of the pen?' Perhaps, but let's leave it and check the other choices." Work through each of the choices as a group. Eliminate answers that don't fit in the sentence.

Question 2: This question asks students to find the main idea. Have students work through each answer choice, eliminating answers that don't make sense. Remind students that the main idea paraphrases the *whole* passage in a few words.

ITBS
Test Preparation and Practice
Grade 4

TERRANOVA
Test Preparation and Practice
Grade 4

Stanford-9
Test Preparation and Practice
Grade 4

ITBS/TEST PREPARATION

TERRANOVA/TEST PREPARATION

SAT 9/TEST PREPARATION

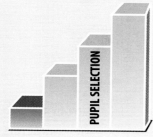

EASY

Phonics

- syllable patterns
- consonant clusters
- ☑ **Comprehension**
- make predictions
- sequence of events
- cause and effect

Answers to Story Questions

Answers will vary and should include examples and details from the stories students have read.

EASY

Story Questions for Selected Reading

1. Who were the main characters in the book?

2. How would you describe your favorite character in the story?

3. What in the story gave you clues to its setting?

4. What was the story mainly about?

5. What other stories have you read that had a similar setting?

Draw a Picture

Draw a picture of the most exciting scene from the book.

Self-Selected Reading
Leveled Books

EASY

UNIT SKILLS REVIEW

Phonics

☑ **Comprehension**

Help students self-select an Easy Book to read and apply phonics and comprehension skills.

Guided Reading

PREVIEW AND PREDICT Discuss the book's title, cover illustration, and table of contents, if present. Ask students to predict what the book is about. List their suggestions on the chalkboard.

SET PURPOSES Have students write a few sentences about why they want to read the book. Encourage them to share their purposes.

READ THE BOOK Use items like the following to guide students' reading or as discussion points after they have read the story independently.

- How did you think the story would end? *Make Predictions*

- Using several main events, tell the story in sequence. *Sequence of Events*

- What caused the characters to act as they did? *Cause and Effect*

- Look back through the story. Can you point out any words beginning with *st, sp, str, spr,* or *thr? Phonics and Decoding*

RETURN TO PREDICTIONS AND PURPOSES Discuss students' predictions. Were they accurate? Why or why not? Have students review their purposes for reading. Did they find out what they wanted to know?

LITERARY RESPONSE Have students discuss questions like the following:

- Think of another ending for the book. Why do you think it would also be a good ending?

- If you could choose to be one of the characters in the book, who would you be? Why?

- Was there another way to solve the problem in the book? Explain.

Self-Selected Reading
Leveled Books

INDEPENDENT

UNIT SKILLS REVIEW

☑ **Comprehension**

Help students self-select an Independent Book to read and apply comprehension skills.

Guided Reading

PREVIEW AND PREDICT Discuss the illustrations at the beginning of the book. Have students predict what the story will be about. List their ideas.

SET PURPOSES Have students write why they want to read the book. Have them share their purposes.

READ THE BOOK Use items like the following to guide students' reading or as discussion points after they have read the book independently.

- After you read the first few pages, what did you think the story would be about? Did you change your mind as you read? *Make Predictions*

- What generalization can you form based on the events in the first part of the story? *Form Generalizations*

- What caused the main problem in the story? *Cause and Effect*

- What happened in the beginning of the story? What happened at the end? *Sequence of Events*

- What is the main idea of the story? *Main Idea*

RETURN TO PREDICTIONS AND PURPOSES Have students review their predictions and discuss whether they were accurate. Ask students whether their purposes were met. Students who read the same book can discuss unanswered questions they may have.

LITERARY RESPONSE The following questions will help focus students' responses:

- If a classmate asked whether you liked the book, what would you say? Why?

- What part of the book did you like most? Explain.

- If you could say one thing to a character in the book or the narrator, what would it be?

Comprehension

- make predictions

- sequence of events

- cause and effect

Answers to Story Questions

Answers will vary and should include examples and details from the stories students have read.

INDEPENDENT

Story Questions for Selected Reading

1. When do the events in the story take place? How can you tell?

2. Why do you think the author wrote this story?

3. How would you summarize the story for a friend?

4. What is this story mainly about?

5. Have you seen a movie or read another book like this one?

Write a Review

Write a book review briefly summarizing the story and explaining why you did or did not like it.

PUPIL SELECTION

CHALLENGE

☑ **Comprehension**

- make predictions
- sequence of events
- cause and effect

Answers to Story Questions

Answers will vary and should include examples and details from the stories students have read.

CHALLENGE

Story Questions for Selected Reading

1. Where does this story take place?

2. What are some of the problems in the story? How are they solved?

3. Do you think the events in the story did or did not happen in real life? Explain.

4. What is this story mainly about?

5. Did this story remind you of some other story you have read or heard? How were they alike?

Write a Letter

Write a letter to a friend telling her or him about the book you just read.

Self-Selected Reading
Leveled Books

CHALLENGE

UNIT SKILLS REVIEW

☑ **Comprehension**

Help students self-select a Challenge Book to read and apply comprehension skills.

Guided Reading

PREVIEW AND PREDICT Discuss the book cover and the illustrations. Have students discuss what the story will be about. List their ideas. If the book has a table of contents, ask students to use it to help them predict.

SET PURPOSES Have students write in their journals why they want to read the book. Have them share their purposes.

READ THE BOOK Use items like the following to guide students' reading or to motivate discussion after they have read the book independently.

- Did the book end the way you thought it would? If not, how was it different? *Make Predictions*

- Can you think of another way of solving the main problem in the book? *Problem and Solution*

- Name one effect in the book and describe its cause. *Cause and Effect*

- In general, was the main problem in the book one that most people encounter in their daily lives? Explain. *Form Generalizations*

- Summarize the story by naming the main events in order. *Sequence of Events*

RETURN TO PREDICTIONS AND PURPOSES Discuss students' predictions. Ask which were closest to what happened in the book and why. Have students review their purposes for reading. Did they find out what they wanted to know?

LITERARY RESPONSE Have students discuss questions like the following:

- What was your favorite part of the book? Why?

- Was the narrator or main character of the book like anyone you know? Explain.

- What would be another good title for the book?

Activities
Anthology and Leveled Books

Connecting Texts

CLASS DISCUSSION Have students discuss connections between the stories. For example, write these story titles horizontally across the tops of two separate charts: *Riding Proud, Jamie the Junkyard Artist, The Uphill Downhill Race, EARS to the Rescue.* Label one chart *Problems* and the other chart *Solutions.* Discuss with students the main problem and solution in each book. Write students' suggestions on the chart.

Problems

Riding Proud	Jamie the Junkyard Artist	The Uphill Downhill Race	EARS to the Rescue
• Krystal's horse escapes just before the parade.	• Jamie's mom doesn't like him collecting so much junk.	• Two men want to get Jamaica involved in the winter Olympics.	• Animals are endangered by disasters.

Solutions

Riding Proud	Jamie the Junkyard Artist	The Uphill Downhill Race	EARS to the Rescue
• Meghan helps her catch the horse.	• Jamie's mom realizes that junk can be recycled into a work of art.	• They train pushcart racers to race bobsleds.	• The Emergency Animal Rescue Service helps.

Viewing/Representing

MAKE POSTERS Have students who have read the same book organize into groups. They should then agree on an exciting scene from the book and create a poster for it.

WRITE A PARAGRAPH Give students time to study the posters. They should then write a paragraph telling which of the books depicted on the posters they would like to read and why.

Research and Inquiry

CHOOSE A TOPIC Have students choose a topic relevant to several books to research, such as ranches, rodeos, recycling, the Dust Bowl, or baseball. Then have them:

- record a few questions about their topics.

- research their topics.

- make notes on index cards as they gather information.

- write a news bulletin to share their findings.

interNET CONNECTION For links to Web pages about ranches, rodeos, recycling, the Dust Bowl, and baseball, have students log on to **www.mhschool.com/reading**

OBJECTIVES

Students will identify and form generalizations.

TEACHING TIP

INSTRUCTIONAL Offer students some examples of generalizations:

• **Most** Americans speak English.

• **Usually**, we study a foreign language in high school.

• **Everyone** knows that Native Americans were here before people from Europe.

Review Form Generalizations

PREPARE

Discuss Generalizations

Explain: A generalization is a broad statement that applies to many examples. Share the following example: Many children are nervous on the first day of school.

Point out that words like *many, most, few, everyone,* and *usually* are clues to identifying generalizations.

TEACH

Read the Passage and Model the Skill

Ask children to listen for generalizations as you read **Teaching Chart 58** with them.

Where to Learn About Native Americans

(Many) museums have information about Native Americans. They (usually) show examples of homes, clothing, and artwork and are (often) good places to learn about Native Americans.
   A powwow is (always) a good place to learn about Native Americans. (Many) states have a powwow each year. At a powwow, people can experience Native American food, dance, art, and customs.
   Visiting a reservation is another way to learn about Native Americans. There, visitors (often) spend time talking to Native Americans to learn about their way of life.

Teaching Chart 58

Guide students to identify the generalizations.

MODEL I'm not sure if the first sentence in the second paragraph is a generalization. Is *always* a clue word? Let me think about the sentence. It does make a broad statement that applies to many examples. That means it is a generalization.

Reread the chart and have students raise their hands when they hear a word that might signal a generalization.

PRACTICE

Identify Generalizations

GROUP

Have students underline the generalizations in the passage and circle the clue words. Then ask small groups to make a list of the clue words they found and brainstorm others to add to the list.

▶ **Linguistic/Interpersonal**

ASSESS/CLOSE

Form Generalizations

PARTNERS

Have partners choose two words that signal generalizations and then use them to write two generalizations about places they have visited. Challenge teams to write a third generalization without using a signal word. Ask volunteers to share their generalizations with the class. Encourage class discussion about the validity of the generalizations.

ALTERNATE TEACHING STRATEGY

FORM GENERALIZATIONS

For a different approach to teaching this skill, see page T62.

SELF-SELECTED Reading

Students may choose from the following titles.

ANTHOLOGY

• Will Her Native Language Disappear?

LEVELED BOOKS

All titles for the unit

Bibliography, pages T76–T77

Meeting Individual Needs for Comprehension

EASY	ON-LEVEL	CHALLENGE	LANGUAGE SUPPORT

EASY — Reteach 70

Name_____ Date_____ Reteach 70

Form Generalizations

Often when you read you can make a **generalization**, or a broad statement, about facts you are given.

Read the paragraphs below. Put a ✔ next to generalizations you can make based on what you read.

At Monk Street Mini Mall, you can shop at Just Pants, the Coat Factory, Socks Ahoy, Completely Clothing, Sam's Sportswear, and Mega Jeans. You can also go to The Bagel Shack or to Cone City. Next to Cone City is Main Bank's automated teller machine.

1. ✔ There are not many choices of food at Monk Street Mini Mall.
2. ___ The mini mall has no banking services.
3. ✔ Most of the stores at the mini mall sell clothes.

On Monday and Wednesday afternoons, Nadine has piano lessons. On Thursday afternoon, she sings in a choir. On Friday, Saturday, and Sunday, Nadine practices piano at least two hours a day. Tuesday afternoon, Nadine has tennis lessons.

4. ___ Nadine spends no time on sports.
5. ✔ Music is a big part of Nadine's life.
6. ___ Nadine's mother forces her to take music lessons.

At Home: Have students tell why items 2, 4, and 6 are not valid generalizations.
Book 4/Unit 2 Will Her Native Language Disappear? 6
70

ON-LEVEL — Practice 70

Name_____ Date_____ Practice 70

Form Generalizations

When you make statements that include words such as *everybody, all, always, many, most, no,* and *none,* you are probably forming a **generalization**.

Read each statement. Write **Yes** if the statement is a generalization and **No** if it is not.

1. No one plays with dolls in high school. — Yes
2. Everyone loves the Fourth of July in our town. — Yes
3. Some people can easily learn a new language. — No
4. Sometimes, when I see that clown, I start to laugh. — No
5. Nobody can memorize new words like Julio. — Yes

Write one sentence that is a generalization and one that is not.

6. Answers will vary but should be written in the correct context and parts of speech. _____

At Home: Have the students write a generalization about their school.
Book 4/Unit 2 Will Her Native Language Disappear? 6
70

CHALLENGE — Extend 70

Name_____ Date_____ Extend 70

Form Generalizations

When you **form generalizations,** you use information in the text to help you make general conclusions about what you read.

Look back at "Will Her Native Language Disappear?" to help you answer the questions. Why does the Endangered Language Fund print books and make recordings of endangered languages? Explain how their work is important.
Answers will vary. Possible answers: They hope to keep endangered languages alive. The books will keep the grammar and vocabulary of the languages alive so that people will not forget them, and the recordings will help keep the pronunciation alive.

Why do you think some young people might not want to speak the language of their older relatives?
Answers will vary. Possible answer: They might not think that it is important and it might take too much time to learn a language that they can only speak with a few people.

Why do you think that it is important to save endangered languages?
Answers will vary. Possible answer: Because they are a part of the background and culture of different groups of people.

At Home: Have students write about a story told to them by an older friend or family member.
Book 4/Unit 2 Will Her Native Language Disappear? 70

LANGUAGE SUPPORT — 78

Name_____ Date_____

Going, Going, Gone

1. Look at the two pictures. Each shows something that is endangered. One is an animal, and one is a human language. 2. On the lines write what the bird and the language have in common that makes them both endangered.

The falcon is endangered because there are very few falcons in the wild today due to gaming and deforestation.

The Choctaw language is endangered because most Choctaw in the United States today speak English.

78 Will Her Native Language Disappear? • Language Support/Blackline Master 38 Grade 4

Reteach, 70	Practice, 70	Extend, 70	Language Support, 78

251F

OBJECTIVES

Students will:

- identify compound words.
- use structural clues to determine the meanings of compound words.

TEACHING TIP

INSTRUCTIONAL Remind students that the combination of the meanings of two small words is often (but not always) a clue to the meaning of a compound.

- Give examples of compound words such as *butterfly, scarecrow,* and *rainbow.*
- Ask them if the meanings of any of these words can be gotten simply by combining the meanings of the words which make them up.

Review Compound Words

PREPARE

Discuss Compound Words

Explain: A word made from two smaller words is called a *compound word.* You can break a compound word into its smaller word parts to help you pronounce it and figure out what it means.

TEACH

Read the Passage and Model the Skill

Display and read **Teaching Chart 59.**

Using My Computer

When I want to learn about <u>anything</u>, from <u>wildlife</u> to languages, I use my computer.

On the Internet, I can find a <u>Web</u> <u>site</u> that gives me the information I need. Web sites have <u>backgrounds</u> with pictures to help me find the information quickly. <u>Sometimes</u> I find facts that I wasn't even looking for!

Last <u>weekend</u> I visited a site about the Choctaw that a <u>classmate</u> had recommended. It made me sad to learn how the Choctaw had been <u>uprooted</u> from their <u>homeland</u> in the 1830s.

Teaching Chart 59

Model using structural clues to understand a compound word.

MODEL The smaller words within the larger word *homeland* help me figure out its meaning. When I put the small words *home* and *land* together, I can build a meaning for the word *homeland.* It probably means "the land where a person or a group of people made their home."

^{TESTED} OBJECTIVES

Students will:

- identify context clues.
- use context clues to understand content-area and specialized vocabulary.

Review Context Clues

PREPARE

Discuss Context Clues

Review: Some reading selections use special words that relate specifically to the topic you're reading about. For example, if you were reading about Native American arts and crafts, you might come across special names for pottery. You can use context, or the words or sentences around an unknown word, to help determine the meaning of unfamiliar words.

TEACH

Read the Passage and Model the Skill

Display and read **Teaching Chart 60.**

Native American Homes

Native Americans had different kinds of homes depending on where they lived. Some Native Americans from the south lived in chikees, <u>open decks with leafy roofs</u> for lots of air.

Most Native Americans from the plains lived in tepees, <u>cone-shaped homes of wood and animal skins.</u>

Native Americans from the Navaho tribe usually lived in hogans, <u>round log houses put together with dried mud.</u> Native Americans used what they found in nature to make homes for themselves.

Teaching Chart 60

Model the use of context clues to decipher the meaning of an unfamiliar word, in this case *chikees*.

MODEL I can use the words before and after *chikees* to help me figure out its meaning. From the phrases *lived in* and *open decks with leafy roofs*, I know that a chikee must be a kind of home. If I want to know more, I can use the dictionary to look up the word.

PRACTICE

Use Context Clues to Determine Meaning

ONE

Ask students to identify two other specialized words that may be unfamiliar to them. (tepees, hogans) Have volunteers underline context clues and then explain how these suggest the meanings for *tepees* and *hogans*. Have students write what they think each word means and then check their work against dictionary definitions.

ASSESS/CLOSE

Create Context Clues for Specialized Vocabulary

Have students read the following definition of *wampum*. Then have them write a sentence containing context clues to suggest a meaning for *wampum*. As a class, review the context clues and build a sentence around the clearest clues.

wampum: small shells and shell beads used for money by Native Americans of the eastern woodlands

ALTERNATE TEACHING STRATEGY

CONTEXT CLUES

For a different approach to teaching this skill, see page T63.

Meeting Individual Needs for Vocabulary

| EASY | ON-LEVEL | CHALLENGE | LANGUAGE SUPPORT |

EASY

Name_____ Date_____ Reteach 72

Use Context Clues

When you read a word you don't know, look at the words and sentences near that word. This is called using **context clues**.

Circle the letter beside the meaning of the underlined word in each sentence.

1. There is a hammock hung between two trees in the backyard. Try it for a nap.
   (a.) a swinging bed made of cloth   b. a sports net

2. In the winter, some Inuit people lived in igloos. They formed the dome-shaped huts from packed snow.
   a. special animal traps   (b.) shelters

3. The family owned a large hacienda where they raised cattle.
   (a.) a ranch   b. a campground

4. I slip on my moccasins when I get home. They comfort my feet.
   (a.) indoor slipper or shoe   b. warm vest

5. Some Native Americans lived in wigwams. They made these by covering poles with hides or bark.
   (a.) places to live   b. means of travel

6. The long flat design of a toboggan makes it great for riding down snow-covered hills.
   a. a type of boat   (b.) a type of sled

At Home: Have students identify the context clues used to help them decide the meaning of hacienda and igloos.

Book 4/Unit 2
Will Her Native Language Disappear? 6

72

ON-LEVEL

Name_____ Date_____ Practice 72

Context Clues

There may be words you don't know in a story you are reading. Sometimes, the sentence holds **context clues** that can help you understand the meaning.

Write a word from the list that makes sense in each sentence.

| shallow | extinct | prediction | century | sturdy |
| value | shrieking | magical | lingered | outburst |

1. Since dinosaurs don't live any more, they are now ___extinct___.

2. The students think highly of, or ___value___, the top speller in their class.

3. The man is 105 years old and has lived for more than a ___century___.

4. The musicians ___lingered___ at the theater long past closing time.

5. The amusement park was an exciting and ___magical___ place.

6. The teacher was surprised at the ___outburst___ of cheering.

7. We could walk far into the lake because the water was so ___shallow___.

8. The monkeys at the baby zoo were crying so loud they were ___shrieking___.

9. The old truck was strong and ___sturdy___ and could carry a heavy load.

10. The boy attempted to say who might win by making a ___prediction___.

At Home: Have students play I'm thinking of a word that means ... with another member of the family.

Book 4/Unit 2
Will Her Native Language Disappear? 10

72

CHALLENGE

Name_____ Date_____ Extend 72

Context Clues

You can often figure out the meaning of a word from the way it is used in a sentence.

| ceremony | pottery | weave | harvest | hunt |
| leather | lodge | moccasin | canoe | legend |

Use as many of the words in the table as you can to write a story. Include **context clues** to help your readers understand the meanings of the words. Answers will vary but should include context clues.

_____
_____
_____
_____
_____
_____
_____
_____
_____
_____
_____
_____
_____
_____

At Home: Have students read their story and point out context clues they've used.

Book 4/Unit 2
Will Her Native Language Disappear?

72

LANGUAGE SUPPORT

Name_____ Date_____

Speaking Choctaw

1. Look at the words in each group below. 2. The English words describe the meaning of the Choctaw words. 3. Draw a line connecting the correct English words with Choctaw words.

Thank you   Ikana

Hello   Chi pisala hakinli

Friend   Yakoke

I'll see you later   Halito

80 Will Her Native Language Disappear? • Language Support/Blackline Master 40   Grade 4

Writing That Compares

GRAMMAR/SPELLING CONNECTIONS

See the 5-Day Grammar and Usage Plan on plurals and possessives, pages 251M–251N.

See the 5-Day Spelling Plan on words from social studies, pages 251O–251P.

TECHNOLOGY TIP

When you want to move sentences and paragraphs around, use the cut and paste functions on your computer instead of deleting and re-inputting.

TEACHING TIP

INSTRUCTIONAL

Organize the class into pairs and have them take turns interviewing each other.

You may want to set the mood for the assignment by describing your own feelings and experiences on your first day of school.

Prewrite

WRITE A DIARY ENTRY Present this writing assignment: LeRoy Sealy's first day of school was perhaps the loneliest day of his life. He couldn't speak English and couldn't understand anyone in his class. Write a diary entry about your first day at school. Compare how you felt then with how you feel now. Clearly state similarities and differences.

BRAINSTORM QUESTIONS Have students work in small groups to brainstorm and share memories of their first day at school. Coach them to explore memories that will bring out thoughts, feelings, and impressions.

Strategy: Make a Chart Have students make a two-column chart. They can jot down memories of their first school day in one column and of their present experiences in the other. Remind them to keep the focus on comparing their first day at school with their present experiences.

Draft

USE YOUR CHART When students finish, have them use their charts to write up the most interesting parts. Remind them to focus on showing specific comparisons, such as feeling scared and lonely the first day and of having friends now because of participation in a school activity or sports team.

Revise

SELF-QUESTIONING Have students examine their drafts for elaboration on comparison points. Ask them to reflect on the following questions:

- Did I write about my real thoughts and feelings?
- Did I compare the first day at school with how I feel now?
- Did I include an interesting beginning and a satisfying ending?

PARTNERS Have partners check each other's writing for accuracy. They can help each other make corrections where necessary.

Edit/Proofread

CHECK FOR ERRORS Students should reread their interviews for spelling, grammar, interview format, and punctuation.

Publish

SHARE THE DIARY ENTRIES Have students exchange diary entries with a partner. They can then discuss experiences and feelings they shared with the interviewee.

My First Day of School

On my first day of school, I was a little nervous because I didn't know anyone and I didn't know what to expect. Everything looked so big and confusing—the halls, the rooms, even the desks!

But now I've been here for four years, and everything seems different. I have lots of friends. I know everybody in my class. I met my best friends, Sherry and Mack, in the Art Club two years ago. Nothing seems new or confusing anymore either. I know my way around. In fact, it's like I've been here forever!

I guess I have to say that this place is really my second home.

Presentation Ideas

ILLUSTRATE THE INTERVIEW Have students illustrate one of their first-day experiences. Create a display of experiences and illustrations. ▶ **Viewing/Representing**

TAPE THE INTERVIEWS Create an archive of first-day-of-school experiences by tape recording the entries. Arrange to play the tapes at a gathering of children about to go to school for the first time.

▶ **Speaking/Listening**

Consider students' creative efforts, possibly adding a plus (+) for originality, wit, and imagination.

Scoring Rubric

Excellent	Good	Fair	Unsatisfactory
4: The writer • vividly describes real thoughts and feelings. • stays focused on specific comparisons. • has a compelling beginning and satisfying conclusion.	**3:** The writer • describes thoughts and feelings. • includes some comparisons. • has a beginning and ending.	**2:** The writer • attempts to describe a first school day. • does not stay focused on comparisons. • may lose track of topic.	**1:** The writer • includes few or no thoughts and feelings. • does not compare. • may present disorganized or unrelated facts.

0: The writer leaves the page blank or fails to respond to the writing task. The response is illegible or incoherent.

For a 6-point or an 8-point scale, see pages T105–T106.

Meeting Individual Needs for Writing

EASY

Chart Have students make a chart showing a few words or phrases they think would be important for a person learning English to know on the first day at school. Have them compare each other's charts in a class discussion.

ON-LEVEL

Interview Have students write an imaginary interview with LeRoy Sealy. They should have him compare his first day at school with his previous life.

CHALLENGE

School Story Students can write a brief story about a student in a new school. Ask them to write from the main character's point of view. Have the character compare the new school with her or his former one. Remind students to use a proper story order.

COMMUNICATION TIPS

REPRESENTING Before they begin to draw, have students close their eyes and focus on what they want their pictures to convey, whether a feeling or a visual impression.

SPEAKING Remind students that good speaking skills include speaking slowly and loudly enough to be understood.

LANGUAGE SUPPORT

ESL Review the format used for written interviews. Suggest that students use the speaker's name, followed by a colon. Remind them to start each new speech on a new line and not to use quotation marks.

Invite students to include their diary entries or another writing project in their portfolios.

PORTFOLIO

5 Day Grammar and Usage Plan

DAILY LANGUAGE ACTIVITIES

Write the Daily Language Activities on the chalkboard each day or use **Transparency 10.** Have students correct the sentences orally. For answers, see the transparency.

Day 1

1. He reads many word's.
2. Ask one of the student's.
3. Many language's are endangered.

Day 2

1. The groups job is to protect languages.
2. LeRoys day was lonely.
3. The picture's are of animals.

Day 3

1. The group prints book's.
2. Jims book is here.
3. Some teacher's speak Choctaw.

Day 4

1. Draw a horses body.
2. A hundred year's is not a long time.
3. I met LeRoy six month's ago.

Day 5

1. LeRoy had many lonely day's.
2. Language's can become extinct.
3. He knows the words meaning.

Daily Language Transparency 10

DAY 1 — Introduce the Concept

Oral Warm-Up Say this sentence aloud: *The girl's foot hurt.* Ask students whether the *-'s* in *girl's* shows that it is possessive or plural.

Introduce Plurals vs. Possessives Do not confuse plurals with possessives. Review the following:

> **Plurals vs. Possessives**
>
> • A **plural noun** names more than one person, place, or thing.
>
> • Add *-s* to most nouns to form the plural. Do not use an apostrophe.

Present the Daily Language Activity and have students correct the sentences orally. Then ask them to write the plural forms of *word, student,* and *language.*

 WRITING Assign the daily Writing Prompt on page 242C.

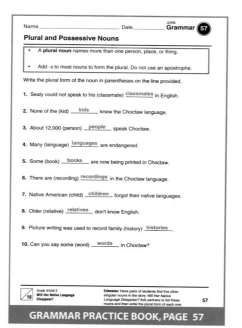

Name_____ Date_____ LEARN **Grammar 57**

Plural and Possessive Nouns

> • A **plural noun** names more than one person, place, or thing.
>
> • Add *-s* to most nouns to form the plural. Do not use an apostrophe.

Write the plural form of the noun in parentheses on the line provided.

1. Sealy could not speak to his (classmate) __classmates__ in English.
2. None of the (kid) __kids__ knew the Choctaw language.
3. About 12,000 (person) __people__ speak Choctaw.
4. Many (language) __languages__ are endangered.
5. Some (book) __books__ are now being printed in Choctaw.
6. There are (recording) __recordings__ in the Choctaw language.
7. Native American (child) __children__ forgot their native languages.
8. Older (relative) __relatives__ don't know English.
9. Picture writing was used to record family (history) __histories__
10. Can you say some (word) __words__ in Choctaw?

GRAMMAR PRACTICE BOOK, PAGE 57

DAY 2 — Teach the Concept

Review Plurals vs. Possessives Ask students how most nouns show that they mean "more than one." Ask whether they should use an apostrophe to show that a word is plural.

Review Adding 's to Show Possession When you want to make a singular noun show possession, add *'s.*

> **Plurals vs. Possessives**
>
> • A **possessive noun** shows who or what owns or has something.
>
> • Add an apostrophe and *-s* to a singular noun to make it possessive.

Present the Daily Language Activity. Then have students write the singular possessive form of *group, LeRoy,* and *picture.*

 WRITING Assign the daily Writing Prompt on page 242C.

Name_____ Date_____ LEARN AND PRACTICE **Grammar 58**

Possessive Nouns

> • A **possessive noun** shows who or what owns or has something.
>
> • Add an apostrophe and *-s* to a singular noun to make it possessive.

Write the possessive form of each singular noun in parentheses.

1. A young (boy) __boy's__ only language was Choctaw.
2. In school, the (teacher) __teacher's__ language was English.
3. One group of people start to speak another (group) __group's__ language.
4. Many of the (world) __world's__ languages could disappear.
5. LeRoy (Sealy) __Sealy's__ goal is to keep Choctaw from disappearing.
6. This Native (American) __American's__ home is in Oklahoma.
7. Today the (man) __man's__ niece is learning Choctaw.
8. A (turtle) __turtle's__ name in Choctaw is *loksi.*

GRAMMAR PRACTICE BOOK, PAGE 58

Plurals vs. Possessives

Learn from the Literature Review plurals and possessives. Read this sentence from page 246 of *Will Her Native Language Disappear?*

> **The smaller group often starts to use the larger group's language and forgets its own.**

Ask students to identify the word that shows possession. Then have them write the plural of *group*.

Form Plurals and Possessives
Present the Daily Language Activity. Then write these words on the board: *telephone, planet, niece, school, book*. Have students divide a sheet of paper into two. They should label the first half *Plurals* and the second *Possessives*. In each section have them write the correct forms of the words.

 Assign the daily Writing Prompt on page 242D.

Review Plurals vs. Possessives
On the chalkboard, make a three-column chart with the headings *singular, plural,* and *singular possessive*. Ask volunteers to fill in the chart with appropriate words. Then present the Daily Language Activity.

Mechanics and Usage Before students begin the daily Writing Prompt on page 242D, review the following:

Plural and Possessive Nouns

- Add -s to most nouns to form the plural. Do not use an apostrophe.

- Add an apostrophe and -s to a singular noun to make it possessive.

 Assign the daily Writing Prompt on page 242D.

Assess Use the Daily Language Activity and page 61 of the **Grammar Practice Book** for assessment.

Reteach On an index card, write each incorrect word in the Daily Language Activity sentences for Days 1, 4, and 5. Put the cards in a pile. Have a volunteer take one and write a sentence showing the correct use of the word. For example, the incorrect word *word's* could be correctly used in the sentence *Look up the word's meaning in the dictionary*.

Have students create a word wall showing words that add -s to form the plural and singular nouns that add 's to form the possessive.

Use page 62 of the **Grammar Practice Book** for additional reteaching.

 Assign the daily Writing Prompt on page 242D.

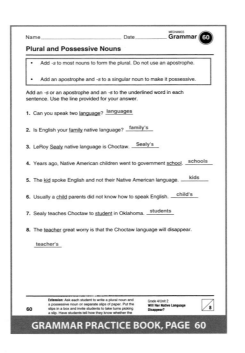

GRAMMAR PRACTICE BOOK, PAGE 59

GRAMMAR PRACTICE BOOK, PAGE 60

GRAMMAR PRACTICE BOOK, PAGE 61

5 Day Spelling Plan

ESL

Review meanings of spelling words with second-language learners. Use photographs, chalkboard drawings, brief explanations, and translations to clarify meanings.

DICTATION SENTENCES

Spelling Words

1. Does he speak just one language?
2. This old house has a long history.
3. We looked for pieces of old pottery.
4. Your room is a good place to study.
5. I have spoken to him about the test.
6. The man spoke with an accent.
7. They belong to the same tribe.
8. Humans lived in this cave.
9. It's not their custom to eat meat.
10. A village is smaller than a city.
11. The folktale was about a talking cat.
12. It takes practice to dance well.
13. My cousins are my relatives.
14. I would like to interview you for the school paper.
15. That region of the country is cold.
16. A flag can be a symbol of a country.
17. Who will guide us through the forest?
18. The totem of her family is the owl.
19. Our state was once a colony.
20. He prints his name in large letters.

Challenge Words

21. This is a fossil of an extinct animal.
22. Are you a native of this state?
23. Tell me about your backgrounds.
24. We have lived here for generations.
25. How long is a century?

DAY 1 — Pretest

Assess Prior Knowledge Use the Dictation Sentences at the left and **Spelling Practice Book** page 57 for the pretest. Allow students to correct their own papers. Students who require a modified list may be tested on the first ten words.

Spelling Words		Challenge Words
1. **language**	11. folktale	21. **extinct**
2. **history**	12. practice	22. **native**
3. **pottery**	13. **relatives**	23. **backgrounds**
4. **study**	14. interview	24. **generations**
5. **spoken**	15. region	25. **century**
6. accent	16. symbol	
7. tribe	17. guide	
8. human	18. totem	
9. custom	19. colony	
10. village	20. **prints**	

*Note: Words in **dark type** are from the story.*

Word Study On page 58 of the **Spelling Practice Book** are word study steps and an at-home activity.

SPELLING PRACTICE BOOK, PAGE 57

WORD STUDY STEPS AND ACTIVITY, PAGE 58

DAY 2 — Explore the Pattern

Sort and Spell Words Say *language* and *spoken*. Ask students whether they hear a short or a long vowel sound in the first syllable of each word. (short, long) Have students read the Spelling Words and sort them as below.

Words with short vowel sounds

language	custom	interview
history	village	symbol
pottery	practice	colony
study	relatives	prints
accent		

Words with long vowel sounds

spoken	folktale	totem
tribe	region	
human	guide	

Word Wall Have students create a word wall based on the word sort and add more words from their reading.

SPELLING PRACTICE BOOK, PAGE 59

DAY 3 — Practice and Extend

Word Meaning: Fill-ins Have students identify the Spelling Word that best completes each sentence.

1. Many people look much like their _____. (relatives)

2. The song was hard for me to play because I was out of _____. (practice)

3. There are only 300 people living in the _____. (village)

Have students write similar sentences for partners to complete.

If students need extra practice, have partners give each other a midweek test.

Glossary Review word histories. Have students read the word history for *century*.

- Write what language the word comes from. (Latin)

- Write the Latin word for 100 men. (centuria)

- Write what *century* means. (a period of 100 years)

DAY 4 — Proofread and Write

Proofread Sentences Write these sentences on the chalkboard, including the misspelled words. Ask students to proofread, circling incorrect spellings and writing the correct spellings. There are two spelling errors in each sentence.

> I want to studie langauges in college. (study, languages)
>
> Her relatifs first settled in the coluny in Virginia. (relatives, colony)

Have students create additional sentences with errors for partners to correct.

WRITING Have students use as many Spelling Words as possible in the daily Writing Prompt on page 242D. Remind students to proofread their writing for errors in spelling, grammar, and punctuation.

DAY 5 — Assess and Reteach

Assess Students' Knowledge Use page 62 of the **Spelling Practice Book** or the Dictation Sentences on page 215O for the posttest.

 Personal Word List If students have trouble with any words in the lesson, have them add the words to their personal lists of troublesome words in their journals. Working in pairs, have students take turns defining each spelling word and having their partners guess the word.

Students should refer to their word lists during later writing activities.

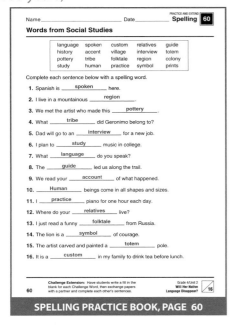

SPELLING PRACTICE BOOK, PAGE 60

SPELLING PRACTICE BOOK, PAGE 61

SPELLING PRACTICE BOOK, PAGE 62

Wrap Up the Theme

Something in Common

Sharing ideas can lead to meaningful cooperation.

REVIEW THE THEME Remind students that all of the selections in this unit relate to the theme Something in Common. Ask students to tell how they have something in common with any of the characters from the stories. Were students able to make any connections to help them understand the characters?

READ THE POEM Read "August 8" by Norman Jordan aloud to students. Ask students to explain how this poem relates to the theme Something in Common. Lead them to understand that the poet suggests we are connected in some way to everyone and everything.

 Listening Library Audiocassettes

MAKE CONNECTIONS Have students work in small groups to brainstorm a list of ways that the stories, poems, and the *Time for Kids* magazine article relate to the theme Something in Common.

Groups can then compare their lists as they share them with the class.

252

LOOKING AT GENRE

Have students review *Just a Dream* and *Baseball Saved Us*. What makes *Just a Dream* a fantasy? What makes *Baseball Saved Us* historical fiction?

Help students list the key characteristics of each literary form or genre. Can they name other fantasies and historical fiction stories that have the same characteristics?

FANTASY *Just a Dream*	HISTORICAL FICTION *Baseball Saved Us*
• Setting is make-believe.	• Characters are placed in a real historical setting.
• The events in the plot could not be real.	• Characters act out a fictional plot.

August 8

There is no break
 between
  yesterday and today
  mother and son
   air and earth
    all are a part
     of the other
      like
       with this typewriter
      I am connected
       with these words
        and these words
         with this paper
          and this paper with you.

by Norman Jordan

253

LEARNING ABOUT POETRY

Literary Devices: Free Verse
Point out that this poem has neither rhythm nor rhyme. It is free verse. Ask students to read the poem aloud, pausing at the end of each line. Discuss how free verse focuses the reader on the words and phrases of the poem. Ask children to give their opinions about poetry written in free verse.

Response Activity Ask a small group of students to move around the room in a clockwise direction as a volunteer reads this poem. Whenever the reader pauses, students must freeze their pose. Experiment by having the reader pause in different places so the students gain a sense of the different rhythms available in free verse.

Activity

Research and Inquiry

Complete the Theme Project
Have student teams work to complete their projects. Guidance needed will vary depending on the projects chosen. Students helping younger students acquire reading skills, for instance, might need instruction about working with younger students. Work to foster cooperation within and between teams.

Make a Classroom Presentation
Once the projects are completed, have teams take turns presenting reports on their projects to the classroom. Have students question presenters about what they learned.

Draw Conclusions Have students draw conclusions about what they learned from researching and preparing their projects. Was the resource chart they made helpful? What other resources did they use? Was the Internet helpful? What conclusions have they made about their topic? Was their project effective? Finally, ask students if doing their projects has helped them see that sharing ideas can lead to meaningful cooperation. What conclusions can they make from this?

Ask More Questions What additional questions do students now have about finding something in common with others? Do students have questions about how to discover commonalities and to share with people from other communities? You might encourage teams to continue their research and prepare other projects.

253

Writing That Compares

CONNECT TO LITERATURE In *Justin and the Best Biscuits in the World,* Justin learns a new way of doing things at Grandpa's ranch. In a class discussion, ask students to compare Justin's way of doing things at the beginning and at the end of the story.

> Frogs and carp living in fresh water ponds have a lot in common. Frogs lay eggs that turn into baby tadpoles. Carp reproduce by laying eggs, too. Carp and frogs are both cold-blooded. Sometimes, they even eat the same kind of bugs.
>
> Once tadpoles grow into frogs, the differences between frogs and carp become more clear. Adult frogs have legs and can breathe air, which allows them to move around on land. Carp, which have gills rather than lungs, must stay in the water, so they don't have as many food sources as frogs.

Prewrite

PURPOSE & AUDIENCE Students will write reports that compare two animals who live in the same ecosystem. Have them focus on how each animal is affected by, or affects, its environment. Have them carefully consider their purpose—to inform—and their audience.

STRATEGY: RESEARCH THE TOPIC On a table, place animal books, encyclopedias, and nature magazines. If possible, show a videotape of an ecosystem you'd like students to focus on. Help them set up comparison charts for their topic animals.

Use **Writing Process Transparency 2A** to model a Venn diagram.

FEATURES OF WRITING THAT COMPARES

- presents similarities and differences, of two topic items
- clearly introduces the main idea, and elaborates on it with facts
- organizes facts and ideas in a logical pattern of comparison
- may have a conclusion based on factual comparative information

TEACHING TIP

ORGANIZATION Help students use their Venn diagrams effectively. Guide them to begin separating research facts under headings marked Likenesses and Differences. Ask them to organize their comparative facts in distinct topic areas, such as food, environment, and physical traits.

PREWRITE TRANSPARENCY

Two Forest Animals

Differences
Likenesses

Animal: Fox
- is small, with long fur and bushy tail
- hunts for and eats meat
- helps to control rodent population

Likenesses:
- live in the forest
- affect the balance of vegetation and animal population
- are affected by weather conditions

Animal: Deer
- is tall, with long legs and brown fur
- eats leaves, nuts and fruit
- helps to control vegetation growth
- may overgraze an area

McGraw-Hill School Division

Grade 4/Unit 2: Writing That Compares/Prewrite 2A

Writing That Compares

Draft

STRATEGY: CONSULT THE VENN DIAGRAM Have students use their diagrams to guide the structure for their first drafts. Invite them to use rich descriptive language to clarify and enliven their factual information. Encourage them to consider whether their essays should have a final conclusion.

Use **Writing Process Transparency 2B** to model a first draft.

LANGUAGE CONTROL Have students start collecting a word bank of adjectives that apply to their topic. Then, guide them to construct descriptive phrases using the articles *a, an,* and *the*; for example: *a* young bear or *the* swift falcon. They can save the adjective banks in their writing portfolios.

LANGUAGE SUPPORT

Some students may need help identifying animal traits. Have students close their eyes and imagine how the animal looks and acts. A partner can help them write lists of descriptive words.

DRAFT TRANSPARENCY

Two Animals That Affect the Forest

Our team has been observing two forest animals, deer and foxes. Obviously, they look very different. Deer are tall, with long legs and short brown fur, while foxes are small with long reddish fur and bushy tails. Deer walk and leap with their heads high. Foxes creep slowly or scurry, but they always stay close to the ground.

Deer roam the forest looking for things to eat. They live on leaves, grasses, and sometimes twigs in the winter months. Foxes have very different tastes. They are meat eaters who hunt for small animals like rodents, birds, and sometimes lizards or snakes. They are more cunning than deer.

These animals each affect the environment in their own way. Deer help to keep forest vegetation from overgrowth. Their grazing allows sunlight to reach all life forms in the forest. But sometimes, too many deer will graze in the same area and use up too much plant life. This can cause problems for other animals who rely on vegetation for their shelter and food.

Foxes help to keep the population of smaller animals under control. This helps to make sure there is enough food and space for other species.

Deer and foxes both help us see that all plants and animals play a role in creating a balanced environment.

McGraw-Hill School Division

Grade 4/Unit 2: Writing That Compares/Publish 2B

Revise

Have students review their own essays for accuracy and clarity. Remind them to be sure that their comparisons are arranged in paragraphs. Ask them to consider whether a reader will have enough facts and details to learn something about their animals.

Use **Writing Process Transparency 2C** for classroom discussion on the revision process. Ask students to comment on how revisions may have improved this writing example.

STRATEGY: ELABORATION Have students examine their first drafts for elaboration on their comparison points, such as environmental challenges, life span, and natural enemies. Ask them to reflect on the following questions:

- Did I show how each animal looks and acts?

- Did I show how each animal affects its environment?

- How should I end my essay? Do I need a conclusion?

TEACHING TIP

TEACHER CONFERENCE

While students are revising, circulate and conference with them individually. You can use these questions as a basis for your conferencing interactions:

- Do your descriptions bring the animals to life?
- What's the best part of your comparison piece?
- What do you want the reader to learn?

REVISE TRANSPARENCY

Two Animals That Affect the Forest

Our team has been ^observing watching two forest animals. deer and foxes. Obviously, they look very diffrent. Deer are tall, with long legs and short brown fur, while foxes are small with reddish fur and bushy tails. Deer walk and leap ^long with their heads high. Foxes creep slow, or scurry close to ,but they always stay the ground.

Deer roam the forest looking for things to eat. They live on leaves, nuts, and sometimes fruit. Foxes have very grasses   twigs in the winter months. different tastes. They were meat eaters who hunt for small animals like rodents, birds and sometimes lizards or snakes. They are most cunning than deer.

These animals affect the environment in their own each way. Deer help to keep forest plants from overgrowth. Their grazeing allows sunlight to reach the forest. But all life forms in sometimes, too many deer will graze in the same area and use up too much plant life. This can cause problem for other animals who rely on vegetation for its shelter and food.

Foxes help to keep the number of smaller animals under control. This helps to make sure that there is enough food and space for other species.

Deer and foxes both show us that all plants and help us see animals play a role in creating the balanced environment.

Grade 4/Unit 2: Writing That Compares/Revise 2C

McGraw-Hill School Division

Writing That Compares

GRAMMAR/SPELLING CONNECTIONS

See the 5-day Grammar and Usage Plans on nouns, pp. 157M–157N, 189M–189N, 215M–215N, 241M–241N, and 251M–251N.

See the 5-day Spelling Plans, pp. 157O–157P, 189O–189P, 215O–215P, 241O–241P, and 251O–251P.

Edit/Proofread

After students finish revising their texts, have them proofread for final corrections and additions.

GRAMMAR, MECHANICS, USAGE

- correct use of adverbs
- correct use of possessive pronouns
- pronoun-verb agreement
- using adverbs *more* and *most* to compare

Publish

TEACHER FOR A DAY Volunteers can read their work aloud to the class. Invite them to pretend they are guest nature professors for a day.

Use **Writing Process Transparency 2D** as a proofreading model, and **Writing Process Transparency 2E** to discuss presentation ideas for their writing.

PROOFREAD TRANSPARENCY

Two Animals That Affect the Forest
                    ^observing
    Our team has been watching two forest animals,
                                              ^e
deer and foxes. Obviously, they look very diffrent. Deer are
        long
tall, with long legs and short brown fur, while foxes are
small with reddish fur and bushy tails. Deer walk and leap
          ^ly, but they always stay
with their heads high. Foxes creep slow, or scurry close to
the ground.
    Deer roam the forest looking for things to eat. They
        grasses   twigs in the winter months.
live on leaves, nuts, and sometimes fruit. Foxes have very
              are
different tastes. They were meat eaters who hunt for small
                      ^,
animals like rodents, birds, and sometimes lizards or
          more ,
snakes. They are most cunning than deer.
          ^each
    These animals affect the environment in their own
      vegetation
way. Deer help to keep forest plants from overgrowth.
                              all life forms in
Their grazing allows sunlight to reach the forest. But
sometimes, too many deer will graze in the same area and
                                          ^ s
use up too much plant life. This can cause problem for
                                          their
other animals who rely on vegetation for its shelter and
food.
      population
    Foxes help to keep the number of smaller animals
under control. This helps to make sure that there is
enough food and space for other species.
              help us see
    Deer and foxes both show us that all plants and
                          ^ a
animals play a role in creating the balanced environment.
      ^

McGraw-Hill School Division

Grade 4/Unit 2: Writing That Compares/Proofread 2D

PUBLISH TRANSPARENCY

Two Animals That Affect the Forest

    Our team has been observing two forest animals, deer and foxes. Obviously, they look very different. Deer are tall, with long legs and short brown fur, while foxes are small with long reddish fur and bushy tails. Deer walk and leap with their heads high. Foxes creep slowly or scurry, but they always stay close to the ground.

    Deer roam the forest looking for things to eat. They live on leaves, grasses, and sometimes twigs in the winter months. Foxes have very different tastes. They are meat eaters who hunt for small animals like rodents, birds, and sometimes lizards or snakes. They are more cunning than deer.

    These animals each affect the environment in their own way. Deer help to keep forest vegetation from overgrowth. Their grazing allows sunlight to reach all life forms in the forest. But sometimes, too many deer will graze in the same area and use up too much plant life. This can cause problems for other animals who rely on vegetation for their shelter and food.

    Foxes help to keep the population of smaller animals under control. This helps to make sure there is enough food and space for other species.

    Deer and foxes both help us see that all plants and animals play a role in creating a balanced environment.

McGraw-Hill School Division

Grade 4/Unit 2: Writing That Compares/Publish 2E

Presentation Ideas

MAKE A NATURE SHOW Have students create a TV-style nature show on the animals they've written about. "Nature Reporters" can also show pictures of the animals and their environments.

▶ **Speaking/Listening**

MAKE A MENAGERIE Have students make animal models from self-drying clay. Make a display of their sculptures, with labels naming each animal and telling where they live. ▶ **Representing/Viewing**

Assessment

- Ask students to self assess their writing. Present the writing that compares features, page 253B, in question form on a chart.

- For a 6-point or an 8-point scale, see pages T105–T106.

COMMUNICATION TIPS

REPRESENTING Have students use nature photos to model their clay animals. They can make shoebox bases painted to show the animal's environment.

SPEAKING Students can create "reporter" personalities. Encourage them to watch a nature reporter on TV.

Scoring Rubric: 6-Trait Writing

4 Excellent

Ideas & Content
- crafts a well-constructed factual comparison of two animals; carefully-selected details clarify each comparison point.

Organization
- careful strategy moves the reader smoothly through each point, from beginning to end; well-placed observations and details strengthen the logic.

Voice
- originality and deep involvement with the topic enlivens the content; writer reaches out to share ideas with an audience.

Word Choice
- makes imaginative use of precise, sophisticated words to describe distinct differences and similarities.

Sentence Fluency
- varied, effective sentences flow naturally; uses both simple and complex sentences creatively; varied beginnings, lengths, and patterns add appeal to the comparisons.

Conventions
- has strong skills in most writing conventions; proper use of the rules of English enhances clarity and cohesion of the comparisons; editing is largely unnecessary.

3 Good

Ideas & Content
- crafts a solid, well-thought-out comparison; details show knowledge of the topic; may make some fresh observations about the animals and their habitat.

Organization
- presents a capable, easy-to-follow strategy; reader can follow the logic from beginning to end; details fit and build on each other.

Voice
- clearly shows who is behind the words; personal style matches the purpose; reaches out to the reader effectively.

Word Choice
- uses a range of precise words to present facts and observations; explores new words, or uses everyday words to state ideas in a fresh way.

Sentence Fluency
- crafts careful sentences that make sense, and are easy to read and understand; sentence lengths and patterns vary, and fit together well.

Conventions
- uses most conventions correctly; some editing may be needed; errors are few and don't make the paper hard to understand.

2 Fair

Ideas & Content
- has some control of the comparison task, but may offer limited or unclear facts and details; makes obvious or predictable observations.

Organization
- tries to structure a comparison, but has trouble sequencing ideas; may not present distinct comparison categories; reader may be confused by poorly-placed facts and details.

Voice
- communicates a main idea, with some hint of who is behind the words; writer may seem personally uninvolved with the topic and an audience.

Word Choice
- gets the argument across, but experiments with few new words; may not use words intended to create a clear picture for the reader.

Sentence Fluency
- sentences are understandable, but may be choppy, rambling, or awkward; some writing is difficult to follow or read aloud, or may interfere with meaning.

Conventions
- makes frequent noticeable mistakes which prevent an even reading of the text; extensive need for editing and revision.

1 Unsatisfactory

Ideas & Content
- does not successfully compare two animals; it is hard to tell what the writer intends to say about the topic.

Organization
- extreme lack of organization makes the text hard to follow; ideas, facts, and details are not connected, out of order, and may not fit the purpose.

Voice
- does not connect with the topic; is not involved in sharing ideas with a reader.

Word Choice
- does not use words that show differences or similarities; some words may detract from the purpose to compare; words do not fit, or are overused.

Sentence Fluency
- uses choppy, rambling, or confusing sentences; does not understand how words and sentences fit together; writing doesn't follow natural sentence patterns, and is hard to read aloud.

Conventions
- has repeated errors in spelling, word choice, punctuation and usage; some parts are impossible to read or understand.

0: This piece is either blank, or fails to respond to the writing task. The topic is not addressed, or the student simply paraphrases the prompt. The response may be illegible or incoherent.

VOCABULARY

ONE Distribute copies of the vocabulary definitions. Have students draw a chart with the headings *Word, Definition,* and *Memory Tips.* Then have them write the words in the first column, cut and paste its definitions in the second, and write or draw meaning clues in the third.

Unit Review

**Justin and
the Best Biscuits in the World**

festival	inspecting	pranced
guilt	lingered	resounded

Just A Dream

bulging	foul	shrieking
crumpled	haze	waddled

Leah's Pony

bidding	county	overflowing
clustered	glistened	sturdy

Baseball Saved Us

crate	endless	inning
ditches	glinting	mound

Will Her Native Language Disappear?

backgrounds	communicate	generations
century	extinct	native

Name_____ Date_____ Practice **73**

Unit 2 Vocabulary Review

A. Read each word in Column 1. Then find the word or words in Column 2 that mean the opposite. Write the letter of the word on the line.

b	1. lingered	a. whispering
e	2. foul	b. left quickly
d	3. sturdy	c. foreign
c	4. native	d. weak
a	5. shrieking	e. fresh

B. Write the correct vocabulary word in the blanks.

haze	pranced	waddled	guilt	crate
ditches	glistened	county	resounded	mound	bidding

1. The fans' loud cheers ___resounded___ in the football stadium.
2. Every year we have a ___county___ fair.
3. The drum major ___pranced___ proudly, leading the marching band.
4. Robert had feelings of ___guilt___ for forgetting his dad's birthday.
5. Water flows in the long ___ditches___ surrounding the corn fields.
6. The vase was shipped to us in a large wooden ___crate___.
7. Pollution sometimes causes a dark ___haze___ to form in the air.
8. The sunlight ___glistened___ brightly on the waters of the lake.
9. The penguins ___waddled___ to the edge of the ice.
10. The auctioneer began the ___bidding___ for the painting at $500.
11. The team's new pitcher stood on the pitcher's ___mound___.

16 Book 4/Unit 2
Unit 2 Vocabulary Review

At Home: Have students write a paragraph using at least four of the vocabulary words. 73

PRACTICE BOOK, 73–74

GRAMMAR

GROUP Ask each student to fold a sheet of paper into fourths. In the top left corner, have groups of four write a proper noun; in the top right a plural common noun; in the bottom left a sentence that includes both nouns, one in possessive form; in the bottom right, draw a picture to go with the sentence. Have groups share their results.

Unit Review

**Justin and
the Best Biscuits in the World**
Common and Proper Nouns

Just a Dream
Singular and Plural Nouns

Leah's Pony
Irregular Plural Nouns

Baseball Saved Us
Possessive Nouns

Will Her Native Language Disappear?
Plurals vs. Possessives

Name_____ Date_____ REVIEW Grammar **63**

Nouns

Read each passage. Choose a word or group of words that belong in each space. Circle your answer.

When Justin visited _____ grandfather, he learned about some famous
(1)
cowboys. One cowboy was _____. Many people thought he rode
(2)
wild horses better than anyone else. Justin said that he had never heard of
Mr. Stahl.

1. A	him	2. F	Mister Jessie stahl
B	he's	G	Mr. Jessie Stahl
C	his	H	Mr Jessie Stahl
D	her	J	Mr. jessie stahl

Walter had a dream about the future. In one part of his dream, his bed was
sitting in the _____ of a tree. Then he was on a factory's smokestack. The
(3)
smoke from the _____ hurt his eyes, nose, and throat.
(4)

3. A	branch's	4. F	ace medicine factory
B	branchs	G	Ace Medicine Factory
C	branches	H	Ace medicine factory
D	branchese	J	Ace Medicine factory

4 Grade 4/Unit 2
Something in Common

63

GRAMMAR PRACTICE BOOK, 63–64

SPELLING

Divide the class into teams, and have one member from each stand with his or her back to the chalkboard. Write a spelling word on the chalkboard, and have team members take turns giving one-word clues. A player earns one point by guessing the word and another point by spelling the word correctly.

Unit Review

Syllable Patterns
clover
razor
biscuit
bandage
fancy

Plurals
soldiers
shovels
eyelashes
ferries
calves

Consonant Clusters
flutter
crack
bridle
among
plank

Social Studies Words
pottery
accent
colony
folktale
totem

Consonant Clusters
stung   spruce
spectacle   thrifty
stress

SPELLING PRACTICE BOOK, 63–64

☑ SKILLS & STRATEGIES

Comprehension
☑ Make Predictions
☑ Form Generalizations
☑ Sequence of Events
☑ Cause and Effect

Vocabulary Strategies
☑ Context Clues
☑ Compound Words

Study Skills
☑ Reference Sources

Writing
☑ Writing That Compares

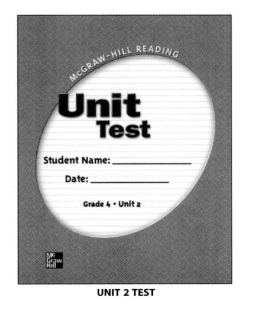

UNIT 2 TEST

Assessment
Follow-Up

Use the results of the informal and formal assessment opportunities in the unit to help you make decisions about future instruction.

SKILLS AND STRATEGIES	Reteaching Blackline Masters	Alternate Teaching Strategies
Comprehension		
Make Predictions	38, 42, 59, 63	T60
Form Generalizations	43, 50, 64, 70	T62
Sequence of Events	45, 49, 57	T64
Cause and Effect	52, 56, 66	T66
Vocabulary Strategy		
Context Clues	44, 58, 72	T63
Compound Words	51, 65, 71	T65
Study Skills		
Reference Sources	41, 48, 55, 62, 69	T61

Writing	Alternate Writing Project—Easy	Unit Writing Process Lesson
Writing That Compares	157L, 189L, 215L, 241L, 251L	253A

McGraw-Hill School
TECHNOLOGY

interNET CONNECTION Research and Inquiry Ideas.
Visit **www.mhschool.com/reading**

Glossary

Introduce students to the Glossary by reading through the introduction and looking over the pages with them. Encourage the class to talk about what they see.

Words in a glossary, like words in a dictionary, are listed in **alphabetical order.** Point out the **guide words** at the top of each page that tell the first and last words appearing on that page.

Point out examples of **entries** and **main entries.** Read through a simple entry with the class, identifying each part. Have students note the order in which information is given: entry words(s), definition(s), example sentence, syllable division, pronunciation respelling, part of speech, plural/verb/adjective forms.

Note that if more than one definition is given for a word, the definitions are numbered. Note also the format used for a word that is more than one part of speech.

Review the parts of speech by identifying each in a sentence:

inter.	*adj.*	*n.*	*conj.*	*adj.*	*n.*
Wow!	A	dictionary	and	a	glossary

v.	*adv.*	*pron.*	*prep.*	*n.*
tell	almost	everything	about	words!

Explain the use of the **pronunciation key** (either the **short key,** at the bottom of every other page, or the **long key,** at the beginning of the glossary). Demonstrate the difference between **primary** stress and **secondary** stress by pronouncing a word with both.

Point out an example of the small triangle signaling a homophone. **Homophones** are words with different spellings and meanings but with the same pronunciation. Explain that a pair of words with the superscripts **1** and **2** are **homographs**—words that have the same spelling, but different origins and meanings, and in some cases, different pronunciations.

The **Word History** feature tells what language a word comes from and what changes have occurred in its spelling and/or meaning. Many everyday words have interesting and surprising stories behind them. Note that word histories can help us remember the meanings of difficult words.

Allow time for students to further explore the Glossary and make their own discoveries.

Glossary

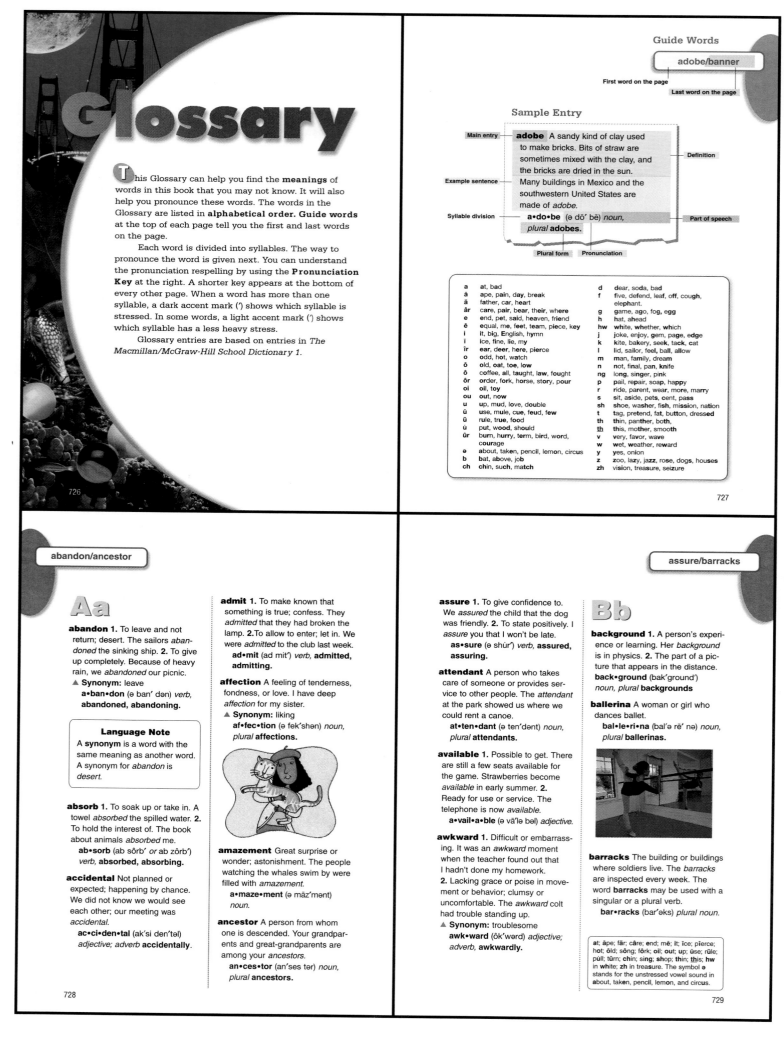

This Glossary can help you find the **meanings** of words in this book that you may not know. It will also help you pronounce these words. The words in the Glossary are listed in **alphabetical order. Guide words** at the top of each page tell you the first and last words on the page.

Each word is divided into syllables. The way to pronounce the word is given next. You can understand the pronunciation respelling by using the **Pronunciation Key** at the right. A shorter key appears at the bottom of every other page. When a word has more than one syllable, a dark accent mark (′) shows which syllable is stressed. In some words, a light accent mark (′) shows which syllable has a less heavy stress.

Glossary entries are based on entries in *The Macmillan/McGraw-Hill School Dictionary 1*.

Guide Words

adobe/banner

First word on the page
Last word on the page

Sample Entry

Main entry — **adobe** A sandy kind of clay used to make bricks. Bits of straw are sometimes mixed with the clay, and the bricks are dried in the sun. Many buildings in Mexico and the southwestern United States are made of *adobe.* — Definition

Example sentence

Syllable division — **a•do•be** (ə dō′ bē) *noun, plural* **adobes.** — Part of speech

Plural form   Pronunciation

a	at, bad	d	dear, soda, bad
ā	ape, pain, day, break	f	five, defend, leaf, off, cough, elephant.
ä	father, car, heart		
âr	care, pair, bear, their, where	g	game, ago, fog, egg
e	end, pet, said, heaven, friend	h	hat, ahead
ē	equal, me, feet, team, piece, key	hw	white, whether, which
i	it, big, English, hymn	j	joke, enjoy, gem, page, edge
ī	ice, fine, lie, my	k	kite, bakery, seek, tack, cat
îr	ear, deer, here, pierce	l	lid, sailor, feel, ball, allow
o	odd, hot, watch	m	man, family, dream
ō	old, oat, toe, low	n	not, final, pan, knife
ô	coffee, all, taught, law, fought	ng	long, singer, pink
ôr	order, fork, horse, story, pour	p	pail, repair, soap, happy
oi	oil, toy	r	ride, parent, wear, more, marry
ou	out, now	s	sit, aside, pets, cent, pass
u	up, mud, love, double	sh	shoe, washer, fish, mission, nation
ū	use, mule, cue, feud, few	t	tag, pretend, fat, button, dressed
ü	rule, true, food	th	thin, panther, both,
u̇	put, wood, should	th	this, mother, smooth
ûr	burn, hurry, term, bird, word, courage	v	very, favor, wave
ə	about, taken, pencil, lemon, circus	w	wet, weather, reward
b	bat, above, job	y	yes, onion
ch	chin, such, match	z	zoo, lazy, jazz, rose, dogs, houses
		zh	vision, treasure, seizure

Aa

abandon 1. To leave and not return; desert. The sailors *abandoned* the sinking ship. **2.** To give up completely. Because of heavy rain, we *abandoned* our picnic.
▲ Synonym: leave
a•ban•don (ə ban′ dən) *verb,* **abandoned, abandoning.**

Language Note
A **synonym** is a word with the same meaning as another word. A synonym for *abandon* is *desert.*

absorb 1. To soak up or take in. A towel *absorbed* the spilled water. **2.** To hold the interest of. The book about animals *absorbed* me.
ab•sorb (ab sôrb′ *or* ab zôrb′) *verb,* **absorbed, absorbing.**

accidental Not planned or expected; happening by chance. We did not know we would see each other; our meeting was *accidental.*
ac•ci•den•tal (ak′si den′təl) *adjective; adverb* **accidentally.**

admit 1. To make known that something is true; confess. They *admitted* that they had broken the lamp. **2.**To allow to enter; let in. We were *admitted* to the club last week.
ad•mit (ad mit′) *verb,* **admitted, admitting.**

affection A feeling of tenderness, fondness, or love. I have deep *affection* for my sister.
▲ Synonym: liking
af•fec•tion (ə fek′shən) *noun, plural* **affections.**

amazement Great surprise or wonder; astonishment. The people watching the whales swim by were filled with *amazement.*
a•maze•ment (ə māz′mənt) *noun.*

ancestor A person from whom one is descended. Your grandparents and great-grandparents are among your *ancestors.*
an•ces•tor (an′ses tər) *noun, plural* **ancestors.**

---

assure 1. To give confidence to. We *assured* the child that the dog was friendly. **2.** To state positively. I *assure* you that I won't be late.
as•sure (ə shu̇r′) *verb,* **assured, assuring.**

attendant A person who takes care of someone or provides service to other people. The *attendant* at the park showed us where we could rent a canoe.
at•ten•dant (ə ten′dənt) *noun, plural* **attendants.**

available 1. Possible to get. There are still a few seats available for the game. Strawberries become *available* in early summer. **2.** Ready for use or service. The telephone is now *available.*
a•vail•a•ble (ə vā′lə bəl) *adjective.*

awkward 1. Difficult or embarrassing. It was an *awkward* moment when the teacher found out that I hadn't done my homework. **2.** Lacking grace or poise in movement or behavior; clumsy or uncomfortable. The *awkward* colt had trouble standing up.
▲ Synonym: troublesome
awk•ward (ôk′wərd) *adjective; adverb,* **awkwardly.**

Bb

background 1. A person's experience or learning. Her *background* is in physics. **2.** The part of a picture that appears in the distance.
back•ground (bak′ground′) *noun, plural* **backgrounds**

ballerina A woman or girl who dances ballet.
bal•le•ri•na (bal′ə rē′ nə) *noun, plural* **ballerinas.**

barracks The building or buildings where soldiers live. The *barracks* are inspected every week. The word **barracks** may be used with a singular or a plural verb.
bar•racks (bar′əks) *plural noun.*

at; āpe; fär; câre; end; mē; it; īce; pîerce; hot; ōld; sông; fôrk; oil; out; up; ūse; rüle; pu̇ll; tûrn; chin; sing; shop; thin; this; hw in white; zh in treasure. The symbol ə stands for the unstressed vowel sound in about, taken, pencil, lemon, and circus.

beloved Loved very much. The dog was *beloved* by the whole neighborhood.
be•lov•ed (bi luv′id *or* bi luvd′) *adjective.*

bid To offer to pay. We *bid* thirty-five dollars for the old desk at the auction. *Verb.*— An offer to pay money. The rug was sold to the person who made the highest *bid. Noun.*
bid (bid) *verb,* **bid,** *or* **bidden, bidding;** *noun, plural* **bids.**

biscuit 1. A small cake of baked dough. For breakfast, he had eggs, bacon, juice, and a *biscuit.* 2. A cracker. Every afternoon, she has tea and *biscuits.*
bis•cuit (bis′kit) *noun, plural* **biscuits.**

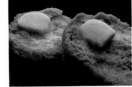

Word History

Cuit is the French word for "cooked." **Biscuit** comes from a 14th-century French word *bescuit,* meaning "twice-cooked bread."

brand-new Completely new. My aunt just bought a *brand-new* car.
brand-new (brand′nū *or* brand′nū) *adjective.*

brilliant 1. Very intelligent. That woman is a *brilliant* scientist. 2. Very bright; sparkling. The North Star is a *brilliant* light in the sky.
bril•liant (bril′yənt) *adjective.*

brisk 1. Quick and lively. She walked at a *brisk* pace. 2. Refreshing; keen; bracing. We walked in the *brisk* winter air.
brisk (brisk) *adjective,* **brisker, briskest.**

broad 1. Large from one side to the other side; wide. The side of the red barn is so *broad* that you can see it from a mile away. 2. Wide in range; not limited. We have a *broad* knowledge of U.S. history.
broad (brôd) *adjective,* **broader, broadest.**

bulge To swell out. Because he put so many clothes in it, the suitcase *bulged. Verb.*— A rounded part that swells out. The rag made a *bulge* in the mechanic's back pocket. *Noun.*
bulge (bulj) *verb,* **bulged, bulging;** *noun, plural* **bulges;** *adjective,* **bulging.**

---

canoe To paddle or ride in a canoe. During the summer, they liked to go *canoeing* on the lake. *Verb.*— A light narrow boat, usually pointed at both ends and moved and steered with a paddle. The *canoe* tipped over when Eddie stood up. *Noun.*
ca•noe (kə nū′) *verb,* **canoed, canoeing;** *noun, plural* **canoes.**

captive A person or animal captured and held by force; prisoner. The police kept the *captive* in jail. *Noun.*—Held prisoner. The *captive* lion was kept in a cage. *Adjective.*
▲ **Synonym:** prisoner
cap•tive (kap′tiv) *noun, plural* **captives;** *adjective.*

captivity The state of being captive. Wolves live longer in *captivity* than in the wild.
cap•tiv•i•ty (kap tiv′ ə tē) *noun.*

celebration 1. The festivities carried on to observe or honor a special day or event. The wedding *celebration* is usually shared by friends and family. 2. The act of celebrating. We went to the *celebration* of my cousin's graduation.
cel•e•bra•tion (sel′ ə brā′ shən) *noun, plural* **celebrations;** *adjective,* **celebratory.**

century A period of one hundred years. The time from 1651 to 1750 is one *century.*
century (sen′ chə rē) *noun, plural* **centuries**

challenge 1. Something calling for work, effort, and the use of one's talents. Chemistry is a real *challenge.* 2. A call to take part in a contest or fight. In the days of duels, only a coward would refuse a *challenge. Noun.*—To question the truth or correctness of. They *challenged* my claim that bats are mammals. *Verb.*
chal•lenge (chal′ənj) *noun, plural* **challenges;** *verb,* **challenged, challenging.**

at; āpe; fär; câre; end; mē; it; īce; pîerce; hot; ōld; sông; fôrk; oil; out; up; ūse; rūle; pùll; tûrn; chin; sing; shop; thin; <u>th</u>is; hw in white; zh in treasure. The symbol ə stands for the unstressed vowel sound in about, taken, pencil, lemon, and circus.

---

chant A singing or shouting of words over and over. *Chants* usually have a strong rhythm. *Noun.* — To sing or shout in a chant. At the election rally, the group *chanted* the name of their favorite candidate. *Verb.*
chant (chant) *noun, plural* **chants;** *verb,* **chanted, chanting.**

Word History

Chant, as it is spelled today, is based on the Middle English word *chaunten.* The Latin word *cantare,* which means "to sing," is the original basis of the word.

circulate 1. To pass from person to person. Bills and coins have *circulated* in the United States since Colonial times. 2. To move around widely among different places. The window fan *circulates* air around the room.
cir•cu•late (sûr′kyə lāt′) *verb,* **circulated, circulating.**

climate The average weather conditions of a place or region through the year. Climate includes average temperature, rainfall, humidity, and wind conditions. Southern California has a warm, mild *climate.*
cli•mate (klī′mit) *noun, plural* **climates.**

cling To stick closely. The wet pants were *clinging* to her legs.
cling (kling) *verb,* **clung, clinging.**

clipper 1. A tool used for cutting. Use *clippers* to cut your fingernails. 2. A fast sailing ship. American *clippers* sailed all over the world.
clip•per (klip′ər) *noun, plural* **clippers.**

clover A small plant with leaves of three leaflets and rounded, fragrant flowers of white, red, or purple.
clo•ver (klō′vər) *noun, plural* **clovers.**

cluster To grow or group in a cluster. We all *clustered* around the campfire. *Verb.*— A number of things of the same kind that grow or are grouped together. Grapes grow in *clusters. Noun.*
clus•ter (klus′tər) *verb,* **clustered, clustering;** *noun, plural* **clusters.**

---

combine To join together; unite. We *combined* eggs, flour, and milk to make the batter. *Verb.* — A farm machine that harvests and threshes grain. *Noun.*
com•bine (kəm bīn′ *for verb;* kom′bin *for noun*) *verb,* **combined, combining;** *noun, plural* **combines.**

commercial An advertising message on radio or television. *Noun.*— Relating to business or trade. I plan to take *commercial* subjects in high school. *Adjective.*
com•mer•cial (kə mûr′shəl) *noun, plural* **commercials.**

communicate To exchange or pass along feelings, thoughts, or information. People *communicate* by speaking or writing.
com•mu•ni•cate (kə mū′ni kāt′) *verb,* **communicated, communicating.**

compare 1. To say or think that something is like something else. The writer *compared* the boom of big guns to the sound of thunder. 2. To study in order to find out how persons or things are alike or different. We *compared* our watches and saw that your watch was five minutes ahead of mine.
com•pare (kəm pâr′) *verb,* **compared, comparing.**

compass 1. An instrument for showing directions; it has a magnetic needle that points to the north. Pilots, sailors, and many other people use compasses. The camper was able to get home because his *compass* showed him which way was west. 2. An instrument for drawing circles or measuring distances, made up of two arms joined together at the top. One arm ends in a point and the other holds a pencil. Using a *compass,* the student was able to create a perfect circle on her drawing paper.
com•pass (kum′pəs) *noun, plural* **compasses.**

at; āpe; fär; câre; end; mē; it; īce; pîerce; hot; ōld; sông; fôrk; oil; out; up; ūse; rūle; pùll; tûrn; chin; sing; shop; thin; <u>th</u>is; hw in white; zh in treasure. The symbol ə stands for the unstressed vowel sound in about, taken, pencil, lemon, and circus.

complicated Hard to understand or do. The directions for putting together the bicycle were too *complicated* for me to follow.
▲ **Synonym:** difficult
com•pli•ca•ted (kom'pli kā'tid) *adjective.*

confusion 1. The condition of being confused; disorder. In my *confusion*, I gave the wrong answer. 2. A mistaking of one person or thing for another. Mistaking John for his twin brother Tom is a common *confusion*.
con•fu•sion (kən fū'zhən) *noun, plural* **confusions.**

connect 1. To fasten or join together. *Connect* the trailer to the car. 2. To consider as related; associate. We *connect* robins with spring.
con•nect (kə nekt') *verb,* **connected, connecting.**

contain 1. To include as a part of. Candy *contains* sugar. 2. To hold. The jar *contains* candy.
con•tain (kən tān') *verb,* **contained, containing.**

coral A hard substance like stone, found in tropical seas. Coral is made up of the skeletons of tiny sea animals. *Coral* is beautiful when growing underwater, and it is very pretty as a decoration out of the water, too. *Noun.*— Having the color coral; pinkish red. She decided to use a *coral* nail polish. *Adjective.*
cor•al (kôr'əl) *noun, plural* **corals;** *adjective.*

county 1. One of the sections into which a state or country is divided. The longest bridge in the whole state is in that *county*. 2. The people living in a county. Most of the *county* came to the fair.
coun•ty (koun'tē) *noun, plural* **counties.**

crate A box made of slats of wood. We broke up the old apple *crates* to use in our bonfire. *Noun.* —To pack in a crate or crates. The farmer *crated* the lettuce. *Verb.*
crate (krāt) *noun, plural* **crates;** *verb,* **crated, crating.**

734

crate

crisscross To mark with crossing lines. The artist *crisscrossed* the paper with fine pencil marks.
criss•cross (kris'krôs) *verb,* **crisscrossed, crisscrossing.**

crumple 1. To press or crush into wrinkles or folds. He *crumpled* up the letter and threw it into the trash can. 2. To fall down or collapse. The old shack *crumpled* when the bulldozer rammed it.
crum•ple (krum'pəl) *verb,* **crumpled, crumpling.**

cultured Having an appreciation of the arts, knowledge, and good taste and manners that are the result of education. The literature professor is a very *cultured* woman.
cul•tured (kul'chərd) *adjective.*

Dd

damage Harm that makes something less valuable or useful. The flood caused great *damage* to farms. *Noun.*— To harm or injure. Rain *damaged* the young plants. *Verb.*
dam•age (dam'ij) *noun, plural* **damages;** *verb,* **damaged, damaging.**

dart To move suddenly and quickly. The rabbit *darted* into the bushes. *Verb.*— A thin, pointed object that looks like a small arrow. He hit the target with each *dart* that he threw. *Noun.*
dart (därt) *verb,* **darted, darting;** *noun, plural* **darts.**

desire A longing; wish. I have always had a great *desire* to travel. *Noun.*—To wish for; long for. My sister *desires* a basketball more than anything. *Verb.*
de•sire (di zīr') *noun, plural* **desires;** *verb,* **desired, desiring.**

at; āpe; fär; câre; end; mē; it; īce; pîerce; hot; ōld; sông; fôrk; oil; out; up; ūse; rüle; püll; tûrn; chin; sing; shop; thin; this; hw in white; zh in treasure. The symbol ə stands for the unstressed vowel sound in about, taken, pencil, lemon, and circus.

735

destroy To ruin completely; wreck. The earthquake *destroyed* the city.
▲ **Synonym:** ruin
de•stroy (di stroi') *verb,* **destroyed, destroying.**

disaster 1. An event that causes much suffering or loss. The flood was a *disaster*. 2. Something that does not go right. My birthday party was a *disaster* because it rained.
▲ **Synonym:** catastrophe
dis•as•ter (di zas'tər) *noun, plural* **disasters.**

display To show or exhibit. The art museum is now *displaying* some of Monet's paintings. *Verb.* —A show or exhibit. A hug is a *display* of affection. *Noun.*
dis•play (dis plā') *verb,* **displayed, displaying;** *noun, plural* **displays.**

ditch A long, narrow hole dug in the ground. Ditches are used to drain off water. After the rain shower, the *ditch* was full. *Noun.*—To make an emergency landing in water. No pilot wants to have to *ditch* an airplane. *Verb.*
ditch (dich) *noun, plural* **ditches;** *verb,* **ditched, ditching.**

736

downstage Toward the front of a theatrical stage. The prop was supposed to land *downstage* left. *Adverb or adjective.*
down•stage (doun'stāj') *adverb; adjective.*

Ee

editor 1. A person who edits. The *editor* made changes in the book after talking with its author. 2. A person who writes editorials. The newspaper *editor* wrote an article in favor of raising city taxes.
ed•i•tor (ed'i tər) *noun, plural* **editors.**

eerie Strange in a scary way; making people frightened or nervous. Walking through that abandoned house was an *eerie* experience.
▲ **Synonym:** creepy
ee•rie (îr'ē) *adjective,* **eerier, eeriest.**

eldest Born first; oldest. I am the *eldest* of three children.
el•dest (el'dist) *adjective.*

elegant Rich and fine in quality. The museum has a major display of *elegant* costumes.
▲ **Synonym:** tasteful
el•e•gant (el'i gənt) *adjective; noun,* **elegance;** *adverb,* **elegantly.**

> **Word History**
> The word *elegant* first appeared in the English language in the 15ᵗʰ century. The word comes from the Latin *eligere,* which means "to select."

endanger 1. To threaten with becoming extinct. Pollution is *endangering* many different species of animals. 2. To put in a dangerous situation. The flood *endangered* the lives of hundreds of people.
▲ **Synonym:** risk
en•dan•ger (en dān'jər) *verb,* **endangered, endangering.**

endless 1. Having no limit or end; going on forever. The drive across the desert seemed *endless*. 2. Without ends. A circle is *endless*.
end•less (end'lis) *adjective.*

enterprise Something that a person plans or tries to do. An *enterprise* is often something difficult or important. The search for the treasure was an exciting *enterprise*.
en•ter•prise (en'tər prīz') *noun, plural* **enterprises.**

entertain 1. To keep interested and amused. The clown *entertained* the children. 2. To have as a guest. They often *entertain* people in their house in the country.
en•ter•tain (en'tər tān') *verb,* **entertained, entertaining.**

at; āpe; fär; câre; end; mē; it; īce; pîerce; hot; ōld; sông; fôrk; oil; out; up; ūse; rüle; püll; tûrn; chin; sing; shop; thin; this; hw in white; zh in treasure. The symbol ə stands for the unstressed vowel sound in about, taken, pencil, lemon, and circus.

737

errand 1. A short trip to do something. I have to run several *errands* this morning. **2.** Something a person is sent to do; the purpose of such a trip. Our *errand* was to buy the newspaper.
er•rand (er'ənd) *noun, plural* **errands.**

exist 1. To be found. Outside of zoos, polar bears *exist* only in arctic regions. **2.** To be real. I do not believe that ghosts *exist.*
ex•ist (eg zist') *verb,* **existed, existing.**

expensive Having a high price; very costly. The town bought an *expensive* new fire engine.
▲ **Synonym:** costly
ex•pen•sive (ek spen'siv) *adjective.*

extinct 1. No longer existing. The dodo became *extinct* because people hunted it for food. **2.** No longer active. The village is built over an *extinct* volcano.
ex•tinct (ek stingkt') *adjective; noun,* **extinction.**

extraordinary Very unusual; remarkable. The teacher said my friend had *extraordinary* talent.
ex•tra•or•di•nar•y
(ek strôr'də ner'ē *or*
ek'strə ôr'də ner'ē) *adjective.*

Ff

fang A long, pointed tooth. When trying to look threatening, a wolf shows its *fangs.*
fang (fang) *noun, plural* **fangs.**

feeble Not strong; weak. That is a *feeble* excuse.
fee•ble (fē'bəl) *adjective,* **feebler, feeblest;** *noun,* **feebleness;** *adverb,* **feebly.**

festival 1. A program of special activities or shows. We saw a foreign film at the film *festival.* **2.** A celebration or holiday. There were plenty of delicious foods to try at the street *festival.*
fes•ti•val (fes'tə vəl) *noun, plural* **festivals.**

738

foggy 1. Full of or hidden by fog; misty. Driving is dangerous on *foggy* days and nights. **2.** Confused or unclear. The ideas were *foggy* and the project needed more research to clear things up.
fog•gy (fôg'ē *or* fog'ē) *adjective,* **foggier, foggiest.**

foothill A low hill near the lower part of a mountain or mountain range. The cabin was in the *foothills* of the Blue Ridge Mountains.
foot•hill (fut'hil') *noun, plural* **foothills.**

foul Very unpleasant or dirty. The water in the old well looked *foul. Adjective.* —A violation of the rules. The basketball player committed a *foul. Noun.*
▲ Another word that sounds like this is **fowl.**
foul (foul) *adjective,* **fouler, foulest;** *noun, plural* **fouls.**

fowl One of a number of birds used for food. Chicken, turkey, and duck are kinds of *fowl.* We always eat *fowl* for Thanksgiving dinner.
▲ Another word that sounds like this is **foul.**
fowl (foul) *noun, plural* **fowl** *or* **fowls.**

fowl

fragrance A sweet or pleasing smell. Roses have a beautiful *fragrance.*
▲ **Synonym:** smell
fra•grance (frā'grəns) *noun, plural* **fragrances.**

fray To separate into loose threads. Many years of wear had *frayed* the cuffs of the coat.
fray (frā) *verb,* **frayed, fraying.**

freeze 1. To harden because of the cold. When water *freezes,* it becomes ice. **2.** To cover or block with ice. The cold weather *froze* the pipes.
freeze (frēz) *verb,* **froze, frozen, freezing.**

739

fret To suffer emotional distress; irritation. My brother *frets* whenever he gets a low grade on a test. *Verb.* —One of the ridges fixed across the fingerboard of a stringed instrument such as a guitar. The notes get higher each time I move my finger up a *fret. Noun.*
fret (fret) *verb,* **fretted, fretting;** *noun, plural* **frets.**

Gg

gallon A unit of measure for liquids. A *gallon* equals four quarts, or about 3.8 liters.
gal•lon (gal'ən) *noun, plural* **gallons.**

garbage Things that are thrown out. All the spoiled food went into the *garbage.*
▲ **Synonym:** trash
gar•bage (gär'bij) *noun.*

generation 1. A group of persons born around the same time. My parents call us the younger *generation.* **2.** One step in the line of descent from a common ancestor. A grandparent, parent, and child make up three *generations.*
gen•er•a•tion (jen'ə rāsh'ən) *noun, plural* **generations.**

gild To cover with a thin layer of gold. The artist *gilded* the picture frame.
▲ Another word that sounds like this is **guild.**
gild (gild) *verb,* **gilded** *or* **gilt, gilding.**

girth The measurement around an object. The *girth* of the old redwood tree was tremendous.
girth (gûrth) *noun, plural* **girths.**

glint To sparkle or flash. Her eyes *glinted* with merriment.
glint (glint) *verb,* **glinted, glinting;** *noun, plural* **glints.**

glisten To shine with reflected light. The snow *glistened* in the sun.
glis•ten (glis'ən) *verb,* **glistened, glistening.**

glum Very unhappy or disappointed. Every member of the losing team looked *glum* after the game.
glum (glum) *adjective.*

740

gourd A rounded fruit related to the pumpkin or squash. Gourds grow on vines and have a hard outer rind. The hollow *gourd* hung above the tub of water.
gourd (gôrd) *noun, plural* **gourds.**

governess A woman who supervises and cares for a child, especially in a private household. The *governess* made sure the children were ready for bed.
gov•ern•ess (guv'ər nis) *noun, plural* **governesses.**

graze 1. To feed on growing grass. The sheep *grazed* on the hillside. **2.** To scrape or touch lightly in passing. The branch *grazed* the house when the wind blew.
graze (gāz) *verb,* **grazed, grazing.**

guilt 1. A feeling of having done something wrong; shame. I felt *guilt* because I got angry at a good friend. **2.** The condition or fact of having done something wrong or having broken the law. The evidence proved the robber's *guilt.*
▲ Another word that sounds like this is **gilt.**
guilt (gilt) *noun; adjective,* **guilty.**

Hh

harbor A sheltered place along a coast. Ships and boats often anchor in a *harbor. Noun.*—To give protection or shelter to. It is against the law to *harbor* a criminal. *Verb.*
har•bor (här'bər) *noun, plural* **harbors;** *verb,* **harbored, harboring.**

haul To pull or move with force; drag. We *hauled* the trunk up the stairs. *Verb.*— The act of hauling. It was an easy *haul* by truck. *Noun.*
▲ Another word that sounds like this is **hall.**
haul (hôl) *verb,* **hauled, hauling;** *noun, plural* **hauls.**

741

haze Mist, smoke, or dust in the air. The bridge was hidden in the *haze*.
haze (hāz) *noun, plural* **hazes**.

headlong 1. With the head first. The runner slid *headlong* into second base. **2.** In a reckless way; rashly. I rushed *headlong* into buying the bicycle.
head•long (hed'lông') *adverb*.

healthy Having or showing good health. She has a *healthy* outlook on life.
health•y (hel'thē) *adjective*, **healthier, healthiest**.

heave 1. To lift, raise, pull, or throw using force or effort. I *heaved* a rock across the stream. **2.** To utter in an effortful way. I *heaved* a sigh of relief.
heave (hēv) *verb*, **heaved, heaving**.

hilltop The top of a hill. From the *hilltop*, the hikers could see the smoke from the campfire.
hill•top (hil'top') *noun, plural* **hilltops**.

horizon 1. The line where the sky and the ground or the sea seem to meet. The fishing boat headed out to sea just as the sun rose above the *horizon*. **2.** The limit of a person's knowledge, interests, or experience. You can widen your *horizons* by reading books.
hor•i•zon (hə rī'zən) *noun, plural* **horizons**.

huddle To gather close together in a bunch. The scouts *huddled* around the campfire to keep warm. *Verb.*—A group of people or animals gathered close together. The football players formed a *huddle* to plan their next play. *Noun.*
hud•dle (hud'əl) *verb*, **huddled, huddling;** *noun, plural* **huddles**.

742

Ii

iceberg A very large piece of floating ice that has broken off from a glacier. Only the tip of the *iceberg* is visible above the surface of the water.
ice•berg (is'bûrg') *noun, plural* **icebergs**.

identify To find out or tell exactly who a person is or what a thing is; recognize. Can you *identify* this strange object?
▲ **Synonym:** recognize
i•den•ti•fy (ī den'tə fī') *verb*, **identified, identifying**.

ignorant 1. Not informed or aware. I wasn't wearing my watch, so I was *ignorant* of the time. **2.** Showing a lack of knowledge. The young cowhands were *ignorant* at first of how to brand cattle, but they learned quickly.
ig•no•rant (ig'nər ənt) *adjective*.

image 1. A person who looks very similar to someone else. That girl is the *image* of her mother. **2.** A picture or other likeness of a person or thing. A penny has an *image* of Abraham Lincoln on one side of it.
im•age (im'ij) *noun, plural* **images**.

importance The state of being important; having great value or meaning. Rain is of great *importance* to farmers, since crops can't grow without water.
im•por•tance (im pôr'təns) *noun*.

ingredient Any one of the parts that go into a mixture. Flour, eggs, sugar, and butter are the main *ingredients* of this cake.
in•gre•di•ent (in grē'dē ənt) *noun, plural* **ingredients**.

injury Harm or damage done to a person or thing. The accident caused an *injury* to my leg.
in•ju•ry (in'jə rē) *noun, plural* **injuries**.

inning One of the parts into which a baseball or softball game is divided. Both teams bat during an inning until three players on each team are put out. Our team won the game by scoring five runs in the last *inning*.
in•ning (in'ing) *noun, plural* **innings**.

at; āpe; fär; câre; end; mē; it; īce; pîerce; hot; ōld; sông; fôrk; oil; out; up; ūse; rüle; pùll; tûrn; chin; sing; shop; thin; this; hw in white; zh in treasure. The symbol ə stands for the unstressed vowel sound in about, taken, pencil, lemon, and circus.

743

inspect To look at closely and carefully. The official *inspected* our car and declared it safe to drive.
▲ **Synonym:** examine
in•spect (in spekt') *verb*, **inspected, inspecting**.

inspire 1. To stir the mind, feelings, or imagination of. The senator's speech *inspired* the audience. **2.** To fill with a strong, encouraging feeling. Success in school *inspired* me with hope for the future.
▲ **Synonym:** encourage
in•spire (in spir') *verb*, **inspired, inspiring**.

instance An example; case. There are many *instances* of immigrants becoming famous Americans.
in•stance (in'stəns) *noun, plural* **instances**.

instinct A way of acting or behaving that a person or animal is born with and does not have to learn. Birds build nests by *instinct*.
in•stinct (in'stingkt') *noun, plural* **instincts**.

Jj

jagged Having sharp points that stick out. Some eagles build nests on *jagged* cliffs.
jag•ged (jag'id) *adjective*.

Kk

keel To fall over suddenly; collapse. The heat in the crowded subway caused two people to *keel* over. *Verb.*— A wooden or metal piece that runs along the center of the bottom of many ships and boats. When we sailed through the shallow waters, the *keel* scraped along the bottom of the lake. *Noun.*
keel (kēl) *verb*, **keeled, keeling;** *noun, plural* **keels**.

744

knapsack A bag made of canvas, leather, nylon, or other material that is used for carrying clothes, books, equipment, or other supplies. A knapsack is strapped over the shoulders and carried on the back. Because she left her *knapsack* on the bus, she couldn't turn in her homework assignment.
▲ **Synonym:** backpack
knap•sack (nap'sak') *noun, plural* **knapsacks**.

knowledge 1. An understanding that is gained through experience or study. I have enough *knowledge* of football to be able to follow a game. **2.** The fact of knowing. The *knowledge* that the car could slide on the icy road made the driver more careful.
knowl•edge (nol'ij) *noun*.

Ll

labor To do hard work. The two women *labored* over the quilt, hoping to finish it in time for the birthday party. *Verb.*—Hard work; toil. The farmers were tired after their *labor*. *Noun.*
la•bor (lā'bər) *verb*, **labored, laboring;** *noun, plural* **labors**.

launch To start something. The company *launched* its store with a big sale. *Verb.*—The act or process of launching. We watched the rocket *launch* on television. *Noun.*
launch (lônch) *verb*, **launched, launching;** *noun, plural* **launches**.

league 1. A number of people, groups, or countries joined together for a common purpose. Those two teams belong to the same *league*. **2.** A measure of distance used in the past, equal to about three miles. The army's camp was only two *leagues* from the city.
league (lēg) *noun, plural* **leagues**.

at; āpe; fär; câre; end; mē; it; īce; pîerce; hot; ōld; sông; fôrk; oil; out; up; ūse; rüle; pùll; tûrn; chin; sing; shop; thin; this; hw in white; zh in treasure. The symbol ə stands for the unstressed vowel sound in about, taken, pencil, lemon, and circus.

745

linger To stay on as if not wanting to leave; move slowly. The fans *lingered* outside the stadium to see the team.
  lin•ger (ling′gər) *verb,* **lingered, lingering.**

lodge A small house, cottage, or cabin. The hunters stayed at a *lodge* in the mountains. *Noun.*—To live in a place for a while. People *lodged* in the school during the flood. *Verb.*
  lodge (loj) *noun, plural* **lodges;** *verb,* **lodged, lodging.**

loft 1. The upper floor, room, or space in a building. The artist cleaned his *loft.* **2.** An upper floor or balcony in a large hall or church. The choir sang in the choir *loft.*
  loft (lôft) *noun, plural* **lofts.**

loosen 1. To make or become looser. *Loosen* your necktie. **2.** To set free or release. The dog had been *loosened* from its leash.
  loosen (lü′sen) *verb,* **loosened, loosening.**

lurk 1. To lie hidden, especially in preparation for an attack. Snakes *lurk* under rocks. **2.** To move about quietly; sneak. Thieves *lurk* in the shadows.
  lurk (lûrk) *verb,* **lurked, lurking.**

Mm

machine 1. A device that does a particular job, made up of a number of parts that work together. A lawn mower, a hair dryer, and a printing press are *machines.* **2.** A simple device that lessens the force needed to move an object. A lever and a pulley are simple *machines.*
  ma•chine (mə shēn′) *noun, plural* **machines.**

malachite A green mineral that is used for making ornaments.
  mal•a•chite (mal′ə kit′) *noun.*

mammal A kind of animal that is warm-blooded and has a backbone. Human beings are *mammals.*
  mam•mal (mam′əl) *noun, plural* **mammals.**

marine Having to do with or living in the sea. Whales are *marine* animals. *Adjective.*—A member of the Marine Corps. She joined the *Marines* after she graduated. *Noun.*
  ma•rine (mə rēn′) *adjective; noun, plural* **marines.**

marketplace A place where food and other products are bought and sold. In old towns the *marketplace* was often in a square.
  mar•ket•place (mär′kit plās′) *noun, plural* **marketplaces.**

marvel To feel wonder and astonishment. We *marveled* at the acrobat's skill. *Verb.*—A wonderful or astonishing thing. Space travel is one of the *marvels* of modern science. *Noun.*
  mar•vel (mär′vəl) *verb,* **marveled, marveling;** *noun, plural* **marvels.**

mature Having reached full growth or development; ripe. When a puppy becomes *mature* it is called a dog. *Adjective.*—To become fully grown or developed. The tomatoes are *maturing* fast. *Verb.*
  ma•ture (mə chür′ *or* mə tür′) *adjective; verb,* **matured, maturing.**

maze A confusing series of paths or passageways through which people may have a hard time finding their way. I got lost in the *maze* of hallways in my new school.
  maze (māz) *noun, plural* **mazes.**

at; āpe; fär; câre; end; mē; it; īce; pîerce; hot; ōld; sông; fôrk; oil; out; up; ūse; rüle; pull; tûrn; chin; sing; shop; thin; this; hw in white; zh in treasure. The symbol ə stands for the unstressed vowel sound in about, taken, pencil, lemon, and circus.

memorize To learn by heart; fix in the memory. You can *memorize* the poem by reciting it over and over.
  mem•o•rize (mem′ə riz′) *verb,* **memorized, memorizing.**

merely Nothing more than; only. Your explanations are *merely* excuses.
  mere•ly (mîr′lē) *adverb.*

messenger A person who delivers messages or runs errands. The *messenger* was delayed by traffic.
  mes•sen•ger (mes′ən jər) *noun, plural* **messengers.**

method 1. A way of doing something. Speaking on the telephone is a *method* of communicating. **2.** Order or system. I could not find what I wanted because the books had been shelved without *method.*
  meth•od (meth′əd) *noun, plural* **methods.**

microscope A device for looking at things that are too small to be seen with the naked eye. It has one or more lenses that produce an enlarged image of anything viewed through it.
  mi•cro•scope (mī′krə skōp′) *noun, plural* **microscopes.**

microscope

mingle 1. To put or come together; mix; join. This stream *mingles* with others to form a river. **2.** To move about freely; join; associate. We *mingled* with the other guests.
  min•gle (ming′gəl) *verb,* **mingled, mingling.**

molar Any one of the large teeth at the back of the mouth. *Molars* have broad surfaces for grinding food.
  mo•lar (mō′lər) *noun, plural* **molars.**

moonscape View of the surface of the moon.
  moon•scape (mün′skāp′) *noun, plural* **moonscapes.**

mound A slightly raised area. The pitcher stands on the *mound* to pitch the ball. *Noun.*—To pile in a hill or heap. I like to *mound* ice cream on top of my pie. *Verb.*
  mound (mound) *noun, plural* **mounds;** *verb,* **mounded, mounding.**

mug A large drinking cup with a handle, often made of pottery or metal. I drink tea out of my purple *mug. Noun.*—To attack and rob someone. A lady was *mugged* of all her belongings. *Verb.*
  mug (mug) *noun, plural* **mugs;** *verb,* **mugged, mugging.**

mutter To speak in a low, unclear way with the mouth almost closed. I *muttered* to myself. *Verb.* —Oral sounds produced in a low, unclear way. There was a *mutter* of disapproval from the audience. *Noun.*
  mut•ter (mut′ər) *verb,* **muttered, muttering;** *noun.*

Nn

native Originally living or growing in a region or country. Raccoons are *native* to America. *Adjective.*—A person who was born in a particular country or place. One of my classmates is a *native* of Germany. *Noun.*
  na•tive (nā′tiv) *adjective; noun, plural* **natives.**

natural 1. Found in nature; not made by people; not artificial. *Natural* rock formations overlook the river. **2.** Existing from birth; not the result of teaching or training. Is your musical talent *natural,* or did you take lessons?
  nat•u•ral (nach′ər əl) *adjective.*

neighbor A person, place, or thing that is next to or near another. Our *neighbor* took care of our dog while we were away.
  neigh•bor (nā′bər) *noun, plural* **neighbors.**

newsletter A small publication containing news of interest to a special group of people. Our chess club publishes a monthly *newsletter.*
  news•let•ter (nüz′let′ər) *noun, plural* **newsletters.**

at; āpe; fär; câre; end; mē; it; īce; pîerce; hot; ōld; sông; fôrk; oil; out; up; ūse; rüle; pull; tûrn; chin; sing; shop; thin; this; hw in white; zh in treasure. The symbol ə stands for the unstressed vowel sound in about, taken, pencil, lemon, and circus.

Glossary

nip 1. To bite or pinch quickly and not hard. The parrot *nipped* my finger. 2. To cut off by pinching. The gardener *nipped* the dead leaves off the plants.
nip (nip) *verb*, **nipped, nipping.**

nursery 1. A baby's bedroom. The baby's *nursery* was painted pink and blue. 2. A place where young children are taken care of during the day.
nurs•er•y (nûr′sə rē) *noun, plural* **nurseries.**

Oo

occasion 1. An important or special event. The baby's first birthday was an *occasion*. 2. A time when something happens. I have met that person on several *occasions*.
oc•ca•sion (ə kā′zhən) *noun, plural* **occasions.**

opponent A person or group that is against another in a fight, contest, or discussion. The soccer team beat its *opponent*.
▲ **Synonym:** enemy
op•po•nent (ə pō′nənt) *noun, plural* **opponents.**

orchard An area of land where fruit trees are grown. We picked apples in the apple *orchard*.
or•chard (ôr′chərd) *noun, plural* **orchards.**

organization 1. A group of people joined together for a particular purpose. The Red Cross is an international *organization*. 2. The act of organizing. Who is responsible for the *organization* of the school dance?
or•gan•i•za•tion (ôr′gə nə zā′shən) *noun, plural* **organizations.**

original Relating to or belonging to the origin or beginning of something; first. The *original* owner of the house still lives there. *Adjective.* —Something that is original; not a copy, imitation, or translation. That painting is an *original* by Monet. *Noun.*
o•rig•i•nal (ə rij′ə nəl) *adjective; noun, plural* **originals.**

750

---

orphan A child whose parents are dead. The little *orphan* was raised by her grandparents. *Noun.* —To make an orphan of. The war *orphaned* many children. *Verb.*
or•phan (ôr′fən) *noun, plural* **orphans;** *verb,* **orphaned, orphaning.**

overalls Loose-fitting trousers with a piece that covers the chest and attached suspenders.
o•ver•alls (ō′vər ôlz′) *plural noun.*

overcome 1. To get the better of; beat or conquer. The tired runner couldn't *overcome* the others in the race. 2. To get over or deal with. I *overcame* my fear of small spaces.
▲ **Synonym:** defeat
o•ver•come (ō′vər kum′) *verb,* **overcame, overcome, overcoming.**

overflow To be so full that the contents spill over. The bathtub *overflowed*. *Verb.*— Something that flows over. We mopped up the *overflow*. *Noun.*
o•ver•flow (ō′vər flō′ *for verb;* ō′vər flō′ *for noun*) *verb,* **overflowed, overflowing;** *noun.*

oxygen A colorless, odorless gas that makes up about one fifth of our air.
ox•y•gen (ok′si jən) *noun.*

Pp

pathway A course or route taken to reach a particular place. This *pathway* leads to the rose garden.
path•way (path′wā′) *noun, plural* **pathways.**

patient A person under the care or treatment of a doctor. The pediatrician had many *patients* to see. *Noun.*—Having or showing an ability to put up with hardship, pain, trouble, or delay without getting angry or upset. I tried to be *patient* while I waited in the line at the post office. *Adjective.*
pa•tient (pā′shənt) *noun, plural* **patients;** *adjective.*

at; āpe; fär; câre; end; mē; it; īce; pîerce; hot; ōld; sông; fôrk; oil; out; up; ūse; rūle; pùll; tûrn; chin; sing; shop; thin; this; hw in white; zh in treasure. The symbol ə stands for the unstressed vowel sound in about, taken, pencil, lemon, and circus.

751

---

peddler One who carries goods from place to place and offers them for sale.
▲ **Synonym:** vendor
ped•dler (ped′lər) *noun, plural* **peddlers.**

percent The number of parts in every hundred. The symbol for *percent* when it is written with a number is %.
per•cent (pər sent′) *noun.*

permit To allow or let. My parents will not *permit* me to play outside after dark. *Verb.*—A written order giving permission to do something. You need a *permit* to fish here. *Noun.*
per•mit (pər mit′ *for verb;* pûr′mit *or* pər mit′ *for noun*) *verb,* **permitted, permitting;** *noun, plural* **permits.**

Word History
Permit comes from the Latin word *permittere*, "to let through."

pesky Troublesome or annoying. If that *pesky* fly does not stop buzzing in my ear, I'll swat it.
▲ **Synonym:** annoying
pes•ky (pes′kē) *adjective,* **peskier, peskiest.**

plantation A large estate or farm worked by laborers who live there. Cotton is grown on *plantations*.
plan•ta•tion (plan tā′shən) *noun, plural* **plantations.**

pod A part of a plant that holds a number of seeds as they grow. Beans and peas grow in *pods*.
pod (pod) *noun, plural* **pods.**

poisonous Containing a drug or other substance that harms or kills by chemical action. Many household chemicals are *poisonous*.
poi•son•ous (poi′zən əs) *adjective.*

poncho A cloak made of one piece of cloth or other material, with a hole in the middle for the head.
pon•cho (pon′chō) *noun, plural* **ponchos.**

752

---

portable Easy to carry from place to place. *Portable* computers are very popular.
port•a•ble (pôr′tə bəl) *adjective.*

portfolio 1. A case for carrying loose pictures, pamphlets, or papers. I placed all the pictures in my *portfolio*. 2. A set of drawings or pictures bound in a book or a folder. I must get my *portfolio* ready for the meeting
port•fo•lio (pôrt fō′lē ō′) *noun, plural* **portfolios.**

pottery Pots, bowls, dishes, and other things made from clay. I made a bowl in *pottery* class.
pot•ter•y (pot′ə rē) *noun.*

pouch 1. A bag; sack. The mail carrier took the letters out of her *pouch*. 2. A pocket of skin in some animals. Kangaroos and opossums carry their young in *pouches*.
pouch (pouch) *noun, plural* **pouches.**

prairie Flat or rolling land covered with grass, and with few or no trees.
prai•rie (prâr′ē) *noun, plural* **prairies.**

prairie

praise An expression of high regard and approval. The teacher had nothing but *praise* for the student's drawing. *Noun.*—To worship. The minister *praised* God in her sermon. *Verb.*
praise (prāz) *noun, plural* **praises;** *verb,* **praised, praising.**

prance 1. To spring forward on the hind legs. The colt *pranced* and leaped about the field. 2. To move in a proud, happy way. The children *pranced* around the house in their fancy costumes.
prance (prans) *verb,* **pranced, prancing.**

at; āpe; fär; câre; end; mē; it; īce; pîerce; hot; ōld; sông; fôrk; oil; out; up; ūse; rūle; pùll; tûrn; chin; sing; shop; thin; this; hw in white; zh in treasure. The symbol ə stands for the unstressed vowel sound in about, taken, pencil, lemon, and circus.

753

G8 *Glossary*

prejudice Hatred or unfair treatment of a particular group, such as members of a race or religion. *Noun.*—To cause to have prejudice. Being hurt once by a dentist *prejudiced* me against all dentists. *Verb.*
   prej•u•dice (prej'ə dis) *noun, plural* **prejudices**; *verb,* **prejudiced, prejudicing.**

preserve To keep from being lost, damaged, or decayed; protect. It is important that we *preserve* our freedoms. *Verb.*—An area set aside for the protection of plants and animals. Rare birds and mammals breed in that nature *preserve. Noun.*
   pre•serve (pri zûrv') *verb,* **preserved, preserving;** *noun, plural* **preserves.**

pressure The force exerted by one thing pushing against another. The *pressure* of his foot on the gas pedal caused the car to go faster. *Noun.*—To urge strongly. The salesperson tried to *pressure* me into buying something I didn't need. *Verb.*
   pres•sure (presh'ər) *noun, plural* **pressures;** *verb,* **pressured, pressuring.**

previously Before; at an earlier time. We had been introduced *previously.*
   ▲ **Synonym:** earlier
   pre•vi•ous•ly (prē'vē əs lē) *adverb.*

quibble A minor dispute or disagreement. It's foolish to have a *quibble* over nothing. *Noun.* To engage in petty arguing. The two sisters *quibbled* for half an hour about who would take out the garbage. *Verb.*
   quib•ble (kwi'bəl) *noun, plural* **quibbles;** *verb,* **quibbled, quibbling.**

Rr

racial Of or relating to a race of human beings. *Racial* prejudice is prejudice against people because of their race.
   ra•cial (rā'shəl) *adjective; adverb,* **racially.**

ramp A sloping platform or passageway connecting two different levels.
   ramp (ramp) *noun, plural* **ramps.**

754

reef A ridge of sand, rock, or coral at or near the surface of the ocean. We like to swim near the beautiful *reefs.*
   reef (rēf) *noun, plural* **reefs.**

reference 1. A person or thing referred to; source of information. The encyclopedia was the *reference* for my report. **2.** A statement that calls or directs attention to something. The authors made a *reference* to their book.
   ref•er•ence (ref'ər əns *or* ref'rəns) *noun, plural* **references.**

reflect 1. To give back an image of something. I saw myself *reflected* in the pond. **2.** To turn or throw back. Sand *reflects* light and heat from the sun.
   re•flect (ri flekt') *verb,* **reflected, reflecting.**

rein One of two or more narrow straps attached to a bridle or bit, used to guide and control a horse. The jockey held tightly to the horse's *reins. Noun.*—To guide, control, or hold back. The rider tried to *rein* in the galloping horse. *Verb.*
   rein (rān) *noun, plural* **reins;** *verb,* **reined, reining.**

related 1. Belonging to the same family. You and your cousins are *related.* **2.** Having some connection. I have problems *related* to school.
   re•la•ted (ri lā'tid) *adjective.*

at; āpe; fär; câre; end; mē; it; īce; pîerce; hot; ōld; sông; fôrk; oil; out; up; ūse; rūle; pùll; tûrn; chin; sing; shop; thin; <u>th</u>is; hw in white; zh in treasure. The symbol ə stands for the unstressed vowel sound in about, taken, pencil, lemon, and circus.

755

release To set free; let go. The hostage was *released* after being held prisoner for ten days. *Verb.*—The act of releasing or the state of being released. The criminal's *release* from prison made headlines. *Noun.*
   re•lease (ri lēs') *verb,* **released, releasing;** *noun, plural* **releases.**

relieve 1. To free from discomfort or pain; comfort. The doctor gave me medicine to *relieve* my cough. **2.** To free from a job or duty. The lifeguards stayed on duty until they were *relieved.*
   re•lieve (ri lēv') *verb,* **relieved, relieving.**

reptile One of a class of cold-blooded animals with a backbone and dry, scaly skin, which move by crawling on their stomachs or creeping on short legs.
   rep•tile (rep'təl *or* rep'tīl) *noun, plural* **reptiles.**

require 1. To have a need of. We all *require* food and sleep. **2.** To force, order, or demand. The law *requires* drivers to stop at a red light.
   re•quire (ri kwīr') *verb,* **required, requiring.**

research A careful study to find and learn facts. I did *research* in the library for my report. *Noun.*—To do research on or for. I *researched* my speech by reading many books on the subject. *Verb.*
   re•search (ri sûrch' *or* rē'sûrch') *verb,* **researched, researching;** *noun, plural* **researches.**

resemble To be like or similar to. That hat *resembles* mine.
   re•sem•ble (ri zem'bəl) *verb,* **resembled, resembling.**

resound 1. To be filled with sound. The stadium *resounded* with cheers. **2.** To make a loud, long, or echoing sound. Thunder *resounded* in the air.
   re•sound (ri zound') *verb,* **resounded, resounding.**

restless 1. Not able to rest. We got *restless* during the long speech. **2.** Not giving rest. The patient spent a *restless* night.
   rest•less (rest'lis) *adjective; adverb,* **restlessly;** *noun,* **restlessness.**

756

rhythm A regular or orderly repeating of sounds or movements. We marched to the *rhythm* of drums.
   rhythm (ri<u>th</u>'əm) *noun, plural* **rhythms.**

roadblock A barrier or obstacle that prevents people or cars from passing through.
   road•block (rōd'blok') *noun, plural* **roadblocks.**

robot A machine that can do some of the same things that a human being can do.
   ro•bot (rō'bət *or* rō'bot) *noun, plural* **robots.**

Ss

sacrifice The giving up of something for the sake of someone or something else. The parents made many *sacrifices* in order to send their children to college. *Noun.*—To offer as a sacrifice. Ancient peoples *sacrificed* animals to their gods. *Verb.*
   sac•ri•fice (sak'rə fīs') *noun, plural* **sacrifices;** *verb,* **sacrificed, sacrificing;** *adjective,* **sacrificial.**

sage A very wise person, usually old and respected. *Noun.*— Having or showing great wisdom and sound judgment. My grandparents often give me *sage* advice. *Adjective.*
   sage (sāj) *noun, plural* **sages;** *adjective,* **sager, sagest.**

sagebrush A plant that grows on the dry plains of western North America.
   sage•brush (sāj'brush') *noun.*

scamper To run or move quickly. The rabbit *scampered* into the woods.
   scam•per (skam'pər) *verb,* **scampered, scampering.**

at; āpe; fär; câre; end; mē; it; īce; pîerce; hot; ōld; sông; fôrk; oil; out; up; ūse; rūle; pùll; tûrn; chin; sing; shop; thin; <u>th</u>is; hw in white; zh in treasure. The symbol ə stands for the unstressed vowel sound in about, taken, pencil, lemon, and circus.

757

Glossary

G9

scribble To write or draw quickly or carelessly. I *scribbled* a note to my friend. *Verb.*—Writing or drawing that is made by scribbling. The paper was covered with messy *scribbles*. *Noun.*
scrib•ble (skrib′əl) *verb,* **scribbled, scribbling;** *noun, plural* **scribbles;** *noun,* **scribbler.**

scuba (Self-Contained Underwater Breathing Apparatus) Equipment used for swimming underwater.
scu•ba (skü′bə) *noun.*

sediment 1. Rocks, dirt, or other solid matter carried and left by water, glaciers, or wind. 2. Small pieces of matter that settle at the bottom of a liquid. There was *sediment* at the bottom of the bottle.
sed•i•ment (sed′ə mənt) *noun.*

segregation The practice of setting one group apart from another.
seg•re•ga•tion (seg′ri gā′shən) *noun.*

settlement 1. A small village or group of houses. During the 1800s, pioneers built many *settlements* in the American West. 2. The act of settling or the condition of being settled. The *settlement* of Jamestown took place in 1607.
set•tle•ment (set′əl mənt) *noun, plural* **settlements.**

758

shanty A small, poorly built house; shack. During the Depression, many poor families lived in *shanties*.
▲ **Synonym:** shack
shan•ty (shan′tē) *noun, plural* **shanties.**

shoreline The line where a body of water and the land meet. My friend has a house near the *shoreline*.
shore•line (shôr′līn′) *noun.*

shortcut 1. A quicker way of reaching a place. I took a *shortcut* to school. 2. A way of doing something faster. Don't use any *shortcuts* in your science experiment.
short•cut (shôrt′cut′) *noun, plural* **shortcuts.**

shriek A loud, sharp cry or sound. The child let out a *shriek* of laughter. *Noun.*—To utter a loud, sharp cry or sound. We all *shrieked* with laughter at her jokes. *Verb.*
shriek (shrēk) *noun, plural* **shrieks;** *verb,* **shrieked, shrieking.**

---

shutter 1. A movable cover for a window, usually attached to the frame by hinges. *Shutters* are used to shut out light 2. The part of a camera that snaps open and shuts quickly to let light onto the film when a picture is taken.
shut•ter (shut′ər) *noun, plural* **shutters.**

siren A device that makes a loud, shrill sound, used as a signal or warning. Ambulances and police cars have *sirens*.
si•ren (sī′rən) *noun, plural* **sirens.**

sketch A rough, quick drawing. The artist made several *sketches* of the model before starting the painting. *Noun.*—To make a sketch of. I *sketched* an old barn for my art class. *Verb.*
sketch (skech) *verb,* **sketched, sketching;** *noun, plural* **sketches.**

> **Word History**
> *Sketch* comes from the Dutch word *schets* and the Italian word *schizzo,* meaning "splash." A sketch is often a rough drawing, a splash of an idea that will later become a detailed finished product.

skill The power or ability to do something. *Skill* comes with practice and experience.
skill (skil) *noun, plural* **skills.**

skillet A shallow pan with a handle. A *skillet* is used for frying.
skil•let (skil′it) *noun, plural* **skillets.**

skim 1. To remove from the surface of a liquid. The cook *skimmed* the fat from the soup. 2. To read quickly. *Skim* the paper for the scores.
skim (skim) *verb,* **skimmed, skimming.**

at; āpe; fär; câre; end; mē; it; īce; pîerce; hot; ōld; sông; fôrk; oil; out; up; ūse; rūle; pull; tûrn; chin; sing; shop; thin; this; hw in white; zh in treasure. The symbol ə stands for the unstressed vowel sound in about, taken, pencil, lemon, and circus.

759

---

smog A combination of smoke and fog in the air. *Smog* is found especially over cities where there are factories and many cars.
smog (smog) *noun.*

> **Word History**
> The word *smog* was made using the first two letters of *smoke* and the last two letters of *fog*.

snout The front part of an animal's head, including nose, mouth, and jaws. My dog has a cute *snout*.
snout (snout) *noun, plural* **snouts.**

soapsuds Water that is bubbly with soap. I like my bath to be filled with *soapsuds*.
soap•suds (sōp′sudz′) *plural noun.*

soggy Very wet or damp; soaked. The soil was *soggy* after the rain.
sog•gy (sog′ē) *adjective,* **soggier, soggiest.**

760

soot A black, greasy powder that forms when such fuels as wood, coal, and oil are burned. The old chimney was caked with *soot*.
soot (sut *or* süt) *noun; adjective,* **sooty.**

spice The seeds or other parts of certain plants used to flavor food. Pepper, cloves, and cinnamon are spices. *Noun.*—To flavor with a spice or spices. I *spiced* the hamburgers. *Verb.*
spice (spis) *noun, plural* **spices;** *verb,* **spiced, spicing;** *adjective,* **spicy.**

spike 1. Any sharp, pointed object or part that sticks out. Baseball shoes have *spikes* on the soles. 2. A large, heavy nail used to hold rails to railroad ties. It was difficult to hammer in the railroad *spike*.
spike (spīk) *noun, plural* **spikes.**

sponge A simple water animal that has a body that is full of holes and absorbs water easily. The dried skeletons of some *sponge* colonies are used for cleaning and washing. *Noun.*—To clean with a sponge. We *sponged* and dried the dirty walls. *Verb.*
sponge (spunj) *noun, plural* **sponges;** *verb,* **sponged, sponging.**

---

squall A strong gust of wind that arises very suddenly. Squalls often bring rain, snow, or sleet. We were forced indoors by a *squall* of snow.
squall (skwôl) *noun, plural* **squalls.**

> **Word History**
> The word *squall* first appeared in the English language in 1699. It is probably based on the Swedish word *skval,* which means "rushing water."

squeal To make a loud, shrill cry or sound. The little pigs *squealed* with excitement. *Verb.* —A loud, shrill cry or sound. The *squeal* of the brakes hurt my ears. *Noun.*
squeal (skwēl) *verb,* **squealed, squealing;** *noun, plural* **squeals.**

stake A stick or post pointed at one end so that it can be driven into the ground. The campers drove in *stakes* and tied the corners of the tent to them. *Noun.* — To fasten or hold up with a stake. The gardener *staked* the beans. *Verb.*
▲ Another word that sounds like this is **steak.**
stake (stāk) *noun, plural* **stakes;** *verb,* **staked, staking.**

sterilize To make free of bacteria and microorganisms. The nurse *sterilized* the scalpels before the operation.
ster•il•ize (ster′ə līz′) *verb,* **sterilized, sterilizing.**

stitch To make, fasten, or mend with stitches; sew. I *stitched* up the tear in my shirt. *Verb.*—One complete movement made with a needle and thread. *Noun.*
stitch (stich) *verb,* **stitched, stitching;** *noun, plural* **stitches.**

strew To spread by scattering. I have to clean my room because my clothes are *strewn* all over the place.
strew (strü) *verb,* **strewed, strewn, strewing.**

at; āpe; fär; câre; end; mē; it; īce; pîerce; hot; ōld; sông; fôrk; oil; out; up; ūse; rūle; pull; tûrn; chin; sing; shop; thin; this; hw in white; zh in treasure. The symbol ə stands for the unstressed vowel sound in about, taken, pencil, lemon, and circus.

761

Glossary

stroll To walk in a slow, relaxed way. We *strolled* through the park. *Verb.* —A slow, relaxed walk. After dinner we took a *stroll. Noun.*
stroll (strōl) *verb,* **strolled, strolling;** *noun, plural* **strolls.**

sturdy Strong; hardy. Heavy trucks can drive on the *sturdy* bridge.
stur•dy (stûr′dē) *adjective,* **sturdier, sturdiest;** *adverb,* **sturdily;** *noun,* **sturdiness.**

success 1. A result hoped for; favorable end. The coach was pleased with the *success* of the game. 2. A person or thing that does or goes well. The party was a big *success.*
suc•cess (sək ses′) *noun, plural* **successes;** *adjective,* **successful.**

sunrise The rising of the sun. We went to the beach to watch the *sunrise.*
sunrise (sun′rīz′) *noun, plural* **sunrises.**

swamp An area of wet land. The *swamp* looked scary and creepy. *Noun.* —To fill with water. High waves *swamped* the boat. *Verb.*
swamp (swomp) *noun, plural* **swamps;** *verb,* **swamped, swamping.**

swamp

Tt

talker One who exchanges spoken words in conversation. The two friends were great *talkers.*
talk•er (tôk′ ər) *noun, plural* **talkers**

teammate A person who is a member of the same team. We're basketball *teammates.*
team•mate (tēm′māt′) *noun, plural* **teammates.**

threat 1. A person or thing that might cause harm; danger. The outbreak of flu was a *threat* to the community. 2. A statement of something that will be done to hurt or punish. The trespassers heeded our *threat.*
threat (thret) *noun, plural* **threats.**

ton A measure of weight equal to 2,000 pounds in the United States and Canada, and 2,240 pounds in Great Britain.
ton (tun) *noun, plural* **tons.**

tractor A vehicle with heavy tires or tracks. *Tractors* are used to pull heavy loads over rough ground.
trac•tor (trak′tər) *noun, plural* **tractors.**

tradition A custom or belief that is passed on from one generation to another.
tra•di•tion (trə dish′ən) *noun, plural* **traditions;** *adjective,* **traditional.**

travel To go from one place to another; to make a trip. We *traveled* through England. *Verb.* —The act of traveling. Camels are used for desert *travel. Noun.*
trav•el (trav′əl) *verb,* **traveled, traveling;** *noun, plural* **travels.**

tricorn A hat with the brim turned up on three sides.
tri•corn (trī′kôrn′) *noun, plural* **tricorns.**

tube A container of soft metal or plastic from which the contents are removed by squeezing. I need a new *tube* of toothpaste.
tube (tüb) *noun, plural* **tubes.**

tusk A long, pointed tooth that sticks out of each side of the mouth in certain animals. Elephants and walruses have *tusks.*
tusk (tusk) *noun, plural* **tusks.**

Ww

waddle To walk or move with short steps, swaying the body from side to side. The duck *waddled* across the yard. *Verb.*—A swaying or rocking walk. The audience laughed at the clown's *waddle. Noun.*
wad•dle (wod′əl) *verb,* **waddled, waddling;** *noun, plural* **waddles.**

at; āpe; fär; câre; end; mē; it; īce; pîerce; hot; ōld; sông; fôrk; oil; out; up; ūse; rüle; pùll; tûrn; chin; sing; shop; thin; *this;* hw in white; zh in treasure. The symbol ə stands for the unstressed vowel sound in about, taken, pencil, lemon, and circus.

weary Very tired. The carpenter was *weary* after the day's hard work. *Adjective.*—To make or become weary; tire. The long walk *wearied* the children. *Verb.*
wea•ry (wîr′ē) *adjective,* **wearier, weariest;** *verb,* **wearied, wearying;** *adverb,* **wearily;** *noun,* **weariness.**

weird Strange or mysterious; odd. A *weird* sound came from the deserted old house.
▲ **Synonym:** peculiar
weird (wîrd) *adjective,* **weirder, weirdest;** *adverb,* **weirdly;** *noun,* **weirdness.**

wharf A structure built along a shore as a landing place for boats and ships; dock. We had to unload the boat once we reached the *wharf.*
wharf (hworf *or* wôrf) *noun, plural* **wharves** *or* **wharfs.**

whicker To neigh or whinny. The horse began *whickering* at the kids. *Verb.*—A neigh or whinny. The horse let out a *whicker. Noun.*
whick•er (hwi′kər) *verb,* **whickered, whickering;** *noun, plural* **whickers.**

whinny A soft neigh. We heard the *whinnies* of the horses. *Noun.* —To neigh in a low, gentle way. My horse *whinnied* when he saw me. *Verb.*
whin•ny (hwin′ē *or* win′ē) *verb,* **whinnied, whinnying;** *noun, plural* **whinnies.**

wildlife Wild animals that live naturally in an area. My favorite part of hiking is observing the *wildlife.*
wild•life (wīld′līf′) *noun.*

windowpane A framed sheet of glass in a window. I placed my candles by the *windowpane.*
win•dow•pane (win′dō pān′) *noun, plural* **windowpanes.**

wondrous Extraordinary; wonderful. The local theater put on a *wondrous* performance.
▲ **Synonym:** marvelous
won•drous (wun′drəs) *adjective;* *adverb,* **wondrously;** *noun,* **wondrousness.**

wrestle 1. To force by grasping. The champion *wrestled* his opponent to the mat. 2. To struggle by grasping and trying to force and hold one's opponent to the ground, without punching. The children *wrestled* on the lawn.
wres•tle (res′əl) *verb,* **wrestled, wrestling.**

wriggle 1. To twist or turn from side to side with short, quick moves; squirm. The bored children *wriggled* in their seats. 2. To get into or out of a position by tricky means. You always try to *wriggle* out of having to wash the dishes.
wrig•gle (rig′əl) *verb,* **wriggled, wriggling;** *adjective,* **wriggly.**

> **Word History**
> The word **wriggle** comes from the Old English word *wrigian,* which means "to turn."

at; āpe; fär; câre; end; mē; it; īce; pîerce; hot; ōld; sông; fôrk; oil; out; up; ūse; rüle; pùll; tûrn; chin; sing; shop; thin; *this;* hw in white; zh in treasure. The symbol ə stands for the unstressed vowel sound in about, taken, pencil, lemon, and circus.

Glossary

G11

Acknowledgments

Cover Illustration: Terry Widener

The publisher gratefully acknowledges permission to reprint the following copyrighted material:

Autobiographical piece by Matt Christopher from PAUSES: AUTOBIOGRAPHICAL REFLECTIONS OF 101 CREATORS OF CHILDREN'S BOOKS by Lee Bennett Hopkins. Copyright © 1995 by Lee Bennett Hopkins. Used by permission of HarperCollins Children's Books, a division of HarperCollins Publishers.

Autobiographical piece by Robert Ballard from TALKING WITH ADVENTURERS by Pat and Linda Cummings. Copyright 1998 by Pat Cummings and Linda Cummings. Used by permission of the National Geographic Society.

"Beezus and Her Imagination" from BEEZUS AND RAMONA by Beverly Cleary. Copyright © 1955 by Beverly Cleary. Used by permission of Dell Publishing, a division of The Bantam Doubleday Dell Publishing Group, Inc.

"The Biggest Problem (Is in Other People's Minds)" from FREE TO BE … YOU AND ME AND FREE TO BE … A FAMILY by Don Haynie. Copyright © 1997, 1987, 1974 by the Free to Be Foundation, Inc. Used by permission of Running Press.

"Birdfoot's Grampa" from ENTERING ONANDAGA by Joseph Bruchac. Copyright © 1978 by Joseph Bruchac. Used by permission.

"Dakota Dugout" from DAKOTA DUGOUT by Ann Turner. Copyright © 1985 by Ann Turner. Reprinted with the permission of Simon & Schuster Books for Young Readers, an imprint of Simon & Schuster Children's Publishing Division.

"The Dentist" from ANOTHER FIRST POETRY BOOK by Judith Nicholls. Copyright © 1987 by Judith Nicholls. Used by permission of Oxford University Press.

"Don't Make a Bargain with a Fox" from THE KING OF THE MOUNTAINS: A TREASURY OF LATIN AMERICAN FOLK STORIES by M. A. Jagendorf and R. S. Boggs. Copyright © 1960 by M. A. Jagendorf and R. S. Boggs. Copyright renewed 1988 by Andre Jagendorf, Merna Alpert and R. S. Boggs. Used by permission of Vanguard Press, a division of Random House, Inc.

"Earth Day Rap" by Doug Goodkin. Copyright © 1995. Used by permission of The McGraw-Hill Co., Inc.

"8,000 Stones" from 8,000 STONES: A CHINESE FOLKTALE retold by Diane Wolkstein. Text copyright © 1972 by Diane Wolkstein. Used by permission.

"Evergreen, Everblue" by Raffi. Copyright © 1990 Homeland Publishing, a division of Troubadour Records Ltd. Used by permission.

ACKNOWLEDGMENTS

The publisher gratefully acknowledges permission to reprint the following copyrighted material.

"Amelia's Road" by Linda Jacobs Altman, illustrated by Enrique O. Sanchez. Text copyright © 1993 by Linda Jacobs Altman. Illustrations copyright © 1993 by Enrique O. Sanchez. Permission granted by Lee & Low Books Inc., 95 Madison Avenue, New York, NY 10016.

"August 8" by Norman Jordan. From MY BLACK ME: A Beginning Book of Black Poetry, edited by Arnold Adoff. Copyright © 1974. Used by permission of Dutton Books, a division of Penguin Putnam, Inc.

"Baseball Saved Us" by Ken Mochizuki, illustrated by Dom Lee. Text copyright © 1993 by Ken Mochizuki. Illustrations copyright © 1993 by Dom Lee. Permission granted by Lee & Low Books Inc., 95 Madison Avenue, New York, NY 10016.

"Final Curve" by Langston Hughes from MY BLACK ME: A Beginning Book of Black Poetry, edited by Arnold Adoff. Copyright © 1974. Used by permission of Dutton Books, a division of Penguin Putnam, Inc.

"The Fox and the Guinea Pig"/"El zorro y el cuy" A traditional Folk Tale translated by Mary Ann Newman, illustrated by Kevin Hawkes. Copyright © 1997 Macmillan/McGraw-Hill, a Division of the Educational and Professional Publishing Group of the McGraw-Hill Companies, Inc.

"The Garden We Planted Together" by Anuruddha Bose from A WORLD IN OUR HANDS. Reprinted with permission of A WORLD IN OUR HANDS by Peace Child Charitable Trust, illustrated by Sanjay Sinha ($15.95). Copyright © 1995 Tricycle Press (800-841-BOOK).

"Gluskabe and the Snow Bird" from GLUSKABE AND THE FOUR WISHES retold by Joseph Bruchac. Copyright © 1995 Cobblehill Books/Dutton.

"Grass Sandals/The Travels of Basho" by Dawnine Spivak, illustrated by Demi. Text copyright © 1997 by Dawnine Spivak, illustrations copyright © 1997 by Demi. Reprinted by permission of Atheneum Books for Young Readers, Simon and Schuster Children's Publishing Division. All rights reserved.

"The Hatmaker's Sign" by Candace Fleming, illustrated by Robert Andrew Parker. Text copyright © 1998 by Candace Fleming. Illustrations copyright © 1998 by Robert Andrew Parker. All rights reserved. Reprinted by permission of Orchard Books, New York.

"How to Tell the Top of a Hill" by John Ciardi from THE REASON FOR THE PELICAN. Copyright © 1959 by John Ciardi. Reprinted by permission of the Estate of John Ciardi.

"I Ask My Mother to Sing" by Li-Young Lee. Copyright © 1986 by Li-Young Lee. Reprinted from Rose with the permission of BOA Editions, Ltd., 260 East Ave., Rochester, NY 14604.

"Just a Dream" is from JUST A DREAM by Chris Van Allsburg. Copyright © 1990 by Chris Van Allsburg. Reprinted by permission of Houghton Mifflin Company.

"Justin and the Best Biscuits in the World" is from JUSTIN AND THE BEST BISCUITS IN THE WORLD by Mildred Pitts Walter. Copyright © 1986 by Mildred Pitts Walter. Published by Lothrop, Lee & Shepard Books and used by permission of William Morrow & Company, Inc. Publishers, New York.

"Leah's Pony" by Elizabeth Friedrich, illustrated by Michael Garland. Text copyright © 1996 by Elizabeth Friedrich. Illustrations copyright © 1996 by Michael Garland. Used by permission of Boyds Mills Press.

"The Lost Lake" by Allen Say. Copyright © 1989 by Allen Say. Reprinted by permission of Houghton Mifflin Company. All rights reserved.

"The Malachite Palace" by Alma Flor Ada, translated by Rosa Zubizarreta, illustrated by Leonid Gore. Text copyright © 1998 by Alma Flor Ada, illustrations copyright © 1998 by Leonid Gore. Reprinted by permission by of Atheneum Books for Young Readers, Simon and Schuster Children's Publishing Division. All rights reserved.

"Meet an Underwater Explorer" by Luise Woelflein. Reprinted from the June 1994 issue of RANGER RICK magazine, with the permission of the publisher, the National Wildlife Federation. Copyright © 1994 by the National Wildlife Federation.

"Mom's Best Friend" by Sally Hobart Alexander, photographs by George Ancona. Text copyright ©1992 by Sally Hobart Alexander. Photographs copyright © 1992 by George Ancona. Reprinted with permission of Simon & Schuster Books for Young Readers, Simon & Schuster Children's Publishing Division.

"My Poems" by Alan Barlow. FROM RISING VOICES: WRITINGS OF YOUNG NATIVE AMERICANS selected by Arlene B. Hirschfelder and Beverly R. Singer. Copyright © 1992. Published by Scribner's. Used by permission.

"On the Bus with Joanna Cole" excerpt from On the Bus with Joanna Cole: A Creative Autobiography by Joanna Cole with Wendy Saul. Copyright © 1996 by Joanna Cole. Published by Heinemann, a division of Reed Elsevier Inc. Reprinted by permission of the Publisher. Illustration on page 447 by Bruce Degen from THE MAGIC SCHOOL BUS INSIDE THE HUMAN BODY by Joanna Cole. Illustration copyright © 1989 by Bruce Degen. Reprinted with permission of Scholastic, Inc. THE MAGIC SCHOOL BUS is a registered trademark of Scholastic, Inc.

"Pat Cummings: My Story" reprinted with the permission of Simon & Schuster Books for Young Readers from TALKING WITH ARTISTS compiled and edited by Pat Cummings. Jacket illustration copyright © 1992 Pat Cummings. Copyright © 1992 Pat Cummings.

"A Place Called Freedom" by Scott Russell Sanders, illustrated by Thomas B. Allen. Text copyright © 1997 by Scott Russell Sanders, illustrations copyright © 1997 by Thomas B. Allen. Reprinted by permission of Atheneum Books for Young Readers, Simon and Schuster Children's Publishing Division. All rights reserved.

"The Poet Pencil" by Jesús Carlos Soto Morfin, translated by Judith Infante. FROM THE TREE IS OLDER THAN YOU ARE: A Bilingual Gathering of Poems and Stories from Mexico, selected by Naomi Shihab Nye. Copyright © 1995 Reprinted by permission of the author.

"The Rajah's Rice" from THE RAJAH'S RICE by David Barry, illustrated by Donna Perrone. Text Copyright © 1994 by David Barry. Art copyright © 1994 by Donna Perrone. Used with permission of W. H. Freeman and Company.

"Sarah, Plain and Tall" text excerpt from SARAH, PLAIN AND TALL by Patricia MacLachlan. Copyright © 1985 by Patricia MacLachlan. Reprinted by permission of HarperCollins Publishers. Cover permission for the Trophy Edition used by permission of HarperCollins Publishers.

"Scruffy: A Wolf Finds His Place in the Pack" by Jim Brandenburg. Copyright © 1996 by Jim Brandenburg. Published by arrangement with Walker Publishing Company, Inc.

"Seal Journey" From SEAL JOURNEY by Richard and Jonah Sobol. Copyright © 1993 Richard Sobol, text and photographs. Used by permission of Cobblehill Books, an affiliate of Dutton Children's Press, a division of Penguin USA, Inc.

"Teammates" from TEAMMATES by Peter Golenbock, text copyright © 1990 by Golenbock Communications, reprinted by permission of Harcourt, Inc.

"To" by Lee Bennett Hopkins from BEEN TO YESTERDAYS: Poems of a Life. Text copyright © 1995 by Lee Bennett Hopkins. Published by Wordsong/Boyds Mill Press. Reprinted by permission.

"The Toothpaste Millionaire" by Jean Merrill. Copyright © 1972 by Houghton Mifflin Company. Adapted and reprinted by permission of Houghton Mifflin Company. All rights reserved.

"Tortillas Like Africa" from CANTO FAMILIAR by Gary Soto. Copyright © 1995 Harcourt, Inc.

"Familiar Friends" from ON THE FARM by James S. Tippett. Compilation copyright © 1991 by Lee Bennett Hopkins. Used by permission of Little, Brown and Company.

"Follow the Drinkin' Gourd," Words and Music by Ronnie Gilbert, Lee Hays, Fred Hellerman and Pete Seeger TRO- © Copyright 1951 (Renewed) Folkways Music Publishers, Inc., New York, New York. Used by permission.

"Fossils" from SOMETHING NEW BEGINS by Lilian Moore. Copyright © 1982 by Lilian Moore. Reprinted with the permission of Atheneum Books for Young Readers, an imprint of Simon & Schuster Children's Publishing Division.

Four haiku from CRICKET NEVER DOES: A COLLECTION OF HAIKU AND TANKA by Myra Cohn Livingston. Text copyright © 1977 by Myra Cohn Livingston. Used by permission of Margaret K. McElderry Books, an imprint of Simon & Schuster Children's Publishing Division.

"Whales" excerpt from WHALES by Seymour Simon. Copyright © 1989 by Seymour Simon. Reprinted by permission of HarperCollins Publishers.

"Yeh-Shen: A Cinderella Story from China" is from YEH-SHEN: A CINDERELLA STORY FROM CHINA by Ai-Ling Louie. Text copyright © 1982 by Ai-Ling Louie. Illustrations copyright © 1982 by Ed Young. Reprinted by permission of Philomel Books. Introductory comments by Ai-Ling Louie and used with her permission.

"Your World" by Georgia Douglas Johnson appeared originally in HOLD FAST TO DREAMS selected by Arna Bontemps. Extensive research has failed to locate the author and/or copyright holder of this work.

Cover Illustration
Terry Widener

Illustration
Roberta Ludlow, 16-17; Jean and Mou-Sien Tseng, 128-129; David Ridley, 130-131; Elizabeth Rosen, 252-253; J. W. Stewart, 254-255; Bruno Paciulli, 372-373; Stefano Vitale, 408-419; Amy Vangsgard, 482-483; Susan Leopold, 484-485; Yoshi Miyake, 612-613; David Catrow, 666-687; B. J. Faulkner, 724-725; George Thompson, 728, 749; Rodica Prato, 732, 739; John Carrozza, 745, 759, 763.

Photography
18-19: c. Fine Art Photographic Library, London/Art Resource, NY. 42-43: c. The Bridgeman Art Library International Ltd. 66: c. Superstock. 94-95: c. Shelburne Museum. 118-119: c. E. A. Barton Collection, England. 132-133: c. Jerry Jacka. 158-159: c. MPTV. 190-191: c. The Museum of Modern Art, New York. 216-217: c. The Bridgeman Art Library International Ltd. 242-243: c. The Bridgeman Art Library International Ltd. 256-257: c. Richard Estes. 282-283: c. Superstock. 298-299: c. The Bridgeman Art Library International Ltd. 332-333: c. The Phillips Collection. The Bridgeman Art Library International Ltd. 360-361: c. Cordon Art B. V. 406-407: c. The Heard Museum. 374-375: c. 424-425: c. Corbis/Bettman. 444-445: c. Private Collection. 472-473: c. The Bridgeman Art Library International Ltd. 486-487: c. Christies Images. 516-517: c. Millenium Pictures. 536-537: c. Art Resource. 568-569: c. Omni-Photo Communications. 600-601: c. The Bridgeman Art Library Ltd. 614-615: c. Jonathan Green. 632-633: c. Chester Beatty Library, Dublin. 664-665: c. Motion Picture and Television Archives. 692/693: c. Superstock. 714-715: c. The Bridgeman Art Library Ltd.

"Hats Off to the Cowboy" from HOME ON THE RANGE: COWBOY POETRY by Red Steagall. Copyright © 1989 by Texas Red Songs. Used by permission of Dial Books, a Division of Penguin Books USA, Inc.

"How It All Began" from THE STORY OF BASEBALL by Lawrence S. Ritter. Copyright © 1983, 1990 by Lawrence S. Ritter. Used by permission of William Morrow and Company, Inc., and Raines and Raines.

"Indians of the Plains" from WORLDS I KNOW AND OTHER POEMS b1y Myra Cohn Livingston. Text copyright © 1985 by Myra Cohn Livingston. Reprinted with the permission of Macmillan Publishing Company, an imprint of Simon & Schuster Children's Publishing Division.

"Jackie Robinson" from FOLLOWERS OF THE NORTH STAR: RHYMES ABOUT AFRICAN AMERICAN HEROES, HEROINES, AND HISTORICAL TIMES by Susan Altman and Susan Lechner. Copyright © 1993 Childrens Press ®, Inc. Used by permission of Childrens Press.

"The Needle in the Haystack" from CRICKET MAGAZINE by John Hamma. Copyright © 1982 by John Hamma. Used by permission of Doris Hamma.

"Pack" text copyright © 1995 by Lee Bennett Hopkins from BEEN TO YESTERDAYS by Lee Bennett Hopkins. Reprinted by permission of Wordsong/Boyds Mills Press, Inc.

"The Paper Garden" from BREAKING THE SPELL: TALES OF ENCHANTMENT by Tony Ramsay. Text copyright © Sally Grindley 1997. Illustrations copyright © Susan Field 1997. Used by permission of Larousse Kingfisher Chambers.

"Rhodopis and Her Golden Sandals" from MULTICULTURAL FABLES AND FAIRY TALES by Tara McCarthy. Published by Scholastic Professional Books. Copyright © 1993 by Tara McCarthy. Reprinted by permission of Scholastic, Inc.

"Seal" from LAUGHING TIME by William Jay Smith. Copyright © 1990 by William Jay Smith. Used by permission of Farrar, Straus & Giroux, Inc.

"Spider in the Sky" by Anne Rose. Copyright © 1978 by Anne Rose. Used by permission of Harper Collins Publishers.

"Super-Goopy Glue" from THE NEW KID ON THE BLOCK by Jack Prelutsky. Text copyright © 1984 by Jack Prelutsky. Used by permission of Greenwillow Books, a division of William Morrow & Company, Inc.

"What's the Big Idea, Ben Franklin?" by Jean Fritz. Text copyright © 1976 by Jean Fritz. Illustrations copyright © 1976 by Margot Tomes. Used by permission of Coward, McCann & Geoghegan.

"When Whales Exhale (Whale Watching)" from WHEN WHALES EXHALE AND OTHER POEMS by Constance Levy. Text copyright © 1996 by Constance King Levy. Used by permission of Margaret K. McElderry Books, an imprint of Simon & Schuster Children's publishing Division.

"Windows of Gold" from WINDOWS OF GOLD AND OTHER GOLDEN TALES by Selma G. Lanes. Text copyright © 1989 retold by Selma G. Lanes. Illustrations copyright © 1989 by Kimberly Bulcken Root. Used by permission of Simon and Schuster Books for Young Readers.

"The Wolf" from THE RANDOM HOUSE BOOK OF POETRY FOR CHILDREN by Georgia Roberts Durston. Copyright © 1983. Used by permission of Random House.

Notes

Backmatter Contents

Hats Off to the Cowboy
by Red Steagall

The city folks think that it's over.
The cowboy has outlived his time—
An old worn-out relic, a thing of the past,
But the truth is, he's still in his prime.

The cowboy's image of freedom,
The hard-ridin' boss of the range.
His trade is a fair one, he fights for what's right,
And his ethics aren't subject to change.

He still tips his hat to the ladies,
Lets you water first at the pond.
He believes a day's pay is worth a day's work,
And his handshake and word are his bond.

Earth Day Rap
Words and Music by Doug Goodkin

The sky is high and the ocean is deep,
But we can't treat the planet like a garbage heap.
Don't wreck it, protect it, keep part of it wild,
And think about the future of your
    great-grandchild.

Recycle, bicycle, don't you drive by yourself,
Don't buy those plastic products on the
    supermarket shelf.
Boycott, petition, let the big bus'ness know,
That if we mess it up here, there's nowhere else
    we can go.

Don't shrug your shoulders, say, "What can I do?"
Only one person can do it and that person is you!

Familiar Friends
by James S. Tippett

The horses, the pigs,
And the chickens,
The turkeys, the ducks
And the sheep!
I can see all my friends
From my window
As soon as I waken
From sleep.

The cat on the fence
Is out walking.
The geese have gone down
For a swim.
The pony comes trotting
Right up to the gate;
He knows I have candy
For him.

The cows in the pasture
Are switching
Their tails to keep off
The flies.
And the old mother dog
Has come out in the yard
With five pups to give me
A surprise.

How It All Began
by Lawrence S. Ritter

Baseball has been providing us with fun and excitement for more than a hundred years. The first *professional* baseball team was the Cincinnati Red Stockings, who toured the country in 1869 and didn't lose a game all year. Soon, baseball began to attract so many fans that in 1876 the National League was organized—the same National League that still exists today.

Although the game as it was played in 1876 was recognizable as baseball—nobody would confuse it with football or basketball—it was quite a bit different from baseball as we know it now. For example, pitchers had to throw underhand, the way they still do in softball; the batter could request the pitcher to throw a "high" or "low" pitch; it took nine balls, rather than four, for a batter to get a base on balls; and the pitching distance was only forty-five feet to home plate.

The rules were gradually changed over the following twenty years, until by about 1900 the game was more or less the same as it is today. In 1884, pitchers were permitted to throw overhand; in 1887, the batter was no longer allowed to request a "high" or "low" pitch; by 1889, it took only four balls for a batter to get a base on balls; and, in 1893, the pitching distance was lengthened to the present sixty feet, six inches.

Players didn't start to wear gloves on the field until the 1880s. At first, they wore only a thin piece of leather over the palm of the hand, with five holes cut out for the fingers to go through. By the 1890s, however, the gloves began to look like today's baseball gloves, although they were not nearly as large.

Gloves remained more or less the same from around 1900 to the mid-1950s. The ball was caught in the "pocket" of the glove, covering the palm of the hand, and it was held with the fingers. The fingers of the glove were short and fairly flexible. The only purpose of the glove was to protect the palm and fingers from injury, although until the

1930s many players insisted on cutting a rather large hole in the palm of the glove in order to grip the ball better.

Nowadays, the glove is much larger than it used to be, and the ball is not caught in the palm of the hand but trapped in the glove's webbing, between the thumb and forefinger. Since the mid-1950s, the glove has become more of a net with which to snare the ball rather than just a protective covering for the hand.

The baseball fields were nowhere near as well taken care of as they are now, so that it was not at all unusual in the old days for the ball to take bad bounces because of pebbles in the infield or uneven ground in the outfield.

Sometimes the ball took a crazy bounce because it was a little lopsided. Since only two or three baseballs would be used for a whole game, by the seventh or eighth inning the ball was often in pretty bad shape. Indeed, this was true until the 1920s. If a ball, like a foul ball or a home run, went into the stands, the ushers would try to get it back, sometimes offering whoever had it a free pass to another game. If the ushers succeeded in getting it back, it would be returned to the field, and the game would resume with the same ball. Now, of course, fifty to sixty baseballs are used in an average big-league game.

Indians of the Plains
by Myra Cohn Livingston

I like the names,
the way they sound—

    Omaha, Iowa, Sioux,
    Pawnee, Winnebago, Potawatomi,

    Indian tribes who knew
    these prairies before we came,
    who lived with the buffalo—
    Illinois, Osage, Sauk
                who lived

on plains of long ago.

Justin and the Best Biscuits in the World • PRACTICE

Name_____ Date_____ **Practice** (38)

Make Predictions

As you read a story, you often ask yourself what will happen next. To answer your question, you think about clues in the story and your own experience. Then you **make a prediction**, or a guess, about what will happen.

Read the first part of the story, and make a prediction. Then check your prediction by reading the next part of the story. **Answers may vary.**

> Mike's aunt often told him not to read scary books before going to bed. But tonight Mike wanted to finish his book. He had to find out what happened next. Mike was well into the final chapter when he heard something. Was it his aunt downstairs? Was it something in the closet? "Probably just the wind," he thought.
> "Lights out, Mike!" called his aunt. Mike put the book down and turned off the light.

1. Why do you think Mike's aunt doesn't want him to read scary stories before going to bed? **Possible answers: Mike will have a hard time going to sleep. Mike will have bad dreams.**

2. What do you predict will happen after Mike turns off the light?
   Possible answer: He will lie awake listening for noises.

3. List the clues in the story that helped you make your prediction.
   Answers will vary, but should mention story clues.

4. Write your own ending to the story using predictions you have made.
   Possible answers: Mike's aunt warns him not to read scary stories before going to bed; Mike thinks he hears something scary.

Book 4/Unit 2
4 Justin and the Best Biscuits in the World
At Home: Have students write the beginning of a one-paragraph story that includes a predictable situation.
38

Name_____ Date_____ **Practice** (39)

Vocabulary

Substitute a vocabulary word for the underlined word or words in each sentence.

guilt	resounded	festival	lingered	pranced	inspecting

1. The food and music were great at the <u>celebration</u>. ___**festival**___

2. People <u>stayed</u> long after the party was over. ___**lingered**___

3. Horses <u>strutted</u> to entertain the crowd at the circus. ___**pranced**___

4. Shouts and whistles <u>echoed</u> through the crowd as the show began.
   ___**resounded**___

5. Children were <u>looking closely at</u> each other's costumes. ___**inspecting**___

6. No one had <u>feelings of having done something wrong</u> for staying up so late. ___**guilt**___

39 **At Home:** Have students write a paragraph using each vocabulary word.
Book 4/Unit 2
Justin and the Best Biscuits in the World 6

Pete's Prize

Every year our school holds a food *festival*. All the food is made by the students. The food is laid out on tables. The judges take turns *inspecting* and tasting it. Judges *lingered* over the little bowls of Pete's Peanut Pudding. They're my entry. I'm Pete.

For the second year in a row, I took first prize for cooking. Clapping and cheering *resounded* in the crowd when I won. So I *pranced* around the room letting everyone shake my hand.

"Stop bragging," said my best friend Angel. "Don't you have any *guilt* about showing off?" I thought for a minute. "No, not really," I said. "I won fairly!"

1. What happens at the school every year?
   The school holds a food festival.

2. What is the job of the judges in the story?
   They inspect and taste the food.

3. What happened in the crowd when Pete won?
   clapping and cheering resounded

4. Why does Angel think Pete should have some guilt?
   He thinks Pete should feel guilty about showing off.

5. Why should Pete feel happy about what he has done?
   He is good at cooking and wins prizes for it.

5 Book 4/Unit 2
Justin and the Best Biscuits in the World
At Home: Have students draw and write a cartoon using some vocabulary words.
39a

Name_____ Date_____ **Practice** (40)

Story Comprehension

Read statements 1 to 6 below. Write **T** for true if the statement describes "Justin and the Best Biscuits in the World." Write **F** for false if it does not.

1. ___T___ Justin felt guilty when he didn't help Grandpa wash the dishes.

2. ___F___ Justin couldn't make his bed, even though he tried.

3. ___F___ "Riding the fence" means "sitting on the fence."

4. ___T___ A baby deer was in trouble and needed Grandpa's help.

5. ___F___ The mother deer attacked Grandpa.

6. ___T___ Grandpa learned to cook the biscuits when he was a boy.

Write to tell why the following statements are not true.
Answers will vary.

7. Grandpa told Justin that one thing cowboys never do is cry.
   Grandpa is a cowboy and he cries. He cried when Justin was born.

8. Justin loves Grandpa, but he didn't learn anything new from him.
   Justin learned that there is no such thing as women's work.
   Everyone has to cook, clean, and make their beds. He also learned
   that everyone cries, even cowboys.

40 **At Home:** Have students write a report about their experiences helping with household chores.
Book 4/Unit 2
Justin and the Best Biscuits in the World 8

Annotated Workbooks

Justin and the Best Biscuits in the World • PRACTICE

Use a Dictionary

A **dictionary** is a book of words listed in alphabetical order. A dictionary entry tells you how to spell a word, how to pronounce it, and what it means. Many words have more than one meaning. A dictionary entry also tells you whether the word is a noun, a verb, or another part of speech.

Read the dictionary entry and answer the questions.

opossum A small, furry animal that lives in trees and carries its young in its pouch. When frightened, the *opossum* lies still as if it were dead. **o•pos•sum** (ə pos´ əm) *noun, plural* **opossums**.

1. Where does an opossum live? __in trees__

2. How many syllables does the word opossum have? __three syllables__

3. Which syllable gets the emphasis? __The second syllable or pos__

4. What part of speech is opossum? __noun__

5. How does looking at the picture help you understand Justin's fear in the story? __It shows you what he saw, an animal as big as a cat with a long rat-like tail.__

Book 4/Unit 2
5 Justin and the Best Biscuits in the World

At Home: Have students use a dictionary to find the meaning of the word *surge* in the sentence *Justin felt a surge of love for Grandpa.*

41

Make Predictions

When you make a **prediction**, you make a logical guess about what will happen next, based on story clues and your own experiences. As you read on, you find out if you were right. Making and confirming predictions can help you understand why characters act as they do.

Think back to your first reading of "Justin and the Best Biscuits in the World." Then answer these questions about predictions you made or might have made at different points in the story. **Answers may vary.**

1. At the beginning of the story, did you think Justin and Grandpa were going to get along? Why? __They wouldn't get along. Justin let Grandpa wash all the dishes.__

2. What did you think would happen when Justin started making his bed while Grandpa watched? __He was going to do a bad job of it. Justin was not used to making beds and didn't know how.__

3. What happened with Justin and the bed? How did it change what you predicted would happen in the rest of the story? __Justin found that making a bed was not hard. Maybe he would try other things.__

4. What did you think Justin would do when he saw the blood from the doe? __Possible answer: He would want to go back to the ranch. He would be upset.__

5. Write a prediction about Justin's future visits to Grandpa's ranch. __Justin will look forward to going. Justin will have a good time visiting Grandpa.__

42

At Home: Have students write a prediction about what will happen at school tomorrow including information used to base their prediction.

Book 4/Unit 2
Justin and the Best Biscuits in the World 5

Form Generalizations

A **generalization** is a broad statement about something. Generalizations often include words such as *always, many, most, almost, all, no,* or *none.*

Complete each sentence starter below by writing a generalization based on details from "Justin and the Best Biscuits in the World."
Answers will vary.

1. Washing dishes __can be easy.__

2. A well-made bed __is always a warm welcome.__

3. None of the wrinkled shirts __had been folded correctly.__

4. The morning sun on the hilltops always __made the foothills appear purple.__

5. A doe's eyes usually __look peaceful and sad.__

6. When Justin's grandpa was a boy, he __helped his father with the cattle.__

7. Cowchips __make the best fuel for a fire.__

8. Diamondback rattlers __are dangerous snakes.__

9. Some of the best cooks in the world __are men.__

10. On the cattle trail __all cooks were men.__

Book 4/Unit 2
10 Justin and the Best Biscuits in the World

At Home: Have students write three sentences beginning: Most students in our class.

43

Context Clues

There may be words you don't know in a story you are reading. Sometimes the sentence, or **context** surrounding a word, holds clues that can help you understand the word's meaning.

Write a word from the list that makes sense in each sentence.

shallow	resounded	mustangs	chores	outburst
broadly	cautiously	lingered	surge	assured

1. The night air __resounded__ with sounds of crickets and bat wings.

2. Hannah __lingered__ in the yard after her parents went into the house.

3. Kevin raked the leaves and finished other outdoor __chores__.

4. Dad showed all his teeth when he smiled __broadly__.

5. Antonio felt a __surge__ of happiness as he rode the horse.

6. Mei-Li tiptoed __cautiously__ so she wouldn't frighten the kittens.

7. When Consuelo spelled the word, she felt __assured__ of the prize.

8. Keeshawn dug __shallow__ holes near the surface for the flower seeds.

9. Tamara used to tame wild ponies called __mustangs__.

10. That was quite an __outburst__ when Chad yelled without thinking.

44

At Home: Have students write sentences with strong context clues for four words.

Book 4/Unit 2
Justin and the Best Biscuits in the World 10

Make Predictions

Name_____ Date_____ **Reteach** 38

> When you think ahead about what may or may not happen next in a story, you **make a prediction**.

Read the sentences. Then circle what you think will happen.

1. Annette gives the cashier a $10 bill for a movie ticket that costs $8.50. What do you think Annette will do next?
   a. look for a place to sit
   b. wait for change from the cashier
   c. buy candy

2. Roger loves to be outdoors and to exercise. Today, he is going to the movies. The theater is 1 mile away from home. How do you think he will get there?
   a. walk   b. take a bus   c. ask his mother for a ride

3. Traci wants to buy a special CD as a gift for a friend. It costs $16 but she has only $10. What do you think Traci might do?
   a. forget about the whole idea
   b. find a way to earn the money that she needs
   c. buy a cheaper CD

4. Nick just remembered that Mia's birthday party is tomorrow. He knows a store that is open for another hour. What do you think Nick will do?
   a. not go to the party
   b. buy a present after the party
   c. hurry to the store

5. Nadine decided to walk rather than take the bus home from school. When she had walked one block, it began to rain. What do you think Nadine will do?
   a. continue walking home
   b. call a friend for a ride
   c. go back and take the bus

Book 4/Unit 2
Justin and the Best Biscuits in the World 5
At Home: Have students watch a favorite television show. At a commercial break, have them predict what will happen next.
38

Vocabulary

Name_____ Date_____ **Reteach** 39

Write a word from the list to complete each sentence.

festival	guilt	inspecting	lingered	pranced	resounded

1. We were _____inspecting_____ the boat to make sure it was safe.
2. Ellen _____lingered_____ at the table long after she had finished her dinner.
3. Jack felt a sense of _____guilt_____ because of the unkind things he had said to his brother.
4. The horses _____pranced_____ restlessly in the corral.
5. The sound of the explosion _____resounded_____ through the night.
6. There will be many bands and good food at the _____festival_____.

6

Story Comprehension

Reteach 40

Write a ✔ next to every sentence that tells about "Justin and the Best Biscuits in the World." For help you may look back at the story.

1. _____ Justin has always liked housework.
2. _____ Justin cleared the table and washed the dishes without being asked.
3. _✔_ Justin learned to fold his shirts and make his bed.
4. _✔_ Justin was impressed by his grandfather's cooking.
5. _____ Justin helped his grandfather inspect the fence.
6. _____ Justin was bored by stories about Black cowboys.
7. _✔_ Justin's grandfather was a cowboy but not a broncobuster.
8. _✔_ Justin learned that it doesn't matter whether women or men do the work when it needs to be done.

At Home: Have students recall two more details from "Justin and the Best Biscuits in the World."
39–40
Book 4/Unit 2
Justin and the Best Biscuits in the World 8

Use a Dictionary

Name_____ Date_____ **Reteach** 41

> A **dictionary** tells you what a word means and how to pronounce it. Each entry also tells you if a word is a noun, a verb, or another part of speech.

Use the sample dictionary entries below to answer the questions.

> **overalls** loose-fitting trousers usually having a piece that covers the chest with suspenders attached. The farmer wore *overalls* while doing his chores. **o•ver•alls** (ō′vər ôlz′) *noun plural*
>
> **overrun** **1.** to swarm or spread over or throughout. The invading army had *overrun* the countryside. **2.** to flow over. The river *overran* its banks. **3.** to run beyond. The player always *overruns* second base. **o•ver•run**, (ō′vər run′) *verb* **o•ver•ran**, **o•ver•run•ning**

1. What does *overalls* mean? _loose-fitting trousers with a piece that covers the chest with suspenders attached_
2. How many syllables does *overalls* have? _3_
3. What part of speech is *overalls*? _noun_
4. How many different definitions does *overrun* have? _3_
5. What meaning does *overran* have in the sentence that follows? *Foxes overran the ranch.* _swarmed or spread over or throughout_
6. What part of speech is *overrun*? _verb_

Book 4/Unit 2
Justin and the Best Biscuits in the World 6
At Home: Have students draw a picture of overalls based on the definition given and then label it.
41

Make Predictions

Name_____ Date_____ **Reteach** 42

> You can use what you know about story characters to **predict**, or think ahead about, what the characters may do.

Read each story below. Then answer the questions.

The horseback riding teacher was curious about why Sandra Sanchez had missed her last three lessons. He knew that the lessons were very important to Sandra's mother. Mrs. Sanchez wanted Sandra to start entering riding contests soon. One day, the riding teacher saw Mrs. Sanchez on the street.

1. What do you think the riding teacher will do?
   He may ask Mrs. Sanchez why Sandra missed her lessons.

2. How do you think Sandra's mother will react?
   Answers will vary. Mrs. Sanchez may be totally surprised to hear about the missed lessons, or she may say that Sandra was sick.

Noah liked every subject but art. Noah's pictures just never looked the way he wanted them to. But a funny thing happened when Noah started painting. Mr. Vass thought that Noah's paintings were good, and asked if Noah would enter them in a contest! Noah smiled with pride. When Noah came home, Noah's parents could see that he was very happy.

3. Do you think that Noah will enter the contest? Explain why.
   Possible answer: Yes. Noah is proud the teacher likes his paintings.

4. Do you think that Noah will stop painting when the art class moves on to a different topic? Explain.
   Possible answer: No. Noah probably feels differently about art class now that he has done well.

At Home: Have students make another prediction based on one of the stories.
42
Book 4/Unit 2
Justin and the Best Biscuits in the World 4

Form Generalizations

> A **generalization** is a broad statement. It can be about many people, many animals, or many things.

Read the paragraphs below. Put a ✔ next to each generalization that you can make from the facts in the paragraph.

Braille is a system of reading that is used by blind people. It is named for its inventor, Louis Braille. The idea came to him when he noticed a system of sending coded wartime messages by using raised dots on cardboard. By placing raised dots in different positions, Braille made an alphabet, a system of punctuation, and music, that blind people read by running their fingers over the dots. Braille was not accepted officially right away. Today, however, it is used in all written languages.

1. _____ All people accepted the Braille system right away.

2. ✔ Today, Braille is widely used in all written languages.

3. _____ There is no system for blind people to read music.

Owning a pet can be a rewarding experience. However you should choose a pet carefully. For example, a large dog might be unhappy in a small apartment. A bird or some fish might be a good choice for someone who wants a pet that does not need to be walked or played with. People who are unwilling or unable to take responsibility for a pet are better off choosing not to have one. A pet is a living being that must be cared for.

4. ✔ Owning a pet is a responsibility.

5. _____ There is only one correct pet for each owner.

6. ✔ To choose a pet, you need to think about how the pet will fit into your home and your life.

Book 4/Unit 2
Justin and the Best Biscuits in the World
`6`

At Home: Have students make a generalization about an article they have read or a television show they have watched.

43

Use Context Clues

> Sometimes when you read, you will come to a word that you don't know. You can use **context clues**, or other words or sentences around the unfamiliar word, to help you figure out the meaning of the word.

Circle the letter beside the meaning of the underlined word in each sentence.

1. Grandfather warmed stew and even fried some bread in the skillet.

   (a.) cooking pan   **b.** type of wagon

2. They see for miles across the treeless, even plains.

   a. hilly green areas   **(b.)** stretch of flat land

3. Fred searched everywhere, scanning the area for stray cattle.

   (a.) looking carefully   **b.** ignoring

4. The foreman told the ranch hands what each should do.

   (a.) boss of a crew   **b.** stranger

5. After tiring, the horse began to canter, and the rider could catch her breath.

   a. run wildly   **(b.)** move at a slow, steady pace

6. On some ranches, calves are branded to let people know who owns them.

   (a.) marked with sign   **b.** kept indoors

At Home: Have students tell what context clues they found to help them identify the meanings of skillet and foreman.

44

Book 4/Unit 2
Justin and the Best Biscuits in the World
`6`

Justin and the Best Biscuits in the World • EXTEND

Make Predictions

A **prediction** is a guess about something that will happen in the future. Use the information in the paragraph below to make predictions about how the students will do on their spelling test Friday.

Carlos reviewed the spelling words every night. Taylor, Natalie, and Julia formed a study group to quiz each other on the words. Jonathan looked over the spelling list on Monday. Chris played video games instead of studying.

Predict who you think will do well on the spelling test.
Carlos, Taylor, Natalie, and Julia

Predict who you think will not do well on the spelling test.
Jonathan and Chris

Predict what you will do to earn a living when you are an adult. Explain how you made your prediction.
Answers will vary.

Book 4/Unit 2
Justin and the Best Biscuits in the World
At Home: Have students make predictions about every day events and how they affect their actions and/or decisions.
38

Vocabulary

festival	guilt	inspecting
lingered	pranced	resounded

Make your own crossword puzzle using the vocabulary words above. Remember to start with **Across** clues and then give the **Down** clues. Then draw numbered boxes for the answers. Exchange your puzzle with a partner's puzzle and try to solve it.

Across
_____
_____
_____
_____
_____

Down
_____
_____
_____
_____
_____

Story Comprehension

Review "Justin and the Best Biscuits in the World." Predict what kind of a grandfather you think that Justin will be. Tell how you used the story to help you make your prediction.
Answers will vary. Possible answer: I think Justin will try to model himself after his own grandfather. He loves his grandfather and learns many things from him.

39–40
At Home: Have students discuss what they think the good and the more difficult aspects of a cowboy's life would be.
Book 4/Unit 2
Justin and the Best Biscuits in the World

Use a Dictionary

If you do not know what a word means, you can use a **dictionary** to find its definition. You can also use a dictionary to check the spelling of a word, to find out what part of speech it is, how many syllables the word has, and how to pronounce it. The dictionary entry may include a sentence that shows how to use the word or it may tell something about the history of the word. Use the dictionary excerpt below to answer the questions.

ro•dent (rō′ dənt) *noun* a mammal with large front teeth used for gnawing. *Rats and squirrels are rodents.*
ro•de•o (rō′ dē ō) *noun* 1. a contest that includes riding broncos and bulls and catching cattle with lassos. *Many cowhands took part in the rodeo.* 2. a cattle roundup. [Rodeo was first used to mean rounding up and counting cattle. From Spanish, *rodear,* to surround.]
roe (rō) *noun* the eggs of a fish. *Certain kinds of fish roe are eaten as a delicacy.*

1. What part of speech is **rodent**? **noun**
2. How many syllables are in each word? **rodent: 2; rodeo: 3; roe: 1**
_____
3. How many meanings are shown for **rodeo**? Which one is currently used the most? Explain. **two meanings; the first one shows the most common use of the word.**
4. What is the meaning of **roe**? **the eggs of a fish**
5. What does the definition of rodeo tell about the history of the word?
It comes from Spanish and is used to mean rounding up cattle.

Book 4/Unit 2
Justin and the Best Biscuits in the World
At Home: Look though a dictionary at home. Discuss common abbreviations used in the dictionary.
41

Make Predictions

Look back at "Justin and the Best Biscuits in the World" to help you answer the questions.

The first morning that Justin was at his grandfather's ranch he did not help prepare breakfast, wash the dishes, or sweep the floor. He also did not have his bed made when his grandfather came into his room.

1. Predict what you think Justin will do on the second morning of his visit. Explain.
Answers will vary. Possible answer: Justin will get up early and make his bed. He'll help with breakfast. He will wash or dry the dishes and offer to sweep the floor. Justin admires his grandfather and will want to be more like him and help out.

Justin did not like to help with household chores at home. He considered them women's work.

2. What do you predict Justin will do about household chores when he returns home? Explain.
Answers will vary. Possible answer: He will probably be more willing to help. Justin's grandfather explained to him that there were no chores that were "women's work."

42
At Home: Have students discuss a favorite story in which they were able to predict the outcome. What clues led to their prediction?
Book 4/Unit 2
Justin and the Best Biscuits in the World

Justin and the Best Biscuits in the World • EXTEND

Form Generalizations

Think about "Justin and the Best Biscuits in the World." When Justin's grandfather showed him how to fold his shirt, Justin was willing to try it on his own. When his grandfather told him to try to make his bed, Justin did so and found that it was not very hard to do.

Do you think that Justin would have responded with the same willingness to similar suggestions from his mother at home? You can use the story to help you form a **generalization**, or a general conclusion, about how Justin might have responded to his mother.

Answers will vary. Possible answer: Probably not, since Justin considered

such chores to be women's work. Justin saw that his grandfather did these

kinds of chores willingly. His way of showing Justin the importance of this

kind of work helped Justin see things differently.

_____

_____

_____

Grandpa told Justin about many African American cowboys. Use the story to form a generalization about the lives of African American cowboys.

Answers will vary. Possible answer: The contributions of African American

cowboys went unrecognized for a long time, but now people are finding out

more about them.

_____

_____

_____

_____

Book 4/Unit 2
**Justin and the Best
Biscuits in the World**

At Home: Have students make generalizations
about what their life will be like years from now.

43

Context Clues

cinch	saddlebags	broncobuster
bale	hitched	branded

Sometimes you can figure out the meaning of a word from its setting and the way it is used in a sentence. The words above are usually used in a western or ranch-related context.

Read each sentence in the box. Use the **context clues** in them to help you match the words with their meaning's below.

> He pulled on the leather strap to *cinch* the saddle.
>
> The *bales* of hay were stacked on the truck.
>
> They *hitched* the horses to a post while they had lunch.
>
> They *branded* the calves with the symbol of the ranch.
>
> The cowboy put his rain gear and a map in the *saddlebags*.
>
> The wild mustang was calmed by the *broncobuster*.

1. marked to indicate identity or ownership branded _____
2. large bundles tied tightly together bales _____
3. fastened with a rope hitched _____
4. a cowboy who tames wild horses broncobuster _____
5. to tighten a saddle girth cinch _____
6. Pouches, usually of leather, hung across a saddle saddlebags _____

Use another sheet of paper to draw a picture that illustrates some of the words above.

At Home: What words do you associate with the
American West? Discuss the reasons why.

44

Book 4/Unit 2
**Justin and the Best
Biscuits in the World**

Justin and the Best Biscuits in the World • GRAMMAR

Common and Proper Nouns

> • A **noun names** a person, place, or thing.
>
> • A **common noun** names any person, place, or thing.
>
> • A **proper noun** names a particular person, place, or thing.
>
> • A proper noun begins with a capital letter.

Underline the common nouns in each sentence. Then double underline the proper nouns in each sentence.

1. Justin and Grapda rode horses across the meadow.
   <u>Justin</u>, <u>Grandpa</u>, horses, meadow

2. Grandpa rode Pal, and Justin rode Black.
   <u>Grandpa</u>, <u>Pal</u>, <u>Justin</u>, <u>Black</u>

3. Justin and Grandpa checked the fence for broken places.
   <u>Justin</u>, <u>Grandpa</u>, fence, places

4. Suddenly, the boy saw a fawn caught in the wire.
   boy, fawn, wire

5. Grandpa mixed dough and cooked delicious biscuits.
   <u>Grandpa</u>, dough, biscuits

6. Justin learned that both men and women can be cooks.
   <u>Justin</u>, men, women, cooks

7. The cardinal made a sound like a whistle.
   cardinal, sound, whistle

8. Anthony had a dog named Pepper.
   <u>Anthony</u>, dog, <u>Pepper</u>

Grade 4/Unit 2
Justin and the Best Biscuits in the World
8

Extension: Ask students to write two sentences about the story using both common and proper nouns. Have partners exchange papers and draw a line under the nouns in each other's sentences.

33

Proper Nouns

> • Some proper nouns contain more than one word. Each important word begins with a capital letter.
>
> • The name of a day, month, or holiday begins with a capital letter.

Capitalize the proper nouns found in each sentence.

1. The rodeo sport bulldogging was invented by bill pickett.
   Bill Pickett

2. He lived on a ranch in the state of oklahoma. **Oklahoma**

3. Some states have cold weather in january. **January**

4. People think jessie stahl rode wild horses better than anyone.
   Jessie Stahl

5. The comedian will rogers was taught how to rope by a cowboy.
   Will Rogers

6. This cowboy was known as clay. **Clay**

7. Another famous cowboy had the nickname deadwood dick.
   Deadwood Dick

8. He got his name from the town of deadwood city.
   Deadwood City

34

Extension: Invite small groups of students to write sentences describing the Black cowboys mentioned in the story. Remind students to capitalize proper nouns.

Grade 4/Unit 2
Justin and the Best Biscuits in the World
8

Common and Proper Nouns

> • A **noun** names a person, place, or thing.
>
> • A **common noun** names any person, place, or thing.
>
> • A **proper noun** names a particular person, place, or thing.
>
> • Some proper nouns contain more than one word. Each important word begins with a capital letter.
>
> • The name of a day, month, or holiday begins with a capital letter.

Write a common noun or proper noun to complete each sentence. For help you may look back at the story.

1. Grandpa showed ____**Justin**____ how to fold a shirt.

2. Grandpa's ____**horses**____ were named Cropper, Pal, and Black.

3. Justin's grandpa lived on a ____**ranch**____.

4. Justin thought of Anthony, his ____**friend**____ back home.

5. The baby ____**deer**____ got caught on the fence.

6. Deadwood ____**Dick**____'s real name was Nate Love.

7. Justin told Grandpa that housework was women's ____**work**____.

8. Instead of chores, Justin wanted to play ball on Saturday and ____**Sunday**____.

Grade 4/Unit 2
Justin and the Best Biscuits in the World
8

Extension: Have students write a paragraph that describes one of the characters from the story. After they have finished, ask students to underline the common nouns and circle the proper nouns in

35

Abbreviations

> • An **abbreviation** is the shortened form of a word.
>
> • An abbreviation begins with a capital letter and ends with a period.
>
> • Abbreviate titles of people before names.
>
> • You can abbreviate days of the week. You can also abbreviate most months.

Write each abbreviation correctly.

A Rancher's Calendar:

1. July -- Look for picture of mr Pickett. ____**Mr.**____

2. aug -- Grandson comes to visit. ____**Aug.**____

3. mon -- Ride fence. ____**Mon.**____

4. wed -- Have dr Jones look at sick cow. ____**Wed.; Dr.**____

5. thurs -- Buy gift for mrs Friend. ____**Thurs.; Mrs.**____

6. sat -- Judge festival. ____**Sat.**____

7. nov -- Buy hay for winter. ____**Nov.**____

8. dec -- Drop hay bales for cattle. ____**Dec.**____

36

Extension: Have students look for abbreviations in newspapers and magazines and circle the ones they find.

Grade 4/Unit 2
Justin and the Best Biscuits in the World
8

Common and Proper Nouns

Find two nouns in each sentence and write them on the lines.

1. The nervous doe watched Grandpa carefully. _____ doe; Grandpa _____

2. A few clouds floated over the foothills. _____ clouds; foothills _____

3. Black drank at the stream first. _____ Black; stream _____

4. Deadwood City was in the Dakota Territory. _Deadwood City; Dakota Territory_

Use the nouns in the box to complete each sentence in a way that makes sense. Don't forget to capitalize any proper nouns.

justin	plain	snake	teddy roosevelt

5. After racing across the _____ plain _____ Black was calm.

6. Justin thought a _____ snake _____ might be in the grass.

7. Grandpa told _____ Justin _____ about Black cowboys.

8. One Black cowboy helped _____ Teddy Roosevelt _____.

Common and Proper Nouns

- A **common noun** names any person, place, or thing.

- A **proper noun** names a particular person, place, or thing.

Mechanics:

- Begin each important word in a proper noun with a capital letter.

- Begin the name of a day, month, or holiday with a capital letter.

Read each sentence. Write the underlined noun correctly on the line.

1. The Rancher is wearing a cowboy hat. _____ rancher _____

2. He carved two pumpkins for halloween and put them on posts.

_____ Halloween _____

3. The name of the ranch, big tree ranch, is on a sign.

_____ Big Tree Ranch _____

4. The girl is dropping Hay over the fence. _____ hay _____

Justin and the Best Biscuits in the World • SPELLING

Syllable Patterns

Pretest Directions

Fold back the paper along the dotted line. Use the blanks to write each word as it is read aloud. When you finish the test, unfold the paper. Use the list at the right to correct any spelling mistakes. Practice the words you missed for the Posttest.

To Parents

Here are the results of your child's weekly spelling Pretest. You can help your child study for the Posttest by following these simple steps for each word on the word list:

1. Read the word to your child.

2. Have your child write the word, saying each letter as it is written.

3. Say each letter of the word as your child checks the spelling.

4. If a mistake has been made, have your child read each letter of the correctly spelled word aloud, and then repeat steps 1–3.

1. _____	1. biscuit
2. _____	2. clover
3. _____	3. public
4. _____	4. oven
5. _____	5. bandage
6. _____	6. cabin
7. _____	7. plastic
8. _____	8. radar
9. _____	9. mitten
10. _____	10. knapsack
11. _____	11. local
12. _____	12. mustard
13. _____	13. pupil
14. _____	14. sofa
15. _____	15. welcome
16. _____	16. razor
17. _____	17. fancy
18. _____	18. limit
19. _____	19. famous
20. _____	20. item

Challenge Words

_____ festival
_____ guilt
_____ inspecting
_____ lingered
_____ resounded

Syllable Patterns

Using the Word Study Steps

1. LOOK at the word.
2. SAY the word aloud.
3. STUDY the letters in the word.
4. WRITE the word.
5. CHECK the word.

Did you spell the word right? If not, go back to step 1.

Spelling Tip
Look for word chunks or smaller words that can help you remember the spelling of a word. Do you see the words *band* and *age* in *bandage*?

Word Scramble

Unscramble each set of letters to make a spelling word.

1. emit	item	11. clipbu	public
2. timil	limit	12. badgean	bandage
3. orzar	razor	13. cutisbi	biscuit
4. faso	sofa	14. clapsit	plastic
5. dratsum	mustard	15. tentim	mitten
6. sankpack	knapsack	16. colla	local
7. darra	radar	17. lippu	pupil
8. binca	cabin	18. cowmele	welcome
9. vone	oven	19. canfy	fancy
10. volcer	clover	20. amusfo	famous

To Parents or Helpers

Using the Word Study Steps above as your child comes across any new words will help him or her learn to spell words effectively. Review the steps as you both go over this week's spelling words.

Go over the Spelling Tip with your child. Help your child find chunks or smaller words in the spelling words to help remember how to spell them.

Help your child complete the spelling activity.

Syllable Patterns

biscuit	bandage	mitten	pupil	fancy
clover	cabin	knapsack	sofa	limit
public	plastic	local	welcome	famous
oven	radar	mustard	razor	item

Write the spelling words with these first syllable spelling patterns.

Vowel sound in the first syllable

long

1. radar
2. famous
3. razor
4. item
5. clover
6. local
7. sofa
8. pupil

short

9. bandage
10. cabin
11. plastic
12. knapsack
13. fancy
14. biscuit
15. mitten
16. limit
17. public
18. mustard
19. oven
20. welcome

Syllable Patterns

biscuit	bandage	mitten	pupil	fancy
clover	cabin	knapsack	sofa	limit
public	plastic	local	welcome	famous
oven	radar	mustard	razor	item

What's the Connection?

Complete each statement with a spelling word.

1. Clothing is to jacket as shelter is to _____ cabin.
2. Cap is to beret as glove is to _____ mitten.
3. Box is to carton as duffel bag is to _____ knapsack.
4. Jam is to toast as butter is to _____ biscuit.
5. Animal is to horse as plant is to _____ clover.
6. Cotton is to nylon as wood is to _____ plastic.
7. Shut is to open as private is to _____ public.
8. Up is to down as plain is to _____ fancy.
9. Educate is to teacher as learn is to _____ pupil.
10. Dig is to shovel as shave is to _____ razor.
11. Tiny is to huge as unknown is to _____ famous.
12. Far is to near as widespread is to _____ local.
13. Fruit is to apple as furniture is to _____ sofa.
14. Salt is to pepper as ketchup is to _____ mustard.
15. Leave is to good-bye as enter is to _____ welcome.

36 Challenge Extension:
Write one sentence for each Challenge Word.
Grade 4/Unit 2
Justin and the Best Biscuits in the World 15

Spelling 37

Syllable Patterns

Proofreading Activity

There are six spelling mistakes in the letter below. Circle the misspelled words. Write the words correctly on the lines below.

Dear Justin,

    Thanks so much for the postcard! I wish I could live in a cabun and ride the range with you and your grandpa. I'd also like to taste some of his stewed raisins and pork, but most of all I'd like a biscut Yummy! I didn't know you could bake without an ovin. By the way, I have a book about Nate Love and some other famus cowboys. They sure did some fancie circle roping and riding. There was no limut to their talents. You can borrow the book when you get home. See you soon.

        Your friend,
        Jamie

1. cabin   3. oven   5. fancy
2. biscuit   4. famous   6. limit

Writing Activity

Suppose you are Justin's friend. Write him a letter describing what you've been doing while he's been away. Use at least four spelling words in your letter.

_____

_____

_____

_____

Spelling 38

Syllable Patterns

Look at the words in each set below. One word in each set is spelled correctly. Use a pencil to fill in the circle next to the correct word. Before you begin, look at the sample sets of words. Sample A has been done for you. Do Sample B by yourself. When you are sure you know what to do, you may go on with the rest of the page.

Sample A
- Ⓐ lemin
- ● lemmon
- Ⓒ lemon
- Ⓓ lemun

Sample B
- Ⓔ razin
- Ⓕ raison
- Ⓖ raizin
- ● raisin

1.
- Ⓐ limmit
- ● limit
- Ⓒ limut
- Ⓓ limitt

2.
- ● welcome
- Ⓕ wellcome
- Ⓖ welcum
- Ⓗ welkcome

3.
- Ⓐ napsac
- Ⓑ knapsac
- Ⓒ knapsak
- ● knapsack

4.
- Ⓔ plastick
- Ⓕ plastik
- ● plastic
- Ⓗ plasic

5.
- ● bandage
- Ⓑ bandadge
- Ⓒ bandidge
- Ⓓ bandudge

6.
- Ⓔ publick
- Ⓕ pubblic
- ● public
- Ⓗ publik

7.
- ● item
- Ⓑ itim
- Ⓒ itum
- Ⓓ ittem

8.
- Ⓔ rayzor
- Ⓕ razer
- Ⓖ raisor
- ● razor

9.
- ● sofa
- Ⓑ soffa
- Ⓒ soafa
- Ⓓ sowfa

10.
- Ⓔ raydar
- ● radar
- Ⓖ raddar
- Ⓗ raidar

11.
- Ⓐ fansy
- Ⓑ fanncy
- ● fancy
- Ⓓ fancie

12.
- Ⓔ musterd
- ● mustard
- Ⓖ mustrad
- Ⓗ musturd

13.
- ● mitten
- Ⓑ miten
- Ⓒ mittin
- Ⓓ mittun

14.
- Ⓔ faymous
- Ⓕ famus
- Ⓖ famis
- ● famous

15.
- Ⓐ cabbin
- Ⓑ cabun
- ● cabin
- Ⓓ caben

16.
- ● pupil
- Ⓕ puppil
- Ⓖ pupill
- Ⓗ puepil

17.
- Ⓐ ofven
- Ⓑ ovin
- Ⓒ ovun
- ● oven

18.
- Ⓔ clofer
- ● clover
- Ⓖ cloaver
- Ⓗ clowver

19.
- Ⓐ biskuit
- Ⓑ biscut
- ● biscuit
- Ⓓ biskit

20.
- Ⓔ lowcal
- Ⓕ loccal
- Ⓖ locul
- ● local

Just a Dream • PRACTICE

Panel 1 (Practice 45)

Name_____ Date_____ Practice **45**

Sequence of Events

The **sequence of events** is the order in which things happen in a story. Keeping track of the order helps you understand the plot. Read this story and then number the events 1 to 5 in the order in which they occurred.

It happened a long time ago on a distant planet called Evergreen. This planet took its name from the beautiful trees that covered much of its land. The special thing about the people on Evergreen was that everything they had was made of paper. The paper was made from trees. They had paper clothes, paper toys, paper houses, and paper cars. The people on Evergreen used a lot of trees.

After a thousand years, great bare spots began to appear in the forests of Evergreen. Many trees had been cut down, but none had been replanted. Next, deer, fox, and other animals disappeared from Evergreen. They had no place to live. Finally, the air began to go bad. The great forests had always cleaned the air. There were no more large forests on the planet. It wouldn't be long until all life on Evergreen disappeared.

__3__ Deer, fox, and other animals disappeared.

__1__ Evergreen was covered with beautiful trees.

__5__ It would not be long before all life on Evergreen would die.

__2__ Houses, clothes, toys, and cars were made of paper.

__4__ The air on Evergreen went bad.

Book 4/Unit 2
Just a Dream 5

At Home: Have students write their own tale and sequence the events in it.

45

Panel 2 (Practice 46)

Name_____ Date_____ Practice **46**

Vocabulary

Label each statement **True** or **False**. If the statement is false, explain why.

1. Objects usually look clear in a morning *haze*.
   False; objects usually look unclear in a morning haze.

2. A police siren makes a *shrieking* sound.
   True

3. A *foul* smell is pleasant.
   False; a foul smell is unpleasant.

4. A word that means the same as *crumpled* is crunched.
   True

5. If groceries are *bulging* out from a bag, a bigger bag is not needed.
   False; the bag is too small if the groceries are bulging out.

6. A duck that *waddled* never swayed from side to side.
   False; a duck that waddled did sway from side to side.

46

At Home: Have students write new sentences using the vocabulary words.

Book 4/Unit 2
Just a Dream 6

Panel 3 (46a)

In Early Spring

A misty *haze* filled the morning sky. The fresh spring air seemed sweet compared to the *foul* air of winter. Baby birds were *shrieking* for food and attention. Baby ducks *waddled* behind their mothers toward the river. A slight breeze blew the fallen and *crumpled* flowers from last year. At the market, people's shopping bags were *bulging* with garden tools, boxes of tiny plants, and flower and vegetable seeds. Spring was really here.

1. What is another name for *haze*? _mist_

2. How is the winter air described? _The air was foul compared to spring air._

3. How are shopper's bags described? _They were bulging with garden tools, boxes of tiny plants, and flower and vegetable seeds._

4. How did the baby ducks walk? _They waddled._

5. Why do you think this story is called "In Early Spring"? _Because it tells of things that occur at that time of year._

Book 4/Unit 2
Just a Dream 5

At Home: Have students draw a picture to illustrate the story.

46a

Panel 4 (Practice 47)

Name_____ Date_____ Practice **47**

Story Comprehension

Complete each sentence with the correct word or phrase. Look back at "Just a Dream" for help.

1. His bed was balancing on the edge of a giant _smokestack_.
2. After the party, Walter and his dad planted the _birthday_ present.
3. Walter _crumpled_ up the empty bag and threw it at the fire hydrant.
4. The sign read Hotel _Everest_.
5. Walter bought a large jelly-filled _doughnut_.
6. This can't be the _future_, Walter thought.
7. The ducks had been looking for the _pond_ for days.
8. Walter couldn't understand why anyone would want a _tree_ for a present.
9. When Walter first woke up, he was in the middle of a huge _dump_.
10. The huge trees seemed very _peaceful_ next to his bed.

47

At Home: Have students take responsibility for a chore at home that involves recycling.

Book 4/Unit 2
Just a Dream 10

T16 *Annotated Workbooks*

Just a Dream • PRACTICE

Use a Thesaurus

A **thesaurus** is a book that lists the synonyms of words. You can use a thesaurus when you want to find different words that have the same, or nearly the same meaning.

Below are two thesaurus entries. Read them, then answer the questions.

> **ridiculous** *adjective* absurd, foolish, laughable, preposterous, unbelievable, silly
>
> **said** *verb* asked, bragged, complained, demanded, exclaimed, mentioned, muttered, questioned, whined, yelled

1. When would you find a thesaurus helpful? __when you want to find a__ __synonym for a word__

2. What are three synonyms for the word ridiculous? __absurd, foolish,__ __preposterous__

3. What part of speech is the word said? __verb__

4. What do we call words that have the same, or nearly the same meaning? __synonyms__

5. What do we call a book that lists synonyms? __thesaurus__

6. Write a sentence using different words for ridiculous and said.

   __Sentences will vary.__

Sequence of Events

The **sequence of events** in a story is the order in which things happen. Keeping track of the sequence of events can help you understand what is happening in a story. Ten events from "Just a Dream" are listed out of order below. Number each event to show the correct sequence.

__3__ 1. Walter watched a television show about the future.

__8__ 2. Walter planted a tree on his birthday.

__1__ 3. Walter threw an empty bag at a fire hydrant.

__6__ 4. Walter saw the fishermen catch one small fish.

__7__ 5. Walter got stuck in traffic on the highway.

__10__ 6. Walter went back to sleep in the shade of two trees.

__2__ 7. Walter dumped all the trash into one can.

__5__ 8. Walter woke up on a mountain of trash.

__4__ 9. Walter wished he had robots to work for him.

__9__ 10. Walter saw a man pushing a motorless lawn mower.

Form Generalizations

A **generalization** is a broad statement about something. Generalizations often include words such as *most, none, everything,* or *all.* Read each passage. Then write a generalization about "Just a Dream" on the line below. **Answers may vary.**

1. When Walter took out the trash, he dumped everything into one can. He didn't care that there were three cans for three different kinds of trash. He wanted to get back to watching television.

   Generalization: __Walter never took the time to sort the garbage.__

2. In the story, Walter wished that he had his own plane, robot, and a machine to make jelly doughnuts.

   Generalization: __Walter wished he had machines to do all the work.__

3. Walter saw houses buried under huge piles of trash. He gasped when he saw the street sign that had the name of his street on it. A man told him no one lived there anymore.

   Generalization: __No one lived on Floral Avenue anymore because of the__ __mountain of trash.__

4. When Walter was on the edge of a smokestack, he coughed and the smoke burned his throat and made his eyes itch.

   Generalization: __All the smoke made it almost impossible to breathe.__

5. When Walter awoke, he ran outside in his pajamas to find the jelly doughnut wrapper he had discarded earlier that day.

   Generalization: __Walter changed all of his old bad habits and__ __stopped polluting.__

Compound Words

A **compound word** is made up of two short words. The two words together may mean something different than what they meant separately. An example would be *head* and *light* making *headlight.*

Put two words from the list together to make a compound word to fill in the blank in each sentence.

skate	book	note	ball	back
flash	thunder	camp	pack	noon
storm	after	fire	board	scraper
basket	sky	brush	light	tooth

1. Ivan wrote stories in her ____notebook____.

2. Bonita delivered papers every ____afternoon____ after school.

3. Teresa carries her books in her ____backpack____.

4. You often have lightning along with a ____thunderstorm____.

5. That ____skyscraper____ has 47 floors.

6. Chan's brother plays guard on the ____basketball____ team.

7. Spyros uses his ____toothbrush____ after every meal.

8. A ____flashlight____ is a good thing to have in the dark.

9. We put more wood on the ____campfire____.

10. I can move really fast when I'm on my ____skateboard____.

Just a Dream • RETEACH

Reteach 45

Name _____ Date _____ **Reteach** 45

Sequence of Events

> **Sequence** is the order in which things happen. Words such as *before*, *first*, and *then* can help you understand sequence.

Read the story. Circle the letter beside the answer to each question.

Jed won the marathon by 10 minutes. But it wasn't as easy as it seemed. Before Jed began running, he read about training. Then he started to run short distances. Jed increased the number of miles he ran each week. After 4 months, Jed ran a half-marathon, or 13 miles. Although Jed lost his first race, he trained for another 8 months until he was ready for a full marathon.

1. Which of these events happened first?
   a. Jed won the marathon.
   b. Jed began running.
   c. Jed read all about training.

2. Which of these events happened last?
   a. Jed trained for another 8 months.
   b. Jed won the marathon.
   c. Jed ran a half-marathon.

3. What is the first thing Jed did after he read about training?
   a. Jed increased the number of miles he ran each week.
   b. Jed ran a half-marathon.
   c. Jed started to run short distances.

4. What did Jed do after he lost the half-marathon?
   a. Jed trained for another 8 months.
   b. Jed read about training.
   c. Jed increased the number of miles that he ran each week.

5. How many months of training did Jed need until he won a marathon?
   a. 4   b. 8   **c.** 12

5 | Book 4/Unit 2 **Just a Dream** | **At Home:** Have students describe five things they have done during the day in the order in which the things happened. | 45

Reteach 46

Name _____ Date _____ **Reteach** 46

Vocabulary

Choose the word that matches the meaning. Then fill in the crossword puzzle.

bulging	crumpled	foul	haze	shrieking	waddled

Across
4. crushed; wrinkled
5. mist, smoke, or dust in the air
6. swelling outwards

Down
1. having a bad smell
2. making a shrill noise
3. walked with short steps, swayed from side to side

(Crossword answers: 4 Across: crumpled; 5 Across: haze; 6 Across: bulging; 1 Down: foul; 2 Down: shrieking; 3 Down: waddled)

6

Story Comprehension
Reteach 47

Circle the letter beside the words that correctly complete each sentence about "Just a Dream." You may look at the story for help.

1. The wish that started Walter's dream trip was _____.
   a. to live in the future   b. to live in the past

2. At the beginning of the story, Walter _____.
   a. cared about litter   **b.** didn't sort garbage

3. When Walter fell asleep, he dreamt about a world that _____.
   a. was dirty and noisy   b. was wonderfully clean

4. Walter's dreams made him change how he _____.
   a. cleaned his room   **b.** felt about the environment

46–47 | **At Home:** Have students retell "Just a Dream" in their own words. | Book 4/Unit 2 **Just a Dream** | 4

Reteach 48

Name _____ Date _____ **Reteach** 48

Use a Thesaurus

> A **thesaurus** is a book that gives synonyms for a word. If you want to add interest to your writing, use a thesaurus.

Use the thesaurus entries to choose the best synonym for the underlined word in each sentence. Circle the correct letter.

> **clean** verb. 1. Volunteers helped *clean* the park.
> *Synonyms:* wash, cleanse, scrub, spruce up, tidy

> **environment** noun. 1. Littering fouls our *environment*.
> *Synonyms:* surroundings, habitat, setting, world, atmosphere

> **trash** noun. 1. Put the *trash* in the can.
> *Synonyms:* waste, garbage, junk, litter
> 2. The expert called the ideas in the report *trash*.
> *Synonyms:* nonsense, foolishness, drivel

1. Norah ignored the article because she thought it was trash.
   a. waste   b. litter   **c.** nonsense

2. The government will clean Wild River.
   a. scrub   **b.** cleanse   c. litter

3. People know that recycling helps the environment.
   a. world   b. setting   c. waste

4. The dump was filled with mountains of trash.
   a. nonsense   **b.** garbage   c. foolishness

5. We had to use a brush to clean the oil off the floor.
   a. tidy   **b.** scrub   c. spruce up

5 | Book 4/Unit 2 **Just a Dream** | **At Home:** Have students explain why scrub is not the best synonym for clean in the second item. | 48

Reteach 49

Name _____ Date _____ **Reteach** 49

Sequence of Events

> Keeping track of **sequence**, or the order in which things happen, can help you better understand and enjoy a story. Look for time clue words to help you identify the sequence.

Read the story and the sentences below. Next to each sentence, write a number from 1 to 8 to show the order in which events happened.

The living room was such a mess! When Mrs. Roper walked in, she couldn't believe that Sam and Janet had cleaned it that afternoon. But they had. Unfortunately, right after they had finished, the first accident happened. Spot jumped up on a table and knocked over the flower pot. That led to the second accident. When Sam tried to vacuum the dirt, the vacuum bag ripped open. Dirt and dust fell all over the floor. Next, Janet slipped on the dirt, and dropped a vase she'd been carrying. A few seconds later, Mrs. Roper walked in.

7 ___ Janet dropped a vase.

8 ___ Mrs. Roper walked in.

1 ___ Sam and Janet cleaned the living room.

5 ___ The vacuum bag ripped open.

3 ___ Spot knocked over the flower pot.

4 ___ Sam tried to vacuum the dirt.

2 ___ Spot jumped up on a table.

6 ___ Janet slipped on the dirt.

49 | **At Home:** Have students think of a few events from "Just a Dream" and list the events in the order in which they happened. | Book 4/Unit 2 **Just a Dream** | 8

Just a Dream • RETEACH

Form Generalizations

> A **generalization** is a broad statement based on a set of facts.

Read the sentences below. Circle the letter next to the generalization that can be drawn from the facts.

1. Mark plays baseball from April to September. He plays football from October to December. However, Mark likes to play basketball year round.
   - **(a.)** Mark enjoys many sports.
   - **b.** Mark likes baseball better than football.
   - **c.** Mark wants to be a professional basketball player.

2. After school every day, Paige walks dogs for her neighbors. On some weekends, Paige babysits. Paige also does errands for pay.
   - **a.** Paige spends a lot of money.
   - **b.** Paige does little when she is not in school.
   - **(c.)** Paige is a hard-working girl.

3. When I told a scary story, Onida yawned. She laughs at horror movies and would skydive, if her mother would let her.
   - **(a.)** Onida is not easy to scare.
   - **b.** Onida likes movies.
   - **c.** Onida is frightened of many things.

4. Mr. Potter built his own computer. After that, he made an alarm system for his house. He also fixed my broken watch.
   - **a.** Mr. Potter breaks a lot of things.
   - **b.** Mr. Potter spends a lot of time at home.
   - **(c.)** Mr. Potter is good at making and fixing mechanical things.

5. Manuel writes in his journal every night. He writes stories for his younger brother all the time. He answers letters from his pen pal every week.
   - **a.** Manuel doesn't like sports.
   - **(b.)** Manuel likes to write.
   - **c.** Manuel does well in math.

At Home: Have students write some facts about themselves and then use the list to make a few generalizations about themselves.

Compound Words

> When two words are put together to make one word, the new word is called a **compound word**. You can usually use the meaning of each of the small words to help you figure out the meaning of the compound word.

Look at the compound words below. Write the two smaller words that make up each compound word. Then write the meaning of the compound word.

clothesline
1. Word 1: clothes
2. Word 2: line
3. Meaning: line that you hang clothes up on

hairbrush
4. Word 1: hair
5. Word 2: brush
6. Meaning: brush used to arrange your hair

underground
7. Word 1: under
8. Word 2: ground
9. Meaning: under the surface or under the ground

shamefaced
10. Word 1: shame
11. Word 2: faced
12. Meaning: showing shame on one's face

At Home: Ask students to name the small words in the compounds storefront, crosswalk, and foghorn and write the meanings for them.

Worksheet 45

Name_____ Date_____ Extend ◆ 45

Sequence of Events

Think about a typical day at school. Do you usually have the same subject at the same time each day? Are recesses and lunch at the same time? Outline a typical day at school. Write each event in the order in which it occurs during the day. Compare the **sequence of events** in your school day with those of classmates. Discuss any differences.

Answers will vary, but events should be in the correct sequence.

_____
_____
_____
_____
_____
_____
_____
_____
_____
_____

Book 4/Unit 2
Just a Dream

At Home: Compare and contrast the sequence of events on a weekday with the sequence of events on a Saturday.

45

Worksheet 46

Name_____ Date_____ Extend ◆ 46

Vocabulary

bulging	crumpled	foul
haze	shrieking	waddled

Make a comic strip in the boxes below. Use the vocabulary words in speech bubbles or in captions in the comic strip. Answers will vary but should show correct use of vocabulary.

Extend ◆ 47

Story Comprehension

In "Just a Dream," Walter's dreams highlight environmental problems. Select two of Walter's dreams that affected you the most. Explain why.
Answers will vary.

_____
_____
_____
_____
_____

46–47

At Home: Have students write about ways they can help the environment.

Book 4/Unit 2
Just a Dream

Worksheet 48

Name_____ Date_____ Extend ◆ 48

Use a Thesaurus

A **thesaurus** is a list of synonyms, or words that have the same or nearly the same meaning. It is usually arranged with words in alphabetical order. Use the thesaurus excerpt below to answer the questions.

> **event** noun 1. incident, occasion, affair. 2. outcome, result.
> **eventful** adjective 1. busy. 2. significant, important.
> **eventually** adverb finally, at last.
> **ever** adverb 1. always, forever. 2. continuously, constantly.
> **everyone** pronoun everybody, all.

1. A thesaurus usually tells what part of speech each entry is. Which words above are adjectives? adverbs? adjectives—eventful; adverb—ever, eventually

2. Write a sentence using an adjective and a sentence using an adverb. Answers will vary.

3. There are two listings for event. Why? Synonyms are given for the two different meanings of the word.

4. Write a sentence using a synonym for event. Answers will vary.

5. What are two synonyms for everyone? everybody, all

6. Write a short 4-line poem using both synonyms. Answers will vary.
_____
_____
_____
_____

Book 4/Unit 2
Just a Dream

At Home: Have students write a thesaurus entry for a word of their choice.

48

Worksheet 49

Name_____ Date_____ Extend ◆ 49

Sequence of Events

The **sequence of events** in a story refers to the order in which the events occurred. Think about the sequence of events in "Just a Dream," and answer the questions.

1. At the beginning of the story Walter litters on his way home from school. What did this tell you about Walter? Answers will vary. Possible answer: He was careless about littering.

2. Why do you think Walter's dream had so many parts? Answers will vary. Possible answer: So he could see the seriousness of the different effects of pollution.

3. What types of pollution does Walter dream about? Answers should include air, water, and noise pollution.

4. How did the illustrations make Walter's dream seem more real to you? Explain. Answers will vary. Possible answer: The pictures show the terrible effects of pollution.

5. At the beginning of the story Walter thinks that Rose's tree is a silly birthday present. By the end of the story, Walter has changed his mind. When do you think Walter asked for his tree? The morning after his first dream when his parents got up.

6. How do you feel about Walter's dreams? How do they make you feel about the environment? Answers will vary but should express an awareness of the problem of environmental pollution.

49

At Home: Have students design a poster showing the sequence of events leading to the pollution of a park.

Book 4/Unit 2
Just a Dream

Just a Dream • EXTEND

Form Generalizations

To **form a generalization** means to think about something in a general way. Form generalizations about "Just a Dream" to answer the questions below. **Answers will vary.**

1. Using Walter's first dream, what generalization can you form about littering?

_____
_____
_____

2. What can you say about most people who like to plant trees?

_____
_____
_____

3. After reading the story, what generalization can you form about pollution?

_____
_____
_____

4. How do you think most people will feel after reading "Just a Dream"?

_____
_____
_____

5. Why do you think the author of "Just a Dream" used dreams to make his points?

_____
_____
_____
_____
_____
_____

Book 4/Unit 2
Just a Dream

At Home: What would you do if clean water did not come out of your faucet at home? Form a generalization about what you would do and how it might affect your life.

50

Compound Words

A **compound word** is a word that is formed by putting two other words together. For example, the word *everyone* is made up of the words *every* and *one*.

Use the words below to write as many compound words as you can on the lines.

birth	be	time	day
air	high	where	light
bed	side	plane	every

Possible answers: birthday, beside, bedtime, airplane, highlight, ___
everywhere, everyday, bedside

_____
_____

Use some of the compound words that you made to write a story about the future.
Answers will vary.

_____
_____
_____
_____
_____
_____
_____
_____
_____
_____

51

At Home: Play a compound word game. Have students think of a compound word. Tell a partner half of the word and give clues as needed. How many clues does it take before your partner guesses the word?

Book 4/Unit 2
Just a Dream

Just a Dream • GRAMMAR

Page 39

Name_____ Date_____
LEARN
Grammar 39

Singular and Plural Nouns

> • A **singular noun** names one person, place, or thing.
>
> • A **plural noun** names more than one person, place, or thing.
>
> • Add -s to form the plural of most singular nouns.

Decide whether each underlined word is a singular or plural noun. Then write an "S" for singular or a "P" for plural on the line.

1. There were three trash <u>cans</u> in the garage. ___P___

2. One can had only <u>bottles</u> in it. ___P___

3. Walter traveled to the future in his <u>bed</u>. ___S___

4. Walter did not like the <u>dream</u> he had. ___S___

5. He put his head under the <u>blankets</u>. ___P___

6. Smoke poured from the <u>smokestack</u> by Walter's bed. ___S___

7. <u>Trucks</u> honked loudly all around the bed. ___P___

8. A woman showed Walter <u>postcards</u> of the Grand Canyon. ___P___

9. A <u>duck</u> that could talk landed on Walter's bed. ___S___

10. Walter was glad to get back to his <u>room</u>. ___S___

10
Grade 4/Unit 2
Just a Dream

Extension: Have students make a list of the underlined singular nouns. Then ask students to add -s to each word and write its plural form.

39

Page 40

Name_____ Date_____
LEARN AND PRACTICE
Grammar 40

Forming Plural Nouns

> • Add -es to form the plural of singular nouns that end in s, sh, ch, or x.
>
> • To form the plural of nouns ending in a consonant and y, change y to i and add -es.
>
> • To form the plural of nouns ending in a vowel and y, add -s.

Find the plural noun in the box for each underlined singular noun in the sentences below. Write the plural noun on the line.

gases	wishes	branches	boxes
bakeries	parties	toys	highways

1. Doughnuts and other sweets are made in <u>bakery</u> ___bakeries___.

2. There were <u>box</u> ___boxes___ of trash in the huge dump.

3. Walter's bed landed on <u>branch</u> ___branches___ in a tree.

4. Deadly <u>gas</u> ___gases___ filled the air.

5. The <u>highway</u> ___highways___ in the future were crowded.

6. Walter's birthday <u>wish</u> ___wishes___ all came true.

7. He got many new <u>toy</u> ___toys___ and a tree.

8. Of all his birthday <u>party</u> ___parties___ he liked this one best.

40

Extension: Have students make a Singular and Plural chart. Ask students to list singular nouns ending in s, sh, ch, x, and y and then write the plurals of these words.

Grade 4/Unit 2
Just a Dream
8

Page 41

Name_____ Date_____
PRACTICE AND REVIEW
Grammar 41

Forming Plural Nouns

> • Add -s to form the plural of most singular nouns.
>
> • Add -es to form the plural of singular nouns that end in s, sh, ch, or x.
>
> • To form the plural of nouns ending in a consonant and y, change y to i and add -es.
>
> • To form the plural of nouns ending in a vowel and y, add -s.

Write the correct plural form of each noun in parentheses.

1. Walter's street was filled with (boxs) ___boxes___ and bags of trash.

2. Two (woodcutteries) ___woodcutters___ cut down a tall tree.

3. In the mountains, Walter saw people wearing (snowshoe) ___snowshoes___.

4. All around Walter, cars and (busies) ___buses___ were honking.

5. The traffic moved slowly, only (inchs) ___inches___ at a time.

6. Walter thought there would be robots in the (citys) ___cities___.

7. Walter felt peaceful outside next to the trees and (bushs) ___bushes___.

8. He enjoyed the blue sky and warm (ray) ___rays___ from the sun.

8
Grade 4/Unit 2
Just a Dream

Extension: Have students brainstorm ideas about the future. Ask them to make a list of singular nouns that name a person, place, or thing of the future. Then have students write the plural form of each singular noun.

41

Page 42

Name_____ Date_____
MECHANICS
Grammar 42

Commas in a Series

> • A **comma** tells the reader to pause between the words that it separates.
>
> • Use commas to separate three or more words in a series.
>
> • Do not use a comma after the last word in a series.

Add commas where they belong in each sentence.

1. An airplane robot and machine were on the TV show Walter watched.
   An airplane, robot, and machine were on the TV show Walter watched.

2. There were trash cans for bottles cans and garbage.
   There were trash cans for bottles, cans, and garbage.

3. Trash traffic smoke and dirt were in Walter's dream.
   Trash, traffic, smoke, and dirt were in Walter's dream.

4. Walter now wants clean air land and water in his future.
   Walter now wants clean air, land, and water in his future.

5. A dinosaur yo-yo and tree were Walter's birthday presents.
   A dinosaur, yo-yo, and tree were Walter's birthday presents.

6. Some day squirrels bugs and birds may live in Walter's tree.
   Some day squirrels, bugs, and birds may live in Walter's tree.

42

Extension: Ask pairs of students to write two sentences, using three or more words in a series, leaving out the commas. Then have partners exchange papers and add missing commas to each other's sentences.

Grade 4/Unit 2
Just A Dream
6

Page 43

Singular and Plural Nouns

Read each sentence. Find the noun that is singular. Circle your answer.

1. The medicine was to help sore throats and itchy eyes.

   a. medicine   **b.** throats   **c.** itchy   **d.** eyes

2. Snowflakes fell as the hikers climbed up to the hotel.

   a. snowflakes   **b.** fell   **c.** hikers   **d. hotel**

3. There were stars and ducks in the black sky.

   a. stars   **b.** ducks   **c.** black   **d. sky**

4. A gentle breeze blew the leaves on two tall trees.

   a. gentle   **b. breeze**   **c.** leaves   **d.** trees

Read each sentence. Find the correct plural form for the noun in parentheses.

5. The (sky) in Walter's dream were filled with smoke or snow or smog.

   a. skys   **b.** skyes   **c. skies**   **d.** skyies

6. Both Walter and Rose planted trees on their (birthday).

   a. birthdays   **b.** birthdayes   **c.** birthdaies   **d.** birthdayies

7. Walter's friends had slices of cake and (dish) of ice cream.

   a. dishs   **b. dishes**   **c.** dishies   **d.** dishyes

8. Walter never saw so many (pastry) on one plate before.

   a. pastrys   **b.** pastres   **c.** pastrees   **d. pastries**

Page 44

Singular and Plural Nouns

- Add -s to form the plural of most singular nouns.
- Add -es to form the plural of singular nouns that end in s, sh, ch, or x.
- To form the plural of nouns ending in a consonant and y, change y to i and add -es.
- To form the plural of nouns ending in a vowel and y, add -s.

Mechanics:

- A comma tells the reader to pause between the words that it separates.
- Use commas to separate three or more words in a series.
- Do not use a comma after the last word in a series.

Correct each sentence below by changing the underlined singular noun to a plural, and by adding the missing commas. With a partner, take turns reading the corrected sentences aloud, pausing when you reach each comma.

1. Walter saw trash covering house streets and trees.

   Walter saw trash covering houses, streets, and trees.

2. Smoke from factory hurt his eyes nose and throat.

   Smoke from factories hurt his eyes, nose, and throat.

3. The only animal Walter saw were a horse a fish and ducks.

   The only animals Walter saw were a horse, a fish, and ducks.

4. Now Walter likes to sort can bottles and box.

   Now Walter likes to sort cans, bottles, and boxes.

Just a Dream • SPELLING

Page 39

Name_____ Date_____

Words with Consonant Clusters

Pretest Directions

Fold back the paper along the dotted line. Use the blanks to write each word as it is read aloud. When you finish the test, unfold the paper. Use the list at the right to correct any spelling mistakes. Practice the words that you missed for the Posttest.

To Parents

Here are the results of your child's weekly spelling Pretest. You can help your child study for the Posttest by following these simple steps for each word on the word list:

1. Read the word to your child.
2. Have your child write the word, saying each letter as it is written.
3. Say each letter of the word as your child checks the spelling.
4. If a mistake has been made, have your child read each letter of the correctly spelled word aloud, then repeat steps 1–3.

1. _____	1. blank
2. _____	2. daring
3. _____	3. claim
4. _____	4. flour
5. _____	5. crack
6. _____	6. bridge
7. _____	7. float
8. _____	8. plank
9. _____	9. classified
10. _____	10. cradle
11. _____	11. brand
12. _____	12. among
13. _____	13. flatter
14. _____	14. clothesline
15. _____	15. bridle
16. _____	16. credit
17. _____	17. darling
18. _____	18. flutter
19. _____	19. clatter
20. _____	20. cruise

Challenge Words

_____ bulging
_____ crumpled
_____ haze
_____ shrieking
_____ waddled

Page 40

Name_____ Date_____

Words with Consonant Clusters

Using the Word Study Steps

1. LOOK at the word.
2. SAY the word aloud.
3. STUDY the letters in the word.
4. WRITE the word.
5. CHECK the word.

Did you spell the word right? If not, go back to step 1.

Spelling Tip

Use words you know how to spell to help you spell new words.

bravery + judge = bridge

Word Scramble

Unscramble each set of letters to make a spelling word.

1. ourfl _____flour_____
2. miacl _____claim_____
3. ackcr _____crack_____
4. ridbeg _____bridge_____
5. ankbl _____blank_____
6. grinda _____daring_____
7. toalf _____float_____
8. fidelassic _____classified_____
9. darcle _____cradle_____
10. dranb _____brand_____
11. knalp _____plank_____
12. gonma _____among_____
13. taterlf _____flatter_____
14. thesenilloc _____clothesline_____
15. dicert _____credit_____
16. dribel _____bridle_____
17. gnarldi _____darling_____
18. rettulf _____flutter_____
19. latertc _____clatter_____
20. resuic _____cruise_____

To Parents or Helpers

Using the Word Study Steps above as your child comes across any new words will help him or her learn to spell words effectively. Review the steps as you both go over this week's spelling words.
Go over the Spelling Tip with your child. Help your child use words he or she knows to figure out how to spell new words on the spelling list.
Help your child complete the spelling activity.

Page 41

Name_____ Date_____

Words with Consonant Clusters

blank	crack	classified	flatter	darling
daring	bridge	cradle	clothesline	flutter
claim	float	brand	bridle	clatter
flour	plank	among	credit	cruise

Write the spelling words with these spelling patterns

words beginning with fl

1. _____flour_____
2. _____float_____
3. _____flatter_____
4. _____flutter_____

words beginning with cl

5. _____claim_____
6. _____classified_____
7. _____clothesline_____
8. _____clatter_____

words beginning with cr

9. _____crack_____
10. _____cradle_____
11. _____credit_____
12. _____cruise_____

words beginning with br

13. _____bridge_____
14. _____brand_____
15. _____bridle_____

words ending with ng

16. _____daring_____
17. _____among_____
18. _____darling_____

words ending with nk

19. _____blank_____
20. _____plank_____

Sounds Alike

Write the spelling word that rhymes with each word below.

21. name _____claim_____
22. sharing _____daring_____
23. track _____crack_____
24. butter _____flutter_____
25. lose _____cruise_____

Page 42

Name_____ Date_____

Words with Consonant Clusters

blank	crack	classified	flatter	darling
daring	bridge	cradle	clothesline	flutter
claim	float	brand	bridle	clatter
flour	plank	among	credit	cruise

Complete each sentence below with a spelling word.

1. When it's windy, the leaves _____flutter_____ and shake.
2. The children helped to hang the laundry on the _____clothesline_____.
3. We mixed milk and _____flour_____ to make biscuits.
4. The horse rider removed the saddle and _____bridle_____.
5. The carpenter replaced a wooden _____plank_____ that had rotted.
6. It took great _____daring_____ to dive into the stormy sea.
7. We read an ad in the _____classified_____ section.
8. Ranchers _____brand_____ their cattle to show who owns them.
9. Did anyone _____claim_____ the ring you found in the parking lot?
10. Our teacher will give us extra _____credit_____ if we read a book.

Word Meaning: Synonyms

Write the spelling word that has the same or almost the same meaning.

11. sweety _____darling_____
12. amid _____among_____
13. overpass _____bridge_____
14. baby bed _____cradle_____
15. voyage _____cruise_____
16. break _____crack_____
17. empty _____blank_____
18. crash _____clatter_____

Challenge Extension: Write one fill-in sentence for each Challenge Word and then exchange papers with a partner to complete them.

Just a Dream • SPELLING

Name_____ Date_____

Words with Consonant Clusters

Proofreading Activity

There are six spelling mistakes in Walter's journal entry below. Circle the misspelled words. Write the words correctly on the lines below.

October 28

What a shocking dream I had! I saw the world in the future. Garbage was piled so high I had to use a (brigde) to get from one side of town to the other. The air was so dirty that the laundry on a (closeline) actually turned black. I got caught (amung) thousands of cars in a gigantic traffic jam, with thousands of horns honking. The (clattur) was so unbearable that I covered my ears to block the noise. The rivers and lakes were so polluted that a person would have to be very (dairing) —or crazy—to go swimming. I was glad when I finally woke up in my room. I hope that the future world will not be like this, as some people (clame) it may be.

1. ___bridge___   3. ___among___   5. ___daring___
2. ___clothesline___   4. ___clatter___   6. ___claim___

Writing Activity

Have you ever had a dream about the future? Write about one of your dreams. Use four spelling words in your writing.

_____

_____

_____

_____

Name_____ Date_____

Words with Consonant Clusters

Look at the words in each set below. One word in each set is spelled correctly. Use a pencil to fill in the circle next to the correct word. Before you begin, look at the sample sets of words. Sample A has been done for you. Do Sample B by yourself. When you are sure you know what to do, you may go on with the rest of the page.

Sample A
- Ⓐ clothez
- ● clothes
- Ⓒ klothes
- Ⓓ clowes

Sample B
- Ⓐ bireak
- Ⓑ brek
- ● break
- Ⓓ breack

1. ● blank
   Ⓑ blangk
   Ⓒ blanck
   Ⓓ blanc

2. Ⓔ cruse
   Ⓕ kruse
   Ⓖ cruize
   ● cruise

3. Ⓐ dareing
   ● daring
   Ⓒ dairing
   Ⓓ darink

4. Ⓔ clattur
   Ⓕ clattir
   ● clatter
   Ⓗ cladder

5. Ⓐ clame
   Ⓑ claim
   Ⓒ klame
   Ⓓ klaim

6. Ⓔ fluttur
   ● flutter
   Ⓖ fluttir
   Ⓗ fluttor

7. Ⓐ flowr
   Ⓑ flourr
   ● flour
   Ⓓ fluor

8. ● credit
   Ⓕ creddit
   Ⓖ kredit
   Ⓗ creditt

9. Ⓐ krak
   Ⓑ crac
   Ⓒ crak
   ● crack

10. Ⓔ bridel
    ● bridle
    Ⓖ briddle
    Ⓗ briddel

11. ● bridge
    Ⓑ brige
    Ⓒ brigde
    Ⓓ bidge

12. Ⓔ clothsline
    Ⓕ closeline
    Ⓖ clozeline
    ● clothesline

13. Ⓐ flote
    Ⓑ flowt
    ● float
    Ⓓ floet

14. Ⓔ flater
    ● flatter
    Ⓖ flattur
    Ⓗ flattir

15. Ⓐ planck
    ● plank
    Ⓒ plang
    Ⓓ plangk

16. Ⓔ amung
    Ⓕ ammong
    Ⓖ amonk
    ● among

17. ● classified
    Ⓑ classifide
    Ⓒ clasiffied
    Ⓓ classfied

18. Ⓔ brande
    Ⓕ branned
    Ⓖ brannd
    ● brand

19. Ⓐ darrling
    ● darling
    Ⓒ darlingk
    Ⓓ darlink

20. Ⓔ cradel
    Ⓕ craddle
    Ⓖ craydel
    ● cradle

Name_____ Date_____ **Practice** 52

Cause and Effect

One event can make or **cause** another event to happen. What happens is the **effect**. Read the following pairs of sentences. In each pair, tell which sentence states a cause and which states an effect. Write **C** for cause and **E** for effect in the blanks.

1. _____C_____ The movie theater charged only $2.00 for tickets on Wednesday evenings.

   _____E_____ There was a large crowd of people at the theater on Wednesday evening.

2. _____E_____ The championship basketball game was cancelled because of bad weather.

   _____C_____ A severe blizzard hit the city on the day of the championship basketball game.

3. _____E_____ There were less than ten people in most classes last week.

   _____C_____ Many students had chicken pox last week.

4. _____E_____ Teachers gave students several extra days to make up the work they missed.

   _____C_____ Students who were sick fell behind in their class work.

5. How can you tell which sentence in each pair describes a cause and which describes an effect? I used the word clues in each sentence.
_____

5 Book 4/Unit 2
Leah's Pony

At Home: Have students write a sentence about the effect of weather on an after school activity.

52

Name_____ Date_____ **Practice** 53

Vocabulary

Choose the correct word from the box to complete each sentence.

sturdy	glistened	overflowing	county	clustered	bidding

1. The old car seemed huge and it was very strong and _____sturdy_____.

2. People from all over the _____county_____ wanted the car.

3. At first small groups of people _____clustered_____ around the car.

4. On the final morning of the fair people were _____bidding_____ on the car.

5. By the time the new owner was announced, the area was _____overflowing_____ with people.

6. The metal on the car _____glistened_____ in the sun.

53

At Home: Have students write a sentence using each vocabulary word.

Book 4/Unit 2
Leah's Pony 6

Auction

The *county* decided to hold an auction to raise money for a swimming pool. The morning of the auction, groups of people clustered near the auctioneer. The stage was *overflowing* with furniture, paintings, and a skateboard. "What will you bid for this used but *sturdy* old skateboard?" called the auctioneer. "I'll start the *bidding* at one dollar."

Tyrone clutched the money he had saved. The quarters *glistened* in the sun. "I bid two dollars," he shouted. Tyrone was hoping to take it home.

"Three dollars," a woman shouted from the crowd.

"Four!" cried Tyrone. That was all the money he had.

Suddenly from the back of the room, a man yelled, "Five hundred dollars,"

Tyrone had lost. As he was about to leave, the man spoke. "This *county* needs a swimming pool. Five hundred dollars is my donation." Then he handed the skateboard to Tyrone. "Enjoy your new skateboard," he said. "And enjoy the new pool."

1. Which part of the government held the auction? _____the county_____

2. Which word describes the auction stage? _____overflowing_____

3. At what amount did the auctioneer start the *bidding*? _____one dollar_____

4. What was the skateboard like? _____used but sturdy_____

5. Why do you think the stage was *overflowing* with so many items?
Possible answer: The people of the county wanted a pool and probably donated a lot of things to be auctioned.
_____

5 Book 4/Unit 2
Leah's Pony

At Home: Have students use the vocabulary words to write a follow up to the story.

53a

Name_____ Date_____ **Practice** 54

Story Comprehension

Answer the questions about "Leah's Pony." Answers may vary.

1. How did the crops grow in the year that Leah got the pony?
They grew tall and straight.

2. What would Mr. B say when Leah rode the pony into town?
That's the finest pony in the whole county.

3. How tall did the corn grow the year the wind was black with dust?
The corn grew no taller than a man's thumb.

4. How did grasshoppers make conditions worse for the farmers?
They ate the trees bare and left only twigs behind.

5. Papa borrowed money from the bank and couldn't pay it back. Why?
He had no corn to sell because of the dust and grasshoppers.

6. What was going to be sold at auction?
The tractor and farm animals including a bull, rooster, and calf.

7. How does Leah try to help?
She sells her pony and uses the money to bid for Papa's tractor.

8. Why was Leah's pony back in the barn the next morning?
Mr. B said it was too small for him or his grandson and that it was the right size for Leah.

54

At Home: Have students retell Leah's story.

Book 4/Unit 2
Leah's Pony 8

Leah's Pony • PRACTICE

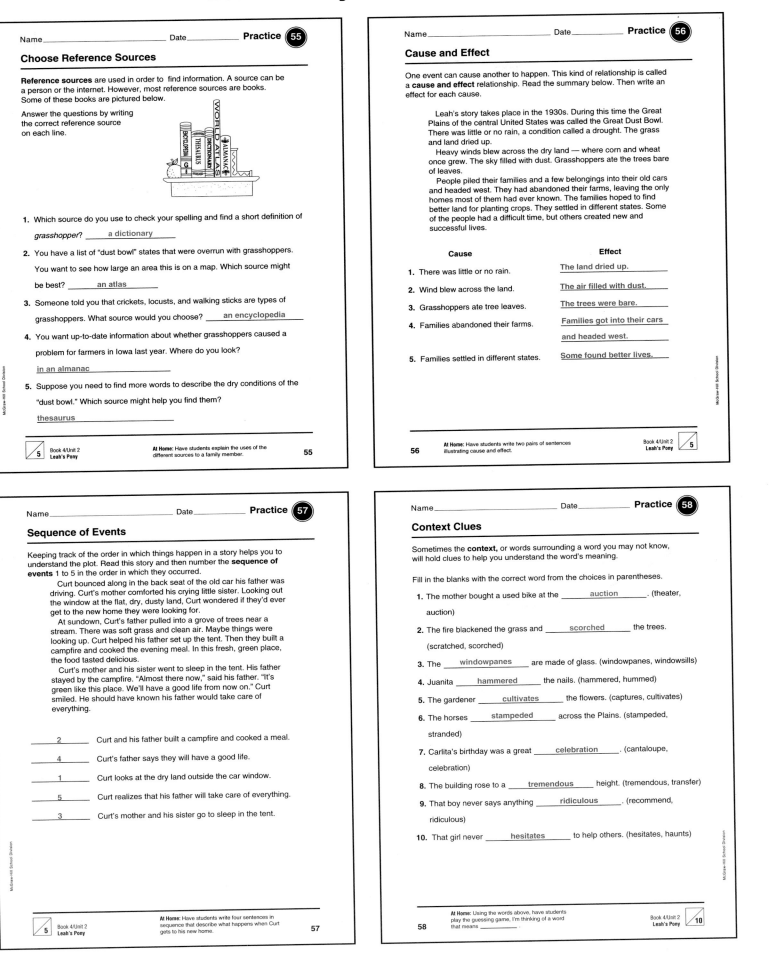

Choose Reference Sources

Reference sources are used in order to find information. A source can be a person or the internet. However, most reference sources are books. Some of these books are pictured below.

Answer the questions by writing the correct reference source on each line.

1. Which source do you use to check your spelling and find a short definition of *grasshopper*? _____a dictionary_____

2. You have a list of "dust bowl" states that were overrun with grasshoppers. You want to see how large an area this is on a map. Which source might be best? _____an atlas_____

3. Someone told you that crickets, locusts, and walking sticks are types of grasshoppers. What source would you choose? _____an encyclopedia_____

4. You want up-to-date information about whether grasshoppers caused a problem for farmers in Iowa last year. Where do you look?

   in an almanac_____

5. Suppose you need to find more words to describe the dry conditions of the "dust bowl." Which source might help you find them?

   thesaurus_____

Cause and Effect

One event can cause another to happen. This kind of relationship is called a **cause and effect** relationship. Read the summary below. Then write an effect for each cause.

Leah's story takes place in the 1930s. During this time the Great Plains of the central United States was called the Great Dust Bowl. There was little or no rain, a condition called a drought. The grass and land dried up.

Heavy winds blew across the dry land — where corn and wheat once grew. The sky filled with dust. Grasshoppers ate the trees bare of leaves.

People piled their families and a few belongings into their old cars and headed west. They had abandoned their farms, leaving the only homes most of them had ever known. The families hoped to find better land for planting crops. They settled in different states. Some of the people had a difficult time, but others created new and successful lives.

Cause	Effect
1. There was little or no rain.	The land dried up.
2. Wind blew across the land.	The air filled with dust.
3. Grasshoppers ate tree leaves.	The trees were bare.
4. Families abandoned their farms.	Families got into their cars and headed west.
5. Families settled in different states.	Some found better lives.

Sequence of Events

Keeping track of the order in which things happen in a story helps you to understand the plot. Read this story and then number the **sequence of events** 1 to 5 in the order in which they occurred.

Curt bounced along in the back seat of the old car his father was driving. Curt's mother comforted his crying little sister. Looking out the window at the flat, dry, dusty land, Curt wondered if they'd ever get to the new home they were looking for.

At sundown, Curt's father pulled into a grove of trees near a stream. There was soft grass and clean air. Maybe things were looking up. Curt helped his father set up the tent. Then they built a campfire and cooked the evening meal. In this fresh, green place, the food tasted delicious.

Curt's mother and his sister went to sleep in the tent. His father stayed by the campfire. "Almost there now," said his father. "It's green like this place. We'll have a good life from now on." Curt smiled. He should have known his father would take care of everything.

2	Curt and his father built a campfire and cooked a meal.
4	Curt's father says they will have a good life.
1	Curt looks at the dry land outside the car window.
5	Curt realizes that his father will take care of everything.
3	Curt's mother and his sister go to sleep in the tent.

Context Clues

Sometimes the **context**, or words surrounding a word you may not know, will hold clues to help you understand the word's meaning.

Fill in the blanks with the correct word from the choices in parentheses.

1. The mother bought a used bike at the _____auction_____. (theater, auction)

2. The fire blackened the grass and _____scorched_____ the trees. (scratched, scorched)

3. The _____windowpanes_____ are made of glass. (windowpanes, windowsills)

4. Juanita _____hammered_____ the nails. (hammered, hummed)

5. The gardener _____cultivates_____ the flowers. (captures, cultivates)

6. The horses _____stampeded_____ across the Plains. (stampeded, stranded)

7. Carlita's birthday was a great _____celebration_____. (cantaloupe, celebration)

8. The building rose to a _____tremendous_____ height. (tremendous, transfer)

9. That boy never says anything _____ridiculous_____. (recommend, ridiculous)

10. That girl never _____hesitates_____ to help others. (hesitates, haunts)

Leah's Pony • RETEACH

Cause and Effect

> A **cause** is the reason something happens. An **effect** is what happens.

Each underlined sentence describes an effect. Circle the letter beside the sentence that tells the cause.

1. After a few minutes, the wind stopped. Terri's sailboat stopped moving. She took out an oar and began to paddle.
   a. Terri began to paddle.
   b. Terri took out an oar.
   c. The wind stopped. *(circled)*

2. Noah was overjoyed! The little park was saved from destruction. The volunteers had raised enough money to buy it from developers.
   a. Noah was overjoyed.
   b. Volunteers raised enough money to buy the park. *(circled)*
   c. Developers donated the park to the volunteers.

3. It was only 2:00 in the afternoon, but Sarah turned on her headlights. Clouds had covered the sun, and it was dark.
   a. Clouds blocked the sun. *(circled)*
   b. Some sun came through the clouds.
   c. It was 2:00 in the afternoon.

4. Snow continued for days. Weather forecasters said it was a record snowfall. Schools were shut for three days. Children had fun sledding and playing in the snow.
   a. Children had fun in the snow.
   b. Weather forecasters said it was a record snowfall.
   c. It had snowed. *(circled)*

`4` Book 4/Unit 2
Leah's Pony

At Home: Have students describe something that happened during the day and tell why it happened.

52

Vocabulary

Write a word from the list to complete each sentence.

bidding	clustered	county	glistened	overflowing	sturdy

1. Reporters ____clustered____ around the baseball star.
2. Meg's eyes ____glistened____ with tears.
3. The laundry hamper was ____overflowing____ with clothes.
4. Mr. Polanski owns the largest farm in the ____county____.
5. The ____bidding____ for the house began at $98,000.
6. Although the table was old and used, it was still ____sturdy____.

`6`

Story Comprehension

Write a ✔ next to every sentence that tells something true about "Leah's Pony." You may look back at the story for help.

1. _____ Leah's family were factory workers.
2. _____ Leah's family always had money problems.
3. __✔__ Some neighbors moved away to find a better place.
4. __✔__ Leah's family had to sell animals and machines.
5. _____ Leah sold her pony because she was told to.
6. __✔__ Neighbors helped buy back the family's things.
7. __✔__ Leah's family was surprised and pleased by her actions.
8. _____ Leah never got back her pony.

At Home: Have students identify their favorite part of "Leah's Pony."

53–54

Book 4/Unit 2
Leah's Pony `8`

Choose Reference Sources

> Knowing in which **reference source** to look for information can save you time and provide you with the best answers to your questions.

Use the descriptions that follow to help you answer the questions.

> **Almanac:** Up-to-date information about people, places, and events. The information often appears in a table or chart.
>
> **Atlas:** Many different kinds of maps.
>
> **Dictionary:** Lists words in alphabetical order. A dictionary gives the meaning, pronunciation, and part of speech of a word.
>
> **Encyclopedia:** Articles on many topics, arranged in alphabetical order.
>
> **Thesaurus:** Synonyms or words with almost the same meaning.

In which reference book would you

1. look for a synonym for a word? ____thesaurus____
2. find the greatest number of maps? ____atlas____
3. find information on how a dairy farm is run? ____encyclopedia____
4. be most likely to find information on how much snow fell in each state last year? ____almanac____
5. look to find the pronunciation and meaning of a word?
   ____dictionary____
6. look to find a list of the ten cities in the world that have the most people?
   ____almanac____

`6` Book 4/Unit 2
Leah's Pony

At Home: Have students give examples of something they would research in each of the resources listed.

55

Cause and Effect

> In stories one thing often **causes** something else to happen. The result is an **effect**. As you read, look for what happens and why.

Read each story. Then write the missing cause or effect.

Mr. Bumper read an article that said "Fish food is brain food!" For four weeks he cooked fish each night. Though Mr. Bumper didn't feel any smarter, he was willing to continue this fish diet. However, Mr. Bumper finally stopped preparing fish. His family simply refused to keep eating fish every night.

1. Cause: Mr. Bumper thought that eating fish would make him smarter.
   Effect: __Mr. Bumper prepared fish every night.__

2. Cause: __Mr. Bumper's family finally refused to eat more fish.__

   Effect: Mr. Bumper stopped making fish.

A magazine article said that doing a headstand for 10 minutes each day was good for a person's health. As a result, Mr. Andreas did a headstand each morning when he got to his office. After a month Mr. Andreas didn't feel much healthier. But now everyone in his company knew who he was. The company newsletter had printed a picture of Mr. Andreas standing on his head.

3. Cause: __An article said headstands were good for your health.__

   Effect: Mr. Andreas did a headstand each morning at his office.

4. Cause: A picture was printed that showed Mr. Andreas standing on his head.
   Effect: __Everyone in the company recognized Mr. Andreas.__

At Home: Have students think of a famous person. Then have students think of causes for that fame.

56

Book 4/Unit 2
Leah's Pony `4`

Leah's Pony • RETEACH

Sequence of Events

> **Sequence** is the order in which things happen. Picturing the events in your mind often helps you understand the order in which events happen.

Each group of sentences below tells a story. The sentences are in the wrong order. Decide the correct order. Write the numbers 1 to 3 on the lines before the sentences to show the order in which events happened.

1. __3__ Nora planted a garden.
   __2__ Nora ordered seeds and got them through the mail.
   __1__ Nora decided to plant a garden.

2. __3__ Ed used his savings to buy a CD player.
   __2__ Ed saved money from the movie theater paycheck.
   __1__ The movie theater hired Ed to collect tickets.

3. __2__ Yolanda started doing extra math homework every night.
   __1__ Yolanda got low grades on two math tests in a row.
   __3__ Yolanda's math grades improved.

4. __3__ Ned used the note cards to give his speech.
   __1__ Ned was asked to talk about his after-school computer business.
   __2__ Ned put the major points of his speech on note cards.

Use Context Clues

> When you read a word you don't know, look at the words and sentences around that word to learn its meaning. This is called using **context clues**.

Read each sentence. Circle the context clues that help you figure out the meaning of each underlined word. Then write the meaning on the line.

1. We work hard to (put the cut hay into piles) The result is a field filled with haystacks. ___piles of cut hay___

2. Mr. Roth and his sons toil in the fields all day. This (hard work) keeps them fit. ___to work hard___

3. Every fall, the farmers harvest their crops. After this (gathering of the food) they have a celebration. ___gathering of food crops___

4. A century ago farmers used a horse to pull a plow through the field (to turn up) (the soil for planting.) ___machine used for turning up the soil___

5. The cows are in the pasture. They eat in (that grassy field) until they are full. ___grassy field___

6. The Beckley farm has pipes and sprinklers (to water) its crops. Many other farms use a similar system to irrigate their land. ___to bring water to crops___

Leah's Pony • EXTEND

Cause and Effect

In a story a particular action, or **cause**, can lead to a result, or **effect**. Think about "Amelia's Road." Write a short paragraph discussing an example of cause and effect. You can look back at the story for help.

Answers will vary. Possible answer: The weather in the story was dry and

hot for a long time. This was a cause. The effects were that the crops didn't

grow, Leah's neighbors packed up and moved away, and Leah's family

held an auction to sell their belongings.

Cause and effect can be used to describe a scientific experiment. Think of a simple experiment you have performed in class or at home. Use cause and effect to write about the experiment.

Answers will vary, but should contain an example of cause and effect.

Book 4/Unit 2
Leah's Pony

At Home: Have students tell about how something that happened at school had an effect on their mood.

52

Vocabulary

bidding	clustered	county
glistened	overflowing	sturdy

Suppose that you are at an auction and overhear a conversation between two people discussing the auction. Write the dialogue between the two people below. Remember to include quotation marks and identify each speaker. Use as many of the vocabulary words from the box as you can.

Answers will vary, but should include some of the vocabulary words and

proper use of grammar.

Story Comprehension

In "Leah's Pony," Leah's parents sell many things even before they have the auction. Why do you think that they never ask Leah to sell her pony?

Answers will vary. Possible answer: They know how important the pony is

to Leah, and selling it might not have made much difference anyway.

53–54

At Home: Discuss how unpredictable the weather can be and the long-term effects of different weather conditions.

Book 4/Unit 2
Leah's Pony

Choose Reference Sources

When you want to find information about something, you can check a **reference source**. The type of reference source you use depends on the information that you need.

Use the descriptions of the reference sources below to answer the questions.

Almanac: Up to date information about people, places, and events.
Atlas: a book of maps.
Dictionary: word spellings, meanings, pronunciations, and parts of speech.
Encyclopedia: a book that has detailed information on a wide variety of subjects.
Thesaurus: a book of synonyms.

1. Suppose you wanted to locate a town in northwestern Kansas. Which reference book would you check?
   atlas

2. In which reference book could you find information on the origins of ponies in America?
   encyclopedia

3. In which reference book(s) could you check the spelling of the word *auctioneer*?
   dictionary or thesaurus

4. In which reference book would you find the population of Kansas?
   almanac

Book 4/Unit 2
Leah's Pony

At Home: Have students list the types of reference books they would use for variety of research needs.

55

Cause and Effect

Cause and effect can be used to describe several different situations in "Leah's Pony." Think about cause and effect to answer the questions below.

1. How does the weather make it possible for Leah to get a pony? When the weather is good the crops are good, and there is money for a pony.

2. How is the weather a cause of the auction? When the weather is so hot, dry, and dusty that crops do not grow, there will be no money from the farm to pay the bills. Then an auction might be held to raise money.

3. What does Leah do when she learns about the auction, and why? She sells her horse to help save the farm.

4. What is the effect of Leah's bidding at the auction? The neighbors decide to bid low and give the items back to Leah's parents.

5. What caused the neighbors to make low bids at the auction? They followed Leah's example.

6. Do you think that Leah intended for the neighbors to bid low prices at the auction? Explain. No. Although she knew how little money she had, Leah did not know that she was setting the example.

56

At Home: Have students recall experiences when their family or school plans were changed because of a cause, such as bad weather.

Book 4/Unit 2
Leah's Pony

Leah's Pony • EXTEND

Sequence of Events

Think about the **sequence of events** in "Leah's Pony." Were you surprised when Leah sold her pony? Write a paragraph describing the sequence of events that made Leah decide to sell her pony.

Answers will vary, but key events in the story should appear in sequence.

_____

_____

_____

_____

_____

_____

_____

Leah's bid at the auction changed the entire course of the auction. Explain how you know this is true.

Answers will vary. Possible answer: Some of the items had already been

sold. If Leah had not made the low bid, the neighbors would not have done

_____

_____

_____

At Home: Discuss situations in which your own actions have been influenced by another person's actions.

Context Clues

Words work together to give meaning to a sentence. If you look closely at how words are used, you can often figure out the meaning of a word from clues in the sentence. These clues are called **context clues**.

All the words below can be used in a country or farm-related context. Use as many of the words as you can to write a short story about what you think a typical day on a farm would be like. Use context clues in your writing.

cornfields	tractor	fertilize	county
cultivate	pasture	gullies	flock
whinny	coop	drooping	galloped

Answers will vary, but should make correct use of the words.

_____

_____

_____

_____

_____

_____

_____

Write a title for your story. Try to include a context clue in your title.
Answers will vary.

_____

_____

_____

At Home: Have students explain the context clues in the story they wrote.

Leah's Pony • GRAMMAR

Irregular Plural Nouns

- Some nouns have special plural forms.

calves	children	feet	geese	gentlemen
lives	men	oxen	teeth	women

Look in the above box for the plural form of each singular noun. Write it on the line provided.

1. man ___men___

2. child ___children___

3. woman ___women___

4. life ___lives___

5. calf ___calves___

6. goose ___geese___

7. ox ___oxen___

8. foot ___feet___

9. tooth ___teeth___

10. gentleman ___gentlemen___

10 Grade 4/Unit 2
Leah's Pony

Extension: Have partners take turns using the singular and plural nouns on this page in oral sentences.

45

Irregular Plural Nouns

- A few nouns have the same singular and plural forms.

Read the sentences below. Then decide whether the underlined word is a singular noun or plural noun and write singular or plural on the line.

1. There was not one <u>sheep</u> on Papa's farm. ___singular___

2. There was no grass in his dry field for <u>sheep</u> to eat. ___plural___

3. Some farms have ponds with <u>fish</u> in them. ___plural___

4. Have you ever seen a <u>fish</u> in a pond? ___singular___

5. Farmers in Maine may see a <u>moose</u> drink from a pond. ___singular___

6. <u>Moose</u> are much bigger animals than cows. ___plural___

7. Moose and <u>deer</u> are not farm animals. ___plural___

8. A <u>deer</u> could jump over a farmer's fence. ___singular___

Extension: Ask students to draw pictures illustrating the singular and plural forms of the words *sheep, fish, moose,* and *deer.* Have students write captions for their pictures.

46

Grade 4/Unit 2
Leah's Pony 8

Plural Nouns

- Some nouns have special plural forms.
- A few nouns have the same singular and plural forms.

Read each sentence. Draw a line under the word in parentheses that is the correct plural form.

1. Of all the (ponys, <u>ponies</u>) in the county, Leah's pony was the finest.

2. Leah waved to the (childs, <u>children</u>) in the truck.

3. (<u>Boxes</u>, Boxs) full of the family's things were piled into the truck.

4. The (lifes, <u>lives</u>) of farmers were hard in these times.

5. The land was too dry for farm animals like (<u>sheep</u>, sheeps) and cattle.

6. There were no (fishes, <u>fish</u>) because the streams had dried up.

7. Several (<u>men</u>, mans) came to the auction.

8. Sometimes (calfs, <u>calves</u>) were sold at an auction.

9. A man in a big hat called out, "Ladies and (gentlemans, <u>gentlemen</u>)."

10. A farmer gave Papa the (<u>keys</u>, keyes) to the truck.

10 Grade 4/Unit 2
Leah's Pony

Extension: Have students name the two nouns in the above sentences that have the same singular and plural forms. Then ask students to name the five nouns that have special plural forms.

47

Capitalization

- A proper noun begins with a capital letter.
- The name of a day, month, or holiday begins with a capital letter.
- Capitalize family names if they refer to specific people.
- Capitalize titles of people before names.

Read the sentences below. Then correct the capitalization mistakes and rewrite the sentences on the line provided.

1. When leah went into town, she always rode by the grocery store.
   When Leah went into town, she always rode by the grocery store.

2. She knew mr. b. liked to see her pony.
   She knew Mr. B. liked to see her pony.

3. Leah's mother always baked coffee cake on saturday.
   Leah's mother always baked coffee cake on Saturday.

4. One day, the neighbors moved to oregon.
   One day, the neighbors moved to Oregon.

5. Because times were hard, papa had to sell his tractor.
   Because times were hard, Papa had to sell his tractor.

6. Papa's tractor was made by a company named farmall.
   Papa's tractor was made by a company named Farmall.

7. The family also had to sell mama's prize rooster.
   The family also had to sell Mama's prize rooster.

8. The story about leah and her pony was written by elizabeth friedrich.
   The story about Leah and her pony was written by Elizabeth Friedrich.

Extension: Ask students to write four sentences that have words beginning with capital letters. The sentences must include the following kinds of names: a month, a holiday, a person's name, and a person's name with a title.

48

Grade 4/Unit 2
Leah's Pony 8

Leah's Pony • GRAMMAR

Irregular Plural Nouns

A. Write *yes* if the noun below has the same singular and plural forms.
Write *no* if the noun does not have the same singular and plural forms.

1. rooster _____no_____

2. deer _____yes_____

3. sheep _____yes_____

4. pony _____no_____

5. moose _____yes_____

6. calf _____no_____

B. Complete each sentence with the plural form of the singular noun in parentheses.

7. Leah's (foot) _____feet_____ were dusty because she walked home.

8. It was hard for (woman) _____women_____ to keep the houses clean.

9. Most (child) _____children_____ on a farm have chores to do.

10. Even the (mouse) _____mice_____ that lived in the fields had little to eat.

Irregular Plural Nouns

- Some nouns have special plural forms.
- A few nouns have the same singular and plural forms.

Mechanics

- A proper noun begins with a capital letter.
- The name of a day, month, or holiday begins with a capital letter.
- Capitalize family names if they refer to specific people.
- Capitalize titles of people before names.

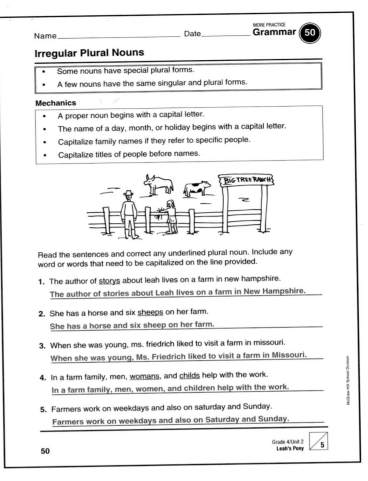

Read the sentences and correct any underlined plural noun. Include any word or words that need to be capitalized on the line provided.

1. The author of <u>storys</u> about leah lives on a farm in new hampshire.
   The author of stories about Leah lives on a farm in New Hampshire.

2. She has a horse and six <u>sheeps</u> on her farm.
   She has a horse and six sheep on her farm.

3. When she was young, ms. friedrich liked to visit a farm in missouri.
   When she was young, Ms. Friedrich liked to visit a farm in Missouri.

4. In a farm family, men, <u>womans</u>, and <u>childs</u> help with the work.
   In a farm family, men, women, and children help with the work.

5. Farmers work on weekdays and also on saturday and Sunday.
   Farmers work on weekdays and also on Saturday and Sunday.

Leah's Pony • SPELLING

Page 45

Words with Consonant Clusters

Pretest Directions

Fold back the paper along the dotted line. Use the blanks to write each word as it is read aloud. When you finish the test, unfold the paper. Use the list at the right to correct any spelling mistakes. Practice the words you missed for the Posttest.

To Parents

Here are the results of your child's weekly spelling Pretest. You can help your child study for the Posttest by following these simple steps for each word on the word list:

1. Read the word to your child.
2. Have your child write the word, saying each letter as it is written.
3. Say each letter of the word as your child checks the spelling.
4. If a mistake has been made, have your child read each letter of the correctly spelled word aloud, then repeat steps 1–3.

1. _____	1. thrill
2. _____	2. spruce
3. _____	3. stand
4. _____	4. speed
5. _____	5. stretch
6. _____	6. sprint
7. _____	7. spare
8. _____	8. threw
9. _____	9. stranger
10. _____	10. springtime
11. _____	11. stern
12. _____	12. spectacle
13. _____	13. strap
14. _____	14. thrifty
15. _____	15. street
16. _____	16. stung
17. _____	17. sparkle
18. _____	18. stress
19. _____	19. special
20. _____	20. steak

Challenge Words

_____ clustered
_____ county
_____ glistened
_____ overflowing
_____ sturdy

Page 46

Words with Consonant Clusters

Using the Word Study Steps

1. LOOK at the word.
2. SAY the word aloud.
3. STUDY the letters in the word.
4. WRITE the word.
5. CHECK the word.

Did you spell the word right? If not, go back to step 1.

Spelling Tip

Make up clues to help you remember the spelling.

"C" the "sh" sound in *special*.

Find and Circle

Find and circle the hidden spelling words.

az**thrill**zxx**spruce**aw**stand**bnu**speed**aa
stretchxx**sprint**xa**spare**zzz**threw**bwxxv
strangeraab**springtime**walmewx**stern**x
z**spectacle**xxv**strap**zzx**thrifty**aab**street**
xxx**stung**kkxxvxxx**sparkle**xxv**stress**xx
z**special**xabhnisnxx**steak**aavxxxvvvvs

To Parents or Helpers

Using the Word Study Steps above as your child comes across any new words will help him or her learn to spell words effectively. Review the steps as you both go over this week's spelling words.

Go over the Spelling Tip with your child. Ask your child if he or she knows other clues to help remember spelling words. Help him or her use the clues and then write the spelling words to remember how to spell them.

Help your child find and circle the hidden spelling words.

Page 47

Words with Consonant Clusters

thrill	stretch	stranger	strap	sparkle
spruce	sprint	springtime	thrifty	stress
stand	spare	stern	street	special
speed	threw	spectacle	stung	steak

Pattern Power

Write the spelling words with these spelling patterns.

words beginning with str

1. stretch
2. stranger
3. strap
4. street
5. stress

words beginning with sp

6. speed
7. spare
8. spectacle
9. sparkle
10. special

words beginning with st

11. stand
12. stern
13. stung
14. steak

words beginning with spr

15. spruce
16. sprint
17. springtime

words beginning with thr

18. thrill
19. threw
20. thrifty

Rhyme Time

Write the spelling word that rhymes with each word.

21. goose   spruce
22. lead   speed
23. shoe   threw
24. among   strung
25. learn   stern

Page 48

Words with Consonant Clusters

thrill	stretch	stranger	strap	sparkle
spruce	sprint	springtime	thrifty	stress
stand	spare	stern	street	special
speed	threw	spectacle	stung	steak

Finish the Word

Write the missing letters to correctly complete the words in the sentences.

"Hurry up," my parents called. "There's not a minute to **1.** sp___are___. We don't want to be late. We'll wait for you in the car."

I grabbed my cap, tightened the **2.** str___ap___ on my fanny pack, and ran out the door to the car.

Every April, our city holds a **3.** spr___ingtime___ festival, beginning with a parade. It is always a very **4.** sp___ecial___ event. This year's parade was an eye-popping **5.** sp___ectacle___. It was a **6.** thr___ill___ for children and adults alike. Dozens of bands and floats made their way down the one-mile **7.** str___etch___ of Fifth Avenue, the main **8.** str___eet___ in our city. My brother and I like to **9.** st___and___ along the curb near City Hall. That's where the parade will slow down for the mayor and then **10.** sp___eed___ up again. This year our sister is in the high school marching band. We watched as she and the other twirlers **11.** thr___ew___ their batons up in the air and then caught them. The sunlight hit the beads and sequins on their outfits and made them **12.** sp___arkle___. What a sight! We cheered loudly as they marched past us.

Word Groups

Write the spelling word that belongs in each group.

13. pierced, pricked, stung
14. fir, pine, spruce
15. strain, pressure, stress
16. economical, penny-wise, thrifty
17. race, run, sprint
18. alien, foreigner, stranger
19. harsh, strict, stern
20. chop, burger, steak

Challenge Extension: Write a sentence for each Challenge Word.

Leah's Pony • SPELLING

Name_____ Date_____

Words with Consonant Clusters

Proofreading Activity

There are six spelling mistakes in this short story. Circle the misspelled words. Write the words correctly on the lines below.

Leah was my best friend. I got a letter from her last month. She told me about the (speshal) way she saved her family's farm. I wish I could have seen the expression on the auctioneer's face when Leah offered him one dollar for her father's tractor!

We lost our farm in the (sprinktime) and then we moved to Oregon. I haven't seen Leah in a year. Whenever I have a few (spair) pennies for a stamp, I write to her.

Life has been difficult for farm families everywhere because of the drought. We had to be as (thirfty) as we could. We (thruw) nothing away, not even empty flour sacks. My mama used the material to make clothes for my sister and me. She could even make a pot of soup (strech) for three or four meals. Times were difficult, but they will get better.

1. ____special____   3. ____spare____   5. ____threw____

2. ____springtime____   4. ____thrifty____   6. ____stretch____

Writing Activity

What do you think Leah said in her letter? Pretend you are Leah. Write a letter telling about the auction. Use four spelling words in your writing.

_____

_____

_____

_____

Name_____ Date_____

Words with Consonant Clusters

Look at the words in each set below. One word in each set is spelled correctly. Use a pencil to fill in the circle next to the correct word. Before you begin, look at the sample sets of words. Sample A has been done for you. Do Sample B by yourself. When you are sure you know what to do, you may go on with the rest of the page.

Sample A
- Ⓐ springkle
- Ⓑ sprinkel
- Ⓒ springle
- ● sprinkle

Sample B
- ● threaten
- Ⓑ threatin
- Ⓒ threten
- Ⓓ threaton

1.
- Ⓐ sturn
- Ⓑ stren
- ● stern
- Ⓓ sternn

2.
- Ⓔ spingtime
- Ⓕ springtime
- Ⓖ sprinktime
- Ⓗ sprngtime

3.
- ● stranger
- Ⓑ strangure
- Ⓒ stanger
- Ⓓ strangur

4.
- Ⓔ specktakle
- Ⓕ spektacle
- Ⓖ specticle
- Ⓗ spectacle

5.
- Ⓐ thrugh
- ● threw
- Ⓒ thriew
- Ⓓ thruw

6.
- Ⓔ strapp
- Ⓕ strape
- Ⓖ starp
- Ⓗ strap

7.
- ● spare
- Ⓑ spair
- Ⓒ spayr
- Ⓓ spaire

8.
- Ⓔ thirfty
- Ⓕ thrifty
- Ⓖ thrfty
- Ⓗ thifty

9.
- ● sprint
- Ⓑ spirnt
- Ⓒ sprnt
- Ⓓ spint

10.
- Ⓔ streat
- Ⓕ streit
- Ⓖ stareet
- ● street

11.
- Ⓐ strech
- Ⓑ stertch
- ● stretch
- Ⓓ sturetch

12.
- Ⓔ spead
- Ⓕ speed
- Ⓖ spede
- Ⓗ speide

13.
- Ⓐ stung
- Ⓑ stong
- Ⓒ stug
- Ⓓ stunge

14.
- Ⓔ stande
- Ⓕ stend
- Ⓖ stanned
- Ⓗ stand

15.
- Ⓐ spurce
- Ⓑ spruse
- ● spruce
- Ⓓ sproose

16.
- ● thrill
- Ⓕ thirll
- Ⓖ thruill
- Ⓗ thril

17.
- Ⓐ stak
- Ⓑ staik
- ● steak
- Ⓓ stacke

18.
- ● sparkle
- Ⓕ spearkle
- Ⓖ sparckle
- Ⓗ sprakle

19.
- Ⓐ streass
- ● stress
- Ⓒ sterss
- Ⓓ stres

20.
- Ⓔ specail
- Ⓕ spacial
- Ⓖ speshal
- ● special

Practice 59

Name_____ Date_____ **Practice** 59

Make Predictions

When you **make a prediction,** you make a logical guess about what will happen next, based on story clues and your own experience. As you continue to read, you find out whether your prediction was right. Read the story below and predict what will most likely happen to Pablo. **Answers may vary.**

> It is rush hour and Pablo is waiting for the train. He has to meet his mother for dinner at 6:30 P.M. During nonrush hours, the train ride from work to the stop near his house is about 20 minutes. It is now 6:00 P.M. A train arrives at the stop, but it is too crowded to let new passengers on. No other trains are in sight.

1. What do you predict will most likely happen? __Possible answer: Pablo__ __will most likely be late.__

2. What information did you use from the story to help make your prediction? __There is no room on the train and there are no trains in__ __sight.__

As you read the following paragraph, think about what will most likely happen.

> Kevin is thinking about leaving his homeland and moving to the United States. Like most of the men in his family, he has always been a coal miner. The mine in which he works is closing. His sister Kate lives in Florida and can get him a job in her company. His brother Tim has just moved to Pennsylvania where he has found work as a miner.

3. What do you predict will most likely happen? __Kevin will most likely__ __move to Pennsylvania and find a job as a miner.__

4. What information did you use to make your prediction? __I thought about__ __the information in the story and thought about what I would do.__

Book 4/Unit 2
Baseball Saved Us — 4

At Home: Have students predict how they will spend their summer vacation.

59

Practice 60

Name_____ Date_____ **Practice** 60

Vocabulary

Substitute a vocabulary word for the underlined word or words in each sentence. Then write your answer in the crossword puzzle.

glinting	ditches	mound	inning	crate	endless

ACROSS

3. We covered Dad's legs with a large pile of sand. ___mound___

4. The sun is shining off the water. ___glinting___

5. Water flows off the road into long narrow holes. ___ditches___

DOWN

1. The fun we had at the beach seemed to have no limit. ___endless___

2. We were listening to the ninth part of the baseball game. ___inning___

6. I had to stand on an old wooden box to see over the heads of the crowd. ___crate___

60

At Home: Have students use the vocabulary words to write their own sentences.

Book 4/Unit 2
Baseball Saved Us — 6

Jenelle's Baseball (60a)

Jenelle's Baseball

"I don't know what the big deal is about baseball," said Jenelle. "It's so boring. One part of the game is called an *inning*. That's fine, but there are nine of those innings! I'm telling you, the game is *endless*. Then there's the pitcher who stands on a little hill of dirt called the *mound*. What's that all about? While a player is batting, the team sits down in one of those *ditches* called a dugout. The team keeps a *crate* of juice bottles down there. They never share it with the other team or with any of us watching the game. Sometimes, the game goes on forever. First it's the sun *glinting* off your glasses. Then, before you know it, it's the moon. As for me, I like kickball — no mounds, no ditches, no innings, just lots of fun!"

1. How many parts or *innings* are there in a game? __nine innings__

2. What is the *mound* used for? __The pitcher stands on it to pitch.__

3. Where does one team sit? __in a ditch called a dugout__

4. What's another word in the story for shining? __glinting__

5. How would you describe Jenelle's general feeling about the game of baseball? __Jenelle finds the game boring, and she really doesn't__ __understand it.__

Book 4/Unit 2
Baseball Saved Us — 5

At Home: Have students write a paragraph using the vocabulary words to explain baseball to a person who is unfamiliar with the game.

60a

Practice 61

Name_____ Date_____ **Practice** 61

Story Comprehension

Read statements 1 to 6 below. Write **T** for true if the statement describes "Baseball Saved Us." Write **F** for false if it does not.

1. __T__ Many of the Japanese Americans in California were born in the United States.

2. __T__ The United States government thought that Japanese Americans couldn't be trusted.

3. __T__ Many Japanese Americans were sent to the camp.

4. __F__ The camp guards provided all the baseball equipment.

5. __T__ The narrator, or person telling the story, hit a home run at the camp's championship game.

6. __F__ The narrator's community welcomed him warmly when his family returned from the camp.

Write to tell why the following statements are not true. **Answers may vary.**

7. The narrator's family went happily to the camp, which was like a summer camp. __The storyteller's mother cried the day they went to the camp.__ __The camp was not like a summer camp. There were armed guards__ __and barbed wire.__

8. The narrator didn't experience any prejudice after he left the camp and returned to school. __He had to eat lunch alone, no one would talk to__ __him, and people called him names.__

Baseball Saved Us • PRACTICE

Use an Encyclopedia

If you want to learn more about Japan or about any other subject, an **encyclopedia** is a good place to start. In most encyclopedias, subject headings appear in alphabetical order. Most encyclopedias also have an index that lists all the topics covered and where to find them. Some information appears under more than one subject heading.

Read the list of topics below. Tell which volume of the encyclopedia you would look in to find them. Usually, each letter in the alphabet is a separate volume. Then write some subject headings under which you might look for information about the topic. Answers may vary.

TOPIC	VOLUME	SUBJECT HEADINGS
1. Japan	11J-K	Japan
2. Japanese bullet train	19T;11J-K	trains, high-speed trains; Japan transportation
3. Baseball in Japan	2B;11J-K 18So-Sz	baseball; Japan, sports
4. Trade in China	19T; 11J-K, 3C-Ch	Trade, China; Trade, China
5. San Francisco	17S–Sn, 3C-Ch	San Francisco; California, cities

---

Make Predictions

To make a **prediction**, you can use story clues and your own experience. Read the following. Think about what might happen and answer the questions. Answers may vary.

Middle West Weather

Weather in the Middle West can change very quickly. A warm spring day can bring sudden hailstones of ice. Sometimes, during spring or early summer, tornadoes swirl quickly through the area, destroying objects in their paths. People in the Middle West know that when a tornado is sighted, they should seek shelter, preferably in the lowest level of their homes.

It is a clear, sunny Saturday afternoon in May. The Bates family decides to have a cookout. During lunch, Mrs. Bates notices a mass of dark clouds in the distance. The breeze turns brisk.

1. What are some of the things that could happen next? There could be a tornado or rainstorm and the Bates will move inside. The Bates could wait out the storm.

2. What do you think will most likely happen next? A storm will come through the area.

3. What clues from the above paragraphs helped you predict what would most likely happen next? The spring weather in the Middle West can change quickly. Mrs. Bates notices the clouds and a change in the breeze.

4. What are some situations in and out of school when you might have predicted something would happen? Answers will vary.

Form Generalizations

A **generalization** is a broad statement about something. Generalizations often include words such as *always, all, everyone, none, everything*. Read each passage. Then write a generalization. Answers may vary.

1. Every Saturday, Maisie goes grocery shopping for her family. As usual, she went next door to ask Mr. Hadley if he needed any milk or other things.

Generalization: Maisie always asks Mr. Hadley if he needs anything.

2. Carlos picked up the newspapers and put them in the trash. He hung up his little brother's jacket and put away the toys. By the time Carlos' father got home from work, Carlos had straightened the whole house.

Generalization: Carlos is very neat and always straightens things up .

3. My brother Bobby likes to eat. The other morning he ate breakfast, then crackers, fruit, and cheese just before lunch.

Generalization: Bobby eats a lot.

4. The coach asked Lee if he would like to have a day off from practice, but Lee said no.

Generalization: Lee would rather practice than take time off.

5. Each fourth grader in Mrs. Freewell's class has the habit of saying "please" and "thank you."

Generalization: Everyone in Mrs. Freewell's class has good manners.

Compound Words

Study the **compound words** below. Write each of the two smaller words that make up each compound. Then write a sentence using the compound word. Sentences will vary. Examples are given.

1. baseball — base / ball
Mom always picks us up after baseball practice.

2. everyone — every / one
Everyone was nervous about the spelling competition.

3. anything — any / thing
Would you like me to bring you anything from the store?

4. bathroom — bath / room
It's my job to clean the bathroom every Saturday.

5. flashlight — flash / light
We were glad we had a flashlight while counting.

6. teammates — team / mates
Each of our teammates is equally important.

7. sunglasses — sun / glasses
Sarah lost her sunglasses at the pool.

8. sidewalk — side / walk
The town has many sidewalk cafes.

9. weekend — week / end
Because of the holiday, we had a long weekend.

10. backyard — back / yard
Sometimes I help my sister garden in the backyard.

Baseball Saved Us • RETEACH

Make Predictions

Reading titles can help you **predict** what a story will be about.

Read each title. Then read the predictions of what the story will be about. Put a ✔ next to the prediction that makes the most sense.

1. "My Life on Stage"
   - _____ a history of movie theaters
   - ✔ the life story of an actor
   - _____ the life story of an athlete

2. "To the Top!"
   - ✔ mountain climbing
   - _____ toy making
   - _____ ocean exploration

3. "All Aboard: Travel on the Iron Tracks"
   - ✔ a history of train travel
   - _____ a history of plane travel
   - _____ a history of the highway system

4. "Beneath the Waves"
   - _____ a man who flies a plane
   - _____ a man who explores caves
   - ✔ a woman who explores the sea

5. "Causes for Celebration"
   - _____ math
   - _____ pet care
   - ✔ holidays

At Home: Choose the title of an unfamiliar story, book, or movie and have students predict what it will be about.

Vocabulary

Write a word from the list to complete each sentence.

crate	ditches	endless	glinting	inning	mound

1. The beach seemed ___endless___ in length.
2. The field was surrounded by deep ___ditches___.
3. Sun was ___glinting___ off the water.
4. My uncle sent us a ___crate___ that was full of oranges.
5. In the eighth ___inning___, Mandy hit a home run.
6. The pitcher stood on the ___mound___.

6

Write sentences to answer the questions about "Baseball Saved Us."

1. Why were the boy and his family sent to a government camp?
   They were Japanese and America was at war with Japan.

2. Why did the boy's father decide to build a baseball field?
   He felt the people needed something to do to get their minds off being
   at the camp.

3. Why did the boy get angry with the guard in the tower?
   The guard was always watching them. He reminded everyone they were
   in camp and couldn't leave.

4. After the boy got out of camp, how did baseball help the boy?
   His experience playing baseball and reacting to the guard helped him fit
   in at his new school.

At Home: Have students use three of the vocabulary words to tell a story of their own.

Use an Encyclopedia

An **encyclopedia** is a set of books with articles about people, places, things, events, and ideas. The articles are arranged in alphabetical order in volumes.

Encyclopedia	Encyclopedia	Encyclopedia	Encyclopedia	Encyclopedia	Encyclopedia	Encyclopedia	Encyclopedia	Encyclopedia	Encyclopedia	Encyclopedia	Encyclopedia	Encyclopedia	Encyclopedia	Encyclopedia	Encyclopedia	Encyclopedia	Encyclopedia	Encyclopedia	Encyclopedia	Encyclopedia	Research Guide & Index
A	B	C–Ch	C–Cz	D	E	F	G	H	I	J–K	L	M	N–O	P	Q–R	S–Sn	So–Sz	T	U–V	W–X Y–Z	
1	2	3	4	5	6	7	8	9	10	11	12	13	14	15	16	17	18	19	20	21	22

Use the sample set of encyclopedias to answer these questions. In which volume would you look for

1. an article on Japan? ___Volume 11, J–K___
2. more information on the city of Tokyo, Japan? ___Volume 19, T___
3. an article on the history of the United States? ___Volume 20, U–V___
4. information about Franklin Delano Roosevelt? ___Volume 16, Q–R___
5. a picture of the Washington Monument? ___Volume 21, W–X–Y–Z___

What are three topics you would like to study? In which encyclopedia volumes would you find the information for your topic?

6. ___Possible answer: Moon, Volume 13, M___
7. ___Possible answer: Reptiles, Volume 16, Q–R___
8. ___Possible answer: Ocean, Volume 14, N–O___

At Home: Have students try to find some of the information listed above in an encyclopedia at home or in the library.

Make Predictions

You can use clues from the story to help you **predict** what may happen next.

Read each story. Then answer the questions.

Emily had always been shy. But her shyness grew worse after her family moved. She tried to avoid talking to any of the people she met. Emily never raised her hand in class, and she walked straight home after school, alone.

Emily had been in school for five weeks and still had no friends. Then one day, she was sitting alone at a small lunch table, when she noticed three girls heading for her table.

1. What do you think Emily will do? ___She will probably try to avoid them.___

2. Why? ___Emily is very shy and has tried to avoid talking with people ever since her family moved.___

Felicia liked her home in town. But sometimes, she thought about the house by the sea. When she was a child, Felicia spent many happy summers there. Felicia had been heartbroken when her grandparents sold the house.

One day, Felicia saw that the house by the sea was for sale. She had saved enough money to allow her to buy it. She hadn't been planning to move. Yet, she felt happier than she'd been in months.

3. What do you think Felicia will decide to do? ___She will move to the house by the sea.___

4. Why? ___She was happy there long ago, and she was excited to be able to afford it.___

At Home: Have students read the first paragraph of a story they choose and predict what will happen next.

Baseball Saved Us • RETEACH

Form Generalizations

> A **generalization** is a broad statement based on a set of facts. Read the facts carefully. Decide what is true based on the facts.

Read each set of facts. Then complete each generalization.

The Steiner Group constructs buildings all over the state. It owns 13 office buildings and 13 shopping malls. The Group also owns 1 apartment building. The company has been in business for 26 years.

1. The Steiner group is a well known company that constructs buildings all over the state.

2. The Steiner Group is a builder that has been respected by businesses for 26 years.

Some people call Marina Del Sol a paradise. The daytime temperature is almost always between 70°F and 80°F, except in January and February. Then it is colder. Last month, there were only six days of rain. Most months, it rains less than that. If you want sunny days and a gentle ocean breeze, pack your bags and come to Marina Del Sol.

3. The daytime temperature in Marina Del Sol is almost never too hot nor too cold.

4. In Marina Del Sol, rainy days are rare; it is almost always sunny and pleasant.

Book 4/Unit 2
Baseball Saved Us
4

At Home: Have students list facts about the town in which they live and then make some generalizations.

64

Compound Words

> A **compound word** is made up of two smaller words. You can usually figure out the meaning of the compound word by looking at the two smaller words and putting their meanings together.

Make a compound word by joining a word in the list to the end of one of the numbered words. Then write a sentence using the compound word. Answers will vary.

brush	boat	pot	place	cloth	flake	coat	light

1. wash ___cloth___
   Sample answer: I folded the washcloth over the towel rack.

2. snow ___flake___
   Sample answer: The snowflakes fell gently.

3. fire ___place___
   Sample answer: After sledding, we built a fire in the fireplace.

4. tooth ___brush___
   Sample answer: I used an old toothbrush to clean grandpa's medal.

5. moon ___light___
   Sample answer: The snow glistened in the moonlight.

6. motor ___boat___
   Sample answer: The motorboat was faster and easier than the canoe.

7. rain ___coat___
   Sample answer: When it started to rain, I remembered my raincoat.

8. flower ___pot___
   Sample answer: He carefully planted tulips in the flowerpot.

At Home: Have students make compound words using each of the following words: horse, horn, shoe, fog.

65

Book 4/Unit 2
Baseball Saved Us
8

Baseball Saved Us • EXTEND

Make Predictions

Suppose that you and your classmates are getting together to play a game. Two classmates are the captains for the two teams. **Predict** how you would feel if you were the last one picked for either team. Explain why.

Answers will vary.

_____
_____
_____
_____
_____
_____

Now suppose that you are the captain of one of the teams. Write a paragraph describing how you would pick the members of your team. Predict how your team would do with those members on it.

Answers will vary.

_____
_____
_____
_____
_____
_____
_____
_____
_____

Book 4/Unit 2
Baseball Saved Us

At Home: Have students write a paragraph in which they predict whether they will become a better athlete, writer, or student.

59

Vocabulary

crate	ditches	endless
glinting	inning	mound

Suppose that you want to recruit some of your friends to play baseball. Write an advertisement that will attract their attention and make them want to play on your team. Use as many of the vocabulary words from the box as you can.

Answers will vary but should use vocabulary correctly.

_____
_____
_____
_____

Story Comprehension

When the boy in "Baseball Saved Us" returned home, most of his friends from camp went to other places. Tell why.

Possible answers: The people in the camp were Japanese Americans from all over the country. People wanted to start their lives again someplace else.

Why did the boy eat lunch alone when he went back to school? Predict how you would feel in a similar situation.

Answers will vary. Possible answers: The other children still resented him for being Japanese. I would feel lonely and sad.

Use an Encyclopedia

Encyclopedias are usually a set of books with detailed information on a wide variety of subjects. The books, or volumes, are arranged alphabetically by subject and usually have an index in a separate volume.

Use the sample set of encyclopedias to answer these questions.
Answers will vary. Possible answers are given.

Encyclopedia	Encyclopedia	Encyclopedia	Encyclopedia	Encyclopedia	Encyclopedia	Encyclopedia	Encyclopedia	Encyclopedia	Encyclopedia	Encyclopedia	Encyclopedia	Encyclopedia	Encyclopedia	Encyclopedia	Encyclopedia	Encyclopedia	Encyclopedia	Encyclopedia	Encyclopedia	Research Guide & Index
A	B	Ca-Cn Co-Cz	D	E	F	G	H	I	J-K	L	M	N-O	P	Q-R	Sa-Sn So-Sz	T	U-V	W-X Y-Z		
1	2	3 4	5	6	7	8	9	10	11	12	13	14	15	16	17 18	19	20	21		

1. In which volumes would you look to find out about Pearl Harbor, Hawaii, during World War II? <u>volume 9–H; volume 15–P; volume 21–W–Z</u>

2. During World War II, Franklin Delano Roosevelt was President of the United States. In which volumes might you find a picture of Roosevelt? <u>volume 16–Q–R; volume 21–W–Z</u>

3. Suppose you wanted to find out who the Allies were during World War II. In which volume would you look? What entry would you look up? <u>vol. 21; World War II</u>

4. Suppose you wanted to find out the history of the Little League. In which volume would you look? <u>volume 12–L; volume 2–B</u>

5. Suppose you wanted to research something, but weren't sure in which encyclopedia volume to look? Where could you begin your research? <u>the encyclopedia's index</u>

Book 4/Unit 2
Baseball Saved Us

At Home: Have students discuss when they would choose to use an encyclopedia rather than a dictionary, thesaurus, or atlas.

62

Make Predictions

In "Baseball Saved Us," the boy made a home run after seeing the sun glinting off the guard's glasses. In the game back home, do you think the sun glinting off glasses helped him focus? Do you think the boy made a home run at the end of the story? Do you think that the glint of the sun on glasses will inspire the boy during other times? How do you think that the children at his school will treat the boy after the baseball game described at the end of the story? Write a paragraph explaining your **predictions**. Include reasons.

Answers will vary. Possible answers: I think that the glasses reminded him of his victory at the camp and made him feel that same determination. I think that he made a home run and helped win the game. The sun on glasses will probably always remind him of what he can do if he is determined. I think that the children will start to accept the boy and realize that he is like them in many ways. They will appreciate his skills at baseball.

_____
_____
_____
_____

63

At Home: Have students predict whether they will reach a goal important to them, then discuss things that might help them focus on a goal and avoid distractions that might interfere with achieving it.

Book 4/Unit 2
Baseball Saved Us

Baseball Saved Us • EXTEND

Form Generalizations

In "Baseball Saved Us," some people **formed a generalization** about Japanese Americans. Tell what the generalization was and why you think people formed it.

Answers will vary. Possible answer: People formed a generalization that Japanese Americans couldn't be trusted. The United States was at war with Japan and some Americans were suspicious of Japanese Americans and thought they might be loyal to Japan rather than to the United States. Other Americans were angry that the Japanese bombed Pearl Harbor without warning, which made them think the Japanese couldn't be trusted.

Form a generalization about why the boy's father decided it was important to have a baseball field at the camp.

Answers will vary. Possible answer: He wanted there to be a positive activity to occupy the time. He was trying to make the best of a terrible situation.

Why was baseball so important to the boy after he returned home?

Answers will vary. Possible answer: He was able to show everyone that he was a valuable member of the team.

At Home: Have students write a paragraph with generalizations on things to remember in order to.

64

Compound Words

Baseball is a **compound word**. It is made up of the words *base* and *ball*. Use the words below to make as many compound words as you can. Write them on the lines.

any	end	no	time
guard	thing	in	less
field	body	day	house
park	out	ball	fit

anybody, anytime, anything, endless, nobody, nothing, daytime, infield,

guardhouse, ballpark, outfit

Suppose that you are a sportscaster for a radio show. You're going to interview a famous baseball player. Use some of the compound words you made above to write questions to ask the player.

Answers will vary, but should include some of the compound words formed above.

Baseball Saved Us • GRAMMAR

Possessive Nouns

- A **possessive noun** is a noun that shows who or what owns or has something.
- A **singular possessive noun** is a singular noun that shows ownership.
- Form a singular possessive noun by adding an **apostrophe (')** and an -s to a singular noun.

Write the possessive form of each underlined singular noun.

1. The <u>boy</u> family had to live in a camp. __boy's__

2. Many of the <u>family</u> things had to be thrown away. __family's__

3. A soldier watched everyone from the <u>Camp</u> tower. __Camp's__

4. The older men were surprised at <u>Teddy</u> words. __Teddy's__

5. Would <u>Dad</u> idea for a baseball field work? __Dad's__

6. Each <u>team</u> uniforms were made from mattress covers. __team's__

7. In the ninth inning, the <u>game</u> score was 3 to 2. __game's__

8. The boy heard the <u>catcher</u> voice. __catcher's__

9. He saw the gleam of the <u>guard</u> sunglasses. __guard's__

10. The ball sailed over the left <u>fielder</u> __fielder's__ head.

Extension: Have students write four sentences, using four of the singular possessive nouns from these sentences. The sentences do not have to be about the story. As students share their sentences, have them check the placement of apostrophes. **51**

Plural Possessive Nouns

- A **plural possessive noun** is a plural noun that shows ownership.
- To form the possessive of a plural noun that ends in s, add an apostrophe.
- To form the possessive of a plural noun that does not end in s, add an apostrophe and an -s.

Write the possessive form of each underlined plural noun. Add an apostrophe or an apostrophe and -s.

1. In Camp, the <u>babies</u> cries kept people awake. __babies'__

2. The <u>soldiers</u> job was to watch everyone. __soldiers'__

3. The sound of the <u>women</u> sewing machines filled the room. __women's__

4. The <u>men</u> work was building the bleachers. __men's__

5. Soon the <u>families</u> children helped pack down the dust. __families'__

6. There were bats, balls, and gloves in the <u>friends</u> sacks. __friends'__

7. The <u>kids</u> teams played all the time. __kids'__

8. After his home run, the boy rode on his <u>teammates</u> shoulders. __teammates'__

Extension: Ask students to write sentences from the story. Have them use the possessive forms of these plural nouns: players, parents, children, teams.

Singular and Plural Possessive Nouns

- A **possessive noun** is a noun that shows who or what owns or has something.
- A **singular possessive noun** is a singular noun that shows ownership.
- A **plural possessive noun** is a plural noun that shows ownership.

Read these sentences. Draw one line under each singular possessive noun. Draw two lines under each plural possessive noun.

1. One day the boy's parents came to his school.

2. Both parents' faces were very sad.

3. In Camp, most of the older boys' time was spent standing around.

4. Teddy's dad asked him to get some water.

5. At first, the field's dirt was dry and cracked.

6. All of the kids' sizes were about the same.

7. Did the man's staring bother the boy?

8. At home, the players' nickname for the boy was Shorty.

Extension: As a class, brainstorm for a list of singular nouns that could show possession. Then arrange students into two teams. In spelling-bee format, have teams challenge each other to form the singular and plural possessive forms of the **53**

Apostrophes

- Add an apostrophe and an -s to a singular noun to make it possessive.
- Add an apostrophe to make most plural nouns possessive.
- Add an apostrophe and an -s to form the possessive of plural nouns that do not end in s.

Read the first sentence in each pair. Use the possessive form of the underlined noun to complete the second sentence.

1. The players thought of a name for their baseball <u>team</u>.

   The __team's__ name is the Mighty Moose.

2. It's easy to tell which kids play for the <u>Moose</u>.

   All the __Moose's__ caps have antlers on them.

3. What color did the <u>players</u> choose for their uniforms?

   The __players'__ uniforms are brown.

4. What a good <u>pitcher</u> the team has!

   The __pitcher's__ fast ball is great.

5. The Mighty Moose have many <u>fans</u>.

   You will see antlers on some of the __fans'__ heads.

Extension: Have students work in pairs. One student lists five nouns; the other writes their possessive forms. Have students reverse their tasks.

Baseball Saved Us • GRAMMAR

Singular and Plural Possessive Nouns

Choose the correct singular possessive form to complete each sentence.

1. The —————— eyes were watching me play ball.

   a. soldier' **b.** soldiers' **c.** soldiers **d.** soldier's ⃝

2. The —————— glove was brown.

   a. fielders' **b.** fielder's ⃝ **c.** fielders's **d.** fielder'

3. The —————— bat was lying on the ground.

   a. boy's ⃝ **b.** boy **c.** boys' **d.** boys's

4. The —————— baseball field needed to be cleaned up.

   a. Camps' **b.** Camp's ⃝ **c.** Camps's **d.** Camps

Choose the correct plural possessive form to complete each sentence.

5. The —————— parents were sad about moving.

   a. brothers' ⃝ **b.** brothers **c.** brother's **d.** brother'

6. The —————— bats came from friends back home.

   a. player' **b.** player's **c.** players' ⃝ **d.** players's

7. The —————— games were fun to watch.

   a. children' **b.** children's ⃝ **c.** children **d.** childrens'

8. Our —————— help is needed to make our lives better.

   a. parents' ⃝ **b.** parent **c.** parents **d.** parent'

Singular and Plural Possessive Nouns

- A **singular possessive noun** is a singular noun that shows ownership.

- A **plural possessive noun** is a plural noun that shows ownership.

Mechanics:

- Add an apostrophe and an -s to a singular noun to make it possessive.

- Add an apostrophe to make most plural nouns possessive.

- Add an apostrophe and an -s to form the possessive of plural nouns that do not end in s.

Work with a partner. Read the sentences aloud. Then make each underlined noun possessive. Be sure to write the possessive forms correctly.

1. Dad mark was the beginning of a baseball field. ———— Dad's

2. Soon both players baseball equipment arrived. ———— players'

3. The other team players made jokes. ———— team's

4. The Camp had a new activity because of many people hard work.

   ———— people's

5. Did the boy hit win the game? ———— boy's

Baseball Saved Us • SPELLING

Plurals

Pretest Directions

Fold back the paper along the dotted line. Use the blanks to write each word as it is read aloud. When you finish the test, unfold the paper. Use the list at the right to correct any spelling mistakes. Practice the words you missed for the Posttest.

To Parents

Here are the results of your child's weekly spelling Pretest. You can help your child study for the Posttest by following these simple steps for each word on the word list:

1. Read the word to your child.

2. Have your child write the word, saying each letter as it is written.

3. Say each letter of the word as your child checks the spelling.

4. If a mistake has been made, have your child read each letter of the correctly spelled word aloud, then repeat steps 1–3.

1. _____	1. cities
2. _____	2. mistakes
3. _____	3. foxes
4. _____	4. babies
5. _____	5. knives
6. _____	6. engines
7. _____	7. soldiers
8. _____	8. ranches
9. _____	9. hobbies
10. _____	10. yourselves
11. _____	11. eyelashes
12. _____	12. uniforms
13. _____	13. batteries
14. _____	14. calves
15. _____	15. shovels
16. _____	16. sunglasses
17. _____	17. groceries
18. _____	18. loaves
19. _____	19. mattresses
20. _____	20. ferries

Challenge Words

_____ crate
_____ ditches
_____ endless
_____ glinting
_____ inning

20 Grade 4/Unit 2
Baseball Saved Us

51

Plurals

Using the Word Study Steps

1. LOOK at the word.

2. SAY the word aloud.

3. STUDY the letters in the word.

4. WRITE the word.

5. CHECK the word.

Did you spell the word right? If not, go back to step 1.

Spelling Tip

Add -s to most words to form plurals.

string + s = strings

Add -es to words ending in x, z, s, sh, or ch.

stretch + es = stretches

When a word ends with a consonant followed by y, change the y to i and add -es.

memory + es = memories

To make plurals of words that end with one f or fe, you often need to change the f or fe to v and add -es.

Find Rhyming Words

Circle the word in each row that rhymes with the spelling word on the left.

1. mistakes	(shakes) taken	6. eyelashes	(flashes) laughs
2. foxes	books (boxes)	7. calves	curves (halves)
3. knives	stoves (wives)	8. sunglasses	grass (masses)
4. ranches	thanks (branches)	9. loaves	(stoves) coats
5. hobbies	cobbles (lobbies)	10. ferries	(berries) furry

To Parents or Helpers

Using the Word Study Steps above as your child comes across any new words will help him or her learn to spell words effectively. Review the steps as you both go over this week's spelling words.

Go over each Spelling Tip with your child. Ask him or her to add -s or -es to form plurals. Ask if he or she knows other words that end with a consonant followed by y. Help your child to use the Spelling Tips to add endings to the words to make them plural.

Help your child find and circle the word in each row that doesn't rhyme with the spelling word.

52

Grade 4/Unit 2
Baseball Saved Us 10

Plurals

cities	knives	hobbies	batteries	groceries
mistakes	engines	yourselves	calves	loaves
foxes	soldiers	eyelashes	shovels	mattresses
babies	ranches	uniforms	sunglasses	ferries

Pattern Power

Write the spelling words that fit each of these plural endings.

-s

1. mistakes
2. engines
3. soldiers
4. uniforms
5. shovels

-es

6. foxes
7. ranches
8. eyelashes
9. sunglasses
10. mattresses

-ies

11. cities
12. babies
13. hobbies
14. batteries
15. groceries
16. ferries

-ves

17. knives
18. yourselves
19. calves
20. loaves

All in Order

Write the following words in alphabetical order: *foxes, cities, babies, ferries, calves, knives, batteries, eyelashes, groceries, hobbies.*

1. babies
2. batteries
3. calves
4. cities
5. eyelashes

6. ferries
7. foxes
8. groceries
9. hobbies
10. knives

30 Grade 4/Unit 2
Baseball Saved Us

53

Plurals

cities	knives	hobbies	batteries	groceries
mistakes	engines	yourselves	calves	loaves
foxes	soldiers	eyelashes	shovels	mattresses
babies	ranches	uniforms	sunglasses	ferries

What's the Word?

Write the spelling words that match the clues below.

1. where some live — cities
2. cans of soup — groceries
3. kinds of ships — ferries
4. newborns — babies
5. tools for snow — shovels
6. work clothes — uniforms

7. on beds — mattresses
8. all of you — yourselves
9. make trains go — engines
10. cut things — knives
11. on eyelids — eyelashes
12. pastimes — hobbies

What's the Word?

Complete each sentence below with a spelling word.

13. I made very few __mistakes__ on my math test.

14. The wild __foxes__ had big, red, bushy tails.

15. The __soldiers__ were trained to fight battles.

16. There are many cattle __ranches__ out West.

17. I got new __batteries__ for my flashlight.

18. The farmer's cows had newborn __calves__ this year.

19. The sun was so bright, I put on my __sunglasses__.

20. He went to the store to buy five __loaves__ of bread.

Challenge Extension: Scramble the letters of each Challenge Word and write the scrambled words down. Exchange papers with a partner and unscramble each word.

54 Grade 4/Unit 2
Baseball Saved Us 20

Baseball Saved Us • SPELLING

Plurals

Writing Activity
There are six spelling mistakes in this paragraph. Circle the misspelled words. Write the words correctly on the lines below.

During World War II, my family and many hundreds of other Japanese-American families from cityes and towns everywhere were forced to live in government camps. We were guarded by soldjers It was a difficult time for all of us. It helped to pass the time by playing baseball. First we had to make a baseball field. We used shovles to clear away plants to make a space for the field. Then we packed down the dust and made it hard. Some men found wood for bleachers. Our mothers used the covers from mattressies to make uniformes for us. Our friends back home sent us bats, balls, and gloves. I was really nervous during the first game. I wasn't a very good player and didn't want to make any misteaks Guess what? I hit a home run!

1. _____cities_____   3. _____shovels_____   5. _____uniforms_____
2. _____soldiers_____   4. _____mattresses_____   6. _____mistakes_____

Writing Activity
If you could interview some of the people who once lived in the government camps, what questions would you ask them? Use four spelling words in your interview questions.

_____

_____

_____

_____

Plurals

Look at the words in each set below. One word in each set is spelled correctly. Use a pencil to fill in the circle next to the correct word. Before you begin, look at the sample sets of words. Sample A has been done for you. Do Sample B by yourself. When you are sure you know what to do, you may go on with the rest of the page.

Sample A
Ⓐ ladees
Ⓑ ladys
Ⓒ ladies
Ⓓ ladees

Sample B
Ⓐ berryes
Ⓑ berries
Ⓒ berrys
Ⓓ berriez

1. Ⓐ ferreez
   Ⓑ ferrys
   Ⓒ ferriez
   Ⓓ ferries

2. Ⓔ loaves
   Ⓕ loafes
   Ⓖ loavz
   Ⓗ loavez

3. Ⓐ songlasses
   Ⓑ sunglasess
   Ⓒ sunglassez
   Ⓓ sunglasses

4. Ⓔ calvs
   Ⓕ calvez
   Ⓖ calves
   Ⓗ claves

5. Ⓐ yuniforms
   Ⓑ uniforms
   Ⓒ unifroms
   Ⓓ uniformz

6. Ⓔ yorselves
   Ⓕ yourselves
   Ⓖ yourselvz
   Ⓗ yuorselves

7. Ⓐ ranchs
   Ⓑ ranchis
   Ⓒ ranches
   Ⓓ ranchez

8. Ⓔ engines
   Ⓕ enginez
   Ⓖ engins
   Ⓗ enginz

9. Ⓐ babees
   Ⓑ babys
   Ⓒ babiez
   Ⓓ babies

10. Ⓔ misteaks
    Ⓕ mistakes
    Ⓖ mistaks
    Ⓗ misstakes

11. Ⓐ cityes
    Ⓑ citees
    Ⓒ cities
    Ⓓ citys

12. Ⓔ foxez
    Ⓕ foxs
    Ⓖ foxies
    Ⓗ foxes

13. Ⓐ knives
    Ⓑ knivez
    Ⓒ knivies
    Ⓓ knifez

14. Ⓔ solders
    Ⓕ soljures
    Ⓖ soldierz
    Ⓗ soldiers

15. Ⓐ hobbies
    Ⓑ hobbyies
    Ⓒ hobbese
    Ⓓ hobbys

16. Ⓔ eyelashs
    Ⓕ eyelashies
    Ⓖ eyelashes
    Ⓗ eyelatches

17. Ⓐ batterys
    Ⓑ battereez
    Ⓒ batteryes
    Ⓓ batteries

18. Ⓔ shovles
    Ⓕ shovlez
    Ⓖ shovels
    Ⓗ shovals

19. Ⓐ grossries
    Ⓑ groceryes
    Ⓒ grocerees
    Ⓓ groceries

20. Ⓔ mattrusses
    Ⓕ mattreses
    Ⓖ mattresses
    Ⓗ mattrasses

T45

Name_____ Date_____ **Practice** (66)

Cause and Effect

One event can cause another event to happen. This kind of relationship is called cause and effect. Read the selection below. Then write an effect for each cause. **Answers may vary.**

The Catawba people lived in the region that is now the Southeastern part of the United States. The warm climate and plentiful forests made this area a good home. The Catawba celebrated the abundance of the land with ceremonies, customs, and skills that have survived for centuries.

One of these skills that has survived to this day is pottery-making. Before Columbus came to the Americas, Catawba women created clay cooking pots and special bowls for important ceremonies. Later on, when the English came, the Catawba traded these beautiful red clay pots for iron tools. Today, Catawba potters continue to use the same techniques that have been handed down from generation to generation for hundreds of years.

Cause	**Effect**
1. The climate was warm and the land was plentiful.	The area was a good home for those who lived there.
2. The Catawba celebrated the abundance of the land.	They celebrated the land with ceremonies, customs, and skills.
3. The Catawba used special bowls for important ceremonies.	Women created special clay bowls for these ceremonies.
4. Techniques were handed down from generation to generation.	Catawba pottery is made today with techniques that have been followed for hundreds of years.

Book 4/Unit 2
Will Her Native Language Disappear? 4

At Home: Have students create a cause and effect chart using information from their lives to fill in the columns.

66

Name_____ Date_____ **Practice** (67)

Vocabulary

A. Complete each sentence with a word from the box.

communicate   extinct   native   backgrounds   generations   century

1. The boy and his dad ____communicate____ by using sign language.

2. The number of years in a ____century____ is one hundred.

3. The students had Spanish, Vietnamese, and French ____backgrounds____.

4. Your ____native____ language is the first language you spoke.

5. Several ____generations____ of the family lived in the village.

6. The volcano is no longer active, so it is ____extinct____.

B. Draw a picture to illustrate a vocabulary word. Then write a caption for your illustration, using as many vocabulary words as you can.

67

At Home: Have students use vocabulary words to describe their backgrounds.

Book 4/Unit 2
Will Her Native Language Disappear? 6

Being Strong

Billy and Mr. Cohales, his next-door neighbor, are from different *generations*. One was born at the beginning of the *century* and the other was born near the end of the century. Their *backgrounds* are different, too. Billy is Polish American. Mr. Cohales is a *Native* American from the Hopi Nation. With the difference in their ages, you wouldn't think that they would *communicate* much with one another. But they did. Mr. Cohales taught Billy a few words in his native language. He explained that it was becoming *extinct*.

One day, as they were talking, Billy said, "When I grow up, I'm going to be very strong. Maybe I'll be a boxer."

"Things were different when I was young," said Mr. Cohales. "The Hopi believed there was a better way to be strong. A man who could make corn seed grow in the desert was strong. I like that idea."

Billy smiled softly. "Me too," he said.

1. Who was born at the beginning of the *century*? ____Mr. Cohales____

2. The fact that Billy is Polish American and Mr. Cohales is Native American means that they have different ____backgrounds____.

3. Having been born at completely different times means that they were from different ____generations____.

4. Why was Mr. Cohales worried about his *native* language? ____He thought it was becoming extinct.____

5. How did Billy and Mr. Cohales communicate? ____They talked.____

6. Why might Billy agree with Mr. Jones that making things in the desert makes someone truly strong? ____You would need to be a strong person to make corn grow where there is no water.____

Book 4/Unit 2
Will Her Native Language Disappear? 6

At Home: Have students use two or three vocabulary words to explain how people from different generations can be friends.

67a

Name_____ Date_____ **Practice** (68)

Story Comprehension

Answer the questions about "Will Her Native Language Disappear?" You may look back at the article.

1. What does the expression "native language" mean? ____A person's native language is the first language he or she speaks.____

2. What is the endangered-language list and why is Choctaw on it? ____Endangered languages are those that may disappear completely. Only about 12,000 people speak Choctaw now, and the number might become smaller.____

3. What does LeRoy Sealy do to keep the Choctaw language from becoming extinct? ____He teaches the Choctaw language at the University of Oklahoma.____

4. What does one picture caption tell you about how LeRoy Sealy is keeping the Choctaw language alive in his family? ____One picture and caption shows him teaching Choctaw to his niece.____

5. What does the group called the Endangered Language Fund do? ____The group makes books and recordings of endangered languages.____

6. How do you say, "Good morning, Friend. I'll see you later," in Choctaw? ____onahinli achukma, ikana. chi pisala hakinli.____

68

At Home: Have students write another Choctaw sentence using the chart in "Will Her Native Language Disappear?".

Book 4/Unit 2
Will Her Native Language Disappear? 6

Will Her Native Language Disappear? • PRACTICE

Conduct an Interview

An **interview** is a meeting between an interviewer who asks questions and a person who is being interviewed. That person has information or an interesting story that the interviewer wants to know more about.

Read the interview plan below. Then answer the quesitons.
Answers will vary but should be in the correct context.

a.	Choose a person to interview who you think is interesting.
b.	Think about the person you will interview and what he or she knows. Write good questions to ask that person.
c.	Begin the interview by stating your purpose for interviewing.
d.	Ask polite, clear questions that use words such as *what? why? where? when? how?*
e.	Listen carefully to the answers to your questions and take good notes.

1. On each blank line below write the name of someone you would like to interview:

   Family member: _____ Famous person: _____

   Neighbor: _____ Owner of a business: _____

2. Choose one person from above. Write what you think would be the most interesting question you could ask that person.

   Person: _____

   Question: _____

3. Write three questions you would like to ask this person in your interview.

   _____

   _____

   _____

4. State your purpose for interviewing this person.

   _____

Form Generalizations

When you make statements that include words such as *everybody, all, always, many, most, no,* and *none,* you are probably forming a **generalization**.

Read each statement. Write **Yes** if the statement is a generalization and **No** if it is not.

1. No one plays with dolls in high school. _____ Yes
2. Everyone loves the Fourth of July in our town. _____ Yes
3. Some people can easily learn a new language. _____ No
4. Sometimes, when I see that clown, I start to laugh. _____ No
5. Nobody can memorize new words like Julio. _____ Yes

Write one sentence that is a generalization and one that is not.

6. Answers will vary but should be written in the correct context and

   parts of speech._____

   _____

   _____

   _____

   _____

Compound Words

A **compound word** is made up of two words. Use the words in the list to make a compound word for each sentence. Then write your own sentence using the word on the lines that follow.

grounds	one	noon	ice
after	skating	some	air
plane	back	times	every

1. Anthony flew on an _____airplane_____ for the first time when his uncle took him to California.

2. Sarah doesn't make lunch often, but _____sometimes_____ she likes to cook for the whole family.

3. The two boys have similar _____backgrounds_____ because they both come from the same small village in Italy.

4. Every _____afternoon_____ just before dinner, our family catches up with one another in our native language, Spanish.

5. We hope _____everyone_____ will take part in Native American Day this September.

6. The new student enjoyed _____ice-skating_____ with her new friends every day after school.

Context Clues

There may be words you don't know in a story you are reading. Sometimes, the sentence holds **context clues** that can help you understand the meaning.

Write a word from the list that makes sense in each sentence.

shallow	extinct	prediction	century	sturdy
value	shrieking	magical	lingered	outburst

1. Since dinosaurs don't live any more, they are now _____extinct_____.

2. The students think highly of, or _____value_____, the top speller in their class.

3. The man is 105 years old and has lived for more than a _____century_____.

4. The musicians _____lingered_____ at the theater long past closing time.

5. The amusement park was an exciting and _____magical_____ place.

6. The teacher was surprised at the _____outburst_____ of cheering.

7. We could walk far into the lake because the water was so _____shallow_____.

8. The monkeys at the baby zoo were crying so loud they were _____shrieking_____.

9. The old truck was strong and _____sturdy_____ and could carry a heavy load.

10. The boy attempted to say who might win by making a _____prediction_____.

Will Her Native Language Disappear? • RETEACH

Cause and Effect

Noting **cause** and **effect** relationships as you read will help you better understand and enjoy the selection.

Read the story. Then fill in the missing causes and effects in the chart.

Almost every day, Richard rode his horse around the edge of his ranch. Two months ago, Richard found a stray dog sleeping near the back gate. Someone had left the gate open by mistake.

The dog had no tags. Richard called his neighbors and the local sheriff. None of them knew about any dogs that were missing. So, Richard decided to take care of the dog himself.

At first, the dog was very weak. He must have been wandering for days without food. But Richard fed the dog and slowly the dog recovered. After a few weeks, the dog was running around and chasing birds. Richard decided to name the dog Birdman.

Effect, or what happened	Cause, or why it happened
1. A dog wandered into the ranch.	Someone left the back gate open by mistake.
2. Richard called his neighbors and the local sheriff.	Richard wanted to find out who the dog belonged to.
3. Richard decided to take care of the dog himself.	No one knew who the dog belonged to.
4. The dog became very weak.	The dog wandered for days without food.
5. Richard decided to name the dog Birdman.	The dog chased birds.

5 Book 4/Unit 2
Will Her Native Language
Disappear?

At Home: Have students identify some effects of a storm, such as a hurricane or tornado.

66

Vocabulary

Choose the word that matches the meaning. Then fill in the crossword puzzle.

communicate	extinct	native
backgrounds	generations	century

Across
2. exchange information; make known
4. gone; dead
5. experiences; environments

Down
1. stages in family history
2. period of 100 years
3. relating to a certain person or place

6

Story Comprehension

Reteach 68

Write **True** or **False** next to each statement about "Will Her Native Language Disappear?" Look back at the article for help.

1. True ___ Not being able to communicate makes people lonely.
2. False ___ All Native American children speak their native languages.
3. True ___ Some people still speak Choctaw.
4. True ___ Languages can become endangered or extinct.
5. True ___ Many young people do not value their native language.
6. True ___ The Endangered Language Fund prints books in languages that are dying out.

67–68

At Home: Have students write a short story using at least four vocabulary words.

Book 4/Unit 2
Will Her Native Language
Disappear?
6

Conduct an Interview

The purpose of an **interview** is to gather information about a person. The person who asks the questions is the *interviewer*. The person who answers the questions is the *interviewee*.

Below are some words to remember when preparing to interview someone.

Key Words for Conducting an Interview:
Purpose—Know It
Prepare
Questions: *Who? What? Where? When? Why? How?*
Listen
Take Notes

A famous Olympic skating champion is coming to your school. You have been chosen to interview her at a school assembly. Answer the following questions about your interview with the champion.

1. How would you begin the interview? Introduce myself and the skater to the audience. Tell the purpose of the interview.

2. What would be the purpose of the interview? Possible responses: to learn how the skater became a champion; to learn about her training and experience; to inspire others to work towards their goals.

3. Write three questions you could ask in the interview. Possible responses: When did you start to skate? Who has helped you in your career? What is the most important thing you have learned from skating?

4. If the skater mentions the jumps and turns she does, but you don't understand the skating terms, what should you do? Possible answer: Ask her to explain more in a follow-up question.

4 Book 4/Unit 2
Will Her Native Language
Disappear?

At Home: Have students think of someone they would like to interview, and then have them write four questions for the interview.

69

Form Generalizations

Often when you read you can make a **generalization**, or a broad statement, about facts you are given.

Read the paragraphs below. Put a ✔ next to generalizations you can make based on what you read.

At Monk Street Mini Mall, you can shop at Just Pants, the Coat Factory, Socks Ahoy, Completely Clothing, Sam's Sportswear, and Mega Jeans. You can also go to The Bagel Shack or to Cone City. Next to Cone City is Main Bank's automated teller machine.

1. ✔ There are not many choices of food at Monk Street Mini Mall.
2. _____ The mini mall has no banking services.
3. ✔ Most of the stores at the mini mall sell clothes.

On Monday and Wednesday afternoons, Nadine has piano lessons. On Thursday afternoon, she sings in a choir. On Friday, Saturday, and Sunday, Nadine practices piano at least two hours a day. Tuesday afternoon, Nadine has tennis lessons.

4. _____ Nadine spends no time on sports.
5. ✔ Music is a big part of Nadine's life.
6. _____ Nadine's mother forces her to take music lessons.

70

At Home: Have students tell why items 2, 4, and 6 are not valid generalizations.

Book 4/Unit 2
Will Her Native Language
Disappear?
6

Name_____ Date_____ **Reteach** `71`

Compound Words

When two words are put together to make one word, the new word is called a **compound word**.

Circle the compound word in each sentence. Write the two words that make up each compound word. Then write the meaning of the compound word.

1. We have the largest (classroom) in the school.
   Word parts: _____ class _____ + _____ room _____
   Meaning: room where classes are held

2. Rosita went on safari to see (wildlife) in its own environment.
   Word parts: _____ wild _____ + _____ life _____
   Meaning: animals living in the wild

3. The (steamboat) was an important invention.
   Word parts: _____ steam _____ + _____ boat _____
   Meaning: boat powered by steam

4. Ken had to work in the (barnyard) every Saturday.
   Word parts: _____ barn _____ + _____ yard _____
   Meaning: yard next to barn or farm building

5. Juan put a (mousetrap) in the cellar.
   Word parts: _____ mouse _____ + _____ trap _____
   Meaning: trap to catch a mouse

`10` Book 4/Unit 2
Will Her Native Language Disappear?

At Home: Ask students if carpet and father are compound words. Why or why not?

71

Name_____ Date_____ **Reteach** `72`

Use Context Clues

When you read a word you don't know, look at the words and sentences near that word. This is called using **context clues**.

Circle the letter beside the meaning of the underlined word in each sentence.

1. There is a hammock hung between two trees in the backyard. Try it for a nap.
   (a.) a swinging bed made of cloth   b. a sports net

2. In the winter, some Inuit people lived in igloos. They formed the dome-shaped huts from packed snow.
   a. special animal traps   (b.) shelters

3. The family owned a large hacienda where they raised cattle.
   (a.) a ranch   b. a campground

4. I slip on my moccasins when I get home. They comfort my feet.
   (a.) indoor slipper or shoe   b. warm vest

5. Some Native Americans lived in wigwams. They made these by covering poles with hides or bark.
   (a.) places to live   b. means of travel

6. The long flat design of a toboggan makes it great for riding down snow-covered hills.
   a. a type of boat   (b.) a type of sled

72

At Home: Have students identify the context clues they used to help them decide the meaning of *hacienda* and *igloos*.

Book 4/Unit 2
Will Her Native Language Disappear? `6`

Will Her Native Language Disappear? • EXTEND

Cause and Effect

Have you ever read a story or watched a movie that was set in another time and place? What things about the characters seemed different to you? Think about **cause and effect** to help you write a description of the different ways of the characters. Tell why you think the characters dressed, acted, or behaved differently.

Answers will vary but should include cause and effect relationships.

_____

_____

_____

_____

_____

_____

_____

_____

_____

_____

_____

_____

_____

_____

_____

_____

_____

_____

_____

_____

Book 4/Unit 2
Will Her Native Language Disappear?

At Home: Talk with an adult family member about how he or she decided what to do to earn a living.

66

Vocabulary

communicate backgrounds	extinct generations	native century

Language allows us to communicate. Use the vocabulary words to write a paragraph about how you think language and communication might change in the next century.

Answers will vary but should include some vocabulary words.

_____

_____

_____

_____

_____

_____

Story Comprehension

What are some of the reasons a language may become endangered? Refer to "Will Her Native Language Disappear?" to help you answer.

Answers will vary. Possible answers: People move to a place where

another language is spoken and they stop using their own language. As

people lose interest in their original language they stop teaching it to their

children. Children may not want to learn the language.

_____

_____

_____

_____

At Home: Discuss why it is important to preserve cultures.

67–68

Book 4/Unit 2
Will Her Native Language Disappear?

Conduct an Interview

In an **interview** usually one person asks another person questions to gain information. To conduct a good interview, it is important to plan carefully before you begin. It's also important to be polite and listen carefully during the interview. Taking notes during it will help you organize what you learn from the interview.

Work with a partner. Suppose you were a talk show host who wanted to do a profile, or a short biography, of a guest. What would you want to know? Write a list of questions on an index card. Then interview your partner in the role of guest. Take notes on a separate sheet of paper. Use the notes to write a paragraph telling what you found out about your guest.

Questions:

Answers will vary but should give a clear biographical profile.

_____

Paragraph:

Answers will vary.

_____

_____

_____

Book 4/Unit 2
Will Her Native Language Disappear?

At Home: Have students listen to an interview. Discuss whether or not the interview was a success.

69

Form Generalizations

When you **form generalizations**, you use information in the text to help you make general conclusions about what you read.

Look back at "Will Her Native Language Disappear?" to help you answer the questions. Why does the Endangered Language Fund print books and make recordings of endangered languages? Explain how their work is important.

Answers will vary. Possible answers: They hope to keep endangered

languages alive. The books will keep the grammar and vocabulary of the

languages alive so that people will not forget them, and the recordings will

help keep the pronunciation alive.

_____

Why do you think some young people might not want to speak the language of their older relatives?

Answers will vary. Possible answer: They might not think that it is

important and it might take too much time to learn a language that they can

only speak with a few people.

_____

Why do you think that it is important to save endangered languages?

Answers will vary. Possible answer: Because they are a part of the

background and culture of different groups of people.

_____

_____

At Home: Have students write about a story told to them by an older friend or family member.

70

Book 4/Unit 2
Will Her Native Language Disappear?

Will Her Native Language Disappear? • EXTEND

Compound Words

| arrowhead | spaceship | downpour | wildlife | sagebrush |
| campfire | racetrack | upstairs | starfish | lighthouse |

Each of the words above is a **compound word**. Write the two words that make up each word on the lines.

arrow, head; space, ship; down, pour; wild, life; sage, brush; camp, fire;

race, track; up, stairs; star, fish; light, house

Use picture writing to show the compound words. Make up your own word signs for each compound word in the space below. Be sure to label the word signs with the corresponding words.

Book 4/Unit 2
Will Her Native
Language Disappear?

At Home: Have students write and speak the Choctaw words in "Will Her Native Language Disappear?".

71

Context Clues

You can often figure out the meaning of a word from the way it is used in a sentence.

| ceremony | pottery | weave | harvest | hunt |
| leather | lodge | moccasin | canoe | legend |

Use as many of the words in the table as you can to write a story. Include **context clues** to help your readers understand the meanings of the words.

Answers will vary but should include context clues.

72

At Home: Have students read their story and point out context clues they've used.

Book 4/Unit 2
Will Her Native
Language Disappear?

Grammar 57 — LEARN

Name _____ Date _____

Plural and Possessive Nouns

- A **plural noun** names more than one person, place, or thing.
- Add -s to most nouns to form the plural. Do not use an apostrophe.

Write the plural form of the noun in parentheses on the line provided.

1. Sealy could not speak to his (classmate) __classmates__ in English.

2. None of the (kid) __kids__ knew the Choctaw language.

3. About 12,000 (person) __people__ speak Choctaw.

4. Many (language) __languages__ are endangered.

5. Some (book) __books__ are now being printed in Choctaw.

6. There are (recording) __recordings__ in the Choctaw language.

7. Native American (child) __children__ forgot their native languages.

8. Older (relative) __relatives__ don't know English.

9. Picture writing was used to record family (history) __histories__.

10. Can you say some (word) __words__ in Choctaw?

Grammar 58 — LEARN AND PRACTICE

Name _____ Date _____

Possessive Nouns

- A **possessive noun** shows who or what owns or has something.
- Add an apostrophe and -s to a singular noun to make it possessive.

Write the possessive form of each singular noun in parentheses.

1. A young (boy) __boy's__ only language was Choctaw.

2. In school, the (teacher) __teacher's__ language was English.

3. One group of people start to speak another (group) __group's__ language.

4. Many of the (world) __world's__ languages could disappear.

5. LeRoy (Sealy) __Sealy's__ goal is to keep Choctaw from disappearing.

6. This Native (American) __American's__ home is in Oklahoma.

7. Today the (man) __man's__ niece is learning Choctaw.

8. A (turtle) __turtle's__ name in Choctaw is *loksi.*

Grammar 59 — PRACTICE AND REVIEW

Name _____ Date _____

Plural and Possessive Nouns

- A **plural noun** names more than one person, place, or thing.
- Add -s to most nouns to form the plural. Do not use an apostrophe.
- A **possessive noun** shows who or what owns or has something.
- Add an apostrophe and -s to a singular noun to make it possessive.

Write a plural noun or a possessive noun to complete each sentence. Use the singular nouns in the box below to help you.

arrow	book	computer	group	kid	picture	tribe	word

1. Two common Choctaw __words__ are *jkana* and *halito.*

2. One __word's__ meaning is "friend."

3. Pictures on rocks and hides told a __tribe's__ history.

4. Native Americans drew __pictures__ to record events.

5. Sometimes they drew __arrows__ to show directions.

6. An __arrow's__ tip might point up or down.

7. Some Native American __kids__ forgot their native language.

8. A group prints __books__ in endangered languages.

9. This __group's__ name is the Endangered Language Fund.

10. Machines like __computers__ have spread English around the world.

Grammar 60 — MECHANICS

Name _____ Date _____

Plural and Possessive Nouns

- Add -s to most nouns to form the plural. Do not use an apostrophe.
- Add an apostrophe and -s to a singular noun to make it possessive.

Add an -s or an apostrophe and an -s to the underlined word in each sentence. Use the line provided for your answer.

1. Can you speak two language? __languages__

2. Is English your family native language? __family's__

3. LeRoy Sealy native language is Choctaw. __Sealy's__

4. Years ago, Native American children went to government school. __schools__

5. The kid spoke English and not their Native American language. __kids__

6. Usually a child parents did not know how to speak English. __child's__

7. Sealy teaches Choctaw to student in Oklahoma. __students__

8. The teacher great worry is that the Choctaw language will disappear.

   __teacher's__

Name________________________ Date__________ TEST Grammar 61

Plurals and Possessives

A. Decide whether each underlined word is a plural noun or a possessive noun. Then write plural or possessive on the line provided.

1. LeRoy Sealy had some lonely days in school. **plural**
2. The boy's problem was that he could not communicate. **possessive**
3. The man's niece is named Patricia. **possessive**
4. Sealy uses pictures to teach his niece Choctaw. **plural**

B. Choose the plural noun or possessive noun that best completes each sentence. Write it on the line provided.

5. Picture writing was one way that (tribes, tribe's) communicated. **tribes**
6. The many (tribes, tribe's) spoke different languages. **tribes**
7. Picture writing told a (tribes, tribe's) history. **tribe's**
8. Some pictures told about important (events, event's). **events**

Name________________________ Date__________ MORE PRACTICE Grammar 62

Plural and Possessive Nouns

- A plural noun names more than one person, place, or thing.
- A possessive noun shows who or what owns or has something.

Mechanics:

- Add *-s* to most nouns to form the plural. Do not use an apostrophe.
- Add an apostrophe and *-s* to a singular noun to make it possessive.

Read the sentences about the picture below. Then find the plural and possessive nouns that are not written correctly. Rewrite the sentences on the lines below, correcting the plural or possessive nouns.

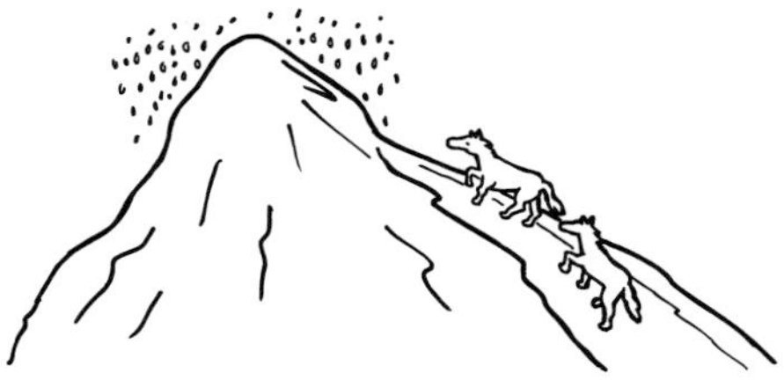

1. What does this pages picture show you?
   What does this page's picture show you?
2. Where are the two horse going?
   Where are the two horses going?
3. There is no saddle on either horse' back.
   There is no saddle on either horse's back.
4. This picture shows rain falling on the mountains top.
   This picture shows rain falling on the mountain's top.

Will Her Native Language Disappear? • SPELLING

Page 57

Words from Social Studies

Pretest Directions

Fold back the paper along the dotted line. Use the blanks to write each word as it is read aloud. When you finish the test, unfold the paper. Use the list at the right to correct any spelling mistakes. Practice the words you missed for the Posttest.

To Parents

Here are the results of your child's weekly spelling Pretest. You can help your child study for the Posttest by following these simple steps for each word on the word list:

1. Read the word to your child.

2. Have your child write the word, saying each letter as it is written.

3. Say each letter of the word as your child checks the spelling.

4. If a mistake has been made, have your child read each letter of the correctly spelled word aloud, then repeat steps 1–3.

1. _____	1. language
2. _____	2. history
3. _____	3. pottery
4. _____	4. study
5. _____	5. spoken
6. _____	6. accent
7. _____	7. tribe
8. _____	8. human
9. _____	9. custom
10. _____	10. village
11. _____	11. folktale
12. _____	12. practice
13. _____	13. relatives
14. _____	14. interview
15. _____	15. region
16. _____	16. symbol
17. _____	17. guide
18. _____	18. totem
19. _____	19. colony
20. _____	20. prints

Challenge Words

_____ extinct
_____ native
_____ backgrounds
_____ generations
_____ century

McGraw-Hill School Division

20 Grade 4/Unit 2
Will Her Native
Language Disappear ?

57

Page 58

Words from Social Studies

Using the Word Study Steps

1. LOOK at the word.

2. SAY the word aloud.

3. STUDY the letters in the word.

4. WRITE the word.

5. CHECK the word.

Did you spell the word right? If not, go back to step 1.

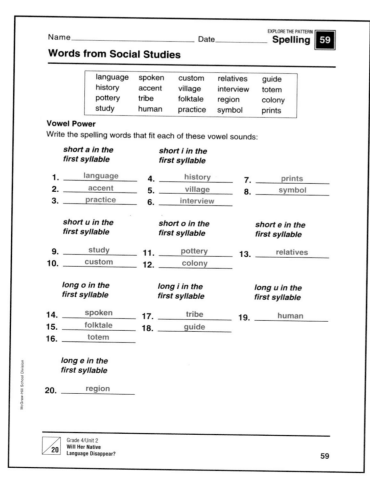

Spelling Tip

Become familiar with the dictionary and use it often.

Word Scramble

Unscramble each set of letters to make a spelling word.

1. skepon ___spoken___
2. idgue ___guide___
3. muhna ___human___
4. coolyn ___colony___
5. anglegau ___language___
6. tolkleaf ___folktale___
7. latesiver ___relatives___
8. blosmy ___symbol___
9. metto ___totem___
10. carpicet ___practice___
11. rhytiso ___history___
12. vieinwert ___interview___
13. biter ___tribe___
14. legliva ___village___
15. strinp ___prints___
16. dyust ___study___
17. engior ___region___
18. mustoc ___custom___
19. rotpety ___pottery___
20. necact ___accent___

To Parents or Helpers

Using the Word Study Steps above as your child comes across any new words will help him or her learn to spell words effectively. Review the steps as you both go over this week's spelling words.

Go over the Spelling Tip with your child. Help him or her look up the spelling words in the dictionary. Help your child unscramble the spelling words.

McGraw-Hill School Division

58

Grade 4/Unit 2
Will Her Native
Language Disappear? 20

Page 59

Words from Social Studies

language	spoken	custom	relatives	guide
history	accent	village	interview	totem
pottery	tribe	folktale	region	colony
study	human	practice	symbol	prints

Vowel Power

Write the spelling words that fit each of these vowel sounds:

short a in the first syllable

1. ___language___
2. ___accent___
3. ___practice___

short i in the first syllable

4. ___history___
5. ___village___
6. ___interview___

7. ___prints___
8. ___symbol___

short u in the first syllable

9. ___study___
10. ___custom___

short o in the first syllable

11. ___pottery___
12. ___colony___

short e in the first syllable

13. ___relatives___

long o in the first syllable

14. ___spoken___
15. ___folktale___
16. ___totem___

long i in the first syllable

17. ___tribe___
18. ___guide___

long u in the first syllable

19. ___human___

long e in the first syllable

20. ___region___

20 Grade 4/Unit 2
Will Her Native
Language Disappear?

59

Page 60

Words from Social Studies

language	spoken	custom	relatives	guide
history	accent	village	interview	totem
pottery	tribe	folktale	region	colony
study	human	practice	symbol	prints

Complete each sentence below with a spelling word.

1. Spanish is ___spoken___ here.

2. I live in a mountainous ___region___.

3. We met the artist who made this ___pottery___.

4. What ___tribe___ did Geronimo belong to?

5. Dad will go to an ___interview___ for a new job.

6. I plan to ___study___ music in college.

7. What ___language___ do you speak?

8. The ___guide___ led us along the trail.

9. We read your ___account___ of what happened.

10. ___Human___ beings come in all shapes and sizes.

11. I ___practice___ piano for one hour each day.

12. Where do your ___relatives___ live?

13. I just read a funny ___folktale___ from Russia.

14. The lion is a ___symbol___ of courage.

15. The artist carved and painted a ___totem___ pole.

16. It is a ___custom___ in my family to drink tea before lunch.

Challenge Extension: Have students write a fill in the blank for each Challenge Word, then exchange papers with a partner and complete each other's sentences.

60

Grade 4/Unit 2
Will Her Native
Language Disappear? 16

Will Her Native Language Disappear? • SPELLING

Words from Social Studies

Proofreading Activity

There are six spelling mistakes in this paragraph. Circle the misspelled words. Write the words correctly on the lines below.

   Did you know that Choctaw is an endangered Native American (langauge)? It is only (spokin) by 12,000 people, today. An organization working to keep alive Choctaw and other Native American languages (prins) books and makes records available for people to use. In (histry) class we are learning Choctaw words and phrases. One of the girls is a member of the Choctaw (trieb) She and her (relitives) speak Choctaw at home. Some of us would like to study Choctaw. I know it will take a lot of practice because it is so different from English.

1. ___language___   3. ___prints___   5. ___tribe___
2. ___spoken___   4. ___history___   6. ___relatives___

Writing Activity

Imagine that the year is 1800 and that you are a Native American child. Write a paragraph about what life is like among your people, using four spelling words.

_____

_____

_____

_____

Words from Social Studies

Look at the words in each set below. One word in each set is spelled correctly. Use a pencil to fill in the circle next to the correct word. Before you begin, look at the sample sets of words. Sample A has been done for you. Do Sample B by yourself. When you are sure you know what to do, you may go on with the rest of the page.

Sample A
- Ⓐ science
- Ⓑ sience
- Ⓒ sciense
- Ⓓ siense

Sample B
- Ⓔ natuve
- Ⓕ native
- Ⓖ nativ
- Ⓗ nattive

1.
- Ⓐ prins
- Ⓑ prints
- Ⓒ printz
- Ⓓ prinz

2.
- Ⓔ language
- Ⓕ langage
- Ⓖ langwage
- Ⓗ langauge

3.
- Ⓐ colny
- Ⓑ colonny
- Ⓒ colony
- Ⓓ coluny

4.
- Ⓔ histry
- Ⓕ histrey
- Ⓖ historie
- Ⓗ history

5.
- Ⓐ totum
- Ⓑ totim
- Ⓒ totem
- Ⓓ tottem

6.
- Ⓔ pottery
- Ⓕ potery
- Ⓖ pottry
- Ⓗ pottary

7.
- Ⓐ guyde
- Ⓑ guide
- Ⓒ giude
- Ⓓ gide

8.
- Ⓔ studie
- Ⓕ studdy
- Ⓖ study
- Ⓗ studie

9.
- Ⓐ simble
- Ⓑ symble
- Ⓒ symbowl
- Ⓓ symbol

10.
- Ⓔ spokin
- Ⓕ spoken
- Ⓖ spocken
- Ⓗ spockin

11.
- Ⓐ region
- Ⓑ regin
- Ⓒ regun
- Ⓓ regon

12.
- Ⓔ acent
- Ⓕ akcent
- Ⓖ acsent
- Ⓗ accent

13.
- Ⓐ intreview
- Ⓑ intrview
- Ⓒ interview
- Ⓓ innerview

14.
- Ⓔ trieb
- Ⓕ tribe
- Ⓖ trybe
- Ⓗ tirbe

15.
- Ⓐ reltives
- Ⓑ relitives
- Ⓒ relutives
- Ⓓ relatives

16.
- Ⓔ humun
- Ⓕ huemin
- Ⓖ human
- Ⓗ humeman

17.
- Ⓐ practice
- Ⓑ practise
- Ⓒ practus
- Ⓓ practise

18.
- Ⓔ costum
- Ⓕ custom
- Ⓖ cusstom
- Ⓗ custim

19.
- Ⓐ foketail
- Ⓑ folktale
- Ⓒ fowktale
- Ⓓ folktail

20.
- Ⓔ villuge
- Ⓕ villige
- Ⓖ vilage
- Ⓗ village

T55

Unit 2 Review • PRACTICE and RETEACH

Practice 73

Name_____ Date_____ **Practice** 73

Unit 2 Vocabulary Review

A. Read each word in Column 1. Then find the word or words in Column 2 that mean the opposite. Write the letter of the word on the line.

b	**1.** lingered	**a.** whispering	
e	**2.** foul	**b.** left quickly	
d	**3.** sturdy	**c.** foreign	
c	**4.** native	**d.** weak	
a	**5.** shrieking	**e.** fresh	

B. Write the correct vocabulary word in the blanks.

haze	pranced	waddled	guilt	crate
ditches	glistened	county	resounded	mound	bidding

1. The fans' loud cheers ____resounded____ in the football stadium.
2. Every year we have a ____county____ fair.
3. The drum major ____pranced____ proudly, leading the marching band.
4. Robert had feelings of ____guilt____ for forgetting his dad's birthday.
5. Water flows in the long ____ditches____ surrounding the corn fields.
6. The vase was shipped to us in a large wooden ____crate____.
7. Pollution sometimes causes a dark ____haze____ to form in the air.
8. The sunlight ____glistened____ brightly on the waters of the lake.
9. The penguins ____waddled____ to the edge of the ice.
10. The auctioneer began the ____bidding____ for the painting at $500.
11. The team's new pitcher stood on the pitcher's ____mound____.

16 Book 4/Unit 2
Unit 2 Vocabulary Review

At Home: Have students write a paragraph using at least four of the vocabulary words.

73

Practice 74

Name_____ Date_____ **Practice** 74

Unit 2 Vocabulary Review

Answer each question with a sentence that includes the underlined word. **Answers will vary. Example sentences are given.**

1. How can we communicate without saying words? We can communicate by using sign language.

2. What animal can you think of that is now extinct? An animal that is extinct is the dinosaur.

3. Why would a county hold a harvest festival? A town would hold a festival to celebrate a good harvest.

4. How many years are there in a century? There are 100 years in a century.

5. Why might a girl be inspecting her bike? She may be inspecting it to find a broken part.

6. How many generations might come together at a family reunion? There were three generations at our family reunion.

7. How would a crunched piece of paper look? A crunched piece of paper would look wrinkled.

8. Why can the last inning of a baseball game be the most exciting. In the last inning, you find out who wins.

9. Why is the bathtub overflowing? It is overflowing because we forgot to turn off the water.

10. Why is your backpack bulging so much? My backpack is bulging with books, video games, and snacks.

74 **At Home:** Have students describe an event at school, using as many vocabulary words as they can.

Book 4/Unit 2
Unit 2 Vocabulary Review 10

Reteach 73

Name_____ Date_____ **Reteach** 73

Unit 2 Vocabulary Review

A. Write the correct word from the list.

native	glinting	lingered	crumpled

1. Claudia ____lingered____ in her seat long after the play was over.
2. Joel ____crumpled____ the wrapper and threw it in the garbage.
3. Light was ____glinting____ off the metal on the building.
4. French is Sabine's ____native____ language.

B. Read each question. Choose a word from the list to answer the question. Write your answer on the line.

county	mound	guilt	foul

1. How might you describe something that smells bad? ____foul____
2. What word names a part of a state? ____county____
3. What might you feel when you do something wrong? ____guilt____
4. What is something that a baseball pitcher stands on? ____mound____

8 Book 4/Unit 2
Unit 2 Vocabulary Review

At Home: Have students look for these vocabulary words in magazines and copy the sentences in which the words appear.

73

Reteach 74

Name_____ Date_____ **Reteach** 74

Unit 2 Vocabulary Review

A. Use the words from the list to complete the crossword puzzle.

inning	clustered	bulging	haze	extinct	crate

Across
3. grouped together
5. wooden box
6. part of a baseball game

Down
1. smoke or dust in the air
2. swelling outwards
4. dead; gone

(crossword grid: c l u s t e r e d, c r a t e, i n n i n g, with h a z e, b u l g i n g, extinct)

B. Write the correct word from the list.

century	endless	overflowing	shrieking

The stadium was 1. ____overflowing____ with fans. The newspapers had called this game of the 2. ____century____.

When the players came on the gigantic field, the fans began

3. ____shrieking____. The noise seemed as if it would be

4. ____endless____.

74 **At Home:** Have students use three of the vocabulary words on this page to write a scary story.

Book 4/Unit 2
Unit 2 Vocabulary Review 10

Unit 2 Review •EXTEND and GRAMMAR

Unit 2 Vocabulary Review

pranced	overflowing	glistened	resounded	endless
shrieking	waddled	backgrounds	inning	glinting

Use the words above to answer the questions.

1. Which words are compound words? overflowing, endless, backgrounds
_____

2. Which words describe a kind of walking or movement? waddled, pranced
_____

3. Which words refer to light on an object or surface? glistened, glinting
_____

4. Which words refer to noise or sound? shrieking, resounded

5. Which word describes a section of a baseball game? inning

Sometimes we associate pictures in our minds with words. For example, you might think of a dog barking if you hear the word *growl*. Describe a picture that you might associate with each word below.

6. waddled Answers may vary. Possible answer: a duck
_____

7. pranced Answers may vary. Possible answer: a horse
_____

8. shrieking Answers may vary. Possible answer: a ghost
_____

Unit 2 Vocabulary Review

bidding	guilt	clustered	inspecting
crate	sturdy	county	extinct
communicate	lingered	native	century
festival	foul	generations	haze
bulging	crumpled	mound	ditches

Use the words above to write a story in which you use the words in alphabetical order. Have fun with your story. Use as many words as you can. Continue your story on a separate piece of paper if necessary.
Answers will vary but should use vocabulary words in alphabetical order.

Nouns

Read each passage. Choose a word or group of words that belong in each space. Circle your answer.

When Justin visited _____ grandfather, he learned about some famous (1) cowboys. One cowboy was _____. Many people thought he rode (2) wild horses better than anyone else. Justin said that he had never heard of Mr. Stahl.

1. A him
   B he's
   (C) his
   D her

2. F Mister Jessie stahl
   (G) Mr. Jessie Stahl
   H Mr Jessie Stahl
   J Mr. jessie stahl

Walter had a dream about the future. In one part of his dream, his bed was sitting in the _____ of a tree. Then he was on a factory's smokestack. The (3) smoke from the _____ hurt his eyes, nose, and throat. (4)

3. A branch's
   B branchs
   (C) branches
   D branchese

4. F ace medicine factory
   (G) Ace Medicine Factory
   H Ace medicine factory
   J Ace Medicine factory

Nouns

Leah's father had to sell his _____ at an auction. Leah sold her (5) pony and bought the tractor. Some farmers at the auction bought the chickens and truck. Then _____ gave them back to the family. (6)

5. (A) chickens, Ford pickup truck, and tractor
   B chickens ford pickup truck and tractor
   C chicken's, Ford pickup truck, and tractor
   D chickens Ford pickup truck, and tractor

6. F these Men
   G the man's
   (H) the men
   J the mens'

Dad decided the Camp needed a baseball field. Grown-ups and kids helped make the field. The _____, made of mattress covers, looked good. (7) When the boy hit his home run, he looked up and saw the _____. (8)

7. (A) players' uniforms
   B players' uniform's
   C players uniform's
   D player's uniform

8. F guards thumb's-up sign
   G guards' thumbs'-up sign
   (H) guard's thumbs-up sign
   J guard thumb-up sign

Many _____ do not know their native language. They speak only English. (9) LeRoy Sealy's native language is Choctaw. He teaches Choctaw to students at the University of Oklahoma. Sealy worries that the _____ (10) _____ will disappear.

9. (A) Native Americans
   B Native American's
   C native americans
   D Native's Americans

10. F worlds languages
    G worlds' languages'
    H world language
    (J) world's languages

Unit 2 Review • SPELLING

Grade 4/Unit 2 Review Test

Read each sentence. If an underlined word is spelled wrong, fill in the circle that goes with that word. If no word is spelled wrong, fill in the circle below NONE. Read Sample A, and do Sample B.

A. She took her <u>sunglasses</u> and a <u>napsack</u> to the <u>cabin</u>.
A · B · C
A. Ⓐ ● Ⓒ Ⓓ NONE

B. We put the <u>sleepy</u> <u>babies</u> in the <u>cradle</u>.
E · F · G
B. Ⓔ Ⓕ Ⓖ ● NONE

1. The explosion <u>amonng</u> the <u>soldiers</u> made a <u>spectacle</u>.
A · B · C
1. ● Ⓑ Ⓒ Ⓓ NONE

2. The <u>colony</u> had <u>clover</u> fields and <u>spruice</u> trees.
E · F · G
2. Ⓔ Ⓕ ● Ⓗ NONE

3. The <u>raizer</u> cut <u>stung</u> so I covered it with a <u>bandage</u>.
A · B · C
3. ● Ⓑ Ⓒ Ⓓ NONE

4. The <u>thrifty</u> man divided one <u>biscit</u> <u>among</u> his friends.
E · F · G
4. Ⓔ ● Ⓖ Ⓗ NONE

5. The men in the <u>colonee</u> used <u>shovels</u> to dig for <u>pottery</u>.
A · B · C
5. ● Ⓑ Ⓒ Ⓓ NONE

6. The <u>thrifty</u> owner repaired the <u>crack</u> in her <u>totim</u> pole.
E · F · G
6. Ⓔ Ⓕ ● Ⓗ NONE

7. When she is under <u>stress</u> her <u>eyelashs</u> <u>flutter</u>.
A · B · C
7. Ⓐ ● Ⓒ Ⓓ NONE

8. This <u>foketale</u> describes a <u>bridle</u> and a <u>totem</u> pole.
E · F · G
8. ● Ⓕ Ⓖ Ⓗ NONE

9. A <u>bandage</u> will not hold the <u>plank</u> between the <u>ferrys</u>.
A · B · C
9. Ⓐ Ⓑ Ⓒ ● NONE

10. Our <u>calves</u> <u>stung</u> from all that <u>fancy</u> dancing.
E · F · G
10. Ⓔ Ⓕ Ⓖ ● NONE

11. We sat in the <u>clover</u> to hear a man with an <u>acent</u> tell a <u>folktale</u>.
A · B · C
11. Ⓐ ● Ⓒ Ⓓ NONE

Grade 4 Unit 2 Review Test

12. The <u>ferries</u> carried <u>soldyiers</u> to the <u>colony</u>.
E · F · G
12. Ⓔ ● Ⓖ Ⓗ NONE

13. The <u>stres</u> on the <u>plank</u> caused it to <u>crack</u>.
A · B · C
13. ● Ⓑ Ⓒ Ⓓ NONE

14. We saw <u>calves</u> eating <u>clovir</u> stuck in a <u>bridle</u>.
E · F · G
14. Ⓔ ● Ⓖ Ⓗ NONE

15. Watching them <u>fluter</u> <u>among</u> the flowers was a <u>spectacle</u>.
A · B · C
15. ● Ⓑ Ⓒ Ⓓ NONE

16. To be <u>fancy</u>, she will <u>spruce</u> up with fake <u>eyelashes</u>.
E · F · G
16. Ⓔ Ⓕ Ⓖ ● NONE

17. The <u>stress</u> on the horse's <u>bridal</u> caused it to <u>crack</u>.
A · B · C
17. Ⓐ ● Ⓒ Ⓓ NONE

18. She ate a <u>biscuit</u> and told a <u>folktale</u> in a French <u>accent</u>.
E · F · G
18. Ⓔ Ⓕ Ⓖ ● NONE

19. We loaded the <u>ferries</u> with <u>potterie</u> and <u>shovels</u>.
E · F · G
19. Ⓐ ● Ⓒ Ⓓ NONE

20. Don't use a <u>razor</u> to cut a <u>plank</u> from that <u>spruce</u>.
E · F · G
20. Ⓔ ● Ⓖ Ⓗ NONE

21. It was a <u>spectacle</u> seeing the <u>calfs</u> share one <u>biscuit</u>.
A · B · C
21. Ⓐ ● Ⓒ Ⓓ NONE

22. He saw her <u>eyelashes</u> <u>flutter</u> after she was <u>stunng</u>.
E · F · G
22. Ⓔ Ⓕ ● Ⓗ NONE

23. A <u>bandage</u> is a <u>thriftie</u> way to hide that <u>fancy</u> ring.
A · B · C
23. Ⓐ ● Ⓒ Ⓓ NONE

24. The boy with the <u>accent</u> engraves <u>pottery</u> with a <u>razor</u>.
E · F · G
24. Ⓔ Ⓕ Ⓖ ● NONE

25. The <u>soldiers</u> used <u>shovles</u> to dig out the <u>totem</u> pole.
A · B · C
25. Ⓐ ● Ⓒ Ⓓ NONE

Make Predictions

OBJECTIVES Students will make and check predictions by listening, observing, and thinking.

Alternate Activities

Visual

PREDICT WITH COMIC STRIPS

PARTNERS **Materials:** comic strip, overhead transparency film, overhead projector, drawing paper, markers

Have students draw a comic strip without the ending. Partners will make predictions about what might happen next.

- Make an overhead transparency film using an age-appropriate comic strip. Display the strip, covering the last frame, which reveals the ending. With students, read and discuss the comic strip.

- Have students make a prediction about the ending of the strip and jot it down. Reveal the rest of the comic strip. Have students compare their predictions to the actual ending.

- Challenge students to generate comic strips of their own. Have them draw several frames on one side of a piece of paper. Then have them draw the ending on the back of the paper.

- Have students switch comic strips with a partner. Ask partners to predict the ending, then check their prediction on the back.
  ▶ **Spatial**

Kinesthetic

PREDICTION SKITS

GROUP Have students work together to perform original skits. Audience members will make predictions about future events.

- Lead students in a discussion of the concept of "cliff-hangers," and share examples.

- Organize students into groups. Ask them to work together to create a brief original skit. Encourage students to end their skit with a cliff-hanger.

- Have audience members make a prediction about the sequel to the skit, basing the prediction on characters and events in the original skit. Encourage students to explain why they think as they do.
  ▶ **Bodily/Kinesthetic**

Auditory

MUSICAL PREDICTIONS

 GROUP **Materials:** musical recordings, cassette player

Have students make predictions about a musical selection after listening to its opening section.

- Play the introduction of a musical selection for students. A classical recording will lend itself well to this activity.

- Stop the tape and guide students in a discussion about the music. Help them identify instruments, pitches, tempos, volume.

- Ask students to make a prediction about the next segment of the selection. Encourage them to describe changes they expect to hear. Have them write their prediction.

- Play more of the selection. Have students compare what they hear to their prediction.
  ▶ **Musical**

See Reteach 38, 42, 59, 63

Reference Sources

OBJECTIVES Students will use reference sources (dictionary, thesaurus, encyclopedia) to practice making reference choices.

Alternate Activities

Kinesthetic

RESOURCE RELAY

 Materials: dictionaries, synonym finders or thesauruses, encyclopedia, index cards, marker

Have students participate in a team game to find information using various resources.

- Prepare cards with simple research questions, such as *What is the meaning of* ambiguous? *What is a synonym for* familiar? *What is the leading export of Brazil?* Make two sets of identical cards.

- Organize students into teams for a research relay. In turn, each student on the team draws a card and uses the appropriate resource to locate the answer. Students jot down the answer, the resource used, and the page.

- As students complete their research, they tag the next member on their team. Check students' answers. If correct, students may be seated. If incorrect, they go to the end of the line to research another answer.

▶ **Bodily/Kinesthetic**

Visual

QUESTION OF THE DAY

 Materials: encyclopedia, paper, pencils, bag

Have each student generate a research question that can be answered by using the encyclopedia. Questions will be compiled and distributed randomly for students to research.

- Have students generate a research question that can be answered by using an encyclopedia. Have students write their question on a slip of paper. Remind students to keep their question narrow. Review students' questions and help them revise as necessary.

- Collect students' questions in a bag. Have students take turns drawing a question out of the bag and completing independent research with the encyclopedia to answer the question.

Have students write a brief report based on their findings.

- Have students share the questions and their research.

▶ **Intrapersonal**

Auditory

LIBRARY TOUR

Have student groups take turns conducting tours of the reference section of the school or classroom library.

- Review with students the reference sources of dictionary, thesaurus or synonym finder, and encyclopedia.

- Lead them in a discussion about choosing the appropriate reference source for a research task.

- Organize students into small groups. Have groups take turns giving a guided tour of the reference section of the school or classroom library.

▶ **Interpersonal**

See Reteach 41, 48, 55, 62, 69

Form Generalizations

TESTED OBJECTIVES Students will form generalizations by creating charts, responding to interviews, and writing a book.

Alternate

Visual

CHARTING IT OUT

Materials: paper, pencils

Have students design a chart that compares two similar things in order to make generalizations.

- Assign students a topic pair to discuss, such as flowers and trees, or schools in two different countries. Encourage students to do some reading on the subject.

- Have students create a chart to compare the things they read about.

- Invite students to share their charts and to make generalizations about the topic. Encourage students to use their information to form generalizations by asking questions such as *What can you say is true about all ___? What seems to be the same about ___ and ___?*
  ▶ **Spatial**

Auditory

GENERAL INTERVIEWS

Have students conduct interviews to ask one another questions about generalizations they formed about a topic.

- Have students read about a nonfiction topic with a broad theme, such as plants, early settlers in America, or the Olympic games.

- Organize students into pairs. Have each pair role-play for classmates a talk-show interview. Have students take turns playing the host and the guest. Encourage the host to ask the guest topic-related questions that require forming generalizations, such as *What do most _____ have in common? What can you say about most _____?* Have partners switch roles.
  ▶ **Interpersonal**

Kinesthetic

FILE FOLDER BOOKS

Materials: file folders, markers

Have students create books to show generalizations they have made about a topic.

- Lead students in a discussion about generalizations they have made about a recent topic of study.

Give each student a manila file folder. Tell them to use the four pages to create a book that focuses on their generalizations about their topic.
  ▶ **Linguistic**

See Reteach 43, 50, 64, 70

Context Clues

OBJECTIVES Students will generate sentences containing clues to content-area and specialized vocabulary. They will read sentences to use context to figure out the meaning of such words.

Alternate Activities

Visual

FLAP BOOK

Materials: construction paper, scissors, markers

PARTNERS

Students will use content and specialized vocabulary in sentences to provide context clues for a partner.

- Show students how to create a flap book. Have them fold a piece of construction paper in half lengthwise. Have them make two cuts to the center to divide the top half of the paper into thirds.

WRITING In each section of the top half of the page, have students write a sentence that contains a content or specialized term and also provides context clues for it.

- Have students lift the flap and write the word's meaning on the bottom half of the page.
- Ask partners to trade flap books and take turns reading and figuring out words using context clues. Have them check the meaning by lifting the flap and reading the definition.

  ▶ **Linguistic**

Kinesthetic

CONTEXT CLUES BOARD GAME

Materials: cardboard, markers

GROUP Students will work together to create a board game to practice reading specialized vocabulary in context.

- Organize students into small groups to work together to design and create a board game to practice reading words in context.
- Provide each group with a list of content-area and specialized vocabulary words.
- Have students establish the theme of their game, springing from the link of the vocabulary words.
- Ask students to write rules and direction cards and gather any necessary game pieces. Instruct students to design the game so that players will get practice figuring out words in context.
- Invite groups to play one another's games.

  ▶ **Spatial**

Auditory

FOCUS ON LISTENING

Materials: cassette tape, cassette recorder

ONE Students will listen for content-area words in an audiotape. They will use context clues to figure out each word's meaning.

- Prepare an audiotape of a reading of content-area material. Write a list of content-area terms students will hear in the tape. Also prepare an answer key that defines each term. Put the tape, list, and answer key in a listening center.
- Have students read the list of words, then listen to the tape to hear the words in context.

  WRITING Have students write a definition for each word, based on the context clues.

  ▶ **Intrapersonal**

See Reteach 44, 58, 72

Sequence of Events

OBJECTIVES Students will arrange story events in order.
They will sing, write, and draw to retell events in order.

Alternate Activities

Kinesthetic

MOVEABLE EVENTS

Materials: butcher paper, markers

Students will wear sandwich boards listing a story event. Students in a group will work together to arrange themselves in order to show the sequence of events.

- Prepare a sandwich board—a large piece of butcher paper to fit over student's head—for each student.

- Organize students into small groups. Have each group select a story and discuss the sequence of events.

Ask students to write an event from their group's story on each sandwich board to summarize the story.

- Have students retell the story to classmates by wearing their sandwich boards and arranging themselves in order from left to right.
  ▶ **Bodily/Kinesthetic**

Visual

SEQUENCE FILMSTRIP

Materials: overhead transparency film, overhead transparency markers, overhead projector

Students will draw a filmstrip that depicts a sequence of events.

- Cut overhead transparency film into filmstrips. Give a strip to each student.

Have students divide the strip into three sections to indicate a beginning, middle, and end. Ask students to write in each section to tell the sequence of events of an original story, or to retell a familiar one. Have students draw illustrations to go with their writing.

- Help students to slide their filmstrip over the overhead projector to show their film. Ask them to read the narration.

- Have students ask audience members questions about the sequence of events.
  ▶ **Spatial**

Auditory

SINGING IN SEQUENCE

Materials: paper, pencils

Students will write and draw to show the sequence of events in ballads and folk songs.

- Lead students in singing songs that tell a story, such as ballads, folk songs, jump-rope rhymes, or clapping games.

Have students make an accordion book to show the sequence of events. Suggest that they write several sentences in each section and draw to enhance their writing.

- Invite students to share their work.
  ▶ **Musical**

See Reteach 45, 49, 57

Compound Words

OBJECTIVES Students will identify and use compound words in "translations" and word games.

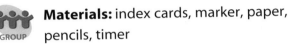
Alternate Activities

Kinesthetic

LITERAL TRANSLATIONS

Materials: index cards, markers, drawing paper

Have students illustrate silly literal translations of compound words.

- Begin a word-wall display of challenging compound words. Encourage students to write the words on index cards and display them on the wall.

- Point out that a new meaning results when two words are joined to form a compound word.

- Have students select a compound word from the word wall to illustrate in a silly way, showing the literal translation. For example, students might choose to illustrate *brainstorm*, *honeymoon*, or *headquarters*.

▶ **Spatial**

Visual

COMPOUND TIC-TAC-TOE

Materials: paper, markers

Have pairs of students play tic-tac-toe by writing compound words.

- Review with students that compound words are two words joined together to form a word with a new meaning.

Have pairs of students play tic-tac-toe by taking turns writing a compound word in a large nine-square grid using an assigned color of marker. As students write their word, encourage them to use it in a sentence.

▶ **Linguistic**

Auditory

COMPOUND RACE

Materials: index cards, marker, paper, pencils, timer

Have groups brainstorm as many words as possible that form a compound with a given word.

- For each group, prepare a set of index cards with one word on each card. Use the following words: *flash, under, water, sun, air*.

- Organize students into small groups. Instruct them to turn over one card at a time and list as many compound words as they can that have the word on the card as the first word in the compound. Groups should have one member act as a recorder.

- Set the timer for two minutes and have students proceed with the race. At the end, have a group read their list of words. Have other groups contribute any words that weren't previously listed.

▶ **Interpersonal**

See Reteach 51, 65, 71

Cause and Effect

OBJECTIVES Students will explore cause-effect relationships through games of skill, listening to and generating riddles, and artistic representations.

Alternate Activities

Auditory

CAUSE-AND-EFFECT RIDDLES

 PARTNERS Students will use cause-effect relationships to write original riddles.

- Present students with *Why?* riddles, such as *Why did the chicken cross the road?* Point out that the answer usually begins with the word *Because.* Call attention to the cause-effect relationship.

WRITING Organize students into pairs. Have partners work together to write *Why?* riddles. Encourage them to share their riddles with classmates.

▶ **Logical/Mathematical**

Kinesthetic

CAUSE-AND-EFFECT GAMES

GROUP **Materials:** commercial games of skill, such as Pick-Up Sticks or Jenga (optional), or building blocks

Have students play games of skill that show cause-effect relationships. These can be commercial games or student-made games, or another activity, such as building and dismantling block towers.

- Organize students into small groups to play the games. As students play, encourage them to focus on and describe the cause-effect relationships. For example, *Because I removed a supporting piece, the tower collapsed.*

▶ **Bodily/Kinesthetic**

Visual

LIFT-THE-FLAP

 ONE **Materials:** construction paper, scissors, glue, crayons or markers

Students will write about and illustrate cause-and-effect relationships in a lift-the-flap format.

- Have students brainstorm examples of cause-and-effect relationships.

- Show students how to create a lift-the-flap page. Have them fold a piece of construction paper from top to bottom. On the front, have them illustrate a cause and cut out a door, or flap, that lifts to reveal the inside of the card.

- Under the flap, have them illustrate the effect. For example, on the outside, students might draw a seedling with sunshine beaming on it and a watering can pouring water. The illustration under the flap would reveal a mature, thriving plant.

WRITING On the back of the card, have students write about the cause-and-effect relationship they illustrated.

▶ **Spatial**

See Reteach 52, 56, 66

A Communication Tool

Although typewriters and computers are readily available, many situations continue to require handwriting. Tasks such as keeping journals, completing forms, taking notes, making shopping or organizational lists, and the ability to read handwritten manuscript or cursive writing are a few examples of practical application of this skill.

BEFORE YOU BEGIN

Before children begin to write, certain fine motor skills need to be developed. Examples of activities that can be used as warm-up activities are:

- **Simon Says** Play a game of Simon Says using just finger positions.
- **Finger Plays and Songs** Sing songs that use Signed English, American Sign Language or finger spelling.
- **Mazes** Mazes are available in a wide range of difficulty. You can also create mazes that allow children to move their writing instruments from left to right.

Determining Handedness

Keys to determining handedness in a child:

- Which hand does the child eat with? This is the hand that is likely to become the dominant hand.
- Does the child start coloring with one hand and then switch to the other? This may be due to fatigue rather than lack of hand preference.
- Does the child cross midline to pick things up or use the closest hand? Place items directly in front of the child to see if one hand is preferred.
- Does the child do better with one hand or the other?

The Mechanics of Writing

DESK AND CHAIR

- Chair height should allow for the feet to rest flat on the floor.
- Desk height should be two inches above the level of the elbows when the child is sitting.
- The chair should be pulled in allowing for an inch of space between the child's abdomen and the desk.
- Children sit erect with the elbows resting on the desk.
- Children should have models of letters on the desk or at eye level, not above their heads.

PAPER POSITION

- **Right-handed children** should turn the paper so that the lower left-hand corner of the paper points to the abdomen.

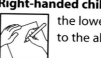

- **Left-handed children** should turn the paper so that the lower right-hand corner of the paper points to the abdomen.

- The nondominant hand should anchor the paper near the top so that the paper doesn't slide.
- The paper should be moved up as the child nears the bottom of the paper. Many children won't think of this and may let their arms hang off the desk when they reach the bottom of a page.

The Writing Instrument Grasp

For handwriting to be functional, the writing instrument must be held in a way that allows for fluid dynamic movement.

FUNCTIONAL GRASP PATTERNS

- **Tripod Grasp** With open web space, the writing instrument is held with the tip of the thumb and the index finger and rests against the side of the third finger. The thumb and index finger form a circle.
- **Quadrupod Grasp** With open web space, the writing instrument is held with the tip of the thumb and index finger and rests against the fourth finger. The thumb and index finger form a circle.

INCORRECT GRASP PATTERNS

- **Fisted Grasp** The writing instrument is held in a fisted hand.

- **Pronated Grasp** The writing instrument is held diagonally within the hand with the tips of the thumb and index finger on the writing instrument but with no support from other fingers.
- **Five-Finger Grasp** The writing instrument is held with the tips of all five fingers.

TO CORRECT WRITING INSTRUMENT GRASPS

- Have children play counting games with an eye dropper and water.
- Have children pick up small objects with a tweezer.
- Do counting games with children picking up small coins using just the thumb and index finger.

FLEXED OR HOOKED WRIST

- The writing instrument can be held in a variety of grasps with the wrist flexed or bent. This is typically seen with left-handed writers but is also present in some right-handed writers. To correct wrist position, have children check their writing posture and paper placement.

Evaluation Checklist

Functional writing is made up of two elements, legibility and functional speed.

LEGIBILITY

MANUSCRIPT

Formation and Strokes

☑ Does the child begin letters at the top?

☑ Do circles close?

☑ Are the horizontal lines straight?

☑ Do circular shapes and extender and descender lines touch?

☑ Are the heights of all upper-case letters equal?

☑ Are the heights of all lower-case letters equal?

☑ Are the lengths of the extenders and descenders the same for all letters?

Directionality

☑ Are letters and words formed from left to right?

☑ Are letters and words formed from top to bottom?

Spacing

☑ Are the spaces between letters equidistant?

☑ Are the spaces between words equidistant?

☑ Do the letters rest on the line?

☑ Are the top, bottom and side margins even?

CURSIVE

Formation and Strokes

☑ Do circular shapes close?

☑ Are the downstrokes parallel?

☑ Do circular shapes and downstroke lines touch?

☑ Are the heights of all upper-case letters equal?

☑ Are the heights of all lower-case letters equal?

☑ Are the lengths of the extenders and descenders the same for all letters?

☑ Do the letters which finish at the top join the next letter?

☑ Do the letters which finish at the bottom join the next letter?

☑ Do letters with descenders join the next letter?

☑ Do all letters touch the line?

☑ Is the vertical slant of all letters consistent?

Directionality

☑ Are letters and words formed from left to right?

☑ Are letters and words formed from top to bottom?

Spacing

☑ Are the spaces between letters equidistant?

☑ Are the spaces between words equidistant?

☑ Do the letters rest on the line?

☑ Are the top, bottom and side margins even?

SPEED

The prettiest handwriting is not functional for classroom work if it takes the child three times longer than the rest of the class to complete work assignments. After the children have been introduced to writing individual letters, begin to add time limitations to the completion of copying or writing assignments. Then check the child's work for legibility.

Handwriting Models—Manuscript

ABCDEFGH
IJKLMNOP
QRSTUVW
XYZ

abcdefgh
ijklmnop
qrstuvw
xyz

Handwriting Models—Cursive

A B C D E F G H I

J K L M N O P Q R

S T U V W X Y Z

a b c d e f g h i j

k l m n o p q r s

t u v w x y z

Selection Titles

Honors, Prizes, and Awards

TO
Unit 1, p. 16
by *Lee Bennett Hopkins*

Poet: Lee Bennett Hopkins, winner of Golden Kite Honor Book Award (1995), Christopher Award (1996) for *Been to Yesterday: Poems of a Life*

THE LOST LAKE
Unit 1, p. 20
by *Allen Say*

Author/Illustrator: Allen Say, winner of Christopher Award (1985) for *How My Parents Learned to Eat*; Boston Globe-Horn Book Award (1988), Caldecott Honor, ALA Notable (1989) for *The Boy of the Three-Year Nap*; Caldecott Medal, Boston Globe-Horn Book Award, ALA Notable, New York Times Best Illustrated (1994) for *Grandfather's Journey*

AMELIA'S ROAD
Unit 1, p. 44
by *Linda Jacobs Altman*
Illustrated by *Enrique O. Sanchez*

Illustrator: Enrique O. Sanchez, winner of Parent's Choice Award (1993) for *Abuela's Weave*

SARAH, PLAIN AND TALL
Unit 1, p. 68
by *Patricia MacLachlan*
Illustrated by *Burton Silverman*

Golden Kite Award for Fiction, IRA-CBC Children's Choice, School Library Best of the Best (1985), Newbery Medal, Christopher Award, Scott O'Dell Historical Fiction Award (1986)

SEAL JOURNEY
Unit 1, p. 96
by *Richard and Jonah Sobol*
Photographs by *Richard Sobol*

Outstanding Science Trade Book for Children (1994)

JUSTIN AND THE BEST BISCUITS IN THE WORLD
Unit 2, p. 134
by *Mildred Pitts Walter*
Illustrated by *Floyd Cooper*

Coretta Scott-King Award (1987)
Author: Mildred Pitts Walter, winner of Coretta Scott King Award for illustration (1984) for *My Mama Needs Me*
Illustrator: Floyd Cooper, winner of Coretta Scott King Award (1995) for *Meet Danitra Brown*

JUST A DREAM
Unit 2, p. 160
by *Chris Van Allsburg*

Author/Illustrator: Chris Van Allsburg, winner of ALA Notable, Caldecott Medal (1982) for *Jumanji*; ALA Notable (1984) for *The Wreck of the Zephyr*; ALA Notable, Boston Globe-Horn Book Honor, Caldecott Medal (1986) for *The Polar Express*; NSTA Outstanding Science Trade Book for Children (1988), IRA-CBC Children's Choice (1989) for *Two Bad Ants*; ALA Notable (1994) for *The Sweetest Fig*

Selection Titles	Honors, Prizes, and Awards
LEAH'S PONY Unit 2, p. 192 by *Elizabeth Friedrich* Illustrated by *Michael Garland*	**National Council of Trade Books Award, Golden Kite Award, Parent's Magazine Best Book of the Year, IRA Teacher's Choice Award (1997), Texas Bluebonnet Award (1997-98)**
BASEBALL SAVED US Unit 2, p. 218 by *Ken Mochizuki* Illustrated by *Dom Lee*	**Parent's Choice Award (1993)**
THE HATMAKER'S SIGN Unit 3, p. 258 by *Candace Fleming* Illustrated by *Robert Andrew Parker*	**Illustrator: Robert Andrew Parker,** winner of Caldecott Honor (1970) for *Pop Corn and Ma Goodness*
PAT CUMMINGS: MY STORY Unit 3, p. 284 by *Pat Cummings*	**Boston Globe-Horn Book Award (1992), ALA Notable (1993)**
GRASS SANDALS: THE TRAVELS OF BASHO Unit 3, p. 300 by *Dawnine Spivak* Illustrated by *Demi*	**National Council of Trade Books Award (1998)** **Illustrator: Demi,** winner of the New York Times Best Illustrated Children's Books of the Year (1985) for *The Nightingale*
A PLACE CALLED FREEDOM Unit 3, p. 334 by *Scott Russell Sanders* Illustrated by *Thomas B. Allen*	**Notable Children's Book in the Field of Social Studies (1998)**
FINAL CURVE Unit 4, p. 372 by *Langston Hughes*	**Poet: Langston Hughes,** winner of Witter Bynner Prize (1926); Harmon Foundation Literature Award (1931); Guggenheim Fellowship (1935); American Academy of Arts and Letters Grant (1946); Spingarn Medal (1960)

Selection Titles

Honors, Prizes, and Awards

SCRUFFY
Unit 4, p. 376
by *Jim Brandenburg*

Author/Photographer: Jim Brandenburg, winner ALA Best Book for Young Adults Award, Orbis Picture Award for Outstanding Non-fiction Honor Book, Minnesota Book Award (1994) for *To the Top of the World: Adventures with Arctic Wolves*; Parent's Choice Award, Outstanding Science Trade Book for Children, John Burroughs List of Outstanding Nature Books for Children (1995) for *Sand and Fog: Adventures in South Africa*; ALA Best Book for Young Adults (1996) for *An American Safari: Adventures on the North American Prairie*

GLUSKABE AND THE SNOW BIRD
Unit 4, p. 408
by *Joseph Bruchac*
Illustrated by *Stefano Vitale*

Author: Joseph Bruchac, winner of the Skipping Stones Honor Award for Multicultural Children's Literature (1997) for *Four Ancestors*

ON THE BUS WITH JOANNA COLE
Unit 4, p. 446
by *Joanna Cole with Wendy Saul*

Author: Joanna Cole, winner of Washington Children's Choice Picture Book Award, Colorado Children's Book Award (1989) for *The Magic School Bus at the Waterworks*; Parenting's Reading Magic Awards (1989) for *The Magic School Bus Inside the Human Body*

TORTILLAS LIKE AFRICA
Unit 4, p. 482
by *Gary Soto*

Poet: Gary Soto, winner of Academy of American Poets Award (1975); American Book Award (1984) for *Living Up the Street*; California Library Association's John And Patricia Beatty Award, Best Books for Young Adults Awards (1991) for *Baseball in April and Other Stories*; Americás Book Award, Honorable Mention (1995) for *Chato's Kitchen*; Americás Book Award, Commended List (1995) for *Canto Familiar*; (1996) for *The Old Man and His Door*; (1997) for *Buried Onions*

HOW TO TELL THE TOP OF A HILL
Unit 5, p. 484
by *John Ciardi*

Poet: John Ciardi, winner of New York Times Best Illustrated Children's Books of the Year (1959) for *The Reason for the Pelican*; (1960) for *Scruffy The Pup*; (1966) for *The Monster Den: Or, Look What Happened at My House—and to It*; ALA Best Book Award (1961) for *I Met a Man*; (1963) for *John Plenty and Fiddler Dan: A New Fable of the Grasshopper and the Ant*; National Council of Teachers of English Award for Excellence in Poetry for Children (1982)

Selection Titles

Honors, Prizes, and Awards

MOM'S BEST FRIEND
Unit 5, p. 518
by *Sally Hobart Alexander*
Photographs by *George Ancona*

Author: Sally Hobart Alexander, winner of Christopher Award (1995) for *Taking Hold: My Journey Into Blindness*

YEH-SHEN
Unit 5, p. 570
retold by **Ai-Ling Louie**
Illustrated by **Ed Young**

ALA Notable, School Library Journal Best Books of the Year (1982), Boston Globe-Horn Book Honor (1983)
Illustrator: Ed Young, winner of Caldecott Honor (1968) for *The Emperor and the Kite*; Boston Globe-Horn Book Honor (1984) for *The Double Life of Pocahontas*; NCSS Notable Children's Book Award (1989), Caldecott Medal, Boston Globe-Horn Book Award, ALA Notable (1990) for *Lon Po Po*; ALA Notable (1991) for *Mice Are Nice*; ALA Notable (1992) for *All Of You Was Singing*; ALA Notable, Boston Globe-Horn Book Award, Caldecott Honor (1993) for *Seven Blind Mice*; ALA Notable (1994) for *Sadako*; National Council for Social Studies Notable Children's Book Awards (1998) for *Genesis* and *Voices of the Heart*

TEAMMATES
Unit 6, p. 616
by *Peter Golenbock*
Illustrated by **Paul Bacon**

Author: Peter Golenbock, winner of National Council of Trade Books in Social Studies Award; Redbook Children's Picture Book Award (1990)

THE MALACHITE PALACE
Unit 6, p. 634
by *Alma Flor Ada*
Illustrated by *Leonid Gore*

Author: Alma Flor Ada, winner of Christopher Award (1992) for *The Gold Coin*

WHALES
Unit 6, p. 694
by *Seymour Simon*

Author: Seymour Simon, winner of ALA Notable (1985) for *Moon*; (1986) for *Saturn*; (1987) for *Mars*; (1993) for *Our Solar System* and *Snakes*; Texas Blue Bonnet Master List (1996–97) for *Sharks*; NSTA Outstanding Science Tradebook for Children (1997) for *The Heart*

DECISIONS
Unit 6, p. 724
by *Angela Shelf Medearis*

Poet: Angela Shelf Medearis, winner IRA-Teacher's Choice Award, Primary Grades (1995) for *Our People*

Trade Books

Additional fiction and nonfiction trade books related to each selection can be shared with students throughout the unit.

JUSTIN AND THE BEST BISCUITS IN THE WORLD

Sitti's Secret
Naomi Shihab Nye (Four Winds Press, 1994)

A young girl in America thinks fondly of her Arab grandmother and the good times they shared in spite of their language barrier and cultural differences.

Mrs. Katz and Tush
Patricia Polacco (Bantam Books, 1992)

An enduring friendship develops between a young African American boy and an elderly Jewish widow when she adopts a kitten he brings her.

Sun & Spoon
Kevin Henkes (Greenwillow Books, 1997)

A sympathetic portrayal of ten-year-old Spoon's struggle to come to terms with his grandmother's death by seeking a memento to keep her memory alive.

JUST A DREAM

Screen of Frogs: An Old Tale
Sheila Hamanaka (Orchard Books, 1993)

A frog brings a life-changing message to a spoiled boy in this imaginatively illustrated retelling of an old Japanese tale.

Aani and the Tree Huggers
Jeannine Atkins, illustrated by Venantius J. Pinto (Lee & Low, 1995)

A young girl in India inspires the women in her village to save their forest from the bulldozers.

Come Back, Salmon: How a Group of Dedicated Kids Adopted Pigeon Creek and Brought It Back to Life
Molly Cone (Sierra Club Books for Children, 1992)

The story of how a group of elementary school students adopt a nearby stream and restore it so that the salmon can return.

Technology

Multimedia resources can be used to enhance students' understanding of the selections.

Justin and the Best Biscuits in the World (Macmillan/McGraw-Hill) CD-ROM Macintosh. An interactive program based on the literature.

Generations (Phoenix/BFA) Video, 11 min. A young boy and an elderly couple befriend each other.

Storm Boy (AIMS Multimedia) Video, 33 min. A young Australian boy learns about life and friendship from an aborigine and a pelican.

Too Much Trash (National Geographic Educational Services) Interactive network Macintosh, Apple II, DOS. Students study the impact of trash and design a program to deal with it.

The Garbage Dump Dilemma (Coronet/MTI) Video or videodisc, 22 min. A look at the problems of and possible solutions to the problem of trash.

The Environment (Tom Snyder Productions) Computer software Macintosh, Apple, MS DOS. Students look at landfills, pollution, recycling, land use, and other environmental issues.

Theme Bibliography

LEAH'S PONY	BASEBALL SAVED US	WILL HER NATIVE LANGUAGE DISAPPEAR?

Dream Jar

Bonnie Pryor (Morrow Junior Books, 1996)

Young Valechka wants to contribute to her family's dream but is not sure how she can earn the money.

The American Family Farm: A Photo Essay

Joan Anderson and George Ancona (Harcourt Brace, 1997)

Informative text and black and white photographs offer insight into the lives of three American farm families in Massachusetts, Georgia, and Iowa.

The Bread Winner

Arvella Whitmore (Houghton Mifflin, 1990)

The Great Depression serves as a backdrop for this story about an enterprising young girl who saves her family from financial ruin.

The Woman Who Outshone the Sun

Alejandro Cruz Martinez, illustrated by Fernando Oliver (Children's Book Press, 1991)

A legend from Mexico tells of a beautiful woman who takes away the river when the village people scorn her.

The Ancestor Tree

T. Obinkaram Echewa, illustrated by Christy Hale (Lodestar Books, 1994)

In this original Nigerian folktale, students persuade the village council to change the tree-planting custom when a beloved old man dies without descendants of his own.

Flood: Wrestling with the Mississippi

Patricia Lauber (National Geographic Society, 1996)

The story of the Mississippi floods of 1927 and 1993 and of the people who worked together to repair the damage.

How Thunder and Lightning Came to Be

Beatrice Orcutt Harrell (Dial Books for Young Readers, 1995)

The author retells the Choctaw legend, passed down from her mother, of how thunder and lightning came to be.

Stories on Stone: Rock Art, Images from Ancient Ones

Jennifer Owings Dewey (Little, Brown, 1996)

Theories on the Native Americans who inscribed and painted their stories on stone long ago. With fascinating illustrations.

The Code Talkers: American Indians in World War II

Robert Daily (Franklin Watts, 1995)

A discussion of the Native Americans who used their native tongue in battle, the Choctaw being the first.

 The Middle West (Phoenix/BFA) Video, 12 min. An introduction to the midwest from earlier times to the present, and the great agricultural resources that it provides.

 SimFarm (ESI) CD-ROM, Macintosh, Windows. In an interactive program, players deal with the day-to-day operations of a farm and manage its resources.

 Yesterday's Farm (Phoenix/BFA) Video, 17 min. This film looks at abandoned farm buildings and tells the story of family farmers, their hopes, dreams, and disappointments.

 From East to West: The Asian American Experience (Zenger Media) Video, 22 min. A look at the historical and cultural elements of the Asian American experience, including the internment of the Japanese during World War II.

Learning to Be a Good Sport (Coronet/MTI) Video, 11 Min. This animated program teaches the elements of good sportsmanship.

Rag-Tag Champs (AIMS) Video, 47 min. A young boy uses his determination to straighten out his own life and make something of his little league baseball team.

 North American Indians (SVE) CD-ROM Macintosh, DOS. A look at the heritage, customs, and history of North American Indians.

Sheena Azak of Canada (United Learning) Video, 12 min. A nine-year-old girl learns about her native Nisga Wolf Tribe through the teachings of her father and the tribe's oral tradition and tribal dances.

Walking with Grandfather (GPN) Videos, 6–15 min. An Indian elder shares the importance of the Native American oral tradition and how stories teach lessons of human values.

Aladdin Paperbacks
(Imprint of Simon & Schuster Children's Publishing)

Alaska Northwest Books
(Division of Graphic Arts Center Publishing Co.)
3019 NW Yeon Ave.
Box 10306
Portland, OR 97296-0306
(503) 226-2402 • (800) 452-3032
Fax (503) 223-1410
www.gacpc.com

Annick Press
(Imprint of Firefly, Ltd.)

Atheneum
(Imprint of Simon & Schuster Children's Publishing)

Avon Books
(Division of Hearst Corp.)
1350 Ave. of the Americas
New York, NY 10019
(212) 261-6800 • (800) 238-0658
Fax (800) 223-0239
www.avonbooks.com

Bantam Doubleday Dell Books for Young Readers
(Imprint of Random House)

Peter Bedrick Books
156 Fifth Ave., Suite 817
New York, NY 10010
(800) 788-3123 • Fax (212) 206-3741

Beech Tree Books
(Imprint of William Morrow & Co.)

Blackbirch Press
1 Bradley Road, Suite 205
Woodbridge, CT 06525
(203) 387-7525 • (800) 831-9183

Blue Sky Press
(Imprint of Scholastic)

Bradbury Press
(Imprint of Simon & Schuster Children's Publishing)

BridgeWater Books
(Distributed by Penguin Putnam Inc.)

Candlewick Press
2067 Massachusetts Avenue
Cambridge, MA 02140
(617) 661-3330 • Fax (617) 661-0565

Carolrhoda Books
(Division of Lerner Publications Co.)

Cartwheel Books
(Imprint of Scholastic)

Children's Book Press
246 First St., Suite 101
San Francisco, CA 94105
(415) 995-2200 • Fax (415) 995-2222

Children's Press (Division of Grolier, Inc.)
P.O. Box 1796
Danbury, CT 06813-1333
(800) 621-1115 • www.grolier.com

Chronicle Books
85 Second Street, Sixth Floor
San Francisco, CA 94105
(415) 537-3730 • (415) 537-4460
(800) 722-6657
www.chroniclebooks.com

Clarion Books
(Imprint of Houghton Mifflin, Inc.)
215 Park Avenue South
New York, NY 10003
(212) 420-5800 • (800) 726-0600
www.hmco.com/trade/childrens/shelves.html

Crabtree Publishing Co.
350 Fifth Ave., Suite 3308
New York, NY 10118
(212) 496-5040 • (800) 387-7650
Fax (800) 355-7166
www.crabtree-pub.com

Creative Education
The Creative Co.
123 S. Broad Street
P.O. Box 227
Mankato, MN 56001
(507) 388-6273 • (800) 445-6209
Fax (507) 388-2746

Crowell (Imprint of HarperCollins)

Crown Publishing Group
(Imprint of Random House)

Delacorte
(Imprint of Random House)

Dial Books
(Imprint of Penguin Putnam Inc.)

Discovery Enterprises, Ltd.
31 Laurelwood Dr.
Carlisle, MA 01741
(978) 287-5401 • (800) 729-1720
Fax (978) 287-5402

Disney Press
(Division of Disney Book Publishing, Inc.,
A Walt Disney Co.)
114 Fifth Ave.
New York, NY 10011
(212) 633-4400 • Fax (212) 633-4833
www.disneybooks.com

Dorling Kindersley (DK Publishing)
95 Madison Avenue
New York, NY 10016
(212) 213-4800 • Fax (800) 774-6733
(888) 342-5357 • www.dk.com

Doubleday (Imprint of Random House)

E. P. Dutton Children's Books
(Imprint of Penguin Putnam Inc.)

Farrar Straus & Giroux
19 Union Square West
New York, NY 10003
(212) 741-6900 • Fax (212) 633-2427
(888) 330-8477

Firefly Books, Ltd.
PO Box 1338
Endicott Station
Buffalo, NY 14205
(416) 499-8412 • Fax (800) 565-6034
(800) 387-5085
www.firefly.com

Four Winds Press
(Imprint of Macmillan, see Simon & Schuster Children's Publishing)

Fulcrum Publishing
350 Indiana Street, Suite 350
Golden, CO 80401
(303) 277-1623 • (800) 992-2908
Fax (303) 279-7111
www.fulcrum-books.com

Greenwillow Books
(Imprint of William Morrow & Co, Inc.)

Gulliver Green Books
(Imprint of Harcourt Brace & Co.)

Harcourt Brace & Co.
525 "B" Street
San Diego, CA 92101
(619) 231-6616 • (800) 543-1918
www.harcourtbooks.com

Harper & Row (Imprint of HarperCollins)

HarperCollins Children's Books
10 East 53rd Street
New York, NY 10022
(212) 207-7000 • Fax (212) 202-7044
(800) 242-7737
www.harperchildrens.com

Harper Trophy
(Imprint of HarperCollins)

Henry Holt and Company
115 West 18th Street
New York, NY 10011
(212) 886-9200 • (212) 633-0748
(888) 330-8477 • www.henryholt.com/byr/

Holiday House
425 Madison Avenue
New York, NY 10017
(212) 688-0085 • Fax (212) 421-6134

Houghton Mifflin
222 Berkeley Street
Boston, MA 02116
(617) 351-5000 • Fax (617) 351-1125
(800) 225-3362 • www.hmco.com/trade

Hyperion Books
(Imprint of Buena Vista Publishing Co.)
114 Fifth Avenue
New York, NY 10011
(212) 633-4400 • (800) 759-0190
www.disney.com

Just Us Books
356 Glenwood Avenue
E. Orange, NJ 07017
(973) 672-0304 • Fax (973) 677-7570

Kane/Miller Book Publishers
P.O. Box 310529
Brooklyn, NY 11231-0529
(718) 624-5120 • Fax (718) 858-5452
www.kanemiller.com

Alfred A. Knopf
(Imprint of Random House)

Lee & Low Books
95 Madison Avenue
New York, NY 10016
(212) 779-4400 • Fax (212) 683-1894

Lerner Publications Co.
241 First Avenue North
Minneapolis, MN 55401
(612) 332-3344 • Fax (612) 332-7615
(800) 328-4929 • www.lernerbooks.com

Little, Brown & Co.
3 Center Plaza
Boston, MA 02108
(617) 227-0730 • Fax (617) 263-2864
(800) 343-9204 • www.littlebrown.com

Lothrop Lee & Shepard
(Imprint of William Morrow & Co.)

Macmillan
(Imprint of Simon & Schuster Children's Publishing)

Mikaya Press
(Imprint of Firefly Books, Ltd.)

Millbrook Press, Inc.
2 Old New Milford Road
Brookfield, CT 06804
(203) 740-2220 • (800) 462-4703
Fax (203) 740-2526
www.millbrookpress.com

William Morrow & Co.
1350 Avenue of the Americas
New York, NY 10019
(212) 261-6500 • Fax (212) 261-6619
(800) 843-9389
www.williammorrow.com

Morrow Junior Books
(Imprint of William Morrow & Co.)

National Geographic Society
1145 17th Street, NW
Washington, DC 20036
(202) 828-5667 • (800) 368-2728
www.nationalgeographic.com

Northland Publishing
(Division of Justin Industries)
P.O. Box 62
Flagstaff, AZ 86002
(520) 774-5251 • Fax (800) 257-9082
(800) 346-3257 • www.northlandpub.com

Orchard Books (A Grolier Company)
95 Madison Avenue
New York, NY 10016
(212) 951-2600 • Fax (212) 213-6435
(800) 621-1115 • www.grolier.com

Oxford University Press, Inc.
198 Madison Ave.
New York, NY 10016-4314
(212) 726-6000 • (800) 451-7556
www.oup-usa.org

Penguin Putnam, Inc.
345 Hudson Street
New York, NY 10014
(212) 366-2000 • Fax (212) 366-2666
(800) 631-8571
www.penguinputnam.com

Philomel Books
(Imprint of Penguin Putnam, Inc.)

Pippin Press
Gracie Station, Box 1347
229 E. 85th Street
New York, NY 10028
(212) 288-4920 • Fax (732) 225-1562

Puffin Books
(Imprint of Penguin Putnam, Inc.)

G.P. Putnam's Sons Publishing
(Imprint of Penguin Putnam, Inc.)

Random House
201 East 50th Street
New York, NY 10022
(212) 751-2600 • Fax (212) 572-2593
(800) 726-0600
www.randomhouse.com/kids

Rising Moon
(Imprint of Northland Publishing)

Scholastic
555 Broadway
New York, NY 10012
(212) 343-6100 • Fax (212) 343-6930
(800) SCHOLASTIC • www.scholastic.com

Sierra Club Books for Children
85 Second Street, Second Floor
San Francisco, CA 94105-3441
(415) 977-5500 • Fax (415) 977-5793
(800) 935-1056 • www.sierraclub.orgbooks

Silver Burdett Press
(Division of Pearson Education)
299 Jefferson Rd.
Parsippany, NJ 07054-0480
(973) 739-8000 • (800) 848-9500
www.sbgschool.com

Simon & Schuster Children's Books
1230 Avenue of the Americas
New York, NY 10020
(212) 698-7200 • (800) 223-2336
www.simonsays.com/kidzone

Gareth Stevens, Inc.
River Center Bldg.
1555 N. River Center Dr., Suite 201
Milwaukee, WI 53212
(414) 225-0333 • (800) 341-3569
Fax (414) 225-0377
www.gsinc.com

Sunburst
(Imprint of Farrar, Straus & Giroux)

Tricycle Press
(Division of Ten Speed Press)
P.O. Box 7123
Berkeley, CA 94707
(510) 559-1600 • (800) 841-2665
Fax (510) 559-1637
www.tenspeed.com

Viking Children's Books
(Imprint of Penguin Putnam Inc.)

Voyager
(Imprint of Harcourt Brace & Co.)

Walker & Co.
435 Hudson Street
New York, NY 10014
(212) 727-8300 • (212) 727-0984
(800) AT-WALKER

Warwick Publishing
162 John St.
Toronto, CAN M5V2E5
(416) 596-1555
www.warwickgp.com

Watts Publishing
(Imprint of Grolier Publishing;
see Children's Press)

Yearling Books
(Imprint of Random House)

Multimedia Resources

AIMS Multimedia
9710 DeSoto Avenue
Chatsworth, CA 91311-4409
(800) 367-2467
www.AIMS-multimedia.com

Ambrose Video and Publishing
28 West 44th Street, Suite 2100
New York, NY 10036
(800) 526-4663 • Fax (212) 768-9282
www.AmbroseVideo.com

BFA Educational Media
(see Phoenix Learning Group)

Boston Federal Reserve Bank
Community Affairs Dept.
P.O. Box 2076
Boston, MA 02106-2076
(617) 973-3459
www.bos.frb.org

Brittanica
310 South Michigan Avenue
Brittanica Center
Chicago, IL 60604-4293
(800) 621-3900 • Fax (800) 344-9624

Broderbund
(Parsons Technology;
also see The Learning Company)
500 Redwood Blvd.
Novato, CA 94997
(800) 521-6263 • Fax (800) 474-8840
www.broderbund.com

Carousel Film and Video
260 Fifth Avenue, Suite 705
New York, NY 10001
(212) 683-1660 • e-mail:
carousel@pipeline.com

CBS/Fox Video
1330 Avenue of the Americas
New York, NY 10019
(800) 457-0686

Cornell University Audio/Video Resource Ctr.
8 Business & Technology Park
Ithaca, NY 14850
(607) 255-2091

Coronet/MTI
(see Phoenix Learning Group)

Direct Cinema, Ltd.
P.O. Box 10003
Santa Monica, CA 90410-1003
(800) 525-0000

Encyclopaedia Britannica Educational Corp.
310 South Michigan Avenue
Chicago, IL 60604
(800) 554-9862 • www.eb.com

ESI/Educational Software
4213 S. 94th Street
Omaha, NE 68127
(800) 955-5570 • www.edsoft.com

Films for the Humanities and Sciences
P.O. Box 2053
Princeton, NJ 08543-2053
(800) 257-5126 • Fax (609) 275-3767
www.films.com

GPN/Reading Rainbow
University of Nebraska-Lincoln
P.O. Box 80669
Lincoln, NE 68501-0669
(800) 228-4630 • www.gpn.unl.edu

Journal Films and Videos
1560 Sherman Avenue, Suite 100
Evanston, IL 60201
(800) 323-9084

Kaw Valley Films
P.O. Box 3900
Shawnee, KS 66208
(800) 332-5060

Listening Library
One Park Avenue
Greenwich, CT 06870-1727
(800) 243-4504 • www.listeninglib.com

Macmillan/McGraw-Hill
(see SRA/McGraw-Hill)

Marshmedia
P.O. Box 8082
Shawnee Mission, KS 66208
(800) 821-3303 • Fax (816) 333-7421
marshmedia.com

MECC
(see The Learning Company)

National Geographic Society Educational Services
P.O. Box 10597
Des Moines, IA 50340-0597
(800) 368-2728
www.nationalgeographic.com

New Jersey Network
1573 Parkside Ave.
Trenton, NJ 08625-0777
(609) 530-5180

PBS Video
1320 Braddock Place
Alexandria, VA 22314
(800) 344-3337 • www.pbs.org

Phoenix Films
(see Phoenix Learning Group)

The Phoenix Learning Group
2348 Chaffee Drive
St. Louis, MO 63146
(800) 221-1274 • e-mail:
phoenixfilms@worldnet.att.net

Pied Piper (see AIMS Multimedia)

Rainbow Educational Video
170 Keyland Court
Bohemia, NY 11716
(800) 331-4047

Social Studies School Service
10200 Jefferson Boulevard, Room 14
P.O. Box 802
Culver City, CA 90232-0802
(800) 421-4246 • Fax (310) 839-2249
socialstudies.com

SRA/McGraw-Hill
220 Daniel Dale Road
De Soto, TX 75115
(800) 843-8855 • www.sra4kids.com

SVE/Churchill Media
6677 North Northwest Highway
Chicago, IL 60631
(800) 829-1900 • www.svemedia.com

Tom Snyder Productions (also see ESI)
80 Coolidge Hill Rd.
Watertown, MA 02472
(800) 342-0236 • www.teachtsp.com

Troll Associates
100 Corporate Drive
Mahwah, NJ 07430
(800) 929-8765 • Fax (800) 979-8765
www.troll.com

United Learning
6633 W. Howard St.
Niles, IL 60714-3389
(800) 424-0362
www.unitedlearning.com

Weston Woods
12 Oakwood Avenue
Norwalk, CT 06850
(800) 243-5020 • Fax (203) 845-0498

Zenger Media
10200 Jefferson Blvd., Room 94
P.O. Box 802
Culver City, CA 90232-0802
(800) 421-4246 • Fax (800) 944-5432
www.Zengermedia.com

UNIT 1

	Vocabulary	Spelling

THE LOST LAKE

brand-new
compass
darted
mug
muttered
talker

Words with Short Vowels

drank	hung	lift	swept
rest	trouble	flock	pleasant
ahead	**magazines**	trust	fist
drink	self	cousin	couple
dock	deaf	cannon	wealth

AMELIA'S ROAD

accidental
labored
occasions
rhythms
shortcut
shutters

Words with long *a* and long *e*

cape	agree	crayon	**rusty**
gray	**teacher**	cable	tray
station	secret	fail	raisin
rail	**family**	tea	bean
freight	cane	zebra	**tidy**

SARAH, PLAIN AND TALL

eerie
huddled
overalls
pesky
reins
squall

Words with long *i* and long *o*

tiger	**crow**	tomato	pine
drive	oak	**stove**	**overhead**
reply	iron	below	chose
roll	alike	groan	hollow
note	supply	title	file

SEAL JOURNEY

assured
horizon
jagged
mature
nursery
squealed

Words with /ū/ and /ü/

ruler	**continue**	**improve**	ruin
avenue	gloomy	beautiful	bugle
raccoon	unit	cube	argue
loose	whose	stool	community
commute	humor	**movement**	tuna

TIME FOR KIDS: OPEN WIDE, DON'T BITE!

broad
fangs
patients
healthy
reptiles
skills

Words from Health

dentist	**gums**	brain	ache
crown	gland	cavity	**dental**
hospital	joint	disease	clinic
medicine	fever	plaque	oral
diet	**chewing**	vitamin	**molars**

Boldfaced words appear in the selection.

UNIT 2

Vocabulary | Spelling

Justin and the Best Biscuits in the World

Vocabulary
- festival
- guilt
- inspecting
- lingered
- pranced
- resounded

Spelling — Syllable Patterns

biscuit	cabin	local	**razor**
clover	plastic	mustard	fancy
public	radar	pupil	limit
oven	mitten	sofa	**famous**
bandage	**knapsack**	**welcome**	item

Just a Dream

Vocabulary
- bulging
- crumpled
- foul
- haze
- shrieking
- waddled

Spelling — Words with Consonant Clusters

blank	bridge	brand	credit
daring	**float**	among	darling
claim	plank	flatter	flutter
flour	classified	**clothesline**	clatter
crack	cradle	bridle	cruise

Leah's Pony

Vocabulary
- bidding
- clustered
- county
- glistened
- overflowing
- sturdy

Spelling — Words with Consonant Clusters

thrill	sprint	stern	stung
spruce	spare	spectacle	sparkle
stand	threw	strap	stress
speed	**stranger**	thrifty	special
stretch	springtime	street	steak

Baseball Saved Us

Vocabulary
- crate
- ditches
- endless
- glinting
- inning
- mound

Spelling — Plurals

cities	engines	eyelashes	**sunglasses**
mistakes	**soldiers**	**uniforms**	groceries
foxes	ranches	batteries	loaves
babies	hobbies	calves	**mattresses**
knives	yourselves	**shovels**	ferries

Time for Kids: Will Her Native Language Disappear?

Vocabulary
- backgrounds
- century
- communicate
- extinct
- generations
- native

Spelling — Words from Social Studies

language	accent	folktale	symbol
history	tribe	practice	guide
pottery	human	**relatives**	totem
study	custom	interview	colony
spoken	village	region	**prints**

Boldfaced words appear in the selection.

T81

UNIT 3

	Vocabulary	Spelling

THE HATMAKER'S SIGN

Vocabulary:
admitted
brisk
displaying
elegantly
strolling
wharf

Spelling: **Words with /ou/ and /oi/**

oily	royalty	**aloud**	**however**
annoy	bounce	tower	appointment
around	**bowing**	avoid	scout
growl	moist	employ	powder
disappoint	enjoyment	**lookout**	noun

PAT CUMMINGS: MY STORY

Vocabulary:
exist
image
inspire
loft
reference
sketch

Spelling: **Words with /u̇/ and /yu̇/**

curious	**should**	**would**	woolen
pure	furious	bulldozer	pudding
fully	cure	soot	goodness
sure	handful	tour	pulley
wooden	crooked	butcher	overlook

GRASS SANDALS: THE TRAVELS OF BASHO

Vocabulary:
chanted
nipped
pouch
restless
scribbled
stitching

Spelling: **Work with Digraphs**

changed	south	**cloth**	whittle
watch	chimney	**themselves**	thoughtful
fresh	scratch	crunch	birch
shoulder	shove	batch	switch
whatever	wheat	harsh	theater

A PLACE CALLED FREEDOM

Vocabulary:
fretted
gourd
plantation
settlement
sunrise
weary

Spelling: **Adding -ed and -ing**

freed	**carried**	shedding	varied
hugged	**believed**	sledding	**arrived**
emptied	dimmed	magnified	plugging
figured	studied	wedged	rising
budding	providing	rotting	**celebrated**

TIME FOR KIDS: TWISTED TRAILS

Vocabulary:
challenge
combine
contained
entertaining
mazes
requires

Spelling: **Words from the Arts**

designs	art	assemble	mold
artist	create	craft	easel
building	**master**	express	plaster
activity	poster	arrange	masterpiece
museum	statue	**professional**	exhibit

Boldfaced words appear in the selection.

UNIT 4

	Vocabulary	Spelling

SCRUFFY: A WOLF FINDS HIS PLACE IN THE PACK

affection
climate
clinging
injury
methods
threat

Words with /ô/ and /ôr/

awful	**toward**	false	dawn
daughter	already	jaw	hoarse
roar	brought	offer	war
order	**form**	sauce	board
office	author	**chorus**	cough

GLUSKABE AND THE SNOW BIRD

confusion
freeze
hilltop
lodge
messenger
praised

Words with /är/ and /âr/

apart	repair	starve	therefore
hardly	**careful**	barber	dairy
yarn	scare	carnival	hare
army	somewhere	carpet	**prepare**
marbles	wear	unfair	pear

MEET AN UNDERWATER EXPLORER

connected
endangered
haul
overcome
poisonous
sponge

Words with /îr/ and /ûr/

fern	mere	**worse**	period
curve	cheer	swirl	insert
worst	serious	**gear**	purpose
shirt	germ	sincerely	twirling
clear	burst	volunteer	spear

ON THE BUS WITH JOANNA COLE

abandon
absorb
available
original
research
traditional

Compound Words

bedroom	backyard	**outline**	**whirlwinds**
anymore	railroad	windowpane	loudspeaker
everybody	forever	**evergreens**	northwest
classroom	bathtub	grandparents	thunderstorm
anyway	homemade	**photocopy**	bedspread

TIME FOR KIDS: EARTH'S FIRST CREATURES

ancestors
disaster
microscope
snout
spikes
weird

Words from Science

shells	**discovered**	mineral	kelp
crabs	cast	dolphin	caterpillar
liquid	lobster	**systems**	depth
fact	**hatch**	clam	skeleton
butterfly	expert	imprint	fungus

Boldfaced words appear in the selection.

T83

UNIT 5

	Vocabulary	**Spelling**

THE FOX AND THE GUINEA PIG

Vocabulary

amazement
destroyed
eldest
fowl
stake
strewn

Spelling — Words with /s/ and /f/

mess	rough	**laughter**	alphabet
sorry	certain	citizen	triumph
balance	telephone	advice	careless
police	**surprise**	photograph	tough
classic	elephant	cider	**enormous**

MOM'S BEST FRIEND

Vocabulary

clippers
errands
instinct
memorizing
relieved
sirens

Spelling — Words with /ər/ and /chər/

brother	**pictures**	member	anchor
honor	odor	nature	pasture
either	enter	tender	chapter
popular	vinegar	visitor	suffer
number	capture	polar	**furniture**

THE RAJAH'S RICE

Vocabulary

attendants
awkwardly
celebration
knowledge
released
spice

Spelling — Words with /əl/ and /ən/

final	pencil	reason	**medical**
uncle	lion	gentle	evil
several	**taken**	total	listen
model	simple	settle	common
terrible	women	level	cotton

YEH-SHEN: A CINDERELLA STORY FROM CHINA

Vocabulary

beloved
bid
desire
heaved
marveled
permit

Spelling — Contractions

that's	there's	they'll	it'll
he'll	couldn't	weren't	hadn't
wasn't	he'd	here's	they'd
what's	could've	she'd	where's
I'd	let's	who's	wouldn't

TIME FOR KIDS: CAN WE RESCUE THE REEFS?

Vocabulary

coral
damage
loosened
percent
reefs
ton

Spelling — Words from Science

rescue	**dying**	**seaweed**	adapt
survive	shelter	**creatures**	locate
channel	extreme	dissolve	assist
vessel	**danger**	motion	future
expose	protect	feature	**divers**

Boldfaced words appear in the selection.

UNIT 6

Vocabulary

Spelling

TEAMMATES

circulated
extraordinary
launched
opponents
organizations
teammate

Words with Silent Letters

knew	writer	knead	stalk
climb	knob	plumber	kneel
calm	numb	chalk	**sought**
although	delight	midnight	thorough
knight	wren	wreck	wrestle

THE MALACHITE PALACE

cultured
feeble
fragrance
mingled
resembled
scampered

Homophones and Homographs

seen	scene	peak	pale
great	beet	post	grave
light	bowl	pail	berry
beat	grate	bury	**peek**
lean	fan	punch	**dates**

THE TOOTHPASTE MILLIONAIRE

brilliant
commercials
expensive
gallon
ingredient
successful

Words with Suffixes

useless	motionless	fairness	hopeless
entertainment	description	government	**production**
construction	measurement	protection	enjoyable
adjustable	adorable	dependable	greatness
darkness	breathless	sickness	

WHALES

identify
mammals
marine
pods
preserve
related

Words with Prefixes

redo	inactive	nonstop	rewind
unkind	**international**	refill	unsure
disappear	unlucky	uncertain	disagree
reread	dislike	interstate	reheat
nonfat	unpack	incomplete	nonsense

TIME FOR KIDS: SAVING THE EVERGLADES

compares
importance
instance
lurk
soggy
wildlife

Words from Math

area	minute	**amount**	quart
hundreds	noon	cylinder	decade
size	cone	zero	rectangle
billions	yard	figure	era
weight	edge	calendar	length

Boldfaced words appear in the selection.

Listening, Speaking, Viewing, Representing

☑ Tested Skill

☐ Tinted panels show skills, strategies, and other teaching opportunities

	K	1	2	3	4	5	6
LISTENING							
Learn the vocabulary of school (numbers, shapes, colors, directions, and categories)							
Identify the musical elements of literary language, such as rhymes, repeated sounds, onomatopoeia							
Determine purposes for listening (get information, solve problems, enjoy and appreciate)							
Listen critically and responsively							
Ask and answer relevant questions							
Listen critically to interpret and evaluate							
Listen responsively to stories and other texts read aloud, including selections from classic and contemporary works							
Connect and compare own experiences, ideas, and traditions with those of others							
Apply comprehension strategies in listening activities							
Understand the major ideas and supporting evidence in spoken messages							
Participate in listening activities related to reading and writing (such as discussions, group activities, conferences)							
Listen to learn by taking notes, organizing, and summarizing spoken ideas							
SPEAKING							
Learn the vocabulary of school (numbers, shapes, colors, directions, and categories)							
Use appropriate language and vocabulary learned to describe ideas, feelings, and experiences							
Ask and answer relevant questions							
Communicate effectively in everyday situations (such as discussions, group activities, conferences)							
Demonstrate speaking skills (audience, purpose, occasion, volume, pitch, tone, rate, fluency)							
Clarify and support spoken messages and ideas with objects, charts, evidence, elaboration, examples							
Use verbal and nonverbal communication in effective ways when, for example, making announcements, giving directions, or making introductions							
Retell a spoken message by summarizing or clarifying							
Connect and compare own experiences, ideas, and traditions with those of others							
Determine purposes for speaking (inform, entertain, give directions, persuade, express personal feelings and opinions)							
Demonstrate skills of reporting and providing information							
Demonstrate skills of interviewing, requesting and providing information							
Apply composition strategies in speaking activities							
Monitor own understanding of spoken message and seek clarification as needed							
VIEWING							
Demonstrate viewing skills (focus attention, organize information)							
Respond to audiovisual media in a variety of ways							
Participate in viewing activities related to reading and writing							
Apply comprehension strategies in viewing activities							
Recognize artists' craft and techniques for conveying meaning							
Interpret information from various formats such as maps, charts, graphics, video segments, technology							
Evaluate purposes of various media (information, appreciation, entertainment, directions, persuasion)							
Use media to compare ideas and points of view							
REPRESENTING							
Select, organize, or produce visuals to complement or extend meanings							
Produce communication using appropriate media to develop a class paper, multimedia or video reports							
Show how language, medium, and presentation contribute to the message							

Reading: Alphabetic Principle, Sounds/Symbols

☑ Tested Skill

▢ Tinted panels show skills, strategies, and other teaching opportunities

	K	1	2	3	4	5	6
PRINT AWARENESS							
Know the order of the alphabet							
Recognize that print represents spoken language and conveys meaning							
Understand directionality (tracking print from left to right; return sweep)							
Understand that written words are separated by spaces							
Know the difference between individual letters and printed words							
Understand that spoken words are represented in written language by specific sequence of letters							
Recognize that there are correct spellings for words							
Know the difference between capital and lowercase letters							
Recognize how readers use capitalization and punctuation to comprehend							
Recognize the distinguishing features of a paragraph							
Recognize that parts of a book (such as cover/title page and table of contents) offer information							
PHONOLOGICAL AWARENESS							
Identify letters, words, sentences							
Divide spoken sentence into individual words							
Produce rhyming words and distinguish rhyming words from nonrhyming words							
Identify, segment, and combine syllables within spoken words							
Identify and isolate the initial and final sound of a spoken word							
Add, delete, or change sounds to change words (such as *cow* to *how*, *pan* to *fan*)							
Blend sounds to make spoken words							
Segment one-syllable spoken words into individual phonemes							
PHONICS AND DECODING							
Alphabetic principle: Letter/sound correspondence	☑	☑	☑				
Blending CVC words	☑						
Segmenting CVC words	☑						
Blending CVC, CVCe, CCVC, CVCC, CVVC words	☑	☑	☑				
Segmenting CVC, CVCe, CCVC, CVCC, CVVC words	☑	☑	☑				
Initial and final consonants: /n/n, /d/d, /s/s, /m/m, /t/t, /k/c, /f/f, /r/r, /p/p, /l/l, /k/k, /g/g, /b/b, /h/h, /w/w, /v/v, /ks/x, /kw/*qu*, /j/j, /y/y, /z/z	☑	☑					
Initial and medial short vowels: *a, i, u, o, e*	☑	☑	☑				
Long vowels: *a-e, i-e, o-e, u-e* (vowel-consonant-e)		☑	☑				
Long vowels, including *ay, ai; e, ee, ie, ea, o, oa, oe, ow; i, y, igh*		☑	☑				
Consonant Digraphs: *sh, th, ch, wh*		☑					
Consonant Blends: continuant/continuant, including *sl, sm, sn, fl, fr, ll, ss, ff*		☑					
Consonant Blends: continuant/stop, including *st, sk, sp, ng, nt, nd, mp, ft*		☑					
Consonant Blends: stop/continuant, including *tr, pr, pl, cr, tw*		☑					
Variant vowels: including /u/oo; /ô/a, aw, au; /ü/ue, ew*		☑	☑				
Diphthongs, including /ou/ou, ow; /oi/oi, oy*		☑	☑				
r-controlled vowels, including /âr/are; /ôr/or, ore; /îr/ear*			☑				
Soft *c* and soft *g*			☑				
nk		☑	☑				
Consonant Digraphs: *ck*	☑	☑					
Consonant Digraphs: *ph, tch, ch*			☑				
Short *e: ea*			☑				
Long *e: y, ey*		☑	☑				
/ü/oo		☑	☑				
/är/ar; /ûr/ir, ur, er*			☑				
Silent letters: including *l, b, k, w, g, h, gh*			☑				
Schwa: /ər/er; /ən/en; /əl/le;			☑				
Reading/identifying multisyllabic words		☑	☑				

Reading: Vocabulary/Word Identification

WORD STRUCTURE	K	1	2	3	4	5	6
Common spelling patterns							
Syllable patterns							
Plurals		☑					
Possessives		☑					
Contractions		☑					
Root, or base, words and inflectional endings (-s, -es, -ed, -ing)	☑	☑	☑		☑		
Compound Words			☑	☑	☑	☑	☑
Prefixes and suffixes (such as un-, re-, dis-, non-; -ly, -y, -ful, -able, -tion)				☑	☑	☑	☑
Root words and derivational endings				☑	☑	☑	☑

WORD MEANING	K	1	2	3	4	5	6
Develop vocabulary through concrete experiences							
Develop vocabulary through selections read aloud							
Develop vocabulary through reading							
Cueing systems: syntactic, semantic, phonetic							
Context clues, including semantic clues (word meaning), syntactical clues (word order), and phonetic clues	☑	☑	☑	☑	☑	☑	☑
High-frequency words (such as *the, a, an, and, said, was, where, is*)							
Identify words that name persons, places, things, and actions							
Automatic reading of regular and irregular words							
Use resources and references (dictionary, glossary, thesaurus, synonym finder, technology and software, and context)							
Synonyms and antonyms			☑	☑	☑	☑	☑
Multiple-meaning words			☑	☑	☑	☑	☑
Figurative language			☑	☑	☑	☑	☑
Decode derivatives (root words, such as *like, pay, happy* with affixes, such as *dis-, pre-, un-*)							
Systematic study of words across content areas and in current events							
Locate meanings, pronunciations, and derivations (including dictionaries, glossaries, and other sources)							
Denotation and connotation							☑
Word origins as aid to understanding historical influences on English word meanings							
Homophones, homographs							
Analogies							☑
Idioms							

Reading: Comprehension

PREREADING STRATEGIES	K	1	2	3	4	5	6
Preview and predict							
Use prior knowledge							
Establish and adjust purposes for reading							
Build background							

MONITORING STRATEGIES	K	1	2	3	4	5	6
Adjust reading rate							
Reread, search for clues, ask questions, ask for help							
Visualize							
Read a portion aloud, use reference aids							
Use decoding and vocabulary strategies							
Paraphrase							
Create story maps, diagrams, charts, story props to help comprehend, analyze, synthesize and evaluate texts							

(continued on next page)

☑ Tested Skill

Tinted panels show skills, strategies, and other teaching opportunities

SKILLS AND STRATEGIES

Skill	K	1	2	3	4	5	6
Recall story details	☑						
Use illustrations	☑	☑					
Distinguish reality and fantasy	☑	☑	☑				
Classify and categorize	☑						
Make predictions	☑	☑	☑	☑	☑	☑	☑
Recognize sequence of events (tell or act out)	☑	☑	☑	☑	☑	☑	☑
Recognize cause and effect			☑	☑	☑	☑	☑
Compare and contrast	☑	☑	☑	☑	☑	☑	☑
Summarize	☑	☑	☑	☑	☑	☑	☑
Make and explain inferences			☑	☑	☑	☑	☑
Draw conclusions			☑	☑	☑	☑	☑
Distinguish important and unimportant information				☑	☑	☑	☑
Recognize main idea and supporting details	☑	☑	☑	☑	☑	☑	☑
Form conclusions or generalizations and support with evidence from text				☑	☑	☑	☑
Distinguish fact and opinion (including news stories and advertisements)				☑	☑	☑	☑
Recognize problem and solution			☑	☑	☑	☑	☑
Recognize steps in a process		☑	☑	☑	☑	☑	☑
Make judgments and decisions				☑	☑	☑	☑
Distinguish fact and nonfact				☑	☑	☑	☑
Recognize techniques of persuasion and propaganda							☑
Evaluate evidence and sources of information							☑
Identify similarities and differences across texts (including topics, characters, problems, themes, treatment, scope, or organization)							
Practice various questions and tasks (test-like comprehension questions)							
Paraphrase and summarize to recall, inform, and organize							
Answer various types of questions (open-ended, literal, interpretative, test-like such as true-false, multiple choice, short-answer)							
Use study strategies to learn and recall (preview, question, reread, and record)							

LITERARY RESPONSE

Skill	K	1	2	3	4	5	6
Listen to stories being read aloud							
React, speculate, join in, read along when predictable and patterned selections are read aloud							
Respond through talk, movement, music, art, drama, and writing to a variety of stories and poems							
Show understanding through writing, illustrating, developing demonstrations, and using technology							
Connect ideas and themes across texts							
Support responses by referring to relevant aspects of text and own experiences							
Offer observations, make connections, speculate, interpret, and raise questions in response to texts							
Interpret text ideas through journal writing, discussion, enactment, and media							

TEXT STRUCTURE/LITERARY CONCEPTS

Skill	K	1	2	3	4	5	6
Distinguish forms of texts and the functions they serve (lists, newsletters, signs)							
Understand story structure							
Identify narrative (for entertainment) and expository (for information)							
Distinguish fiction from nonfiction, including fact and fantasy							
Understand literary forms (stories, poems, plays, and informational books)							
Understand literary terms by distinguishing between roles of author and illustrator							
Understand title, author, and illustrator across a variety of texts							
Analyze character, character's point of view, plot, setting, style, tone, mood		☑	☑	☑	☑	☑	☑
Compare communication in different forms							
Understand terms such as *title, author, illustrator, playwright, theater, stage, act, dialogue,* and *scene*							
Recognize stories, poems, myths, folktales, fables, tall tales, limericks, plays, biographies, and autobiographies							
Judge internal logic of story text							
Recognize that authors organize information in specific ways							
Identify texts to inform, influence, express, or entertain							
Describe how author's point of view affects text				☑	☑	☑	☑
Recognize biography, historical fiction, realistic fiction, modern fantasy, informational texts, and poetry							
Analyze ways authors present ideas (cause/effect, compare/contrast, inductively, deductively, chronologically)							
Recognize flashback, foreshadowing, symbolism							

(continued on next page)

☑ Tested Skill

Tinted panels show skills, strategies, and other teaching opportunities

VARIETY OF TEXT	K	1	2	3	4	5	6
Read a variety of genres							
Use informational texts to acquire information							
Read for a variety of purposes							
Select varied sources when reading for information or pleasure							
FLUENCY							
Read regularly in independent-level and instructional-level materials							
Read orally with fluency from familiar texts							
Self-select independent-level reading							
Read silently for increasing periods of time							
Demonstrate characteristics of fluent and effective reading							
Adjust reading rate to purpose							
Read aloud in selected texts, showing understanding of text and engaging the listener							
CULTURES							
Connect own experience with culture of others							
Compare experiences of characters across cultures							
Articulate and discuss themes and connections that cross cultures							
CRITICAL THINKING							
Experiences (comprehend, apply, analyze, synthesize, evaluate)							
Make connections (comprehend, apply, analyze, synthesize, evaluate)							
Expression (comprehend, apply, analyze, synthesize, evaluate)							
Inquiry (comprehend, apply, analyze, synthesize, evaluate)							
Problem solving (comprehend, apply, analyze, synthesize, evaluate)							
Making decisions (comprehend, apply, analyze, synthesize, evaluate)							

Study Skills

INQUIRY/RESEARCH	K	1	2	3	4	5	6
Follow directions							
Use alphabetical order							
Identify/frame questions for research							
Obtain, organize, and summarize information: classify, take notes, outline							
Evaluate research and raise new questions							
Use technology to present information in various formats							
Follow accepted formats for writing research, including documenting sources							
Use test-taking strategies							
Use text organizers (book cover; title page—title, author, illustrator; contents; headings; glossary; index)		☑	☑	☑	☑	☑	☑
Use graphic aids, including maps, diagrams, charts, graphs		☑	☑	☑	☑	☑	☑
Read and interpret varied texts including environmental print, signs, lists, encyclopedia, dictionary, glossary, newspaper, advertisement, magazine, calendar, directions, floor plans		☑	☑	☑	☑	☑	☑
Use reference sources, such as glossary, dictionary, encyclopedia, telephone directory, technology resources		☑	☑	☑	☑	☑	☑
Recognize Library/Media center resources, such as computerized references; catalog search—subject, author, title; encyclopedia index		☑	☑	☑	☑	☑	☑

Writing

	K	1	2	3	4	5	6
MODES AND FORMS							
Interactive writing							
Personal narrative (Expressive narrative)			☑	☑	☑	☑	☑
Writing that compares (Informative classificatory)			☑	☑	☑	☑	☑
Explanatory writing (Informative narrative)		☑	☑	☑	☑	☑	☑
Persuasive writing (Persuasive descriptive)			☑	☑	☑	☑	☑
Writing a story		☑	☑	☑	☑	☑	☑
Expository writing		☑	☑	☑	☑	☑	☑
Write using a variety of formats, such as advertisement, autobiography, biography, book report/report, comparison-contrast, critique/review/editorial, description, essay, how-to, interview, invitation, journal/log/notes, message/list, paragraph/multi-paragraph composition, picture book, play (scene), poem/rhyme, story, summary, note, letter							
PURPOSES/AUDIENCES							
Dictate messages such as news and stories for others to write							
Write labels, notes, and captions for illustrations, possessions, charts, and centers							
Write to record, to discover and develop ideas, to inform, to influence, to entertain							
Exhibit an identifiable voice in personal narratives and stories							
Use literary devices (suspense, dialogue, and figurative language)							
Produce written texts by organizing ideas, using effective transitions, and choosing precise wording							
PROCESSES							
Generate ideas for self-selected and assigned topics using prewriting strategies							
Develop drafts							
Revise drafts for varied purposes							
Edit for appropriate grammar, spelling, punctuation, and features of polished writings							
Proofread own writing and that of others							
Bring pieces to final form and "publish" them for audiences							
Use technology to compose text							
Select and use reference materials and resources for writing, revising, and editing final drafts							
SPELLING							
Spell own name and write high-frequency words							
Words with short vowels (including CVC and one-syllable words with blends CCVC, CVCC, CCVCC)							
Words with long vowels (including CVCe)							
Words with digraphs, blends, consonant clusters, double consonants							
Words with diphthongs							
Words with variant vowels							
Words with r-controlled vowels							
Words with /ər/, /əl/, and /ən/							
Words with silent letters							
Words with soft c and soft g							
Inflectional endings (including plurals and past tense and words that drop the final e when adding -ing, -ed)							
Compound words							
Contractions							
Homonyms							
Suffixes including -able, -ly, or -less, and prefixes including dis-, re-, pre-, or un-							
Spell words ending in -tion and -sion, such as station and procession							
Accurate spelling of root or base words							
Orthographic patterns and rules such as keep/can; sack/book; out/now; oil/toy; match/speech; ledge/cage; consonant doubling, dropping e, changing y to i							
Multisyllabic words using regularly spelled phonogram patterns							
Syllable patterns (including closed, open, syllable boundary patterns)							
Synonyms and antonyms							
Words from Social Studies, Science, Math, and Physical Education							
Words derived from other languages and cultures							
Use resources to find correct spellings, synonyms, and replacement words							
Use conventional spelling of familiar words in writing assignments							
Spell accurately in final drafts							

(continued on next page)

☑ Tested Skill

Tinted panels show skills, strategies, and other teaching opportunities

GRAMMAR AND USAGE

	K	1	2	3	4	5	6
Understand sentence concepts (word order, statements, questions, exclamations, commands)							
Recognize complete and incomplete sentences							
Nouns (common; proper; singular; plural; irregular plural; possessives)							
Verbs (action; helping; linking; irregular)							
Verb tense (present, past, future, perfect, and progressive)							
Pronouns (possessive, subject and object, pronoun-verb agreement)							
Use objective case pronouns accurately							
Adjectives							
Adverbs that tell how, when, where							
Subjects, predicates							
Subject-verb agreement							
Sentence combining							
Recognize sentence structure (simple, compound, complex)							
Synonyms and antonyms							
Contractions							
Conjunctions							
Prepositions and prepositional phrases							

PENMANSHIP

	K	1	2	3	4	5	6
Write each letter of alphabet (capital and lowercase) using correct formation, appropriate size and spacing							
Write own name and other important words							
Use phonological knowledge to map sounds to letters to write messages							
Write messages that move left to right, top to bottom							
Gain increasing control of penmanship, pencil grip, paper position, beginning stroke							
Use word and letter spacing and margins to make messages readable							
Write legibly by selecting cursive or manuscript as appropriate							

MECHANICS

	K	1	2	3	4	5	6
Use capitalization in sentences, proper nouns, titles, abbreviations and the pronoun I							
Use end marks correctly (period, question mark, exclamation point)							
Use commas (in dates, in addresses, in a series, in letters, in direct address)							
Use apostrophes in contractions and possessives							
Use quotation marks							
Use hyphens, semicolons, colons							

EVALUATION

	K	1	2	3	4	5	6
Identify the most effective features of a piece of writing using class/teacher generated criteria							
Respond constructively to others' writing							
Determine how his/her own writing achieves its purpose							
Use published pieces as models for writing							
Review own written work to monitor growth as writer							

For more detailed scope and sequence including page numbers and additional phonics information, see McGraw-Hill Reading Program scope and sequence (K-6)

T99

Scoring Chart

The Scoring Chart is provided for your convenience in grading your students' work.

- Find the column that shows the total number of items.
- Find the row that matches the number of items answered correctly.
- The intersection of the two rows provides the percentage score.

TOTAL NUMBER OF ITEMS

NUMBER CORRECT

N.C. \ Items	1	2	3	4	5	6	7	8	9	10	11	12	13	14	15	16	17	18	19	20	21	22	23	24	25	26	27	28	29	30
1	100	50	33	25	20	17	14	13	11	10	9	8	8	7	7	6	6	6	5	5	5	5	4	4	4	4	4	4	3	3
2		100	67	50	40	33	29	25	22	20	18	17	15	14	13	13	12	11	11	10	10	9	9	8	8	8	7	7	7	7
3			100	75	60	50	43	38	33	30	27	25	23	21	20	19	18	17	16	15	14	14	13	13	12	12	11	11	10	10
4				100	80	67	57	50	44	40	36	33	31	29	27	25	24	22	21	20	19	18	17	17	16	15	15	14	14	13
5					100	83	71	63	56	50	45	42	38	36	33	31	29	28	26	25	24	23	22	21	20	19	19	18	17	17
6						100	86	75	67	60	55	50	46	43	40	38	35	33	32	30	29	27	26	25	24	23	22	21	21	20
7							100	88	78	70	64	58	54	50	47	44	41	39	37	35	33	32	30	29	28	27	26	25	24	23
8								100	89	80	73	67	62	57	53	50	47	44	42	40	38	36	35	33	32	31	30	29	28	27
9									100	90	82	75	69	64	60	56	53	50	47	45	43	41	39	38	36	35	33	32	31	30
10										100	91	83	77	71	67	63	59	56	53	50	48	45	43	42	40	38	37	36	34	33
11											100	92	85	79	73	69	65	61	58	55	52	50	48	46	44	42	41	39	38	37
12												100	92	86	80	75	71	67	63	60	57	55	52	50	48	46	44	43	41	40
13													100	93	87	81	76	72	68	65	62	59	57	54	52	50	48	46	45	43
14														100	93	88	82	78	74	70	67	64	61	58	56	54	52	50	48	47
15															100	94	88	83	79	75	71	68	65	63	60	58	56	54	52	50
16																100	94	89	84	80	76	73	70	67	64	62	59	57	55	53
17																	100	94	89	85	81	77	74	71	68	65	63	61	59	57
18																		100	95	90	86	82	78	75	72	69	67	64	62	60
19																			100	95	90	86	83	79	76	73	70	68	66	63
20																				100	95	91	87	83	80	77	74	71	69	67
21																					100	95	91	88	84	81	78	75	72	70
22																						100	96	92	88	85	81	79	76	73
23																							100	96	92	88	85	82	79	77
24																								100	96	92	89	86	83	80
25																									100	96	93	89	86	83
26																										100	96	93	90	87
27																											100	96	93	90
28																												100	97	93
29																													100	97
30																														100

Writing That Compares

6-Point Writing Rubric

6 Exceptional	5 Excellent	4 Good	3 Fair	2 Poor	1 Unsatisfactory
• **Ideas & Content** crafts a clearly detailed comparison between two animals; shares fresh observations about the animals and their habitat.	• **Ideas & Content** crafts a cohesive, carefully detailed comparison of two animals; makes some fresh observations of the habitat.	• **Ideas & Content** presents a solid, clear comparison; details help to bring the main idea into focus.	• **Ideas & Content** attempts to compare two animals; some ideas or details are not clear, or do not fit the task.	• **Ideas & Content** has little control of task to compare, or seems unsure of the topic; ideas are vague; facts and details are few, repeated, or inaccurate.	• **Ideas & Content** does not compare two animals; writer is unfocused or unsure of what s/he wants to say.
• **Organization** presents a logically devised sequence of facts and ideas; strong beginning and effective conclusion; carefully placed details clarify the information.	• **Organization** presents a well-planned strategy, in a sequence that helps the reader follow and understand the comparisons; facts and details are evenly connected.	• **Organization** presents facts and observations in a logical order; has a clear beginning and ending; reader can follow the writer's logic.	• **Organization** tries to structure a comparison, but the logic is sometimes hard to follow; ideas, sentences, and paragraphs may need more transition or connection.	• **Organization** has no clear structure; the order of ideas is hard to follow; few connections are made between ideas; details don't fit where they are placed.	• **Organization** shows extreme lack of organization; ideas are not connected; details, if any, are incomplete, irrelevant, or do not fit.
• **Voice** shows originality and deep involvement with the topic; a genuine personal style enlivens the facts.	• **Voice** shows originality and strong involvement with the topic; personal style helps bring the animal habitat to life.	• **Voice** tries to convey an authentic personal touch to the reader; shows involvement with the topic; message style matches the comparison purpose.	• **Voice** may not be involved with the topic; message comes across, but does not clearly connect to the purpose and audience.	• **Voice** is not involved in sharing observations with a reader; writing may be lifeless, with no sense of who is behind the words.	• **Voice** does not address an audience; does not have a sense of sharing a personal message or style.
• **Word Choice** imaginative use of specific language brings the animal habitat to life; careful choices make the comparisons unusually precise and interesting.	• **Word Choice** thoughtful use of precise, colorful language makes comparisons clear and interesting; explores new words, or uses everyday words in a fresh way.	• **Word Choice** communicates the main idea; uses a variety of words that fit the comparison task; explores some new words, or may try to use everyday words in a new way.	• **Word Choice** compares two animals in an obvious way; may try to use a range of words, but some do not fit; may overuse some words/expressions.	• **Word Choice** does not choose words that paint strong pictures of animals or a habitat; some words are overused, or may confuse the comparison points.	• **Word Choice** uses words that do not compare, or are vague and confusing; no new words are attempted; may overuse familiar words.
• **Sentence Fluency** simple and complex sentences flow in a natural rhythm; writing is easy to follow and read aloud; fragments or other devices, if used, strengthen the comparisons.	• **Sentence Fluency** well-paced simple and complex sentences flow naturally; a variety of lengths, beginnings, and patterns fit together and enhance the text.	• **Sentence Fluency** creates careful, easy-to-follow sentences that vary in length, beginnings, and patterns; uses simple and complex constructions, with stronger control of simple sentences.	• **Sentence Fluency** most sentences are readable, but are limited in lengths and patterns; some rereading may be necessary to follow the meaning; choppy or awkward sentences make the text hard to read aloud.	• **Sentence Fluency** sentences may be choppy or awkward; patterns are similar or monotonous; text may be hard to follow or read aloud.	• **Sentence Fluency** sentences are incomplete, rambling, or confusing, and make the text hard to follow and read aloud.
• **Conventions** is skilled in most writing conventions; proper use of the rules of English enhances clarity, meaning, and style; editing is largely unnecessary.	• **Conventions** shows skills in most writing conventions; proper use of the rules of English enhances clarity, meaning, and style; editing is largely unnecessary.	• **Conventions** may make some errors in spelling, capitalization, punctuation, or usage, which do not interfere with understanding the text; some editing is needed.	• **Conventions** has basic control of conventions; makes noticeable errors that interfere with an easy reading of the text; significant editing is needed.	• **Conventions** frequent errors in spelling, word choice, punctuation, and usage make the paper difficult to read; requires extensive editing.	• **Conventions** makes severe errors in most conventions; spelling errors may make it hard to guess what words are meant; some parts of the text may be impossible to follow or understand.

0: This piece is either blank, or fails to respond to the writing task. The topic is not addressed, or the student simply paraphrases the prompt. The response may be illegible or incoherent.

Writing That Compares

8-Point Scoring Rubric

8	7	6	5	4	3	2	1
The writer	The writer	The writer	The writer	The writer	The writer	The writer	The writer
• has used many facts from a variety of research sources, as well as interesting personal observations, to construct a superb comparison of two things.	• has used research sources and personal observation to present a factual, well-organized comparison of two things.	• has used research and some personal observation to construct an organized comparison of two things.	• has used some basic research and articulated a few strong personal observations to construct a fairly well-organized comparison of two things.	• has attempted to compare two things using mostly personal observations.	• may attempt to compare two things, but uses no factual research and limited personal observations.	• has made a poor attempt at comparing two things.	• has not successfully compared two things.
• presents an appealing introductory paragraph or statement, as well as an original conclusion.	• constructs a clear introductory statement and a good conclusion.	• presents introductory and concluding statements.	• presents basic introductory and concluding statements.	• may have constructed an opening or closing statement, but not both.	• includes distracting digressions and demonstrates a lack of strong overall structure.	• has not clearly presented an opening or concluding statement.	• exhibits problems with language serious enough to detract from overall readability.
• consistently and thoroughly constructs comparisons using elaborative details and sophisticated verbs and adjectives.	• has made many colorful comparisons using a variety of elaborative details and well-chosen verbs and adjectives.	• creates comparisons that include strong elaborations and numerous adjectives and verbs.	• creates solid comparisons using some elaboration with grade-level adjectives and verbs.	• creates a few comparisons that may lack elaboration.	• may have failed to develop clear opening and closing statements.	• exhibits serious problems with organization, word choice, and conventions.	• has not demonstrated a grasp of the characteristics of comparative writing.
• has consistently maintained a fluid, logical order of events, linked by a variety of transitional words and phrases.	• maintains a clear sequence of events linked by transition words.	• demonstrates a sound organizational structure with few digressions.	• constructs an overall organizational structure that may include some irrelevant facts and digressions that do not seriously detract from overall readability.	• has not successfully maintained a cohesive organizational structure. The piece contains a few digressions that distract somewhat from its overall readability.	• creates comparisons using few details to elaborate main points.	• has not applied his or her understanding of the genre to the assignment.	

0: This piece is either blank, or fails to respond to the writing task. The topic is not addressed, or the student simply paraphrases the prompt. The response may be illegible or incoherent.

Notes

Notes

Notes

Notes

Notes

Notes